This book comes with access to more content online.

Watch videos, take practice tests,
and study with flashcards!

Redeem your book or ebook at
www.dummies.com/go/getaccess.

Select your product, and then follow the prompts
to validate your purchase.

2025/2026 ASVAB

by Angie Papple Johnston

for dummies
A Wiley Brand

2025/2026 ASVAB For Dummies®

Published by: **John Wiley & Sons, Inc.,** 111 River Street, Hoboken, NJ 07030-5774, www.wiley.com

Copyright © 2025 by John Wiley & Sons, Inc. All rights reserved, including rights for text and data mining and training of artificial technologies or similar technologies.

Media and software compilation copyright © 2025 by John Wiley & Sons, Inc. All rights reserved, including rights for text and data mining and training of artificial technologies or similar technologies.

Published simultaneously in Canada

No part of this publication may be reproduced, stored in a retrieval system or transmitted in any form or by any means, electronic, mechanical, photocopying, recording, scanning or otherwise, except as permitted under Sections 107 or 108 of the 1976 United States Copyright Act, without the prior written permission of the Publisher. Requests to the Publisher for permission should be addressed to the Permissions Department, John Wiley & Sons, Inc., 111 River Street, Hoboken, NJ 07030, (201) 748-6011, fax (201) 748-6008, or online at http://www.wiley.com/go/permissions.

Trademarks: Wiley, For Dummies, the Dummies Man logo, Dummies.com, Making Everything Easier, and related trade dress are trademarks or registered trademarks of John Wiley & Sons, Inc. and may not be used without written permission. All other trademarks are the property of their respective owners. John Wiley & Sons, Inc. is not associated with any product or vendor mentioned in this book.

LIMIT OF LIABILITY/DISCLAIMER OF WARRANTY: THE PUBLISHER AND THE AUTHOR MAKE NO REPRESENTATIONS OR WARRANTIES WITH RESPECT TO THE ACCURACY OR COMPLETENESS OF THE CONTENTS OF THIS WORK AND SPECIFICALLY DISCLAIM ALL WARRANTIES, INCLUDING WITHOUT LIMITATION WARRANTIES OF FITNESS FOR A PARTICULAR PURPOSE. NO WARRANTY MAY BE CREATED OR EXTENDED BY SALES OR PROMOTIONAL MATERIALS. THE ADVICE AND STRATEGIES CONTAINED HEREIN MAY NOT BE SUITABLE FOR EVERY SITUATION. THIS WORK IS SOLD WITH THE UNDERSTANDING THAT THE PUBLISHER IS NOT ENGAGED IN RENDERING LEGAL, ACCOUNTING, OR OTHER PROFESSIONAL SERVICES. IF PROFESSIONAL ASSISTANCE IS REQUIRED, THE SERVICES OF A COMPETENT PROFESSIONAL PERSON SHOULD BE SOUGHT. NEITHER THE PUBLISHER NOR THE AUTHOR SHALL BE LIABLE FOR DAMAGES ARISING HEREFROM. THE FACT THAT AN ORGANIZATION OR WEBSITE IS REFERRED TO IN THIS WORK AS A CITATION AND/OR A POTENTIAL SOURCE OF FURTHER INFORMATION DOES NOT MEAN THAT THE AUTHOR OR THE PUBLISHER ENDORSES THE INFORMATION THE ORGANIZATION OR WEBSITE MAY PROVIDE OR RECOMMENDATIONS IT MAY MAKE. FURTHER, READERS SHOULD BE AWARE THAT INTERNET WEBSITES LISTED IN THIS WORK MAY HAVE CHANGED OR DISAPPEARED BETWEEN WHEN THIS WORK WAS WRITTEN AND WHEN IT IS READ.

For general information on our other products and services, please contact our Customer Care Department within the U.S. at 877-762-2974, outside the U.S. at 317-572-3993, or fax 317-572-4002. For technical support, please visit https://hub.wiley.com/community/support/dummies.

Wiley publishes in a variety of print and electronic formats and by print-on-demand. Some material included with standard print versions of this book may not be included in e-books or in print-on-demand. If this book refers to media that is not included in the version you purchased, you may download this material at http://booksupport.wiley.com. For more information about Wiley products, visit www.wiley.com.

Library of Congress Control Number: 2025931345

ISBN 978-1-394-32346-3 (pbk); ISBN 978-1-394-32348-7 (ebk); ISBN 978-1-394-32347-0 (ebk)

SKY10106193_052825

Contents at a Glance

Introduction 1

Part 1: Getting Started with the ASVAB 5
CHAPTER 1: Putting the ASVAB under a Microscope 7
CHAPTER 2: Knowing What It Takes to Get Your Dream Job 19
CHAPTER 3: Strategizing Your Way to a Good Score 25

Part 2: Words to Live By: Communication Skills 39
CHAPTER 4: Word Knowledge 41
CHAPTER 5: Paragraph Comprehension 65

Part 3: Making the Most of Math: Arithmetic Skills 89
CHAPTER 6: Mathematics Knowledge and Operations 91
CHAPTER 7: Algebra 121
CHAPTER 8: Geometry 147
CHAPTER 9: Arithmetic Reasoning: Math Word Problems 175

Part 4: Examining General Science under a Microscope 197
CHAPTER 10: General Science and Life Science 199
CHAPTER 11: Physical Sciences 225
CHAPTER 12: Earth and Space Sciences 249

Part 5: The Whole Ball of Facts: Technical Skills 275
CHAPTER 13: Auto Information 277
CHAPTER 14: Shop Information 299
CHAPTER 15: Mechanical Comprehension 313
CHAPTER 16: Electronics Information 339
CHAPTER 17: Assembling Objects 363

Part 6: Practice ASVAB Exams 373
CHAPTER 18: Practice Exam 1 375
CHAPTER 19: Practice Exam 1: Answers and Explanations 407
CHAPTER 20: Practice Exam 2 427
CHAPTER 21: Practice Exam 2: Answers and Explanations 459
CHAPTER 22: Practice Exam 3 477
CHAPTER 23: Practice Exam 3: Answers and Explanations 509
CHAPTER 24: AFQT Practice Exam 1 529
CHAPTER 25: AFQT Practice Exam 1: Answers and Explanations 547
CHAPTER 26: AFQT Practice Exam 2 557
CHAPTER 27: AFQT Practice Exam 2: Answers and Explanations 575

Part 7: The Part of Tens 587
CHAPTER 28: Ten Surefire Ways to Fail the ASVAB 589
CHAPTER 29: Ten Tips for Doing Well on the AFQT 593
CHAPTER 30: Ten Ways to Boost Your Math and English Skills 597

Appendix: Word Knowledge Resources 601

Index 619

Table of Contents

INTRODUCTION 1
    About This Book 1
    Foolish Assumptions 2
    Icons Used in This Book 2
    Beyond the Book 2
    Where to Go from Here 3

PART 1: GETTING STARTED WITH THE ASVAB 5

CHAPTER 1: Putting the ASVAB under a Microscope 7
    Knowing Which Version You're Taking 7
    Mapping Out the ASVAB Subtests 8
    Eyeing Easy, Medium, and Hard Questions 10
    Deciphering ASVAB Scores 10
        Defining all the scores 11
        Understanding the big four: Your AFQT scores 12
    Do-Over: Retaking the ASVAB 15
        U.S. Army retest policy 16
        U.S. Air Force and U.S. Space Force retest policy 16
        U.S. Navy retest policy 16
        U.S. Marine Corps retest policy 16
        U.S. Coast Guard retest policy 17

CHAPTER 2: Knowing What It Takes to Get Your Dream Job 19
    Eyeing How ASVAB Scores Determine Military Training Programs and Jobs 20
    Understanding How Each Branch Computes Line Scores 20
        Line scores and the Army 21
        Line scores and the Navy and Coast Guard 22
        Line scores and the Marine Corps 22
        Line scores and the Air Force and Space Force 22

CHAPTER 3: Strategizing Your Way to a Good Score 25
    Taking the Test: Computerized or Paper? 25
        Going paperless: The pros and cons of the computerized test 26
        Writing on hard copy: The advantages and disadvantages of the paper version 27
    Tackling Multiple-Choice Questions 28
    When You Don't Know an Answer: Guessing Smart 29
    Studying and Practicing for the ASVAB 30
    Getting Access to the Online Test Bank 32
    Personalizing Your Own Study Plan 32
    Outlining Your ASVAB Study Strategy 33
        Sharpening your skills with 12 weeks to prepare 34
        Studying up with 6 weeks to test day 35
        Mapping your review 3 weeks out 36
        Heading into crunch time with 1 week to prepare 37
    Making Last-Minute Preparations: 24 Hours and Counting ... 37

PART 2: WORDS TO LIVE BY: COMMUNICATION SKILLS 39

CHAPTER 4: Word Knowledge 41
Grasping the Importance of Word Knowledge 42
Checking Out the Word Knowledge Question Format 42
Building Words from Scratch: Strategies to Help You Decipher Word Meanings 43
    From beginning to end: Knowing prefixes and suffixes 43
    Determining the root of the problem 45
    Word families: Finding related words 46
    Deconstructing words 47
Yin and Yang: Understanding Synonyms and Antonyms 48
ASVAB Word Knowledge Strategy: Finding the Answer When You Just Don't Know 49
    Creating your own context 49
    How's it feel? Letting the words speak to you 49
    Compare and contrast: Picking up on signals 50
    One of these things is not like the other: Ruling out wrong answers 51
    Mind filling in? Replacing the word with the answer choices 51
    Say what? Parts of speech matter 52
    If all else fails, break your word 53
    Guess what! It's okay on the ASVAB 54
You Are What You Speak: Improving Your Vocabulary, Improving Yourself 54
    Reading your way to a larger vocabulary 55
    Keeping a list and checking it twice 55
    Crosswords: Making vocabulary fun 56
    Sounding off by sounding it out 56
Word Knowledge Practice Questions 58
    Easy Word Knowledge practice questions 58
    Medium Word Knowledge Practice Questions 59
    Hard Word Knowledge Practice Questions 60
Answers and Explanations 62

CHAPTER 5: Paragraph Comprehension 65
Understanding the Importance of Paragraph Comprehension for Military Jobs 65
Eyeing the Physique of the Paragraph Comprehension Subtest 66
Sampling the Four Types of Comprehension Questions 66
    Treasure hunt: Finding specific information 67
    Cutting to the chase: Recognizing the main idea 68
    If the shoe fits: Determining word meaning in context 69
    Reading between the lines: Understanding implications 70
Do You Get My Point? Breaking down Paragraphs 71
    What's the big idea? Determining the main idea in a paragraph . 71
    Extra, extra! Identifying subpoints 73
Analyzing What You've Read: Guessing at What the Writer Really Means 74
Faster than a Speeding Turtle: Tips for Slow Readers 75
    Read more, watch less 75
    Become a lean, mean word machine 76
    Build your confidence 76
Test-Taking Tips for Reading and Gleaning 77
Paragraph Comprehension Practice Questions 78
    Easy Paragraph Comprehension practice questions 78
    Medium Paragraph Comprehension practice questions 81
    Hard Paragraph Comprehension practice questions 83
Answers and Explanations 86

PART 3: MAKING THE MOST OF MATH: ARITHMETIC SKILLS ... 89

CHAPTER 6: Mathematics Knowledge and Operations ... 91

Just When You Thought You Were Done with Vocab: Math Terminology ... 92
Operations: What You Do to Numbers ... 93
    First things first: Following the order of operations ... 94
    Completing a number sequence ... 95
    Averaging mean, median, and mode in a range ... 96
Working on Both Sides of the Line: Fractions ... 97
    Common denominators: Preparing to add and subtract fractions ... 97
    Multiplying and reducing fractions ... 99
    Dividing fractions ... 100
    Converting improper fractions to mixed numbers ... and back again ... 101
    Expressing a fraction in other forms: Decimals and percents ... 101
    Showing comparisons with ratios ... 104
A Powerful Shorthand: Writing in Scientific Notation ... 106
Getting to the Root of the Problem ... 106
    Perfect squares ... 106
    Irrational numbers ... 107
    Other roots ... 108
Test-Taking Techniques for Your Mathematical Journey ... 108
    Knowing what the question is asking ... 108
    Figuring out what you're solving for ... 109
    Solving what you can and guessing the rest ... 109
    Using the process of elimination ... 110
Math Knowledge and Operations Practice Questions ... 111
    Easy Math Knowledge questions ... 111
    Medium Math Knowledge questions ... 112
    Hard Math Knowledge questions ... 114
Answers and Explanations ... 115

CHAPTER 7: Algebra ... 121

Coming to Terms with Basic Algebra Lingo ... 121
Solving for x ... 123
When All Things Are Equal: Keeping an Algebra Equation Balanced ... 124
    Solving one-step equations involving addition and subtraction ... 124
    Multiplying and dividing ... 125
    Solving multistep equations ... 125
    Simplifying equations ... 126
    Using FOIL ... 127
Tackling Two-Variable Equations ... 127
    Substitution ... 127
    Combining equations ... 128
Explaining Exponents in Algebra ... 129
A Step Back: Factoring Algebra Expressions to Find Original Numbers ... 129
    Pulling out the greatest common factor ... 130
    Factoring a three-term equation $\left(x^2 + bx + c\right)$ ... 130
Making Alphabet Soup: Solving Quadratic Equations ... 131
All Math Isn't Created Equal: Solving Inequalities ... 132
Algebra Practice Questions ... 134
    Easy algebra practice questions ... 134
    Medium algebra practice questions ... 135
    Hard algebra practice questions ... 137
Answers and Explanations ... 138

CHAPTER 8: **Geometry**..147
- Perusing Perimeter and Area...148
- Outlining Angles...148
  - Parallel lines...149
  - Naming angles..150
- Pointing Out Triangle Types...150
- Back to Square One: Quadrilaterals....................................151
- Going around in Circles...153
  - Navigating the circumference.......................................153
  - Mapping out the area of a circle...................................154
- Fillin' It Up: Calculating Volume.....................................154
  - Scratching the surface area of solids..............................155
  - Breaking down combined figures.....................................157
- Mapping Out Coordinates...159
- Hammering Down Helpful Geometry Formulas..............................160
- Geometry Practice Questions...162
  - Easy geometry practice questions...................................162
  - Medium geometry practice questions.................................164
  - Hard geometry practice questions...................................167
- Answers and Explanations..169

CHAPTER 9: **Arithmetic Reasoning: Math Word Problems**...................175
- Tackling the Real World of Word Problems..............................176
  - Reading the entire problem...176
  - Figuring out what the question is asking...........................176
  - Digging for the facts..177
  - Setting up the problem and working your way to the answer.........178
  - Drawing a diagram..178
  - Reviewing your answer..179
- The Guessing Game: Putting Reason in Your Guessing Strategy...........179
  - Using the process of elimination...................................180
  - Solving what you can and guessing the rest........................180
  - Making use of the answer choices..................................180
- Arithmetic Reasoning (Math Word Problems) Practice Questions..........182
  - Easy Arithmetic Reasoning questions................................182
  - Medium Arithmetic Reasoning questions..............................184
  - Hard Arithmetic Reasoning questions................................187
- Answers and Explanations..189

PART 4: EXAMINING GENERAL SCIENCE UNDER A MICROSCOPE....197

CHAPTER 10: **General Science and Life Science**..........................199
- There's a Scientific Method to the Madness............................200
- Understanding Forms of Measurement....................................201
- Uncovering Biology, from Big to Small.................................202
  - Relating to your world through ecology.............................202
  - Variety is the spice of life: Biodiversity.........................203
  - Categorizing Mother Nature...203
- Perusing the Human Body Systems.......................................206
  - Picking your brain: The nervous system.............................207
  - Flowing through the heart, blood, and circulatory system..........207
  - Are you kidney me? The renal system................................208
  - Breathing in and out: The respiratory system......................208
  - You are what you eat: The digestive system........................208

- Muscling your way through life 209
- Taking the skeletons out of the closet 209
- Ending up in the endocrine system 210
- The lymphatic system: When things go haywire 210
- Damage control through the integumentary system 211
- Continuing the species through the reproductive system 211
- Keeping the body in peak operating condition 211
- Digging through Plant Physiology 212
  - Types of plants 212
  - Where plant processes take place 212
  - Plant reproduction 214
- Thinking Small: A Look at Cells 214
  - Inspecting cell structure 214
  - Profiting from cell processes 216
- Swimming in the Gene Pool: Genetics 216
  - Copying genes 216
  - Determining your sex with two little letters 216
  - Knowing which genes get passed down the family line 217
- Using Common Sense to Hypothesize about Answers 217
- General and Life Science Practice Questions 218
  - Easy life science questions 218
  - Medium life science questions 219
  - Hard life science questions 221
- Answers and Explanations 222

CHAPTER 11: Physical Sciences 225

- Chemistry: Not Blowing Up the Lab 226
  - How chemists look at things 226
  - Understanding the elements, my dear Watson 227
  - Building molecular structures 227
  - Sitting down at the periodic table 227
  - Changing states: Physical and chemical moves for molecules 228
  - Boiling and freezing 229
  - Compounds, mixtures, and reactions: When atoms and elements get together 230
  - Covering all the bases (and the acids, too) 232
- Physics: It Matters (and It's Matter) 233
  - Keeping track with SI units of measurement 233
  - Weight and mass 233
  - Newton's laws: The science of motion 234
  - Measuring work, force, energy, and power 236
  - Did you hear that? Understanding sound waves 237
  - The rainbow of frequencies on the electromagnetic spectrum 238
  - Heating things up with energy 239
  - Opposites attract: Magnetism and polarization 241
- Physical Science Practice Questions 242
  - Easy physical science practice questions 242
  - Medium physical science practice questions 243
  - Hard physical science practice questions 245
- Answers and Explanations 246

CHAPTER 12: Earth and Space Sciences 249

- Staying Down to Earth with Geology 249
  - Peeling back the layers of the planet 250
  - Sedimentary, metamorphic, and igneous rocks 251
  - What's shakin'? A word on earthquakes 251

Sinking or Swimming: Oceanography...252
    Filling the ocean, one drop at a time 252
    Swirling around the currents...253
    Making waves in the atmosphere......................................253
    Tugging on the moon with tides 254
    Diving into basins, coasts, and estuaries 254
Outta This World: Checking the Atmosphere 254
    Gases in the atmosphere 255
    The magnetosphere: A polarizing force 255
    Warming up to cold fronts 256
    We're not in Kansas anymore: Understanding what causes extreme weather events..257
    Keeping track of weather patterns 257
    Classifying clouds..257
    Figuring out temperature conversions.................................258
Paleontology: Can You Dig It? 259
    Plants, germs, dinosaurs, and humans 260
    Dating a caveman 261
Where Few Have Gone Before: Astronomy...................................262
    Taking a bite out of the Milky Way 262
    Taking a quick glimpse at the sun.....................................262
    Perusing the planets 263
    Shooting for the moons 264
    Watching for meteors, comets, and asteroids 265
Getting Back to Your Latin Roots to Improve Your Test Score 266
Earth and Space Science Practice Questions.................................268
    Easy Earth and space science practice questions.....................268
    Medium Earth and space science practice questions 269
    Hard Earth and space science practice questions 271
Answers and Explanations...272

PART 5: THE WHOLE BALL OF FACTS: TECHNICAL SKILLS 275

CHAPTER 13: Auto Information 277
Checking under the Hood 277
    Chassis and frame: Holding it all together............................278
    The engine: Different strokes 278
    Electrical and ignition systems: Starting up 282
    Cooling systems: Preventing a meltdown 283
    Lubrication systems: Keeping the engine moving smoothly.........283
    Exhaust systems: Where byproducts go to die.......................284
    Emissions-control systems: Filtering out pollutants..................284
    Drive systems: Taking it for a spin....................................284
    Suspension and steering systems: Keeping it on the road 285
    Brake system: Pulling out all the stops...............................287
Cruising toward a Better Score 287
Auto Information Practice Questions..289
    Easy Auto Information practice questions............................289
    Medium Auto Information practice questions 291
    Hard Auto Information practice questions 293
Answers and Explanations...295

CHAPTER 14: Shop Information 299
Picking Up the Tools of the Trade...299
    Measuring tools..300
    Leveling and squaring tools..300

Striking tools...301
Fastening tools...301
Soldering and welding tools...303
Cutting tools...303
Drilling, punching, and gouging tools...303
Finishing tools...305
Clamping tools...306
Sticking Materials Together with Fasteners...306
Nails...306
Screws and bolts...307
Nuts and washers...307
Rivets...308
Building a Better Score...308
Shop Information Practice Questions...310
Answers and Explanations...312

CHAPTER 15: **Mechanical Comprehension**...313
A-mass-ing Knowledge on Matter, Weight, Density, and Relativity...314
Understanding the Forces of the Universe...315
You hit me first! The basics of action and reaction...315
Equilibrium: Finding a balance...316
Under pressure: Spreading out the force...316
Looking at kinds of forces...316
You Call That Work?!...320
Contrasting the difference between potential and kinetic energy...320
Exerting force to make things happen...321
Overcoming resistance...321
Powering through work...321
Relying on Machines to Help You Work...322
Using levers to your advantage...322
Ramping up the inclined plane...323
Easing your effort: Pulleys and gears...324
Multiplying your effort: Wheels and axles...328
Opening up the door to torque...328
Getting a grip on things with vises...329
Magnifying your force with liquid: Hydraulic pressure...330
Working Your Way to a Better Test Score...331
Using your observations and common sense...331
Using the mathematics of mechanics...332
Guessing with a mechanical mind...332
Mechanical Comprehension Practice Questions...333
Answers and Explanations...336

CHAPTER 16: **Electronics Information**...339
Uncovering the Secrets of Electricity...340
Going subatomic...341
Earning the good conduct(or) medal...342
Examining the current of the electrical river...342
Resistance: Putting the brakes on electrical flow...342
Measuring voltage: Do you have the potential?...343
Getting around to circuits...344
Measuring power...348
Producing electrical effects...349
Switching Things Up with Alternating and Direct Current...350
Figuring out frequency...350
Impedance: Join the resistance!...351

Table of Contents **xiii**

Rectifying the situation: Going direct 352
  Turning up the transistor radio. 352
 Picture It: Decoding Electrical Circuit Codes 352
 Coming in Hot: Wire Color Codes Used in the U.S.. 356
 Eyeing Some Electronics Information Test Tips 357
  Memorizing simple principles 357
  Playing the guessing game. 358
 Electronics Information Practice Questions 359
 Answers and Explanations 361

CHAPTER 17: Assembling Objects. 363
 Getting the Picture about Assembling Objects 363
 Two Types of Questions for the Price of One 364
  Putting tab A into slot B: Connectors 364
  Solving the jigsaw puzzle: Shapes 366
 Tips for the Assembling Objects Subtest 367
  Comparing one piece or point at a time 368
  Visualizing success: Practicing spatial skills ahead of time 368
 Assembling Objects Practice Questions. 369
 Answers and Explanations 371

PART 6: PRACTICE ASVAB EXAMS. 373

CHAPTER 18: Practice Exam 1 375
 Answer Sheet for Practice Exam 1 377
 Subtest 1: General Science. 379
 Subtest 2: Arithmetic Reasoning. 381
 Subtest 3: Word Knowledge. 385
 Subtest 4: Paragraph Comprehension. 388
 Subtest 5: Mathematics Knowledge 391
 Subtest 6: Electronics Information 394
 Subtest 7: Auto & Shop Information. 396
 Subtest 8: Mechanical Comprehension 399
 Subtest 9: Assembling Objects 404

CHAPTER 19: Practice Exam 1: Answers and Explanations. 407
 Subtest 1: General Science Answers. 407
 Subtest 2: Arithmetic Reasoning Answers 409
 Subtest 3: Word Knowledge Answers. 412
 Subtest 4: Paragraph Comprehension Answers 414
 Subtest 5: Mathematics Knowledge Answers 415
 Subtest 6: Electronics Information Answers 418
 Subtest 7: Auto & Shop Information Answers. 420
 Subtest 8: Mechanical Comprehension Answers 421
 Subtest 9: Assembling Objects Answers 423

CHAPTER 20: Practice Exam 2 427
 Answer Sheet for Practice Exam 2 429
 Subtest 1: General Science. 431
 Subtest 2: Arithmetic Reasoning. 433
 Subtest 3: Word Knowledge. 437
 Subtest 4: Paragraph Comprehension. 440
 Subtest 5: Mathematics Knowledge 443
 Subtest 6: Electronics Information 446
 Subtest 7: Auto & Shop Information. 448

Subtest 8: Mechanical Comprehension 451
Subtest 9: Assembling Objects 456

CHAPTER 21: **Practice Exam 2: Answers and Explanations** 459
Subtest 1: General Science Answers 459
Subtest 2: Arithmetic Reasoning Answers 461
Subtest 3: Word Knowledge Answers 463
Subtest 4: Paragraph Comprehension Answers 465
Subtest 5: Mathematics Knowledge Answers 466
Subtest 6: Electronics Information Answers 469
Subtest 7: Auto & Shop Information Answers 470
Subtest 8: Mechanical Comprehension Answers 472
Subtest 9: Assembling Objects Answers 473

CHAPTER 22: **Practice Exam 3** 477
Answer Sheet for Practice Exam 3 479
Subtest 1: General Science 481
Subtest 2: Arithmetic Reasoning 484
Subtest 3: Word Knowledge 487
Subtest 4: Paragraph Comprehension 490
Subtest 5: Mathematics Knowledge 493
Subtest 6: Electronics Information 496
Subtest 7: Auto & Shop Information 498
Subtest 8: Mechanical Comprehension 501
Subtest 9: Assembling Objects 506

CHAPTER 23: **Practice Exam 3: Answers and Explanations** 509
Subtest 1: General Science Answers 509
Subtest 2: Arithmetic Reasoning Answers 511
Subtest 3: Word Knowledge Answers 515
Subtest 4: Paragraph Comprehension Answers 516
Subtest 5: Mathematics Knowledge Answers 518
Subtest 6: Electronics Information Answers 520
Subtest 7: Auto & Shop Information Answers 522
Subtest 8: Mechanical Comprehension Answers 523
Subtest 9: Assembling Objects Answers 525

CHAPTER 24: **AFQT Practice Exam 1** 529
Answer Sheet for AFQT Practice Exam 1 531
Subtest 1: Arithmetic Reasoning 533
Subtest 2: Word Knowledge 537
Subtest 3: Paragraph Comprehension 540
Subtest 4: Mathematics Knowledge 544

CHAPTER 25: **AFQT Practice Exam 1: Answers and Explanations** 547
Subtest 1: Arithmetic Reasoning Answers 547
Subtest 2: Word Knowledge Answers 550
Subtest 3: Paragraph Comprehension Answers 552
Subtest 4: Mathematics Knowledge Answers 553

CHAPTER 26: **AFQT Practice Exam 2** 557
Answer Sheet for AFQT Practice Exam 2 559
Subtest 1: Arithmetic Reasoning 561
Subtest 2: Word Knowledge 565

  Subtest 3: Paragraph Comprehension................................568
  Subtest 4: Mathematics Knowledge................................571

CHAPTER 27: AFQT Practice Exam 2: Answers and Explanations............575
  Subtest 1: Arithmetic Reasoning Answers............................575
  Subtest 2: Word Knowledge Answers................................579
  Subtest 3: Paragraph Comprehension Answers........................581
  Subtest 4: Mathematics Knowledge Answers..........................582

PART 7: THE PART OF TENS 587

CHAPTER 28: Ten Surefire Ways to Fail the ASVAB..........................589
  Choosing Not to Study at All 589
  Failing to Realize How Scores Are Used 590
  Studying for Unnecessary Subtests 590
  Losing Focus..590
  Panicking over Time 591
  Deciding Not to Check the Answers 591
  Making Wild Guesses or Not Guessing at All........................591
  Changing Answers...592
  Memorizing the Practice Test Questions 592
  Misunderstanding the Problem......................................592

CHAPTER 29: Ten Tips for Doing Well on the AFQT..........................593
  As Soon as the Test Starts, Write Down What You're Likely to Forget....593
  Read All the Answer Choices before Deciding.......................593
  Don't Expect Perfect Word Matches 594
  Read the Passages before the Questions 594
  Reread to Find Specific Information 594
  Base Conclusions Only on What You Read 594
  Change Percents to Decimals 594
  Understand Inverses...595
  Remember How Ratios, Rates, and Scales Compare 595
  Make Sure Your Answers Are Reasonable.............................595

CHAPTER 30: Ten Ways to Boost Your Math and English Skills...............597
  Practice Doing Math Problems 597
  Put Away Your Calculator..597
  Memorize the Order of Operations 598
  Know Your Geometry Formulas 598
  Keep a Word List 599
  Study Latin and Greek...599
  Use Flashcards..600
  Read More, Watch TV Less..600
  Practice Finding Main and Supporting Points 600
  Use a Study Guide...600

APPENDIX: WORD KNOWLEDGE RESOURCES 601

INDEX 619

Introduction

If you're reading this book, there's a good chance that you want to join the United States military. Perhaps it's been your lifelong dream to drive a tank, fire a machine gun, or blow things up (legally). Maybe you've always wanted to learn how to cook for 2,000 people at a time. Possibly you were attracted to the military because of education and training opportunities, the chance to travel, or huge enlistment bonuses. In any event, by now you've discovered that you can't just walk into a recruiter's office and say, "Hey, I'm here. Sign me up!" These days, you have to pass the ASVAB.

The ASVAB (short for Armed Services Vocational Aptitude Battery) is unlike any test you've ever taken. It covers standard academic areas, such as math and English, but it also measures your knowledge of mechanics, electronics, science, and assembling objects.

The good news is that you need to do well on some of the subtests but not necessarily all of them. In this book, you find out what you need to know to do well on *all* the subtests. You also get the information you need to figure out which subtests require good scores for your dream job. I include charts and tables that tie together military jobs and test scores, information you may see on the test, and even practice questions in each area to help you determine how much you need to study to get the right scores for your personal goals.

About This Book

The computer enlistment version of the ASVAB has ten separate subtests that result in a total of nine scores, and the paper version of the test has nine subtests to provide you with those same nine scores (two of the subtests are combined). This book shows you what to expect on each subtest, offers strategies for studying each subject area, gives you test-taking (and guessing) tips, and provides three full-length practice tests that help you determine your strengths and weaknesses. These practice tests also help you prepare mentally for taking the real test — you can use them to get in the zone. I've thrown in two extra tests that cover the four most important subtests of the ASVAB that make up the AFQT (Armed Forces Qualification Test) score at no extra cost.

Although much of the material covered on the ASVAB is taught in practically every high school in the country, you may have slept through part of the info or performed a major brain-dump as soon as the ink was dry on your diploma. For that reason, you also get a basic review of the relevant subject areas to help refresh your memory, as well as some pointers on where to find more information if you need it. This book also includes detailed, point-by-point study plans you can use as test day approaches; you can find them in Chapter 3.

Foolish Assumptions

While writing and revising this book, I made a few assumptions about you — namely, who you are and why you picked up this book. I assume the following:

- » You've come here for test-taking tips and other helpful information. You may be a nervous test-taker.
- » You want to take a few ASVAB practice tests to measure your current knowledge in various subject areas to help you develop a study plan.
- » You want the military job of your dreams, and passing the ASVAB (or certain sections of it) is really important to you.
- » You're in a high school that participates in the ASVAB Career Exploration Program, and you want to know what to expect on the test.

Icons Used in This Book

Throughout this book, you find icons that help you use the material in this book. Here's a rundown of what they mean:

TIP This icon alerts you to helpful hints regarding the ASVAB. Tips can help you save time and avoid frustration.

REMEMBER This icon reminds you of important information you should read carefully.

WARNING This icon flags actions and ideas that may prove hazardous to your plans of conquering the ASVAB. Often, this icon accompanies common mistakes or misconceptions people have about the ASVAB or questions on the test.

TECHNICAL STUFF This icon points out information that is interesting, enlightening, or in-depth but that isn't necessary for you to read.

EXAMPLE This icon points out sample test questions that appear in review chapters.

Beyond the Book

In addition to what you're reading right now, this book comes with a free access-anywhere Cheat Sheet that includes tips to help you prepare for the ASVAB. To get this Cheat Sheet, simply go to www.dummies.com and type **ASVAB For Dummies Cheat Sheet** in the Search box.

You also get access to seven full-length online practice tests (six ASVAB and one AFQT) and hundreds of flashcards. To gain access to the online practice, all you have to do is register. Just follow these simple steps:

1. Go to www.dummies.com/go/getaccess.
2. **Create a new account or log in to an existing account.**

   If you create a new account you'll receive an email confirmation. Click through to finish creating a new account.

   Note: If you do not receive a confirmation email after creating your account, please check your spam folder before contacting us through our Technical Support website at http://support.wiley.com or by phone at 877-762-2974.

3. **After you've logged into your new or existing account, select "Dummies" under the "Select the brand for your product" header.**
4. **Select your title from the drop-down list. Choose "2025/2026 ASVAB For Dummies (+7 Practice Tests, Flashcards, & Videos Online)."**
5. **Answer a validation question about the product, and then click "Redeem."**

You must choose the correct title and edition from the drop-down list. Select the option that says **"2025/2026 ASVAB For Dummies (+7 Practice Tests, Flashcards, & Videos Online)."**

Now you're ready to go! You can come back to the practice material as often as you want — simply log on with the username and password you created during your initial login.

Your registration is good for one year from the day you redeem your product.

But wait! There's more! This book also comes with some helpful online videos that cover all the topics that you need to study to do well on the ASVAB. Check them out at www.dummies.com/go/asvabvideos.

Where to Go from Here

You don't have to read this book from cover to cover to score well. I suggest that you begin with Chapters 1 and 2. That way, you can get a feel for how the ASVAB is organized (along with the most up-to-date changes on the test) and which subtests may be important for the military service branch and job of your choice. This plan of attack helps you set up logical and effective goals to maximize your study efforts.

You may want to start by taking one of the practice tests in Part 6. By using this method, you can discover which subjects you're strong in and which subjects you could spend a little more time reviewing. If you choose this technique, you can use the other practice tests to measure your progress after reading through and studying the subject chapters.

If you're taking the ASVAB for the purpose of enlisting in the U.S. military, you may want to skip entire chapters, depending on your career goals. For example, if the military careers you're interested in don't require a great score on the Mechanical Comprehension subtest, you may want to spend less time studying that topic and concentrate your study time on chapters focusing on developing knowledge or skills that your dream job does require.

I wish you luck on taking this battery of tests, and if you want to join the military, I hope you have a tremendously successful journey!

1
Getting Started with the ASVAB

IN THIS PART . . .

Get the details about what topics are covered on the ASVAB, how your score is calculated, and the policies on retaking the test if you didn't do so well on your first try.

Check out how line scores relate to military jobs and how each branch of the military computes those scores.

Review test-taking strategies and get some last-minute preparation tips.

IN THIS CHAPTER

» Checking out the different versions of the ASVAB

» Figuring out what each subtest covers

» Computing the Armed Forces Qualification Test (AFQT) score

» Taking the ASVAB again

Chapter 1
Putting the ASVAB under a Microscope

The Armed Services Vocational Aptitude Battery (ASVAB) consists of ten tests that cover subjects ranging from general science principles to vocabulary. Your ASVAB test results determine whether you qualify for military service and, if so, which jobs you qualify for. The ASVAB isn't an IQ test. The military isn't trying to figure out how smart you are. The ASVAB specifically measures your ability to be trained to do a specific job. Although you don't see the same questions in this book that appear on the test — ASVAB materials are tightly controlled items — you do see the same concepts. (Read that as "Don't waste your time memorizing the answers to these questions. Focus on the concepts instead.")

The famous Chinese general Sun Tzu said, "Know your enemy." To develop an effective plan of study (check out Chapter 3) and score well on the ASVAB, it's important to understand how the ASVAB is organized and how the military uses the scores from the subtests. This chapter describes the different versions of the ASVAB, the organization of the subtests, how the AFQT score is calculated, and the various services' policies for retaking the ASVAB.

Knowing Which Version You're Taking

Regardless of the military branch you want to join, you take the same ASVAB everyone else takes. That goes for the Army, Air Force, Navy, Marine Corps, Coast Guard, and Space Force. Every test-taker gets questions from the same pool, so you and every other potential enlistee are all on equal ground.

However, the ASVAB comes in five versions, depending on where and why you take it. The varieties of the test are essentially the same; they're just administered differently. Table 1-1 boils them down.

TABLE 1-1 Versions of the ASVAB

Version	How You Take It	Format	Purpose
Student	Given to juniors and seniors in high school; it's administered through a cooperative program between the Department of Education and the Department of Defense at high schools across the United States	Paper	Its primary purpose is to provide a tool for guidance counselors to use when recommending civilian career areas to high school students (though it can be used for enlistment if taken within two years of enlistment). For example, if a student scores high in electronics, the counselor can recommend electronics career paths. If a student is interested in military service, the counselor then refers them to the local military recruiting offices.
Enlistment	Given through a military recruiter at a Military Entrance Processing Station (MEPS) or at a satellite testing site	Usually computer, may be paper	This version of the ASVAB is used by all the military branches for the purpose of enlistment qualification and to determine which military jobs a recruit can successfully be trained in.
Enlistment Screening Test (EST)	Given at the discretion of a military recruiter for a quick enlistment qualification screening	Computer	These mini-ASVABs aren't qualification tests; they're strictly recruiting and screening tools. The EST contains about 50 questions similar but not identical to questions on the AFQT portion of the ASVAB. The test is used to help estimate an applicant's probability of obtaining qualifying ASVAB scores.
Pre-screening, internet-delivered Computerized Adaptive Test (PiCAT)	Online, on your own time after receiving an access code from your recruiter	Computer	The PiCAT is an unproctored, full version of the ASVAB. You take it on your own time, but you must take a verification test at a MEPS to validate your score. The verification test typically takes 25 to 30 minutes to complete.
Armed Forces Classification Test (AFCT)	Given at installation educational centers to people already in the military through the Defense Manpower Data Center	Computer	At some point during your military career, you may want to retrain for a different job. If you need higher ASVAB scores to qualify for such retraining, or if you're a commissioned officer who wants to become a warrant officer, you can take the AFCT. The AFCT is essentially the same as the other versions of the ASVAB.

The vast majority of military applicants are processed through a MEPS, where they take the computerized format of the ASVAB (called the CAT-ASVAB, short for *computerized-adaptive testing ASVAB*), undergo a physical exam, and run through a security screening, many times all in one trip. The paper-and-pencil (P&P) version is most often given in high school and at Mobile Examination Test (MET) sites located throughout the United States. Most MET sites use paper versions of the test.

Mapping Out the ASVAB Subtests

The computerized format of the ASVAB contains ten separately timed subtests, with the Auto & Shop Information subtest split in two. The paper format of the test has nine subtests (the Auto & Shop Information subtests are combined). The two formats differ in the number of questions in each subtest and the amount of time you have for each one. The CAT-ASVAB now often contains *tryout questions.* These questions haven't been used on an officially scored ASVAB; test-makers use your responses to them to ensure the questions are good enough to use on future versions of the test. Each tester sees 15 tryout questions in two, three, or four of the subtests. These questions don't count toward your score, but you still have to answer them. The tryout questions are only on the computerized version of the test; they're not on the paper version. When you get tryout questions in a subtest, you get extra time to complete it.

Table 1-2 outlines the ASVAB subtests in the order that you take them in the enlistment (computerized or paper) and student (paper only) versions of the test; you can also see which chapters to turn to when you want to review that content.

TABLE 1-2 The ASVAB Subtests in Order

Subtest	Questions/Time without Tryout Questions (CAT-ASVAB)	Possible Questions/Time with Tryout Questions (CAT-ASVAB)	Questions/Time (Paper Version)	Content	Chapter
General Science (GS)	15 questions, 12 minutes	30 questions, 25 minutes	25 questions, 11 minutes	General principles of biological and physical sciences	Chapters 10, 11, and 12
Arithmetic Reasoning (AR)	15 questions, 55 minutes	30 questions, 113 minutes	30 questions, 36 minutes	Word problems involving high school math concepts that require calculations	Chapter 9
Word Knowledge (WK)	15 questions, 9 minutes	30 questions, 18 minutes	35 questions, 11 minutes	Correct meaning of a word; occasionally antonyms (words with opposite meanings)	Chapter 4
Paragraph Comprehension (PC)	10 questions, 27 minutes	25 questions, 75 minutes	15 questions, 13 minutes	Questions based on passages (usually a couple of hundred words) that you read	Chapter 5
Mathematics Knowledge (MK)	15 questions, 31 minutes	30 questions, 65 minutes	25 questions, 24 minutes	High school math, including algebra and geometry	Chapters 6, 7, and 8
Electronics Information (EI)	15 questions, 10 minutes	30 questions, 21 minutes	20 questions, 9 minutes	Electrical principles, basic electronic circuitry, and electronic terminology	Chapter 16
Auto & Shop Information (AS)	10 Auto Information questions, 7 minutes; 10 Shop Information questions, 7 minutes	25 Auto Information questions, 18 minutes; 25 Shop Information questions, 17 minutes	25 questions, 11 minutes	Knowledge of automobiles, shop terminology, and tool use	Chapters 13 and 14
Mechanical Comprehension (MC)	15 questions, 22 minutes	30 questions, 42 minutes	25 questions, 19 minutes	Basic mechanical and physical principles	Chapter 15
Assembling Objects (AO)*	15 questions, 18 minutes	30 questions, 38 minutes	25 questions, 15 minutes	Spatial orientation	Chapter 17

*The Assembling Objects subtest isn't part of the student version of the test.

CHAPTER 1 **Putting the ASVAB under a Microscope** 9

Eyeing Easy, Medium, and Hard Questions

The questions on the ASVAB range in difficulty from easy to hard, with most falling somewhere in the middle. On the paper-and-pencil version of the test, questions are presented in random order. For instance, you may see a hard question right off the bat, followed by a pair of easy questions and then a medium question. On the CAT-ASVAB, which I cover in more detail in Chapter 3, the questions you have to answer depend on how well you're performing on the test. If you answer an easy question correctly, the computer will most likely give you a question of medium difficulty next; if you answer that one right, the next question is probably going to be harder.

TIP The CAT-ASVAB is designed to figure out what you know in the shortest amount of time possible. That's why some people believe the ASVAB is harder (or in some cases, easier) than they thought it would be. Essentially, the test says, "This applicant knows that 5 + 5 = 10, so let's see whether they know what x represents in the equation $5x = 10$. No? Okay — let's see whether they know what 10 − 5 equals."

Deciphering ASVAB Scores

The Department of Defense is an official U.S. government agency, so (of course) it provides plenty of detail regarding your scores. When you receive your ASVAB score results, you don't see just one score; you see several. Figure 1-1 shows an example of an ASVAB score card used by high school guidance counselors (for people who take the student version — see "Knowing Which Version You're Taking" for details).

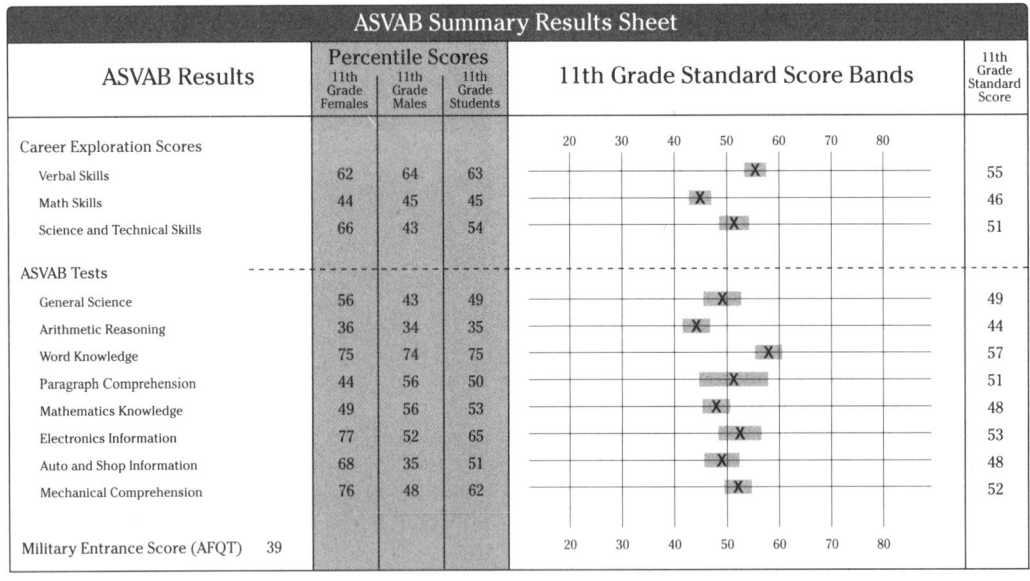

ASVAB Results	11th Grade Females	11th Grade Males	11th Grade Students	11th Grade Standard Score Bands	11th Grade Standard Score
Career Exploration Scores					
Verbal Skills	62	64	63		55
Math Skills	44	45	45		46
Science and Technical Skills	66	43	54		51
ASVAB Tests					
General Science	56	43	49		49
Arithmetic Reasoning	36	34	35		44
Word Knowledge	75	74	75		57
Paragraph Comprehension	44	56	50		51
Mathematics Knowledge	49	56	53		48
Electronics Information	77	52	65		53
Auto and Shop Information	68	35	51		48
Mechanical Comprehension	76	48	62		52
Military Entrance Score (AFQT)	39				

FIGURE 1-1: A sample ASVAB score card used by high school guidance counselors.

© John Wiley & Sons, Inc.

Figure 1-2 depicts an example of an ASVAB score card used for military enlistment purposes.

So what do all these different scores actually mean? Check out the following sections to find out.

SAMPLE CAT-ASVAB TEST SCORE REPORT

Testing Site ID: 521342   Service: AF

Testing Session: Date: 2013/05/18   Starting Time: 15:30

Applicant: Jane P. Doe   SSN: 333-33-3333

Test Form: 02E   Test Type: Initial

Standard Scores:	GS	AR	WK	PC	MK	EI	AS	MC	AO	VE
	63	59	60	52	56	81	64	62	52	58

COMPOSITE SCORES:

Army:	GT	CL	CO	EL	FA	GM	MM	OF	SC	ST
	118	121	128	130	127	132	134	129	128	125

Air Force:	M	A	G	E
	91	76	83	96

Navy/CG:	GT	EL	BEE	ENG	MEC	MEC2	NUC	OPS	HM	ADM
	117	259	234	120	185	173	235	225	177	114

Army:	MM	GT	EL
	139	122	134

SAMPLE CAT-ASVAB TEST SCORE REPORT

FIGURE 1-2: A sample ASVAB score card used for military enlistment purposes.

© John Wiley & Sons, Inc.

Defining all the scores

When you take a test in high school, you usually receive a score that's pretty easy to understand — A, B, C, D, or F. (If you do really well, the teacher may even draw a smiley face on the top of the page.) If only your ASVAB scores were as easy to understand.

In the following list, you see how your ASVAB test scores result in several different kinds of scores:

» **Raw score:** This score is the total number of points you receive on each subtest of the ASVAB. Although you don't see your raw scores on the ASVAB score cards, they're used to calculate the other scores.

You can't use the practice tests in this book (or any other ASVAB study guide) to calculate your probable ASVAB score. ASVAB scores are calculated by using raw scores, and raw scores aren't determined by adding the number of right or wrong answers. On the actual ASVAB, harder questions are worth more points than easier questions are.

» **Standard scores:** The various subtests of the ASVAB are reported on the score cards as standard scores. A *standard score* is calculated by converting your raw score based on a standard distribution of scores with a mean of 50 and a standard deviation of 10.

Don't confuse a standard score with the graded-on-a-curve score you may have seen on school tests — where the scores range from 1 to 100 with the majority of students scoring between 70 and 100. With standard scores, the majority score is between 30 and 70. That means that a standard score of 50 is an average score and that a score of 60 is an above-average score.

CHAPTER 1 **Putting the ASVAB under a Microscope**   11

» **Percentile scores:** These scores range from 1 to 99. They express how well you did in comparison with another group called the *norm.* On the student version's score card, the norm is fellow students in your same grade (except for the AFQT score).

On the enlistment and student score cards, the AFQT score is presented as a percentile with the score normed using the *1997 Profile of American Youth,* a national probability sample of 18-to-23-year-olds who took the ASVAB in 1997. For example, if you receive a percentile score of 72, you can say you scored as well as or better than 72 out of 100 of the norm group who took the test. (And by the way, this statistic from 1997 isn't a typo. The ASVAB is occasionally re-normed; the last time was in 2004, and the sample group used for the norm was those folks who took the test in 1997. There's no official word on when the next re-norming will happen.)

» **Composite scores (line scores):** *Composite scores* are individually computed by each service branch. Each branch has its own particular system when compiling various standard scores into individual composite scores. These scores are used by the different branches to determine job qualifications. Find out much more about this topic in Chapter 2.

Understanding the big four: Your AFQT scores

The ASVAB doesn't have an overall score. When you hear someone say, "I got an 80 on my ASVAB," that person is probably talking about their percentile on the Armed Forces Qualification Test (AFQT) score, not an overall ASVAB score. The AFQT score determines whether you even qualify to enlist in the military, and only four subtests are used to compute it:

» Word Knowledge (WK)

» Paragraph Comprehension (PC)

» Arithmetic Reasoning (AR)

» Mathematics Knowledge (MK)

Each job in the military, from food service positions to specialty jobs in the medical field, requires a certain combination of line scores that can include the scores you get on the AFQT. The subtests that aren't part of the AFQT are used only to determine the jobs you qualify for. (See Chapter 2 for information on how the military uses the individual subtests.)

TIP Figure out which areas to focus on based on your career goals. If you're not interested in a job that requires a great score on the Mechanical Comprehension subtest, you don't need to invest a lot of time studying for it. As you're preparing for the ASVAB, remember to plan your study time wisely. If you don't need to worry about the Assembling Objects subtest, don't bother with that chapter in this book. Spend the time on Word Knowledge or Arithmetic Reasoning. Keep in mind, though, if you don't have a desired job or aren't sure about your options, it's best to study this book and take the practice tests, focusing on all areas of the ASVAB. Doing well on each subtest will broaden your available job choices and make you a more desirable candidate.

Calculating the AFQT score

The military brass (or at least its computers) determines your AFQT score through a very particular process:

1. **Add the value of your Word Knowledge score to your Paragraph Comprehension score.**
2. **Convert the result of Step 1 to a scaled score, ranging from 20 to 62.**

    This score is known as your *Verbal Expression* or VE score.

3. **To get your raw AFQT score, double your VE score and then add your Arithmetic Reasoning (AR) score and your Mathematics Knowledge (MK) score to it.**

   The basic equation looks like this:

   Raw AFQT Score = 2VE + AR + MK

4. **Convert your raw score to a percentile score, which basically compares your results to the results of thousands of other ASVAB test-takers.**

   For example, a score of 50 means that you scored as well as or better than 50 percent of the individuals the military is comparing you to.

Looking at AFQT score requirements for enlistment

AFQT scores are grouped into six main categories based on the percentile score ranges in Table 1-3. Category III and Category IV are divided into subgroups because the services sometimes use this chart for internal tracking purposes, enlistment limits, and enlistment incentives. Based on your scores, the military decides how trainable you may be to perform jobs in the service.

TABLE 1-3 AFQT Scores and Trainability

Category	Percentile Score	Trainability
I	93–99	Outstanding
II	65–92	Excellent
III A	50–64	Above average
III B	31–49	Average
IV	10–30	Below average
V	1–9	Not trainable

The U.S. Congress has directed that the military can't accept Category V recruits or more than 4 percent of recruits from Category IV, although the Secretary of Defense may increase that number to 20 percent if necessary. People without high school diplomas must score at or above the 31st percentile (that is, be in Category III B or higher) to be eligible for enlistment, and even then, they must have an alternative credential, such as a General Educational Development (GED) certificate or another high school equivalency certificate. If your score falls in Category III B or anywhere in Category IV, your chances of being able to enlist are smaller (especially if other Category III B recruits beat you to it) because at least 60 percent of recruits must score above average on the AFQT.

Depending on whether you have a high school diploma or a passing score on your state's approved high school equivalency test (such as the GED), the military has different AFQT score requirements. Check out Table 1-4.

The minimum scores required in each branch can — and do — change frequently because the military has different needs at different times. For example, at the height of Operation Iraqi Freedom, the Army accepted recruits with GEDs who scored 31 on the AFQT.

TABLE 1-4 AFQT Score Requirements

Branch of Service	Minimum AFQT Score with High School Diploma	Minimum AFQT Score with High School Equivalency Test Certificate	Special Circumstances
Air Force and Space Force	31	50	The Air Force allows less than 1 percent of its enlistees each year to have a high school equivalency test certificate instead of a high school diploma. If you have a high school equivalency certificate, you must have at least 15 hours of college credits to gain the same eligibility as a high school graduate and wait for an applicant slot to become available.
Army	31	50	The Army sometimes approves waivers for applicants with high school equivalency test certificates and AFQT scores below 31.
Coast Guard	40	Varies	If you have a high school equivalency certificate, the minimum AFQT score doesn't apply. If your ASVAB line scores qualify you for a specific job and you're willing to enlist in that job, your recruiter may be able to put in a waiver. Very few people (about 5 percent) each year are allowed to enlist with a high school equivalency certificate.
Marine Corps	31	50	Sometimes the Marines issue waivers for people with scores below the minimum thresholds, particularly when the Corps is struggling to fill enlistment goals.
Navy	31	50	If you enlist with a high school equivalency certificate, you must have at least 15 college credits.
Space Force	60		You may be able to enlist in the Space Force with a high school equivalency certificate; in some cases, enlistees with equivalency certificates must have at least 15 college credits.

Checking out the military's AFQT requirements for special programs

Achieving the minimum required AFQT score established by an individual branch gets your foot in the door, but the higher you score, the better. For example, if you need a medical or criminal history waiver in order to enlist, the military personnel who make those decisions are more likely to take a chance on you if they think you're a pretty smart cookie than they would be if you barely made the minimum qualifying score.

REMEMBER

Enlistment programs are subject to change without notice based on the current recruiting needs of the service. Your recruiter can give you the most up-to-date information.

TIP

If you don't know which kind of job you want to do in the military, the ASVAB helps you and the military determine your potential ability for different types of jobs. If you're in this situation, review all the chapters in this book, brushing up on the basic principles of everything from science to electronics, but focus on the four subtests that enable you to qualify for enlistment: Word Knowledge, Paragraph Comprehension, Arithmetic Reasoning, and Mathematics Knowledge. Following this plan ensures a relatively accurate appraisal of your aptitude for various military jobs.

> **MILITARY OPENS COMBAT ROLES TO WOMEN**
>
> Jobs that were traditionally open only to male members of the U.S. Armed Forces are now open to women — but it took 378 years for the military to change the way it does business.
>
> The first militias in the New World began organizing in 1636, and men were the only ones who served. Even after June 14, 1775, the official "birthday" of the U.S. Army, the military denied women the opportunity to enlist. However, females sometimes traveled with the troops to act as nurses, laundresses, and cooks if they could prove their usefulness to troop commanders.
>
> History occasionally reveals a woman who disguised herself as a man to join the fight between 1776 and 1948. (During the Civil War, a nominal number of females served as spies while others continued to fight on the front lines disguised as men.)
>
> Congress passed the Women's Armed Services Integration Act on June 12, 1948, which gave women the right to enlist during peacetime and to collect veteran benefits.
>
> Sixty-seven years later, on December 3, 2015, Secretary of Defense Ash Carter ordered the full integration of women in the Armed Forces. Under that order, all military occupational specialties are now open to women — including ground combat roles and special operations, such as Navy SEALs, Army Special Forces and Rangers, and Air Force Special Tactics.
>
> New, gender-neutral job titles replaced traditional titles such as "artilleryman" and "reconnaissance man." Now those jobs are referred to as *artillery technician* and *reconnaissance Marine*.

Do-Over: Retaking the ASVAB

An AFQT score between 0 and 9 tells the military that you're not trainable, so no branch of the service accepts people who score in that range. Even if you score higher than that, you can fail to achieve a score high enough to enlist in the service branch you want. This means you need to work on one (or more) of the four core areas: Mathematics Knowledge, Arithmetic Reasoning, Paragraph Comprehension, and Word Knowledge. Parts 2 and 3 of this book are specifically designed to help you improve your scores on these four subtests.

When you're sure you're ready, you can apply (through your recruiter) to take the ASVAB. After you take the ASVAB for the first time, you can retake the test after one month (taking the ASVAB in high school does count for retest purposes). After the first retest, you must wait another month to test again. From that point on, you must wait at least six months before taking the ASVAB again.

You can't retake the ASVAB on a whim or whenever you simply feel like it. Each of the services has its own rules concerning whether it allows a retest, and I explain them in the following sections.

REMEMBER ASVAB test results are valid for two years, as long as you aren't in the military. In most cases, after you join the military, your ASVAB scores remain valid as long as you're in. In other words, except in a few cases, you can use your enlistment ASVAB scores to qualify for retraining years later.

U.S. Army retest policy

The Army allows a retest in one of the following instances:

- The applicant's previous ASVAB test has expired.
- The applicant failed to achieve an AFQT score high enough to qualify for enlistment.
- Unusual circumstances occur, such as if an applicant, through no fault of their own, is unable to complete the test.

REMEMBER: Army recruiters aren't authorized to have applicants retested for the sole purpose of increasing aptitude area scores to meet standards prescribed for enlistment options or programs.

U.S. Air Force and U.S. Space Force retest policy

For the U.S. Air Force, the intent of retesting is for an applicant to improve the last ASVAB scores so the enlistment options increase. Before any retest is administered, the recruiting flight chief must interview the applicant in person or by telephone and then give approval for the retest.

Here are a few other policies to remember:

- The Air Force doesn't allow retesting for applicants after they've enlisted in the Delayed Entry Program (DEP).
- Current policy allows retesting of applicants who aren't holding a job/aptitude area reservation and/or who aren't in DEP but already have qualifying test scores.
- Retesting is authorized when the applicant's current line scores (mechanical, administrative, general, and electronic) limit the ability to match an Air Force skill with their qualifications.

U.S. Navy retest policy

The Navy allows retesting of applicants

- Whose previous ASVAB tests have expired
- Who fail to achieve a qualifying AFQT score for enlistment in the Navy

In most cases, individuals in the Delayed Entry Program (DEP) can't retest.

U.S. Marine Corps retest policy

The Marine Corps authorizes a retest if the applicant's previous test has expired. Otherwise, recruiters can request a retest if the initial scores don't appear to reflect the applicant's true capability, considering the applicant's education, training, and experience.

REMEMBER: For the Marine Corps, the retest can't be requested solely because the applicant's initial test scores didn't meet the standards prescribed for enlistment options or programs.

TRACING THE TESTING TRAIL

In 1948, Congress made the Department of Defense develop a uniform screening test to be used by all the services. The Defense Department came up with the Armed Forces Qualification Test (AFQT). This test consisted of 100 multiple-choice questions in areas such as math, vocabulary, spatial relations, and mechanical ability. The military used this test until the mid-1970s. Each branch of the service set its own minimum qualification (AFQT) score.

When the military decides to do something, it often acts with the lightning speed of a snail carrying a 30-pound rucksack. In the 1960s, the Department of Defense decided to develop a standardized military selection and classification test and to administer it in high schools. That's where your old buddy, the ASVAB, came from. The first ASVAB test was given in 1968, but the military didn't use it for recruiting purposes for several years. In 1973, the draft ended, and the nation entered the contemporary period in which all military recruits are volunteers. In 1976, the ASVAB became the official entry test used by all services.

The ASVAB remained unchanged until 1980, when it underwent its first revision. The subtest areas remained the same, but several of the questions were updated to keep up with changes in technology.

In 1993, the computerized version was released for limited operational testing, but it didn't begin to see wide-scale use until 1996. The questions on the computerized version of the ASVAB were identical to the questions on the paper version. It wasn't until the end of 2002 that the ASVAB finally underwent a major revision. Two subtests (Coding Speed and Numerical Operations) were eliminated, and a new subtest (Assembling Objects) was added to the computerized version. Also during the 2002 revision, all the questions were updated, and the order of the subtests was changed. The revised ASVAB was first rolled out in the computerized format, and the paper versions of the test were updated during the next year. Today, the Department of Defense is considering adding new subtests, including one called "Complex Reasoning" and some form of a cyber test to produce a "computational thinking" composite score. The Department of Defense currently updates the computerized version of the ASVAB on a rolling basis.

U.S. Coast Guard retest policy

For Coast Guard enlistments, six months must have elapsed since an applicant's last test before they may retest solely for the purpose of raising scores to qualify for a particular enlistment option.

The Coast Guard Recruiting Center may authorize retesting after one calendar month has passed from an initial ASVAB test if substantial reason exists to believe the initial test scores or subtest scores don't reflect an applicant's education, training, or experience.

IN THIS CHAPTER

» Finding out there's more to life than the AFQT score

» Making sense out of line scores

» Discovering how each military branch uses line scores

Chapter 2
Knowing What It Takes to Get Your Dream Job

The Armed Forces Qualification Test (AFQT) portion of the ASVAB is your most important score because it determines whether you can join the service branch of your choice. However, qualifying to join is only part of the picture. Unless you'd be content to spend your military career performing a job you didn't choose, you need to understand how the ASVAB relates to various military job opportunities.

Civilian employers generally use a person's education and experience level when selecting candidates for a job position, but in the military, the vast majority of all enlisted jobs are entry-level positions. The military doesn't require you to have a college degree in computer science before you're hired to become a computer programmer. You don't even have to have any previous computer experience, nor does the military care if you do. The military sends you to advanced individual training (the school you must complete after basic training) to teach you everything it wants you to know.

Sounds like a good deal, right? So what's the catch? Well, believe me — the military spends big bucks turning high school graduates into highly trained and skilled aircraft mechanics, language specialists, and rescue divers. In an average year, the services aim to enlist about 150,000 new recruits. Each and every recruit has to be sent to a military school to train for a job. Uncle Sam needs a way to determine whether these recruits have the mental aptitude to succeed at that job — preferably before he spends people's hard-earned tax dollars.

Enter the ASVAB. The services combine various ASVAB subtest scores into groupings called composite scores or line scores. Through years of trial and error, each individual military service has determined what minimum composite scores are required to successfully complete its various job-training programs. In this chapter, you discover how those test scores translate into finding the military job of your dreams.

Eyeing How ASVAB Scores Determine Military Training Programs and Jobs

Each service branch has its own system of scores. Recruiters and military job counselors use these scores, along with factors such as job availability, security clearance eligibility, and medical qualifications, to match up potential recruits with military jobs.

REMEMBER

During the initial enlistment process, your service branch determines your military job or enlistment program based on established minimum *line scores:* various combinations of scores from individual subtests (see the next section for details). If you get high enough scores in the right areas, you can get the job you want — as long as that job is available and you meet other qualification factors.

For active duty, the Army is the only service that looks at the scores and offers a guaranteed job for all its new enlistees, aside from those enlisting in the infantry or trying out for Special Forces. In other words, nearly every single Army recruit knows what their job is going to be before signing the enlistment contract. The other active duty services use a combination of guaranteed jobs or guaranteed aptitude and career areas:

- **Air Force:** About 40 percent of active duty Air Force recruits enlist with a guaranteed job. The majority enlists in one of four guaranteed aptitude areas, and during basic training, these recruits are assigned to a job that falls into that aptitude area.
- **Coast Guard:** The Coast Guard rarely, if ever, offers a guaranteed job in its active duty enlistment contracts. Instead, new Coast Guardsmen spend their first year or so of service doing general work ("Paint that ship!") before finally applying for specific job training.
- **Marine Corps:** A vast majority of Marine Corps active duty enlistees are guaranteed one of several job fields, such as infantry, avionics, logistics, vehicle maintenance, aircraft maintenance, munitions, and so on. Each of these fields is further divided into specific sub-jobs, called Military Occupational Specialties (MOSs). Marine recruits often don't find out their actual MOSs until about halfway through basic training.
- **Navy:** Most Navy recruits enlist with a guaranteed job, but several hundred people each year also enlist in a guaranteed career area and then *strike* (apply) for the specific job within a year of graduating boot camp.
- **Space Force:** For the Space Force, you take the ASVAB and then meet with a counselor who gives you placement options based on your scores. Then you enter the Delayed Entry Program and wait until officials select you for a job. When that's done, you ship off to basic military training.

All enlistment contracts for the National Guard and reserve forces (regardless of branch) contain guarantees for a specific job. Why? Because reserve recruiters recruit for vacancies in specific reserve units, usually located within 100 miles of where a person lives.

Understanding How Each Branch Computes Line Scores

A *line score* combines various standard ASVAB scores to see which jobs or training programs you qualify for. The *standard scores* are your scores on the individual ASVAB subtests (with Word Knowledge and Paragraph Comprehension combined as a Verbal Expression score):

- General Science (GS)
- Arithmetic Reasoning (AR)
- Auto & Shop Information (AS)
- Mathematics Knowledge (MK)
- Mechanical Comprehension (MC)
- Electronics Information (EI)
- Assembling Objects (AO)
- Verbal Expression (VE), the sum of Word Knowledge (WK) and Paragraph Comprehension (PC)

Each of the military services computes its line scores differently. Some calculations even include *dummy scores* — average scores received by thousands of test-takers — for Numerical Operations (NO) and Coding Speed (CS), subtests that are no longer part of the ASVAB. The following sections outline how each branch comes up with its line scores.

Line scores and the Army

To compute line scores for job qualification, the Army combines the various scores into ten separate areas by simple addition of the ASVAB standard scores. Table 2-1 shows the line scores and the ASVAB subtests that make them up.

TABLE 2-1 The U.S. Army's Ten Line Scores

Line Score	Standard Scores Used	Formula Used
Clerical (CL)	Verbal Expression (VE), Arithmetic Reasoning (AR), and Mathematics Knowledge (MK)	VE + AR + MK
Combat (CO)	Arithmetic Reasoning (AR), Coding Speed (CS), Auto & Shop Information (AS), and Mechanical Comprehension (MC)	AR + CS + AS + MC
Electronics (EL)	General Science (GS), Arithmetic Reasoning (AR), Mathematics Knowledge (MK), and Electronics Information (EI)	GS + AR + MK + EI
Field Artillery (FA)	Arithmetic Reasoning (AR), Coding Speed (CS), Mathematics Knowledge (MK), and Mechanical Comprehension (MC)	AR + CS + MK + MC
General Maintenance (GM)	General Science (GS), Auto & Shop Information (AS), Mathematics Knowledge (MK), and Electronics Information (EI)	GS + AS + MK + EI
General Technical (GT)	Verbal Expression (VE) and Arithmetic Reasoning (AR)	VE + AR
Mechanical Maintenance (MM)	Numerical Operations (NO), Auto & Shop Information (AS), Mechanical Comprehension (MC), and Electronics Information (EI)	NO + AS + MC + EI
Operators and Food (OF)	Verbal Expression (VE), Numerical Operations (NO), Auto & Shop Information (AS), and Mechanical Comprehension (MC)	VE + NO + AS + MC
Surveillance and Communications (SC)	Verbal Expression (VE), Arithmetic Reasoning (AR), Auto & Shop Information (AS), and Mechanical Comprehension (MC)	VE + AR + AS + MC
Skilled Technical (ST)	General Science (GS), Verbal Expression (VE), Mathematics Knowledge (MK), and Mechanical Comprehension (MC)	GS + VE + MK + MC

Line scores and the Navy and Coast Guard

The Navy and Coast Guard use the standard scores directly from the ASVAB: the individual subtest scores and Verbal Expression (VE) score, which is the sum of Word Knowledge (WK) and Paragraph Comprehension (PC).

Although the Navy and Coast Guard don't use their line scores for officially determining jobs, the scores provide recruiters, job counselors, and recruits with a snapshot of which broad career areas recruits may qualify for. For example, the Navy regulation that lists the qualifications to become an Air Traffic Control Specialist states that an ASVAB score of VE + AR + MK + MC = 220 (or higher) is required for that job.

Table 2-2 shows the Navy and Coast Guard line scores that show up on the ASVAB score sheet.

TABLE 2-2 The U.S. Navy and Coast Guard's Line Scores

Line Score	Standard Scores Used	Formula Used
Engineman (ENG)	Auto & Shop Information (AS) and Mathematics Knowledge (MK)	AS + MK
Administrative (ADM)	Mathematics Knowledge (MK) and Verbal Expression (VE)	MK + VE
General Technical (GT)	Arithmetic Reasoning (AR) and Verbal Expression (VE)	AR + VE
Mechanical Maintenance (MEC)	Arithmetic Reasoning (AR), Auto & Shop Information (AS), and Mechanical Comprehension (MC)	AR + AS + MC
Health (HM)	General Science (GS), Mathematics Knowledge (MK), and Verbal Expression (VE)	GS + MK + VE
Mechanical Maintenance 2 (MEC2)	Assembling Objects (AO), Arithmetic Reasoning (AR), and Mechanical Comprehension (MC)	AO + AR + MC
Electronics (EL)	Arithmetic Reasoning (AR), Electronics Information (EI), General Science (GS), and Mathematics Knowledge (MK)	AR + EI + GS + MK
Nuclear Field (NUC)	Arithmetic Reasoning (AR), Mechanical Comprehension (MC), Mathematics Knowledge (MK), and Verbal Expression (VE)	AR + MC + MK + VE
Engineering and Electronics (BEE)	Arithmetic Reasoning (AR), General Science (GS), and two times Mathematics Knowledge (MK)	AR + GS + 2MK
Operations (OPS)	Arithmetic Reasoning (AR) and Mathematics Knowledge (MK)	AR + MK

Line scores and the Marine Corps

The Marine Corps computes its three line scores for job qualification by adding scores from various ASVAB subtests, as Table 2-3 shows.

Line scores and the Air Force and Space Force

The U.S. Air Force and Space Force use standard scores from the ASVAB subtests to derive scaled scores in four aptitude areas called MAGE (mechanical, administrative, general, and electronics). MAGE scores are calculated as *percentiles*, ranging from 0 to 99, that show your relationship to thousands of others who've taken the test. In other words, a percentile score of 51 indicates you scored better in this aptitude area than 50 percent of the testers who were used to establish the norm.

TABLE 2-3 **The Marine Corps's Line Scores**

Line Score	Standard Scores Used	Formula Used
Mechanical Maintenance (MM)	General Science (GS), Auto & Shop Information (AS), Mathematics Knowledge (MK), and Mechanical Comprehension (MC)	GS + AS + MK + MC
General Technical (GT)	Verbal Expression (VE) and Arithmetic Reasoning (AR)	VE + AR
Electronics (EL)	General Science (GS), Arithmetic Reasoning (AR), Mathematics Knowledge (MK), and Electronics Information (EI)	GS + AR + MK + EI

Table 2-4 lays out the four areas, the subtests used, and the formula used to calculate the score for each particular area. After calculating the score for a particular area, the test-scorer converts that score to a percentile.

TABLE 2-4 **The U.S. Air Force and Space Force's MAGE Scores**

Line Score	Standard Scores Used	Formula Used
Mechanical	General Science (GS), Mechanical Comprehension (MC), and two times Auto & Shop Information (AS)	GS + MC + 2AS
Administrative	Numerical Operations (NO), Coding Speed (CS), and Verbal Expression (VE)	NO + CS + VE
General	Arithmetic Reasoning (AR) and Verbal Expression (VE)	AR + VE
Electronics	General Science (GS), Arithmetic Reasoning (AR), Mathematics Knowledge (MK), and Electronics Information (EI)	GS + AR + MK + EI

SCORE! SPEAKING THE LINGO

When you sit down with your recruiter or military career counselor at the Military Entrance Processing Station (MEPS) to discuss your ASVAB scores and what you qualify for, you may think they suddenly decided to speak in a foreign language. For job-qualification purposes, remember three key terms and their definitions:

AFQT score: Calculated from the math and English subtests of the ASVAB, the Armed Forces Qualification Test (AFQT) score is used by the military to determine overall enlistment qualification. Chapter 1 explains exactly how this critical score is computed.

- **Line score:** A line score combines various standard scores and is used by the services for job qualification purposes.
- **Standard score:** A standard score refers to individual ASVAB subtest scores (that is, Verbal Expression, Arithmetic Reasoning, Mathematics Knowledge, and so on).

IN THIS CHAPTER

» Differentiating the computer and paper tests

» Developing multiple-choice strategies

» Making educated guesses

» Getting some studying and test tips

» Personalizing your own study plan

Chapter 3
Strategizing Your Way to a Good Score

How many times have you heard someone say (or even said yourself), "I just can't take tests."? A lot of people feel that way, but that mind-set isn't an option on the ASVAB or in the military. In basic training, your drill sergeant will convince you that the words "I can't" don't even *exist* in the military. If you don't believe me, try telling your drill sergeant, "I just can't do push-ups." You'll find that with sufficient practice — and your drill sergeant will ensure you get a lot of practice — you can do push-ups just as well as the next person. (Actually, I don't recommend testing this, for reasons that should be obvious.) The truth is that those who do well on tests are those who've figured out how to study efficiently and how to use a dash of test-taking psychology.

This chapter includes information on how to prepare for the test. I explain how to study, as well as how and why you should take the practice exams. In addition, you get some inside info, such as secrets for guessing when you don't know the answer to a question (although if you study for the test, you won't need to guess, right?). You can even use this chapter to create a personalized study plan based on how much time you have before test day.

Taking the Test: Computerized or Paper?

Many versions of the ASVAB exist, but you don't have any say in which one you take. The versions primarily boil down to two basic differences: the computerized version and the paper version. Each version has advantages and disadvantages, which I discuss in the following sections.

If you're taking the ASVAB as part of the student program in high school, you'll take the paper version of the test — the one that doesn't include the Assembling Objects subtest.

If you're taking the ASVAB to enlist in any branch of the military, you'll take the enlistment ASVAB. This version comes in two formats: computerized (CAT-ASVAB) and paper-and-pencil (P&P). You may even take the Pre-screening, internet-delivered Computerized Adaptive Test (PiCAT) on your own time. In any event, there's a great chance that you'll take a computerized version, because to save time and money, recruiters often accompany their applicants to the nearest Military Entrance Processing Station (MEPS) for testing, medical examination, and enlistment (one-stop shopping). MEPS only uses the computerized version, and the P&P version is offered only at Military Entrance Test (MET) sites that aren't within an easy traveling distance to MEPS. If your high school schedules a testing event, you'll most likely take the P&P version as well. Your recruiter might be able to schedule an ASVAB-only test session and bring you back in for a follow-on physical (and to sign your contract) if you can't complete everything in one day. There are 65 MEPS locations in the United States and in Puerto Rico, and MET sites are located in each state (often at National Guard armories or local high schools).

WARNING Cheating gets you thrown out of the testing location. But even if you were able to get away with looking at your neighbor's paper or computer screen, you'd fail the test. There are several versions of the test, and the people sitting around you have different questions presented in different orders.

Going paperless: The pros and cons of the computerized test

The computerized version of the ASVAB uses *computerized adaptive testing* to make sure each applicant gets questions tailored to their ability level. This version, called the CAT-ASVAB, presents test questions in a different format. It adapts the questions it offers you based on your level of proficiency (that's why it's called *adaptive*). Translation: The first test item is of average difficulty. If you answer this question correctly, the next question may be more difficult. If you answer that first question incorrectly, the computer will most likely follow with an easier question. By contrast, on the paper ASVAB, easy and hard questions are presented randomly.

The CAT-ASVAB also has fewer questions than the paper-and-pencil version has — the people who designed it did that on purpose. With this type of testing, the computer can quickly determine how much you know without asking you a full range of very easy to very hard questions.

REMEMBER Maybe it's because people today are more comfortable in front of a computer than with a pencil, but military recruiters have noted that among applicants who've taken both the paper-based and computerized versions of the ASVAB, many applicants tend to score slightly higher on the computerized version of the test.

You don't have to be a computer guru to appreciate the advantages of the computerized version of the ASVAB:

>> **It's impossible to record your answer in the wrong space on the answer sheet.** Questions and possible answers are presented on the screen, and you press the key that corresponds to your answer choice before moving on to the next question. Often, only the A, B, C, and D keys are activated when you take the test.

>> **The difficulty of the test items presented depends on whether you answered the previous question correctly.** On the two math subtests of the ASVAB, harder questions are worth more points than easier questions are, so this method helps maximize your AFQT score.

> » **You get your scores right away.** The computer automatically calculates and prints your standard scores for each subtest and your line scores for each service branch. (For more on line scores, see Chapter 2.) This machine is a pretty smart cookie — it also calculates your AFQT percentile score on the spot. You usually know whether you qualify for military enlistment on the same day you take the test and, if so, which jobs you qualify for.

On the downside, you can't skip questions or change your answers after you enter them on the CAT-ASVAB. Instead of being able to go through and immediately answer all the questions you're sure of, you have to answer each question as it comes. This can make it difficult to judge how much time to spend on a tough question before guessing and moving on. Also, if you have a few minutes at the end of the test, you can't go back and make sure you marked the correct answer to each question. Finally, the CAT-ASVAB is the only version of the test that includes tryout questions (see Chapter 1 for more information), which can stretch out your total test-taking time — but on a positive note, the tryout questions don't affect your score.

Writing on hard copy: The advantages and disadvantages of the paper version

The questions on the CAT-ASVAB are the same questions you get on the paper version. Some people feel that the P&P ASVAB provides certain advantages:

> » **You can skip questions that you don't know the answer to and come back to them later.** This option can help when you're racing against the clock and want to get as many answers right as possible. You can change an answer on the subtest you're currently working on, but you can't change an answer on a subtest after the time for that subtest has expired.
>
> » **You may not make any marks in the exam booklet; however, you may make notes on your scratch paper.** If you skip a question, you can lightly circle the item number on your answer sheet to remind yourself to go back to it. If you don't know the answer to a question, you can mentally cross off the answers that seem unlikely or wrong to you and then guess based on the remaining answers. Be sure to erase any stray marks you make on your answer sheet before time is called for that subtest.

THE PiCAT: THE ASVAB'S STAY-AT-HOME COUSIN

The Pre-screening, internet-delivered Computer Adaptive Test, or PiCAT, is the military's way of operating more efficiently and speeding up the enlistment process. It allows recruiters to give applicants a special access code to take a full-length, unproctored ASVAB on any computer. After a recruit completes the PiCAT — provided their scores are high enough to enlist in the military — the recruiter can take the recruit to MEPS for verification testing. Verification testing takes 25 to 30 minutes, and its purpose is simple: to make sure the recruit wasn't at home looking up answers to ASVAB test questions. When PiCAT scores are verified (meaning the recruit most likely didn't cheat on the test), the recruit is good to go for enlistment. When the scores *aren't* verified (meaning the recruit scored poorly on the verification test compared to how they scored on the PiCAT), the recruit must take a full-length ASVAB at MEPS. The resulting ASVAB score will be the score of record. Not all recruiters use the PiCAT, and those who do may not use it for all applicants.

Killing trees isn't the only disadvantage of the paper-based test. Other drawbacks include the following:

- **Harder questions are randomly intermingled with easier questions.** This means you can find yourself spending too much time trying to figure out the answer to a question that's too hard for you and may miss answering some easier questions at the end of the subtest, thereby lowering your overall score.

- **The paper answer sheets are scored by using an optical mark scanning machine.** The machine has a conniption when it comes across an incompletely filled-in answer circle or a stray pencil mark and will often stubbornly refuse to give you credit, even if you answered correctly.

- **Getting your scores may seem like it takes forever.** The timeline varies; however, your recruiter will have access to your score no later than 72 hours (3 days) after you finish the test (not counting days MEPS personnel don't work, such as weekend days or holidays).

Tackling Multiple-Choice Questions

Both the computerized and paper versions of the ASVAB are multiple-choice tests. You choose the correct (or most correct) answer from among the four available choices. Here are some tips to keep in mind as you approach the choices:

- **Read the directions carefully.** Most ASVAB test proctors agree — the majority of the time when there's an issue with an applicant's scores, misreading directions is a prime offender. Each subtest is preceded by a paragraph or two describing what the subtest covers and instructions on how to answer the questions.

- **Make sure you understand the question.** If you don't understand the question, you're naturally not going to be able to make the best decision when selecting an answer. Understanding the question requires attention to three particular points:

  - **Take special care to read the questions correctly.** Most questions ask something like, "Which of the following equals 2 x 3?" But sometimes, a question may ask, "Which of the following does not equal 2 x 3?" You can easily skip right over the word *not* when you're reading, assume that the answer is 6, and get the question wrong.

  - **On the math subtests, be especially careful to read the symbols.** When you're in a hurry, the + sign and the ÷ sign can look very similar. Blowing right by a negative sign or another symbol is just as easy.

  - **Make sure you understand the terms being used.** When a math problem asks you to find the product of two numbers, be sure you know what finding the product means (you have to multiply the two numbers). If you add the two numbers, you arrive at the wrong answer. If you're having a tough time remembering what equals what in math terminology, check out Chapter 6.

- **Take time to review all the answer options.** On all the subtests, you select the correct answer from only four possible answer options. On the ASVAB, you're supposed to choose the answer that is most correct. (Now and then you do the opposite and choose the answer that's least correct.) Sometimes several answers are reasonably correct for the question at hand, but only one of them is the best answer. If you don't stop to read and review all the answers, you may not choose the one that's most correct. Or if you review all the answer options, you may realize that you misread the question.

Often, a person reads a question, decides on the answer, glances at the answer options, chooses the option that agrees with their answer, marks it on the answer sheet, and then moves on. Although this approach usually works, it can sometimes lead you astray.

» **If you're taking a paper test, mark the answer carefully.** A machine scores the paper-based ASVAB answer sheets. You have to mark the answer clearly so the machine knows which answer you've selected. This means carefully filling in the space that represents the correct letter. You've done this a million times in school, but it's worth repeating: Don't use a check mark, don't circle the answer, and don't let your mark wander into the next space. If you must erase, make sure all evidence of your prior choice is gone; otherwise, the grading machine may credit you with the wrong choice or disregard your correct answer and give you no credit at all.

Incorrectly marking the answer sheet (answering Question 11 on the line for Question 12, Question 12 on the line for Question 13 — you get the idea) is a very real possibility. Be especially careful if you skip a question that you're going to return to later.

Incorrectly marking the answers can cause a real headache. If you fail to get a qualifying score, the minimum amount of time you must wait before retaking the ASVAB is one month. Even then, your journey to military glory through ASVAB torment may not be over. If within six months of a previous test, your retest AFQT score increases by 20 points or more, you'll be required by MEPCOM regulation to take an additional ASVAB test, called a *confirmation test*. (Confirmation tests can be taken only at MEPS facilities, by the way.) If you're not careful, you'll be taking three ASVABs when all you really needed to take was one. Sound fun? Chapter 1 discusses how and when you can retake the ASVAB.

When You Don't Know an Answer: Guessing Smart

On the ASVAB, guessing is sometimes okay. Guessing can help you on the paper-and-pencil version because of how the test is scored. Here's how the point system breaks down:

» If you choose the correct answer, you get one point (or more, depending on how the question is weighted).

» If you don't answer a question, you get nada.

» If you guess on a question and get the question wrong, you get nada — no worrying about losing points or getting any sort of penalty!

Don't make wild guesses if you can make educated guesses. However, if you're nearing the end of a subtest on the CAT-ASVAB and you know you won't have time to finish, try to select answers for every question. If you fail to complete a subtest, you'll be penalized; the system will score the items you didn't complete as though you answered them randomly.

The ASVAB's computer system rarely has to penalize a test-taker. On average, the computerized test takes about two hours to complete, and most people have enough time to finish (or at least come very close to finishing) the test.

Because ASVAB questions have four possible answers, you have at least a 25 percent chance of guessing correctly, which means you have chances to increase your score. There's nearly always at least one answer that isn't even close to the correct answer, so by using simple deduction, you can often narrow your choices down to three answers or fewer. Here are some things to keep in mind when eliminating answer choices:

- Don't eliminate an answer based on how frequently that answer comes up. For example, if Choice (B) has been the correct answer for the last five questions, don't assume that it must be the wrong answer for the question you're on just because that would make it six in a row.

- An answer that has *always, all, everyone, never, none,* or *no one* is usually incorrect.

- The longer the answer, the more likely that it's the correct answer. The test-makers have to get all those qualifiers in there so you can't find an example to contradict the correct answer. If you see phrases like "in many cases" or "frequently," that's often a clue that the test-makers are trying to make the answer most correct.

- If two choices are very similar in meaning, neither of them is probably the correct choice. On the other hand, if two answer options contradict each other, one of them is usually correct.

If you have to guess, never, ever go back and change the answer, unless you're absolutely, 100 percent, positively convinced that you're changing it to the correct answer and you answered incorrectly only because you had sweat in your eyes and didn't read the choices properly. The United States Air Force Senior NCO Academy conducted an in-depth study of several Air Force multiple-choice test results, taken over several years, and found that when students changed answers on their answer sheets, they changed from a right answer to a wrong answer more than 72 percent of the time!

In each of the chapters in Parts 3, 4, and 5, you find more hints for making educated guesses that are specific to those topics.

If you guess on more than one question throughout the test, choosing the same answer for every guess is a smart way to go. For example, all your guesses could be Choice (B). This technique slightly increases your chances of getting more answers correct. However, if you can eliminate Choice (B) as a wrong answer, then, by all means, choose a different answer option for that question.

Studying and Practicing for the ASVAB

The practice tests that come with this book are valuable study aids. Before you begin studying, take one of the tests. Try to duplicate the testing environment — take the entire exam at one time, time yourself, and don't allow interruptions.

The military has a saying, "Train as you fight." The same is true of the ASVAB. If you'll be taking the CAT-ASVAB, spend most of your time practicing with online tests (check out the later section "Getting Access to the Online Test Bank" for details on unlocking the online tests that come with this book). If you plan to take the paper-and-pencil version of the ASVAB, concentrate most of your efforts on the written practice tests in this book.

Get a sense of how long it takes you to complete each subtest so you know how much time you have to spend on educated guessing. After you complete each practice test, check your answers to see where you need improvement.

When you study for the ASVAB, fall in line with these study habits to make the most of your time:

- **Focus on the subtests that matter to you.** If you have a clear interest in pursuing a career in electronics, the Electronics Information subtest should be at the top of your list to ace. Although you'll want to make sure all your line scores are good (in case your desired job isn't available or you want to retrain later in your career), focusing on your expertise in certain areas of interest makes you a more desirable candidate. (See Chapter 2 for lists of the subtests that affect your acceptance into the job areas you're pursuing.)

- **Concentrate on subject areas that need improvement.** It's human nature to find yourself spending your study time on subject areas that you have an interest in or that you're good at. If you're a whiz at fixing cars, don't waste your time studying for the Auto & Shop Information subtests. You're already going to ace that part of the test, right? On the other hand, if you had a hard time in math during your high school years, you need to spend extra time brushing up on your arithmetic skills.

- **Be a loner.** You may want to study with a partner now and then so the two of you can brainstorm answers and quiz each other, but most of your studying should be done on your own.

- **Try to reduce distractions.** Always study in a well-lit, quiet area away from pets, loud music, and the TV.

- **Study in long blocks of time.** Studying for an hour or two once or twice a day is much more effective than studying 15 minutes six times a day.

- **Schedule your study times when you are rested.** Don't try to cram studying into your schedule. Quality over quantity!

- **Keep study breaks short.** A few minutes every hour is sufficient. Don't ignore breaks completely, however. Studies show that taking short breaks while you study improves how well you're able to remember information.

- **Practice the actual act of test-taking.** Practice marking answers correctly on the answer key and time yourself to see how long it takes you to answer questions.

If you're unsure of how to begin studying for the ASVAB, check out the study strategies in the later section "Outlining Your ASVAB Study Strategy." Depending on how much time you have before you take the test, the plans there can help you zero in on what's most important.

After you do some additional studying, take the second practice exam. Again, try to duplicate testing conditions. Check your answers. Compare your scores to the scores from your first test. Have you improved? If so, continue studying as you have been. If not, reconsider how you're studying or whether you're setting aside enough time to study. A school counselor or teacher can give you additional study pointers. Continue practicing with the next few tests.

A couple of weeks before the ASVAB, take the next-to-last practice test. Brush up on any of those nagging areas that still give you fits. Check to see which areas you need help with and spend more time studying those areas.

A week before your test date, take the last test. This test helps you calm your nerves before taking the ASVAB — how the test works will be fresh in your mind.

REMEMBER: Don't waste time memorizing the practice questions in this guide or any other ASVAB study guide. You won't see the same questions on the ASVAB. Use this guide and the sample tests for two purposes:

- **To determine the subject areas in which you need to improve:** Use the tips and techniques, along with standard study materials (like high school textbooks), to improve your knowledge of each specific subject.

- **To familiarize yourself with the types of test questions and the way they're presented on the test:** Getting a good idea of what all the subtests look like will improve your test-taking speed. You won't have to spend time trying to figure out how a question looks. You can spend your time answering the question.

Getting Access to the Online Test Bank

Accessing the online test bank that comes with this book is as easy as clicking a few buttons. First, visit www.dummies.com/go/getaccess. Then select the name of the book from the drop-down menu (it's listed as 2025/2026 ASVAB For Dummies). You may need to scroll all the way down to the bottom of the drop-down menu to find it. Follow the onscreen prompts to validate your purchase and enter your email address. You'll receive an email with your PIN and instructions on getting to the test bank (plus hundreds of flashcards you can use to practice your skills) by visiting www.dummies.com and looking for the text that says "Have a book PIN? Activate Now."

Personalizing Your Own Study Plan

Provided you meet the baseline AFQT score your branch requires (see Chapter 1), the ASVAB can determine the course of your entire military career. The military uses carefully calculated line scores as I explain in Chapter 2 to determine which jobs will be a good fit for you within the branch you choose. That means you need to tailor your study plan for the job you want *and* the amount of time you have left before test day.

First, determine what scores you need to get the job you want. *Note:* Minimum scores are subject to change with no notice, so your best bet is to call a recruiter to ask what the most current requirements are.

TIP: Having a backup job in mind is also a good idea in case your first choice isn't available. The military's needs change on an almost daily basis, so even if your recruiter is fairly certain your dream job will be available when you sign on the dotted line, I recommend you get used to adapting to the unexpected; you'll face it often during the course of your military career.

Your recruiter will call MEPS to find out when you can take the ASVAB, but ultimately, you control when you take it. If you need more time to prepare, ask for it. Studying at your own pace so you can absorb all the information you need is important. And don't try to put off studying until the night before you take the test; you'll end up being frazzled on test day, and your scores will show it. The recommendations in the following section can help you put together a plan of attack whatever your timeline.

32   PART 1 **Getting Started with the ASVAB**

REMEMBER: Make sure you give each subtest the necessary study time. The AFQT is one of the most important scores, but every section of the ASVAB is important. Each branch gauges your overall ability based on various combinations of your scores, so you need to do as well as possible on each subtest. Besides, scoring your best now means that if you want to switch jobs after you get some rank on your chest, you won't have to retake the ASVAB to score high enough to make the change.

Outlining Your ASVAB Study Strategy

Plan your study strategy according to the subjects you need to work on and how much time you have left. As I note in the preceding section, if you only recently met with a recruiter (or haven't met with a recruiter at all) and you're still weighing your options, you can stretch out your timeline to give yourself plenty of time to prepare. The following sections can help you map out a study plan if you know how much time you have to prepare for the test.

Before you start to study, take Practice Exam 1 in Chapter 18 so you get a good idea of which areas need a little spit-and-polish (that's an old military term that refers to shining boots). I remind you to take the first practice exam in the following sections because it's important to establish your baseline scores; it lets you see how much you know so you can decide which topics to study. Make sure you're in a quiet place where others are unlikely to disturb you, and keep a stack of scratch paper and a pencil handy.

REMEMBER: Though you won't find the questions in this book (or in any other study guide) on the test, you will see the same concepts; knowing how to solve problems, decipher complex words, and dig up facts you may have learned long ago will help you perform your best on test day.

Score each subtest according to the answers in Chapter 19. Take an objective look at your scores and determine which subtests you performed well on. If they correspond with the job you want in the military, that's great. But as the military always says, don't become complacent. You still need to study, right up to the day before the test, to make sure you're on the right track to ace the ASVAB.

If you didn't perform very well on some of the subtests, you know exactly where to focus. However, at this point, determining how you stack up against military standards on the AFQT portion of the test is most important. The scores that matter most are

- Word Knowledge
- Paragraph Comprehension
- Arithmetic Reasoning
- Mathematics Knowledge

These four subtests determine whether you're even eligible to enlist in the military. If you performed poorly on one (or more) of them, head to Parts 2 (language arts) and 3 (math) to zero in on the topics you need.

TIP: You may find creating your own flashcards with blank index cards helpful. Studies have shown that flashcards help people memorize new information, and even the act of writing down information can go a long way toward helping you remember.

Sharpening your skills with 12 weeks to prepare

Write down your scores in each subtest that matters for your first- and second-choice jobs. You can find each job's minimum score requirements by talking to your recruiter. Because you have around three months to get ready for the test, you can prioritize by studying the most critical areas early. Keep studying them right up until test day, and introduce other topics you feel are important along the way.

For example, if you've waited your whole life to become a track vehicle mechanic in the military but you're not so hot on mechanical skills or electronics, you need to spend plenty of time poring over Chapters 15 and 16; those are two of the subtests that will help the military determine whether it'll let you turn a wrench on those types of vehicles.

After you know what score you need, run through the practice questions at the end of each chapter you're studying. That's a good way to gauge your existing knowledge (and it helps you decide whether you should pick up some additional study materials at your local library). Then, if you haven't already, take the first practice test in Chapter 18. Take the whole test in one sitting, and try to replicate normal testing conditions by turning off the TV and silencing your phone; make sure you have scratch paper and a pencil, and give yourself some privacy.

Soon after you finish the test, grade your answers by using the key in Chapter 19. Read over each answer explanation so you understand what you got right or wrong. Your score on the first practice test lets you know where you stand on *all* the subtests. You may find that you need to brush up on other areas or discover that you know more than you think. In either case, you find out where to focus most of your energy over the next three months or so.

If you're so inclined, head back to Chapter 18 and highlight the questions you got wrong the first time around. Those questions can help you piece together a pattern that lets you identify which topic areas you need to brush up on.

Because there are three full practice exams in this book and online (the remaining two are in Chapters 20 and 22), aim to take one about every four weeks between now and test day. If you need to work on the topics on the AFQT (Reading Comprehension, Word Knowledge, Mathematics Knowledge, or Arithmetic Reasoning), take the AFQT practice tests between full practice tests. Here's a quick look at what your schedule may look like:

- 12 weeks out: Practice Exam 1
- 10 weeks out: AFQT Practice Exam 1
- 8 weeks out: Practice Exam 2
- 6 weeks out: AFQT Practice Exam 2
- 4 weeks out: Practice Exam 3
- 2 weeks out: AFQT Practice Exam online

Take at least one practice test online. (Find instructions for accessing this book's online test bank in the earlier section "Getting Access to the Online Test Bank" and inside the front cover of this book.) That way, you can get familiar with computerized testing — especially if you haven't taken a test for a while.

Between practice tests, read the text in the chapters you need to study. Each chapter also points you to additional resources that can help you take a more in-depth look at the subject, and sometimes you can get creative. For example, if you know you need to work on you download a crossword app on your phone or — you guessed it — read as often Fortunately, free apps are available to help you find out about nearly any topic u ranging from mechanics and physics to math and English.

TIP

Use a physical calendar to map out your study plan. After you schedule your test date, plan backward and choose which days to test yourself. Circling or underlining important dates on the calendar will help keep you accountable. Think of it as a contract with yourself.

Studying up with 6 weeks to test day

Six weeks is plenty of time to get ready for the ASVAB if you have a little knowledge under your belt. The first step is to outline your goals, so write down the scores you need for your top two dream jobs (talk to your recruiter to find the required minimums). For example, if you want to be an air traffic controller in the U.S. Air Force, you need to score at least 55 in the General category, which covers Arithmetic Reasoning and Verbal Expression, and at least 55 in its Mechanical category, which includes General Science, Mechanical Comprehension, and Auto & Shop Information. (Discover what types of skills go into each branch's line or composite scores in Chapter 2.)

After you know what scores you need, take the first practice exam in Chapter 18 (if you haven't already). Score your answers to determine what you need to study most. If you performed poorly in science as a whole, flip through Part 4; if you did just fine in chemistry but poorly in Earth science, only spend time on Chapter 12. If you didn't do so well in Auto & Shop Information, Chapters 13 and 14 are right there waiting for you.

Study for at least a week, setting aside an hour or so each day based on your schedule, before you take the next practice test. Part of your study should include taking advantage of the online flashcards that come with this book. Get instructions for creating your online account, which is completely free, inside the book's front cover or in the earlier section "Getting Access to the Online Test Bank."

A week after your first full practice exam, take the first AFQT practice exam in Chapter 24; that lets you double-check that you can at least pass the test and qualify for military service.

Take the second full practice exam (Chapter 20) when you have about four weeks left to study. If you don't have time to take an entire test, answering only questions in the topic areas you've been studying is okay; I won't tell. If you take the paper version of the test in the book, grade your answers and see how much you've improved since you took the last test. If your scores haven't increased much, check out some of the additional resources I mention at the beginning of each chapter. Usually, I refer you to other *For Dummies* books that let you take a deeper dive into very specific subjects, but I also point out other tools (such as websites, apps, and games) that can help you pick up what you need to know before test day.

Here's a sample schedule you can use as you hurtle through time and space toward the ASVAB:

- 6 weeks out: Practice Exam 1
- 5 weeks out: AFQT Practice Exam 1
- 4 weeks out: Practice Exam 2
- 3 weeks out: AFQT Practice Exam 2 (if necessary)
- 2 weeks out: Practice Exam 3

Use your remaining two weeks to circle back to the questions you missed in the practice exams, and if you're up for it, create a customized test online covering only the topics you need most. You should also use that time to read and study as much as you can in those topics; remember, the practice questions you see in this book and in the online test bank aren't the same questions you see on the test. ASVAB test questions change often, and test-prep authors aren't allowed to see them. (If you do see a question in this book and on the ASVAB, it's just luck, and you should probably buy two lottery tickets — one for you and one for me.)

Mapping your review 3 weeks out

I get it — you like to live on the edge. That's why you're taking the ASVAB three weeks from now and just now picking up this book. That, or your recruiter has told you that you're going to MEPS for testing in a few weeks without giving you much say in the matter. Either way, you're looking at about 21 days to tap-dance your way to the military job of your dreams.

First things first: Figure out what scores you need to qualify for that job (and a second choice, while you're at it). Write down those scores so you have a goal you can look at as you study. Then roll up your sleeves, grab a pencil, and take the first practice exam in Chapter 18. Score your answers as soon as you can (preferably right after you take the test) so you can identify your weak spots. If you take the practice test online, the software scores your answers for you.

REMEMBER

Taking a full practice test immediately is important. That way, if you have a blind spot — that is, an area you're a little rusty in — you notice it and can start studying right away.

TIP

If you take the first practice exam and realize that you need more time to study before taking the ASVAB, that's okay — even if your recruiter wants you to move faster. It's *your* career, not your recruiter's, and earning the scores you need to get a job you actually want pays off. If you don't reach the minimum scores you need for your dream job, the military will try to funnel you into a job it wants you to perform. That job may not match your interests, which will definitely affect your quality of life after you sign up. Tell your recruiter that you need a few extra weeks (or more) to make sure you're ready; a good recruiter will understand. And don't forget that you aren't under any obligation to stick with the same recruiter. You can work with someone else in the office or even go to another Armed Forces Career Center. You can even talk to recruiters from other branches. Often, recruiters are direct reflections of the branches they serve.

Even if you score well on the subtests you need to ace for your dream job, you still need to head to those chapters in this book and study. Try to limit your study sessions to an hour or two a day to avoid burnout.

A week after you take the first practice exam, take the second one. If you're very confident in some areas, skipping them is okay. You have to use your time wisely right now. That also means bypassing tests that don't contribute to your goals. For example, only the Navy actually uses scores from the Assembling Objects test, and even then only for a handful of jobs, so practicing on it may well be a waste of your time if you aren't after one of those gigs.

Regardless of whether you skip certain subtests, score your answers right away. Then look at the questions you answered incorrectly. They may help you pinpoint specific areas of knowledge you need to work on. If you can't tell the difference between calipers and needle-nose pliers but the job you want requires a decent level of shop knowledge, you probably need to spend time studying tools (which you can do in Chapter 14).

Before you complete your study, it's a good idea to take at least one AFQT practice exam, just to ensure you have enough basic knowledge to qualify for enlistment. After you take the first and second practice exams, as well as an AFQT practice exam, you should have about a week left before test day. Take that time to revisit your most important topics and, if necessary, check out the additional resources I point out in the beginning of each chapter.

Heading into crunch time with 1 week to prepare

If you have only a week before your ASVAB testing appointment, ask your recruiter to find out what line or composite scores you need to land the job you want. For example, if you've wanted to be a sonar technician on a submarine for as long as you can remember, you need to score well in Arithmetic Reasoning, Mathematics Knowledge, Electronics Information, and General Science.

After you know what scores you need, sit down and take a full practice test. Taking an online practice test to familiarize yourself with computerized testing is a good idea. You can use the online exams that come with this book by activating your online account (find instructions on how to do so in the earlier section "Getting Access to the Online Test Bank" or inside the front cover of the book). Take the *entire test* — not just part of it — so you aren't blindsided if you don't perform as well as you thought you would in other topics.

If you don't perform as well as you need to for your dream job, tell your recruiter you need more time. You're taking a huge step by joining the military, and a good recruiter will understand that you're mapping out your future career.

If you find that you're in pretty good shape to take the ASVAB, spend the next several days reading over the chapters in your most critical topic areas. Run through the practice questions in each chapter, and take one more full practice test before you show up on test day. That way, you can become more comfortable with the types of questions you encounter on the ASVAB, as well as how they're presented, so you know what to expect when you sit down at MEPS.

Making Last-Minute Preparations: 24 Hours and Counting

Set yourself up for one final study session the day before you're scheduled to take the test — but don't be too hard on yourself. Break up your time into two 1-hour blocks, and during the first hour, focus on the subjects you need to ace to get your dream job. During the second hour, review all the notes you've taken, flip through this book to look for highlights, and make sure you're familiar with the time constraints you'll face when you're sitting in front of the computer at MEPS (see Chapter 1).

WARNING: Whatever you do, *don't* spend the night before the test cramming. The day before the test is for light review.

Before you settle in for your last study session, pack up everything you need to bring to MEPS: your ID card, your glasses, and anything else your recruiter has told you to bring.

TIP: Most MEPS locations adhere to a specific dress code, even for those taking the ASVAB. Ask your recruiter beforehand what the facility allows. Crop tops, cutoff shorts, open-toed shoes, and other super-casual wear may be off-limits. (Welcome to the military! Here are some rules to get you started.)

These pointers may help you do your best on test day:

- **Get some sleep.** A full night's rest (at least eight hours) before the test prepares your body and mind to perform their best during the test. When you get enough sleep, your brain actively organizes information so you can remember it more easily during the test.

  While you're thinking about sleep, consider maintaining a regular sleep schedule at least two or three nights before the test; sticking to a healthy pattern helps ensure your mind is sharp when you need to recall facts, formulas, and vocabulary words during the ASVAB.

- **On the morning of the test, eat a light meal.** Anything too heavy will make you drowsy, but not eating enough will make it hard for you to concentrate.

  Try to avoid eating a breakfast high in carbohydrates and sipping energy drinks. Although the carbs and caffeine will initially make you feel energetic, a couple of hours into the test, you may come crashing down. Select foods high in protein instead.

- **Get exercise the day before and even the morning of the test.** Doing so gets your blood pumping and helps you remain mentally sharp. And here's a bonus tip: If you're not already used to working out every morning, there's no time like the present to get there. You exercise as a group every morning (and noon and night) in basic training.

- **If you're sick, upset, or injured, consider rescheduling the test.** Right before the test starts, the proctor asks if there's anything, such as sickness or injury, that may affect your test performance. After the test actually starts, it's considered an "official test," and you have to wait a certain time period before any possibility of a retest. See Chapter 1 for details.

- **Don't bring personal supplies to the test.** Your test administrator will provide you with pencils and scratch paper. Don't bring calculators, personal electronic devices (smartphones, tablets), backpacks, or a cooler of munchies to the testing site. You won't be allowed to have them with you. (But if you wear eyeglasses, bring them.)

- **Bring a watch to help you keep track of time if you're taking the paper version.** The computerized version has a clock on the screen.

- **Don't drink a lot of liquids just before the test.** You don't want to waste valuable test time in the restroom!

- **Make sure you arrive at the test site with plenty of time to spare.** In the military, arriving on time means you're 5 minutes late. You should plan to be in your seat at least 15 minutes before the scheduled testing time. Unless your recruiter is driving you (which is often the case), you may want to do a test run a day or two before your testing date to make sure you know where the entrance is, check parking availability, and figure out where to meet your recruiter.

- **Bring your ID.** You have to show proof of your identity when you arrive at MEPS.

2 Words to Live By: Communication Skills

IN THIS PART . . .

Brush up on vocabulary lessons that will help you ace the Word Knowledge subtest. Review prefixes, suffixes, and roots, and distinguish between synonyms and antonyms.

Get help tackling the Paragraph Comprehension subtest, and check out the different types of questions you'll encounter.

Work some practice questions at the end of each chapter to help you determine where you excel and where you could use some more review.

IN THIS CHAPTER

» Being well-spoken in the military

» Seeing some example questions

» Keeping a word list

» Knowing the difference between synonyms and antonyms

» Improving your overall vocabulary

Chapter 4
Word Knowledge

To make it to basic combat training, you need a pretty decent vocabulary that helps you score well on the Word Knowledge subtest of the ASVAB. Not only do you have to know how to spell to some degree (so you can differentiate among words), but you also need to know what the words on the test mean. The military wants to know how big your vocabulary is so it can determine whether you'll be able to communicate with other troops, understand written and spoken instructions, report to higher-ups, and lead junior servicemembers.

But what if you don't know the difference between a carbine and a carbon? Don't stress too much; I'm here to help (or deluge you with expressions to help you flex your lexicon, if you prefer). With the help of this chapter and a little work on your part, you can whip your word-knowledge skills right into shape. And then at the end of the chapter, you can check out the practice questions to test those skills.

When you take the Word Knowledge subtest on the computerized version of the ASVAB, you have 9 minutes to answer only 15 questions, which means you have 36 seconds to answer each question. (If your Word Knowledge subtest includes tryout questions, which I explain in Chapter 1, you have 18 minutes to answer 30 questions.) On the paper version, the schedule's a little tighter. You have 11 minutes to answer 35 questions (or less than 20 seconds for each question). Either way, it's plenty of time, as long as you stay focused and don't waste time daydreaming about your future in the military (sorry, I mean becoming lost in reverie as you consider your impending enlistment).

These days, most candidates take the computerized version of the ASVAB, which is designed to ask you questions that gauge your ability quickly. You start with a question of medium difficulty. If you answer correctly, you see a harder question next; if you answer incorrectly, you see an easier question next. Some people find that the ASVAB is easier — or harder — than they expect, but that's sometimes because the test adapts itself to the test-taker's ability.

Grasping the Importance of Word Knowledge

Word Knowledge is included on the ASVAB because words represent ideas, and the more words you understand, the better you can communicate with others. The military wants to be sure that you can follow directions for using and maintaining equipment, rules and regulations outlined in military manuals, and all the things your superiors are telling you — and that you can communicate with the troops working under you. Whether you're trying to get more supplies (submit necessary logistical requisitions) or get the assignment you want (via application for personnel career-enhancement programs), you need to develop a good vocabulary. The military considers clear communication so important that it's taught and graded at all levels of training (including basic training).

REMEMBER

The Word Knowledge subtest is one of the four most important subtests on the ASVAB (along with Paragraph Comprehension, Mathematics Knowledge, and Arithmetic Reasoning). This subtest makes up a significant portion of the AFQT score — the score that determines your eligibility for military service. You also need to do well on the Word Knowledge subtest to qualify for many military jobs, such as air traffic controller, military intelligence, and even firefighting.

Table 4-1 shows the military line scores that are calculated by using your Word Knowledge subtest score.

TABLE 4-1 Military Line Scores That Use the Word Knowledge Score

Branch of Service	Line Score
U.S. Army	Clerical, Combat, General Technical, Operators and Food, Skilled Technical, and Surveillance and Communications
U.S. Air Force/Space Force	Administrative, General, and Mechanical
U.S. Navy/Coast Guard	Administrative, General Technician, Hospital, Nuclear, and Operations
U.S. Marine Corps	Clerical and General Technician

Chapter 2 has more information about military line scores.

Checking Out the Word Knowledge Question Format

The Word Knowledge portion of the ASVAB measures your vocabulary. The questions usually come in one of two types:

>> The first type asks for a straight definition.
>> The second type gives you an underlined word used in the context of a sentence.

When you're asked for a straight definition, your task is quite simple: Choose the answer closest in meaning to the underlined word. Look at the following example:

EXAMPLE

Abate most nearly means

(A) encourage.

(B) relax.

(C) obstruct.

(D) terminate.

Abate means to suppress or terminate. In this case, the correct answer is Choice (D).

When you see an underlined word in a sentence, your goal is to choose the answer closest in meaning to the underlined word. **Remember:** *Closest in meaning* doesn't mean *the exact same thing.* You're looking for similar or related words. For example:

EXAMPLE

The house was derelict.

(A) solid

(B) run-down

(C) clean

(D) inexpensive

Here, the answer is Choice (B).

TIP

Keep in mind that although you may know the word in the question, you may not know one or more of the words in the multiple-choice answers. If this is the case, use the process of elimination to help you narrow down your choices. Eliminate the words that you know are wrong and then choose the one that's most likely correct from what's left.

Building Words from Scratch: Strategies to Help You Decipher Word Meanings

Merriam-Webster currently defines more than 300,000 words online. Fortunately, you don't need to study all of them. It's possible to decipher English word meanings even if you've never heard a particular word before.

Developing a large vocabulary takes time — often years. However, just because you have a limited amount of time to study doesn't mean you should give up hope. Instead, focus on the tips throughout this section to help you improve your Word Knowledge score.

From beginning to end: Knowing prefixes and suffixes

Prefixes, roots, and suffixes are the main parts that make up words. Not every word has all three, but most have at least one. A word's *prefix* — the first syllable — affects its meaning. A *suffix* is the last syllable in a word, and it, too, affects the word's meaning. *Roots* are the parts that lie in the middle of a word. Think of roots as the base of the word and prefixes and suffixes as word parts that are attached to the base to modify its meaning. (Check out the following section for more info on — you guessed it — roots.)

CHAPTER 4 **Word Knowledge** 43

These basic word parts generally have the same meaning in whatever word they're used. For instance, the prefix *pro-* means *in favor of, forward,* or *positive,* whether you use it in the word *pro*ton or the word *pro*ceed.

Tables 4-2 and 4-3 list some common prefixes and suffixes. Each list has the word part, its meaning, and one word that uses each word part. Write down additional words that use each word part to help you memorize the list. You can find even more prefixes, suffixes, and roots in the appendix.

TABLE 4-2 **Prefixes**

Prefix	Meaning	Sample Word
a-	no, not	atheist
ab- or abs-	away, from	absent
anti-	against	antibody
bi-	two	bilateral
circum-	around	circumnavigate
com- or con-	with, together	conform
contra- or counter-	against	contradict
de-	away from	detour
deca-	ten	decade
extra-	outside, beyond	extracurricular, extraordinary
fore-	in front of	foretell
geo-	earth	geology
hyper-	above, over	hyperactive
il-	not	illogical
mal- or male-	evil, bad	malediction
multi-	many	multiply
ob-	blocking	obscure
omni-	all	omnibus
out-	external	outside
que-, quer-, or ques-	ask	question, query
re-	back, again	return
semi-	half	semisweet
super-	over, more	superior
tele-	far	telephone
trans-	across	transatlantic
un-	not	uninformed

TABLE 4-3 **Suffixes**

Suffix	Part of Speech It Indicates	Meaning	Original Word: Suffixed Word
-able or -ible	Adjective	capable of	agree: agreeable
-age	Noun	act of	break: breakage
-al	Adjective	relating to	function: functional
-ance or -ence	Noun	instance of an action	perform: performance
-ation	Noun	action, process	liberate: liberation
-en	Adjective, verb	made from	silk: silken
-ful	Adjective	full of	help: helpful
-ic	Adjective	relating to, like	anemia: anemic
-ical	Adjective	possessing a quality of	magic: magical
-ion	Noun	result of, act of	legislate: legislation
-ish	Adjective, noun	resembling	child: childish
-ism	Noun	condition or manner	hero: heroism
-ist	Noun	one who or that which does	anarchy: anarchist
-ity	Noun	quality of or state of	dense: density
-less	Adjective, noun	not having	worth: worthless
-let	Noun	small one	book: booklet
-ly	Adjective, adverb	like	fearless: fearlessly
-ment	Noun	act or process of	establish: establishment
-ness	Adjective, noun	possessing a quality	good: goodness
-or, -er	Noun	one who does a thing	orate: orator
-ous	Adjective	state of	danger: dangerous

Suffixes are busy little word segments. They affect the meaning of a word and usually tell you what part of speech a word is (which comes in handy when you're navigating through Word Knowledge questions that you can't answer immediately).

If you memorize prefixes, suffixes, and roots, you have a better chance of figuring out the meaning of an unfamiliar word when you see it on the ASVAB. Figuring out the meaning of unfamiliar words is how people with large vocabularies make them even larger. (They look up words in the dictionary, too.)

Determining the root of the problem

Root words are word parts that serve as the base of a word. In English, one root word can be changed slightly to perform all sorts of roles — it can act as a noun, a verb, an adjective, or an adverb with just a little modification. If you recognize a root, you can generally get an idea of what the word means, even if you're not familiar with it. For example, if you know what the root word *attach* means, you can figure out what the word *attachment* means. If you know *adhere*, you can deduce what *adherence* means.

Table 4-4 lists some common roots. Memorize them. When you sit down to take the ASVAB, you'll be glad you did.

TABLE 4-4 Roots

Root	Meaning	Sample Word
anthro or anthrop	relating to humans	anthropology
bibl	relating to books	bibliography
brev	short	abbreviate
cede or ceed	go, yield	recede
chrom	color	monochrome
cogn	know	cognizant
corp	body	corporate
dict	speak	diction
domin	rule	dominate
flu or fluc	flow	influx
form	shape	formulate
fract or frag	break	fragment
graph	writing	biography
junct	join	juncture
liber	free	liberate
lum or lumen	light	illuminate
oper	work	cooperate
path or pathy	suffer, feeling	pathology
port	carry	portable
press	squeeze	repress
scrib or script	write	describe
sens or sent	feel	sentient
tract	pull	traction
voc or vok	call	revoke

TIP: When you see an unfamiliar word, try dropping a couple of letters from the beginning and/or the end of the word to see whether you recognize what's left — the root. If so, you can make a good guess about the meaning of the word. You can find more root words to help maximize your vocabulary in the appendix.

Word families: Finding related words

When you see an unfamiliar word on the Word Knowledge section, don't get upset and pound on the computer (they make you pay for those things if you break them). You may know the word after all — just in a different form. Suppose you run across the word *beneficent* on the Word Knowledge portion:

Beneficent most nearly means

(A) kind.

(B) beautiful.

(C) unhappy.

(D) troubled.

You sit there and begin to sweat. You've never seen the word before, and it's all over for you, right? Well, maybe not. Take a closer look. What other word starting with the letters *benefi* do you know? How about the word *benefit*? A *benefit* is something that helps or aids. It'd be a good bet that the word *beneficent* is related to helping or aiding. So, when you look over the possible choices, you can choose the one that has something to do with helping.

But wait! None of the answers states help or aid. Now what? Just use the process of elimination. If someone is helpful (beneficent), they probably aren't troubled or unhappy. They may be beautiful, but more likely, they're kind. So, the best answer would be Choice (A).

Remember when your high school guidance counselor recommended that you take French or Spanish? You should thank them when you score well on this subtest. Why? Because knowledge of other languages can help you puzzle out the meaning of many English words. For example, if you know that *salud* means "health" in Spanish, you may be able to puzzle out the meaning of the English word *salutary* (favorable to or promoting health). Knowing that *sang* means "blood" in French may help you figure out what the English word *sanguine* means (try to puzzle this one out on your own; then check a dictionary to see how close you are).

Deconstructing words

Pulling apart words is a great strategy when you're not sure what something means. Even knowing what part of a word means can help you make a smarter choice — and on the ASVAB, every question counts.

Try to pull apart the word in this question to see whether you can figure out its meaning.

Detractor most nearly means

(A) critic.

(B) driver.

(C) expert.

(D) adulatory.

Take apart the word *detractor*:

- *de-* is the prefix
- *tract* is the root
- *-or* is the suffix

If you've learned what any part of the word means, whether it's the prefix, root, or suffix, finding the correct answer is easier. (Check Tables 4-2, 4-3, and 4-4 if you're not sure yet.)

The prefix *de-* means "away from," *tract* means "pull," and the suffix *-or* means "one who does a thing." After you've broken down the word *detractor*, you can see that it means a person who pulls away from something.

Remember, too, that the suffix *-or* often makes a word a noun (a word that names a person, place, thing, or idea), so you can immediately rule out Choice (D). That leaves three choices: *critic, driver,* and *expert.*

If you guessed that *detractor* most nearly means *critic,* Choice (A), you're right. It's the only one that makes sense when you know what each part of the word means.

Yin and Yang: Understanding Synonyms and Antonyms

A *synonym* is a word that has the same meaning as or a very similar meaning to another word. *Smile* and *grin* are synonyms. They may not mean exactly the same thing, but their meanings are very similar. An *antonym* is a word that has an opposite or nearly opposite meaning as another word. *Smile* and *frown* are antonyms.

TIP: To help remember the definitions of synonym and antonym, think of a synonym as the *same* (both also start with an *s*) and an antonym as the *antithesis* (that's another word for opposite).

The ASVAB may ask you to find the word that most nearly means the same thing as a given word, which is a synonym. Or you may be asked to find the word that most nearly means the opposite of a given word, which is an antonym. Most of the questions on the Word Knowledge subtest ask you to find synonyms, although a few may ask you to find antonyms.

TIP: How can you study and find the synonym of a word (or the antonym, for that matter)? Take a look at these suggestions:

>> **Start in the dictionary.** Many dictionary entries include the abbreviation *syn.*, which means synonym. The words that follow this abbreviation are synonyms of the entry word. You may also see the abbreviation *ant.*, which stands for antonym; the word or words that follow it mean the opposite of the entry word.

>> **Make a list of synonyms and antonyms of the words you learn.** As you study vocabulary words for the Word Knowledge subtest, add them to your list.

>> **Use the root-word list from Table 4-4 (earlier in the chapter).** Using a dictionary and/or thesaurus, come up with a list of synonyms and antonyms for each word listed in the Sample Word column. (Of course, not every word has synonyms and antonyms, but many do.)

Many of the ASVAB Word Knowledge questions require you to know a one-word definition for another word. There's no better study aid for this concept than a thesaurus, a book of synonyms.

ASVAB Word Knowledge Strategy: Finding the Answer When You Just Don't Know

Although it's helpful to have a massive vocabulary at your disposal, you can still ace the Word Knowledge subtest if you have a few strategies up your sleeve. Read through this section and then practice these strategies as you answer the Word Knowledge questions at the end of this chapter and on the practice tests in Part 6.

Creating your own context

Some of the Word Knowledge questions you'll see on the ASVAB don't have any context that can offer you clues about their meaning (some are in sentences, which can make them easier to decode). The good news: You may be able to give a word *your own* context, and when you do, you may find that you actually know the answer.

When you see a word you don't know, try to place it in context. Ask yourself, "Have I heard this word before?"

Afoul most nearly means

(A) correctly.

(B) wrongly.

(C) easily.

(D) disgusting.

Have you heard the word *afoul* in a sentence before? If you've heard of someone "running afoul of the law," you can surmise that the word doesn't mean correctly, easily, or disgusting — and that leaves you with Choice (B), which happens to be the right answer. It might be a fuzzy definition, but sometimes that's all you need.

Think of phrases you've heard that include these words (or variations of them), and then see whether you can guess their meanings.

» **Abstain:** "We had abstinence-only education in school."

» **Deduce:** "I'll try to deduce the answer based on what I know."

» **Malignant:** "The tumor is malignant."

» **Credible:** "Can you back that up with a credible source?"

(*Abstain* is a verb that means to restrain oneself from doing something. *Deduce* is a verb that means to arrive at a conclusion by reasoning. *Malignant* is an adjective that means life-threatening, spiteful, or mean. *Credible* is an adjective that means believable.)

How's it feel? Letting the words speak to you

Words can be positive or negative, and you can often tell which they are through context. In Word Knowledge questions that require you to find a word's meaning based on the sentence it's in, you can use the warm-fuzzy or cold-prickly feeling you get to rule out incorrect answers.

EXAMPLE

David hoped that going to the amusement park would help him shake his <u>melancholy</u> mood.

(A) joyful

(B) sorrowful

(C) thoughtful

(D) excited

As long as it's not raining, most people have fun at an amusement park (it's nearly as much fun as basic training, where "If it ain't raining, you ain't training" is often the motto of the day). The sentence also says that David wants to "shake his melancholy mood," which means *melancholy* can't be a very good feeling. It must have a negative connotation (that cold-prickly feeling). You can rule out Choices (A) and (D), then, and think about what's the opposite of fun — and that's most likely Choice (B), because *sorrowful* means "down in the dumps."

Words and phrases such as "dread," "looking forward to," and "shied away from" all give you hints about a sentence's tone, which can help you pick the right answer when you're unsure. Even ruling out one or two incorrect answers can make a big difference in your score.

Compare and contrast: Picking up on signals

Many sentence-based Word Knowledge questions have context clues that can help you decipher the underlined word's meaning. If you can pick up on the signal words that tell you about contrast and similarity, you'll be able to boost your score *and* your vocabulary.

Signal words can be especially helpful in helping you predict a word's meaning. Table 4-5 lists some common signal words and whether they indicate similarity or contrast.

TABLE 4-5 Signal Words

Signal Word	Indicates	Example
indeed	Similarity	"The children were happy; *indeed*, they couldn't control their excitement."
like	Similarity	"When I shook the soda bottle, it erupted *like* a volcano."
too	Similarity	"The seniors were upset, and they were angry, *too*."
although	Contrast	"*Although* she was hesitant, Cheryl voted to reopen the school."
but	Contrast	"The class is difficult *but* fun."
despite	Contrast	"The dog ate the ice cream *despite* having eaten 10 minutes before."
however	Contrast	"Sadie applied at several colleges. *However*, only one accepted her."
rather than	Contrast	"The movie is boring *rather than* enjoyable."
while	Contrast	"Many troops are resourceful, *while* others are unimaginative."

EXAMPLE

They <u>recoiled</u> as if they had just seen a ghost.

(A) cringed

(B) laughed

(C) shouted

(D) endured

The signal phrase in the question is "as if," which is very similar to "like." Knowing that, what's the most likely answer? If you saw a ghost, you probably wouldn't laugh, shout, or endure. (I'd run.) The most correct answer is Choice (A), *cringed,* because that's far more likely to be your response than any of the other choices are.

One of these things is not like the other: Ruling out wrong answers

One of the most successful ASVAB strategies involves ruling out answers that aren't likely to be correct before settling on the one you think is right. When two answer choices mean almost the same thing, or when some choices don't match the prefix, suffix, or root word, you can cross them off as possibilities.

Inhabit most nearly means

(A) vacate.

(B) reside.

(C) depart.

(D) leave.

Choices (A), (C), and (D) are all very similar in meaning, leaving only Choice (B), *reside,* as the clear front-runner.

On the ASVAB, your choices aren't likely to be this obvious, but you may be able to rule out two choices and give yourself a 50-50 chance of finding the correct answer.

Deform most nearly means

(A) cure.

(B) heal.

(C) contort.

(D) tragedy.

Choices (A) and (B) are essentially the same, so you can eliminate those two. Now look at the prefix, *de-,* and compare it to what you find in Table 4-2 or other words that begin with the same prefix. *De-* means "away from." In Table 4-4, you can see that the root word *form* means "shape." That means Choice (C), *contort,* is the right answer for this question. (Combining ASVAB test-taking strategies gives you an extra edge!)

Mind filling in? Replacing the word with the answer choices

When you encounter a Word Knowledge question that asks you to define a word in a sentence, you may find that swapping out the underlined word with each of your choices leads you to the correct answer.

The CDC hasn't been able to identify the pathogen that these people ingested before turning into zombies.

(A) person

(B) carrier

(C) event

(D) bacteria

CHAPTER 4 **Word Knowledge** 51

Replace *pathogen* with *person, carrier, event,* and *bacteria*. (The word *ingested* is a big clue. The words *person, carrier,* and *event* just don't make sense in the sentence.)

This strategy can work in conjunction with other strategies, too:

EXAMPLE

Maria was worried that the cockroaches in the apartment would have a <u>deleterious</u> effect on her daughter's health.

(A) helpful

(B) harmful

(C) erasing

(D) backward

Replace *deleterious* with each of the answer choices. Choice (B), *harmful,* is the only one that makes sense — especially because the sentence says, "Maria was worried," which shows you that the correct answer won't be something positive.

Say what? Parts of speech matter

When you see a Word Knowledge question that asks you to define a word in a sentence, you might be able to weed out one or two incorrect choices by knowing the parts of speech. Table 4-6 lists the eight parts of speech, notes what roles they play in sentences, and gives you some examples.

TABLE 4-6 Parts of Speech

Part	Role	Examples
Noun	Names a person, place, thing, or idea	Mr. Hall, lawyer, United States, suffix
Verb	Expresses an action or state of being	to write, to read, to eat, to play, to be
Adjective	Describes a noun	green, sleepy, hungry, fast, beautiful
Adverb	Modifies a verb, adjective, or another adverb	tremendously, very, cautiously, dangerously, sneakily
Pronoun	Replaces a noun	he, she, they, it, this, I, you
Preposition	Relates a noun or pronoun to another word	in, on, around, after, under
Conjunction	Connects clauses to sentences	and, but, if
Interjection	Expresses emotions or feelings	cool, awesome, holy cow, uh-oh, eek

REMEMBER

A suffix can tell you what part of speech a word is, so when you encounter a word you don't know, you'll be able to eliminate possible answer choices that you *do* know by looking at the suffixes.

Suffixes are usually only part of nouns, verbs, and adjectives. If the ASVAB asks you to define *analogous,* but you don't know what it means, you can use your knowledge of the suffix to help you rule out answers that don't make any sense. Because the suffix *-ous* typically modifies nouns and turns words into adjectives, you know that the correct answer probably won't be a noun.

EXAMPLE

Analogous most nearly means

(A) inclusive.

(B) danger.

(C) write.

(D) comparable.

Of those answer choices, *inclusive* and *comparable* are the only adjectives. *Danger* is a noun, and *write* is a verb. You can rule out Choices (B) and (C) to make a more educated choice — and improve your chances of answering the question correctly — if you know that the suffix *-ous* usually refers to adjectives. Choice (D) is correct here; *analogous* means comparable in certain respects, especially when it clarifies the relationship between two things that are being compared ("The relationship between a drill sergeant and a new recruit is analogous to the relationship between a hungry fish and a worm on a hook").

EXAMPLE

Cameron knew that the only viable option was to invest 10 percent of his savings.

(A) succeed

(B) glowing

(C) reasonable

(D) life

The underlined word, *viable,* describes Cameron's option; *option* is a noun in this sentence, so that makes *viable* an adjective. Look through the answer choices and figure out what part of speech each word is. Choice (A), *succeed,* is a verb because it describes an action (the action of succeeding). Choice (B), *glowing,* is an adjective because it modifies a noun (for example, "the glowing candle"), so that's a possible answer. Choice (C), *reasonable,* is also an adjective because it modifies nouns (as in, "That's a reasonable alternative"), so that's another option. Choice (D), *life,* is a noun (and it wouldn't make any sense in this sentence), so it's off the table.

Choices (B) and (C) are the most likely of the four to be correct. If you haven't tried it yet, replace *viable* with each choice. You'll see that Choice (C), *reasonable,* makes the most sense in the sentence.

If all else fails, break your word

If you're stumped on a Word Knowledge question, you can resort to breaking apart the word (read about that in "Deconstructing words" earlier in this chapter). Even taking off a prefix or suffix can point you in the right direction, especially if you've studied Tables 4-2 and 4-3 and the extensive lists in the appendix.

Predict the meanings of these words to test your skills:

» Desensitize

» Decode

» Deplume

These words all have something in common, and it's the prefix *de-*. Knowing that *de-* usually means "away from," you can guess what each word will mean.

Predict the meanings of these words:

- Approachable
- Serviceable
- Governable

The common theme with these words is the suffix *-able*, which typically signifies "capable of." You can use that to your advantage when you're taking the ASVAB, too.

Guess what! It's okay on the ASVAB

In some cases, it's okay to guess on the ASVAB — but only if you do it strategically.

You won't be penalized for guessing on the paper-and-pencil version of the ASVAB (aside from choosing the wrong answers, that is). You can complete each section at your own pace within the time limits, and you're allowed to review and change your answers in the current section. After time expires and the test proctor tells you to close your booklet, you won't be permitted to go back to that portion of the test.

You *will* be penalized for guessing on the CAT-ASVAB (the computerized version of the test) that new recruits take at MEPS. If you look at the clock and start clicking random answers in a rush because you're almost out of time for that section, your score will go down. You can take the entire CAT-ASVAB at your own pace, but you can't review or change any answers after you've submitted them. You can't go back to the beginning of the subtest after you start. If you're running out of time, *do not guess!* Keep trying to answer each question to the best of your ability, using the test-taking strategies outlined in this chapter.

REMEMBER: You'll have 9 minutes to answer 15 questions if you're taking the CAT-ASVAB and your subtest has no tryout questions, which leaves you about 36 seconds for each one. If you're taking the paper-and-pencil version, you'll have 11 minutes to answer 35 questions. That's about 18 seconds per question (if you want to check the math, refer to Chapter 6).

TIP: If you *must* guess on the ASVAB, eliminate choices that you know are incorrect first. You have a 25 percent chance of getting each question right without reading it, but you can increase those chances if you eliminate even one incorrect choice. That's why these test-taking strategies are so important — the better you perform on the Word Knowledge section, the higher your score will be, which opens doors to more desirable jobs and helps you get your military career off to a good start.

You Are What You Speak: Improving Your Vocabulary, Improving Yourself

Having an extensive vocabulary can help you do well on the Word Knowledge subtest. But even if you don't have a huge vocabulary, the strategies in this section can help you make up for that.

REMEMBER: You can acquire vocabulary words in the short term as well as over a long period of time. Combining both approaches is best, but if you're pressed for time, focus on short-term memorization and test-taking skills.

Reading your way to a larger vocabulary

In a world of constant social media updates and 17 billion streaming platforms, the pastime of reading for enjoyment is quickly fading. To build your vocabulary, you have to read — it's that simple. Studies consistently show that those who read for enjoyment have a much larger vocabulary than those who dislike reading. You have to see the words in print, not just hear someone say them. Besides, people can read and understand many more words than they could ever use in conversation.

That doesn't mean you have to start with *Advanced Astrophysics*. In fact, if you don't read much, you can start with your daily newspaper, a news magazine, or any type of reading material that's just a notch or two above what you ordinarily read. Choose topics that interest you. If you're interested in the subject matter, you'll enjoy reading more. Plus, you may learn something new!

When you encounter a word you don't know, try to understand what it means by looking at the context in which the word is used. For example, if you read, "The scientist extrapolated from the data," and you don't know what *extrapolated* means, you can try substituting words you do know to see whether they'd make sense. For example, the scientist probably didn't hide from the data. They probably used the data to make some sort of decision, judgment, or guess. To confirm your understanding of the word, check your dictionary. Making predictions like this can help you remember a definition for the long term.

You may even consider keeping a running list of terms you come across as you read, along with their definitions (see the following section). On the Word Knowledge subtest of the ASVAB, you often won't be able to guess what a word means from its context (in many cases, there's no context in the test because the words aren't used in sentences). You also won't be able to look the word up in the dictionary. But considering context and consulting a dictionary are two great ways to discover vocabulary words during your test preparation.

Keeping a list and checking it twice

Not long ago, an 11-year-old girl went through the entire dictionary and made a list of all the words she didn't know. (The process took several months.) She then studied the list faithfully for a year and went on to win first place in the National Spelling Bee finals. You don't have to go to this extent, but even putting in a tenth of her effort can dramatically improve your scores on the Word Knowledge subtest.

One way to improve your vocabulary is to keep a word list. Here's how that list works:

1. **When you hear or read a word that you don't understand, jot it down or make note of it in your phone.**

2. **When you have a chance, look up the word in the dictionary and then write the meaning on your list.**

3. **Use the word in a sentence that you make up.**

   Write the sentence down, too.

4. **Use your new word in everyday conversation.**

   Finding a way to work the word *zenith* into a description of last night's basketball game requires creativity, but you won't forget what the word means.

TIP: Arrange your list by related items so the words are easier to remember. For example, list the words having to do with your work on one page, words related to mechanical knowledge on another page, and so on.

You can also find websites that offer lists of words if you spend a few minutes surfing. Try using search phrases such as "vocabulary words" and "SAT words." Here are a few resources:

- **Vocabulary.com:** This site (`www.vocabulary.com`) offers thousands of vocabulary words and their definitions, as well as interactive, adaptive games to help you learn.
- **Dictionary.com and Thesaurus.com:** Dictionary.com (`www.dictionary.com`) includes a great online dictionary and word of the day. The related site Thesaurus.com (`www.thesaurus.com`), which links back to the dictionary, gives you the same word of the day as well as lists of synonyms and antonyms.
- **Merriam-Webster online:** Merriam-Webster online (`www.merriam-webster.com`) is another useful site with a free online dictionary, thesaurus, and word of the day.

Crosswords: Making vocabulary fun

My grandma always kept a book of crossword puzzles in the center of her kitchen table — and she always kept an ink pen inside to complete the puzzles. (You know somebody's good if she's doing crossword puzzles in ink!) So, what was her secret? She'd been doing crosswords since the 1940s, long before you could play word games on a smartphone.

One of the great things about crossword puzzles (other than fun) is that you can find them at all levels of difficulty. Start with one that has a difficulty level consistent with your word-knowledge ability and then work your way up to more difficult puzzles. Before you know it, you'll be a lean, mean word machine and have loads of fun in the process. Dozens of free crossword apps are available for smartphones, so you don't even need to buy a book in the checkout lane at the supermarket.

Sounding off by sounding it out

Sometimes you actually know a word because you've heard it in conversation, but you don't recognize it when you see it written down. For instance, a student who'd heard the word *placebo* (pronounced "plah-*see*-bow") knew that it meant an inactive substance, like a sugar pill. But when she came across it in writing, she didn't recognize it. She thought it was a word pronounced "plah-*chee*-bow," which she'd never heard before.

TIP: When you see a word on the ASVAB that you don't recognize, try pronouncing it (not out loud, please) a couple of different ways. The following pronunciation rules can help you out:

- Sometimes letters are silent, like the *b* in *subtle* or the *k* in *knight*. A letter at the end of a word may be silent, especially if the word is French; for instance, *coup* is pronounced *coo*.
- Some sounds have unusual pronunciations in certain contexts. Think of the first *l* in *colonel*, which is pronounced like *kernel*.
- The letter *c* can sound like *s* (*lice*) or *k* (*despicable*).
- The letter *i* after a *t* can form a sound like *she*. Think of the word *initiate*.

- » The letter *x* at the beginning of a word is generally pronounced like *z (xylophone)*.

- » A vowel at the end of a word can change the pronunciation of letters in the word. The word *wag* has a different *g* sound than the word *wage*.

- » When several vowels are right next to each other, they can be pronounced many different ways (consider *boo, boa,* and *bout*). Try a couple of different possibilities. For instance, if you see the word *feint,* you may think that it should be pronounced *feent* or *fiynt,* but it in fact sounds like *faint*. It means fake or pretend.

Word Knowledge Practice Questions

In the stem of each of the following Word Knowledge practice questions, you see an underlined word. Select the choice that best answers the question in relation to the underlined word.

REMEMBER

Pay attention to the wording of each question. Some questions ask you to select the choice closest in meaning to the underlined word. Some questions may ask you to select the word most opposite in meaning. On other questions, you see the underlined word used in a sentence. In that case, your task is to select the choice most similar in meaning to the underlined word as it is used in the context of the sentence.

Easy Word Knowledge practice questions

1. Estrange most nearly means
   - (A) sharp.
   - (B) small.
   - (C) alienate.
   - (D) shiny.

2. Momentous most nearly means
   - (A) significant.
   - (B) small.
   - (C) reality.
   - (D) postpone.

3. Pollute most nearly means
   - (A) eliminate.
   - (B) contaminate.
   - (C) clean.
   - (D) confuse.

4. The loving couple celebrated their fidelity over the years on their anniversary.
   - (A) complications
   - (B) faithfulness
   - (C) regrets
   - (D) treachery

5. The Army commander decided to avert trouble by heading back to headquarters.
   - (A) help
   - (B) complicate
   - (C) prevent
   - (D) attack

6. Authority most nearly means
   - (A) power
   - (B) disadvantage
   - (C) lack
   - (D) weakness

7. Terry assumed his friend would turn left, but instead, they turned right.
   - (A) misunderstood
   - (B) confused
   - (C) pretended
   - (D) supposed

8. The detective turned away from the gruesome sight.
   - (A) cartoonish
   - (B) pleasant
   - (C) man-made
   - (D) unpleasant

9. Conclusion most nearly means
   - (A) evidence
   - (B) end
   - (C) story
   - (D) influence

10. The driving instructor told the student to merge into the right lane.
    - (A) turn abruptly
    - (B) blend in
    - (C) ignore
    - (D) return

Medium Word Knowledge Practice Questions

11. The college student met with the bursar to discuss tuition payment options.
    (A) planner
    (B) treasurer
    (C) politician
    (D) ghost

12. The mother chastised her child.
    (A) comforted
    (B) carried
    (C) lectured
    (D) supervised

13. We often wondered why Daniel lived in such an opulent apartment.
    (A) run-down
    (B) lavish
    (C) far away
    (D) hideous

14. Paul sent all of his friends a salutary message on the internet.
    (A) beneficial
    (B) profane
    (C) funny
    (D) interesting

15. The word most opposite in meaning to reflect is
    (A) ponder.
    (B) consider.
    (C) ignore.
    (D) speculate.

16. The word most opposite in meaning to forthright is
    (A) honest.
    (B) polite.
    (C) blunt.
    (D) outspoken.

17. The witness was happy to corroborate the man's explanation.
    (A) exaggerate
    (B) destroy
    (C) confirm
    (D) question

18. Barry thought he could forge the paperwork without getting caught.
    (A) trash
    (B) destroy
    (C) fabricate
    (D) forget

19. Acclaim most nearly means
    (A) enthusiastic approval.
    (B) religion.
    (C) help.
    (D) program.

20. Quell most nearly means
    (A) launch.
    (B) support.
    (C) enrich.
    (D) suppress.

21. The kinetic energy was converted to electricity.
    (A) regulated
    (B) disbursed
    (C) frantic
    (D) moving

22. This year, unlike last year, the Paris fashion industry has decided to eschew short skirts and high heels.
    (A) favor
    (B) manufacture
    (C) shun
    (D) sell

23. The attendant charged Karen a nominal fee to park in the crowded lot.
    (A) expensive
    (B) insignificant
    (C) large
    (D) crazy

24. You can't circumvent the process; you have to follow the procedure.
    (A) connive
    (B) regale
    (C) overcome
    (D) face

25. The general relinquished command and retired.
    (A) gave up
    (B) continued
    (C) reclaimed
    (D) asserted

26. Repugnant most nearly means
    (A) accessible
    (B) political
    (C) distasteful
    (D) doglike

27. The new recruits had backpacks full of illicit materials.
    (A) required
    (B) common
    (C) adult
    (D) banned

28. If you work for the federal government, you may be entitled to a public transit subsidy.
    (A) forfeiture
    (B) grant
    (C) write-off
    (D) loss

29. Kai asked the salesperson to expedite delivery.
    (A) explore
    (B) entropy
    (C) speed up
    (D) reform

30. The nation faced heavy sanctions from the United States.
    (A) artillery
    (B) disapproval
    (C) reward
    (D) penalties

Hard Word Knowledge Practice Questions

31. Obtrude most nearly means
    (A) condition.
    (B) absorb.
    (C) prepare.
    (D) impose.

32. Now that you've read through it once, it's time to recapitulate the Word Knowledge chapter.
    (A) discuss
    (B) summarize
    (C) test
    (D) reread

33. Clemency most nearly means
    (A) mercy.
    (B) force.
    (C) imprisonment.
    (D) compliment.

34. Latent most nearly means
    (A) hidden.
    (B) dull.
    (C) pretentious.
    (D) active.

35. The word most opposite in meaning to blame is

(A) attribute.

(B) reprove.

(C) muster.

(D) exalt.

36. Amenable most nearly means

(A) amended.

(B) prepared.

(C) guided.

(D) cooperative.

37. Calamity most nearly means

(A) desert.

(B) disaster.

(C) remorse.

(D) overeating.

38. The word most opposite in meaning to profound is

(A) thorough.

(B) mild.

(C) absolute.

(D) intense.

39. The word most opposite in meaning to keen is

(A) fervent.

(B) reluctant.

(C) zealous.

(D) appetent.

40. Truncate most nearly means

(A) shorten.

(B) fixate.

(C) pretend.

(D) turn.

Answers and Explanations

Use this answer key to score the Word Knowledge practice questions.

1. **C.** *Estrange* means to alienate, Choice (C). Note that *estrange* is a verb, and the only answer choice that's also a verb is Choice (C); the others are adjectives.

2. **A.** *Momentous* is an adjective and means very significant, Choice (A).

3. **B.** *Pollute* means to contaminate, Choice (B).

4. **B.** *Fidelity* is a noun meaning faithfulness and loyalty in a relationship. (If you've heard the Marine Corps's motto, *semper fidelis*, which means "always faithful," this one may have been easy for you to figure out.)

5. **C.** *Avert* is a verb meaning to turn something away or prevent it from happening.

6. **A.** *Authority* is a noun that means the power or right to give orders and make decisions.

7. **D.** *Assume* is a verb that means to suppose to be the case, even without proof.

8. **D.** *Gruesome* is an adjective that means grisly; it's something that causes horror or repulsion.

9. **B.** *Conclusion* is a noun that means the end of an event or process; it also means a judgment or decision reached by reasoning.

10. **B.** *Merge* is a verb that means to combine or to blend into something else.

11. **B.** *Bursar* is similar to the word *reimburse*. The question gives context clues about tuition payment, and that should give you enough clues to select the correct answer, Choice (B).

12. **C.** *Chastised* means disciplined or punished, so Choice (C) is the most correct choice. Choices (A), (B), and (D) are unrelated.

13. **B.** *Opulent* is an adjective that means wealthy, rich, or affluent. Choice (B) is the answer closest in meaning. The other choices are unrelated or opposite of the meaning.

14. **A.** *Salutary* is an adjective meaning beneficial, so Choice (A) is correct. If you took Spanish in high school, you may remember that a related word, *salud*, relates to health and well-being, making Choice (A) a good guess.

15. **C.** *Reflect* is a verb that means to think deeply about, demonstrate, or give back. *Ignore* would be most opposite in meaning from the choices given.

16. **B.** *Forthright* is an adjective meaning straightforward and honest, so of the choices given, *polite* is the closest to the opposite.

17. **C.** *Corroborate* is a verb meaning to back up or confirm a story.

18. **C.** *Forge* is a verb meaning to counterfeit or fabricate.

19. **A.** Used as a noun, *acclaim* means a shout of approval, so the answer is Choice (A).

20. **D.** *Quell* is a verb meaning to defeat or suppress.

21. **D.** *Kinetic* is an adjective meaning relating to or characterized by motion.

22. **C.** *Eschew* is a verb that means to avoid or keep away from. Choice (C) is the correct answer, and the other answers are unrelated.

23. **B.** *Nominal* is an adjective meaning insignificant or lower than the actual or expected value.

24. **C.** *Circumvent* is a verb that means to find a way around an obstacle or challenge.

25. **A.** *Relinquish* is a verb that means to voluntarily give up.

26. **C.** *Repugnant* is an adjective that means gross, extremely distasteful, or unacceptable.

27. **D.** *Illicit* is an adjective that means forbidden by custom, rules, or law.

28. **B.** *Subsidy* is a noun that means the grant of a sum of money from the government or a public body to help keep prices affordable or competitive.

29. **C.** *Expedite* is a verb meaning to speed up or make something happen sooner.

30. **D.** *Sanction* is a noun meaning a threatened penalty for breaking a rule or law.

31. **D.** The correct answer is Choice (D). *Obtrude* means to intrude or to impose oneself on another. The other choices are unrelated.

32. **B.** *Recapitulate* is a verb that means to summarize. It's also the longer version of the word *recap*. The correct answer is Choice (B). Choice (A) is somewhat close, but Choice (B) is the closest in meaning.

33. **A.** *Clemency* means forgiveness or leniency in punishing a person. Choice (A) is the correct answer. The other choices are unrelated.

> **TIP** Knowing prefixes can be useful when determining the definitions of many words. For example, you may have heard the word *inclement* used to describe stormy, severe weather. If you know that the prefix *in-* can mean *not*, you can conclude that *clement* is likely to be mild and gentle, traits related to mercy.

34. **A.** *Latent* means present but not visible or noticeable, so Choice (A) is the correct answer. *Latent* can also mean dormant, but none of the answer choices relates to that definition.

35. **D.** *Blame* can be both a noun and a verb; as a verb, it means to condemn, place responsibility, or accuse. So, *exalt* is most opposite in meaning.

36. **D.** *Amenable* is an adjective meaning willing and cooperative.

37. **B.** *Calamity* is a noun meaning disaster.

38. **B.** *Profound* is an adjective meaning thoughtful, intellectual, and intense, so *mild* is the most opposite in meaning.

39. **B.** *Keen* is an adjective meaning interested and enthusiastic, so *reluctant* is the choice most opposite in meaning.

40. **A.** *Truncate* is a verb meaning to shorten or abbreviate.

IN THIS CHAPTER

» Knowing what to expect of the Paragraph Comprehension subtest

» Pumping up your comprehension

» Maxing out your reading speed

» Improving your odds at test time

Chapter 5
Paragraph Comprehension

One thing you learn as soon as you step off the bus at basic training is that understanding orders is important. But perhaps more important than making sense of drill instructors barking commands is being able to read and understand *written* directions, which can save you and your buddies hundreds of push-ups (trust me on this one).

When you're the biggest federal agency in the United States, you get to name sections of your entrance exam anything you want to name them — so the Department of Defense calls this subtest Paragraph Comprehension. It's no different from any other reading comprehension test. It measures your ability to understand what you read and draw conclusions from that material. It contains a number of written passages and questions about those passages. After you enlist, you'll discover that the military runs on paperwork. If you can't read and understand a regulation, how are you going to follow it?

On the paper-and-pencil version, you have 13 minutes to answer 15 questions. If you're taking the computerized version of the ASVAB, you have 15 minutes to read the passages and answer 10 questions. If you get tryout questions in the Paragraph Comprehension subtest of the CAT-ASVAB, you have 75 minutes to complete 27 questions. I cover tryout questions in Chapter 1.

Understanding the Importance of Paragraph Comprehension for Military Jobs

The Paragraph Comprehension subtest contributes to your AFQT score, which is the most important score because it determines whether a particular branch of service lets you join. The score is so important that I plan to keep on repeating it until you're mumbling "The AFQT is the most important score" in your sleep.

The vast majority of military jobs require a decent score on the Paragraph Comprehension subtest. In fact, you'll have a hard time qualifying for any branch if the ASVAB shows the military that you won't understand the written orders you'll receive. For example, if the directions in a military recipe make your head spin, how are you going to use it to cook an edible meal for 2,000 troops? (Assuming you want to become a military cook, that is.) Table 5-1 shows the military job qualification line scores that are calculated by using your Paragraph Comprehension subtest score.

TABLE 5-1 **Military Line Scores That Use the Paragraph Comprehension Score**

Branch of Service	Line Score
U.S. Army	Clerical, General Technical, Operators and Food, Surveillance and Communications, and Skilled Technical
U.S. Air Force/Space Force	Administrative and General
U.S. Navy/Coast Guard	Administrative, General Technical, Health, and Nuclear
U.S. Marine Corps	General Technical and Clerical

Chapter 2 has more information about military line scores.

Eyeing the Physique of the Paragraph Comprehension Subtest

When you get to the Paragraph Comprehension subtest, you have several passages to read. Most passages are only one paragraph long, and rarely are they longer than two paragraphs. Each passage contains between 50 and 200 words. (Look at it this way: At least you won't be required to read *War and Peace*!)

The ASVAB test authors may ask you to answer only one question about a given reading passage, or they may ask you to answer as many as five questions about one passage. Unfortunately, this subtest doesn't consist of the most interesting passages you'll ever read. (You won't find paragraphs from your favorite sci-fi novel here.) It's important that you set your attention span dial to the maximum setting.

In order to understand what you read — which is what the Paragraph Comprehension subtest is all about — you need to develop several abilities, which I cover later in this chapter:

- Finding the main idea or argument that the author is making
- Remembering specific details about the reading
- Drawing conclusions from what you've read
- Understanding relationships between ideas
- Paraphrasing or summarizing what you've read

Sampling the Four Types of Comprehension Questions

The Paragraph Comprehension questions on the ASVAB usually take one of four forms:

» Finding specific information

» Recognizing the main idea

» Determining word meaning in context

» Drawing an implication from a stated idea

Each type of question asks you to perform a different kind of analysis of the reading passage. If a passage has more than one question associated with it, chances are each question falls under a different category. The following sections spell out the differences among these four types of questions.

Treasure hunt: Finding specific information

This type of Paragraph Comprehension question asks you to pick out (you guessed it) specific information from a passage. Sounds easy, right? Take a look at the following passage, which clearly states the answer to the question that directly follows it:

> An `13,000 martial arts schools exist in the United States with nearly 6 million active members. Of the 13,000 schools, nearly 7,000 offered tae kwon do lessons.

According to this passage, how many people actively participated in martial arts lessons?

(A) 13,000

(B) 7,000

(C) 6 million

(D) It can't be determined.

The correct answer is Choice (C).

At times, the information that a question asks about isn't directly stated in the question, but you can infer the information from the text. Remember, in the military, the only easy day was yesterday.

Ready to go on a fact-finding mission of your own? Underline the facts in the following passages.

> Surveys say that around 45 percent of dogs sleep in their owners' beds, and as many as 70 percent of people sign their dog's name in holiday cards. Still, some people are "cat people" who won't give dogs a second thought.

> The average astronaut makes under $150,000 per year. But it's a tough job that's not for the faint of heart. The training is very rigorous. It's no wonder so few people try to become astronauts; it's just not worth the meager payoff.

> Remodeling your kitchen may cost more than $10,000, but how much you spend is up to you. You may only want to put in a new sink, which costs less than buying new counters and laying a new floor do. Don't let anyone pressure you into spending more than you can afford.

> Mark Twain didn't smile in pictures. In fact, he once said, "A photograph is a most important document, and there is nothing more damning to go down to posterity than a silly, foolish smile caught and fixed forever." Most people during Twain's time took photos very seriously.

If you underlined the following facts in these four passages, you're on the right track:

- "45 percent of dogs sleep in their owners' beds"
- "as many as 70 percent of people sign their dog's name in holiday cards"
- "The average astronaut makes under $150,000 per year"
- "The training is very rigorous"
- "Remodeling your kitchen may cost more than $10,000"
- "a new sink, which costs less than buying new counters and laying a new floor do"
- "Mark Twain didn't smile in pictures"
- "Most people during Twain's time took photos very seriously"

WARNING: When questions are phrased in the negative, you may be confused about what the question is asking. (This is especially true when the information being sought isn't directly stated in the passage.) Misreading a negative question is also easy. Research has shown that people often skip over a negative word, such as *not*, when they read. Questions on the Paragraph Comprehension portion of the ASVAB are sometimes stated in the negative. When you see a negative word, an alarm should go off in your head to remind you to read the question more carefully.

Cutting to the chase: Recognizing the main idea

Some Paragraph Comprehension questions ask you to identify the main point of a passage. Sometimes the passages directly state the main point, and sometimes they only imply it. The *main idea* of a passage is really just a summary. Think about when you explain why a friend should see a movie; you tell them what it's about without giving away too much detail.

Want to see if your skills are on point? Write the main point below each of the following passages.

> He had the best clothes and great grades, and he could score a touchdown without putting in much effort at all. But the phone never rang. Nobody ever asked him how he was doing. He just wasn't popular.

> Vikings often hunted and traveled in sub-freezing temperatures. To keep warm and cook food while they were on the move, Vikings needed fire, so they often used wood shavings, dry string, and unprepared wool to quickly ignite campfires. Even more impressively, they discovered that boiling a tree fungus called touchwood in urine made it smolder rather than burn. They often carried smoldering touchwood with them to start fires with dry materials.

> Many reality shows take place in unreal environments. It's not unusual for a reality show to feature a group of young adults temporarily living in an oceanside mansion, forming relationships with each other based on their proximity, and having to re-stage events to make for more captivating television. None of these things would happen in the real world.

If you determined the main points are something like the following, you're heading in the right direction:

- He was unpopular.
- Vikings found ways to start fires quickly.
- Reality TV isn't always reflective of the reality most people experience.

TIP If you're not sure what the main point of a paragraph is, reread the first sentence and the last sentence. Chances are one of these two sentences contains the main point. (Flip to "What's the big idea? Determining the main idea in a paragraph" later in this chapter for more information on identifying main ideas.)

If the shoe fits: Determining word meaning in context

Sometimes the Paragraph Comprehension subtest asks you to determine the meaning of a word when it's used in a passage. The correct definition that the question is looking for can be the most common meaning of the word, or it can be a less well-known meaning. In either case, you have to read the passage, make sure you understand how the word is being used, and select the answer option that's closest in meaning to the word as it's used in the passage. Consider this example:

> In the 18th century, it was common for sailors to be pressed into service in Britain. Young men found near seaports could be kidnapped, drugged, or otherwise hauled aboard a ship and made to work doing menial chores. They weren't paid for their service, and they were given just enough food to keep them alive.

EXAMPLE In this passage, <u>pressed</u> means

(A) hired.
(B) ironed.
(C) enticed.
(D) forced.

The descriptions of the conditions these sailors found themselves in should help you decide that they weren't hired or enticed; ironed is one meaning of the word *pressed*, but it isn't correct in this context. The correct answer is Choice (D). Here's another example:

> Since the 1980s, computers have become an indispensable part of American business. Computers can be used for thousands of applications, from word processing and running spreadsheets to keeping one's checkbook updated.

EXAMPLE In this passage, <u>applications</u> means

(A) functions.
(B) sizes.
(C) requests.
(D) types.

Try putting the answer choices in this sentence: "Computers can be used for thousands of applications." You can see that *functions* is closest in meaning to applications, although in a different context, some of the other answer choices may be correct. The correct answer is Choice (A).

CHAPTER 5 **Paragraph Comprehension** 69

Head to Chapter 4 if you need to brush up on your vocabulary. Otherwise, try your hand at using context to figure out the meanings of the following underlined words:

Word in Context	Meaning
The court had no jurisdiction over the case.	
You may be able to redeem yourself if you perform community service.	
The author is reclusive and never makes public appearances.	
We get so tired of the mendacious propaganda in TV commercials during election years.	

Answers: *Jurisdiction* is a noun that means the official power to make legal decisions or judgments. *Redeem* is a verb that means to compensate for faults or to atone for something. *Reclusive* is an adjective that means solitary or avoiding other people's company. *Mendacious* is an adjective that means lying or characterized by deception.

Reading between the lines: Understanding implications

Some Paragraph Comprehension questions ask you to draw an inference from a stated idea. This simply means that you may need to draw a conclusion from what you've read. This conclusion should always be based on the reading, not your own particular opinions about a subject.

REMEMBER

The conclusion — which may be called an *inference* or *implication* — must be reasonably based on what the passage says. You have to use good judgment when deciding which conclusions can be logically drawn from what you've read. Give it a shot:

> Twenty-five percent of all automobile thefts occur when the doors of a car are left unlocked. People often forget to lock their doors, find it inconvenient, or tell themselves, "I'll only be a minute." But it only takes a minute for an accomplished car thief to steal a car. And thieves are always alert to the opportunities that distracted or rushed people present them with.

EXAMPLE

To prevent auto theft, it's a person's responsibility to

(A) leave the doors unlocked.

(B) never be in a rush.

(C) prevent the opportunity.

(D) be willing to perform a citizen's arrest.

Although the paragraph doesn't state, "It's your own responsibility to prevent car thieves from having an opportunity to break into your car," this idea is certainly implied. The correct answer is Choice (C). There's no implication that people should be willing to (or can) perform a citizen's arrest. Leaving the doors unlocked is the opposite of what one should do, and never being in a rush is probably unlikely.

An example of an unreasonable conclusion drawn from the passage would be something like "if everyone locked their doors, there would be no crime" or "all car thieves should be sentenced to 30 years in prison." Nothing in this particular passage supports such a conclusion.

TIP: One way to help determine whether you've drawn a reasonable conclusion is to ask yourself, "Based on what I've just read, would the author agree with the conclusion I've reached?" If the answer is yes, your conclusion is probably reasonable. If the answer is no, it's time to think up a new conclusion.

Check out another example:

> Boiler technicians operate main and auxiliary boilers. They maintain and repair all parts, including pressure fittings, valves, pumps, and forced-air blowers. Technicians may have to lift or move heavy equipment. They may have to stoop and kneel and work in awkward positions.

EXAMPLE: According to this job description, a good candidate for this job would be

(A) a person with joint problems.

(B) an individual unaccustomed to heavy lifting.

(C) a person who isn't mechanically minded.

(D) a person who's physically fit.

Although the passage doesn't state, "This job requires a physically fit person," the duties listed imply that this is so. The correct answer is Choice (D). A person with joint problems may not be able to stoop or kneel or work in awkward positions. A person who's unaccustomed to heavy lifting may not be able to lift or move the heavy equipment as needed. A person who isn't mechanically minded may not have the knowledge necessary to maintain and repair boilers and all their parts. This leaves Choice (D) as the answer, and it's true that a person who's physically fit would be a good choice for the job.

Do You Get My Point? Breaking down Paragraphs

All good writing has a point. Some writing has more than one point. *Points* are ideas that the writer is trying to convey to the reader. The primary purpose of the writing is known as the main point or main idea. Points used to support or clarify the main point are called *subpoints* or *supporting points*. You should know how to identify main points and subpoints when you practice reading.

What's the big idea? Determining the main idea in a paragraph

Questions on the Paragraph Comprehension subtest frequently ask you to identify the main point of a reading passage. How do you get better at identifying main ideas? Practice. The main idea, which is the most important point the author is making, is sometimes stated and sometimes implied in a piece of writing.

Finding a topic sentence

Often, the author begins or ends a paragraph or passage with the main idea, which is located in what's called a *topic sentence*. A topic sentence, reasonably enough, describes the topic that the author is writing about.

CHAPTER 5 **Paragraph Comprehension** 71

TIP If you're looking for the main idea, start off by checking the first and last sentences of the passage. (No, this doesn't mean that you should skip the rest of the passage.) For example, suppose you read the following paragraph:

> The local school district is facing a serious budgetary crisis. The state, suffering a revenue shortfall of more than $600 million, has cut funding to the district by $18.7 million. Already, 65 teachers have been laid off, and more layoffs are expected.

No, the primary theme of this passage isn't "schools in our area suck." You can find the main point of this paragraph in the opening sentence, "The local school district is facing a serious budgetary crisis." What follows are details regarding the budget crisis.

Sometimes a passage builds up to its main idea, and sometimes the main idea is implied instead of stated. Consider the following paragraph:

> The farmers' market reopened on the second weekend of May. Amid the asparagus and flowers, shoppers chatted about the return of temperatures in the 70s. Across the street, children (and their dogs) played Frisbee in the park. Finally, spring has come to town.

In this paragraph, you may think that the farmers' market's reopening is the main point, but the other information about the temperature and the kids playing Frisbee tells you that the main idea is something a bit broader than the market's opening. The main idea is stated in the last sentence: "Finally, spring has come to town."

TIP In boot camp, your drill instructor may say, "Some of you better check to see that your bunks are properly made." Or they may rip your bunk bed apart and say, "Now make this bunk the right way!" Both comments mean the same thing. In the first statement, the drill instructor implies the meaning (and you'd better go check your bunk); the second statement is a bit more direct.

In other words: Rephrasing passages

TIP One of the best ways to identify the main point of a paragraph is to put the paragraph into your own words (*paraphrase* it) or to sum up the basic idea of the paragraph (*summarize* it). By quickly doing this when you take the Paragraph Comprehension portion of the ASVAB, you can be confident that you're answering the question correctly. In other words (to paraphrase), you'll know you understand *what* the paragraph is talking about.

You likely won't have time to write down the main point or to jot down your paraphrase or summary. Instead, as you're reading, simply try to mentally keep track of what's being said by putting it into your own words.

Look at the following paragraph:

> The local school district is facing a serious budgetary crisis. The state, suffering a revenue shortfall of more than $600 million, has cut funding to the district by $18.7 million. Already, 65 teachers have been laid off, and more layoffs are expected.

Now put down this book and spend a few moments paraphrasing the preceding paragraph. When you're done, come back to this page and compare your ideas to the passage. If you wrote something like the following, you're right on track:

> The school district has a budget crunch because the state has a budget crunch. The state cut funding to the school district. Some teachers have been laid off already. More may be laid off soon.

Now, if you wrote something like, "It's finally May, and shoppers and kids-at-play are out and about, enjoying the warmer temperatures of spring," then you're not paying attention.

As you study for the ASVAB, practice paraphrasing reading passages. You can paraphrase or summarize any short passage you read — a few sentences or a paragraph or two. Read different passages from a book or magazine and then set them aside. Get a pencil and jot down your paraphrases. (Remember, you won't have time to do this on the test itself, but the practice helps you mentally prepare for when you take the test.)

Extra, extra! Identifying subpoints

If a writer stuck to just one point, the Paragraph Comprehension subtest would be a breeze. However, an author usually doesn't make just one point in a piece of writing, so you also need to understand the other points the author makes. These details, or *subpoints*, may include facts or statistics, or they may be descriptions that support the passage's main point. Subpoints help you see what the author's saying. For instance, look at this passage:

> The local school district is facing a serious budgetary crisis. The state, suffering a revenue shortfall of more than $600 million, has cut funding to the district by $18.7 million. Already, 65 teachers have been laid off, and more layoffs are expected.

The subpoints help you understand the main point, which is that the school district is facing a severe budgetary crisis. The subpoints help you understand why: "The state, suffering a revenue shortfall of more than $600 million, has cut funding to the district by $18.7 million." You can see that the budgetary crisis is part of a larger problem, which is the state is suffering a severe revenue shortfall. The subpoints also help you understand what this crisis means: "Already, 65 teachers have been laid off, and more layoffs are expected." By using these facts and figures, the author helps you grasp the main point *and* its implications.

Practice identifying subpoints by underlining facts that support the main idea in the following passages.

> A 1943 copper penny may be worth as much as $50,000. During that year, most pennies were made out of steel because the U.S. government needed copper to support World War II efforts, so it was pretty precious. These rare pennies are very valuable to collectors.

> Wildlife is abundant in the Grand Canyon. There are bighorn sheep, California condors, mule deer, elk, cougars, bald eagles, and even bats. Don't forget about reptiles! Grand Canyon National Park is home to 41 species of reptiles, including gila monsters, gopher snakes, rattlesnakes, short-horned lizards, and desert tortoises.

> More than 5.17 billion people use social media. That's 63.7 percent of the total global population, which has grown by about 5.8 percent. An average of 8.9 new users sign up for social media sites every second.

If you underlined the following subpoints, you picked up what I was laying down:

- "During that year, most pennies were made out of steel" and "the U.S. government needed copper to support World War II efforts."
- "Bighorn sheep, California condors, mule deer, elk, cougars, bald eagles, and even bats" and "41 species of reptiles, including gila monsters, gopher snakes, rattlesnakes, short-horned lizards and desert tortoises."
- "63.7 percent," "5.8 percent," and "8.9 new users sign up for social media sites every second."

Analyzing What You've Read: Guessing at What the Writer Really Means

The Paragraph Comprehension subtest of the ASVAB also requires you to analyze what you've read. Analysis is more than simply picking out the point of the text. Analyzing a passage requires you to draw conclusions from what you've read and understand relationships among the ideas presented in the text.

By drawing conclusions about the meaning of a passage, you reach new ideas that the author implies but doesn't come right out and state. You must analyze the information the author presents in order to make inferences from what you've read. For instance, look at the following paragraph:

> The local school district is facing a serious budgetary crisis. The state, suffering a revenue shortfall of more than $600 million, has cut funding to the district by $18.7 million. Already, 65 teachers have been laid off, and more layoffs are expected.

Although the author doesn't say so, you can draw the conclusion that if the state revenue shortfall could somehow be corrected — by increasing state sales tax, for example — the local school district's budgetary crisis could be resolved. The $18.7 million cut from the school budget could be restored. The author never actually makes this point in the paragraph, but by using logic, you can draw this conclusion from the facts presented.

REMEMBER Making inferences and drawing conclusions requires you to use your judgment. You don't want to read too much into a passage. For example, nothing in the example paragraph suggests that electing a new governor is necessary or that increasing federal income taxes would help the problem.

Look at the next paragraph:

> The farmers' market reopened on the second weekend of May. Amid the asparagus and flowers, shoppers chatted about the return of temperatures in the 70s. Across the street, children (and their dogs) played Frisbee in the park. Finally, spring has come to town.

Suppose you're asked the following question about this paragraph:

EXAMPLE You can infer from the passage that

(A) Frisbee playing in the park doesn't happen in winter.

(B) the warm weather is unusual for this time of year.

(C) the shoppers were disappointed in the farmers' market produce.

(D) rain is imminent.

If the point of the passage is that spring has come to town and the author uses Frisbee playing as evidence of the arrival of spring, then it's likely that Frisbee playing doesn't occur in the winter but does begin again in spring. The answer is Choice (A).

Practice inferring what the author's trying to say in the following passages.

> The handcuffs chafed her skin, and she was filled with a sense of dread. She didn't want to hear the heavy clink of the door behind her, but she knew it was coming.
>
> From this passage, you can infer that the woman is _____.

74 PART 2 **Words to Live By: Communication Skills**

The bag got heavier as the day wore on. The backs of Mason's shoes, which seemed to fit first thing in the morning, now rubbed against his Achilles tendon — or maybe it was the socks. Maybe the socks were slipping just a fraction of a millimeter with every step he took. He was sure he'd put a million miles under his heels, but it still wasn't far enough.

From this passage, you can infer that Mason is _____.

The thunder made Jack very nervous. It reminded him of the fireworks on the Fourth of July, when mom and dad put him in his crate and left the house. They were so loud! His tail sagged a little, and he laid his head down on the blanket. Then he heard keys jingling, and his ears perked up as he tilted his head to get a better grasp on the sound. He was so relieved to see mom and dad walk through the door seconds later. Now he didn't have to face the storm alone.

From this passage, you can infer that Jack is _____.

If you figured out that the woman is in jail, Mason's been walking away from something all day, and Jack is a dog who's scared of storms, you're on the right track to solving Paragraph Comprehension problems that involve inference.

Faster than a Speeding Turtle: Tips for Slow Readers

REMEMBER Today's military is much more complex than attending basic training, learning how to shoot a gun, and shipping off to war. After boot camp, you attend intensive classroom training to learn your military job. If you can't read well, you're going to have a very hard time. But the good news is that it's never too late to work on improving your reading skills.

For many people, 13 to 27 minutes is enough time to read all the passages, understand the questions, and choose the correct answers. But slow readers may have more difficulty answering all the questions before time is up. Don't despair: Take the suggestions in this section to help build your reading speed. Of course, they require work, but you knew the mission came with its challenges, right?

Read more, watch less

If you're a slow reader, chances are you don't do a lot of reading. If you have plenty of time before you're due to take the ASVAB, start reading more — right now. It's in your best interest.

TIP You don't have to pick up *A Tale of Two Cities* or *War and Peace*; you can start with the newspaper, a biography of a person you admire, or magazines you find at the library. All reading counts! If you devote at least one hour a day simply to reading, you'll see your reading comprehension and speed increase within a month or so.

TECHNICAL STUFF Several studies have shown that folks who enjoy reading as a pleasurable pastime score better on reading comprehension tests than individuals who dislike reading. Sounds obvious, right? So why study it? The idea is if you grow to enjoy reading, you'll want to read more. You'll become a better reader and thereby score better on reading comprehension tests. How do you discover an enjoyment of reading? Simple — choose reading material in subject areas that interest you.

Become a lean, mean word machine

People sometimes read slowly because they don't have a large vocabulary and don't understand everything they read. If you can identify with this situation, improving your vocabulary is your first step toward increasing your reading comprehension and your reading speed. (Chapter 4 gives you info on building your word knowledge. Check it out.)

Keep a pocket dictionary or a dictionary app handy while reading so you can look up words you don't know. If you're reading articles on the Internet, keep a tab open to one of the online dictionaries (such as www.dictionary.com, www.yourdictionary.com, or www.m-w.com) so you can quickly find the definition of words you find confusing. Your reading will become more enjoyable, and you'll be adding to your vocabulary knowledge to boot.

Build your confidence

Another reason people read slowly is that they don't have confidence in themselves. They're not convinced that they understand what they're reading, so they read a passage several times, trying to make sure they haven't missed anything. But just like people who check that the front door is locked 15 times before leaving for vacation and still lie awake at night wondering whether they locked the door, you'll find that reading and rereading a passage doesn't give you confidence that you understand the text. You get confidence from proving that you understand it.

How do you prove to yourself that you understand what you're reading? Here are a few tips:

» **Get out a textbook or reference book (preferably one that contains some subject matter that interests you) and read one or two paragraphs straight through without going back and rereading anything.** Then set the book aside (keeping your place marked) and write, in your own words, a brief description of what you've read. Finally, turn back to the passage and compare your description to the information on the page.

» **Play the 20-questions game.** Read an article from a magazine, reference book, or textbook. Then ask someone to pick out facts from the article and ask you questions.

» **Create motivation and interest by reading the daily newspaper or news magazines.** Discuss news events with your classmates, friends, or co-workers. Stronger interest equals greater comprehension.

Is your written version of the article close in meaning to the original? Are you getting most of the 20 questions correct? Do you feel comfortable discussing current events with others? If so, you understand what you're reading, and that should build your confidence. If not, keep working on it, and your comprehension will improve. Do the preceding confidence-building drills a few times a day until you feel like you can read any paragraph or two and understand the content without having to reread the information.

The Paragraph Comprehension subtest checks your ability to understand what you read, not how quickly you can read. When you sit down to take this subtest, try to go as quickly as you can without sacrificing accuracy. Being methodical in your reading isn't a bad thing as long as you're getting the answers right. Just try to read a little faster than normal without panicking or missing the point. It's better to read the paragraphs carefully and answer the questions correctly on half of the questions and guess on the other half of the questions than it is to speed through all the reading and get none of the answers right.

Test-Taking Tips for Reading and Gleaning

Although no shortcuts exist for improving your reading comprehension skills (besides practice), you can do a few things on test day to make sure you score as high as possible on this part of the ASVAB.

REMEMBER

If you're running out of time on this subtest or you're not sure whether you can identify the main idea of a passage, take a guess. (But be careful: Guessing and getting too many questions wrong at the end of the subtest may result in a penalty against your score.) If you think that's a good piece of advice, check out these tried-and-true tactics for test day:

- **Read first, ask questions later.** Read the passage all the way through before glancing at the question and answer options.

- **Take it one question at a time.** Some passages have more than one question associated with them, but look at only one question at a time.

- **Understand each question.** What's the question asking you to do? Are you supposed to find the main point? Draw a conclusion? Find a word that's nearest in meaning? Make sure you know what the question is asking before you choose among the answer options. This tip may seem obvious, but when you're in a hurry, you can make mistakes by misunderstanding the questions.

- **Read each answer option carefully.** Don't just select the first answer that seems right. Remember, on the Paragraph Comprehension subtest, one answer is often most right and others are almost right. You want to choose the most right answer, not the almost right answer. And to do that, you have to read all the answers.

- **Check your feelings at the door.** Answer each question based on the passage, not your own opinions or views on the topic.

- **Don't choose vague answer options.** They're incorrect 99.99 times out of 100. (Oh heck, call it 100 times out of 100.) If an answer strikes you as not quite true but not totally false, that answer is incorrect. The ASVAB test authors have put those answers in there to throw you off. Don't give them the satisfaction of falling for their trap!

- **(Almost) never select *never*.** For the most part, answer options that are absolutes are incorrect. *Never, always,* and related words are often a sign that you should select a different answer. Words like *generally* and *usually* are more likely to be correct.

Paragraph Comprehension Practice Questions

The following questions are designed to present you with an opportunity to practice your Paragraph Comprehension skills. Read each short paragraph, followed by one or more questions regarding information contained in that passage. Make sure to read the paragraph carefully before selecting the choice that most correctly answers the question.

Easy Paragraph Comprehension practice questions

Passage one

Mercedes was dismayed to find out that her final exam fell on her birthday — and Russian exams were *hard*. Still, after nearly a year at the Defense Language Institute, she was ready to wrap things up and begin her Air Force career outside the schoolhouse. The whole day would be a mess, though. The test began at 8:00 a.m., and each airman was allowed exactly 90 minutes to complete all the questions. Then, at 10:00 a.m., everyone had to begin writing a 1,000-word essay. Mercedes pressed her fingers to her temples; just thinking about what kind of topics were in the pool (and the fact that she had to finish the essay by noon) conjured a familiar ache. She knew she was ready, and she knew the language inside and out, but test-taker anxiety started to creep in.

1. How does Mercedes feel about taking her final exam?

    (A) She is anxious.
    (B) She's angry.
    (C) She's overconfident.
    (D) She wants to celebrate her birthday instead.

2. Why does Mercedes press her fingers to her temples?

    (A) It helps her concentrate.
    (B) She's beginning to get a headache.
    (C) It's an old habit.
    (D) All of the above.

Passage two

Some people argue that baking is an art, but Chef Debra Dearborn says that baking is a science. She says that if you follow a recipe carefully, assembling the ingredients accurately, cooking at the specified temperature for the specified period of time, your cookies will always turn out right. Chef Dearborn says the best baking is like the best experiment — anyone can duplicate it.

3. In this passage, the word *assembling* most nearly means

    (A) measuring.
    (B) putting together.
    (C) buying.
    (D) storing.

4. According to the passage, if you follow cooking instructions,

    (A) you should experiment more in the kitchen.
    (B) you're an artist.
    (C) your baked goods will come out just right.
    (D) you're Chef Dearborn.

Passage three

At dinner-time tonight I was feverish to do three things at once: write out my day's journal, eat my food, and read *The Journal of Marie Bashkirtseff*. Did all three — but unfortunately not at once, so that when I was occupied with one I would surreptitiously cast a glance sideways at the other — and repined.

5. Which of the following was the author NOT planning to do?

   (A) go shopping
   (B) eat food
   (C) write a journal
   (D) read a journal

Passage four

To motivate your people, give them tasks that challenge them. Get to know your people and their capabilities, so you can tell just how far to push each one. Give them as much responsibility as they can handle and then let them do the work without looking over their shoulders and nagging them. When they succeed, praise them. When they fall short, give them credit for what they've done and coach or counsel them on how to do better next time.

6. According to the paragraph, if your subordinates fail to adequately perform their tasks, you should

   (A) punish them.
   (B) praise them.
   (C) counsel them.
   (D) both B and C.

7. After assigning responsibility for the tasks at hand to your subordinates, you should

   (A) supervise them closely to ensure the tasks are performed correctly.
   (B) let them do the work on their own.
   (C) check their progress at the end of each day.
   (D) schedule sufficient work-breaks to avoid job burnout.

Passage five

Approximately 15,000 years ago the first Native Americans may have appeared in Colorado. The earliest inhabitants were hunters and nomadic foragers on the plains, as well as the western plateau. Agricultural settlements began appearing along river valleys in the eastern part of Colorado from approximately 5,000 B.C. as people learned farming techniques from the Mississippi River Native Americans.

8. The first Native Americans in Colorado were

   (A) farmers.
   (B) traders.
   (C) hunters and gatherers.
   (D) originally from the Mississippi River region.

Passage six

The Tuskegee Airmen were the first Black military pilots in the United States, and they were called that because they trained at Tuskegee University's airfield in Alabama under the only school that trained Black pilots. During World War II, the Tuskegee Airmen formed the 332nd Fighter Group and the 477th Bombardment Group. There were only about a thousand of these courageous men; they're still known today for their unparalleled successes in escorting bombers, but they also served as technicians, radio operators, medical personnel, meteorologists, and more. You can find a beautiful memorial to these heroes at the Tuskegee Airmen National Historic Site.

9. The Tuskegee Airmen formed the

   (A) 472nd Fighter Group and 337th Bombardment group.
   (B) Tuskegee University's Flight School for Black Americans.
   (C) Tuskegee Airmen National Historic Site at Tuskegee University.
   (D) 332nd Fighter Group and 477th Bombardment Group.

10. The Tuskegee Airmen also served as

    (A) technicians.
    (B) medical personnel.
    (C) radio operators.
    (D) all of the above.

Passage seven

His name is Frank Clarke, but his real name isn't really as real as the one the children gave him — The Toyman — because he's always making the kids things, such as kites and tops, sleds and boats, jokes and happiness and laughter. His face is as brown as saddle leather, with a touch of apple red in it from the sun. His face is creased, too, because he laughs and jokes so much. Sometimes when The Toyman appears to be solemn you want to laugh most, for he's only pretending to be solemn. And, best of all, if you hurt yourself or if your pet doggie hurts himself, The Toyman knows how to fix it to make it all well again.

11. Frank Clarke's face could best be described as
    (A) rugged.
    (B) pink and smooth.
    (C) fair.
    (D) feminine.

12. Clarke received his nickname because he was always
    (A) fixing toys.
    (B) making toys for the children.
    (C) telling stories about toys.
    (D) playing with toys.

Passage eight

The third leading cause of unintentional injury death the world over is drowning. Sad to say, most of these deaths can be prevented if the simple rules of water safety are applied. Most drownings are preventable if the victim does not become panicked; therefore, the first and most important safety rule is to remain calm. The ability to swim may save your life, but even an experienced swimmer can panic with fear and stop making rational decisions and begin to flounder. When this happens, the swimmer has taken the first step to drowning. The key to preventing panic is relaxation. When confronted with an emergency, the swimmer must remain calm and in charge, making conscious efforts to escape the situation.

13. According to this passage, what is the first step in drowning?
    (A) going underwater
    (B) giving in to fear
    (C) not wearing a life preserver
    (D) not knowing how to swim

14. The word *flounder*, as used in this passage, most nearly means
    (A) a fish.
    (B) a building foundation.
    (C) to splash about helplessly.
    (D) to float.

15. According to the passage, what is the best prevention for drowning?
    (A) staying out of the water
    (B) learning how to swim
    (C) having a buddy nearby
    (D) remaining calm

Medium Paragraph Comprehension practice questions

Passage nine

Let me now take you on to the day of the assault. My cousin and I were separated at the outset. I never saw him when we forded the river; when we planted the English flag in the first breach; when we crossed the ditch beyond, and, fighting every inch of our way, entered the town.

It was only at dusk, when the place was ours, and after General Baird himself had found the dead body of Tippoo under a heap of the slain, that Herncastle and I met.

16. What would be a good title for the passage?

    (A) "Attacking Japan"
    (B) "War without Violence"
    (C) "Moving to the Mountains"
    (D) "My Account of the War"

17. How long was the main character fighting in the area?

    (A) two hours
    (B) from day to dusk
    (C) a few days
    (D) none of the above

18. In this passage, what is the meaning of the word *heap*?

    (A) pile
    (B) rubbish
    (C) marker
    (D) note

19. According to the passage, you can assume the main character is

    (A) at a community function.
    (B) in a war.
    (C) dreaming.
    (D) moving to a new town.

Passage ten

Braille was based on a military code called *night writing*, developed in response to Napoleon's demand for a means for soldiers to communicate silently at night and without light. A soldier invented a tactile system of raised dots. Napoleon rejected it as too complicated, but Louis Braille simplified it for use by the blind. Braille is still used today, consisting of one to six raised dots, representing the alphabet, that a person can feel with their fingertips.

20. Why was Napoleon interested in Braille?

    (A) He was blind.
    (B) He wanted to help the blind.
    (C) He couldn't read.
    (D) He wanted a code that could be read at night.

21. How many raised dots are used to form each letter of the alphabet in Braille?

    (A) three
    (B) six
    (C) one to six
    (D) none of the above

22. What was Louis Braille's contribution to the invention of this reading system?

    (A) He taught blind people how to read.
    (B) He urged Napoleon to have it developed.
    (C) He named it.
    (D) He simplified someone else's complicated idea.

23. The word *tactile*, as used in this passage, most nearly means

    (A) a sharp object.
    (B) words on a printed page.
    (C) something that is sticky.
    (D) something that can be felt with the fingers.

Passage eleven

There seem to be abundant job opportunities for nurses these days. Plus, nurses receive decent salaries and benefits. Nursing jobs are very flexible with work schedules. There is an array of specialties when it comes to nursing positions in a variety of settings. It is true that nursing offers room for advancement and raises. Overall, the biggest advantage to being a nurse must be the satisfaction you get from knowing you are helping others.

24. According to the paragraph, what is the best part about being a nurse?

    (A) getting good benefits
    (B) helping people
    (C) having three days off in a row
    (D) having room for advancement

25. According to the passage, which of the following is not a benefit of being a nurse?

    (A) room for advancement
    (B) array of specialties
    (C) convenient uniforms
    (D) flexible scheduling

26. What is the main idea of the paragraph?

    (A) There are a lot of nurses.
    (B) There are a lot of nursing jobs.
    (C) Nursing pays well.
    (D) Nursing has many benefits.

27. In this paragraph, what is the meaning of the word *abundant*?

    (A) excellent
    (B) plenty
    (C) few
    (D) competitive

Passage twelve

Immigration and Customs Enforcement, commonly called ICE, has four directorates: Homeland Security Investigations, Enforcement and Removal Operations, the Office of the Principal Legal Advisor, and Management and Administration. An additional component, the Office of Professional Responsibility, is part of the agency but isn't considered a directorate. All the directorates, components, and program offices are part of ICE, which itself falls under a larger agency — the Department of Homeland Security. ICE conducts some deportation operations, but it also focuses on threats to homeland security involving wildlife trafficking, sex trafficking, human trafficking, and the importation of illegal goods. The agency has been responsible for investigations leading to high-level convictions, such as those of famous musicians and actors inappropriately involved with minors, and the repatriation of historic artifacts to their home countries (such as the stone tablet containing the Epic of Gilgamesh).

28. What's the passage's main idea?

    (A) Department of Homeland Security operations
    (B) sex trafficking and human trafficking
    (C) what Immigration and Customs Enforcement does
    (D) directorates of Homeland Security

29. Which of the following is not a directorate of ICE?

    (A) the Office of Professional Responsibility
    (B) Homeland Security Investigations
    (C) the Office of the Principal Legal Advisor
    (D) Enforcement and Removal Operations

30. Based on context, what does *repatriation* mean?

    (A) deportation
    (B) trafficking
    (C) return
    (D) theft

Hard Paragraph Comprehension practice questions

Passage thirteen

Black hat search engine optimization is an unethical practice that goes against search engine guidelines; it's called "black hat" in contrast to white hat, which is ethical and above-board. Some website developers use black hat techniques to try to manipulate search engines and show up higher in search results. Tactics like keyword stuffing (packing a page with irrelevant keywords), using private link networks (building multiple websites with the sole purpose of linking them all together), and tricking users by delivering content they don't expect are all considered black hat techniques. Sadly, many developers make a fortune selling black hat services, but on the bright side, it usually doesn't take long for major search engines to discover what they're doing and blacklist their sites.

31. What can you infer from the passage?

    (A) You should never try to manipulate search engines.
    (B) Most people use black hat techniques to get their websites to show up online.
    (C) Search engine guidelines are arbitrary and rarely enforced.
    (D) Tricking users may be a good idea.

32. Which of the following is not a black hat practice?

    (A) keyword stuffing
    (B) using private link networks
    (C) adding videos to your pages
    (D) deceiving users

Passage fourteen

Washington, D.C., isn't your average American city; it was established in 1790 with the U.S. Constitution, which designated it as the nation's capital. Though it's packed with businesses, homes, museums, and other attractions, it's the most political city in the country — and it's been estimated that there are around 10,000 spies in D.C. at any given time. A representative from the Federal Bureau of Investigation once said, "A spy is nondescript. A spy is going to be someone that's going to be a student in a school, a visiting professor, your neighbor. It could be a colleague or someone that shares the soccer field with you." With tens of thousands of international students, more than 175 foreign embassies, and uncountable numbers of businesspeople linked to foreign intelligence agencies, you'd never know if you were sitting beside a spy on the subway or standing in the checkout line behind someone bent on stealing America's secrets.

33. Which of the following is true about Washington, D.C.?

    (A) The U.S. Constitution established it as the nation's capital.
    (B) There are approximately 10,000 spies in the city.
    (C) There are over 175 foreign embassies in D.C.
    (D) All of the above are true.

34. What's the passage's main idea?

    (A) There are tremendous numbers of spies in D.C.
    (B) You should be wary of your neighbors if you live in the city.
    (C) Politics rule everything in D.C.
    (D) Don't play soccer with strangers.

35. What does the word *bent* mean in this context?

    (A) crooked
    (B) curved
    (C) determined
    (D) talented

Passage fifteen

Dorisa Temple is often called the birthplace of Korean Buddhism. With an ancient, five-story stone pagoda that was built to house a hexagonal reliquary with 17-centimeter-tall sides that contained the Buddha Shaykamuni's ashes, it's considered a very holy site. The reliquary is one of Korea's national treasures. Dorisa is rumored to be the former home of the famed Monk Ado, who meditated and practiced Zen on a stone seat after discovering the site around the year 418. Some monks say that Ado built the temple there because unlike most other places in Korea, peach and plum trees blossomed year-round on the site. The temple had been in place for centuries before monks eventually built the five-story stone pagoda during the Goryeo Period (918 to 1392 CE).

36. What does the word *reliquary* mean?

   (A) temple

   (B) container

   (C) pagoda

   (D) none of the above

37. When was Korea's Goryeo Period?

   (A) Before the Monk Ado built the temple

   (B) Before 918 CE

   (C) 418 CE

   (D) Between 918 and 1392 CE

38. Which of the following is a sensible inference from the passage?

   (A) Buddhism began in Japan before the year 400.

   (B) The Buddha Shaykamuni is an important figure in Korean Buddhism.

   (C) Monk Ado primarily ate fruits from the trees at Dorisa Temple.

   (D) Seventeen centimeters is very small for a reliquary.

Passage sixteen

Don't run drain lines, water lines, or electrical wiring where they may interfere with or contact the dishwasher's motor or legs. Make sure there's plenty of clearance between the motor and the floor; the motor should *never* touch the floor. Never install the dishwasher over carpeted flooring. Connect the drain hose to a waste tee or disposer inlet above a drain trap in house plumbing at least 20 inches above the floor. Drill a hole for the power supply cord and route the cable from the power supply through it. Drill a hole for the water line and route the water line through it. After your hoses are connected and routed, check the air gap (if necessary), install a moisture barrier, and remove the dishwasher panels. Put the dishwasher on its back, install the strain relief, and connect the ground wire before connecting remaining wires. Adjust the wheels and legs, add shims as needed, and install the door handle. Finally, install the countertop attachment.

39. What's the main idea of this passage?

   (A) Where and how to install a dishwasher

   (B) Getting the most from your dishwasher warranty

   (C) How to get side panel kits for dishwashers

   (D) none of the above

40. According to the passage, in what order should you perform these steps?

   (A) Connect the drain hose to a waste tee; route the water line through the hole; route the power supply through the hole.

   (B) Check the air gap; install a moisture barrier; drill a hole for the water line.

   (C) Install the strain relief; connect the ground wire; connect remaining wires.

   (D) Add shims; install the countertop attachment; adjust the wheels and legs.

Passage seventeen

Ensure the gunner restraint harness is properly worn at all times to prevent the gunner from falling. It should be free from twists, which can cause injury when the gunner moves suddenly in the harness. The gunner must hold on tightly to the vehicle-mounted weapon or other supports to assist them in maintaining stability at all times. Failure to comply with this basic safety instruction can result in serious injury or death to personnel. Ensure the straps are not knotted, damaged, kinked, cut, or frayed before fastening them to the platform. If the straps are cut, damaged, or frayed, notify your vehicle maintenance team to order replacement straps. Failure to comply may result in serious injury or death to personnel. When adjusting the gunner's seat for use, ensure both feet are square on the gunner platform and the seat is at a comfortable height for the gunner, providing visibility and promoting mobility in the turret. Failure to comply may result in serious injury or death to personnel.

41. This passage is most likely from
    - (A) a military instruction manual.
    - (B) an email to a military unit.
    - (C) a book on military history.
    - (D) none of the above.

42. This passage's main idea is
    - (A) failing to comply with instructions can result in injury or death.
    - (B) how to manage a gunner's harness and seat.
    - (C) what to do about cut, damaged, or frayed straps on a gunner's harness.
    - (D) ensuring gunners are comfortable so they can perform their jobs while deployed.

43. According to the passage, does the gunner restraint harness provide stability on its own?
    - (A) Yes, it prevents the gunner from falling.
    - (B) Yes, while wearing the harness, the gunner will be stable by placing their feet on the gunner platform.
    - (C) No, the gunner should hold the vehicle-mounted weapon and other supports for stability.
    - (D) No, the gunner should use their feet for stability.

Passage eighteen

Organizational leaders influence several hundred to several thousand people. They do this indirectly, generally through more levels of subordinates than do direct leaders. The additional levels of subordinates can make it more difficult for them to see results. Organizational leaders have staffs to help them lead their people and manage their organizations' resources. They establish policies and the organizational climate that support their subordinate leaders.

44. Organizational leaders provide
    - (A) direct leadership.
    - (B) general policies.
    - (C) organizational budgets.
    - (D) daily work schedules.

45. In order to become more efficient, organizational leaders make significant use of
    - (A) computer technology.
    - (B) rules and regulations.
    - (C) efficiency and management reports.
    - (D) staffs.

Answers and Explanations

Use this answer key to score the Paragraph Comprehension practice questions.

1. **A.** The correct answer is Choice (A). Mercedes is anxious about taking the test, which you can tell with context clues such as "The whole day would be a mess" and "test-taker anxiety started to creep in."

2. **B.** The correct answer is Choice (B). The passage says, "just thinking about what kind of topics were in the pool (and the fact that she had to finish the essay by noon) conjured a familiar ache."

3. **B.** Although measuring is something you do when baking, it doesn't most nearly mean the same thing as *assembling*. Putting together does. Therefore, Choice (B) is the correct answer.

4. **C.** The passage states that if you follow a recipe carefully, "your cookies will always turn out right." The correct answer is Choice (C).

5. **A.** The passage's first sentence tells you everything you need to know — it mentions writing and reading journals and eating food. Shopping isn't mentioned, so the correct answer is Choice (A).

6. **D.** If you didn't read the passage, praising someone who didn't measure up may seem like a bad idea. However, the last sentence states you should give your subordinates credit for the parts of the task they performed correctly and counsel them how to do better the next time. Although that sentence doesn't use the word *praise*, you can infer that giving someone credit means the same thing. The correct answer is Choice (D).

7. **B.** Choices (C) and (D) sound like good ideas, but they aren't suggestions discussed in the paragraph. Remember to avoid the trap of answering based on your personal feelings. Choice (A) is the opposite of what the passage suggests — the writer says to "let [employees] do the work without looking over their shoulders." Choice (B) is the correct answer.

8. **C.** The second sentence states that the original inhabitants "were hunters and nomadic foragers," and because none of the other answer options include hunters, you can deduce that *nomadic foragers* means gatherers. The correct answer is Choice (C).

9. **D.** The passage says that the Tuskegee Airmen formed the 332nd Fighter Group and the 477th Bombardment Group during World War II.

10. **D.** You can read in the passage that the Tuskegee Airmen "also served as technicians, radio operators, medical personnel, meteorologists, and more."

11. **A.** According to the passage, Frank's face is "brown as saddle leather," and he has wrinkles from laughing often. Choice (A) is the correct answer.

12. **B.** The first sentence in the passage explains why the children gave Frank the nickname of The Toyman. Frank knows how to fix things, but that's not how he got his name. The correct answer is Choice (B).

13. **B.** The passage states that fear leads a swimmer to stop making rational decisions, the first step in drowning.

14. **C.** To *flounder* in the water is to splash around helplessly.

15. **D.** The paragraph doesn't discourage the reader from going in the water, nor does it mention having someone nearby. It says knowing how to swim can save your life, but the main focus of the passage is on the importance of remaining calm when trouble strikes.

16. **D.** Choice (A) doesn't make much sense because the group put up an English flag in the first breach. Choice (B) doesn't work because the passage talks about fighting and dead bodies. Choice (C) isn't the best answer because it doesn't directly relate to the passage. Choice (D) is correct because the main character is speaking of his experiences of a particular war.

17. **B.** The passage states in the beginning that the assault began in the day. Later in the passage, the author explains that the town was theirs by dusk, so you can conclude the time frame was from daytime into dusk.

18. **A.** *Heap* is a noun meaning a group of things placed, thrown, or lying one on another — in other words, a pile — so Choice (A) is the correct answer.

19. **B.** The main character is describing a scene relative to that of a war, even mentioning an English flag, a general, and dead bodies. The paragraph never states he is doing something for the community, is planning to stay at the town, or is in a dream, so you can conclude that the main character is in some sort of war.

20. **D.** Napoleon wanted to devise a code that could be read at night, so one of his soldiers invented a system of raised dots that later became Braille.

21. **C.** The passage states that each letter of the alphabet is represented in Braille by raised dots and that each letter uses from one to six dots.

22. **D.** Napoleon rejected the idea for a code that could be read at night because it was too complicated. Louis Braille took that idea and simplified it for use by blind people.

23. **D.** The word *tactile* refers to something that can be felt with one's hands.

24. **B.** According to the last sentence, the biggest satisfaction of being a nurse comes from knowing you make a difference in people's lives, so Choice (B), helping people, is correct.

25. **C.** The passage describes many benefits of being a nurse, but it doesn't talk about the uniforms nurses may wear.

26. **D.** The passage says that nursing has not only good monetary and work benefits but also rewarding self-satisfaction benefits.

27. **B.** *Abundant* is an adjective meaning marked by great plenty. The passage describes abundant job opportunities, meaning there are a lot of jobs from which a nurse can choose.

28. **C.** Though it touches on the other topics, the passage's main idea covers ICE's responsibilities.

29. **A.** The passage says that the Office of Professional Responsibility is part of the agency but isn't considered a directorate, and the other three are.

30. **C.** *Repatriation* is a noun that means to return someone or something to its own country.

31. **A.** The passage concludes by saying, "it usually doesn't take long for major search engines to discover what they're doing and blacklist their sites." That means you can safely infer that trying to manipulate search engines is probably a bad idea.

32. **C.** The paragraph doesn't mention anything about adding video to website pages, but it explicitly points out that keyword stuffing, using private link networks, and deceiving users are black hat practices.

33. **D.** The passage notes that the U.S. Constitution established Washington, D.C.; around 10,000 spies are in the area at any given time, and the city has more than 175 foreign embassies.

34. **A.** The passage says that Washington, D.C., has about 10,000 spies, and it goes on to quote an FBI representative who says just about everyone's a suspect.

35. **C.** In this context, *bent* is an adjective that means determined to do something. (It also means crooked or curved, but in this passage, that definition doesn't make any sense.)

36. **B.** A *reliquary* is a container for holy relics, and as you may have inferred from the passage, the Buddha's ashes fit that bill.

37. **D.** The passage says that Korea's Goryeo Period lasted between 918 and 1392 CE.

38. **B.** Because Dorisa Temple features a five-story stone pagoda that was built just to contain the *container* holding Buddha Shaykamuni's ashes, you can surmise that he's a very important figure in Korean Buddhism. (Another hint is that the reliquary is one of the country's national treasures.)

39. **A.** The passage explains where to install a dishwasher and begins covering installation instructions.

40. **C.** Though it's not the most interesting passage you'll ever read, it's packed with facts that you have to sort through. The passage says, "Put the dishwasher on its back, install the strain relief, and connect the ground wire before connecting remaining wires," which is the only correctly ordered set of instructions among the answer choices.

41. **A.** The thorough and detailed instructions that relate to a gunner indicate that it most likely comes from a military instruction manual.

42. **B.** Although it's very clear that failing to follow the instructions can lead to injury or death, the passage's main idea is how to manage the gunner's harness and seat.

43. **C.** The passage says "The gunner must hold on tightly to the vehicle-mounted weapon or other supports to assist them in maintaining stability at all times," which means the harness alone doesn't provide stability.

44. **B.** The passage mentions direct leaders but only to contrast them with organizational leaders, so Choice (A) is wrong. According to the passage, organizational leaders "establish policies and the organizational climate that support their subordinate leaders." The correct answer is Choice (B).

45. **D.** Organizational leaders have staffs to help them efficiently lead their subordinates and manage the organization. Therefore, Choice (D) is the correct answer.

3 Making the Most of Math: Arithmetic Skills

IN THIS PART . . .

Review math concepts that you'll encounter on the ASVAB, including operations, fractions and decimals, algebra, and geometry.

Find strategies for deciphering the questions on the Arithmetic Reasoning subtest and discover how to solve them correctly.

Answer some practice questions at the end of each chapter to help you determine where you're strong and which topics you should study further.

IN THIS CHAPTER

» Getting more terminology under your belt

» Tackling basics like operations, fractions, and roots

» Performing calculations without the calculator

» Working your way to a higher score

Chapter 6
Mathematics Knowledge and Operations

Rumor has it that Albert Einstein once wrote to a fan, "Do not worry about your problems with mathematics. I assure you mine are far greater." The good professor obviously never had to worry about taking the ASVAB! But you don't have to be a mathematical theoretician to score well on the Mathematics Knowledge subtest. This subtest asks questions about basic high school mathematics — no college or graduate degrees needed.

On the computerized version of the ASVAB, the Mathematics Knowledge subtest consists of 15 questions, and you have 31 minutes to complete it. The paper-and-pencil ASVAB serves up 25 questions that you have to answer in 24 minutes. If you're one of the lucky ones who gets tryout questions on this subtest (see Chapter 1), you answer 30 questions in 65 minutes. You don't necessarily have to rush through each calculation, but the pace you need to set doesn't exactly give you time to daydream. If you're taking the P&P version of the test, you can skip questions you're not sure of and come back to them after answering other, easier questions (just be careful to fill in the right blanks on your answer sheet). You have to focus and concentrate to solve each problem quickly and accurately. And no calculators allowed! Test proctors give you all the scratch paper you can handle, though, and they'll make sure you have plenty of sharpened pencils on hand.

REMEMBER

You don't have the luxury of skipping questions when you're taking the CAT-ASVAB because you have to answer the question you're on before moving to the next. Remember, too, that you may find the CAT-ASVAB harder (or easier) than you thought you would. That's because the program is designed to adapt to your ability. It does that by offering you a medium-difficulty question to kick things off and then chooses the difficulty of the next question based on whether you answer the first correctly. If you're knee-deep in the test and you find yourself saying, "This is harder than what the book covered," that most likely means you're getting a lot of the questions right.

Most of the time, the Mathematics Knowledge subtest contains only one or two questions testing each specific mathematical concept. For example, one question may ask you to multiply fractions, the next may ask you to solve a mathematical inequality, and the question after that may ask you to find the value of an exponent. (If you're freaked out by the last sentence, calm down. I cover each of these concepts in this book.)

All this variety forces you to shift your mental gears quickly to deal with different concepts. You can look at this situation from two perspectives. These mental gymnastics can be difficult and frustrating, especially if you know everything about solving for *x* but nothing about finding a square root. But variety can also help save you on the test. If you don't know how to solve a specific type of problem, that oversight may cause you to get only one or two questions wrong.

You can get more practice for the Mathematics Knowledge subtest — and the rest of the AFQT subtests — with *1,001 ASVAB AFQT Practice Questions For Dummies* by yours truly (Wiley).

REMEMBER: To qualify for military enlistment, you have to score well on this subtest (it's part of the AFQT discussed in Chapter 1). You also have to perform well in Mathematics Knowledge to land certain jobs in the military.

In this chapter, I go over the basic arithmetic you need to know. This info also comes in handy when solving word problems on the Arithmetic Reasoning subtest, which I cover in Chapter 9.

Just When You Thought You Were Done with Vocab: Math Terminology

Math has its own vocabulary. In order to understand what each problem on the Mathematical Knowledge subtest asks, you need to understand certain mathematical terms:

» **Integer:** An *integer* is any positive or negative whole number or zero. The ASVAB often requires you to work with integers, such as –6, 0, or 27.

» **Numerical factors:** Factors are integers (whole numbers) that can be divided evenly into another integer. To *factor* a number, you simply determine the numbers that you can divide into it. For example, 8 can be divided by the numbers 2 and 4 (in addition to 1 and 8), so 2 and 4 are factors of 8. The *prime factorization* of the number 30 is written $2 \times 3 \times 5$.

Numbers may be either composite or prime, depending on how many factors they have:

- **Composite number:** A *composite* number is a whole number that can be divided evenly by itself and by 1, as well as by one or more other whole numbers; in other words, it has more than two factors. Examples of composite numbers are 6 (whose factors are 1, 2, 3, and 6), 9 (whose factors are 1, 3, and 9), and 12 (whose factors are 1, 2, 3, 4, 6, and 12).

- **Prime number:** A *prime* number is a whole number that can be divided evenly by itself and by 1 but not by any other number, which means that it has exactly two factors. The number 1 is not a prime number. Examples of prime numbers are 2 (whose factors are 1 and 2), 5 (whose factors are 1 and 5), and 11 (whose factors are 1 and 11).

» **Base:** A *base* is a number that's used as a factor a specific number of times — it's a number raised to an exponent. For instance, the term 4^3 (which can be written $4 \times 4 \times 4$, and in which 4 is a factor three times) has a base of 4.

» **Exponent:** An exponent is a shorthand method of indicating repeated multiplication. For example, 15×15 can also be expressed as 15^2, which is also known as "15 squared" or "15 to the second power." The small number written slightly above and to the right of a number is the *exponent,* and it indicates the number of times you multiply the base by itself. Note that 15^2 (15×15), which equals 225, isn't the same as 15×2 (which equals 30).

To express $15 \times 15 \times 15$ using this shorthand method, simply write it as 15^3, which is also called "15 cubed" or "15 to the third power." Again, 15^3 (which equals 3,375) isn't the same as 15×3 (which equals 45).

» **Square root:** The *square root* of a number is the number that, when multiplied by itself (in other words, *squared*), equals the original number. For example, the square root of 36 is 6. If you square 6, or multiply it by itself, you produce 36. (Check out "Getting to the Root of the Problem" later in this chapter.)

» **Factorial:** A *factorial* is an operation represented by an exclamation point (!). You calculate a factorial by finding the product of (multiplying) a whole number and all the whole numbers less than it down to 1. That means 6 factorial (6!) is $6 \times 5 \times 4 \times 3 \times 2 \times 1 = 720$.

A factorial helps you determine *permutations* — all the different possible ways an event may turn out. For example, if you want to know how many different ways six runners could finish a race (permutation), you would solve for 6!: $6 \times 5 \times 4 \times 3 \times 2 \times 1$.

» **Reciprocal:** A *reciprocal* is the number by which another number can be multiplied to produce 1; if you have a fraction, its reciprocal is that fraction turned upside down. For example, the reciprocal of 3 is $\frac{1}{3}$. If you multiply 3 times $\frac{1}{3}$, you get 1. The reciprocal of $\frac{1}{6}$ is $\frac{6}{1}$ (which is the same thing as 6); $\frac{1}{6} \times 6 = 1$. The reciprocal of $\frac{2}{3}$ is $\frac{3}{2}$. The number 0 doesn't have a reciprocal. Get the idea?

» **Rounding:** *Rounding* is limiting a number to a certain number of significant digits (replacing some digits with zeros). You perform rounding operations all the time — often without even thinking about it. If you have $1.97 in change in your pocket, you may say, "I have about two dollars." The rounding process simplifies mathematical operations.

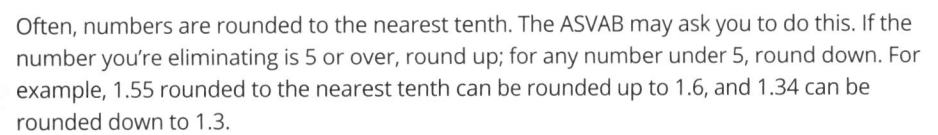

Often, numbers are rounded to the nearest tenth. The ASVAB may ask you to do this. If the number you're eliminating is 5 or over, round up; for any number under 5, round down. For example, 1.55 rounded to the nearest tenth can be rounded up to 1.6, and 1.34 can be rounded down to 1.3.

Many math problems require rounding — especially when you're doing all this without a calculator. For example, pi (π) represents a number approximately equal to 3.1415926535897932384626433838 (and on and on and on). However, in mathematical operations and on the ASVAB, it's common to round π to 3.14.

Operations: What You Do to Numbers

When you toss numbers together (mathematically speaking), you perform an *operation*. When you add or multiply, you perform a *basic operation*. But because math functions according to yin-yang-like principles, each of these basic operations also has an opposite operation called an *inverse operation*. Thus, the additive inverse (of addition) is subtraction, and the multiplicative inverse (of multiplication) is division. And of course, the inverse of subtraction is — you got it — addition. The inverse of division is multiplication.

Don't confuse *opposite* with *inverse*. When you're doing mathematical operations, such as adding and multiplying, the inverse operation is the opposite operation. But when you're talking numbers, *opposite* and *inverse* don't mean the same thing. The opposite of a positive number is a negative number, so the opposite of x is $-x$. But the multiplicative inverse of a number is its reciprocal — that number turned on its head. The reciprocal of x is $\frac{1}{x}$. The inverse of $\frac{1}{5}$ is $\frac{5}{1}$ (or just 5).

NAMING THE ANSWERS

The result of each operation — addition, subtraction, multiplication, or division — goes by a different name:

- When you add two numbers together, you arrive at a *sum*.
- When you subtract, all that remains is a *difference*.
- When you multiply, you come up with a *product*.
- When you divide, you're left with a *quotient*.

First things first: Following the order of operations

Operations must be performed in a certain order. For example, when you have parentheses in a math problem, you must do the calculation in the parentheses before you do any calculations outside of the parentheses. In the equation $2 \times (16 + 5) = ?$, you first add 16 to 5 to arrive at 21, and then you multiply by 2 to come up with a total of 42. You get a different (and wrong) answer if you simply calculate from left to right: $2 \times 16 = 32$, and $32 + 5 = 37$. And you better believe that both results will be choices on the test!

To figure out which mathematical operation you should perform first, second, third, and so on, follow these rules, otherwise known as the *order of operations*:

REMEMBER

1. **Parentheses take precedence.**

    You should do everything contained in parentheses first. In cases where parentheses are contained within parentheses, do the innermost parentheses first. This rule also goes for brackets and braces.

    Note: If you're dealing with a fraction, treat the top as though it were in parentheses and the bottom as though it were in parentheses, even if the parentheses aren't written in the original state. Suppose you have the problem $\frac{3}{1+2} =$. Add the numbers below the fraction bar before dividing. The answer is $\frac{3}{3} = 1$. (For more on fractions, see the later section "Working on Both Sides of the Line: Fractions.") The square root sign $(\sqrt{\ })$ is also a grouping symbol, so you solve for whatever's under the top bar of the square root sign before doing any other operation in the problem.

2. **Exponents come next.**

    Remember that the exponent goes with the number or variable that it's closest to. If it's closest to a parenthesis, then you already should've performed the calculation inside the parentheses in Step 1. For example, $(5 \times 2)^2 = 10^2 = 100$. The square root sign $(\sqrt{\ })$ is also treated as an exponent, so you take the square root during this step.

3. **Multiplication and division are next.**

    Do these operations in left-to-right order (just like you read).

4. **Addition and subtraction are last.**

    Perform these operations from left to right as well.

Check out the following example for a little practice with order of operations:

$$(15 \div 5) \times 3 + (18 - 7) = ?$$

Do the work in parentheses and then remove the parentheses:

$3 \times 3 + 11 = ?$

No exponents are present, so division and multiplication come next (in this problem, only multiplication is needed):

$9 + 11 = ?$

Finally, do the addition and subtraction (in this problem, only addition is needed). Your final answer is 20.

TIP Use the acronym PEMDAS, or "Please Excuse My Dear Aunt Sally," to remember the order of operations. It stands for "parentheses, exponents, multiplication, division, addition, subtraction" to show you which calculations to perform in order.

Check out these order of operations practice problems and see what you come up with.

Problem	Your Solution
$7 \div (5 \times 2 - (6 \div 3)) = ?$	
$7(4 + 13) = ?$	
$16 - 5 + (7 - 3) \times 3 = ?$	
$23 \times (8 \times 4) \div 5 = ?$	

The answers, in order from top to bottom, are 0.875, 119, 23, and 147.2.

Completing a number sequence

The Arithmetic Reasoning (AR) subtest often includes questions that test your ability to name what comes next in a sequence of numbers. Generally, these problems are the only AR questions that aren't word problems (which I cover in Chapter 9). However, sequence questions do test your ability to do arithmetic and to reason, because you have to determine how the numbers relate to each other. And to do this, you must be able to perform mathematical operations quickly.

Suppose you have a sequence of numbers that looks like this: 1, 4, 7, 10, ?. Each new number is reached by adding 3 to the previous number: $1 + 3 = 4$, $4 + 3 = 7$, and so on. So the next number in the sequence is $10 + 3 = 13$, or 13.

But of course, the questions on the ASVAB aren't quite this simple. More likely, you'll see something like this: 2, 4, 16, 256, ?. In this case, each number is being multiplied by itself, so $2 \times 2 = 4$, $4 \times 4 = 16$, and so on. The next number in the sequence is 256×256, which equals 65,536 — the correct answer.

You may also see sequences like this: 1, 2, 3, 6, 12, ?. In this sequence, the numbers are being added together: $1 + 2 = 3$, and $1 + 2 + 3 = 6$. The next number is $1 + 2 + 3 + 6 = 12$. So the next number would be 24.

CHAPTER 6 Mathematics Knowledge and Operations   95

Finding the pattern

To answer sequence questions correctly, you need to figure out the pattern as quickly as possible. Some people, blessed with superior sequencing genes, can figure out patterns instinctively. The rest of the population has to rely on a more difficult, manual effort.

Finding a pattern in a sequence of numbers requires you to think about how numbers work. For instance, seeing the number 256 after 2, 4, 16 should alert you that multiplication is the operation, because 256 is so much larger than the other numbers. On the other hand, because the values in 1, 2, 3, 6, 12 don't increase by much, you can guess that the pattern requires addition.

Dealing with more than one operation in a sequence

Don't forget that more than one operation can occur in a sequence. For example, a sequence may be "add 1, subtract 1, add 2, subtract 2." That would look something like this: 2, 3, 2, 4, ?.

Because the numbers in the sequence both increase and decrease as the sequence continues, you should suspect that something tricky is going on.

Make sure to use your scratch paper! Jot down notes while you're trying to find the pattern in a sequence. Writing down your work helps you keep track of which operations you've tried.

Try your hand at predicting the next numbers in the following sequence problems.

Problem	Your Solution
6, 13, 27, 55, . . .	
5, 16, 27, 38, . . .	
8, 14, 22, 36, 58, . . .	
$\frac{16}{4}, \frac{4}{2}, \frac{2}{2}, \frac{1}{2}, \ldots$	

The answers are, in order from top to bottom, 111, 49, 94, and $\frac{1}{4}$.

Averaging mean, median, and mode in a range

An average number is one that expresses a typical value in a set of data. In plain English, that means what you can expect as an outcome. For example, if you take the ASVAB three times and get an AFQT score of 80, 85, and 90, respectively, your average score is 85. (I advise against retaking the ASVAB to practice your averaging skills; I just want you to take it once and score really well!) Things get a little sticky when the numbers aren't so nicely rounded, though. If someone's scores are 35, 35, and 50, their average is 40.

This type of average is technically called the *arithmetic mean*, or just *mean* for short. To figure out a mean, add all the numbers in a data set (in this case, that's 35, 35, and 50). Divide the sum by how many numbers there are. Because there are three numbers in this data set, your math looks like this:

$$35 + 35 + 50 = 120$$
$$120 \div 3 = 40$$

You might also counter other types of averages on the ASVAB, including *median* and *mode*.

> **Median:** The median is the middle value in a set of ordered numbers. You can find it by putting your numbers in numerical order, from smallest to largest. In the data set 47, 56, 58, 63, 100, the median is 58.

> **Mode:** Mode is the value or values that occur most often in a list of numbers. If no numbers are repeated, there's no mode. But in the earlier data set with the test scores — 35, 35, and 50 — the mode is 35 because it appears most often.

Working on Both Sides of the Line: Fractions

I don't know why, but it seems almost all math textbooks explain fractions in terms of pies. (I think most mathematicians must have a sweet tooth.) But I like pizza, so I'm going to use pizza instead. If a *whole number* is a pizza, a *fraction* is a slice of pizza. A fraction also illustrates the slice's relationship to the whole pizza. For example, consider the fraction $\frac{3}{5}$. If you accuse your cousin of eating $\frac{3}{5}$ of the pizza when they come over for movie night, you're saying that the pizza is divided into five equal-sized slices — fifths — and your cousin ate three of those five slices.

REMEMBER The number above the fraction bar — the three slices your cousin ate — is called the *numerator*. The number written below the fraction bar — the total number of slices the pizza is divided into — is called the *denominator*.

Common denominators: Preparing to add and subtract fractions

To add and subtract fractions, the fractions must have the same denominator (bottom number), which is called a *common denominator*. If the fractions don't have a common denominator, you have to find one. There are two basic methods to use. Sound fun? Read on.

Method one

Finding a common denominator can be easy, or it can be as hard as picking off anchovies.

Suppose you want to add $\frac{3}{5}$ and $\frac{3}{10}$. Getting a common denominator is easy here, and you use this process whenever you can evenly divide one denominator by another. Follow these steps:

1. **Divide the larger denominator by the smaller denominator.**

   If there's a remainder, then you can't use this method, and you have to use method two (see the next section). In this case, 10 can be divided evenly by 5. The quotient (answer) that results is 2.

2. **Take the fraction with the smaller denominator $\left(\frac{3}{5}\right)$; multiply both the numerator (top number) and the denominator (bottom number) by the answer that resulted in Step 1.**

   Multiply 3 by 2, and the result is 6 — that's your new numerator. Multiply 5 by 2, and the result is 10 — that's your new denominator.

3. **Replace the numerator and denominator with the numbers from Step 2.**

   You can also express $\frac{3}{5}$ as $\frac{6}{10}$. (If you cut the pizza into 10 slices instead of 5 and your cousin eats 6 slices instead of 3, they've eaten exactly the same amount of pizza.)

After you've found a common denominator, you add the two fractions by simply adding the numerators together: $\frac{6}{10} + \frac{3}{10} = \frac{9}{10}$. Think of it this way: If your cousin eats $\frac{6}{10}$ of the pizza (which is just another way of saying $\frac{3}{5}$) and you eat $\frac{3}{10}$ of the pizza, together you've eaten $\frac{9}{10}$ of the pizza.

Method two

Suppose your cousin eats $\frac{3}{5}$ of one pizza and your sister eats $\frac{1}{6}$ of another pizza (one that was cut into 6 slices instead of 5), and you want to know how much pizza has been eaten. In this case, you need to add $\frac{3}{5}$ and $\frac{1}{6}$.

Adding these fractions is a bit more difficult because you can't divide either denominator by the other. You have to find a common denominator that both 5 and 6 divide into evenly. Here's how:

1. **Multiply the denominator of the first fraction by the denominator of the second fraction.**

    In the preceding example, $5 \times 6 = 30$. The common denominator for both fractions is 30.

2. **Express the first fraction in terms of the new common denominator.**

    $\frac{3}{5} = \frac{?}{30}$

3. **Multiply the numerator by the number that you multiplied by to result in the new denominator.**

    To convert the denominator (5) to 30, you multiply by 6, so multiply the numerator (3) by 6. The result is 18. Therefore, the fraction $\frac{3}{5}$ can be expressed as $\frac{18}{30}$.

    When you're trying to find an equivalent fraction for a fraction, always multiply the numerator and the denominator by the same number. Otherwise, you change the value of the fraction.

    REMEMBER

    With this example, you multiply the numerator and the denominator by 6, discovering that $\frac{3}{5}$ is the same thing as $\frac{18}{30}$. But if you were to multiply only the denominator by 6, you'd have a new number; $\frac{3}{5}$ and $\frac{3}{30}$ don't have the same value.

4. **Next, express the second fraction in terms of the new common denominator.**

    $\frac{1}{6} = \frac{?}{30}$

5. **Multiply the numerator of the second fraction by the number you used to result in the denominator.**

    To get 30, you have to multiply 6 by 5. Multiply the numerator by the same number: You find that $1 \times 5 = 5$, so the fraction $\frac{1}{6}$ can be expressed as $\frac{5}{30}$.

    After all that work, you can finally add the fractions: $\frac{18}{30} + \frac{5}{30} = \frac{23}{30}$. Now pause and take a bite of pizza.

Finding common denominators for three or more fractions

If you have more than two fractions with different denominators, you have to find a common denominator that all the denominators divide into. Suppose you need to add $\frac{1}{2} + \frac{2}{3} + \frac{3}{5}$.

A simple way to find a common denominator is to take the largest denominator (in this case, 5) and multiply it by whole numbers, starting with 1, 2, 3, 4, and so on until you find a denominator that the other denominators also divide into evenly.

If you multiply 5 by 2, you get 10, but 3 doesn't divide evenly into 10. So keep going: $5 \times 3 = 15$, $5 \times 4 = 20$, and so on until you find a number that 2, 3, and 5 can divide into evenly. In this case, 30 is the first number you can find that 2, 3, and 5 can divide into evenly, so 30 is your common denominator.

Practice your own fraction addition and subtraction with the following problems.

Problem	Your Solution
$\frac{5}{9} + \frac{1}{2} = ?$	
$\frac{3}{16} + \frac{3}{4} = ?$	
$\frac{7}{9} - \frac{1}{2} = ?$	
$\frac{11}{20} - \frac{4}{60} = ?$	

The answers from the top down are $1\frac{1}{18}, \frac{15}{16}, \frac{5}{18}, \frac{29}{60}$.

Multiplying and reducing fractions

REMEMBER

Multiplying fractions is easy. You just multiply the numerators and then multiply the denominators. So look at the following equation: $\frac{1}{2} \times \frac{3}{4} \times \frac{3}{5} = ?$. You multiply $1 \times 3 \times 3 = 9$ (the numerators) and then $2 \times 4 \times 5 = 40$ (the denominators) to result in $\frac{9}{40}$.

Occasionally, when you multiply fractions, you end up with an extremely large fraction that can be simplified or reduced. To express a fraction in its *lowest terms* means to put it in such a way that you can't evenly divide the numerator and the denominator by the same number (other than 1).

A number that you can divide into both the numerator and the denominator is called a *common factor*. If you have the fraction $\frac{6}{10}$, both the numerator (6) and the denominator (10) can be divided by the same number, 2. If you do the division, $6 \div 2 = 3$ and $10 \div 2 = 5$, you find that $\frac{6}{10}$ can be expressed in the simpler terms of $\frac{3}{5}$. You can't reduce (simplify) $\frac{3}{5}$ any further; the only other number that both the numerator and denominator can be divided by is 1, so the result would be the same, $\frac{3}{5}$.

TIP

Remember, you can't use a calculator on the ASVAB, so multiplying large numbers can take extra steps and valuable time. You can make your work easier by *canceling out* common factors before multiplying.

For example, suppose you have the problem $\frac{20}{21} \times \frac{14}{25}$. Multiplying the numerators $(20 \times 14 = 280)$, then multiplying the denominators $(21 \times 25 = 525)$, and finally reducing the fraction $\left(\frac{280}{525} = \frac{8}{15}\right)$ may require you to write out three or more separate multiplication/division problems. But you can save time if a numerator and denominator have common factors. Here, the numerator of the first fraction (20) and the denominator of the second (25) have a common factor of 5, so you can divide both of those numbers by 5: Your problem becomes $\frac{4}{21} \times \frac{14}{5}$. The numerator of the second fraction (14) and the denominator of the first fraction (21) are both divisible by 7, so you can cancel out a 7: Divide 14 and 21 by 7. This changes the equation to $\frac{4}{3} \times \frac{2}{5} = \frac{8}{15}$, a much simpler math problem.

Work out your own solutions by multiplying the following fractions.

Problem	Your Solution
$\frac{3}{4} \times \frac{2}{8} = ?$	
$\frac{7}{8} \times \frac{1}{10} = ?$	
$\frac{4}{32} \times \frac{3}{11} = ?$	
$\frac{2}{26} \times \frac{6}{6} = ?$	

From top to bottom, the answers are $\frac{3}{16}, \frac{7}{80}, \frac{3}{88}, \frac{1}{13}$.

Dividing fractions

Dividing fractions is simple if you remember this rule: Dividing a fraction by a number is the same as multiplying it by the multiplicative inverse (reciprocal) of that number. Of course, there are always exceptions. You can't use this operation on zero. Zero has no multiplicative inverse.

REMEMBER

You obtain the reciprocal of a number by flipping the number. That means that if you want to divide a fraction by 5, you simply multiply the fraction by the inverse of 5, which is $\frac{1}{5}$. You can understand this process more easily if you remember that 5 is the same thing as $\frac{5}{1}$. In other words, 5 divided by 1 equals 5 (that is, $5 \div 1 = 5$). And the reciprocal of $\frac{5}{1}$ is $\frac{1}{5}$. To come up with the reciprocal of a number, simply stand the number on its head.

To divide a fraction, use the inverse of the number that follows the division symbol (÷) and substitute a multiplication symbol (×) for the division symbol. Therefore, $\frac{1}{3} \div 2$ is expressed as $\frac{1}{3} \times \frac{1}{2}$, and you already know how to multiply fractions. (If not, check out the "Multiplying and reducing fractions" section earlier in the chapter.) $1 \times 1 = 1$ and $3 \times 2 = 6$, so the product of $\frac{1}{3} \times \frac{1}{2} = \frac{1}{6}$. Therefore, $\frac{1}{3} \div 2 = \frac{1}{6}$.

Try your hand at divvying up fractions using the following problems.

Problem	Your Solution
$\frac{5}{6} \div \frac{3}{4} = ?$	
$\frac{1}{2} \div \frac{3}{4} = ?$	
$\frac{10}{11} \div \frac{10}{11} = ?$	
$\frac{7}{8} \div \frac{14}{15} = ?$	

The answers, from top to bottom, are $1\frac{1}{9}, \frac{2}{3}, 1, \frac{15}{16}$.

Converting improper fractions to mixed numbers ... and back again

If you have a fraction with a numerator larger than or equal to its denominator, you have an *improper fraction*. For example, $\frac{7}{3}$ is an improper fraction. To put an improper fraction into simpler (proper) terms, you can change $\frac{7}{3}$ into a *mixed number* (a number that includes a whole number and a fraction). Simply divide the numerator by the denominator: 7 divided by 3 gives you a quotient of 2 with a remainder of 1. There's something left over because 3 doesn't divide evenly into 7. The remainder becomes a numerator over the original denominator, so $\frac{1}{3}$ is left over. Therefore, $\frac{7}{3}$ is the same as $2\frac{1}{3}$.

REMEMBER: If you want to multiply or divide a mixed number, you need to convert it into a fraction — an improper fraction. To make the change, convert the whole number into a fraction and add it to the fraction you already have. Here's how:

1. **Multiply the whole number by the denominator (bottom number) of the existing fraction to arrive at a new numerator.**

    Suppose you have $7\frac{2}{3}$. Multiply 7 by 3: $7 \times 3 = 21$.

2. **Place this new numerator over the existing denominator.**

    $\frac{21}{3}$

3. **Add that fraction to the original fraction to get the final answer.**

    $\frac{21}{3} + \frac{2}{3} = \frac{23}{3}$

    Check out the "Common denominators: Preparing to add and subtract fractions" section earlier in this chapter for the complete scoop on adding fractions.

Or if you want to get technical, you can look at the whole process this way, too:

$$7\frac{2}{3} = \frac{7 \times 3 + 2}{3} = \frac{23}{3}$$

Expressing a fraction in other forms: Decimals and percents

A fraction can also be expressed as a decimal and as a percent. Here's how to convert between forms:

- **To change a fraction into a decimal:** Divide the numerator (top number) by the denominator (bottom number). Given that handy explanation, $\frac{3}{5}$ (or $3 \div 5$) converted into decimal form is 0.6. (Refer to the section "Dividing decimals" later in this chapter.)

    Some fractions convert to *repeating decimals* — a decimal in which one digit is repeated infinitely. For instance, $\frac{2}{3}$ is the same as 0.66666 (with the sixes never stopping).

    Repeating decimals are often rounded to the nearest hundredth; therefore, $\frac{2}{3}$ rounds to 0.67.

    (**Remember:** The first space to the right of the decimal is the *tenths* place, the second space is the *hundredths* place, and the third is the *thousandths,* and so on.)

- **To make a decimal into a percent:** Move the decimal point two spaces to the right and add a percent sign. For example, 0.6 becomes 60%.

See the following sections for more thorough discussions of decimals and percents.

Adding and subtracting decimals

To add and subtract decimals, put the numbers in a column and line up the decimal points. Then add or subtract as if the decimals were whole numbers, keeping the decimal point in the same position in your answer.

Here are two examples:

$$\begin{array}{r} 1.4583 \\ +0.5500 \\ \hline 2.0083 \end{array} \qquad \begin{array}{r} 1.4583 \\ -0.5500 \\ \hline 0.9083 \end{array}$$

TIP You can add zeros to the end of a decimal if performing the calculations this way is easier for you. So 0.1 can be 0.100 without changing its value. In the preceding problems, 0.55 can be 0.5500 to help you line up the decimal points and perform the operation.

Multiplying decimals

Multiplying a decimal is like multiplying a regular, everyday whole number, except that you have to place the decimal point in the correct position after you reach an answer.

1. **Multiply as though you were multiplying whole numbers, without the decimal points.**

   Suppose you're multiplying 3.77×2.8. In this example, $377 \times 28 = 10,556$.

2. **Count and add the number of decimal places (to the right of the decimal point) in the numbers being multiplied.**

   If one of the numbers you're multiplying is 3.77, you have two decimal places. If the other number you're multiplying is 2.8, you have one more decimal place, so the total number of decimal places in your answer will be three.

   REMEMBER If you're multiplying a number that has only zeros to the right of the decimal point, then those decimals don't count. For instance, 3 can also be expressed as 3.0, but you wouldn't count the 0 as a decimal place. All the zeros to the right of the decimal point don't count unless a number other than zero comes after them. For instance, 3.000007 has six decimal spaces, 3.0070 has three decimal spaces, and 3.000 has none, at least not for the purpose of multiplying (and as long as you're not including those 0s in the multiplication).

3. **In the answer, move the decimal point back to the left by the number of places you counted in Step 2.**

   This time, zeros do count. You counted three total decimal places in 3.77 and 2.8, so you move the decimal point in 10566 back to the left three places. The resulting product is 10.556.

   REMEMBER If your answer doesn't include enough numbers for the decimal spaces you need, then add as many zeros as necessary to the left of the answer. Suppose your answer is 50, and you have to move the decimal point to the left three spaces. There aren't three spaces in 50, so you add a zero to the left to make it 050 and put the decimal point in its proper position: 0.050 is your answer.

Here's another example: 0.04×0.25. Multiply the decimals as if they were whole numbers: $4 \times 25 = 100$. Count and add the number of decimal places in the original two numbers; there are four. Then put the decimal point in the correct place in the answer. For 100, count from right to left four places, and put the decimal point there: 0.0100, or 0.01. Here's the method behind the madness:

$$\frac{4}{100} \times \frac{25}{100} = \frac{100}{10,000} = \frac{1}{100} = 0.01 \text{ (or } 0.0100\text{)}$$

Dividing decimals

Decimals are divided according to slightly different rules, depending on whether both numbers in the problem are decimals.

DIVIDING DECIMALS BY WHOLE NUMBERS

Here's how to divide a decimal by a whole number:

1. **Move the decimal point over to the right until the decimal is a whole number, counting the number of decimal places.**

   For example, if you want to find $1.25 \div 4$, change 1.25 to 125 by moving the decimal two decimal places to the right. Remember how many places you moved the decimal — you need that info later.

2. **Perform the division operation on the whole number.**

   $125 \div 4 = 31.25$

3. **In your answer, move the decimal point to the left the number of places you moved it in Step 1.**

   To make up for moving the decimal point two places to the right when you made 1.25 into a whole number, move the decimal point two places to the left in 31.25. Your answer is 0.3125.

DIVIDING DECIMALS BY DECIMALS

Here's how to divide a decimal by another decimal in which there are the same number of places after the decimal point:

1. **Make the *divisor* (the decimal going into the other number) into a whole number: Move the decimal point all the way to the right, counting the number of places you move it.**

   Suppose you want to divide 0.15 by 0.25 (that is, $0.15 \div 0.25$). Move the decimal point in 0.25 two places to the right: It then becomes 25.

2. **Move the decimal in the *dividend* (the number being divided) the same number of decimal places.**

   Move the decimal point in 0.15 two places: 0.15 becomes 15.

3. **Divide.**

   When you divide 15 by 25, the result is 0.60. You don't need to move any more decimals around — 0.60 is your final answer.

Unlike multiplying decimals, where you place the decimal point after the computation, when dividing decimals you place the decimal point first. If your problem is $0.42\overline{)2.394}$, move the decimal point to the right in the divisor until you have a whole number. In this case, you have to move the decimal point two places to the right in both the divisor and the dividend:

$$0.42_{\wedge}\overline{)2.39_{\wedge}4}$$

When you move both decimal points to the right two places, the problem now reads $42\overline{)239.4}$. When you divide, put your decimal point in the quotient above its place in the divisor, like this:

$$42\overline{)239.4}^{\,5.7}$$

Playing with percents

A percent is a fraction based on one-hundredths. Five percent (5%) is the same as $\frac{5}{100}$ or 0.05. The ASVAB often asks you to calculate "10% off" or "an increase of 15%" on the Arithmetic Reasoning subtest. You need to be able to convert percents to fractions or decimals to answer these questions correctly.

To add, subtract, multiply, or divide using percents, change the percent to a fraction or a decimal. Here are some helpful hints for figuring percents:

- » Remember, a percent is just hundredths, so 3% is $\frac{3}{100}$ or 0.03, 22% is $\frac{22}{100}$ or 0.22, and 110% is $\frac{110}{100}$ or 1.10.
- » To convert a percent to a decimal, just drop the percent sign and move the decimal point two places to the left, adding zeros as needed.
- » The decimal point always starts to the right of a whole number, so 60 is the same thing as 60.0. Moving the decimal point two spaces to the left leaves you with 0.6.

After you do the conversion, follow the rules outlined in the earlier sections for performing specific operations on fractions or decimals.

Showing comparisons with ratios

A *ratio* shows a relationship between two things. For example, if Margaret invested in her tattoo parlor at a 2:1 (or 2 to 1) ratio to her business partner, Julie, then Margaret put in $2 for every $1 that Julie put in. You can express a ratio as a fraction, so 2:1 is the same as $\frac{2}{1}$.

Or suppose you fill up your shiny, brand-new SUV, and you want to compute your gas mileage — miles per gallon. You drive for 240 miles and then refill the tank with 15 gallons of gas, so the ratio of miles to gallons is 240:15. You can compute your gas mileage by dividing the number of miles by the number of gallons: 240 miles ÷ 15 gallons. You're getting 16 miles per gallon. Time for a tuneup!

In this section, I cover some uses for ratios, including scale drawings and rates such as speed.

Navigating scale drawings

Scale, particularly when used on the ASVAB, relates to scale drawings. For example, a map drawn to scale may have a 1-inch drawing of a road that represents 1 mile of physical road in the real world. The Arithmetic Reasoning portion of the ASVAB often asks you to calculate a problem based on scale, which can be represented as a standard ratio (1 inch : 1 mile) or a fraction $\left(\frac{1 \text{ inch}}{1 \text{ mile}}\right)$.

On a map with a scale of 1 inch to 1 mile, the ratio of the scale is represented as 1:1. But questions are never this easy on the ASVAB. You're more likely to see something like, "If a map has a scale of 1 inch to every 4 miles . . ." That scale is expressed as the ratio 1 : 4, or $\frac{1}{4}$.

Try your hand with the following common scale problem:

If the scale on a road map is 1 inch = 250 miles, how many inches would represent 1,250 miles?

The problem wants you to determine how many inches on the map represent 1,250 miles if 1 inch is equal to 250 miles. You know that 1 inch = 250 miles, and you also know that some unknown number of inches, which you can call *x*, equals 1,250 miles. The problem can be expressed as two ratios set equal to each other, known as a proportion: $\frac{1}{250} = \frac{x}{1,250}$. Now all you have to do is solve for x by multiplying each side of the equation by 1,250:

$$\frac{1}{250} = \frac{x}{1,250}$$
$$\frac{1}{250} \times 1,250 = \frac{x}{1,250} \times 1,250$$
$$\frac{1,250}{250} = x$$
$$x = 5$$

So if 1 inch is equal to 250 miles, then 5 inches would be equal to 1,250 miles. If this problem causes you to scratch your head, check out Chapter 7 for info on solving for x.

REMEMBER: Almost every military job makes use of scales, which is why scale-related questions are so common on the ASVAB. Whether you're reading maps at Mountain Warfare School or organizing trash pickup (what the military calls "area beautification") around the base, you need to use and interpret scales frequently.

Playing with proportions

Proportion is a mathematical comparison between two ratios. When you see math (or real-world) problems that say things like "3 parts vinegar, 1 part water," you're dealing with a ratio (and in this case, it's 3:1). But when you compare two ratios (3 parts vinegar, 1 part water and 9 parts vinegar, 3 parts water), you're dealing with a proportion.

If two sets of numbers increase or decrease in the same ratio, they're *directly proportional* to each other. You can identify proportions by the symbol :: or ∝ (just like the vinegar and water recipe I describe in the previous paragraph). You use direct proportions when an ASVAB question asks you to determine how much to increase or decrease a recipe, how long takes one vehicle takes to travel a certain distance at a certain speed, and a few other scenarios.

Inverse proportions occur when one value increases and the other decreases. For example, more workers on a job reduce the amount of time necessary to complete a task. You may see inverse proportions on ASVAB questions about multiple people filling up a swimming pool, time to complete a job, or something similar.

Remembering important rates

A *rate* is a fixed quantity — a 5% interest rate, for example. It can mean the speed at which someone or something works (John reads at the rate of one page per minute), or it can mean an amount of money paid based on another amount (life insurance may be purchased at a rate of $1 per $100 of coverage). A rate is often a speed — something per a unit of time.

REMEMBER: Word problems often ask you to solve problems that involve speed or simple interest rates. Here are two rate formulas you should commit to memory:

» **Simple interest:** $I = Prt$, where I represents the amount of interest, P is the principal (the initial amount invested), r is the interest rate written as a decimal, and t is the length of time in years the money is invested.

» **Distance:** $d = rt$, where d represents the distance traveled, r is the rate (speed) of travel, and t is the amount of time traveled.

TIP: In a rate, you can generally think of the word *per* as a division sign. For instance, suppose someone drives 141 miles in 3 hours, and you have to find the average speed. You want the rate of speed in miles per hour, so you take miles (distance) divided by hours (time): 141 miles ÷ 3 hours = 47 miles/hour. Using algebra, you can rearrange the distance formula to say the same thing: $d \div t = r$.

A Powerful Shorthand: Writing in Scientific Notation

Scientific notation is a compact format for writing very large or very small numbers. Although it's most often used in scientific fields, you may find a question or two on the Mathematics Knowledge subtest of the ASVAB asking you to covert a number to or from scientific notation.

Scientific notation separates a number into two parts: a number between 1 and 10 and a power of ten (such as 10^7, 10^{21}, or 10^{-18}; see the earlier section "Just When You Thought You Were Done with Vocab: Math Terminology" for info on powers and exponents). Therefore, 1.25×10^4 means 1.25×10 to the fourth power, or 12,500; 5.79×10^{-8} means $5.79 \div 10$ to the eighth power, or 0.0000000579. The exponent tells you how many places to move the decimal point and whether to move it left (if it's negative) or right (if it's positive).

Getting to the Root of the Problem

A *square root* is the factor of a number that, when multiplied by itself, produces the number. Take the number 36, for example. One of the factors of 36 is 6. If you multiply 6 by itself (6×6), you come up with 36, so 6 is the square root of 36. The number 36 has other factors, such as 18. But if you multiply 18 by itself (18×18), you get 324, not 36. So 18 isn't the square root of 36.

All whole numbers are grouped into one of two camps when it comes to roots:

» **Perfect squares:** Only a few whole numbers, called *perfect squares*, have exact square roots. For example, the square root of 25 is 5.

» **Irrational numbers:** Other whole numbers have square roots that are decimals that go on forever and have no pattern that repeats (nonrepeating, nonterminating decimals), so they're called *irrational numbers*. The square root of 30 is 5.4772255 with no end to the decimal places, so the square root of 30 is an irrational number.

REMEMBER: The sign for a square root is called the *radical sign*. It looks like this: $\sqrt{}$. Here's how you use it: $\sqrt{36}$ means "the square root of 36" — in other words, 6.

Perfect squares

Square roots can be difficult to find at times without a calculator, but because you can't use a calculator during the test, you're going to have to use your mind and some guessing methods. To find the square root of a number without a calculator, make an educated guess and then verify your results.

To use the educated-guess method (see the next section), you have to know the square roots of a few perfect squares. One good way to do this is to memorize the squares of the square roots 1 through 12:

- 1 is the square root of 1 $(1 \times 1 = 1)$
- 2 is the square root of 4 $(2 \times 2 = 4)$
- 3 is the square root of 9 $(3 \times 3 = 9)$
- 4 is the square root of 16 $(4 \times 4 = 16)$
- 5 is the square root of 25 $(5 \times 5 = 25)$
- 6 is the square root of 36 $(6 \times 6 = 36)$
- 7 is the square root of 49 $(7 \times 7 = 49)$
- 8 is the square root of 64 $(8 \times 8 = 64)$
- 9 is the square root of 81 $(9 \times 9 = 81)$
- 10 is the square root of 100 $(10 \times 10 = 100)$
- 11 is the square root of 121 $(11 \times 11 = 121)$
- 12 is the square root of 144 $(12 \times 12 = 144)$

Irrational numbers

When the ASVAB asks you to figure square roots of numbers that aren't perfect squares, the task gets a bit more difficult. In this case, the ASVAB usually asks you to find the square root to the nearest tenth.

Suppose you run across this problem:

$$\sqrt{54}$$

Think about what you know: You know that the square root of 49 is 7, and 54 is slightly greater than 49. You also know that the square root of 64 is 8, and 54 is slightly less than 64. So if the number 54 is somewhere between 49 and 64, the square root of 54 is somewhere between 7 and 8. Because 54 is closer to 49 than to 64, the square root will be closer to 7 than to 8, so you can try 7.3 as the square root of 54.

Multiply 7.3 by itself: $7.3 \times 7.3 = 53.29$, which is very close to 54. Now try multiplying 7.4 by itself to see if it's any closer to 54: $7.4 \times 7.4 = 54.76$, which isn't as close to 54 as 53.29. Therefore, 7.3 is the square root of 54 to the nearest tenth without going over.

Other roots

The wonderful world of math is also home to concepts like cube roots, fourth roots, fifth roots, and so on. A *root* is a factor of a number that when cubed (multiplied by itself three times), taken to the fourth power (multiplied by itself four times), and so on produces the original number. A couple of examples seem to be in order:

» The cube root of 27 is 3. If you cube 3 (also known as raising it to the third power or multiplying $3 \times 3 \times 3$), the product is 27.

» The fourth root of 16 is the number that, when multiplied by itself four times, equals 16. Any guesses? Drumroll, please: 2 is the fourth root of 16 because $2 \times 2 \times 2 \times 2 = 16$.

Test-Taking Techniques for Your Mathematical Journey

As with all the other subtests on the ASVAB, guessing on the Mathematics Knowledge subtest may be a good idea — especially if you're taking the paper-and-pencil version. If you're unsure of an answer (and you're not rushing at the end of the subtest), pick an answer, any answer. If you don't, your chances of getting that answer right are zero. But if you take a shot at it, your chances increase to 25%, or 1 in 4. In the following sections, you find some tips that can help you improve those odds, even when you don't know how to solve the problem.

If you're not confident in your math skills, you may want to invest some extra study time. Check out *Algebra I For Dummies* by Mary Jane Sterling, *Geometry For Dummies* by Mark Ryan, and *SAT Math For Dummies* by Mark Zegarelli — all published by Wiley.

Knowing what the question is asking

The Mathematics Knowledge subtest presents the questions as straightforward math problems, not word problems, so knowing what the question is asking you to do is relatively easy. However, reading each question carefully, paying particular attention to plus (+) and minus (−) signs (which can really change the answer), is still important. Finally, make sure you do all the calculations needed to produce the correct answer. Check out this example:

Find the value of $\sqrt{81^2}$.

(A) 9

(B) 18

(C) 81

(D) 6,561

If you're in a hurry, you may put 9 down as an answer because you remember that the square root of 81 is 9. Or, in a rush, you may multiply 9 (the square root of 81) by 2 instead of squaring it, as the exponent indicates you should. Or you may just multiply 81 by 81 to get 6,561 without remembering that you also need to then find the square root, which gives you the correct answer, Choice (C). So make sure you perform all the operations needed (and that you perform the correct operations) to find the right answer. Here, noticing that you're both squaring 81 and taking the square root of 81^2 should make it easy for you to recognize that the answer is actually just 81 without having to work out the multiplication.

Figuring out what you're solving for

Read the question carefully right out of the gate. Some questions can seem out of your league at first glance, but if you look at them again, a light may go on in your brain. Suppose you get this question:

EXAMPLE

Solve for s: $s = \frac{2}{5} \times \frac{1}{2}$

(A) $2\frac{1}{2}$

(B) 2

(C) $\frac{1}{5}$

(D) $\frac{1}{10}$

At first glance, you may think, "Oh, no! Solve for an unknown, s. I don't remember how to do that!" But if you look at the question again, you may see that you're simply multiplying a fraction. So you take $\frac{2}{5}$ times $\frac{1}{2}$ and arrive at $\frac{2}{10}$, but you should reduce that fraction to get $\frac{1}{5}$. The correct answer is Choice (C).

Solving what you can and guessing the rest

Sometimes a problem requires multiple operations for you to arrive at the correct answer. If you don't know how to do all the operations, don't give up. You can still narrow down your choices by doing what you can.

Suppose this question confronts you:

EXAMPLE

What's the value of $(0.03)^3$?

(A) 0.0027

(B) 0.06

(C) 0.000027

(D) 0.0009

Say you don't remember how to multiply decimals. All isn't lost! If you remember how to use exponents, you know that you have to multiply $0.03 \times 0.03 \times 0.03$. So if you simplify the problem and just multiply $3 \times 3 \times 3$, without worrying about those pesky zeros, your answer will have a 27 in it. With this pearl of wisdom in mind, you can see that Choice (B), which adds 0.03 to 0.03, is wrong. It also means that Choice (D), which multiplies 0.03 and 0.03, is wrong. Now you have two possible answers, and you've improved your chances of guessing the right one to 50 percent! Multiply $3 \times 3 \times 3$ to get 27, and don't forget to put the decimal points back in. You have six places to make up, so move the decimal from 27 six places to the left to get 0.000027. The correct answer is Choice (C).

Using the process of elimination

Another method for when you run into questions and draw a total blank is to plug the possible answers into the equation and see which one works. Say the following problem is staring you right in the eyes:

Solve for x: $x - 5 = 32$

(A) $x = 5$
(B) $x = 32$
(C) $x = -32$
(D) $x = 37$

If you're totally stumped and can't think of any possible way of approaching this problem, simply plugging in each of the four answers to see which one is correct is your best bet.

Choice (A): $5 - 5 = 32$, which you know is wrong

Choice (B): $32 - 5 = 32$, which is wrong

Choice (C): $-32 - 5 = 32$, which is wrong

Choice (D): $37 - 5 = 32$, which is correct

Don't forget that plugging in all the answers is time-consuming, so save this tactic for when you've answered all the problems you can answer on the pencil-and-paper ASVAB. If you're taking the computer version, you can't skip a question, so remember to budget your time wisely. If you don't have much time, just make a guess and move on. You may be able to solve the next question easily.

Math Knowledge and Operations Practice Questions

Run through these practice questions to flex your math muscles. You'll be able to check your answers and figure out how much time you need to devote to studying basic mathematical concepts before you move on to tougher calculations. I've grouped these questions by difficulty (easy, medium, and hard). Remember, you're likely to see a question of medium difficulty first on the ASVAB; the questions that follow depend on whether you answer questions correctly.

Easy Math Knowledge questions

1. Solve: $(4 \times 3) \times 3 - 6 \times (9 \div 3)$

   (A) 54
   (B) 14
   (C) 18
   (D) 28

2. Which of the following fractions is the largest?

   (A) $\frac{2}{3}$
   (B) $\frac{5}{8}$
   (C) $\frac{11}{16}$
   (D) $\frac{3}{4}$

3. Which of the following is expressed as an improper fraction?

   (A) $1\frac{5}{28}$
   (B) $\frac{9}{7}$
   (C) $\frac{1}{2}$
   (D) $\frac{345}{346}$

4. Continue the pattern:

   . . . 5, 10, 9, 15, 20, 19, 25 . . .

   (A) 30, 35, 41
   (B) 30, 29, 35
   (C) 26, 30, 35
   (D) 26, 30, 31

5. $27.65 \times 31.3 =$

   (A) 865.445
   (B) 835.556
   (C) 867.5309
   (D) 842.1

6. $\frac{1}{4} \times \frac{2}{3} =$

   (A) $\frac{3}{4}$
   (B) $\frac{1}{4}$
   (C) $\frac{1}{6}$
   (D) $\frac{1}{3}$

7. $\frac{1}{5} \cdot \frac{2}{3} =$

   (A) $\frac{2}{15}$
   (B) $\frac{3}{15}$
   (C) $\frac{2}{5}$
   (D) $\frac{1}{15}$

8. $3 \div \frac{3}{4} =$

   (A) $2\frac{1}{4}$
   (B) 4
   (C) $3\frac{3}{4}$
   (D) 5

9. Round 27.534 to the nearest whole number.

   (A) 27.5
   (B) 27.53
   (C) 27
   (D) 28

10. An integer is

    (A) any positive or negative whole number or zero.
    (B) a number that can be divided evenly by itself and by 1, but no other numbers.
    (C) a shorthand method of indicated repeated multiplication.
    (D) the number by which another number can be multiplied to produce 1.

Medium Math Knowledge questions

11. What is the average of the following?

    101, 15, 62, 84, and 55

    (A) 55
    (B) 63.4
    (C) 75.5
    (D) 56.25

12. Find the mode:

    46, 29, 47, 22, 100, 47, 157, 138, 47, 22, 184

    (A) 22
    (B) 47
    (C) 76.3
    (D) 184

13. Express the ratio of 48 privates to 2 drill instructors.

    (A) 1:24
    (B) 2:48
    (C) 48:2
    (D) 48:1

14. If the scale on a military map is 1 inch = 1,000 kilometers, how many inches represent 4,500 kilometers?

    (A) 4.5
    (B) 0.5
    (C) $2\frac{1}{8}$
    (D) 0.45

15. How many miles per gallon does a military truck get if you drive 300 miles on 12 gallons of gas?

    (A) 24
    (B) 25
    (C) 30
    (D) 60

16. What is the prime factorization of 4?

    (A) 2×2
    (B) 1×4
    (C) $1 \times 2 + 2$
    (D) 2×4

17. What is the prime factorization of 147?

    (A) $2 \times 2 \times 3 \times 3 \times 3$
    (B) $2 \times 3 \times 4 \times 5$
    (C) $3 \times 7 \times 9$
    (D) $3 \times 7 \times 7$

18. What is the prime factorization of 37?

    (A) $2 \times 2 \times 3 \times 3$
    (B) $2 \times 3 \times 5$
    (C) 37
    (D) $1 \times 3 \times 4 \times 7.5$

19. What are the factors of 158?

    (A) 1, 2, 79, 158
    (B) 1, 2, 58, 100, 158
    (C) 1, 5, 8, 10, 79, 158
    (D) 2, 79, 158

20. Find the unknown in the proportion $\frac{7}{10} :: \frac{28}{?}$

    (A) 4
    (B) 40
    (C) 400
    (D) 21

21. To make 6 holiday wreaths, you need 48 large flowers and 60 small flowers. How many large flowers do you need to make 18 wreaths?

    (A) 96
    (B) 108
    (C) 144
    (D) 180

22. A recipe to feed 9 troops calls for 9 pounds of chicken, 6 tablespoons of garlic, 8 tablespoons of oil, and 12 potatoes. Given this recipe, express the proportion of pounds of chicken to potatoes you'd need to feed 3 troops.

    (A) $\frac{9}{12} :: \frac{3}{4}$
    (B) $\frac{9}{12} :: \frac{6}{6}$
    (C) $\frac{6}{12} :: \frac{3}{6}$
    (D) $\frac{3}{6} :: \frac{3}{4}$

23. A composite number

   (A) is an even or odd number that can only be divided by itself and 1.
   (B) is a whole number that can be divided evenly by itself and by 1, as well as by one or more other whole numbers.
   (C) can have only two factors or it becomes a different type of number.
   (D) is a whole number or a fraction that can be divided evenly by itself and by 1, as well as by one or more other numbers or fractions.

24. A prime number

   (A) is any positive integer.
   (B) can be divided evenly by itself and by 1, but not by any other numbers.
   (C) is any number that can be divided, but not by a multiple of 2.
   (D) can have multiple factors.

25. 15 percent off a dinner order totaling $75.50 is

   (A) $71.18
   (B) $69.20
   (C) $65
   (D) $64.18

26. If you want to tip your server 22 percent on a dinner bill that totals $98.40, how much money would you leave on the table?

   (A) $21.65
   (B) $21.64
   (C) $20.30
   (D) $19.87

27. Solve: $6 \times 4 \div 12 + (182 \div 7)^2$

   (A) 15.79
   (B) 706.04
   (C) 678
   (D) 654

28. Solve: $\frac{1}{3} \times \frac{2}{3}^2 - \frac{1}{9}$

   (A) $\frac{1}{27}$
   (B) $3\frac{8}{9}$
   (C) $\frac{4}{27}$
   (D) $3\frac{7}{9}$

29. Solve: $7.12 \div 0.005$

   (A) 3,560
   (B) 356
   (C) 142.4
   (D) 1,424

30. An irrational number is

   (A) negative with decimal places.
   (B) any number with decimal places.
   (C) a number that has no end of decimal places.
   (D) a number that has no square root.

Hard Math Knowledge questions

31. What's the product of $\sqrt{36}$ and $\sqrt{49}$?

    (A) 1,764
    (B) 42
    (C) 13
    (D) 6

32. $2^3 \times 2^4 =$

    (A) 16
    (B) 108
    (C) 128
    (D) 148

33. Express 403,000,000,000,000 in scientific notation.

    (A) 4.03×10^{14}
    (B) 4.03×10^{-14}
    (C) 4.03×10
    (D) 0.43×10

34. What's the prime factorization of 90?

    (A) $2 \times 3 \times 5$
    (B) $2 \times 3^2 \times 5$
    (C) $2^2 \times 3^2$
    (D) $2 \times 3 \times 5^2$

35. $\sqrt{121} =$

    (A) 12
    (B) 9
    (C) 21
    (D) 11

36. Jayce is saving up to buy a luxury car that costs $120,000. He puts $80,000 in the bank and will earn a return of 5 percent per year. If he only earns interest on his initial investment of $80,000, how many years does he have to wait to pay for the luxury car (as long as the car's price doesn't increase)?

    (A) 12
    (B) 9
    (C) 10
    (D) 4

37. How much interest will you pay if you take out a loan for $2,500 at a 9 percent interest rate for a term of 9 months?

    (A) $125.75
    (B) $168
    (C) $175.25
    (D) $168.75

38. A bus traveling at 50 miles per hour makes a trip to Los Angeles in 6 hours. If it had traveled at 45 miles per hour, how much longer would it have taken to arrive in Los Angeles?

    (A) 40 minutes
    (B) 45 minutes
    (C) 60 minutes
    (D) 75 minutes

39. Ilhan drove to work at an average speed of 36 miles per hour. On the way home, she traveled an average of 27 miles per hour. She spent an hour and 45 minutes in the car. How far does Ilhan live from work?

    (A) 18 miles
    (B) 22 miles
    (C) 25 miles
    (D) 27 miles

40. Ayanna and Cori live 270 miles apart. They drive toward each other to meet. Ayanna drives an average speed of 65 miles per hour, and Cori drives an average speed of 70 miles per hour. How long do they drive before they meet?

    (A) 1.5 hours
    (B) 2 hours
    (C) 2 hours, 10 minutes
    (D) 2.5 hours

Answers and Explanations

Use this answer key to score the practice questions.

1. **C.** Solve by using the order of operations:

    $(4 \times 3)3 - 6(9 \div 3)$
    $= (12)3 - 6(3)$
    $= 36 - 18$
    $= 18$

2. **D.** To arrive at the answer, find a common denominator that all the denominators divide into evenly. In this case, the common denominator is 48. Next, convert all fractions to 48ths. In the case of Choice (A), multiply $\frac{2}{3} \times \frac{16}{16}$ to reach $\frac{32}{48}$. Perform the same type of calculation for all the other fractions, figuring out what number times the denominator gives you 48, and then multiplying each numerator by that number; then compare numerators. The largest numerator is the largest fraction. The other fractions are equal to $\frac{30}{48}, \frac{33}{48}$, and $\frac{36}{48}$. Choice (D) is the correct answer.

3. **B.** An *improper fraction* is a fraction in which the numerator is larger than or equal to the denominator.

4. **B.** The pattern is the next two multiples of 5, minus 1:

    . . . 5, 10, 9, 15, 20, 19, 25, 30, 29, 35, 40 . . .

5. **A.** When you multiply decimals, you move the decimal directly back into its spot after the ones place.

6. **C.** $\frac{1}{4} \times \frac{2}{3} = \frac{2}{12} = \frac{1}{6}$. The correct answer is Choice (C).

7. **A.** To multiply fractions, go straight across the numerator and denominator, like this:

    $\frac{1}{5} \cdot \frac{2}{3} = \frac{1 \cdot 2}{5 \cdot 3} = \frac{2}{15}$.

8. **B.** Find the reciprocal of the fraction first, then multiply and simplify:

    $3 \div \frac{3}{4} = \frac{3}{1} \cdot \frac{4}{3} = \frac{3 \cdot 4}{1 \cdot 3} = \frac{12}{3} = 4$.

9. **D.** A whole number is a number without any fractions (or decimals). Because you round 0.5 or greater to the next-higher whole number, Choice (D) is correct.

10. **A.** An integer is any positive or negative whole number, or zero.

11. **B.** To find the average, add the numbers and divide by 5 (the total number of items in the set):

    $101 + 15 + 62 + 84 + 55 = 317$
    $317 \div 5 = 63.4$

12. **B.** The mode in a number range is the value that appears most frequently. In this case, it's the number 47, which shows up three times. If you added all the numbers and divided by 11, you were looking for the mean — and you would've chosen Choice (C), which isn't what the question asked for.

13. **C.** There are 48 privates for every 2 drill instructors, so you express that ratio 48:2. Your drill instructor would say, "These privates outnumber us 48 to 2." If you were going to simplify the ratio, you could divide both sides by two to arrive at 24:1, but the question doesn't ask you to do that.

14. **A.** Scale problems ask you to determine how many inches represent a certain distance. If 1 inch is equal to 1,000 kilometers on a military map, then 4 inches represents 4,000 kilometers; the remaining 500 kilometers can be represented by adding 0.5 inches, which you may be able to do in your head. However, you can express this mathematically by letting x represent the number of inches you need to determine:

$$\frac{1}{1,000} = \frac{x}{4,500}$$
$$\frac{1}{1,000} \times 4,500 = \frac{x}{4,500} \times 1,250$$
$$\frac{4,500}{1,000} = x$$
$$x = 4.5$$

15. **B.** The truck gets 25 miles per gallon if you can drive 300 miles on 12 gallons of gas. This is a ratio or division problem; you can express the ratio of distance to gallons as 300:12, and you can compute the gas mileage by dividing the number of miles by the number of gallons: 300 miles ÷ 12 gallons, which equals 25.

16. **A.** Prime factorization is the act of finding out which prime numbers (whole numbers greater than 1 that you can't make by multiplying other whole numbers) you can multiply together to make the original number. The only prime number you can multiply together to create 4 is 2, so the prime factorization of 4 is 2×2.

17. **D.** When you need to find prime factors of a larger number, start with a low prime (2 is the best) and figure out if you can divide the larger number by it. You can't divide 147 by 2 and get a whole number, but you can divide it by 3 and get 49. Keep that 3 in your back pocket, then find the prime factorization of 49 (it's 7×7). That means the prime factorization of 147 is $3 \times 7 \times 7$.

18. **C.** The number 37 is a prime number, so that's as far as you can go.

19. **A.** Factors are numbers that you can multiply together to reach a certain number. In this case, you can multiply 1×158 or 2×79 to get a product of 158; those are the only whole numbers you can multiply to land exactly on 158, so they're each its factors.

20. **B.** If 7 is directly proportional to 28, that means you must multiply the remaining known proportional by 4 (because $7 \times 4 = 28$) to find out what the unknown proportional is. Doing so tells you that the answer is 40, because $10 \times 4 = 40$.

21. **C.** This is a proportion problem in disguise. Because you need 48 large flowers to make 6 wreaths, you can express the ratio of wreaths to flowers as 48:6 (which you can also express as $\frac{48}{6}$ if that's the way your brain works best). Your proportion for 18 wreaths looks like this: $\frac{48}{6} :: \frac{?}{18}$. Because 6×3 is 18, you know that you have to multiply 48 by 3 to keep the

expression directly proportional. 48×3 is 144, so you need 144 large flowers. (The number of small flowers is irrelevant, and I just put it there to keep you on your toes.)

22. **A.** The ratio of chicken to potatoes you need to feed nine troops is 9:12, but you're feeding just a third of those troops. That means you have to decrease the recipe by two-thirds, and you do that by finding how the two ratios are directly proportional; $\frac{9}{12} \div 3 = \frac{3}{4}$, so the proportion is 9:12 = 3:4 or $\frac{9}{12} :: \frac{3}{4}$.

23. **B.** A composite number is a whole number that you can divide evenly by itself and by 1, as well as by one or more other whole numbers.

24. **B.** A prime number is a whole number that can be divided evenly by itself and by 1, but not by any other number. Prime numbers have only two factors (such as the number 5, which has factors of 1 and 5, or the number 17, which has factors of 1 and 17).

25. **D.** When you get 15 percent off your dinner order for a meal that costs $75.50, you still pay 85 percent of that total. Your math should look like this: $75.5 \times 0.85 = 64.175$. Because no business is going to charge you a fraction of a penny, your meal will cost $64.18 (before the tip).

26. **A.** Leaving your server a 22 percent tip is a nice thing to do — and if your bill was $98.40, multiply that by 0.22 to figure out that you should leave $21.65. (You'd actually leave $21.648, but you'd round up because you can't deal in fractions of pennies.)

27. **C.** Using the correct order of operations, which you can remember with the acronym PEMDAS, tackle the parentheses first; then follow the rest of the order. In this expression, your math looks like this:

$$6 \times 4 \div 12 + (182 \div 7)^2 = ?$$
$$6 \times 4 \div 12 + (26)^2 = ?$$
$$6 \times 4 \div 12 + 676 = ?$$
$$24 \div 12 + 676 = ?$$
$$2 + 676 = 678$$

28. **A.** The order of operations (PEMDAS) still applies when you're working with fractions. In this case, you add your own parentheses to solve:

$$\frac{1}{3} \times \frac{2}{3}^2 - \frac{1}{9} = ?$$
$$\frac{1}{3} \times \left(\frac{2}{3} \times \frac{2}{3}\right) - \frac{1}{9} = ?$$
$$\frac{1}{3} \times \frac{4}{9} - \frac{1}{9} = ?$$
$$\frac{4}{27} - \frac{3}{27} = \frac{1}{27}$$

29. **D.** The simplest way to divide decimals without a calculator is to move the decimal point. Because you want to work with whole numbers, turn 0.005 into 5 by moving the decimal point three spaces to the right. What you do to one part, you must do to the other, so $7.12 \div 0.005$ becomes $7120 \div 5$. Regular long division shows you that the answer is 1,424 — and when both parts of your problem involve moved decimals, you don't have to put them back.

30. **C.** An irrational number is one that you can't make by dividing two integers (whole numbers) and has a forever-repeating decimal (like pi, which is 3.14159265359 . . .).

31. **B.** The square root of 36 is 6, and the square root of 49 is 7. The product of those two numbers (6×7) is 42. The correct answer is Choice (B). *Remember:* Product indicates you multiply.

32. **C.** $2^3 \times 2^4 = 2^7 = 2 \times 2 \times 2 \times 2 \times 2 \times 2 \times 2 = 128$. Choice (C) is the correct answer.

33. **A.** The correct way to write the number in scientific notation is 4.03×10^{14}. When the exponent is positive, the decimal point moves said number of places to the right. When the exponent is negative, the decimal point moves said places to the left. The exponent in Choice (A) is a positive 14, which means you move the decimal point 14 places to the right. Choice (A) is the correct answer.

34. **B.** When you figure which prime numbers you need to multiply together to get the original number, you're using *prime factorization*. Here, $90 = 9 \times 10 = 3 \times 3 \times 2 \times 5 = 2 \times 3^2 \times 5$. The correct answer is Choice (B). If you don't know how to solve this problem, you can guess by finding the value of each answer choice. Choice (A) is 30, Choice (B) is 90, Choice (C) is 36, and Choice (D) is 150.

35. **D.** The square root of 121 is 11, because 11^2, or $11 \cdot 11 = 121$.

36. **C.** This is an interest problem that tells you Jayce needs to earn $40,000 in interest. First, find out how much interest he'll earn on his $80,000 savings in one year: $80,000 \times 0.05 = 4,000$. Then, to find the total number of years Jayce needs to wait, divide the total amount he needs ($40,000) by the interest for one year: $40,000 \div 4,000 = 10$.

37. **D.** This simple interest problem requires you to calculate time in months, which means you need to convert 9 months into 0.75 years before you do anything else. Then, use *I = Prt* to solve:

    $I = 2,500 \times 0.09 \times 0.75$
    $I = 168.75$

38. **A.** For the first scenario, you know the rate and time from the problem (50 miles per hour and 6 hours, respectively). The distance is the variable, and the equation to figure it out is *d = rt* (with *r* representing rate and *t* representing time). Multiplying 50 by 6 tells you that the distance between the bus's original location and Los Angeles is 300 miles. Use that information for the second scenario, which tells you the bus traveled at 45 miles per hour to travel a distance of 300 miles. In the second scenario, the variable is time *(t)*. Your equation looks like this: $300 = 45t$. Do the math:

    $300 = 45t$
    $\dfrac{300}{45} = \dfrac{45t}{45}$
    $6\dfrac{2}{3} = t$

    That tells you it took $6\dfrac{2}{3}$ hours for the bus to make it to LA. Because the problem asked you how many minutes it would take, convert $\dfrac{2}{3}$ of an hour into 40 minutes.

39. D. It's often helpful to use a table to create equations for round-trip problems. In this case:

	Rate	Time	Distance
Scenario 1 (to work)	36 miles per hour	t	
Scenario 2 (from work)	27 miles per hour	$1.75 - t$	

The table tells you that $36t$ = Ilhan's distance to work, and you can represent her distance from work as $d = 27(1.75 - t)$. The two are going to be the same number; she travels the same distance to and from work. Combine the two equations by working out the trip *from* work to solve for *t*:

$$d = 27(1.75 - t)$$
$$36t = 27(1.75 - t)$$
$$36t = 47.25 - 27t$$
$$63t = 47.25$$
$$t = 0.75$$

Then, replace t in the other equation to find out how far Ilhan lives from work: $d = 36 \times 0.75$. After you perform the calculation, you'll see that Ilhan lives 27 miles from work.

40. B. A table like this can help you organize your equations:

	Distance	Rate	Time
Ayanna	d	65	t
Cori	$270 - d$	70	t

Together, they will have covered the total distance (*d*) at the time they meet. They drive the same amount of time, so the equation for Ayanna's travel is $d = 65t$ and the equation for Cori's travel is $270 - d = 70t$. Combine the equations by replacing the *d* in Cori's equation with Ayanna's $65t$:

$$270 = 65t = 70t$$
$$270 = 135t$$
$$2 = t$$

IN THIS CHAPTER

» Getting familiar with algebra terms

» Reviewing algebraic concepts such as linear systems, term factorization, and inequalities

» Keeping things simplified

» Quantifying quadratic equations

Chapter 7
Algebra

The Mathematics Knowledge subtest on the computerized version of the ASVAB requires you to answer 15 questions in 31 minutes (or 30 questions in 65 minutes if your subtest includes tryout questions, which I cover in Chapter 1). If you're taking the paper-and-pencil version, you'll have to answer 25 questions in 24 minutes. You can't use a calculator on the test, but you can use as much scratch paper as you need.

Some people freak out just hearing the word *algebra*. But algebra is just a way to put problems into mathematical language using the simplest mathematical terms possible. In fact, solving most word problems is almost impossible without some use of algebra. In this chapter, I cover all the basic algebra knowledge you need to nail the Mathematics Knowledge subtest of the ASVAB — and the concepts you review here will also come in handy on the Arithmetic Reasoning subtest, which I cover in Chapter 9. You won't see these exact questions when you take the ASVAB, but knowing how to tackle these types of problems will help you answer the questions that do pop up during the test.

REMEMBER The questions on the Mathematics Knowledge subtest aren't all algebra-related. Many involve basic math concepts like fractions, percentages, scientific notation, and square roots (see Chapter 6 for more information). And some are related to geometry, which you can brush up on in Chapter 8.

REMEMBER The CAT-ASVAB adapts to your ability as you answer questions, so it may not meet your expectations as far as difficulty goes.

Coming to Terms with Basic Algebra Lingo

Algebra has its own language, and knowing how to speak it can take you a long way on the ASVAB. Some of the most common algebraic terms you encounter, both in this book and on the test, include the following:

» **Term:** One or more numbers and/or letters all connected by multiplication or division.

» **Algebraic expression:** An *algebraic expression* is one or more terms in a phrase. It's not a whole "sentence," so an expression doesn't include an equal sign. Here's an example: $4x + 2y + 38c$.

- **Equation:** An *equation* is a mathematical statement that states that two mathematical expressions are equal. An equation always includes an equal sign, like this example: $7a + 3b = 588$.

- **Variable:** A *variable* is a number in disguise. In this expression, *x* and *y* are the variables: $7x + 10y = 27$. They're called variables because the numbers they represent can vary from problem to problem. When you write your own equations, you can use any letters that make sense to you.

  REMEMBER

  If the same letter appears more than once in a given equation or expression, it stands for the same number in all instances in that equation/expression. In $3x + 2x = 10$, the first *x* doesn't represent a different number from the second *x*. In this case, $x = 2$ (both times).

- **Coefficient:** A *coefficient* is the number part of an algebraic term. In this equation, 8 and 12 are the coefficients: $8a - 12b = -4$.

- **Constant:** A *constant* is a term in an algebraic expression that contains only a number; it's a term without a variable attached to it. In this equation, 5 is the constant: $14d + 12a + 5$.

- **Real numbers:** *Real numbers* are actual quantities, like amounts, ages, distances, and temperatures. A real number can be an integer, fraction, or decimal, and it can be rational or irrational. They're numbers that appear on a number line, like this:

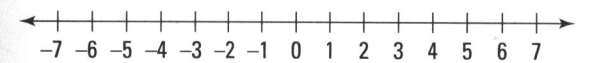

  ←|—|—|—|—|—|—|—|—|—|—|—|—|—|—|→
  −7 −6 −5 −4 −3 −2 −1 0 1 2 3 4 5 6 7

- **Rational numbers:** *Rational numbers* are the set of real numbers, fractions, and terminating decimals. Rational numbers can always be written as the ratio or quotient of two integers. These are examples of rational numbers: $\frac{1}{2}$, 5, 0.25.

- **Irrational numbers:** *Irrational numbers* can't be expressed as a quotient or ratio of two integers. With irrational numbers, the decimal form is nonrepeating and nonterminating, like pi. You can't write pi as a quotient of two integers, and its decimal form goes on forever. The same goes for square root and other roots.

- **Exponents:** An *exponent* tells you how many times to use a value (its *base*) in multiplication. In this equation, 2 and *x* are both exponents: $s^2 + 3^x = 470$.

- **Polynomial:** A *polynomial* is an expression that contains one or more terms, like constants, variables, and exponents. The exponents on the variables in a polynomial are always whole numbers. Here's an example of a polynomial: $3ab - 2x^2 + 2y^3 - 7$. Other special names for polynomials signal whether they have one, two, or three terms. For example, $2ab^7$ is a monomial because it has one term. $6x - 3$ is a binomial because it has two terms, and $4a + 7b^3 - 5$ is a trinomial because it has three terms.

- **Like terms:** In algebra, you combine *like terms* — terms that have matching variables in the expression or equation. The variables must have the same power to be *like terms*. These are all like terms: 4*xy*, 7*xy*, 32*xy*. Because *xy* is the same, you can combine them if you're working with an equation, like this:

  $4xy + 7xy + 32xy = 215$
  $\qquad 43xy = 215$

WHAT'S IN A NAME? ARITHMETIC, ALGEBRA, AND CALCULUS

Don't get spooked by all the names. *Arithmetic* is simply the combination of numbers (which I cover in Chapter 6). *Algebra* builds on arithmetic by including variables that allows math to describe a situation for all possible numbers in a place. *Calculus* is a deeper mathematic topic that describes how situations (and their equations) will change over time. Although calculus is important for many advanced professions, it is not tested on the ASVAB.

Solving for x

In algebra, you often hear about "solving for *x*" or "solving for the unknown," but what's the unknown? The *unknown* is the answer you want to find. Check out this example:

EXAMPLE

Rod's mom worked up a powerful thirst solving a ton of math problems and asked Rod to run to the corner store and get her a large fountain drink. If a regular-sized fountain drink costs $0.50 and the large size costs three times the price of the regular size, how much will Rod have to spend?

You can express this problem in terms of *x*, with *x* being the cost of the largest drink: *x* equals 3 (the price difference) $\times 50$ cents. Written a bit more formally, the equation looks like this: $x = 3(0.50)$ or $3(0.50) = x$.

What if you don't know how much the regular-sized soft drink costs? You can express this missing piece of information in an equation as well: *x* (how much it will cost to buy the large drink) equals 3 (the cost increase) times *p* (the price of one regular-sized drink). Once again, written a bit more formally, the equation looks like this: $x = 3p$ or $x = 3 \times p$.

TIP

You can remove the multiplication symbol in algebraic expressions when using a combination of letters and numbers. Therefore, the equation $x = 3 \times p$ can also be written $x = 3p$. The multiplication symbol is implied. It's also common to use parentheses or the dot multiplication symbol, $\cdot$, to indicate multiplication. Most people avoid using the $\times$ because it looks so close to the letter *x*.

Try your hand at creating your own algebraic equations using the information in the following table. You may have to create formulas to solve ASVAB questions.

Problem	Your Equation
Kathy sold 10 more carnival tickets than Bonnie did. Together, they sold 480 tickets. How many tickets did Bonnie sell?	
Half a number plus 5 is 11. What is the number?	
Five years ago, Cheryl's age was half the age she will be in 8 years. How old is she now?	
Ryan's volleyball team won three times as many matches as it lost. If the team won 15 matches, how many did it lose?	

The answers, from top to bottom, are $t + (t + 10) = 480$; $0.5x + 5 = 11$; $x - 5 = 0.5(x + 8)$; and $3x = 15$.

When All Things Are Equal: Keeping an Algebra Equation Balanced

Algebra problems can be equations, which means that the quantities on both sides of the equal sign are equal — they're the same. For instance, $2 = 2$, $1+1 = 2$, and $3-1 = 2$. In all these cases, the quantities are the same on both sides of the equal sign. To solve an algebra equation, you find out what the variable equals by getting it by itself on one side of the equal sign. So if $x = 2$, then x is 2 because the equal sign says so.

REMEMBER You can perform any calculation on either side of an equation as long as you do the same thing to both sides of the equation. That keeps the equation equal.

You can also combine like terms lying on one side of the equation when operating on algebraic expressions: $3x + 3x = (3+3)x = 6x$. However, $3x + 3y$ doesn't equal $6xy$, nor does $x^2 + x^3 = x^5$. (See the earlier section "Coming to Terms with Basic Algebra Lingo" for more on like terms and the later section "Explaining Exponents in Algebra" to find out more about algebra involving exponents.)

Solving one-step equations involving addition and subtraction

If $x + 1 = 2$, then x must be 1, because only 1 added to 1 is 2. So far, so simple, so good. But what if the equation is a little more complicated?

$$x + 47{,}432 = 50{,}000$$

To solve the problem, you need to isolate x on one side of the equal sign. To get that job done, move any other numbers on the x side of the equal sign to the other side of the equal sign.

By looking at the x side of the equation, you can see that it's an addition problem. To move the number on the x side to the opposite side, you have to perform the inverse operation. The inverse operation of addition is subtraction. (For a full rundown on inverse operations, check out Chapter 6.) So to move 47,432 from the x side to the non-x side of the equation, simply subtract that number from both sides:

$$x + 47{,}432 - 47{,}432 = 50{,}000 - 47{,}432$$

Performing these operations removes the 47,432 from the x side of the equation ($47{,}432 - 47{,}432 = 0$, so that side of the equation is $x + 0$ or simply x) and gives you 2,568 on the non-x side of the equation ($50{,}000 - 47{,}432 = 2{,}568$). You're left with the final answer:

$$x = 2{,}568$$

To double-check that this answer is correct, you can plug your answer into the original problem:

$$x + 47{,}432 = 50{,}000$$
$$2{,}568 + 47{,}432 = 50{,}000$$

If you plug in the answer and it doesn't work, you've made an error in your calculations. Start again; remember that you're trying to isolate x on one side of the equation.

Multiplying and dividing

REMEMBER

In multiplication and division, if the two terms being operated on (on either side of the equal sign) are both positive numbers or both negative numbers, the answer will be a positive number. If one number is negative and the other is positive, the answer will be negative.

To solve the problem $-6x = 36$ (don't forget, $6x$ is the same thing as $6 \times x$), you need to isolate x. So perform an inverse operation; the inverse operation of multiplication is division. Division in algebra is usually represented with a fraction bar:

$$\frac{-6x}{-6} = \frac{36}{-6}$$
$$x = -6$$

The answer is a negative number because the two terms, 36 and –6, have different signs.

Need some hands-on practice? Work on balancing and solving with the following four sample problems.

Problem	Your Solution
$135 - 36b = 9b$	
$x + 14,500 = 57,500$	
$3d = 24$	
$5x - 2 = 3x + 4$	

The answers, from top to bottom, are 3; 43,000; 8; and 3.

Solving multistep equations

Not all algebra problems have one-step solutions. (That would be too easy, and you wouldn't sweat nearly as much.) Solving algebra problems on the ASVAB often requires you to perform several steps.

An example of a multistep equation is one in which x shows up on both sides of the equal sign. Then you have to get rid of x on one side of the equation by moving x terms from one side to the other. You do this by performing the inverse operation.

Suppose you want to solve this equation: $3x + 3 = 9 + x$. To remove the x from one side of the equation, perform the inverse operation. The right side of the equation adds an x, so subtract x from both sides of the equation:

$$3x + 3 - x = 9 + x - x$$
$$3x + 3 - 1x = 9 + 0$$
$$2x + 3 = 9$$

To get the x term, $2x$, by itself, subtract 3 from each side of the equation:

$$2x + 3 - 3 = 9 - 3$$
$$2x = 6$$

Divide both sides of the equation by 2 to isolate x:

$$\frac{2x}{2} = \frac{6}{2}$$
$$x = 3$$

Ready for some practice? Solve the following equations as if you saw them on the ASVAB.

Problem	Your Solution
$20 - x = 4 + 3$	
$19a - 8 = 600$	
$4x + 10 = 30$	
$3(x + 1) = -6$	

The answers, top to bottom, are 13; 32; 5; and −3.

REMEMBER: When you have a variable by itself, such as *x*, it's always equal to 1 times that variable (or one of that variable), like 1*x*, even if the 1 isn't written out. In fact, any number is equal to 1 times itself, so you could also say $2 = 2 \times 1$.

Simplifying equations

Before you evaluate or solve an algebraic expression or equation, you need to simplify it. Simplifying makes your calculations a lot easier — and it saves you valuable time on the ASVAB. Here are the basic steps to simplify an expression:

1. **Remove whatever parentheses you can by multiplying factors.**

   If your expression is $3(2 + x) + 4(4x + 3) - (x^2)^2$, the first thing to do is get rid of the parentheses. Using the distributive property, which lets you multiply the factors times the terms inside the parentheses, you can get rid of two sets right off the bat.

   The first set works like this: After you multiply the factors times the terms inside the parentheses, $3(2 + x)$ is equal to $6 + 3x$ because $3 \cdot 2 = 6$ and $3 \cdot x = 3x$. Now the original expression is $6 + 3x + 4(4x + 3) - (x^2)^2$.

   Remove the second set of parentheses the same way: $4(4x + 3) = 4 \cdot 4x = 16x$ and $4 \cdot 3 = 12$, so $4(4x + 3) = 16x + 12$. Now the original expression is $6 + 3x + 16x + 12 - (x^2)^2$.

2. **Use exponent rules to remove any remaining parentheses (if applicable).**

   When a term with an exponent is raised to a power, you multiply the exponents. That means $(x^2)^2 = x^4$. All the parentheses are gone. The original expression is now $6 + 3x + 16x + 12 - x^4$.

3. **Combine like terms.**

   The like terms in the original equation are 3*x* and 16*x*, which together are 19*x*. The original expression is now $6 + 19x + 12 - x^4$.

4. **Combine constants.**

   The constants in this expression are 6 and 12, and together, they add up to 18. The original expression is now $19x + 18 - x^4$.

Try your hand at simplifying the following expressions.

Problem	Your Solution
$20x - 6 - 13x + 10$	
$8x^2 + 5x - 3x^2 - 9x + 14$	
$\dfrac{x^2 + 4x - 45}{x^2 + x - 30}$	
$4xy - 2y - 3(xy + 1) - 2$	

The answers, from top to bottom, are $7x + 4$; $5x^2 - 4x + 14$; $\dfrac{x+9}{x+6}$; and $xy - 2y - 5$.

You may see questions on the ASVAB that ask you to simplify expressions, so knowing how to get rid of all the excess can help you sail right through.

Using FOIL

FOIL is a technique for distributing two binomials in algebra. FOIL stands for First, Outer, Inner, and Last, and it refers to problems like this one: $(x+2)(x+5)$.

Here's what each part of FOIL means:

- **First** means multiply the terms that occur first in each binomial.
- **Outer** means multiply the terms that occur on the outermost ends of the product (the first and last).
- **Inner** means multiply the innermost terms of the product (the second and third).
- **Last** means multiply the last terms in each binomial.

FOIL looks like this: $(x+2)(x+5)$, where First is $x \cdot x$, Outer is $x \cdot 5$, Inner is $2 \cdot x$, and Last is $2 \cdot 5$.

That means $(x+2)(x+5) = x \cdot x + x \cdot 5 + 2 \cdot x + 2 \cdot 5$. Combine like terms to further simplify the problem: $x^2 + 7x + 10$.

Tackling Two-Variable Equations

When you have two-variable equations, which you'll see when you're working with graphs and in some other instances, there are usually multiple solutions. When you have two or more of these equations and they all have exponents of 1, the equations are called *linear systems*, and to solve them, you have to either use substitution or combine equations.

Substitution

When a system is simple, like this one, substitution is the way to go.

$x + 3 = y$
$3x + y = 7$

In this system, you know that $y = x + 3$. Plug $x + 3$ into the second equation, in place of y, to find the value of x, and then simplify and solve:

$$3x + x + 3 = 7$$
$$4x + 3 = 7$$
$$4x + 3 - 3 = 7 - 3$$
$$4x = 4$$
$$\frac{4x}{4} = \frac{4}{4}$$
$$x = 1$$

Because $x = 1$, substitute that value into the original equation, $y = x + 3$, to determine that $y = 4$.

Combining equations

When a system is more complicated, like this one, you need to combine them.

$$12x - 9y = 37$$
$$8x + 9y = 23$$

You have to add these two equations to figure out just one of the variables, like this:

$$12x - 9y = 37$$
$$+8x + 9y = 23$$
$$\overline{20x = 60}$$

When you solve for x, you see that $x = 3$. Plug 3 in for the value of x in either of the original equations to figure out the value of y.

$$8(3) + 9y = 23$$
$$24 + 9y = 23$$
$$9y + 24 - 24 = 23 - 24$$
$$9y = -1$$
$$y = -\frac{1}{9}$$

Combining equations may require you to change one equation entirely to figure out the answer. Here's another system as an example:

$$7x + 10y = 36$$
$$2x - y = -9$$

To solve by combining, multiply the bottom equation by 10. The equation becomes $20x - 10y = -90$. Add it to the first equation to eliminate y. The result is $27x = -54$. Divide to find the value of x:

$$\frac{27x}{27} = \frac{-54}{27}$$
$$x = -2$$

Take the value of x, which is -2, and substitute it into one of the original equations to solve for y (I use the second):

$$2x - y = 9$$
$$2(-2) - y = 9$$
$$-4 - y = 9 - 4$$
$$y = 5$$

Test your two-variable equation skills here.

Problem	Your Solution
$x + 3y = 6$ $2x + 8y = -12$	
$2x + 3y = 16$ $5x - 4y = -6$	
$3x + 2y = 2$ $y + 8 = 3x$	
$2x + 3y = -2$ $4x - 3y = 14$	

The answers, from top to bottom, are x = 42 and y = –12; x = 2 and y = 4; x = 2 and y = –2; and x = 2 and y = –2.

Explaining Exponents in Algebra

Exponents are an easy way to show that a number is to be multiplied by itself a certain number of times. For example, 5^2 is the same as 5×5, and y^3 is the same as $y \times y \times y$. The number or variable that's multiplied by itself is called the base, and the number or variable showing how many times it is to be multiplied by itself is called the exponent or power.

Here are important rules when working with exponents in algebra:

REMEMBER

>> Any base raised to the power of one equals itself: $x^1 = x$.
>> Any base raised to the zero power (except 0) equals 1: $x^0 = 1$.
>> To multiply terms with the same base, add the exponents: $x^2(x^3) = x^{2+3} = x^5$.
>> To divide terms with the same base, subtract the exponents: $x^5 \div x^2 = x^{5-2} = x^3$.
>> If a base has a negative exponent, it's equal to its reciprocal (inverse) with a positive exponent: $x^{-3} = \frac{1}{x^3}$.
>> When a product has an exponent, each factor is raised to that power: $(xy)^3 = x^3 y^3$.

A Step Back: Factoring Algebra Expressions to Find Original Numbers

Now and then, the ASVAB gives you a product (the answer to a multiplication problem), and you have to find the original numbers that were multiplied together to produce that product. This process is called *factoring*. You use factors when you combine like terms and add fractions.

Pulling out the greatest common factor

Your task may be to pull out the greatest common factor from two or more terms. Take, for example, this product: $4xy + 2x^2$. To factor this product, follow these steps:

1. **Find the greatest common factor — the highest number that evenly divides all the terms in the expression and the lowest power of each variable.**

   Look at both the constants (numbers) and variables. In this case, the highest number that divides into 4 and 2 is 2. And the highest variable that divides into both xy and x^2 is x. You can see that the greatest common factor is $2x$.

2. **Divide both terms in the expression by the greatest common factor.**

   When you have a fraction, such as $\dfrac{4xy + 2x^2}{2x}$, the resulting terms are $2y + x$.

3. **Multiply the entire expression (from Step 2) by the greatest common factor (from Step 1) to set the expression equal to its original value.**

   Doing so produces $2x(2y + x)$.

Factoring a three-term equation $\left(x^2 + bx + c\right)$

Time to try something a little more complicated: factoring a trinomial (an expression with three terms). Suppose you start with $x^2 - 12x + 20$. Follow these steps:

1. **Find the factors of the first term of the trinomial.**

   The factors of the first term, x^2, are x and x $\left(x \cdot x = x^2\right)$. Put those factors (x and x) on the left side of two sets of parentheses: $(x \quad)(x \quad)$.

2. **Determine whether the parentheses will contain positive or negative signs.**

   You can see that the last term in the trinomial (+20) has a plus sign. That means the signs in the parentheses must be either both plus signs or both minus signs.

   REMEMBER: Two positive numbers multiplied by each other equal a positive number, and two negative numbers multiplied by each other equal a positive number. A negative number times a positive number equals a negative number.

   Because the second term (–12x) is a negative number, both factors must be negative: $(x-\quad)(x-\quad)$.

3. **Find the two numbers that go into the right sides of the parentheses.**

   This part can be tricky. The factors of the third term, when added together or subtracted, must equal the second term of the trinomial.

   In this example, the third term is 20 and the second term is –12x. You need to find the factors of 20 (the third term) that add to give you –12. The two factors you want are –2 and –10, because $(-2)(-10) = 20$ (the third term) and $-2 + -10 = -12$ (the second term). Plug in these numbers: $(x-2)(x-10)$.

   Thus, the factors of $x^2 - 12x + 20$ are $(x-2)$ and $(x-10)$.

130 PART 3 **Making the Most of Math: Arithmetic Skills**

Making Alphabet Soup: Solving Quadratic Equations

REMEMBER

A *quadratic equation* is an equation that includes the square of a variable. The exponent in these equations is never higher than 2 (because it would then no longer be the square of an unknown; it would be a cube or something else). Here are some examples of quadratic equations:

» $x^2 - 4x = -4$
» $2x^2 = x + 6$
» $x^2 = 36$

REMEMBER

Simple quadratic equations (those that consist of just one squared term and a number) can be solved by using the square root rule:

If $x^2 = k$, then $x = \pm\sqrt{k}$, as long as k isn't a negative number.

Remember to include the $\pm$ sign, which indicates the answer is a positive or negative number. Take the following simple quadratic equation: $7y^2 = 28$.

First, get rid of the 7 by dividing both sides by 7: $y^2 = 4$. Using the square root rule, take the square root of both sides of the equation. You know that $\sqrt{y^2} = y$ and $\sqrt{4} = \pm 2$, so $y = \pm 2$.

When you're solving a complex quadratic equation, you put all the terms on one side of the equal sign, making the equation equal zero. In other words, get the quadratic equation into this form: $ax^2 + bx + c = 0$, where a, b, and c are numbers and x is unknown. Take a look at the following equation: $x^2 - 2x = 15$. You can convert this equation to standard form by subtracting 15 from both sides of the equation: $x^2 - 2x - 15 = 0$.

The most efficient way to solve most quadratic equations is by factoring the equation and then setting each separate factor equal to zero. See the section "A Step Back: Factoring Algebra Expressions to Find Original Numbers" earlier in this chapter for info on factoring.

Look at the factored equation:

$$x^2 - 2x - 15 = 0$$
$$(x-5)(x+3) = 0$$

For the left side of the equation to equal zero, one of the quantities in parentheses has to equal zero (because zero times any number equals zero). That means you can split the equation in two, setting each factor equal to zero:

$x - 5 = 0$ or $x + 3 = 0$
$x = 5$ $x = -3$

The solution for $x^2 - 2x - 15$ is $x = 5$ or -3.

Ready to give quadratic equations your best shot? Practice them here.

Problem	Your Solution
$x^2 - 5x - 14 = 0$	
$x^2 + 15x = -50$	
$y^2 = 11y - 28$	
$x^2 - 16x + 61 = 2x - 20$	

The answers, from the top down, are x = –2 and x = 7; x = –5 and x = –10; y = 4 and y = 7; and x = 9.

All Math Isn't Created Equal: Solving Inequalities

Some algebra problems state that two quantities aren't equal to each other; thus, they're *inequalities*. Just like with equations, the solution to an inequality is a value that makes (or values that make) the inequality true. For the most part, you solve inequalities the same as you would solve a normal equation. You need to keep some facts of inequality life in mind, however. Short and sweet, here they are:

» Negative numbers are less than zero.

» Zero is less than positive numbers but greater than negative numbers.

» Positive numbers are greater than zero.

A regular algebraic equation includes the equal sign (=), because the very basis of the equation is that one side of the equation must equal the other. Quite the opposite is true with inequalities, and they have their own special symbols, used to express the differences:

» ≠ means "does not equal" in the way that 3 does not equal 4, or $3 \neq 4$.

» > means "greater than" in the way that 4 is greater than 3, or $4 > 3$.

» < means "less than" in the way that 3 is less than 4, or $3 < 4$.

» ≤ means "less than or equal to" in the way that x may be less than or equal to 4, or $x \leq 4$.

» ≥ means "greater than or equal to" in the way that x may be greater than or equal to 3, or $x \geq 3$.

To solve an inequality, you follow the same rules you would for solving an equation. For example, check out this inequality: $3 + x \geq 4$.

To solve it, simply isolate x by subtracting 3 from both sides of the equation:

$3 + x - 3 \geq 4 - 3$

$x \geq 1$

Therefore, 1 or any number greater than 1 makes this inequality true.

REMEMBER The only special rule for inequalities takes effect when you multiply or divide both sides of the inequality by a negative number. In that case, the inequality sign is reversed. So if you multiply both sides of the inequality $3 < 4$ by -4, your answer is $-12 > -16$. And if you divide both sides of $-2x < 14$ by -2, your answer is $x > -7$.

When you're itching to even the score by solving inequalities, give the following problems a try.

Problem	Your Solution
$2x < x - 4 \leq 3x + 8$	
$4(x+2) - 1 > 5 - 7(4-x)$	
$5x + 7 \leq 22$	
$-2(x+3) < 10$	

From top to bottom, the answers are $-6 \leq x < -4$; $x < 10$; $x \leq 3$; and $x > -8$.

TIP You may encounter ASVAB questions that ask you to identify the correct number line for an inequality. Inequalities are characterized by one of these symbols: $>, <, \geq, \leq$ and $\neq$, although you're not likely to see any number line questions featuring the $\neq$ symbol on the ASVAB (I'm only including that symbol because technically, it means two expressions are inequal). Here's how each looks on a number line:

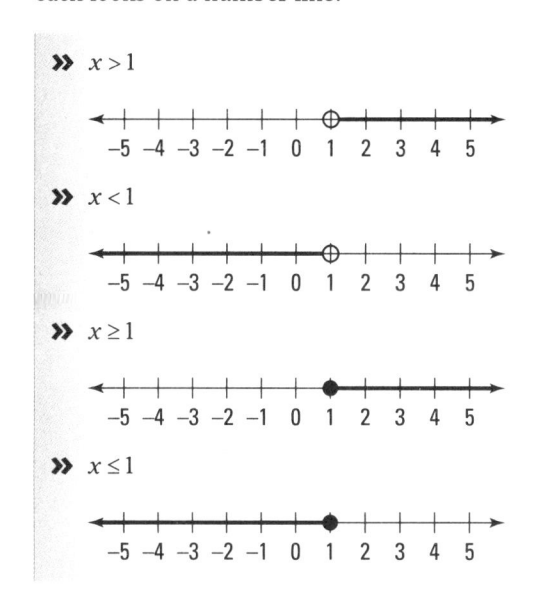

» $x > 1$

» $x < 1$

» $x \geq 1$

» $x \leq 1$

CHAPTER 7 **Algebra** 133

Algebra Practice Questions

The practice questions here are straightforward math; no word problems. Remember, these questions are designed for high school level and below. You won't be solving equations to calculate the orbit of Mars around the sun — you're just doing basic algebra.

Easy algebra practice questions

1. Solve for x: $2x - 3 = x + 7$
   - (A) 10
   - (B) 6
   - (C) 21
   - (D) −10

2. Combine like terms: $4a + 3ab + 5ab + 6a$
   - (A) $10a + 8ab$
   - (B) $18ab$
   - (C) $8a + 10ab$
   - (D) $2ab - 2a$

3. Solve for s: $30s + s = 62$
   - (A) $30s^2$
   - (B) 30
   - (C) 2
   - (D) 5

4. Solve for x: $3x = 9$
   - (A) 30
   - (B) 18
   - (C) 9
   - (D) 3

5. Solve for a: $3x + 2 = 14$
   - (A) 5.8
   - (B) 5
   - (C) 4
   - (D) 3.8

6. What is the value of $8x - 6$ when $x = -1$?
   - (A) 14
   - (B) −14
   - (C) 2
   - (D) −2

7. What is the value of $5a + 2b$ when $a = 2$ and $b = 6$?
   - (A) 34
   - (B) 30
   - (C) 28
   - (D) 22

8. Choose the expression or equation that best represents the statement "three times a number plus 6 is 12."
   - (A) $3x + 6 = 12$
   - (B) $x^3 + 6 = 12$
   - (C) $\frac{1}{3}x + 6 = 12$
   - (D) $3x + 6 + 12$

9. Choose the expression or equation that best represents the statement "the product of four times a number and nine."
   - (A) $\frac{1}{4}x = 9$
   - (B) $4x = 9$
   - (C) $4x + 9$
   - (D) $4(x) \times 9$

10. Solve for j: $2j - 5 = 11$
    - (A) 2
    - (B) 3
    - (C) 5
    - (D) 8

Medium algebra practice questions

11. Simplify $8x^2 - 3x + 4xy - 9x^2 - 5x - 20xy$.

(A) $5x^2 + 9xy$
(B) $8x - 9x^2$
(C) $-x^2 - 8x - 16xy$
(D) $8x + 9x^2$

12. Evaluate $3x^2$, if $x = -2$.

(A) 12
(B) −12
(C) 6
(D) −6

13. Solve for x: $4x + 8 > 2x + 7$

(A) $x > 1$
(B) $x > -1$
(C) $x > -\frac{1}{2}$
(D) $x > \frac{2}{3}$

14. Which number line illustrates the answer to $2a > 4$?

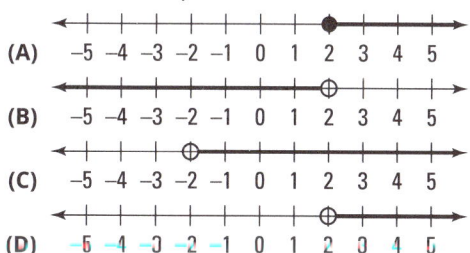

(A) [number line with closed circle at 2, shaded right]
(B) [number line with open circle at 2, shaded right]
(C) [number line with open circle at −2, shaded right]
(D) [number line with open circle at 1, shaded right]

15. Solve for y: $3y + 25y = 145 - y$

(A) 5
(B) 9
(C) 130
(D) 27

16. There are 25 males in your platoon. There are three more males than two times the number of females. How many females are in your platoon?

(A) 8
(B) 11
(C) 16
(D) 22

17. Jesse has taken four tests in his English class and scored 89, 83, 78, and 92 percent. His final exam is worth two test grades. What score does he need on the final exam to get 90 percent in the class?

(A) 94
(B) 95
(C) 97
(D) 99

18. The 22 students in Ms. Burton's fifth-grade class each have a sibling and/or a pet. If 14 have a sibling and 18 have a pet, how many students have both?

(A) 10
(B) 12
(C) 13
(D) 18

19. Bianca's cellular carrier charges a monthly rate of $12.95 and $0.25 per minute for international calls. If the bill is $21.20, how many minutes did Bianca spend on international calls?

(A) 30
(B) 33
(C) 43
(D) 48

20. Charles has $60 and is saving $7 per week. David has $120 and is saving $5 per week. How long will it be before David and Charles have the same amount of money?

(A) 18 weeks
(B) 22 weeks
(C) 26.5 weeks
(D) 30 weeks

21. Angie is 6 years older than Heather. Six years ago, Angie was twice as old as Heather was. How old is Heather now?

    (A) 12
    (B) 18
    (C) 24
    (D) 25

22. When added together, two numbers equal 108. One number is twice the other. What are the numbers?

    (A) 32 and 77
    (B) 33 and 75
    (C) 36 and 72
    (D) 39 and 69

23. Bellamy has dimes, nickels, and pennies in his pocket. He has two more nickels than dimes, and three times as many pennies as nickels. How many pennies does he have if he has $0.52 in his pocket?

    (A) 20
    (B) 14
    (C) 19
    (D) 12

24. Jayden rented a small moving van for $30 per day, plus $0.50 per mile. It took him two days to move, and the van cost $360. How many miles did Jayden drive?

    (A) 580
    (B) 600
    (C) 601.5
    (D) 602.5

25. Chief Hall and Sergeant First Class Aziz both donated money to the Army Emergency Relief Fund. Chief Hall gave three times as much as Sergeant First Class Aziz did. Between the two of them, they donated $280. How much money did Chief Hall give?

    (A) $70
    (B) $120
    (C) $190
    (D) $210

26. Three senior citizens decide to take a wakeboarding lesson. Each person has to pay for the cost of their own lesson, plus a $15 rental fee for the equipment. If the total cost is $120, how much does the lesson cost each person?

    (A) $20
    (B) $22.50
    (C) $25
    (D) $27.50

27. Ava spent $42 on a skateboard, which was $14 less than twice what she spent on skating shoes. How much were the shoes?

    (A) $28
    (B) $35
    (C) $26
    (D) $18

28. The pet daycare center has 31 dogs, which is three more than four times the number of cats. How many cats are in the pet daycare center?

    (A) 4
    (B) 6
    (C) 7
    (D) 12

29. The sum of two consecutive numbers is 37. What are the two numbers?

    (A) 13 and 14
    (B) 14 and 15
    (C) 16 and 17
    (D) 18 and 19

30. Divide $80 between Simon, Alberto, and Paloma so that Alberto has twice as much as Simon and Paloma has $5 less than Alberto. How much does Paloma get?

    (A) $17
    (B) $34
    (C) $29
    (D) 38

Hard algebra practice questions

31. Solve for x: $\begin{array}{l} x+5=y \\ 3x+y=12 \end{array}$

(A) 1
(B) $1\frac{5}{8}$
(C) 12
(D) $1\frac{3}{4}$

32. Simplify: $7y^2 \cdot 8y^7 \cdot 8y^5$

(A) 448^{14}
(B) $447y^{15}$
(C) $448y^{14}$
(D) $448y^{70}$

33. One number is 10 more than another. The sum of twice the smaller number plus three times the larger number is 55. What is the larger number?

(A) 15
(B) 5
(C) 50
(D) 55

34. The price of a pair of jeans has increased by 15 percent. The original price of the jeans was $20. What is the new price?

(A) $23
(B) $23.50
(C) $24.75
(D) $25

35. It takes 2 minutes for a chef to wrap 3 burritos. What equation expresses this rate if x is the number of minutes and y is the number of burritos?

(A) $x = \frac{2}{3}y$
(B) $y = mx + b$
(C) $x = \frac{3}{2}y$
(D) $\frac{2}{3}xy$

36. Abby is one-third her mom's age. In 12 years, she'll be half her mom's age. How old is Abby now?

(A) 8
(B) 10
(C) 12
(D) 13

37. You have 25 coins in nickels and dimes that total $1.65. How many nickels do you have?

(A) 10
(B) 17
(C) 18
(D) 21

38. The vending machine at the zoo has $17 in it. It only accepts $1 coins and quarters, and it has a total of 26 coins inside. How many $1 coins does the vending machine contain?

(A) 8
(B) 9
(C) 14
(D) 22

39. Private Joe Snuffy spent $35 at the post exchange. That was $7 less than three times what he spent at the commissary. How much did he spend at the commissary?

(A) $14
(B) $32
(C) $48
(D) $51

40. The sum of two numbers is 72, and one of the numbers is five times the other. What are the two numbers?

(A) 12 and 60
(B) 5 and 35
(C) 2 and 36
(D) 14 and 21

Answers and Explanations

Use this answer key to score the practice questions.

1. **A.** Isolate the *x*'s on the left side of the equation by subtracting *x* from both sides: $2x - 3 - x = x + 7 - x$, or $x - 3 = 7$. Continue to perform operations to isolate *x*: Add 3 to both sides of the equation to get rid of the −3 on the left: $x - 3 + 3 = 7 + 3$, or $x = 10$. The correct answer is Choice (A).

2. **A.** Group the two term categories (*a* and *ab*):

    $$3ab + 5ab = 8ab$$
    $$4a + 6a = 10a$$

3. **C.** First, combine like terms: $30s + s = 62$ is really $31s = 62$. Then solve for *s*:

    $$31s = 62$$
    $$\frac{31s}{31} = \frac{62}{31}$$
    $$s = 2$$

4. **D.** Isolate *x*:

    $$3x = 9$$
    $$\frac{3x}{3} = \frac{9}{3}$$
    $$x = 3$$

5. **C.** Get *x* by itself to solve:

    $$3x + 2 = 14$$
    $$3x + 2 - 2 = 14 - 2$$
    $$3x = 12$$
    $$\frac{3x}{3} = \frac{12}{3}$$
    $$x = 4$$

6. **B.** The question tells you that the value of *x* is −1, so multiply 8 by −1 to get −8. Then, subtract 6 for a total of −14.

7. **D.** The question tells you that $a = 2$ and $b = 6$, so plug those values into the problem to solve: $5(2) + 2(6)$, which means $10 + 12 = 22$.

8. **A.** Work through what the problem tells you one step at a time. "Three times a number" is best represented by $3x$, and the problem tells you that you need to add 6 to reach 12.

9. **C.** *Product* means you need to multiply, so the product of three times a number is best represented by $3x$. Because the problem says "and nine," adding is the proper way to work the number 9 into your expression.

10. D. Isolate j by balancing the equation and then solve:

$$2j - 5 = 11$$
$$2j - 5 + 5 = 11 + 5$$
$$2j = 16$$
$$\frac{2j}{2} = \frac{16}{2}$$
$$j = 8$$

11. C.

$$8x^2 - 3x + 4xy - 9x^2 - 5x - 20xy$$
$$= (8x^2 - 9x^2) + (-3x - 5x) + (4xy - 20xy)$$
$$= -x^2 - 8x - 16xy$$

The correct answer is Choice (C).

12. A. Just substitute -2 for x:

$$3x^2 = 3(-2)^2$$
$$= 3(4)$$
$$= 12$$

13. C. Solve an inequality just like you'd solve an equation, by isolating the variable:

$$4x + 8 > 2x + 7$$
$$4x + 8 - 2x > 2x + 7 - 2x$$
$$2x + 8 > 7$$
$$2x + 8 - 8 > 7 - 8$$
$$2x > -1$$
$$\frac{2x}{2} > -\frac{1}{2}$$
$$x > -\frac{1}{2}$$

14. D. Solve the inequality and choose the number line that corresponds with it:

$$2a > 4$$
$$\frac{2a}{2} > \frac{4}{2}$$
$$a > 2$$

The number line that corresponds with $a > 2$ is Choice (D).

15. A. Combine like terms and then solve for y:

$$3y + 25y = 145 - y$$
$$28y + y = 145 - y + y$$
$$29y = 145$$
$$\frac{29y}{29} = \frac{145}{29}$$
$$y = 5$$

16. B. Let f represent the number of females in your platoon. The problem tells you that 25 is three more than two times f, so your equation looks like this: $25 = 2f + 3$. Solve for f:

$$25 = 2f + 3$$
$$25 - 3 = 2f - 3$$
$$22 = 2f$$
$$\frac{22}{2} = \frac{2f}{2}$$
$$11 = f$$

You can check your math by working through the problem with 11 females. Multiply 11 by 2 to get 22, then add 3 to get 25. That means you found the correct answer choice.

17. D. This weighted average problem requires you to find the value of an unknown, so let x represent the score for one test grade. Because Jesse's final exam counts as two test grades, use $2x$ to represent the score he needs. Set up your math like this: $\frac{89 + 83 + 78 + 92 + 2x}{6} = 90$. (The denominator 6 represents the fact that the final score, 90, needs to be the average of six test scores.) Solve for x:

$$\frac{89 + 83 + 78 + 92 + 2x}{6} = 90$$
$$\frac{89 + 83 + 78 + 92 + 2x}{\cancel{6}} \cdot \frac{\cancel{6}}{1} = 90 \cdot 6$$
$$342 + 2x = 540$$
$$2x + 342 - 342 = 540 - 342$$
$$2x = 198$$
$$\frac{2x}{2} = \frac{198}{2}$$
$$x = 99$$

Jesse needs to score 99 percent on his test to get a 90 in the class.

18. A. Ten of Ms. Burton's students have both a sibling and a pet. Use x to represent the number of students who have both and create an equation that includes all the students who have a sibling and all the students who have a pet, plus the total number of students in the class:

$$14 + 18 - x = 22$$
$$32 - x = 22$$
$$32 - x - 32 = 22 - 32$$
$$-x = -10$$
$$\frac{-x}{-1} = \frac{-10}{-1}$$
$$x = 10$$

19. B. Let m represent the number of minutes the cellular carrier billed and then solve for m:

$$0.25m + 12.95 = 21.20$$
$$0.25m + 12.95 - 12.95 = 21.20 - 12.95$$
$$\frac{0.25m}{0.25} = \frac{8.25}{0.25}$$
$$m = 33$$

20. **D.** Let *x* represent the number of weeks Charles and David will save their money. Write an equation that represents Charles's money with 7*x* + 60 and David's money with 5*x* + 120:

$$7x + 60 = 5x + 120$$
$$7x + 60 - 60 = 5x + 120 - 60$$
$$7x = 5x + 60$$
$$7x - 5x = 5x + 60 - 5x$$
$$2x = 60$$
$$\frac{2x}{2} = \frac{60}{2}$$
$$x = 30$$

21. **A.** Let *x* represent Heather's age and *x* + 6 represent Angie's age now:

$$(x+6) - 6 = 2(x-6)$$
$$x = 2x - 12$$
$$-x = -12$$
$$x = 12$$

22. **C.** Rule out Choice (D) right off the bat; those two numbers don't add up to 108. Then, let *x* represent the smaller number and 2*x* represent the larger number. You know that *x* + 2*x* = 108, so perform the calculations:

$$3x = 108$$
$$\frac{3x}{3} = \frac{108}{3}$$
$$x = 36$$

The lower number is 36. Because the sum of the two numbers is 108, subtract that from 108: 108 − 36 = 48. The two numbers are 36 and 72.

23. **D.** Let *x* represent the number of dimes Bellamy has (always choose the group with the fewest; in this case, it's dimes). Then, *x* + 2 equals the number of nickels he has, and 3(*x* + 2) represents the number of pennies in Bellamy's pocket. Add all the amounts (and work in pennies so you don't have to worry about decimals):

$$10x + 5(x+2) + 3(x+2) = 52$$
$$10x + 5x + 10 + 3x + 6 = 52$$
$$18x = 36$$
$$\frac{18x}{18} = \frac{36}{18}$$
$$x = 2$$

Remember, *x* represents the number of dimes Bellamy has (and the answer is two). The question asks you how many pennies he has, so replace *x* in the expression 3(*x* + 2) to determine that he has 12 pennies in his pocket.

24. **B.** Let *m* represent the number of miles Jayden drove, create an equation that includes two days of van rental at $30 each, and solve for *m*:

$$30(2) + 0.5m = 360$$
$$60 + 0.5m - 60 = 360 - 60$$
$$0.5m = 300$$
$$\frac{0.5m}{0.5} = \frac{300}{0.5}$$
$$m = 600$$

25. **D.** Chief Hall donated $210, but to figure that out, you must first let x represent how much money Sergeant First Class Aziz donated. That means $3x$ represents Chief Hall's donation, and that $x + 3x = \$280$. Solve:

$$x + 3x = 280$$
$$4x = 280$$
$$\frac{4x}{4} = \frac{280}{4}$$
$$x = 70$$

If Sergeant First Class Aziz donated $70, Chief Hall ponied up $210, three times that.

26. **C.** There are three people taking lessons and renting equipment, so let $3x$ represent the total cost of the lessons; for three people to rent equipment costs $45 (the three people each pay $15). Your equation looks like this:

$$3x + 45 = 120$$
$$3x + 45 - 45 = 120 - 45$$
$$3x = 75$$
$$\frac{3x}{3} = \frac{75}{3}$$
$$x = 25$$

27. **A.** Let x represent how much Ava spent on the skate shoes and create an equation that expresses the information in the problem:

$$2x - 14 = 42$$
$$2x - 14 + 14 = 42 + 14$$
$$2x = 56$$
$$\frac{2x}{2} = \frac{56}{2}$$
$$x = 28$$

28. **C.** Let c represent the number of cats in the daycare center. The center has 31 dogs, which is three more than four times the number of cats; that tells you that your equation should look like this: $4c + 3 = 31$. Solve:

$$4c + 3 = 31$$
$$4c + 3 - 3 = 31 - 3$$
$$4c = 28$$
$$\frac{4c}{4} = \frac{28}{4}$$
$$c = 7$$

29. **D.** You can take a shortcut and simply add the numbers in each answer choice — or you can solve this problem algebraically (which may make more sense with a more complicated problem). Let x be the first number; the number after it is $x + 1$. Because the sum is 37, your equation looks like this:

$$x + x + 1 = 37$$
$$2x + 1 - 1 = 37 - 1$$
$$2x = 36$$
$$\frac{2x}{2} = \frac{36}{2}$$
$$x = 18$$

The second number is $x + 1$, which gives you 18 and 19 to work with.

PART 3 **Making the Most of Math: Arithmetic Skills**

30. C. Let *x* represent the amount of money Simon gets. Let 2*x* represent Alberto's money and 2*x* − 5 represent Paloma's money. The sum of all the money is $80:

$$x + 2x + 2x - 5 = 80$$
$$5x - 5 = 80$$
$$5x - 5 + 5 = 80 + 5$$
$$5x = 85$$
$$\frac{5x}{5} = \frac{85}{5}$$
$$x = 17$$

That tells you that Simon has $17. Because Paloma's cash is represented by the expression 2*x* − 5, she has 2($17) − 5, which is $29.

31. D. In this system, use substitution to find the value of *x*. Start by replacing *y* in the second equation with *x* + 5. Then combine like terms, simplify, and solve:

$$x + 5 = y$$
$$3x + (x + 5) = 12$$
$$4x + 5 - 5 = 12 - 5$$
$$\frac{4x}{4} = \frac{7}{4}$$
$$x = 1\frac{3}{4}$$

If you needed to solve for *y*, you'd plug in the *x* value to either one of the equations and solve. Some questions on the ASVAB will require you to do that, so be ready!

32. C. Simplify this expression with exponents by adding the exponents together and then multiplying like terms. Because the variable attached to each number is *y*, you can multiply them in order.

33. A. Let *x* represent the smaller number. The larger number is 10 more, or *x* + 10. Create an equation to figure out what numbers you're dealing with based on what the problem tells you:

$$2x + 3(x + 10) = 55$$
$$2x + 3x + 30 = 55$$
$$5x = 55 - 30$$
$$5x = 25$$
$$x = 5$$

This tells you that the smaller number is 5, so the larger number — which is 10 more than the smaller number — is 15.

34. A. You can solve this problem in two ways. First, you can find 15 percent of the original price by converting 15 percent into a decimal and performing these calculations:

$$x = \$20 + (0.15 \cdot 20)$$
$$x = \$20 + \$3$$
$$x = \$23$$

You can also multiply the original amount ($20) by 1.15, because the new price is 100 percent of the original price plus 15 percent. Either way, the correct answer is $23.

35. **A.** Write an equation that relates the number of burritos the chef can wrap in 3 minutes: $\frac{2 \text{ minutes}}{3 \text{ burritos}} = \frac{\text{how many minutes}}{1 \text{ burrito}}$. Let x represent the number of minutes and y represent the number of burritos, and then simplify your equation:

$$\frac{2}{3} = \frac{x}{1y}$$
$$3x = 2y$$
$$x = \frac{2}{3}y$$

36. **C.** Let a represent Abby's age. Because her mom is three times as old as Abby is, let $3a$ represent her age. The problem asks you to calculate Abby's age 12 years in the future, when she'll be half her mom's age, so set up your equation like this and solve for a:

$$a + 12 = \frac{1}{2}(3a + 12)$$
$$2 \cdot (a + 12) = 3a + 12$$
$$2a + 24 = 3a + 12$$
$$3a - 2a = 24 - 12$$
$$a = 12$$

Abby is 12 years old now, and her mom is 36. In 12 years, Abby will be 24 and her mom will be 48 — and that's exactly what the problem said would happen (she'll be half her mom's age).

37. **B.** Let n represent the number of nickels you have and let d represent the number of dimes you have. Together, $n + d = 25$ because you have 25 coins. Describe each coin using its value, like this: $(0.05)(n) + (0.10)(d) = 1.65$. Then find the value for one of the variables so you can work through the equation. Because $n + d = 25$, $d = 25 - n$. You can multiply both sides of the equation by 100 to get $5n + 10(25 - n) = 165$ so you don't have to work with decimals. Then, combine one n with the other:

$$5n + 250 - 10n = 165$$
$$-5n + 250 = 165$$
$$-5n = 165 - 250$$
$$-5n = -85$$
$$\frac{-5n}{-5} = \frac{-85}{-5}$$
$$n = 17$$

If the problem had asked you to figure out how many dimes you had, $25 - 17 = 8$ would tell you that you have 8 dimes. (I'd just take the coins out of my pocket and count them, but that's the easy way out.)

38. **C.** Let q represent quarters and d represent dollars so that $26 - q = d$ (the machine has 26 coins in total). Use $25q$ to represent the value in cents of all the quarters together. Because the dollar coins have a value of 100 cents each, you have to determine how many cents the machine has from the dollar coins. That's $100(26 - q)$. Create a table to help you keep all these coins straight, like this:

144 PART 3 Making the Most of Math: Arithmetic Skills

	Number of Coins	Cents per Coin	Total Cents
Quarters	q	25	$25q$
Dollars	$(26-q)$	100	$100(26-q)$
Total	26		1,700

Add the total value of the quarters to the dollar coins' value:

$$\begin{aligned} 25q + 100(26-q) &= 1{,}700 \\ 25q + 2{,}600 - 100q &= 1{,}700 \\ -75q + 2{,}600 &= 1{,}700 \\ -75q &= -900 \\ q &= 12 \end{aligned}$$

The machine contains 12 quarters but a total of 26 coins. That means the 14 remaining coins are $1 coins.

39. A. Private Snuffy spent x dollars at the commissary. To figure out just how much lighter his bank account is, create an equation that shows he spent three times as much at the post exchange, less $7: $3x - 7 = \$35$. Then solve for x:

$$\begin{aligned} 3x - 7 &= 35 \\ 3x - 7 + 7 &= 35 + 7 \\ 3x &= 42 \\ \frac{3x}{3} &= \frac{42}{3} \\ x &= \$14 \end{aligned}$$

40. A. The problem tells you that one number is five times the other and that the sum of both numbers is 72, so there's only one variable. Set up an equation like this: $x + 5x = 72$. Remember that $5x$ is standing in for the second number. Then solve for x:

$$\begin{aligned} x + 5x &= 72 \\ 6x &= 72 \\ \frac{6x}{6} &= \frac{72}{6} \\ x &= 12 \end{aligned}$$

That tells you that the first number is 12. Multiply that by 5 (that's where the $5x$ comes in) to find the second number, which is 60. The two numbers are 12 and 60.

IN THIS CHAPTER

» Looking at things from a different angle

» Shaping up for calculations involving common forms

» Zeroing in on coordinates and graphs

Chapter 8
Geometry

Geometry is the branch of mathematics that deals with the properties of shapes, lines, points, angles, and other such objects and the relationships among them.

The computerized ASVAB's Mathematics Knowledge subtest consists of 15 questions, and you have 31 minutes to complete them all; if your test includes tryout questions, which I explain in Chapter 1, you have 65 minutes to complete 30 questions. The paper-and-pencil ASVAB has 25 questions, and you have 24 minutes to answer them all. Not all those questions deal with geometry, but you're very likely to encounter at least a few that do. You may finish a question about algebra and head right into a question that asks you to find the volume of a cylinder, the circumference of a circle, or the slant of an angle. Or you may have to deal with something entirely different, like adding fractions, messing with percentages, or working with scientific notation (but don't worry — I cover all those things in Chapter 7).

You're not allowed to use a calculator, but you can use as much scratch paper as you need — the test proctors hand it out like candy.

REMEMBER: The CAT-ASVAB is designed to test how much you know and do it quickly. The test usually kicks off with a question of medium difficulty. If you answer correctly, you get a harder question, but if you answer incorrectly, you get an easier question. The whole test works like that, which means you may not see very many "easy" questions at all — or you may not see any "hard" questions at all and think that the practice exams in Part 6 are much harder than they need to be.

REMEMBER: Before you read any further, you should note a few things:

» Arcs of a circle and sizes of angles are measured in *degrees* and (not very often) in *minutes* or even *seconds;* 1 degree equals 60 minutes, and 1 minute equals 60 seconds.

» A *circle* has 360 degrees (360°). Any arc that isn't a complete circle measures less than 360°.

» A *quadrilateral* (a shape with four sides, such as a square or rectangle) has angles that add up to 360°.

Perusing Perimeter and Area

Flat shapes — I'm talking squares, rectangles, circles, and triangles — are called *two-dimensional*, or 2D, because they have only two dimensions you can measure: length and width. Solid objects that have height or depth are *three-dimensional* (3D); some examples are cubes, cuboids, spheres, and cones. The *perimeter* of a shape is the distance around it (you can view it as the shape's boundary), and its *area* is all the flat space within that boundary.

The perimeter of a 2D object is always the sum of the length of all its sides (even a circle has a side, though just one), and its area is usually the object's length times its width or something pretty similar. Check out these and other important geometry formulas in the later section, "Hammering Down Helpful Geometry Formulas."

Outlining Angles

Angles are formed when two lines intersect (cross) at a point. You typically measure angles in degrees. The greater the number of degrees, the wider the angle is:

» A *straight line* is 180°.
» A *right angle* is exactly 90°. (**Note:** Right angles are marked by a right angle square; that is, a small, square-shaped figure that sits at the vertex where two lines meet at 90°. You can see a right angle square in action in Figure 8-1. It's in the images of the right and complementary angles.)
» An *acute angle* is more than 0° but less than 90°.
» An *obtuse angle* is more than 90° but less than 180°.
» A *reflex angle* measures more than 180°.
» *Complementary angles* are two angles that equal 90° when added together.
» *Supplementary angles* are two angles that equal 180° when added together.

An angle's *vertex* is the point where two rays intersect to form an angle.

Take a look at the different types of angles in Figure 8-1.

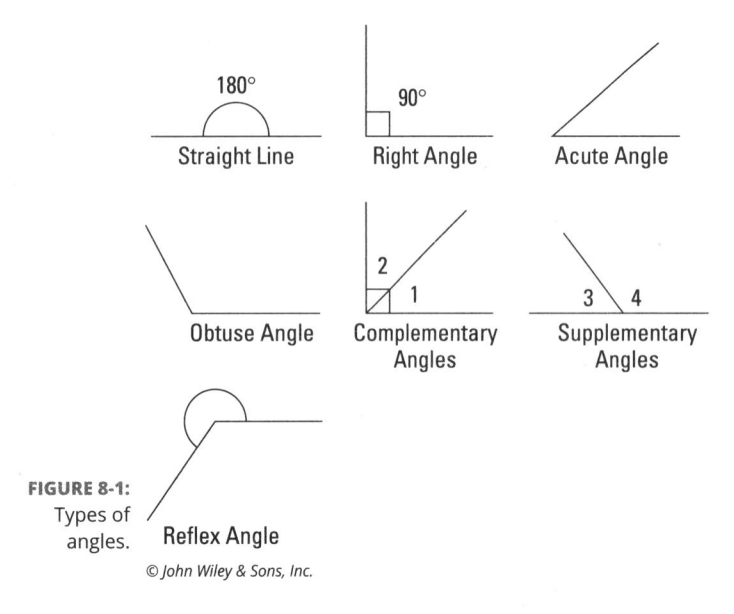

FIGURE 8-1: Types of angles.

© John Wiley & Sons, Inc.

Vertical angles oppose each other when two lines cross. They're always equal, like they are in Figure 8-2. Angles *a* and *b* are equal, and angles *x* and *y* are equal. In this case, the term *vertical* refers to where the lines cross each other; it has nothing to do with direction.

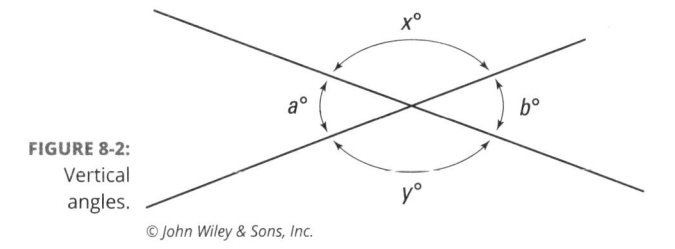

FIGURE 8-2: Vertical angles.

© John Wiley & Sons, Inc.

Parallel lines

Parallel lines never intersect. Lines are considered *parallel* if they're always the same distance apart (the technical term for this attribute is *equidistant*) and they'll never meet. They also point in the same direction. When another line, called a *transversal*, crosses parallel lines, the angles formed make pairs that have the same measure, just as they are in Figure 8-3. Each type of angle in this situation has its own name.

- » **Corresponding angles** have the same measure. They're on the same side of the transversal and both are either above or below the parallel lines. The pairs in Figure 8-3 are *a* and *w, d* and *z, b* and *x,* and *c* and *y.* These angles have to be equal if the lines are parallel.

- » **Alternate interior angles** are on opposite sides of the transversal and between the parallel lines, like *d* and *x* are in Figure 8-3. Equality between these angles means you have parallel lines on your hands.

- » **Alternate exterior angles** are on opposite sides of the transversal, like *a* and *y* are in Figure 8-3. When these angles are equal — you guessed it — parallel lines.

- » **Consecutive interior angles** are on the same side of the transversal, between the parallel lines, like *d* and *w* are in Figure 8-3. If these two angles add up to 180°, you're dealing with parallel lines.

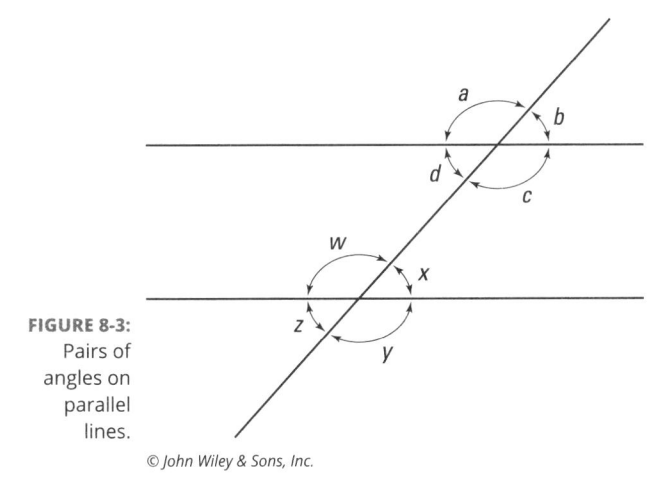

FIGURE 8-3: Pairs of angles on parallel lines.

© John Wiley & Sons, Inc.

CHAPTER 8 **Geometry** 149

Naming angles

Angles have descriptors like acute, obtuse, and complementary, but you can also name angles by using the vertex point and a point on each of the angle's rays. You may see problems where angles are named $\angle ABC$, $\angle CMZ$, or $\angle DRJ$. The middle letter in this type of label is the vertex. Also, angles can be named using only the vertex, as long as it's clear which angle you're talking about (not two angles sharing the same vertex).

Here's what an angle labeled $\angle DRJ$ may look like:

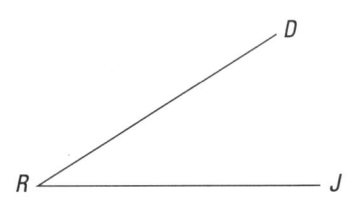

Pointing Out Triangle Types

A *triangle* consists of three straight sides that intersect at the three vertices. All three angles always add up to 180°. Triangles can be classified according to the relationship among their angles or the relationship among their sides:

- **Isosceles triangle:** An *isosceles triangle* has two equal sides; the angles opposite the equal sides are also equal.

- **Equilateral triangle:** An *equilateral triangle* has three equal sides; each of the angles measures 60°.

- **Right triangle:** A *right triangle* has one right angle (90°); therefore, the remaining two angles are complementary (add up to 90°). The side opposite the right angle is called the *hypotenuse*, which is the longest side of a right triangle. The other two sides are called *legs*.

- **Obtuse triangle:** An *obtuse triangle* has an angle greater than 90°.

- **Scalene triangle:** A *scalene triangle* has three unequal sides.

Check out Figure 8-4 to see what these triangles look like.

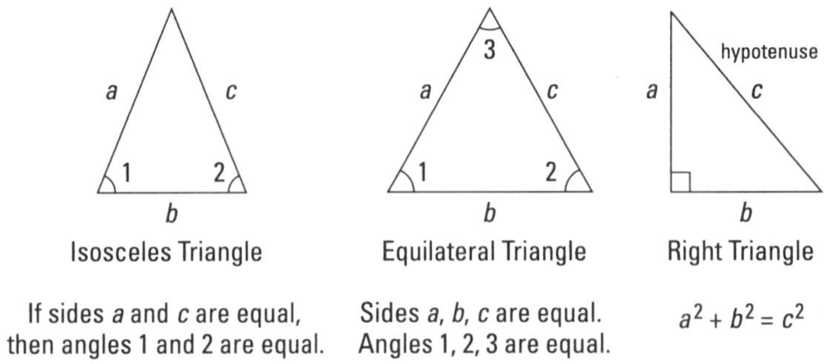

FIGURE 8-4: The three basic types of triangles.

Isosceles Triangle — If sides *a* and *c* are equal, then angles 1 and 2 are equal.

Equilateral Triangle — Sides *a*, *b*, *c* are equal. Angles 1, 2, 3 are equal.

Right Triangle — $a^2 + b^2 = c^2$

© John Wiley & Sons, Inc.

REMEMBER You can find the perimeter of a triangle by adding together the lengths of the three sides. The area of a triangle is one-half the product of the base (*b*, the bottom or the length) and the height (*h*, the distance drawn perpendicular from the base to the opposite vertex), or $A = \frac{1}{2}bh$.

The *Pythagorean theorem* (also known as Pythagoras's theorem) says that when a triangle has a right angle and you make squares on all three sides, the biggest square has the exact same area as the other two squares put together. It doesn't sound like something you'll ever use, but it really comes in handy when you know the lengths of two sides of a triangle and need to figure out the third.

The Pythagorean theorem only works with right-angled triangles.

The formula for this theorem is $a^2 + b^2 = c^2$, where a and b are the triangle's legs and c is its longest side. On paper, it looks like Figure 8-5.

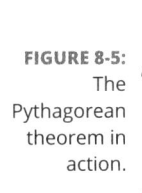

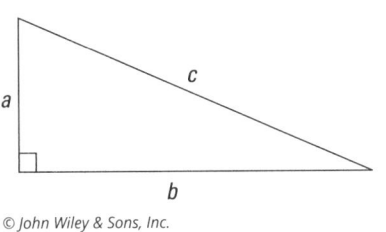

FIGURE 8-5: The Pythagorean theorem in action.

© John Wiley & Sons, Inc.

Find the length of c.

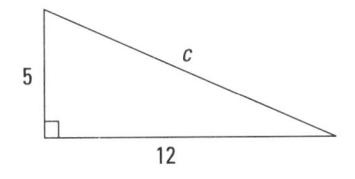

(A) 13
(B) 17
(C) 26
(D) 169

Remember that c is always the hypotenuse, which is what you need to find. Take the measurements from the figure and apply them to the Pythagorean theorem:

$$a^2 + b^2 = c^2$$
$$5^2 + 12^2 = c^2$$
$$25 + 144 = c^2$$
$$169 = c^2$$

The square root of 169 is 13, so the triangle's hypotenuse is 13. The correct answer is Choice (A).

Back to Square One: Quadrilaterals

Quadrilaterals — shapes with four sides — all contain angles totaling 360°. Many types of quadrilaterals exist (see Figure 8-6):

» *Squares* have four sides of equal length, and all the angles are right angles.

» *Rectangles* have all (four) right angles, and the opposite sides have equal lengths.

» *Parallelograms* have opposite sides that are parallel, and their opposite sides and angles are equal. The angles don't have to be right angles.

» *Rhombuses* have four sides of equal length, but the angles don't have to be right angles.

» *Trapezoids* have exactly two sides that are parallel.

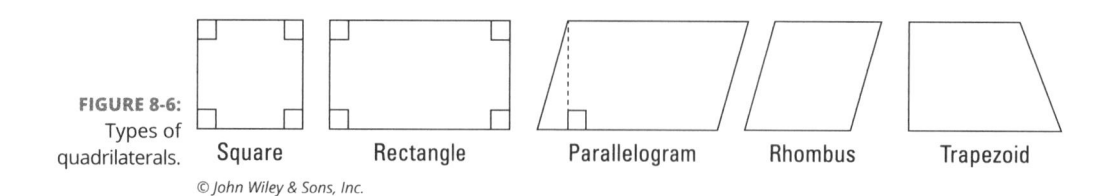

FIGURE 8-6: Types of quadrilaterals. Square, Rectangle, Parallelogram, Rhombus, Trapezoid
© John Wiley & Sons, Inc.

You can find the area of a square and a rectangle with the formula $A = lw$, where A represents area, l represents length of one side, and w represents width.

To find the area of a parallelogram, you need the formula $A = bh$, where A represents area, b represents base, and h represents height. The height is measured from the base perpendicular to the parallel side.

The area of a rhombus is a bit trickier. It's $A = \frac{pq}{2}$, where A represents area, p represents the length of one diagonal, and q represents the length of the other diagonal. The variables in this formula look like this:

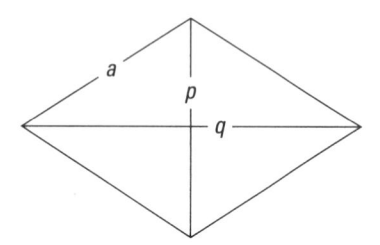

The formula to find the area of a trapezoid is $A = \frac{a+b}{2}h$, where A represents area, a represents the length of one base (one of its parallel lines), and b represents the length of the other base (the other parallel line). In this formula, h represents height as measured between the two parallel lines, like this:

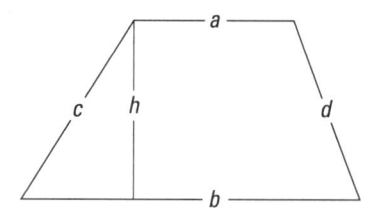

REMEMBER

Knowing these formulas may come in handy if you're answering "hard" Mathematics Knowledge or Arithmetic Reasoning questions on the ASVAB. But the test doesn't have that many questions (15 if you're taking the CAT-ASVAB without tryout questions and 25 if you're taking the pencil-and-paper version). Most people only see a handful of geometry-related questions.

Going around in Circles

A *circle* is formed when its points are all located an equal distance from its center. A circle always has 360°. Here are some key circle terms (see Figure 8-7, which shows the parts of a circle):

» **Circumference (C):** The points forming the circle — that is, the distance around the circle — is called its *circumference*.

» **Radius (r):** The *radius* of a circle is the straight-line measurement from the center of the circle to any point on the circumference of the circle.

» **Diameter (d):** The *diameter* of the circle is measured as a line passing through the center of the circle, from a point on one side of the circle all the way to a point on the other side of the circle. Any line that passes through a circle and connects two points on the circle is called a *chord*. The diameter is the longest chord.

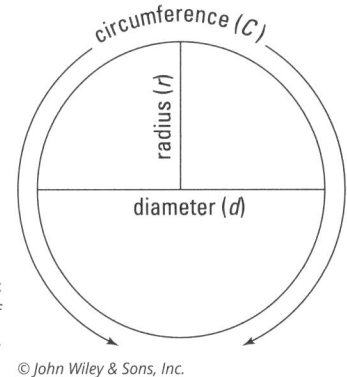

FIGURE 8-7: The parts of a circle.

© John Wiley & Sons, Inc.

The diameter of a circle is always twice as long as the radius of a circle: $d = 2r$.

Navigating the circumference

To measure the circumference of a circle, use the number pi (π). Although π is a lengthy number, it's generally rounded to 3.14 or approximated as $\frac{22}{7}$. If you round π so you can solve a problem, you don't use the equal sign because the answer isn't equal to the actual length. You use the approximation symbol ($\approx$) instead.

The formula for circumference is circumference = $\pi \times$ diameter, or $C = \pi d$. Because the radius of a circle is half its diameter, you can also use the radius to determine the circumference of a circle. Here's the formula: $C = 2\pi r$.

Suppose you know that the pie you just baked has a diameter of 9 inches. You can determine its circumference by using the circumference formula:

$C = \pi d$
$C \approx 3.14 \times 9$
$C \approx 28.26$ inches

CHAPTER 8 **Geometry** 153

Mapping out the area of a circle

REMEMBER

Determining the area of a circle also requires the use of π. Area = π × the square of the circle's radius, or $A = \pi r^2$.

To determine the area of a 9-inch-diameter pie, multiply π by the square of 4.5. Why 4.5 and not 9? Remember, the radius is always half the diameter, and the diameter is 9 inches.

$A = \pi r^2$
$A \approx 3.14 \times 4.5^2$
$A \approx 3.14 \times (4.5 \times 4.5)$
$A \approx 3.14 \times 20.25$
$A \approx 63.585$ square inches

Fillin' It Up: Calculating Volume

Volume is the space a solid (three-dimensional) shape takes up. You can think of volume as how much a shape would hold if you poured water into it. Volume is measured in cubic units. The formula for finding volume depends on the object, which, when the sides are all polygons (flat figures), is a *prism*:

» **Rectangular prisms:** For rectangular prisms, you multiply length × width (depth) × height. You can do so because the length, width, and height of a rectangle are consistent throughout the whole shape. The formula looks like this: $V = lwh$.

Remember that a cube is also a box; its sides are all the same length, and you use the same formula as you would with a rectangular box.

» **Cylinders:** A cylinder has two circles for its bases. The volume equals π × the radius squared × height, or $V = \pi r^2 h$.

Basically, you're multiplying the area of the cylinder's circular base $\left(A = \pi r^2\right)$ times the height *(h)* of the cylinder.

» **Spheres:** Finding the volume of a sphere (a ball-shaped object) requires this formula: $V = \frac{4}{3}\pi r^3$, where *V* represents volume and *r* represents the sphere's radius. (Like circles, spheres have diameter and radius.)

EXAMPLE

Find the volume of this rectangular prism:

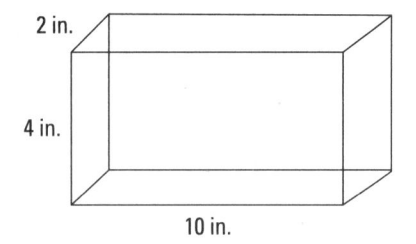

2 in.
4 in.
10 in.

(A) 40 in.³
(B) 80 in.²
(C) 80 in.³
(D) 160 in.³

154 PART 3 Making the Most of Math: Arithmetic Skills

Use the formula for the volume of a rectangular object, $V = lwh$, where V represents volume, l represents length, w represents width, and h represents height. Plug in the values to solve:

$V = lwh$
$V = 10 \cdot 2 \cdot 4$
$V = 80$

Volume is measured in cubic inches (represented by in.³), so don't let Choice (B) mess you up. The answer is Choice (C).

EXAMPLE

Find the volume of this cylinder:

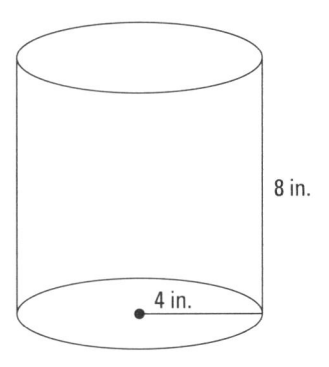

8 in.

4 in.

(A) 401.92 in.³
(B) 396.56 in.³
(C) 403.12 in.³
(D) 112.8 in.³

Replace the variables in the formula for the volume of a cylinder with what you see in the diagram:

$V \approx \pi r^2 h$
$V \approx (3.14) \cdot 4^2 \cdot 8$
$V \approx 3.14 \cdot 16 \cdot 8$
$V \approx 401.92$

The variables fit right into the formula, and using 3.14 to represent pi, you can perform the calculations on your scratch paper. The correct answer on this question is Choice (A).

If you start seeing questions like these on the ASVAB, it's because you've answered previous questions correctly. These — and other math questions involving 3D shapes — are considered "hard" questions, and you may not see them on the test at all.

Scratching the surface area of solids

Surface area is all the area on the exterior of a solid, and some questions on the Mathematics Knowledge or Arithmetic Reasoning subtests of ASVAB may ask you to calculate it. The surface area of an object is the sum of all the areas of all the shapes that cover the surface of it.

The formula for surface area is different for different objects:

» **Surface area of a cube:** $SA = 6s^2$, where s represents the length of the side of each edge

» **Surface area of a rectangular prism:** $SA = 2ab + 2bc + 2ac$, where a, b, and c represent the lengths of the three sides

» **Surface area of any prism:** $SA = 2B + ph$, where B represents the area of the base, p represents the perimeter of the base, and h represents height

» **Surface area of a cylinder:** $SA = 2\pi r^2 + 2\pi rh$, where r represents radius and h represents height

EXAMPLE

Find the surface area of this cube:

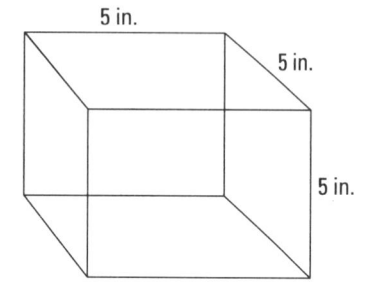

5 in.
5 in.
5 in.

(A) 100 in.²
(B) 150 in.²
(C) 300 in.²
(D) 900 in.²

Each side of the cube is 5 inches long, and the formula for the surface area of a cube is $SA = 6s^2$. Replace s in the formula with 5 and work through the equation:

$SA = 6s^2$
$SA = 6(5 \cdot 5)$
$SA = 6(25)$
$SA = 150$

The correct answer is Choice (B). Remember that surface area is measured in square inches, which is abbreviated in.².

EXAMPLE

Find the surface area of this rectangular prism:

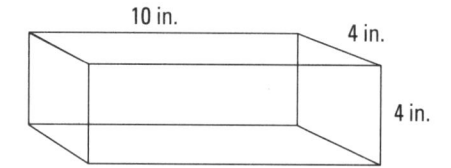

10 in.
4 in.
4 in.

(A) 150 in.²
(B) 172 in.²
(C) 192 in.²
(D) 215 in.²

156 PART 3 Making the Most of Math: Arithmetic Skills

The formula for the surface area of a rectangular prism is $SA = 2ab + 2bc + 2ac$, so choose what you want to fill in for a, b, and c (any side will do) from the figure. Put it into the formula:

$$SA = 2ab + 2bc + 2ac$$
$$SA = (2 \cdot 4 \cdot 4) + (2 \cdot 4 \cdot 10) + (2 \cdot 4 \cdot 10)$$
$$SA = 32 + 80 + 80$$
$$SA = 192$$

The answer, Choice (C), is a measurement of every square inch of the outside of the rectangular prism in the figure.

Breaking down combined figures

On the ASVAB, you may come across nonstandard shapes — they're like a mashup of two (or more) shapes. When you have to find the area, volume, or surface area of one of these figures, you have to break apart the figure and perform multiple sets of calculations (one for each shape you're left with). Figure 8-8 shows some examples of combined figures.

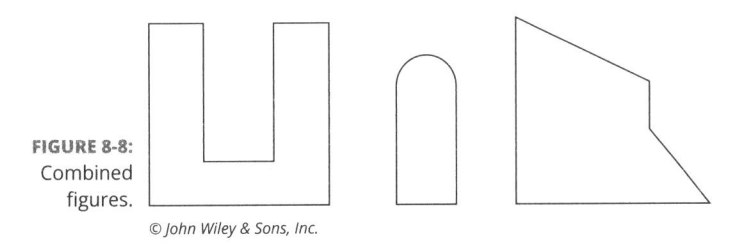

FIGURE 8-8: Combined figures.

© John Wiley & Sons, Inc.

Find the area of this figure:

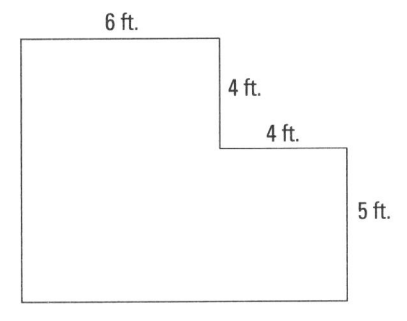

(A) 54 ft.²
(B) 16 ft.²
(C) 70 ft.²
(D) 74 ft.²

You can solve this problem two ways: You can find the area of the figure as if it were one whole figure, subtracting the part that's missing (the 4-foot-by-4-foot segment in the upper right corner), or you can find the sum of the areas of two rectangles stuck together (one that measures 4 feet by 5 feet and one that measures 6 feet by 9 feet). On the ASVAB, you have a limited amount of time to answer each question, so do what's easiest for you.

In this case, it may be easier to figure out what the area would be if this figure were a whole rectangle, and then subtract the area of the missing part. If this shape were a whole rectangle, its measurements would be 10 feet by 9 feet, so use the formula for the area of a rectangle: $A = lw$. Because $10 \cdot 9 = 90$, the whole rectangle's area would be 90 ft.² Subtract the area of the missing piece, which is 16 ft.² (because $4 \cdot 4 = 16$). $90 - 16 = 74$, so the answer is Choice (D).

Find the area of this figure:

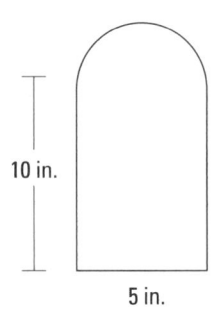

EXAMPLE

10 in.

5 in.

(A) 65.32 in.²
(B) 59.81 in.²
(C) 45.23 in.²
(D) 31.41 in.²

The figure depicts two shapes: a half-circle and a rectangle. You have to perform calculations to find the area of a circle, divide your answer in half (because it's a half-circle), and also find the area of the rectangle. You can perform the calculations in whatever order is easiest for you.

The rectangle's area is 50 in.² because the formula for the area of a rectangle is $A = lw$, and the diagram says one side is 5 inches long and the other is 10 inches long.

The formula for the area of a circle is $A \approx \pi r^2$. Radius is half a circle's diameter, and the figure shows that the circle's diameter is 5 inches. That means this circle's radius is 2.5 inches, so replace r in the formula to find the first part of the answer:

$$A \approx \pi (2.5)^2$$
$$A \approx 3.14(6.25)$$
$$A \approx 19.625$$

That gives you the area of the whole circle, but you have to cut it in half. $19.625 \div 2 = 9.8125$, and because the answer choices only have two numbers to the right of the decimal, you can round that down to 9.81.

The last step in this problem is adding the areas of the two shapes together: $50 + 9.81 = 59.81$. The correct answer is Choice (B).

A good guessing strategy on the ASVAB is to rule out answer choices you know can't be correct. In this case, Choices (C) and (D) are impossible — they're both smaller than what you know the area of the rectangle is. If you were going to guess on this question, you'd have a 50-50 chance of getting it right by eliminating those two choices.

TIP

PART 3 Making the Most of Math: Arithmetic Skills

Mapping Out Coordinates

Geometry coordinates are a little different from what you'll experience on a military Land Navigation Course, but chances are pretty good you'll use this skill to get from Point A to Point B on a military map — and you may need to use it on the ASVAB, too.

In geometry, a *coordinate grid* is a grid that includes a horizontal *x*-axis and a vertical *y*-axis. The two axes meet at the *origin*, and its coordinates are (0, 0). Every point on the grid has a pair of coordinates. In this figure, Point A's coordinates are (−8, 8), Point B's coordinates are (3, 4), and Point C's coordinates are (−5, −2). Coincidentally, you read these grids just like you read military maps. Whenever the *x*- or *y*-coordinate is the same within a set of points, those points are what's called *colinear*.

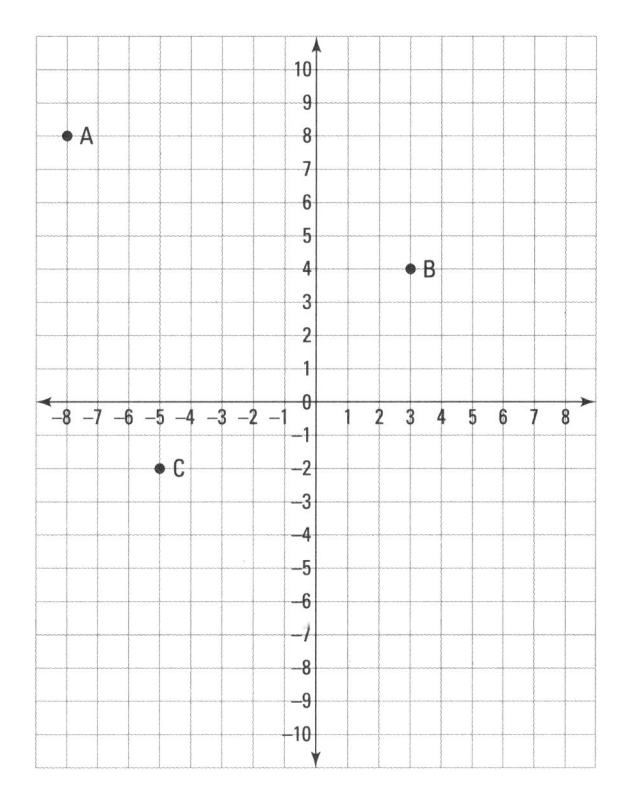

You can represent a line on a coordinate grid by using a formula called the *slope-intercept form* of a linear equation. That formula is $y = mx + b$, where *m* represents the line's slope, *b* represents the point where the line crosses the *y*-axis, and *x* and *y* represent coordinates of points that lie on the line.

Find the *y*-intercept of the straight line that has a slope of 4 and passes through the point (−1, −6).

EXAMPLE
(A) −2
(B) −3
(C) 2
(D) 3

Using slope-intercept form, plug in what you know. Remember to read coordinates the right way, which is (x, y).

$$y = mx + b$$
$$-6 = (4 \cdot -1) + b$$
$$-6 = -4 + b$$
$$-6 + 4 = b$$
$$-2 = b$$

The correct answer is Choice (A). The line crosses the y-axis at the point −2, and it travels through points −1 and −6. The equation of the line is $y = 4x - 2$.

The x and y axes divide the plane into four regions called *quadrants.* Each quadrant has its own number, beginning with the Roman numeral I on the upper right and working counterclockwise with II, III, and IV.

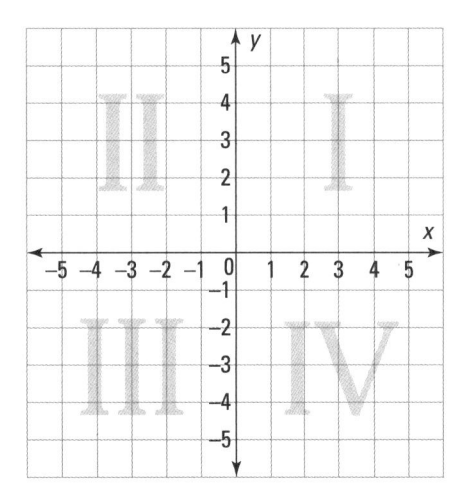

Hammering Down Helpful Geometry Formulas

Just about every operation in geometry comes with its own formula. If you know the formula that applies to the problem in front of you, you can replace its variables and solve for the answer. Get acquainted with the formulas outlined in Table 8-1. They may come in handy on test day.

You're unlikely to see problems that require you to perform complex calculations, because you're not allowed to use a calculator on the test. The people who write ASVAB test questions aren't trying to send you into full meltdown mode! However, the ASVAB may ask you to give estimates on things like the surface area or volume of a sphere if you're powering through all the easy and medium questions. Remember, the test is designed to determine what you know quickly and efficiently. If you incorrectly answer a question of medium difficulty, you see an easier question next; if you give the right answer on a medium-difficulty question, the next question that pops up on your screen is more difficult.

TABLE 8-1 **Common Geometry Formulas**

Operation	Formula
Perimeter of a square or rectangle	$P = 4s$ or $2s + 2s$
Area of a square or rectangle	$A = lw$
Perimeter of a triangle	$P = a + b + c$
Area of a triangle	$A = \frac{1}{2}bh$
Pythagorean theorem	$a^2 + b^2 = c^2$
Sum of angles for all triangles	$A + B + C = 180°$
Diameter of a circle	$d = 2r$
Circumference of a circle	$C = 2\pi r$
Area of a circle	$A = \pi r^2$
Area of a trapezoid	$A = \frac{a+b}{2}h$
Volume of a cube	$V = a^3$
Volume of a rectangular solid	$V = lwh$
Surface area of a rectangular solid	$SA = 2hw + 2lh + 2lw$
Volume of a cylinder	$v = \pi r^2 h$
Surface area of a cylinder	$SA = 2\pi rh + 2\pi r^2$
Volume of a sphere	$V = \frac{4}{3}\pi r^3 \frac{7}{2}$
Surface area of a sphere	$SA = 4\pi r^2$

Geometry Practice Questions

On the ASVAB's mathematics knowledge subtest, you're very likely to encounter problems that include figures and formulas. If you're taking the computerized version of the test, you'll probably kick off with a question of medium difficulty; if you get it right, the questions will get harder until you get one wrong, and if you get that first question wrong, the questions will get easier until you get one right. You may see a lot of difficult questions, a lot of easy questions, or a mix — it all depends on how you're doing on the test.

Easy geometry practice questions

1. Find the perimeter:

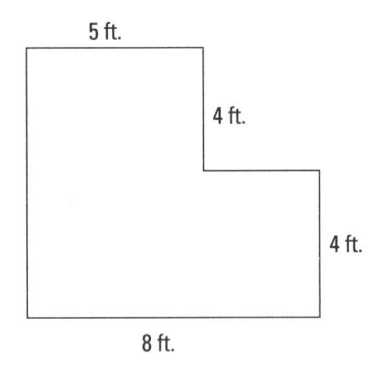

   5 ft.
   4 ft.
   4 ft.
   8 ft.

   (A) 32 ft.
   (B) 33 ft.
   (C) 34 ft.
   (D) 35 ft.

2. Find the area of the rectangle:

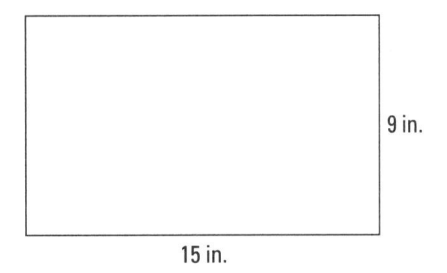

   9 in.
   15 in.

   (A) 48 in.²
   (B) 65 in.²
   (C) 90 in.²
   (D) 135 in.²

3. Identify the angle:

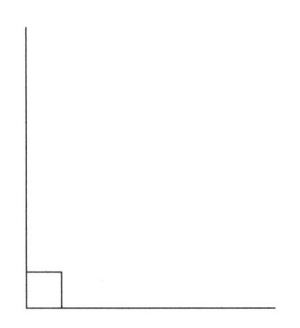

   (A) acute
   (B) obtuse
   (C) complementary
   (D) right

4. At 3:00 p.m., the angle between the hands of the clock is

   (A) 90 degrees
   (B) 180 degrees
   (C) 120 degrees
   (D) 360 degrees

5. In any triangle, the sum of the interior angles adds up to how many degrees?

   (A) 90
   (B) 180
   (C) 270
   (D) 360

6. What letter represents the vertex?

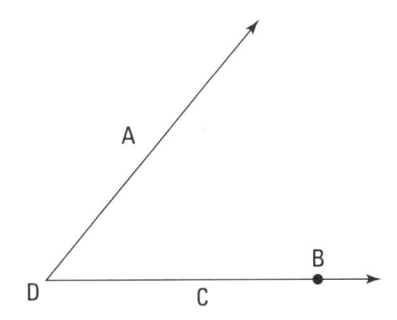

(A) A
(B) B
(C) C
(D) D

7. What is the angle of a straight line?

(A) 90 degrees
(B) 145 degrees
(C) 180 degrees
(D) 360 degrees

8. What is the perimeter of a square that has 9-inch sides?

(A) 9 inches
(B) 18 inches
(C) 27 inches
(D) 36 inches

9. What is the formula to identify the area of a rectangle?

(A) $A = \frac{1}{2}bh$
(B) $A = lw$
(C) $P = 4s$
(D) $A = \pi r^2$

10. Which of the following is true of parallel lines?

(A) Parallel lines never intersect.
(B) The points on a parallel lines may be different distances apart.
(C) Parallel lines aren't usually equidistant.
(D) Both (A) and (C) are true.

Medium geometry practice questions

11. The radius of a circle is 2 inches. What is its approximate circumference?

(A) 12 inches

(B) 12.56 inches

(C) 23.23 inches

(D) 26.2 inches

12. What is the value of YZ? (*Note:* This figure is not drawn to scale.)

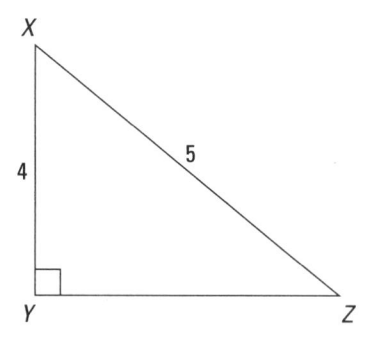

(A) 3

(B) 2

(C) 6

(D) 5

13. What is the area of the trapezoid?

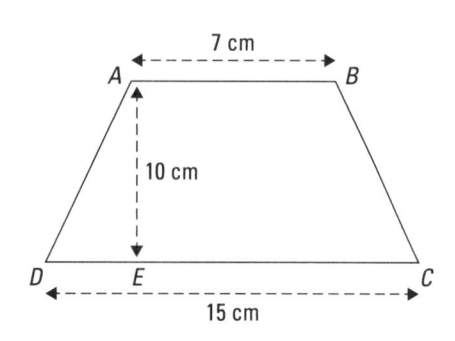

(A) 32 cm²

(B) 157 cm²

(C) 110 cm²

(D) 220 cm²

14. A circle has a radius of 15 feet. What's most nearly its circumference?

(A) 30 feet

(B) 225 feet

(C) 94 feet

(D) 150 feet

15. Find the area of a circle with a radius of 5 cm.

(A) 87.5 cm²

(B) 78.5 cm²

(C) 17.5 cm²

(D) 8.5 cm²

16. One complementary angle is 62 degrees. What is measure of the other angle?

(A) 158 degrees

(B) 28 degrees

(C) 62 degrees

(D) 26 degrees

17. In which quadrant does the point (7, −8) lie?

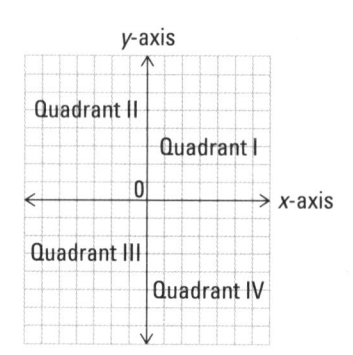

(A) Quadrant I

(B) Quadrant II

(C) Quadrant III

(D) Quadrant IV

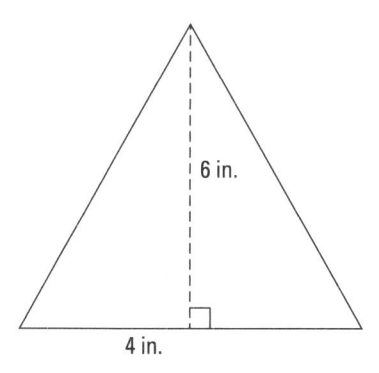

18. Find the area:

(A) 12 in.²
(B) 15 in.²
(C) 24 in.²
(D) 48 in.²

19. Find the circumference:

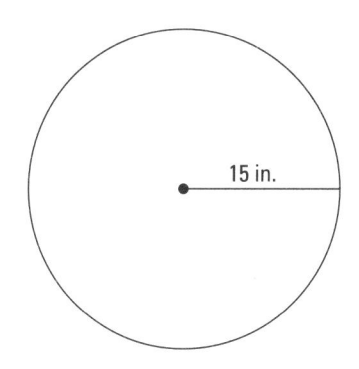

(A) 92.5 in.
(B) 94.2 in.
(C) 143.2 in.
(D) 150 in.

20. What is the measurement of Angle D?

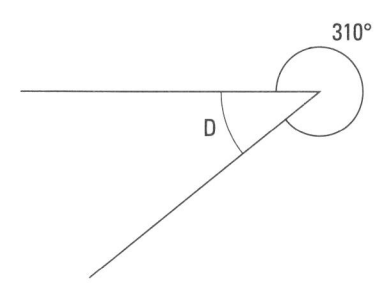

(A) 50°
(B) 60°
(C) 45°
(D) 310°

21. Evelyn is measuring a 50-foot, triangular perimeter in the corner of her yard so she can plant a persimmon tree. If two sides of the triangle are equal and the third side is 5 feet longer than the equal sides, what is the length of the third side?

(A) 15 feet
(B) 17.5 feet
(C) 20 feet
(D) 22.5 feet

22. Two angles are equal in a quadrilateral. The third angle is equal to the sum of the two equal angles, and the fourth angle is 60° less than twice the sum of the other three angles. What are the measures of the four angles?

(A) 50°, 75°, 35°, 180°
(B) 60°, 65°, 75°, 160°
(C) 35°, 35°, 75°, 215°
(D) 35°, 35°, 70°, 220°

23. You have half a cherry pie left after your holiday party. You cut a slice with a 30° angle and put it in the refrigerator for your roommate. You eat the rest of the pie. What is the measure of your piece of the pie in degrees?

(A) 150°
(B) 160°
(C) 145°
(D) 310°

24. David eats half a pizza. Of the remaining amount, Angie wants to eat twice what Sadie eats, but she also needs to save some for Jeff. Angie cuts a 30° slice for Jeff. What is the measure of Angie's piece of pizza in degrees?

(A) 50°
(B) 60°
(C) 85°
(D) 100°

25. The measure of one supplementary angle is twice the measure of the second. What is the measure of each angle?

(A) 60°, 120°
(B) 60°, 130°
(C) 45°, 90°
(D) 31°, 62°

26. Identify the set of colinear points.

    (A) (2, 4), (2, 0), (3, 2)
    (B) (3, 3), (2, 3), (3, 2)
    (C) (2, 5), (2, 7), (2, 9)
    (D) (3, 2), (3, 9), (9, 3)

27. A right triangle's acute angles measure at the ratio 1:3. What is the measure of the acute angles?

    (A) 22.5°, 67.5°, 70°
    (B) 22.5°, 67.5°, 90°
    (C) 23.5°, 66.5°, 90°
    (D) 100°, 0°, 90°

28. A penny's diameter is 0.75 inches, and a quarter's diameter is 0.955 inches. If you place a penny on top of a quarter, what area of the quarter's surface is still showing?

    (A) 0.299 in.²
    (B) 0.3 in.²
    (C) 0.274 in.²
    (D) 0.374 in.²

29. The bases of a trapezoid are 5 cm and 6 cm, respectively. If the trapezoid is 4 cm high, what's it's area?

    (A) 11 cm²²
    (B) 22 cm²
    (C) 22.5 cm²
    (D) 27 cm²

30. If a circle's radius is 1.5 inches, what is its circumference?

    (A) approximately 9.42 inches
    (B) approximately 10.3 inches
    (C) approximately 14 inches
    (D) approximately 15 inches

Hard geometry practice questions

31. What is the measure of *x*?

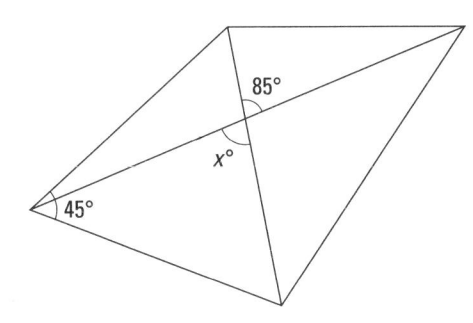

(A) 85°
(B) 135°
(C) 95°
(D) 20°

32. Find the slope of the line $y = 2x + \frac{2}{7}$.

(A) 2
(B) $\frac{7}{2}$
(C) $\frac{2}{7}$
(D) $2\frac{2}{7}$

33. Find the surface area:

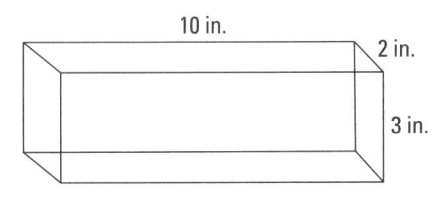

(A) 58 in.²
(B) 96 in.²
(C) 112 in.²
(D) 200 in.²

34. What is the area of the larger circle less the area of the smaller circle?

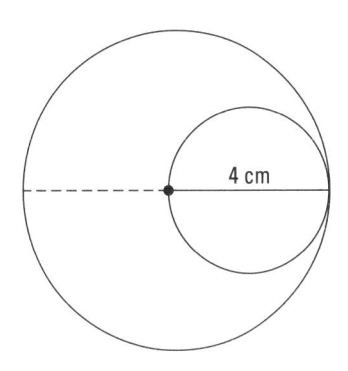

(A) 50.24 cm²
(B) 40 cm²
(C) 37.68 cm²
(D) 12.56 cm²

35. Find the height of a rectangular prism that has a rectangular base measuring 10 mm in length and 8 mm in width if its volume is 3,200 mm³.

(A) 40 mm
(B) 36 mm
(C) 88.88 mm
(D) 120 mm

36. If the area of one face of a cube is 64 cm², what's the cube's volume?

(A) 8 cm³
(B) 64 cm³
(C) 128 cm³
(D) 512 cm³

37. What is the surface area of a box that measures 14 centimeters long, 17 centimeters high, and 9 centimeters wide?

(A) 517 cm²
(B) 600 cm²
(C) 689.9 cm²
(D) 1,034 cm²

38. Jakson is filling up an empty tube that's 5 centimeters high and has a radius of 3 centimeters. How many cubic inches of sand can Jakson fit inside the tube?

(A) 120 in³
(B) 131.4 in³
(C) 141.3 in³
(D) 147.7 in³

39. What is the surface area of a cylinder that has a base radius of 4 centimeters and a height of 13 centimeters? Estimate pi to be 3.14.

(A) 427 cm²
(B) 427.04 cm²
(C) 427.08 cm²
(D) 434 cm²

40. Julian is coloring a trapezoid that measures 3 inches high, 4 inches across on its first base, and 2 inches across on its second base. What's the area he'll cover in crayon?

(A) 6 square inches
(B) 6.5 square inches
(C) 9 square inches
(D) 12 square inches

Answers and Explanations

Use this answer key to score your performance on geometry practice questions.

1. **A.** Perimeter is the total of the length of each side. Although not all the segments are labeled, every side totals 8 feet in length. That makes Choice (A) the correct answer.

2. **D.** The formula for the area of a rectangle is $A = lw$, and this rectangle is 15 inches long by 9 inches wide. $15 \cdot 9 = 135$, so the answer is Choice (D).

3. **D.** The angle depicted in the figure is a right angle, which has a measurement of 90° (you can tell because of the small square in the corner). An acute angle has a measurement that's more than 0° but less than 90°, an obtuse angle measures more than 90° but less than 180°, and complementary angles add up to 90°.

4. **A.** At 3:00 p.m., one hand is on the 12, and the other is on the 3. This creates a right angle — a 90° angle. The correct answer is Choice (A).

5. **B.** All angles of a triangle always add up to 180°.

6. **D.** The vertex of an angle is where the two rays converge. In this case, it's Choice (D).

7. **C.** The angle of a straight line is always 180 degrees. (A right angle is 90 degrees, and a circle is 360 degrees.)

8. **D.** Calculate the perimeter of a square by multiplying the length of one side by 4. Because the square in this problem has 9-inch sides, the answer is 36 inches.

9. **B.** Find a rectangle's area by multiplying its length by its width. Bonus: This works for squares, too. The formula is $A = lw$, where A represents area, l represents length, and w represents width.

10. **A.** Parallel lines never intersect. No matter how long the lines are, all their points are always *equidistant* — that is, they're always equal distances apart.

11. **B.** The formula for the circumference of a circle is $C = 2\pi r$, and the problem tells you the circle's radius is 2 inches. Plug in the numbers you know and solve:

    $$C \approx 2\pi r$$
    $$C \approx 2 \cdot 3.14 \cdot 2$$
    $$C \approx 12.56$$

    Use 3.14 as an approximation of pi, and you should come up with the correct answer, which is Choice (B).

12. **A.** Use the Pythagorean theorem:

    $$a^2 + b^2 = c^2$$
    $$4^2 + b^2 = 5^2$$
    $$16 + b^2 = 25$$
    $$16 + b^2 - 16 = 25 - 16$$
    $$b^2 = 9$$
    $$b = \sqrt{9}$$
    $$b = 3$$

13. C. The area of a trapezoid is

$$A = \frac{a+b}{2}h$$

Plug in the values and solve:

$$A = \left(\frac{7+15}{2}\right)10$$
$$A = \left(\frac{22}{2}\right)10$$
$$A = (11)10$$
$$A = 110 \text{ cm}^2$$

14. C. The circumference of a circle is π times the diameter; the diameter equals two times the radius. Therefore, $3.14 \times 30 \approx 94.2$ feet. The correct answer is Choice (C).

15. B. The formula for the area of a circle is $A = \pi r^2$. Plug in the values and solve:

$$A \approx (3.14)(5)^2$$
$$A \approx (3.14)(25)$$
$$A \approx 78.5 \text{ cm}^2$$

16. B. Complementary angles are angles that add up to 90°: $90° - 62° = 28°$.

17. D. The coordinates (7, −8) are read "7 right, 8 down," so the point lies in Quadrant IV.

18. A. The formula to find the area of a triangle is $A = \frac{1}{2}bh$, and the diagram says the base is 4 inches and the height is 6 inches. Work out the math like this:

$$A = \frac{1}{2}bh$$
$$A = \frac{1}{2}(4 \cdot 6)$$
$$A = \frac{1}{2}(24)$$
$$A = 12$$

The answer is Choice (A).

19. B. Find the circumference of a circle with the formula $C \approx 2\pi r$. The radius of the circle in the diagram is 15 inches, so fill in the formula and use 3.14 for pi:

$$C \approx 2\pi r$$
$$C \approx 2\pi(15)$$
$$C \approx 2 \cdot 3.14 \cdot 15$$
$$C \approx 94.2$$

20. A. A circle has 360 degrees, and this angle cuts into a circle. The reflex angle is 310 degrees, as shown in the diagram, which means the only possible measurement of Angle D is 50 degrees.

21. **C.** Two of the sides of Evelyn's triangle are equal, so represent them with x. The third side is 5 feet longer, so that's x + 5. The problem tells you that the entire perimeter measures 50 feet. The perimeter of a triangle (or any other shape with sides) is simply the sum of all the sides' lengths, so your formula and solution should look like this:

$$50 = x + x + x + 5$$
$$50 = 3x + 5$$
$$45 = 3x$$
$$x = 15$$

But wait! There's more! The question asks you for the length of the third side (that was x + 5 in your calculations), so the answer is Choice (C) — 20 feet.

22. **D.** First, assign variables to your problem (and if it helps, sketch a diagram). Let x represent the size of one of the two equal angles. That way, x + x represents the third angle, and $2(x + x + x) - 60$ represents the fourth angle. The sum of the angles in a quadrilateral is always 360°, so plug in the variables, combine like terms, and solve for x:

$$360 = x + x + (x + x) + 2(x + x + x) - 60$$
$$360 = 12x - 60$$
$$420 = 12x$$
$$\frac{420}{12} = \frac{12x}{12}$$
$$x = 35$$

Because the question asks for the values of all the angles, replace x with 35 to determine that the measurements are 35°, 35°, 70°, and 220°.

23. **A.** A circle has 360 degrees, but you don't have a circle; you have half a circle, and that means you have to work with 180 degrees. After putting a 30° slice in the refrigerator, you're left with a slice that measures 150° on your plate. (For the record, this question is based on my life.)

24. **D.** A half-circle measures 180°, so that's the foundation of the problem. Let x represent the smallest unknown slice of pizza; that's Sadie's piece. Angie's piece is twice as big as Sadie's, so 2x represents her slice. Jeff's piece of the pizza measures 30°, so your equation is x + 2x + 30° = 180°. Combine like terms and solve for x:

$$3x + 30 = 180$$
$$3x = 150$$
$$\frac{3x}{3} = \frac{150}{3}$$
$$x = 50$$

Angie's slice of pizza is twice as large as Sadie's is, so hers measures 100°.

25. **A.** Supplementary angles always add up to 180°. Let x represent the measure of the first angle, which means 2x represents the measure of the second angle. Your equation looks like this: x + 2x = 180°. Run through the math to determine that the first angle, x, measures 60°. Because the second angle is twice that, it measures 120°.

26. **C.** The x-coordinate of all the points in Choice (C) is the same, which means they're colinear. Any time the x- or y-coordinate is the same within a set of points, the points are colinear.

27. B. The angles inside a triangle always add up to 180°, and the problem tells you that you're dealing with a right triangle; that means one of the angles is 90°. The ratio lets you know that the second acute angle is three times bigger than the first acute angle, so let x represent the first angle, and 3x represent the second angle. Your equation should look like this:

$$x + 3x + 90 = 180$$
$$4x + 90 = 180$$
$$4x = 90$$
$$\frac{4x}{4} = \frac{90}{4}$$
$$x = 22.5$$

The first angle is 22.5°. Triple that to find out that the second angle is 67.5° and you arrive at the answer in Choice (B).

28. C. Both coins are circles, so the right formula for this job is $A = \pi r^2$. Let B represent the area of a quarter minus the area of the penny and figure out the radius (it's 0.375 inches for the penny and 0.4775 for the quarter). Using 3.14 for pi, your work looks like this:

$$B = (3.14 \cdot 0.4775 \cdot 0.4775) - (3.14 \cdot 0.375 \cdot 0.375)$$
$$B = 0.715 - 0.441$$
$$B = 0.274$$

29. B. The formula to determine the area of a trapezoid is $A = \frac{a+b}{2}h$, where a represents one base, b represents the other, and h represents height. That means $\frac{5+6}{2} \cdot 4 = 22$.

30. A. The formula to determine the circumference of a circle is $C = 2\pi r$, so replace the variable r with 1.5 and use 3.14 for pi:

$$C = 2 \cdot 3.14 \cdot 1.5$$
$$C \approx 9.42$$

31. A. Angle x and the angle marked 85° are vertical angles — they're opposite each other where two lines cross. Vertical angles are always equal. It doesn't matter what other angles are labeled in the figure. You don't need to do any math to find out that the answer is Choice (A).

32. A. The formula to find the slope of a line is $y = mx + b$, where m represents the slope. The formula in the problem has 2 in place of the m variable, so you don't need to do any math — the answer is right in the question.

33. C. The formula to find the surface area of a prism is $SA = 2ab + 2bc + 2ac$. Choose a variable for each measurement in the diagram, such as $a = 10$ in., $b = 2$ in., and $c = 3$ in. Then fill in what you know from the diagram:

$$SA = 2ab + 2bc + 2ac$$
$$SA = (2 \cdot 10 \cdot 2) + (2 \cdot 2 \cdot 3) + (2 \cdot 10 \cdot 3)$$
$$SA = 40 + 12 + 60$$
$$SA = 112$$

The surface area of the rectangular prism depicted in the question is 112 in.²

34. C. Determine the area of both circles using $A \approx \pi r^2$. The radius of the circle is 4 centimeters, as shown in the diagram. Use 3.14 for pi and figure out the large circle's area:

$$A \approx \pi r^2$$
$$A \approx 3.14 \cdot 4^2$$
$$A \approx 50.24$$

The large circle's area is 50.24 cm². Now figure out the smaller circle's area the same way:

$$A \approx \pi r^2$$
$$A \approx 3.14 \cdot 2^2$$
$$A \approx 12.56$$

Subtract the smaller circle's area from the larger circle's area: $50.24 - 12.56 = 37.68$. The correct answer is Choice (C).

35. A. The formula for finding the volume of a rectangular prism is $V = bh$, where V represents volume, b represents the base's area, and h represents the prism's height. This question tells you that $V = 3{,}200$ and leaves you to figure out that the base's area is 80 mm. After you know that, it's plug-and-play to solve for h:

$$3{,}200 = 80h$$
$$\frac{3{,}200}{80} = \frac{80h}{80}$$
$$40 = h$$

36. D. The problem tells you that one square face of the cube measures 64 cm², which means the length of the base of just one side has to be 8 cm long. The formula to find the volume of a cube is $V = a^3$, where a represents the length of one edge. You can input what you know into the formula to determine that the cube's volume is 512 cm³, which is Choice (D).

37. D. The formula to find the surface area of a rectangular solid — in this case, the box — is $S = 2hw + 2lh + 2lw$. The problem tells you the box's height (17 cm), length (14 cm), and width (9 cm), so it's just a matter of math:

$$SA = 2(17 \cdot 9) + 2(14 \cdot 17) + 2(14 \cdot 9)$$
$$SA = 306 + 476 + 252$$
$$SA = 1{,}034$$

38. C. You can figure out how many cubic inches are in a tube, which is technically a right circular cylinder, by using the formula $V = \pi r^2 h$. You already know that the cylinder's height is 5 cm and its radius is 3 cm, so estimate pi as 3.14 and calculate:

$$V \approx (3.14)3^2 \cdot 5$$
$$V \approx 141.3$$

39. B. The problem tells you to use 3.14 for pi, so no guesswork there. The formula to find the surface area of a cylinder is $SA = 2\pi rh + 2\pi r^2$, where r represents the base's radius and h represents the cylinder's height. When you put the information into the problem, your math looks like this:

$$SA \approx \left(2(3.14) \cdot 4 \cdot 13\right) + \left(2(3.14) \cdot 4^2\right)$$
$$SA \approx 427.04$$

40. C. The formula to find the area of a trapezoid is $A = \frac{a+b}{2}h$, so replace the variables in the equation to solve for A:

$$A = \frac{a+b}{2}h$$
$$A = \frac{2+4}{2} \cdot 3$$
$$A = 9$$

IN THIS CHAPTER

» Solving life's little (math) problems

» Multiplying your chances for a better score

Chapter 9
Arithmetic Reasoning: Math Word Problems

How many miles per gallon does your brand-new SUV get? How long does it take to go over the river and through the woods to Grandmother's house? How much wood would a woodchuck chuck? These are examples of everyday questions that can be answered by arithmetic reasoning. (Okay, maybe not the woodchuck situation.)

The rest of the world calls this type of question math *word problems*. The ASVAB calls them *Arithmetic Reasoning*. No matter what they're called, these problems help you apply mathematical principles to the real world (at least the real world according to the people who think up word problems). Your job is to read a word problem, determine what the question asks, and select the correct answer.

Arithmetic Reasoning is an important part of the Armed Forces Qualification Test (AFQT) score, which is used to determine your general qualification for enlistment in all the service branches (see Chapter 1 for more information). Also, certain military jobs require that you score well on this subtest.

The test administrator will supply you with scratch paper and a trusty No. 2 pencil, but one thing they won't give you (or even let you bring) is a calculator. You can use your paper and graphite to clarify the data, write formulas, and mathematically solve the problems. You can even use them to draw pretty pictures to help you understand the problem. Don't get too artistic, though — you have 55 minutes to answer 15 questions if you're taking the CAT-ASVAB (or 113 minutes to answer 30 questions if your subtest includes tryout questions, which I explain in Chapter 1). You have 36 minutes to answer 30 questions if you're taking the paper version. As long as you're focused on problem-solving, you should have plenty of time.

To do well on the Arithmetic Reasoning subtest, you have to remember that there are two parts: arithmetic and reasoning. You usually have to use both skills for each problem. The arithmetic part comes in when you have to perform mathematical operations such as addition, subtraction, multiplication, and division. The reasoning comes in when you figure out which formulas and numbers to use in your calculations. In other words, Arithmetic Reasoning tests how you apply your ability to perform calculations to real-life problems. If you slept through high school math, don't worry. This chapter helps you decipher these math problems, focusing on the reasoning part. For additional info on the arithmetic, flip to Chapter 6.

REMEMBER: The CAT-ASVAB, which most people take, gives you questions based on whether you answer previous questions correctly or incorrectly.

Tackling the Real World of Word Problems

Test-takers often waste a lot of time reading and rereading word problems as if the answer might reveal itself to them by some miracle; however, correctly solving math word problems requires you to perform a series of organized steps:

1. **Read the problem completely.**
2. **Figure out what the question is asking.**
3. **Dig out the relevant facts.**
4. **Set up one or more equations to arrive at a solution and then solve the problem.**
5. **Review your answer.**

I cover these steps in detail throughout this section.

Reading the entire problem

The first step in solving a word problem is reading the entire problem to discover what it's all about. Try forming a picture about the problem in your mind or — better yet — draw a sketch of the problem on your scratch paper. Ask yourself whether you've ever seen a problem like this before. If so, what's similar about it, and what did you do to solve it in the past?

Figuring out what the question is asking

The second and most important step in solving a word problem is to determine exactly what the question is asking. Sometimes the question is asked directly. At other times, identifying the actual question may be a little more difficult. Suppose you're asked the following question:

EXAMPLE

What's the volume of a cardboard box measuring 12 inches long by 14 inches wide by 10 inches tall?

(A) 52 cubic inches
(B) 88 cubic inches
(C) 120 cubic inches
(D) 1,680 cubic inches

The problem directly asks you to determine the volume of a cardboard box. Recall from your high school algebra and geometry classes that the volume of a rectangular container is length × width × height, or $V = lwh$. So $12 \times 14 \times 10 = 1,680$. The correct answer is Choice (D).

Now take a look at the next example:

EXAMPLE

How many cubic inches of sand can a cardboard box measuring 12 inches long by 14 inches wide by 10 inches tall contain?

(A) 52 cubic inches

(B) 88 cubic inches

(C) 120 cubic inches

(D) 1,680 cubic inches

This is the same problem, but the question you need to answer isn't as directly stated. Therefore, you have to use clues embedded in the problem to figure out what the actual question is. Would figuring out the perimeter of the box help you with this question? Nope. Would figuring out the area of one side of the box help you? Nope — you're not painting the box; you're filling it. The question wants you to determine the volume of the container.

TIP

Clue words can be a big help when trying to figure out which question is being asked. Look for the following clue words:

» **Addition:** Sum, total, in all, perimeter, increased by, combined, added

» **Division:** Share, distribute, ratio, quotient, average, per, out of, percent

» **Equals:** Is, was, are, were, amounts to

» **Multiplication:** Product, total, area, cubic, times, multiplied by, of

» **Subtraction:** Difference, how much more, exceed, less than, fewer than, decreased

Digging for the facts

After you figure out what question you're answering, the next step is to figure out which data is necessary to solve the problem and which data is extra. Start by identifying all the information and variables in the problem and listing them on your scratch paper. Make sure you attach units of measurement contained in the problem (miles, feet, inches, gallons, quarts, and so on). After you've made a list of the facts, try to eliminate those facts that aren't relevant to the question. Look at the following example:

EXAMPLE

To raise money for the school yearbook project, Tom sold 15 candy bars, Becky sold 12 candy bars, Debbie sold 17 candy bars, and Jane sold the most at 50. How many candy bars did Becky, Debbie, and Jane sell?

The list of facts may look something like this:

$$Tom = 15 \text{ bars}$$
$$Becky = 12 \text{ bars}$$
$$Debbie = 17 \text{ bars}$$
$$Jane = 50 \text{ bars}$$
$$? = \text{total Becky, Debbie, and Jane sold}$$

Because the question is the total number of candy bars sold by Becky, Debbie, and Jane, the number of bars Tom sold isn't relevant to the problem and can be scratched off the list. Just add the remaining bars from your list. The answer is 79.

CHAPTER 9 **Arithmetic Reasoning: Math Word Problems** 177

Setting up the problem and working your way to the answer

You need to decide how the problem can be solved and then use your math skills to arrive at a solution. For instance, a question may ask the following:

Joan just turned 37. For 12 years, she's dreamed of traveling to Key West to become a beach bum. To finance this dream, she needs to save a total of $15,000. How much does Joan need to save each year if she wants to become a beach bum by her 40th birthday?

Write down, in mathematical terms, what the question is asking you to determine. Because the question is asking how much money Joan needs to save per year to reach $15,000, you can say y (years Joan has to save) × m (money she needs to save each year) = $15,000. (Assume she saves the same amount each year.) Or to put it more mathematically,

$$ym = \$15{,}000$$

You don't know the value of m (yet) — that's the unknown you're asked to find. But you can find out the value of y — the number of years Joan has to save. If she's 37 and wants to be a beach bum by the time she's 40, she has 3 years to save. So now the formula looks like this:

$$3m = 15{,}000$$

To isolate the unknown on one side of the equation, you simply divide each side by 3, so $3m \div 3 = 15{,}000 \div 3$. (If you don't remember how to isolate unknowns, flip to Chapter 6.) Therefore, your answer is

$$m = 5{,}000$$

Joan needs to save $5,000 each year for 3 years to reach her goal of $15,000 by the time she's 40. You may be tempted to include the 12 years Joan has been dreaming of this trip in your formula. This number was put into the problem as a distraction. It has no bearing on solving the problem.

Drawing a diagram

Sometimes it's easier to work through a problem when you can visualize it. You can use as much scratch paper as you need on the ASVAB, so you may want to draw diagrams to help work out some of the questions.

For example, if you encounter a question that asks you how much tile you need to floor a six-walled room that measures 15 feet on one side, 14 feet on another, 8 feet on another, and 6 feet on a fourth, it can be really helpful to draw a diagram like this:

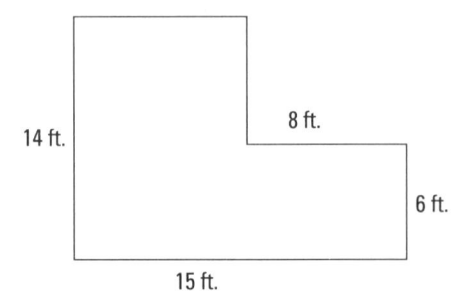

As you work through the practice questions in this book and complete the practice tests, use scratch paper to help you visualize what you're working through — that way, you'll know when drawing a quick sketch or creating a diagram will help you when you take the ASVAB.

Reviewing your answer

Before marking your answer sheet or punching in that choice on the computer, review your answer to make sure it makes sense. Review by asking yourself the following questions:

- **Does your solution seem probable?** Use your common sense. If you determine that a 12-by-16-foot roof is covered in only 12 shingles, you've probably made a mistake in your calculations.

- **Does it answer the question asked?** Reread the problem. For example, if a question asks you to calculate the number of trees *remaining* after 10% of the total was cut down, the correct answer wouldn't be 10% of the trees but rather the 90% still standing. Both answers will most likely be choices.

- **Are you sure?** Double-check your answer. To keep you on your toes, test-makers often supply false answers that are very, very close to the correct answer.

- **Is your answer expressed using the same units of measurement as used in the problem?** A question may ask how many cubic feet of concrete are required to cover a driveway. Your answer in cubic yards would have to be converted to cubic feet so you can select the correct answer choice.

Although you may have been taught in school to round up for 5 or more and down for less than 5, rounding real-world problems requires a different mindset. For example, if someone needs 2.2 cans of paint for a particular job, they really need 3 cans of paint to make sure they have enough, even though you'd generally round down. And if someone gets a 15-minute break for every 4 hours of work but works only 7 hours, they'd get only one break, even though 7 divided by 4 equals 1.75, which is generally rounded up to 2.

You may find that the solution you arrived at doesn't fit the facts presented in the problem. If this is the case, back up and go through the steps again until you arrive at an answer that seems probable.

The Guessing Game: Putting Reason in Your Guessing Strategy

Guessing wrong on any of the ASVAB subtests doesn't count against you, unless you guess incorrectly on a bunch of questions in a row at the end of the subtest when taking the CAT-ASVAB. If you don't guess, your chances of getting that answer right are zero, but if you take a shot at it, your chances increase to 25%, or 1 in 4. Eliminate two wrong answers, and you have a 50-50 shot.

If you're taking the paper version of the ASVAB, you can always skip the tough questions and come back to them after you've finished the easier ones. If you're taking the computerized version of the ASVAB, the software won't let you skip questions, so you need to make your guess right then and there.

WARNING: If you're taking the paper version of the test and elect to skip questions until later, make sure you mark the next answer in the correct space on the answer sheet. Otherwise, you may wind up wearing out the eraser on your pencil when you discover your error at the end of the test. Or even worse, you may not notice the error and wind up getting several answers wrong because you mismarked your answer sheet.

Using the process of elimination

Guessing doesn't always mean "pick an answer, any answer." You can increase your chances of picking the right answer by eliminating answers that can't be right. To eliminate some obvious wrong answers, you can do the following:

» **Make sure the answer is realistic in relation to the question asked.** For example, if a question asks you how much water would be required to fill a child's wading pool, 17,000 gallons isn't a realistic answer. You can save time by eliminating this potential answer choice immediately.

» **Pay attention to units of measurement.** If a question asks how many feet of rope you'll need, answer choices listed in inches or cubic feet are probably incorrect.

» **Consider easier answer choices first.** Remember, you're not allowed to use a calculator on the ASVAB, so math answers that you'd arrive at by using complicated formulas are probably not correct.

Solving what you can and guessing the rest

Sometimes you may know how to solve part of a problem but not all of it. If you don't know how to do all the calculations — or don't have time for them — don't give up. You can still narrow down your choices by doing what you can. Here's how partially solving problems can help:

» When adding mixed numbers (a whole number and a fraction), add the whole-number parts first; then immediately eliminate answer choices that are too low. Or when adding lengths, add full feet first and cross off choices that are too small, even before considering the inches.

» Multiply just the last digits and cross off all answers that don't end in the right numbers (assuming the answers aren't rounded).

Making use of the answer choices

If you're stuck on a particular problem, sometimes plugging possible answers into an equation can help you find the right answer. Here's how using the answer choices can improve your guessing:

» **Plug in each remaining answer choice until you get the right answer.** Plugging in all the answer choices is time-consuming, so make sure you eliminate obviously wrong choices first.

» **Estimate and plug in numbers that involve easy mental calculations.** For instance, if Choice (A) is 9 and Choice (B) is 12, plug in 10 and solve the equation in your head. Think about whether the right answer has to be higher or lower than 10, and choose from there.

» **Using a little logic, do calculations with an obviously wrong answer choice.** Sometimes a wrong answer choice — especially one that differs drastically from the other answers — represents an intermediate step in the calculations, so you can use it to solve the problem. For instance, take this example:

EXAMPLE

A security guard walks the equivalent of six city blocks when they make a circuit around the building. If they walk at a pace of eight city blocks every 30 minutes, how long will it take them to complete a circuit around the building, assuming they don't run into any thieves?

(A) 20.00 minutes

(B) 3.75 minutes

(C) 22.50 minutes

(D) 24.00 minutes

Choice (B) is obviously way too low to be the right answer, but it would be a logical guess for the security guard's rate for a single block. Multiply 3.75 minutes/block by 6 blocks, and you probably have a good candidate for the right answer — 22.50 minutes, Choice (C).

Arithmetic Reasoning (Math Word Problems) Practice Questions

Arithmetic Reasoning questions are math problems expressed in a story format. Your goal is to determine what the question is asking by picking out the relevant factors needed to solve the problem, set up mathematical equations as needed, and arrive at the correct solution. Sounds easy, right? Try your hand at the following questions.

Easy Arithmetic Reasoning questions

1. If apples are on sale at 15 for $3, what's the cost of each apple?

   (A) 50 cents
   (B) 25 cents
   (C) 20 cents
   (D) 30 cents

2. An Army battalion in Hawaii has four companies. Two of the companies, Alpha and Charlie, each have 70 soldiers. Bravo Company has 44 soldiers, while Delta Company has 84. What is the average number of soldiers in a company in this battalion?

   (A) 67 soldiers
   (B) 45 soldiers
   (C) 70 soldiers
   (D) 62 soldiers

3. Terry got paints for $32.50, canvas for $112.20, and paintbrushes for $17.25. How much total money did she spend at the art supply store?

   (A) $167.45
   (B) $144.70
   (C) $161.95
   (D) $156.95

4. If mailing the first ounce of a letter costs $0.49, and it costs $0.21 to mail each additional ounce, how much does it cost to mail a 5-ounce letter?

   (A) $1.85
   (B) $1.05
   (C) $1.54
   (D) $1.33

5. Joe ran around a pentagon-shaped track with sides each measuring 1,760 feet. If he made three complete trips around the track, how far did he run?

   (A) 37,500 feet
   (B) 15,300 feet
   (C) 20,150 feet
   (D) 26,400 feet

6. Mike took Jen bowling for the first time. He bowled two games with scores of 157 and 175. Jen had never bowled before and scored 78 and 98. What was Mike's average score?

   (A) 88
   (B) 127
   (C) 156
   (D) 166

7. Billy left the house without his wallet. When he went to purchase his lunch, he had to dig into his change stash to buy it. How much did he have left if he had 15 quarters, 15 dimes, 22 nickels, and 12 pennies and the lunch cost $5.52?

   (A) $0.45
   (B) $1.15
   (C) $0.95
   (D) $1.03

8. Jack eats three hot dogs per minute, while Jeff eats two hot dogs per minute. How many total hot dogs do they eat in 12 minutes?

   (A) 35
   (B) 40
   (C) 60
   (D) 65

9. How far will your platoon go if you march for 3 hours at 6 miles per hour?

   (A) 9 miles
   (B) 6 miles
   (C) 18 miles
   (D) 12 miles

10. Your convoy has to travel a straight line across 4.7 grid squares on a military map. Every grid square equals 1,000 meters. How many meters will your convoy travel?

    (A) 4.7 meters
    (B) 470 miles
    (C) 470 meters
    (D) 4,700 meters

Medium Arithmetic Reasoning questions

11. A noncommissioned officer challenged 11 soldier friends to perform a 26-mile training run in 4 hours. If all the noncommissioned officer's friends complete the challenge, how many total miles will the friends have run?

    (A) 71.5 miles
    (B) 6.5 miles
    (C) 286 miles
    (D) 312 miles

12. Diane takes her client to an expensive restaurant in town to discuss new legal strategies. The restaurant adds a 15% gratuity for the server. If her meal and drinks cost $85 and her client's meal and drinks cost $110, how much does the restaurant add as a gratuity?

    (A) $22.50
    (B) $29.25
    (C) $20.00
    (D) $224.25

13. Farmer Beth has received an offer to sell her 320-acre farm for $3,000 per acre. She agrees to give the buyer $96,000 worth of land. What fraction of Farmer Beth's land is the buyer getting?

    (A) $\frac{1}{4}$
    (B) $\frac{1}{10}$
    (C) $\frac{1}{5}$
    (D) $\frac{2}{3}$

14. A large wall map is drawn so that 1 inch equals 3 miles. On the map, the distance from Kansas City to Denver is $192\frac{1}{2}$ inches. How far is the round trip from Kansas City to Denver in miles?

    (A) $192\frac{1}{2}$ miles
    (B) $577\frac{1}{5}$ miles
    (C) 385 miles
    (D) 1,155 miles

15. Mr. Cameron purchased a shirt for $20. He sold it for $26. By what percentage did he increase the price?

    (A) 5
    (B) 20
    (C) 30
    (D) 25

16. In the military, $\frac{1}{4}$ of an enlisted person's time is spent sleeping and eating, $\frac{1}{12}$ is spent standing at attention, $\frac{1}{6}$ is spent exercising, and $\frac{2}{5}$ is spent working. The rest of the time is spent at the enlisted person's own discretion. How many hours per day does this discretionary time amount to?

    (A) 6.0 hours
    (B) 1.6 hours
    (C) 2.4 hours
    (D) 3.2 hours

17. A designer sells a square yard of carpet for $15.00. The same carpet can be purchased at the carpet outlet store for $12.50. As a percentage, how much more expensive is the designer's carpet?

    (A) The designer's carpet costs 17% more than the outlet-store carpet.
    (B) The designer's carpet costs 20% more than the outlet-store carpet.
    (C) The designer's carpet costs 25% more than the outlet-store carpet.
    (D) The designer's carpet costs 12% more than the outlet-store carpet.

18. It takes Steve 56 hours to paint his fence. If his 3 children each work 7 hours per day with him, how many days will it take Steve and the children to paint the fence, assuming they all work at the same rate?

    (A) 2
    (B) 4
    (C) 2.5
    (D) 1

19. What is the width of a rectangular vegetable garden whose perimeter is 150 feet and length is 50 feet?

    (A) 100 feet
    (B) 25 feet
    (C) 200 feet
    (D) 50 feet

20. What will it cost to carpet a room 10 feet wide and 12 feet long if carpet costs $12.51 per square yard?

    (A) $166.80
    (B) $213.50
    (C) $186.23
    (D) $165.12

21. Five students take a math test, scoring 97, 92, 81, 90, and 73. What is the median score in the group?

    (A) 90
    (B) 86.6
    (C) 73
    (D) 92

22. David's dogs, Cujo and Achilles, got into a bag containing 250 dog treats. Together, the dogs ate 200 of the treats. What percentage of the treats remains?

    (A) 75
    (B) 25
    (C) 80
    (D) 20

23. Crisean is five times as old as Sailor is. The sum of their ages is 18, so how old is Sailor?

    (A) 3
    (B) 4
    (C) 5
    (D) 6

24. A train leaves its station and travels toward Seoul averaging 40 kilometers per hour. An hour later, a train on another track leaves from the same station and also travels toward Seoul at an average rate of 50 kilometers per hour. How many hours will it take the second train to overtake the first?

    (A) 4 hours
    (B) 5 hours
    (C) 6 hours
    (D) The second train will not overtake the first before it arrives in Seoul.

25. A coin collector has $25 in nickels and dimes. There are three times as many nickels as there are dimes. How many of each coin are there?

    (A) 125 dimes and 300 nickels
    (B) 100 dimes and 300 nickels
    (C) 300 dimes and 100 nickels
    (D) 150 dimes and 150 nickels

26. Karl buys a pair of sunglasses that's been marked down to a 15%-off sale price of $25.50. The next week, the same pair of sunglasses is marked down 25% from its original price. How much would the sunglasses have cost Karl if he had waited until the second sale?

    (A) $30
    (B) $26.50
    (C) $22.50
    (D) $20

27. A rectangular window frame measures 24 inches by 36 inches. If window trim costs $2.75 per linear foot, how much will it cost to put trim around the entire window?

    (A) $27.50
    (B) $30
    (C) $30.50
    (D) $35

CHAPTER 9 Arithmetic Reasoning: Math Word Problems

28. Genesis bought 5 pints of ice cream and a punch bowl for a total of $45. If the punch bowl was $25, how much is one pint of ice cream?

(A) $3.50
(B) $3.75
(C) $3.90
(D) $4

29. India pays $80 for bulk candy at her favorite shop, which has a minimum purchase of 20 pounds. The candy costs $2.50 per pound. By how much did India's purchase exceed the minimum?

(A) 32 pounds
(B) 25 pounds
(C) 15 pounds
(D) 12 pounds

30. If $2x^2 = 50$, what could be the value of x?

(A) −5
(B) 5
(C) 10
(D) Both Choice (A) and Choice (B).

Hard Arithmetic Reasoning questions

31. A bag of sand holds 1 cubic foot of sand. How many bags of sand are needed to fill a square sandbox measuring 5 feet long and 1 foot high?

    (A) 25 bags
    (B) 5 bags
    (C) 10 bags
    (D) 15 bags

32. Margaret and Julie can sell their tattoo parlor for $150,000. They plan to divide the proceeds according to the ratio of the money they each invested in the business. Margaret put in the most money at a 3:2 ratio to Julie's contribution. How much money should Julie get from the sale?

    (A) $50,000
    (B) $30,000
    (C) $60,000
    (D) $90,000

33. Larry travels 60 miles per hour going to a friend's house and 50 miles per hour coming back, using the same road. He drives a total of 5 hours. What is the distance from Larry's house to his friend's house, rounded to the nearest mile?

    (A) 110
    (B) 126
    (C) 136
    (D) 154

34. To buy a new car priced at $32,000, Martha takes out a five-year loan with a simple interest rate of 6.5%. By the time she owns the car, how much will she have paid including principal and interest?

    (A) $45,000
    (B) $41,500
    (C) $40,000
    (D) $42,400

35. The cost of 4 shirts, 4 pairs of dress pants, and 2 ties is $560. A shirt costs twice as much as a tie, and a pair of pants costs $70 more than a tie. What is the total cost of 1 shirt, 1 pair of dress pants, and 1 tie?

    (A) $150
    (B) $230
    (C) $175
    (D) $195

36. A can of pork and beans has a radius of 3 inches and a height of 7 inches. What is the volume of the can?

    (A) 198 cubic inches
    (B) 156 cubic inches
    (C) 21 cubic inches
    (D) 42 cubic inches

37. Edward's electric bill for the month of July was $90.12. The electric company charges a flat monthly fee of $20.00 for service plus $0.14 per kilowatt-hour of electricity used. Approximately how many kilowatt-hours of electricity did Edward use in July?

    (A) 361.11
    (B) 424.12
    (C) 500.86
    (D) 567.17

38. The simple interest on Jerry's fixed sum of money depends on the length of time the money is invested. If it draws $60 in 4 months, how much will it draw in 1.5 years?

    (A) $320
    (B) $240
    (C) $270
    (D) $200

CHAPTER 9 Arithmetic Reasoning: Math Word Problems   187

39. A rancher is driving along the edge of a circular sinkhole on their property. The sinkhole's diameter is 14 kilometers. If the rancher walked around the sinkhole, how far would they walk?

(A) 34 kilometers

(B) 54 kilometers

(C) 44 kilometers

(D) 35 kilometers

40. What is the price of a $200 item after successive discounts of 10% and 15%?

(A) $75

(B) $175

(C) $153

(D) $150

Answers and Explanations

Use this answer key to score the Arithmetic Reasoning practice questions.

1. **C.** Divide $3 by 15. The answer is $0.20, so the correct answer is Choice (C). Remember to simplify; 15 for $3 is the same as 5 for $1.

2. **A.** Add all the soldiers in the battalion: $70 + 70 + 84 + 44 = 268$. Divide 268 by 4 to find the average, which is 67. The average company in the battalion has 67 soldiers.

3. **C.** Simply add the amounts together: $\$32.50 + \$112.20 + \$17.25 = \$161.95$. Choice (C) is the correct answer.

4. **D.** The first ounce costs $0.49. The next 4 ounces cost $0.21 each. Multiply $\$0.21 \times 4$ and then add $0.49 to determine how much mailing a 5-ounce letter costs: $\$0.21 \times 4 = \$0.84$, and $\$0.84 + \$0.49 = \$1.33$, the cost of mailing a 5-ounce letter. Choice (D) is the correct answer.

5. **D.** A pentagon has 5 sides. If each side measures 1,760 feet, the formula for finding the total feet Joe ran looks like this:

    $$1,760(5)(3) = 8,800(3) = 26,400 \text{ feet}$$

6. **D.** Don't let Jen's scores throw you off. They're completely irrelevant. To solve this problem, first add up Mike's scores and then divide by 2:

    $$157 + 175 = 332$$
    $$332 \div 2 = 166$$

7. **C.** Add the change to see how much Billy has before he buys lunch:

    $$15(\$0.25) + 15(\$0.10) + 22(\$0.05) + \$0.12$$
    $$= \$3.75 + \$1.50 + \$1.10 + \$0.12$$
    $$= \$6.47$$

    Subtract the cost of the lunch:

    $$\$6.47 - \$5.52 = \$0.95$$

8. **C.** If Jack eats 3 hot dogs in 1 minute, you know he eats $3(12) = 36$ in 12 minutes. If Jeff eats 2 per minute, he eats $2(12) = 24$ in 12 minutes. Add $36 + 24 = 60$ and you have your answer. That's a lot of hot dogs.

9. **C.** Using the distance formula, which is $d = rt$, where d represents distance, r represents rate (speed), and t represents time, you can figure out how far your platoon will get: $d = 3 \cdot 6$ $d = 18$.

10. **D.** The problem tells you that each grid square measures 1,000 meters, and your convoy must travel across 4.7 of them. Multiply 4.7 by 1,000 meters, which equals 4,700 meters.

11. **C.** Multiply 26×11. The other information in the question is irrelevant — it's there to throw you off. The correct answer is Choice (C). You can immediately eliminate Choice (B) because it isn't a reasonable answer. Identifying unreasonable answers (through the process of elimination) can help you choose the correct answer choice faster.

12. B. Add 85 and 110 to get the cost of the services ($85 + $110 = $195); then multiply the answer by 0.15 (15%) to find the gratuity. The question asks for the amount of the tip, so the correct answer is Choice (B), $29.25. You can immediately eliminate Choice (D), because the amount is far too high to make sense.

13. B. The buyer's price, $96,000, divided by $3,000 (price per acre) equals 32 acres. Thirty-two acres divided by 320 acres (total of the farm) equals 10%, or $\frac{1}{10}$, of the land. The correct answer is Choice (B).

14. D. Multiply 192.5×3 to get the distance in miles, and then double the answer to account for both legs of the trip. Choice (D) is the correct answer. *Note:* A quick approach here involves rounding. The distance is about 200 inches, or 400 inches round trip. Multiply that by 3, and you get 1,200 miles. The only choice that comes close is Choice (D).

15. C. Let *x* = the percentage of profit. Set up the following proportion and solve for *x* by cross-multiplying:

$$\frac{x}{100} = \frac{6}{20}$$
$$20x = 600$$
$$x = 30$$

Mr. Cameron increased the price by 30% on the shirt he sold.

16. C. Calculate this answer by first assigning a common denominator of 60 to all the fractions and adjusting the numerators accordingly: $\frac{15}{60}, \frac{5}{60}, \frac{10}{60},$ and $\frac{24}{60}$. Add the fractions to find out how much time is allotted to all of these tasks. The total time is $\frac{54}{60}$, which leaves $\frac{6}{60}$ or $\frac{1}{10}$ of the day to the enlisted person's discretion. One-tenth of 24 hours is 2.4 hours. Therefore, Choice (C) is the correct answer.

17. B. You want the cost of the designer's carpet in terms of the outlet-store carpet, so divide the difference in costs by the lower price: $15.00 − $12.50 = $2.50, and $2.50 ÷ $12.50 = 0.20 = 20%. The correct answer is Choice (B) — the designer's carpet is 20% more expensive.

18. A. Four people are working on the fence for 7 hours a day; therefore, the family is spending $(4)(7) = 28$ person-hours on the job each day. Divide the total number of hours needed to complete the job by the total number of person-hours to find the total number of days: $56 \div 28 = 2$. It will take 2 days for the team to finish painting the fence.

19. B. Use the formula for perimeter to find the answer; *w* = width and *l* = length:

$$\text{Perimeter} = 2w + 2l$$
$$150 = 2w + 2(50)$$
$$150 = 2w + 100$$
$$50 = 2w$$
$$25 \text{ feet} = w$$

20. A. The room measures $10 \times 12 = 120$ square feet. Because there are 3 feet in a yard, 1 square yard = 9 square feet. Use this conversion factor to find out how many square yards you need to carpet:

$$\frac{120}{9} = 13\frac{1}{3} \text{ square yards}$$

Estimate $13\frac{1}{3}$ to be 13.333 and multiply that by the cost per square yard ($12.51):

$13.333 \times 12.51 = 166.80$.

21. **A.** Median is the middle number in a series when the numbers are in order. Putting the list in order from smallest to largest, you have: 73, 81, 90, 92, 97. In this case, the median number is 90.

22. **D.** The two dogs ate 200 out of the 250 treats that were in the bag, or $\frac{200}{250}$. You can solve it in your head or go through the math, dividing 200 by 250, but the ASVAB only allows you a limited time to solve math problems, and you can't use a calculator. First, simplify the fraction: $\frac{200}{250} = \frac{20}{25}$. You need the denominator to equal 100 when you're figuring out a percent, so multiply by 4: $\frac{20}{25} \cdot 4 = \frac{20 \cdot 4}{25 \cdot 4} = \frac{80}{100}$. That tells you that the dogs ate 80 percent of the treats, but the question asks you what percentage of the treats remain. The dogs left only 20 percent of the treats behind.

23. **A.** Let x represent Sailor's age. Because Crisean is 5 times as old as Sailor is, let 5x represent his age. Set up your equation and solve for x:

$$x + 5x = 18$$
$$6x = 18$$
$$x = 3$$

24. **A.** The second train will overtake the first after 4 hours. (For the record, Choice (D) can't be correct because the problem doesn't tell you the distance the trains have to travel to reach Seoul.) The best way to figure out this problem is to set up a table and figure out an equation, letting x represent the time the first train leaves and x − 1 represent the time the second train leaves:

	Rate	Time	Distance
Train 1	40 km/hour	x	40x
Train 2	50 km/hour	x − 1	$50(x-1)$

Your equation needs to compare the two trains, so use $40x = 50(x-1)$. Solve:

$$40x = 50(x-1)$$
$$40x = 50x - 50$$
$$40x - 50x = -50$$
$$-10x = -50$$
$$\frac{-10x}{-10} = \frac{-50}{-10}$$
$$x = 5$$

That tells you that the first train traveled 5 hours by the time the second train overtook it — but the question asks how many hours the *second* train traveled. Because x = 5 and 5 − 1 = 4, the correct answer is Choice (A).

25. **B.** There are 100 dimes and 300 nickels. To figure that out, let x represent the number of dimes and $3x$ represent the number of nickels (the problem tells you that there are three times as many nickels as there are dimes). Convert the amount the collector has to 2,500 cents and write an equation using the value of each coin:

$$10x + 5(3x) = 2,500$$
$$25x = 2,500$$
$$x = 100$$

Because the collector has three times as many nickels as dimes (and has 100 dimes), there are 300 nickels in the collection.

26. **C.** Karl would have paid $22.50 for the sunglasses if he'd waited until the second markdown. First, determine the sunglasses' original price by letting x represent the original price and multiplying it by the percentage of the original price Karl paid:

$$25.50 = (1 - 0.15)x$$
$$25.50 = 0.85x$$
$$30 = x$$

That tells you that the sunglasses' original price was $30, but the question asks how much he would have paid if he'd waited for the 20 percent discount. Find 25 percent of 30 and subtract: $30 \times 0.25 = 7.5$, so subtract $7.50 from $30 to determine that he would've paid $22.50.

27. **A.** Find the perimeter of the window using $P = 2(l + w)$ or by adding its two 24-inch sides and two 36-inch sides. The window's perimeter is 120 inches. The trim costs $2.75 per 12 inches (there are 12 inches in a foot), so multiply $2.75 by 10 to find that it costs $27.50 to put trim around the entire window.

28. **D.** Let x represent the price of a pint of ice cream; that means the price of five pints is $5x$. The problem tells you that the punch bowl cost $25 and that Genesis spent a total of $45; that leaves $20 for the ice cream. Your equation looks like this:

$$5x = 20$$
$$\frac{5x}{5} = \frac{20}{5}$$
$$x = 4$$

29. **D.** Let x represent the number of pounds of candy India bought at $2.50 per pound:

$$2.5x = 80$$
$$x = 32$$

This tells you India bought 32 pounds of candy. The shop's minimum purchase is 20 pounds, and the question wants you to figure out how much *more* than the minimum she bought. Take 32 − 20 to get 12 pounds. (Hopefully India has dental insurance.)

30. **D.** Both Choice (A) and Choice (B) are correct. Solve for x:

$$2x^2 = 50$$
$$x^2 = 25$$
$$\sqrt{x^2} = \sqrt{25}$$
$$x = \pm 5$$

31. **A.** To find the volume of the sandbox, you take length times width times height ($V = lwh$). Don't forget that the measurements are for a square sandbox, so you can assume that if the box is 5 feet long, then it's also 5 feet wide. So $5 \times 5 \times 1$ is 25 cubic feet. Each bag holds 1 cubic foot of sand, and $25 \div 1 = 25$. Choice (A) is the correct answer. If you were thinking answer Choice (B) sounded good, remember that the answer should make sense. Five cubic feet of sand would not fill a very large sandbox, would it?

32. **C.** According to the ratio, Margaret should get $\frac{3}{5}$ of the money and Julie should get $\frac{2}{5}$ of the money. You calculate the fractions by adding both sides of the ratio together ($3 + 2 = 5$) to determine the denominator — Margaret gets 3 parts of the total, and Julie gets 2 parts, so there are 5 total parts. Each side of the ratio then becomes a numerator. Multiply the total amount of money by the fraction representing Julie's share: Multiply $150,000 by 2, and then divide the answer by 5 to determine Julie's share of the money. The correct answer is Choice (C). (You can also divide $150,000 by 5 and then multiply that total by 2 to get the same answer.)

33. **C.** Let *x* be the distance traveled to Larry's friend's house. The time it takes to drive to the house looks like this:

    $$\frac{\text{distance}}{\text{speed}} = \frac{x}{60}$$

    The time it takes to return looks like this:

    $$\frac{\text{distance}}{\text{speed}} = \frac{x}{50}$$

    The total time to travel and return is 5 hours. Therefore,

    $$\frac{x}{50} + \frac{x}{60} = 5$$

    Next, find the common denominator in order to add the fractions and solve for *x*:

    $$\frac{6x}{300} + \frac{5x}{300} = 5$$
    $$\frac{11x}{300} = 5$$
    $$11x = 1,500$$
    $$x \approx 136.36$$

    The answer is 136 miles (rounded to the nearest mile), Choice (C).

34. **D.** The formula for interest is Interest = Principal × Rate × Time. Simply substitute what you know to solve this problem:

    $$\text{Interest} = 32,000(0.065)(5)$$
    $$\text{Interest} = 10,400$$

    Now add the interest to the principal: $32,000 + 10,400 = 42,400$

    Martha is paying $42,400 for her new car.

35. **A.** Let *s* = the price of one shirt.

    Let *p* = the price of one pair of dress pants.

    Let *t* = the price of one tie.

    Here's what you know: A shirt costs twice as much as a tie, so the value of one shirt is 2*t*, which means $s = 2t$. A pair of pants costs $70 more than a tie, so the value of one pair of pants is $t + 70$, which means $p = t + 70$. To find out how much 1 shirt, 1 pair of dress pants, and 1 tie costs, multiply these values by 2, 4, and 4, respectively, to get a sum of 560, which corresponds with the number of clothing items in the original problem:

$$(2t)+(2t \times 4)+((t+70)4)=560$$
$$2t+8t+4t+280=560$$
$$14t+280=560$$
$$14t=280$$
$$\frac{14t}{14}=\frac{280}{14}$$
$$t=20$$

Now you know that a tie costs $20, so a shirt ($20 × 2) costs $40, and a pair of dress pants ($20 + 70) is $90. The cost of 1 shirt, 1 pair of dress pants, and 1 tie is $20 + $40 + $90, which adds up to $150.

36. **A.** To solve this problem, you have to know the formula for volume of a cylinder:

$$V = \pi r^2 h$$

where h is the height and r is the radius. Simply plug in the numbers from the question to solve:

$$V \approx 3^2(3.14)(7)$$
$$V \approx 9(3.14)(7)$$
$$V \approx 63(3.14)$$
$$V \approx 197.82$$

Round to the nearest whole number to get Choice (A).

37. **C.** First, subtract the monthly fee from the bill to find the total amount actually spent on electricity:

$$\$90.12 - \$20.00 = \$70.12$$

Now divide your answer by the charge per kilowatt-hour:

$$\frac{70.12}{0.14} \approx 500.857$$

Choice (C) is the winner here.

38. **C.** Let i = the interest earned in 1.5 years and convert 1.5 years to months ($12 \times 1.5 = 18$ months). Then set up a proportion that represents the ratios of interest earned to time invested:

$$\frac{60}{i} = \frac{4}{18}$$
$$\frac{60}{i} = \frac{2}{9}$$

Cross-multiply to solve:

$$2i = 540$$
$$i = \$270$$

Jerry will make $270, Choice (C).

39. C. Use the formula Circumference = πd, where d is the diameter, to solve this problem:

$$C = \pi(14)$$
$$C \approx 3.14(14)$$
$$C \approx 43.96$$

Rounded to the nearest whole number, the sinkhole's circumference is 44 kilometers, Choice (C).

40. C. The item originally sold for $200. The first reduction was 10%, taking the item down to $180:

$$200 - 0.1(200)$$
$$= 200 - 20$$
$$= 180$$

The second reduction was 15%, taking the item down to $153:

$$180 - 0.15(180)$$
$$= 180 - 27$$
$$= 153$$

Choice (C) is the right answer.

4
Examining General Science under a Microscope

IN THIS PART . . .

Explore biological processes and figure out what makes plants and animals tick under the umbrella of life sciences.

Pour yourself into a chemistry mindset to come up with solutions to common questions. Work through physics principles and leverage a better ASVAB score.

Dig into earth science topics that you may encounter on the General Science subtest. Zero in on space science topics that can help you ace the test.

Answer some practice questions at the end of each chapter to help you determine where you excel and where you could use some more review.

IN THIS CHAPTER

» Figuring out the scientific method

» Grasping measurements

» Examining human and plant biology

» Considering cell structures and processes

» Getting into genetics

» Using scientific strategies to improve your score

Chapter 10
General Science and Life Science

The General Science subtest asks questions about topics you learned in various high school science classes. Getting the answers right depends on how many facts and figures you have stashed away in your brain. The questions you see on this subtest should be pretty diverse, covering Earth and space sciences, chemistry, biology, and a splash of physics.

You have 12 minutes to answer 15 General Science questions on the CAT-ASVAB (25 minutes to answer 30 questions if your subtest includes tryout questions, which I cover in Chapter 1). If you take the paper version, you get 11 minutes to answer 25 questions. That comes out to a maximum of 40 seconds per question, so you have no time to daydream. For the most part, you either know the answer or you don't. If you don't know the answer, you can always guess (check out Chapter 3 for tips on guessing on the ASVAB).

You can relax this time around . . . well, just a little. The General Science subtest has no bearing on your Armed Forces Qualification Test (AFQT) score. On the other hand, your score on this subtest is used to calculate some of the military composite scores that are used for job qualification purposes.

TIP Instead of trying to remember 9 million individual facts, spend some time reviewing the general principles behind the facts. Think about how the facts relate to each other. Looking at the big picture is an effective learning technique.

Dedicate yourself to the information in this chapter, Chapter 11, and Chapter 12 to boost your General Science score if the job you want requires a good mark here. You can also log in and access the online flashcards that come with this book (find instructions for getting access in the front cover of the book). If you find yourself struggling with taxonomies, human physiology, and plant life, check out *Biology For Dummies* (Wiley) by René Fester Kratz, PhD, for more information.

REMEMBER: The computerized version of the ASVAB is designed to ferret out your scientific knowledge quickly and efficiently. Like all the other parts of the computerized test, the General Science subtest is responsive to your answers. That means it chooses question difficulty based on whether you've answered the preceding question correctly. If you get a question of medium difficulty wrong, the test throws you an easier question; if you get the right answer to a medium-difficulty question, it gives you a harder one. This approach helps the military figure out the probable extent of your knowledge without keeping you at a testing site for weeks on end. The questions are the same for every branch, too (Army, Navy, Marine Corps, Air Force, Space Force, Coast Guard, and reserve components).

There's a Scientific Method to the Madness

Scientists are pretty skeptical. They don't necessarily believe anything said by anyone else unless it's been shown to be true (time after time after time) using a process called the *scientific method*. Scientists know that personal and cultural biases may influence perceptions and interpretations of data, so they've derived a standard set of procedures and criteria to minimize those influences when developing a theory. Because the scientific method is prevalent in all fields of science, you can expect to see a few questions about the process on the General Science subtest.

Here are the usual steps to solving a problem using the scientific method:

1. **Observe some aspect of the universe.**
2. **Ask a question about why this thing is happening.**
3. **Develop a testable explanation *(hypothesis)* based on the theory.**
4. **Make a prediction based on the hypothesis.**
5. **Experiment and observe to test the prediction.**
6. **Use the results of the experiment to create new hypotheses or predictions.**

If a theory holds up to repeated testing, scientists gain confidence in it, and a hypothesis that's supported consistently over time eventually comes to be considered a law, fact, or principle.

The terms *law* and *theory* mean different things to scientists than they do to the average person. Scientifically speaking, a *law* is a statement about something that happens: When you jump off a diving board, you're going to travel in a downward direction. A scientific law doesn't say *why* you fall toward the pool — only that you *do* fall toward the pool. Laws usually rely on a mathematical equation, and they're always true. (In case you were wondering, the formula for gravity is $F = \dfrac{G(m_1 m_2)}{r^2}$, where F represents the force due to gravity between two masses, which are represented by m_1 and m_2, and G represents the gravitational constant.)

A *theory* is a detailed explanation of the phenomenon. It consists of one or more hypotheses that have been supported through repeated testing. Theories are widely accepted as true in the scientific community, but in order to hold that status, they must never have been proven wrong. If a theory doesn't hold up, it's been disproved. Theories can also evolve based on new evidence, which doesn't mean the original theory was wrong; it simply means it was incomplete.

SCIENTIFIC LAWS AND THEORIES YOU ALREADY KNOW

Every moment you're awake, you observe scientific laws in action. You're holding this book in your hands, which means you're an active participant in Newton's third law: The book is exerting force on your hands, while your hands are exerting equal and opposite force on the book. You're not floating on the ceiling right now, which means the law of gravity is working on you. The fact that you aren't identical to your parents, who aren't identical to their parents (and on and on) is part of the theory of evolution, which states that living things on Earth have origins in other, preexisting types and that the ways you're different from your ancestors are due to modifications in your DNA over generations. *Remember:* Scientific laws are statements about things that happen, and theories are explanations of why they happen.

Understanding Forms of Measurement

Because science is based on developing objective facts — evidence and results that are measurable and experiments that can be reproduced — measurements are an important part of science. And because this subtest is all about science, you can expect to run into a few questions about measuring scientifically on the ASVAB.

The metric system, or SI (abbreviated for the French *le Système International d'Unités*, which translates to the International System of Units), is based on a decimal system of multiples and fractions of ten. Scientists almost always use the metric system for precise measurement so a standard exists among scientists around the world. In fact, the majority of countries around the globe use the metric system — the United States is one of the few countries that still teach and use the Imperial (non-metric) system.

Here are some units of measurement you need to know for the General Science subtest of the ASVAB:

» The meter (m) is a unit of length.

» The liter (L) is a unit of volume.

» The gram (g) is a unit of mass (similar to weight).

You can attach prefixes to these base units to indicate units that are larger or smaller. Check out Table 10-1 for metric prefixes and Table 10-2 for some abbreviations of common metric measurements. Table 10-3 has the most common conversion formulas.

TABLE 10-1 Metric Prefixes

Prefix	Symbol	What It Means
milli-	m	One-thousandth (0.001)
centi-	c	One-hundredth (0.01)
deci-	d	One-tenth (0.1)
deca-	da	10
hecto-	h	100
kilo-	k	1,000
mega-	M	1,000,000

TABLE 10-2 **Common Metric Units and Their Abbreviations**

Length	Liquid Volume	Mass
millimeter (mm)	milliliter (mL)	milligram (mg)
centimeter (cm)	centiliter (cL)	centigram (cg)
meter (m)	liter (L)	gram (g)
kilometer (km)	kiloliter (kL)	kilogram (kg)

TABLE 10-3 **Imperial to Metric Conversions**

Imperial	Conversion Formula	Metric
Inches	inches × 2.54 = centimeters	1 inch = 2.54 centimeters
Feet	feet × 0.3 = meters	1 foot = 0.3 meters
Yards	yards × 0.9 = meters	1 yard = 0.9 meters
Miles	miles × 1.6 = kilometers	1 mile = 1.6 kilometers
Square inches	square inches × 6.45 = square centimeters	1 square inch = 6.45 square centimeters
Square feet	square feet × 0.09 = square meters	1 square foot = 0.09 square meters
Quarts	quarts × 0.94 = liters	1 quart = 0.94 liters
Gallons	gallons × 3.78 = liters	1 gallon = 3.78 liters
Ounces	ounces × 28.3 = grams	1 ounce = 28.3 grams
Pounds	pounds × 0.45 = kilograms	1 pound = 0.45 kilograms

Uncovering Biology, from Big to Small

It would be impossible to cover all the areas of biology in this book, and I'm not going to try. Luckily, the General Science subtest of the ASVAB measures your knowledge of scientific disciplines at the average high school level. You remember studying the Animal kingdom, the human body, plant physiology, and cell structures in high school, right? If not, the following sections can serve as a short refresher course. You're likely to see a handful of biology questions on the ASVAB.

Relating to your world through ecology

Ecology is the study of the environment — more specifically, the relationship between organisms and the world around them. All plants and animals are part of an *ecosystem* (a biological community of interacting organisms and their environment). An ecosystem includes producers that make their own food and consumers that eat other things. An ecosystem also has decomposers, such as bacteria, that break down dead plants, animals, and the waste of all organisms.

REMEMBER

Animals can't produce their own food, so they're consumers, which are classified in three categories:

» **Carnivores** eat only meat. Some examples include lions, tigers, polar bears, snakes, crocodiles, hawks, and eagles.

> » **Herbivores** eat only plants. Cows, moose, giraffes, and elk are herbivores.

> » **Omnivores** eat both plants and other animals. People are omnivores, and so are pigs, mice, raccoons, chickens, crows, and foxes.

Conditions in the world either encourage or prevent the establishment of individual ecosystems. For plants (producers) to grow, adequate sunlight, good soil, moderate temperatures, and water must be part of the environment. If plants aren't around, plant-eating consumers can't be sustained, which means predators (who eat other animals) can't be sustained, either. For consumers, mates are as essential as a food supply. Diseases and enemies can prevent an animal from establishing itself in an ecosystem. Human actions, such as wasting natural resources and polluting the air, water, or soil, can disrupt or destroy an entire ecosystem.

Variety is the spice of life: Biodiversity

Biodiversity is the term scientists use to talk about the variety of life in the world-at-large or in specific habitats and ecosystems. Scientists have already named and classified just under 2 million species of plants and animals, but experts suspect between 8 and 10 million haven't been discovered yet. Every species has an important role to play in natural sustainability, from the smallest bacterium to the biggest animal.

The continuation of life on this planet depends on biodiversity; if one species that was food for another species dies out, it creates a domino effect that disrupts the entire food chain (all the way up to humans). It's not only about food, though. It's also about depending on other organisms to perform functions that keep the world turning (such as bees pollinating plants or big trees taking carbon dioxide out of the air and replacing it with oxygen).

When any species has good genetic diversity, it has a larger gene pool to pull from during the process of evolution — and that makes organisms more adaptable to changing conditions over time so species can survive. About 40 percent of the medicines we use today come from natural compounds in plants, fungi, and animals, too. Biodiversity is nature's checks-and-balances system, and without it, conditions for every species on Earth would quickly go downhill.

Categorizing Mother Nature

A long time ago, scientists looked at the world, noticed the hundreds of thousands of plants and animals around them, and decided that all these organisms (living things) needed to be labeled and grouped. To effectively study and discuss plants, animals, and other living creatures, all scientists needed to use the same names. Thus, a system of scientific classification was developed.

The most common classification system was created by Swedish botanist Carl Linnaeus, who published ten editions of his works from 1753 to 1758. Scientists often refer to this system as *taxonomy.* Not only does taxonomy provide official names for every plant and animal, but it also helps scientists understand how living creatures are related to one another. Modern-day taxonomy has its roots in the Linnaean taxonomic system.

REMEMBER

No one is privy to the actual questions asked on the ASVAB (test materials are considered "controlled items" and are locked up in safes when not in use). In this category, questions can range anywhere from "How many kingdoms are there?" to "What's the genus for *Canis familiaris?*"

CHAPTER 10 **General Science and Life Science** 203

Counting down the classification system

The scientific classification system notes the relationships and similarities among organisms. It consists of eight main levels:

- **Domain:** A *domain* is a group of organisms that are similar based on characteristics such as chemistry and cell structure. The three domains are the broadest classifications and include the most kinds of organisms.

- **Kingdom:** *Kingdoms* group organisms by developmental characteristics and whether they make their own food. The relationships between organisms in a kingdom can be extremely loose, so members may share only a few characteristics. According to scientists, five or six kingdoms exist.

- **Phylum:** *Phylum* (plural *phyla*) is the next major taxonomic group. Within the kingdoms, organisms are divided into 36 phyla by general characteristics. For example, in the Animal kingdom, animals with backbones (vertebrates) are placed in a separate phylum from animals without backbones.

- **Class:** Organisms in a phylum are divided into *classes.* In the Animal kingdom, for example, birds, mammals, and fish all go in their own classes. Among plants, all flowering plants comprise the *Angiosperm* class, and all trees that bear cones, such as pines and spruces, comprise the *Conifer* class.

- **Order:** Scientific groupings create *orders,* which separate organisms based on the characteristics of the major groups in their class. For example, humans, chimps, gorillas, and gibbons are all part of the order *Primate* because they all share large brains and opposable thumbs, use tools, and have social groups. The order *Rodentia* includes gnawing mammals with continuously growing teeth, like squirrels, hamsters, and rats.

- **Family:** Families further divide organisms of the same order by similar characteristics. For example, humans are part of the *Hominidae* family, where gibbons split off into their own family: *Hylobatidae*.

- **Genus:** Two or more species that share unique body structures or other characteristics are closely related enough to be placed in a single *genus.* A genus may include only a single species if no other organism has characteristics similar enough for it to be considered the same genus. Here's where humans split from gorillas; we're part of the genus *Homo,* while they're in the genus *Gorilla.*

- **Species:** A *species* is the most specific level, so it contains the fewest types of organisms. Organisms of the same species have very similar characteristics. The human species is *sapiens,* while a gorilla's species is *gorilla* (and yes, that means they're classified as *Gorilla gorilla,* because species are conventionally written with the genus and the species together).

TIP

If the classification system gets you mixed up, try the mnemonic "Dear King Phillip, come over for good spaghetti." The first letter of each word represents part of the classification system, in order from broadest (domain) to most narrow (species). Figure 10-1 shows you the taxonomic system in action.

TECHNICAL STUFF

To get a better idea of how the scientific classification system works, Table 10-4 shows you how a few species are classified.

FIGURE 10-1: The Linnaean taxonomic classification system.

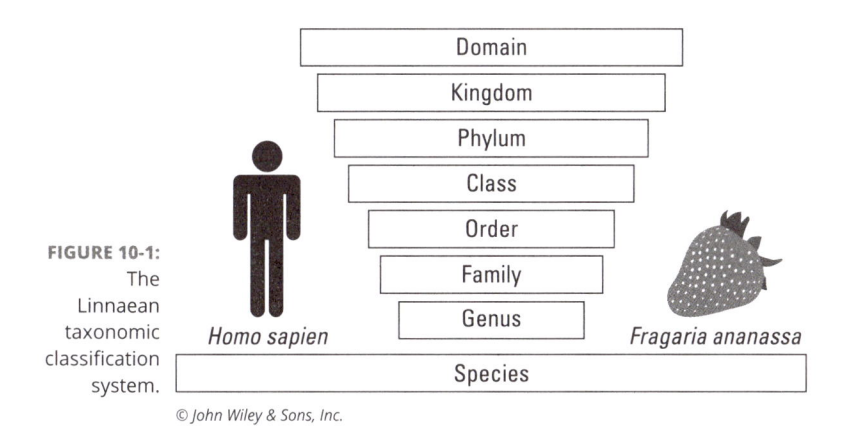

Homo sapien — Domain, Kingdom, Phylum, Class, Order, Family, Genus, Species — *Fragaria ananassa*

© John Wiley & Sons, Inc.

TABLE 10-4 Taxonomy of Different Organisms

Taxonomic Group	Human	Strawberry	House cat	Staphylococcus aureus
Domain	Eukarya	Eukarya	Eukarya	Bacteria
Kingdom	Animalia	Plantae	Animalia	Eubacteria
Phylum	Chordata	Spermatophyta	Chordata	Firmicutes
Class	Mammalia	Dicotyledonae	Mammalia	Bacilli
Order	Primate	Rosales	Carnivora	Bacillales
Family	Hominidae	Rosaceae	Felidae	Staphylococcaceae
Genus	Homo	Fragaria	Felis	Staphylococcus
Species	sapiens	ananassa	silvestris	aureus

Visiting the kingdoms

Most scientists agree that there are five or six kingdoms. Check out the kinds of organisms that fall under each:

>> **Animals:** This is one of the two largest kingdoms, and it includes many-celled organisms that, unlike plants, don't have cell walls, chlorophyll, or the capacity to use light to make energy (photosynthesis). Members of this kingdom can move. The Animal kingdom includes more than one million species. (Check out Figure 10-3 later in the chapter for a better look at cells.)

>> **Plants:** Plants are also one of the two largest kingdoms. This kingdom includes organisms that can't move, don't have obvious nervous or sensory systems (the Venus flytrap is one exception), and possess cell walls made of cellulose. More than 250,000 species belong to the Plant kingdom.

>> **Fungi:** Examples of common fungi are mushrooms and yeast. Fungi don't *photosynthesize* (use light to create energy) like plants do, but they do have cell walls made of a carbohydrate called *chitin*. More than 100,000 species belong to the Fungi kingdom.

>> **Protists:** Protists include one-celled organisms that do have a nucleus, such as the protozoan, which you may remember from biology class. This kingdom consists of more than 250,000 species.

>> **Eubacteria:** This kingdom, which used to be considered Monerans, is made up of single-celled organisms that don't have distinct nuclei or *organelles* (small, specialized structures within cells that act like organs). Bacteria are found everywhere, including your body and the depths of the ocean.

>> **Archaebacteria:** Archaea is a kingdom comprising single-celled organisms that have no distinct nuclei or organelles; they have different genetic structures and metabolic processes than bacteria do. (Archaebacteria was originally part of Eubacteria in the Monera kingdom, which is why some biologists believe there are five, rather than six, kingdoms.)

Just name it: Showing off your genius about the species

Each organism is given a scientific name that consists of two words (usually derived from Latin) — the genus and the species of the organism. The genus is the first word, and the species is the second. Thus, *Homo sapiens* refers to humans. *Canis familiaris* is your dog, and *Canis lupus* is a wolf. Because dogs and wolves share many similarities, they share the same genus (no, no, not the same genes, the same genus).

TECHNICAL STUFF: When writing a scientific name, the genus name is capitalized, and the species name is all lowercase. Both names are italicized.

Perusing the Human Body Systems

Your body consists of several major systems that work together to keep you alive. (And staying alive is a good thing, so be sure to thank your circulatory system and all the rest!) These systems include the ones listed in Table 10-5 and described in the following sections.

TABLE 10-5 Human Body Systems

System	Components	What the System Does
Nervous system	Cerebrum, cerebellum, medulla, spinal cord, and nerves	Receives, processes, and responds to all physical stimuli; for example, if you burn your hand on the stove, this system prompts you to remove your hand from the stove
Cardiovascular and circulatory systems	Heart, arteries, veins, capillaries, and blood	Delivers oxygenated blood and nutrients from the heart to the rest of the body, whisks away waste products, and returns the blood to the heart to oxygenate it again
Renal system and urinary system	Kidneys, bladder, and urethra	Filters toxins from the blood and sends them out with urine
Respiratory system	Nose, nasal cavity, trachea, and lungs	Inhales air, uses the oxygen in the air to release energy, and exhales the carbon dioxide that results from this process
Digestive system and excretory system	Mouth, esophagus, stomach, and intestines	Breaks down food into smaller substances that the body can absorb and process into energy; eliminates waste from the body
Muscular system	Smooth, cardiac, and skeletal muscles	Allows organs to contract and allows bodily movement
Skeletal system	Bones, joints, tendons, and cartilage	Supports the body's muscles and organs; allows bones and joints to move
Endocrine system	Thyroid, pituitary, adrenal, pineal, and reproductive glands; pancreas; and hormones	Communicates through hormones

System	Components	What the System Does
Lymphatic system and immune system	Lymph nodes, spleen, tonsils, and lymph	Helps rid the body of toxins, waste, and other materials the body doesn't need; fights infection
Integumentary system and exocrine system	Skin, hair, nails, and exocrine glands such as sweat glands	Protects the body from damage, such as overheating, injuries, abrasion, and loss of water from the outside
Reproductive system	Sex organs and reproductive organs	Enables and controls the production of offspring

Your nervous system is at the wheel, controlling everything that happens in your body. Your cardiovascular system pumps blood to spread oxygen to all your organs and tissues — but it couldn't do that if your respiratory system wasn't bringing in the oxygen in the first place. Your musculoskeletal system enables you to keep bringing in food by eating, and your digestive system turns the food into fuel for your nervous system (and all your other systems).

Some of these functions are involuntary, like breathing and pumping blood through your body. Others, such as eating, running, and scratching the itch on your foot, are voluntary — they require you to actively choose to do something (even if it happens within a split second) and then act on your impulse. When your nervous system takes in stimuli (either through one of your external senses or through an internal stimulus, like hunger), it kicks into high gear. It sends chemical and electrical signals out to the organs that need to participate in what's happening next, and they take action.

Picking your brain: The nervous system

The human brain is part of the *nervous system,* which also includes the spinal cord and billions of nerve cells called neurons. The *central nervous system* contains the cerebrum, which is responsible for thinking, hearing, seeing, and other functions. The cerebellum is also part of the central nervous system; it's the group of nerves responsible for your balance and muscle coordination. The medulla connects your brain to your spinal cord, and it handles all your involuntary actions (including your heartbeat). The spinal cord — the last major component of the central nervous system — is the highway that carries nerve impulses so your brain and organs can communicate. The *peripheral nervous system* is everything else, and it includes every other neuron in your body.

Flowing through the heart, blood, and circulatory system

The *circulatory system* keeps blood with oxygen and nutrients flowing to all your organs so they continue to work. At its core is the *heart,* a four-chambered organ that contracts and relaxes several times each minute. Two chambers collect blood coming in (each is called an atrium, but together, they're atria), and two, called ventricles, pump it back out. Heart valves close after blood leaves, preventing it from coming back in the Exit door.

When blood leaves the heart, it rushes through *arteries* — the largest and thickest tunnels in the circulatory system. These blood-carrying tubes have to be thick and strong, because the heart pumps out oxygenated blood fast, which creates a lot of pressure. Arteries branch out several times (each branch is called an *arteriole*) to send blood into the tissues through tiny tunnels called *capillaries.* Capillaries let out oxygen and nutrients while they take in carbon dioxide and waste in a process called *diffusion* (arteries and veins don't).

Veins carry blood back to the heart, and they don't have thick walls because they don't need them; when blood makes its return trip, it's not under a lot of pressure to get there quickly. The blood going back to the heart is dark red because it's deoxygenated (it drops off all its oxygen to organs and systems when it travels from the heart).

Blood is made up of cells suspended in plasma. Red blood cells carry oxygen, white blood cells fight infection, and platelets are pieces of cells that cause blood to clot. The cells for blood are made in *bone marrow* (the spongy stuff inside the cavities of bones). Types A, B, AB, and O are all the types of blood, which can be positive or negative.

TECHNICAL STUFF

When you donate blood, or when someone donates it to you, your blood types need to match. The exceptions to this rule are Type O negative and Type AB positive. Type O negative blood is considered the *universal donor;* it can be donated to anyone. Type AB positive is the *universal recipient,* which means a person with this blood type can receive any other kind of blood.

Are you kidney me? The renal system

The *renal system,* home to the kidneys, ureters, bladder, and urethra, is the main toxin-filtering component of your body. The kidneys filter blood to remove waste, and they produce urine. Together, the ureters, bladder, and urethra form the *urinary tract* — the pathway that carries urine from the body.

The kidneys control excretion of several minerals, so if the body has too many, the kidneys get rid of them. These wonder-organs also monitor and control blood pressure, and they help maintain *homeostasis* (the body's ability to regulate its inner environment so it remains stable, even when outside conditions aren't).

Breathing in and out: The respiratory system

The process of bringing in oxygen and getting rid of carbon dioxide is respiration, and all the magic happens in your nose, mouth, throat, and lungs (with support from your muscles and heart). When you breathe in — a result of your chest cavity expanding, which causes your lungs to suck in air — your nasal cavity filters, warms, and moistens the air. Another filter in the *pharynx* (what usually hurts when you have a sore throat) catches pathogens before they go through your *epiglottis* (the bit that makes a mistake when you choke on food). The final filter is in your *trachea,* which is the area right below the hard lump you can feel in your throat (that's the *larynx,* or voice box).

After all that, the air you breathe goes into your lungs through the left and right bronchi. The bronchi separate into smaller tunnels, called *bronchioles,* and each one ends in a tiny sac, or alveolus (plural alveoli), that puts oxygen into your bloodstream.

You are what you eat: The digestive system

When you pick up an apple, a bag of chips, or a glass of milk, your *digestive system* is gearing up to do its job. This essential system lets you break down food into fuel your body can use. It all starts when you think about food: Your mouth starts to water, and your stomach may start to growl. Those are the signs your digestive system is up and running.

When you eat, your teeth and tongue break the food into smaller parts while your saliva starts to break down starch. Your chewed-up food moves into your esophagus when you swallow, and the esophagus contracts to push the food into your stomach. Gastric acids and a chemical called *pepsin* break the food down further, but the most intense part of the process doesn't start until the food reaches your small intestine.

The small intestine in a normal adult is about 23 feet long, and it produces enzymes that work with other enzymes made in the pancreas and liver to turn fat, carbs, and proteins into useful substances for your body. The large intestine is about 5 feet long; it reabsorbs water and minerals into your body. The kidneys filter liquid waste and secrete it through urine. The solid waste matter left over stays in your rectum until you evacuate it.

Muscling your way through life

Your body has three types of muscles: cardiac, smooth, and skeletal. Some of them you choose to move, while others don't give you any say in the matter. (Remembering to tell your heart to beat would be a pain, anyway.)

- **Cardiac muscle** is only present in your heart. The fibers of these cylindrical, involuntary muscles interlock with each other so that your heart can pump blood. Your heart muscles contract involuntarily — they act on their own, outside your control.
- **Smooth muscle** is the muscle of choice for hollow organs (such as your stomach, lungs, and intestines). These muscles are arranged in parallel lines to form sheets of tissue. Like cardiac muscles, smooth muscles contract involuntarily.
- **Skeletal muscle** is what makes you run, jump, and use the remote control to stream your favorite TV shows. They're *striated* (they appear striped under a microscope) and cylindrical. These muscles are voluntary because you can consciously decide to use them.

Taking the skeletons out of the closet

Your *skeletal system* is the frame that holds your body together, keeps you upright, and in some ways protects you from injury. Humans have an *endoskeleton* — one that's inside the body and covered by soft tissue. Other animals (such as armadillos, grasshoppers, and lobsters) have *exoskeletons* that protect their soft tissues. Some animals, such as jellyfish, don't have skeletons at all.

The skeletal system includes bones, cartilage, ligaments, and tendons. Bones start their lives as cartilage, but over time, the cartilage is replaced by calcium and phosphorus in a process called *ossification.* (That's the technical term for bone formation.) Cartilage is much more flexible than bone is, but because bone is still living tissue, it can repair itself when it's damaged or broken.

The human body has several types of joints, but they all share one thing in common: They enable two or more bones to move relative to each other. Here are the seven major types of joints:

- **Hinge joints,** such as those at your elbows and knees, work like a door hinge or the binding of a book.
- **Ball and socket joints,** like those in your shoulders and hips, consist of a ball-like end that fits into a bowl-shaped receptacle. They work like a joystick, allowing you a wide range of motion.
- **Pivot joints** allow you to rotate one bone around another because one bone fits into a ring formed by another bone. You find them in your neck's first and second vertebrae (that's what allows you to move your head back and forth).
- **Fixed joints** are places where two separate bones meet, but there's no room or ability for movement. Your skull has fixed joints.
- **Saddle joints** are joints that let you move one bone in an oval motion. Rotate your thumb to see a saddle joint in action.

> **Condyloid joints** allow back-and-forth and side-to-side movement. You find condyloid joints in your knuckles (the ones connected to your hand bones, not the ones halfway up your fingers). They give you the range of motion you need to signal that you want five cheeseburgers and to make a fist.
>
> **Gliding joints** occur between the surfaces of two bones held together by ligaments. They're in your wrists and ankles and between the tiny bones in your feet.

Ligaments and tendons help your bones move so you can move. *Ligaments* join the bones (think of them like rubber bands), while *tendons* connect muscle tissue to bones and other structures in your body (like your eyeballs).

Ending up in the endocrine system

The glands that produce hormones to regulate reproduction and sexual function, growth and development, tissue function, sleep, mood, and a whole host of other actions are part of the *endocrine system.* This system uses hormones to communicate with organs and other glands.

The lymphatic system: When things go haywire

The body's *lymphatic* and *immune systems* include *lymph* (a fluid that contains white blood cells that fight infection). These systems can fight off many bacteria and viruses, which are everywhere. *Bacteria* are single-celled organisms that cause illnesses such as pneumonia and staph infections, and *viruses* cause illnesses like colds, COVID-19, and HIV. The bacteria and viruses that cause diseases evolve — sometimes very quickly, such as when antibiotic resistance pops up — and the lymphatic system responds quickly to new challenges from newly evolved organisms.

Antibiotics can be used to treat bacterial infections, but they don't work on viruses. Scientists have had a tough time defeating most viruses, except through prevention by way of vaccines. Vaccinations prevent disease by teaching the immune system how to fight specific viruses before they have a chance to reproduce.

THE FIRST TROOP INOCULATION: SMALLPOX

General George Washington, the commander-in-chief of the Continental Army, was also the first person ever to command his troops to be inoculated against disease. In 1777, Washington ordered that his soldiers be exposed to mild forms of the smallpox virus to prevent them from getting a more serious version of the disease. His decision was based on the fact that about 5,000 Continental soldiers came down with smallpox after a skirmish near Quebec — but most of the British, Canadians, and Native Americans who were also involved didn't even get sick. Some historians believe that if Continental troops had been inoculated earlier, the Revolutionary War would've ended sooner (and the spoils may have included some or all of Canada). The actual smallpox vaccine wasn't invented until 1796, 13 years after the revolution ended.

Today, troops are tested for immunity to a variety of diseases as soon as they arrive at basic training. Any who aren't immune receive vaccinations to protect them against diseases they can pick up here or overseas, from the flu and chickenpox to smallpox and anthrax.

TECHNICAL STUFF

Human bodies are always in a balancing act between staying healthy and falling apart. Some illnesses and diseases are caused by diet and lifestyle, so they're preventable. Others are genetic and ingrained in DNA. Still others come through pathogens, such as bacteria and viruses; sometimes these illnesses and diseases are preventable, too. Disease-carrying organisms are called *vectors*, and they include mosquitoes, rats, and ticks.

Damage control through the integumentary system

The *integumentary system* protects you from getting scuffed up, losing all the water in your body, and smashing your bones when you miss the nail and hit your thumb with a hammer. The largest organ in your body — your skin — is part of this essential system. It also includes your fingernails, hair, and sweat glands, as well as *sebaceous* glands (the ones responsible for oily skin) and *ceruminous* glands (the purveyors of earwax). The whole system protects you from more severe injuries, but it's also there to produce vitamin D that your body needs.

Continuing the species through the reproductive system

Like any species, humans have to reproduce to ensure long-term survival. Sex organs, including external organs and internal ones like testes, ovaries, fallopian tubes, the uterus, sperm, and eggs (ova), work together to pass the genes down to the next generation. I discuss how genetics and DNA combine to make new humans (the tiny kind) in the later section "Swimming in the Gene Pool: Genetics."

Human reproduction can't occur unless a male's sperm fertilizes a female's ovum. Women release an egg from an ovary approximately once every 28 days. The egg travels down the fallopian tube and into the uterus, where it waits for fertilization. If it's not fertilized, the endometrial lining comes off in a process called menstruation — but if sperm does fertilize it, the egg turns into a zygote. If conditions are right, the zygote can implant itself in the uterus and eventually develop into a fetus.

Keeping the body in peak operating condition

In order to work properly (so all those functions can keep on keepin' on), your body needs plenty of fuel — and that comes in the form of food, vitamins, minerals, and water. You need the following:

- **Carbohydrates for energy:** Carbohydrates come from starches and sugars, such as bread, pasta, fruit, and candy bars.

- **Fats for energy:** Too much fat is bad, but you do need some in your diet. Fats fall into three categories: saturated, monounsaturated, and polyunsaturated. Polyunsaturated fats are required for normal body functions, but your body can't make them, so you have to eat foods that contain them (such as many vegetable oils, walnuts, and some fish). Saturated fats come from meat, shellfish, eggs, and dairy. Monounsaturated fats come from olives, avocados, and some nuts.

- **Fiber for getting rid of waste products:** Leafy green vegetables, beans, potatoes, and fruits have plenty of fiber.

- **Minerals for various bodily functions:** A few necessary minerals include iron to develop red blood cells, calcium to keep your bones strong, and potassium to keep your heart's electrical activity in check. A well-balanced diet ensures you're getting the minerals you need, but some people need supplements.

- **Protein for growth, maintenance, and repair:** Humans consume protein through meat, fish, beans, nuts, and a handful of other sources.
- **Vitamins for various bodily functions:** You can usually get all the 13 essential vitamins from fruits, veggies, and the sun. Your body uses them for things such as blood clotting, processing food, and regulating your hormones.
- **Water to keep your cells from shriveling up and withering away:** Most foods contain water, but you still need to drink water as well. Humans lose about four pints of water each day, and you have to replace it or face serious health consequences, such as headaches, cramps, and even death.

TECHNICAL STUFF

While you're in basic training, your diet is extremely balanced. You may not have time to actually *taste* your food (which can be a good thing in some military dining facilities), but rest assured that the military is making sure you get what you need to become a lean, mean, fighting machine.

Digging through Plant Physiology

Plants, like animals, are made from cells and tissues. Plants have organs, too, but they're quite a bit different from humans' organs. Most plants have two organ systems. One consists of its underground roots, and the other consists of above-ground shoots (stems, leaves, flowers, and seeds).

The roots bring in nutrients and anchor the plant to the ground. The stem is like the plant's spine, supporting it above ground and serving as a highway for nutrients and water between roots and leaves. The leaves collect energy from the sun and host the processes that make food for the plant through photosynthesis.

Types of plants

Scientists usually put plants in one of four major groups based on the types of tissues they have and how they reproduce. Plants fall under the Linnaean taxonomic system, too (which you can read about in the "Categorizing Mother Nature" section earlier in this chapter).

- **Angiosperms** are flowering plants. These plants have vascular tissue (tissue that transports fluid and nutrients internally, which is similar to human veins) and produce flowers and seeds. Angiosperms include roses and all the flowers in your garden; palm trees; and apple trees.
- **Bryophytes** are plants that don't have a vascular system and don't produce flowers or seeds. They reproduce by releasing spores. Lichen, liverwort, and many types of mosses are bryophytes.
- **Ferns** are plants with vascular tissue, but they don't produce seeds.
- **Gymnosperms** are plants that produce cones and seeds rather than flowers, and they have vascular tissue, too. Your Christmas tree is a gymnosperm, as are California's giant sequoias and most non-flowering shrubs.

Where plant processes take place

Plants sustain themselves by pulling nutrients and water from the soil, capturing energy from the sun, and taking carbon dioxide from the air. Table 10-6 shows how plants use their organs to stay alive and well, and Figure 10-2 shows the basic anatomy of a plant.

TABLE 10-6 **Plant Systems and Functions**

System	Components	What the System Does
Root	Vascular tissue, primary roots, and secondary roots (branches)	Absorbs water and nutrients from the soil, holds the plant in place, and stores nutrients
Shoot	Vascular tissue, stem or stalk, leaves, flowers, cones	Allows the plant to grow taller, absorbs light energy from the sun, converts energy, absorbs carbon dioxide, and releases oxygen

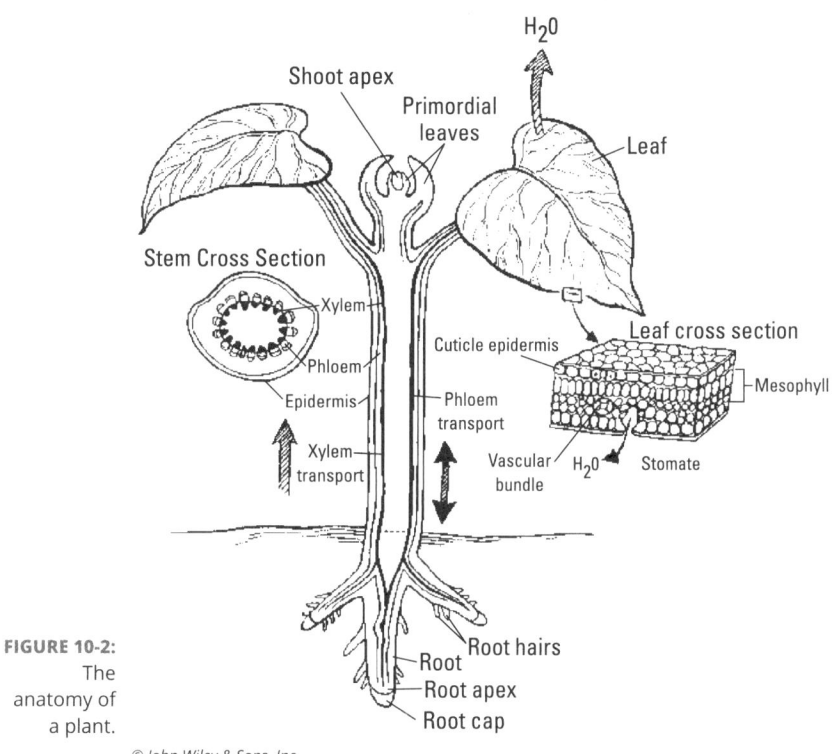

FIGURE 10-2: The anatomy of a plant.

© John Wiley & Sons, Inc.

A plant's stem is technically part of its shoot system, but it has several big jobs. It moves water and nutrients between roots and leaves, holds the plant upright so it can grow taller (and access more sun so it can grow even taller), and redirects the plant's growth.

Plants make their own food through *photosynthesis*, which takes place in the leaves. All they need are carbon dioxide, water, and sunlight. Photosynthesis occurs in two stages: light-dependent reactions and the Calvin cycle.

Light-dependent reactions happen when chlorophyll (the chemical substance that makes plants green) and other pigments absorb energy from sunlight. The energy splits water molecules into hydrogen and oxygen (I explain molecular structures in Chapter 11), and the oxygen evaporates into the atmosphere when temperatures heat up. The hydrogen that's left behind combines with carbon dioxide the plant absorbs to form glucose — that's what plants "eat."

The Calvin cycle is a series of chemical reactions that take place during photosynthesis. These reactions can only happen after the plant has captured energy from sunlight.

TECHNICAL STUFF

Every living organism on earth is carbon-based. Carbon atoms form the backbone of nearly every molecule that makes up creatures and plants that can live in Earth's environment. Carbon, as an element, is really, *really* good at bonding to other elements. It's so good that it can bond with itself to create long carbon chains and rings — and without it, DNA wouldn't be possible.

Plant reproduction

Plants, like all other organisms, need to reproduce. They can do so sexually (when two cells carrying half the DNA necessary for a new, whole cell join) or asexually (when one cell splits into two identical cells).

TECHNICAL STUFF

More advanced plants are angiosperms or gymnosperms; bryophytes and ferns are considered primitive plants. Angiosperms and gymnosperms produce seeds to reproduce, but bryophytes and ferns reproduce through spores.

- » **Angiosperms** are the most advanced types of plants when it comes to sexual reproduction. They create flowers that contain *stigma,* which produces pollen, and *carpels,* which catch pollen. A bug, a bird, or even the wind can pick up pollen from one flower and deposit it on the stigma of the same species (or on another stigma of the same plant). Each particle of pollen grain contains sperm that fertilizes an *ovule* (egg) in the flower.

- » **Gymnosperms** sexually reproduce in ways similar to angiosperms. They produce naked seeds — seeds that aren't wrapped in a fruit or seed pod — that develop on the upper surfaces of cone scales (pine trees are gymnosperms, and pine cones are where seeds develop). Wind carries the seeds where they need to be for fertilization.

- » **Bryophytes and ferns** reproduce sexually and asexually. They use spores, which contain male and female reproductive organs. Fertilization occurs before the plant ever releases a spore. After a plant releases a spore, the spore can grow where it lands (as long as conditions are right). Scientists believe that all plants were once spore-bearing, and only after plants evolved and adapted to live on land did they begin to form seeds.

Thinking Small: A Look at Cells

Living things are made up of cells that share certain characteristics. Cells come in different sizes and shapes, depending on what they do. In the human body, a muscle cell looks very different from a brain cell. Cells combine to create tissues, which form structures like bones and skin.

Inspecting cell structure

Nearly all cells have four things in common. Each has a nucleus, cytoplasm, a membrane, and ribosomes.

TECHNICAL STUFF

- » **Nucleus:** The *nucleus* (plural *nuclei*) controls cellular activity. It's like the brains behind the cell, and it holds the cell's genetic material — DNA.

  Bacteria are *prokaryotes,* which means their cells don't have nuclei. Their genetic material floats in the cytoplasm instead of being held inside a membrane *(nuclear envelope).*

- » **Cytoplasm:** The *cytoplasm* is a gel-like substance, composed mostly of water, that's inside the cell membrane and outside the nucleus. Cytoplasm contains many chemicals that carry out the life processes in the cell.

- » **Cell membrane (plasma membrane):** This thin membrane holds the cell together, protecting the nucleus and cytoplasm.

- » **Ribosomes:** *Ribosomes* manufacture proteins that the cell uses to perform work. They're necessary for biochemical reactions inside cells that allow them to survive.

See Figure 10-3 for a description of other cell structures.

Plant Cell

1. Chloroplast: Contains chlorophyll, which produces food
2. Cell wall: Protects the cell
3. Nucleus: The "brain" of the cell
4. Chromatin: Thin fibers containing genes
5. Nucleoplasm: Protoplasm (living material) in the nucleus
6. Ribosome: Combines amino acids into proteins
7. Cytoplasm: The cell's factory
8. Mitochondria: Produce the energy for cellular activity
9. Cell membrane: Contains the cellular material within it
10. Vacuole: Storage area

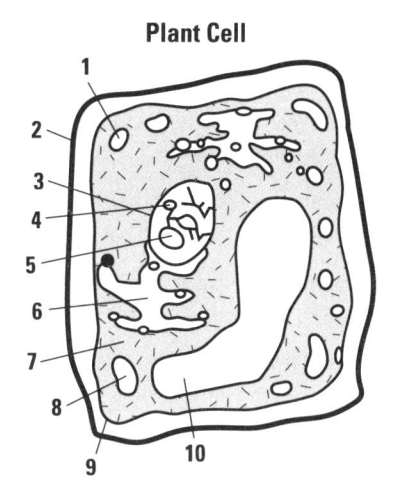

Animal Cell

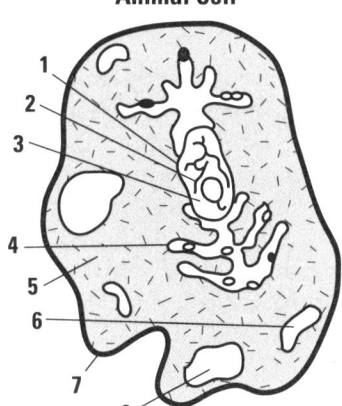

1. Nucleus
2. Chromatin
3. Nucleoplasm
4. Ribosome
5. Cytoplasm
6. Mitochondria
7. Cell membrane
8. Vacuole

FIGURE 10-3: Basic structures of plant and animal cells.

© John Wiley & Sons, Inc.

Plant cells differ from animal cells in several ways:

REMEMBER

- Plant cells have a firm cell wall that supports and protects the cell. Animal cells don't have such a structure.

- Plant cells have larger *vacuoles* (storage areas) than those found in animal cells.

- Unlike animal cells, many plant cells contain *chloroplasts,* which contain *chlorophyll,* a chemical that helps plants create food with the help of sunlight.

- Animal cells contain *centrioles* (cylindrical structures involved in cell division). Most plant and fungus cells don't.

- Animal cells have *lysosomes* (sacs of enzymes), which aren't found in plant cells.

Profiting from cell processes

Cells perform various processes to function at an optimum level. Here are a few of these processes:

- » **Metabolism:** Chemical processes within a cell that are necessary to maintain life
- » **Osmosis:** Movement of liquid through the cell membrane (and the main way that water goes in and out of cells)
- » **Phagocytosis:** Acquisition of particles of material from outside the cell; it's accomplished by surrounding the particles and passing them through the cell membrane
- » **Photosynthesis:** Conversion of light energy from the sun to chemical energy that the cell can use
- » **Cellular respiration:** Process in which biochemical energy from nutrients turns into products the cell can use; one of the ways a cell releases chemical energy to fuel its activity

Swimming in the Gene Pool: Genetics

You might have your grandma's eyes, your great-grandpa's nose, or your great-great-grandfather's height. Whether you like it or not, it happens because parents pass their traits on to their offspring. Understanding *genetics* — how traits are physically passed from parents to offspring and what happens when the process goes wrong — helps scientists pinpoint the causes of diseases and disorders and can help them develop treatments and cures.

REMEMBER

In human genetics, a standard person has 23 pairs of *chromosomes* (the structure that contains the genes). The mother and the father each supply one chromosome per pair. Genes contained in the chromosomes determine many characteristics of the resulting child.

Copying genes

When body cells multiply to produce tissues and organs (and eventually a complete living thing), they reproduce their genetic material. Most cells reproduce by *mitosis*, in which the nucleus of a cell divides, forming two cells and two identical sets of chromosomes.

However, sex cells (eggs and sperm) reproduce differently. Through *meiosis*, each cell divides into four cells, each containing only half the number of chromosomes as a nonsex cell. This process takes place so the sex cells of one person (with 23 chromosomes) can hook up with the sex cells of another person (with 23 chromosomes) to produce 46 chromosomes, or 23 pairs. Otherwise, way too many chromosomes would be floating around.

Sometimes cells don't copy themselves and divide perfectly and a genetic difference occurs. This frequently results in a fetus who doesn't live or in a fetus with a genetic condition. For example, Down syndrome is the result of a fetus having 47 rather than 46 chromosomes.

Determining your sex with two little letters

The genes on one pair of chromosomes, called the *sex chromosomes*, determine whether a child will be a biological male or female. In females, the two sex chromosomes are alike, and they're labeled XX. In males, the chromosomes are different and are labeled XY.

The child always receives an X chromosome from the mother (who has only XX chromosomes). The father (who has XY chromosomes) can contribute either an X or a Y chromosome, so Dad actually determines the sex of the child.

Knowing which genes get passed down the family line

Many characteristics that you possess (from the way your nose turns up at the end to the color of your eyes) are determined by a pair of genes (or multiple pairs of genes). These two genes may be alike, or they may not.

Some genes are dominant, and some genes are recessive. If you have two unlike genes, the characteristic that they produce comes from the *dominant gene;* the gene that doesn't overshadow the other is called the *recessive gene.* If each parent has two unlike genes, both parents will have the dominant trait, but they can have a child with the recessive trait — because each parent contributes a gene to the offspring, each parent may contribute a recessive gene to the child. Whew!

Using Common Sense to Hypothesize about Answers

If you don't know the answer to a question right off the bat, don't panic. You can often eliminate a few incorrect choices simply by using common sense. Even if you can't determine the answer, keep in mind that this subtest doesn't penalize you for guessing (unless you guess incorrectly on several questions in a row at the end of the subtest when taking the CAT-ASVAB). Guessing makes sense; you have a 25 percent chance of guessing the right answer even if you can't eliminate any obviously wrong answers. If you can eliminate just one wrong answer, you improve your chances to 33 percent.

Most people don't have to rush to finish the General Science subtest, but then again, you don't have much leisure time to stop and think about all the questions at length, either. If you don't know the answer to a question right away, do your best to eliminate wrong answers quickly, make your best guess, and move along. (For help on making these eliminating decisions, check out Chapter 3.)

Try the process of elimination on the following question:

The knee joint is known as a

(A) pivot joint.

(B) fixed joint.

(C) ball-and-socket joint.

(D) hinge joint.

Looking at the choices, you can eliminate Choice (A), pivot joint, because if you picture something that pivots, you think of it moving in a circular or at least a semi-circular manner. Your knee doesn't do that, so that choice is out the window. Choice (B), fixed joint, can't be right either; your knee isn't stuck in one position (or if it is, it shouldn't be). A ball-and-socket joint is one that permits limited movement in any direction (your shoulder joint is a ball-and-socket joint). Your knee doesn't do that, so you can strike off Choice (C) and choose Choice (D), hinge joint, as the most likely answer. Your knee moves like a door on a hinge.

CHAPTER 10 **General Science and Life Science** 217

General and Life Science Practice Questions

General science and life science are both broad topics. To score well on this subtest, you pretty much have to wade through the textbooks and memorize the facts. See how well you do on the following 40 practice questions, which I've classified as easy, medium, and hard.

Easy life science questions

1. The human circulatory system
   (A) uses air to release energy.
   (B) processes food and eliminates waste.
   (C) moves oxygenated blood throughout the body.
   (D) controls movement of joints.

2. The process plants use to make their own food is called
   (A) photosynthesis.
   (B) respiration.
   (C) digestion.
   (D) osmosis.

3. The organ that pumps blood through the body is the
   (A) liver.
   (B) kidney.
   (C) heart.
   (D) lung.

4. Animals that eat only plants are called
   (A) vegivores.
   (B) carnivores.
   (C) omnivores.
   (D) herbivores.

5. What is the hereditary material that passes genetic information from parent to offspring?
   (A) protein
   (B) DNA
   (C) RNA
   (D) mitochondria

6. What type of organism decomposes organic matter?
   (A) producer
   (B) consumer
   (C) decomposer
   (D) carnivore

7. The part of the plant responsible for absorbing water and nutrients from the soil is the
   (A) stem.
   (B) leaves.
   (C) roots.
   (D) flowers.

8. The waste product of animal respiration is
   (A) oxygen.
   (B) nitrogen.
   (C) carbon dioxide.
   (D) hydrogen.

9. The largest organ in the human body is the
   (A) heart.
   (B) skin.
   (C) liver.
   (D) kidney.

10. An animal that eats plants and other animals is a(n)
    (A) herbivore.
    (B) carnivore.
    (C) omnivore.
    (D) detritivore.

Medium life science questions

11. A cell nucleus is often referred to as the
    - (A) control center.
    - (B) cytoskeleton.
    - (C) cell membrane.
    - (D) chromosome.

12. Proteins come from all the following sources except
    - (A) beans.
    - (B) water.
    - (C) meat.
    - (D) eggs.

13. The nasal cavity is part of which system?
    - (A) respiratory
    - (B) cardiac
    - (C) muscular
    - (D) lymphatic

14. The gram is a unit of
    - (A) liquid measurement.
    - (B) mass.
    - (C) distance.
    - (D) temperature.

15. The first step in the scientific method is to
    - (A) ask questions.
    - (B) test hypotheses.
    - (C) make observations.
    - (D) create a theory.

16. Where would you find a hinge joint in the human body?
    - (A) the neck
    - (B) the elbow
    - (C) the hip
    - (D) none of the above

17. What is the process by which cells divide to produce new cells?
    - (A) osmosis
    - (B) mitosis
    - (C) photosynthesis
    - (D) fermentation

18. A group of similar cells that perform a specific function is called
    - (A) a tissue.
    - (B) an organ.
    - (C) an organism.
    - (D) a compound.

19. Which blood cells are responsible for fighting infections?
    - (A) red blood cells
    - (B) white blood cells
    - (C) platelets
    - (D) plasma cells

20. Which part of the human digestive system is primarily responsible for water absorption?
    - (A) stomach
    - (B) small intestine
    - (C) large intestine
    - (D) esophagus

21. Which system in the human body is responsible for removing waste from the blood through urine?
    - (A) respiratory
    - (B) digestive
    - (C) renal
    - (D) circulatory

22. The pigment that gives leaves a green color and absorbs light for photosynthesis is
    - (A) carotene.
    - (B) chlorophyll.
    - (C) anthocyanin.
    - (D) xanthophyll.

23. Which bodily system includes the spleen, thymus, and lymph nodes?
    - (A) endocrine
    - (B) immune
    - (C) nervous
    - (D) muscular

24. What part of a cell contains its genetic material?

    (A) cytoplasm
    (B) cell membrane
    (C) nucleus
    (D) mitochondria

25. Organisms maintain a stable internal environment through

    (A) metabolism.
    (B) homeostasis.
    (C) osmoregulation.
    (D) thermoregulation.

26. What type of muscle is found in the heart?

    (A) cardiac
    (B) skeletal
    (C) smooth
    (D) voluntary

27. The main structural component of plant cell walls is

    (A) cellulose.
    (B) chitin.
    (C) keratin.
    (D) collagen.

28. What organ detoxifies chemicals and metabolizes drugs in the body?

    (A) heart
    (B) kidneys
    (C) pancreas
    (D) liver

29. What type of blood vessel carries blood away from the heart?

    (A) vein
    (B) artery
    (C) capillary
    (D) valve

30. What term describes the variety of life in the world, a particular habitat, or an ecosystem?

    (A) ecology
    (B) conservation
    (C) symbiosis
    (D) biodiversity

Hard life science questions

31. In the term *Homo sapiens,* the word *sapiens* describes the organism's

  (A) genus.
  (B) domain.
  (C) species.
  (D) phylum.

32. Most cells reproduce by

  (A) meiosis.
  (B) mitosis.
  (C) photosynthesis.
  (D) osmosis.

33. Which kingdom includes mushrooms, mold, and yeast?

  (A) Plantae
  (B) Animalia
  (C) Fungi
  (D) Protista

34. Which of these isn't a function of the skeletal system?

  (A) support the body
  (B) protect internal organs
  (C) produce blood cells
  (D) conduct impulses

35. Which classification group to lions belong to?

  (A) Reptilia
  (B) Amphibia
  (C) Mammalia
  (D) Aves

36. The alveoli are essential parts of which human body system?

  (A) digestive
  (B) respiratory
  (C) circulatory
  (D) nervous

37. In the hierarchy of biological classification, which rank immediately follows the domain?

  (A) phylum
  (B) class
  (C) order
  (D) kingdom

38. Which of the following best describes the process of digestion as it begins in the human body?

  (A) The kidneys filter liquid waste from food to start the digestive process.
  (B) The stomach immediately breaks down food with gastric acids as soon as you eat.
  (C) The digestive process begins when the mouth waters.
  (D) Enzymes in the small intestine break down food as soon as you eat.

39. What does the body need for energy?

  (A) vitamins and minerals
  (B) carbohydrates and fats
  (C) only fiber
  (D) minerals and fats

40. Which characteristic is unique to the Plant kingdom?

  (A) ability to move
  (B) presence of cell walls made of cellulose
  (C) lack of a distinct nucleus
  (D) ability to photosynthesize

Answers and Explanations

Use this answer key to score the life science practice questions.

1. **C.** The respiratory system uses air to release energy, the digestive system processes food and eliminates waste, and the musculoskeletal system controls the movement of joints. The correct answer is Choice (C).

2. **A.** Green plants and some other organisms use sunlight to synthesize foods with carbon dioxide and water in a process called photosynthesis, which has a byproduct everyone needs: oxygen.

3. **C.** The heart is a muscular organ that pumps blood through the circulatory system, which then supplies the body with oxygen and nutrients.

4. **D.** An herbivore is an animal that eats only plants, so Choice (D) is correct. Carnivores eat meat, and omnivores eat both meat and plants. (And for the record, vegivores aren't a thing.)

5. **B.** DNA, or deoxyribonucleic acid, is the hereditary material common to humans and almost all other organisms. Almost every cell in your body has the same DNA, which is passed from parents to their offspring.

6. **C.** Decomposers are organisms that break down dead or decaying organisms; they make the decomposition process possible. Fungi and bacteria are the most common of their kind.

7. **C.** A plant's roots typically lie below the soil's surface (or, in some cases, the water's surface) and are responsible for soaking up water and nutrients, anchoring the plant in place, and storing food.

8. **C.** Animals absorb oxygen from inhaled air and release carbon dioxide (and some unused oxygen) as a waste product of respiration. Ambient air contains about 21% oxygen, 78% nitrogen, 1% other gases, and trace amounts of carbon dioxide, while an exhaled breath contains around 16% oxygen and 5% carbon dioxide (the rest is 1% other gases and 78% nitrogen).

9. **B.** The skin is the body's largest organ, and it keeps the inside of the body safe from all the things outside; it's a protective barrier that helps prevent injury and regulate temperature, and it helps you feel sensations like hot and cold.

10. **C.** Animals that eat plants and other animals are omnivores. (*Omni-* is a prefix that generally means "all," and knowing that can also help you on your Word Knowledge subtest.)

11. **A.** The nucleus contains most of the cell's genetic material and is often referred to as the control center of the cell, so the correct answer is Choice (A).

12. **B.** Beans, meat, and eggs all contain protein necessary for body functions, but water doesn't contain proteins. That makes Choice (B) the right answer.

13. **A.** The nasal cavity, where air enters your body, is part of the respiratory system. Other parts of this system include the nose, lungs, and trachea.

14. **B.** The gram is a unit of mass in the metric system, making Choice (B) the only right answer.

15. **C.** The scientific method starts with observation. Scientists then ask questions, develop a hypothesis, make predictions about what will happen, and test the hypothesis.

16. **B.** Hinge joints are found at the elbows, fingers, toes, and knees, and they allow bones to move back and forth (like a door that opens and closes).

17. **B.** Cells divide to produce two new cells in a process called mitosis. When that happens, each cell has the same number and kind of chromosomes that the parent nucleus has.

18. **A.** Tissue is a grouping of similar cells that work together to perform a specific function. Animals' bodies have all kinds of tissue, including muscle tissue, nervous tissue, and connective tissue.

19. **B.** White blood cells are part of the immune system, and their main job is to fight off infection and protect the body against invaders.

20. **C.** The large intestine is primarily responsible for absorbing water from indigestible food matter and transmitting waste from the body.

21. **C.** The renal system, which consists of the kidneys, ureters, bladder, and urethra, removes waste from blood and excretes it as urine.

22. **B.** Chlorophyll is the green pigment found in plants' chloroplasts. It absorbs light for use in photosynthesis.

23. **B.** The immune system, which helps protect the body against disease and infection, includes the spleen, thymus, and lymph nodes.

24. **C.** The part of the cell containing genetic material — by way of DNA — is the nucleus.

25. **B.** Living things maintain a stable internal environment through homeostasis; it keeps organisms functioning effectively.

26. **A.** The heart is made of a specialized muscle called cardiac muscle. It's characterized by interconnected fibers that let it contract so it can pump blood.

27. **A.** Green plants have cell walls made primarily of an organic compound called cellulose.

28. **D.** The liver has many jobs, and two of them are detoxifying chemicals and metabolizing drugs. It also secretes bile that ends up back in the intestines.

29. **B.** Arteries are blood vessels that carry blood away from the heart so it can travel to other parts of the body.

30. **D.** Biodiversity refers to the variety of life in any system, including the diversity of species, ecosystems, and even genetic diversity within species.

31. **C.** Species is the most specific classification in the Linnaean taxonomic system, and *sapiens* is a species. Domain is the broadest, and phylum and genus are between the two. (*Homo* in this question is the genus.)

32. **B.** Most cells reproduce by mitosis, the process of dividing into two separate cells with identical DNA, so Choice (B) is correct. By contrast, meiosis is the process of cells separating into four separate cells. Photosynthesis refers to plants making energy from light, and osmosis is the transfer of liquid between cell walls.

33. **C.** The kingdom Fungi includes mushrooms, molds, and yeasts — all of which are very distinct from plants, animals, and bacteria.

34. **D.** The skeletal system supports the body, protects delicate internal organs, and produces blood cells — but it doesn't conduct impulses. That's the nervous system's job.

35. **C.** Lions are mammals, which are characterized by the presence of mammary glands and a neocortex. *Mammary glands* produce milk for feeding their young, and the *neocortex* is a region of the brain that's involved in higher-level brain function like sensory perception, cognition, spatial reasoning, and language.

36. **B.** Alveoli are tiny air sacs in the lungs where the exchange of oxygen and carbon dioxide takes place. They're essential parts of the respiratory system.

37. **D.** In the Linnaean system of biological classification, the broadest category is domain, and the narrowest is species. The rank that follows domain is kingdom (and then phylum, class, order, family, genus, and species, in case you were wondering).

38. **C.** The digestive process begins before you start eating; sometimes thinking about food can cause your mouth to water and your stomach to growl, which signal that the digestive system is gearing up to start work.

39. **B.** The body needs carbohydrates and fats for energy. You find carbs in foods such as bread and pasta, while fats are in oils, nuts, and fish.

40. **B.** Organisms in the Plant kingdom are generally stationary and don't have a nervous or sensory system, but they do have cell walls made of cellulose. (Their fungi counterparts have cell walls made of chitin, and animals don't have any cell walls at all.)

> **IN THIS CHAPTER**
>
> » Unearthing elements
>
> » Compounding chemistry facts
>
> » Seeing what's up with SI units
>
> » Studying matter, mass, and motion
>
> » Finding out about physics topics like frequencies and magnets

Chapter 11
Physical Sciences

Brushing up on your chemistry and physics knowledge for the General Science subtest on the ASVAB is essential if you want to snag a good score for a particular job. And don't worry — this subtest doesn't factor into your Armed Forces Qualification Test (AFQT) score, so you can still join the military if you don't know an atom from Adam.

As you study, remember that understanding the principles behind the facts is what's important. You don't see these exact questions (or questions from any other test-prep book) on the ASVAB, but you do encounter the principles I cover in this chapter. You'll most likely see a mix of chemistry, physics, biology, Earth science, and space science when you sit down to take the test.

You have 12 minutes to answer 15 questions on the General Science subtest if you're taking the CAT-ASVAB (and 25 minutes for 30 questions if your test includes the tryout questions I describe in Chapter 1). If you're going the old-fashioned paper-and-pencil route, you get 11 minutes to answer 25 questions. As long as you focus on finding the right answers (and you've checked out the tips for guessing in Chapter 3), you should have plenty of time. The questions in this subtest are pretty cut-and-dried, which means you know the answers or you don't.

WARNING
When you answer an easy question correctly on the CAT-ASVAB, you're most likely going to get a question of medium difficulty next. Get that one right, and you'll be facing down a hard question. If you get hard questions right, you see more of them, but if you get them wrong, the computer dials back to medium and easy questions. Making sure you have the basics nailed down before you start studying (or even brushing up on) more advanced subjects is usually a good idea.

If the job you want requires a good score on the General Science subtest, this chapter is one you need to bookmark. You can also check out *Chemistry For Dummies* by John T. Moore, along with *Physics I For Dummies* and *Physics II For Dummies* by Steven Holzner, PhD (all from Wiley), as well as the online flashcards that come with this book (see the first page in the book for instructions to access them).

Chemistry: Not Blowing Up the Lab

Chemists study matter, and everything that has mass and takes up space — including your old Chevy that's up on blocks and the mosquito buzzing around the room — is matter. All matter is made up of basic substances (building blocks) called *atoms*. Atoms are the basic particles of the chemical elements that make up everything on Earth.

REMEMBER

In order to study matter, chemists use exactly what scientists in other fields use: the scientific method, which I discuss in Chapter 10. The careful steps scientists follow help ensure they cover all their bases. Figure 11-1 shows the way the scientific method works in a loop so scientists can continue learning (even when they think they already know the answers).

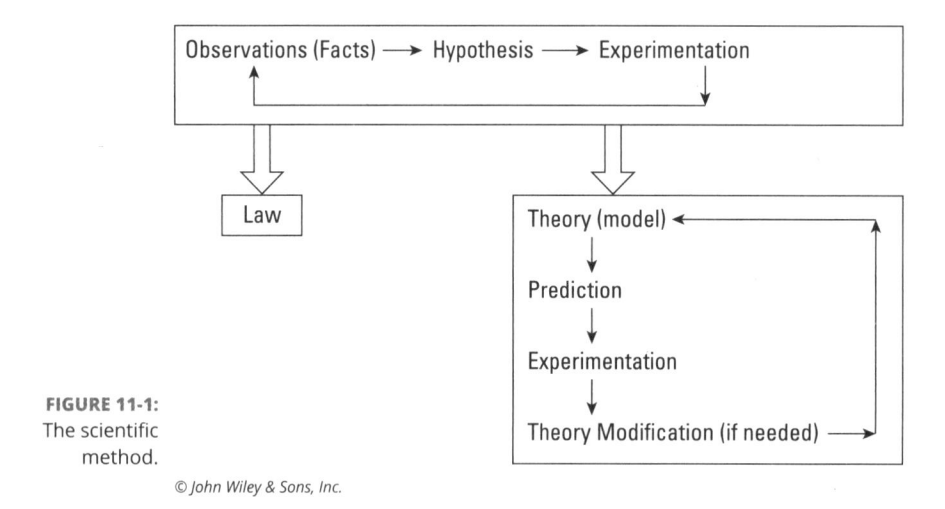

FIGURE 11-1: The scientific method.

© John Wiley & Sons, Inc.

How chemists look at things

Chemists see the world two ways: on a macroscopic level and on a microscopic level. *Macroscopic* refers to the world-at-large — all the stuff you can see right now. *Microscopic* refers to a much smaller level, where gas particles bump into each other and atoms bind together.

They use the information they gather to analyze substances, create compounds (a process called *synthesis*), create models and test theories, and measure substances' physical properties.

EVERYDAY CHEMISTRY

Everything on Earth is made from chemical elements — your desk, this book, your dog, and even your body. In fact, your body contains a significant amount of a chemical called dihydrogen oxide, and the same substance covers about 71 percent of the Earth.

Dihydrogen oxide is just water, but in scientific terms, it's still a chemical. Many of the things around you are made from chemicals that have been engineered to make your life better (the result of the scientific method). Look under your kitchen sink at the cleaning supplies — all engineered to kill germs and cut through grime. What about your clothes? Chemists worked in a lab to develop nylon, rayon, and polyester. Even your food is made up of chemical elements (some natural, some concocted in a lab).

Chemists typically use the SI system for measurements (flip to Chapter 10 for details) so they can communicate in the same scientific language as other chemists around the world. The base unit for length in the SI system is the *meter,* the unit for mass is the *kilogram,* and the main units of volume are the *cubic meter* and *liter.* Temperature is measured in *kelvins,* and pressure is measured in *pascals* and *newtons.* Finally, energy is measured in *joules* and *calories.*

Understanding the elements, my dear Watson

The *atom* is the smallest part of an element that still retains the characteristics of that element. Every atom contains *subatomic particles* — very, very small pieces of matter. *Electrons* are negatively charged subatomic particles that float around the atom's *nucleus,* or core, in an electron cloud made up of *neutrons* (subatomic particles with no charge) and *protons* (positively charged subatomic particles).

REMEMBER

Each element has its own atomic number that's equal to the number of protons it has. If an atom has one proton in its nucleus, it has the atomic number 1. Hydrogen is the only element with just one proton in its nucleus. Magnesium, which has 12 protons in its nucleus, has the atomic number 12.

Building molecular structures

Atoms can connect with each other to form *molecules. Chemical bonds* are strong, attractive forces that hold together the atoms in most molecules. Look at it this way: Like many people, atoms want to reach the most stable state they can. This *ground state* occurs when all an atom's electrons occupy the lowest possible energy levels around its nucleus.

In nature, opposites attract. An atom can form a bond when it overlaps or interacts with a different atom. The positive charge in an atom's nucleus attracts the negatively charged electrons in another atom's electron cloud, which creates the force that holds the atoms together to create a molecule.

If those atoms are of two or more different elements, the molecule is called a *compound.* A compound can have very different properties from the elements that make it up. For example, table salt, which is mostly harmless, consists of two lethal elements — sodium and chlorine. But when combined, these elements make a compound that people ingest every day: salt.

When atoms bond and form compounds, their structures and characteristics don't change. For example, when the chemical bond for water (H_2O) forms, its atoms — hydrogen and oxygen — remain the same. An oxygen atom has a slightly negative charge that attracts hydrogen's slightly positive charge. When an oxygen atom is lucky enough to attract two hydrogen atoms and shares electrons with each, voilà: It becomes a water molecule.

Every atom's bond makes a difference. When two oxygen atoms bond together with two hydrogen atoms, you end up with H_2O_2, which is hydrogen peroxide. Many compounds exist, and you can find out more about them in the later section "Compounds, mixtures, and reactions: When atoms and elements get together."

Sitting down at the periodic table

The *periodic table* (also known as the table of elements) classifies all elements, because scientists love to classify things. It lists elements according to their atomic numbers (number of protons) and arranges them into *families* of similar elements.

The periodic table lists the atomic number, the abbreviation for each element, and its *atomic weight,* which is the average mass of one atom of the element. Looking at Figure 11-2, you can see that copper (Cu, atomic number 29) has an atomic weight of 63.546, which means that copper is much, much heavier than helium (He, atomic number 2), which has an atomic weight of 4.0026.

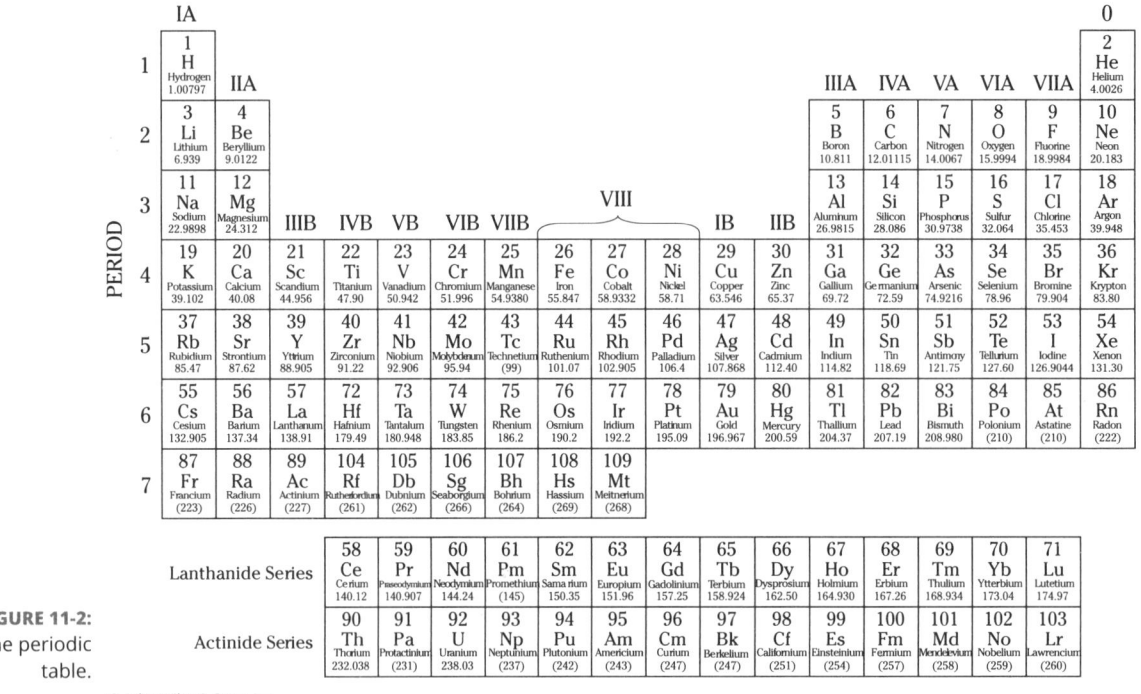

FIGURE 11-2: The periodic table.

© John Wiley & Sons, Inc.

You don't have to memorize the periodic table to do well on the ASVAB, but knowing the atomic numbers for common elements such as hydrogen (1), helium (2), carbon (6), nitrogen (7), and oxygen (8) can't hurt.

Changing states: Physical and chemical moves for molecules

Particles of matter are always in motion. How much kinetic energy (motion energy) a particle has determines whether the matter is a solid, liquid, or gas in its normal state. (The later section "Measuring work, force, energy, and power" has more on kinetic energy.) Gas particles move around very quickly, liquid particles move more slowly, and solid particles move much more slowly than either of the other two.

When heat or cold is applied to matter, the kinetic energy of the matter changes; therefore, the nature of the substance can change. Heat applied to water changes the water from a liquid to a gas (steam), and cold applied to water changes it from a liquid to a solid (ice). When physical changes occur, the molecule itself remains the same. For example, water is still made of hydrogen and oxygen, no matter which state it's in.

Scientists can distinguish these states (shown in Figure 11-3) at the macroscopic level *and* the microscopic level.

>> **Solids** have particles or molecules that are close together and don't move much, and they have a definite shape. In many cases, that's because the molecules are bound together in a

very rigid structure of repeating patterns. The structure is called *crystal lattice*. The molecules are still moving, but not much.

» **Liquids** have particles that are a bit more spread out than they are in solids. The big difference? They move around a lot more. Liquids don't have definite shapes, but they do have a definite volume. (Picture one cup of orange juice in a plastic box and one cup of orange juice in a coffee mug. They both have the same volume — one cup — but they definitely have different shapes.)

» **Gases** have particles that are much more spread out than they are in solids or liquids, and they move faster, too. Gases have no definite shape and no definite volume. The molecules move independently of one another, so gases expand to fill the area that contains them. You can compress gases (such as in a SCUBA tank) or release them (like when you turn the knob and release the gas from the same SCUBA tank).

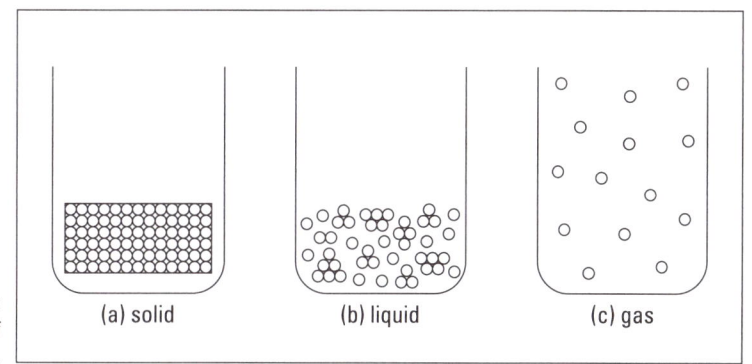

FIGURE 11-3: States of matter.

(a) solid   (b) liquid   (c) gas

© John Wiley & Sons, Inc.

Matter can — and does — change states. It usually takes extreme conditions to change the state of matter, like boiling or freezing. For example, an ice cube is a solid, but it quickly becomes a liquid when you leave it on the sidewalk in the sun. Soon after that, it evaporates into a gas. As molecules heat up, they move more quickly and become more spread out.

Boiling and freezing

When you're making spaghetti for dinner, the first thing you do is boil a pot of water so you have an environment that's hot enough to change the spaghetti from a very solid piece of pasta to a softer (and much tastier) piece of pasta without catching it on fire. You eat the pasta while it's transitioning between states; it's still a solid, but it's a much *softer* solid. If you leave the pasta in boiling water for too long, it'll turn into mush and eventually become a liquid.

Heating water changes its state. The molecules begin to move faster as they absorb heat, and the temperature rises until water reaches its boiling point. (Water's boiling point varies based on atmospheric pressure, but if you're at sea level, it's 100 degrees Celsius or 212 degrees Fahrenheit.) The temperature stays constant until all the liquid *evaporates* into a gas (water turns into steam). Steam contains the same molecules water does (H_2O), but in each state, the molecules are at different distances and moving at different speeds.

Cooling water changes its state, too. *Condensation* — the process of a substance changing from a gas to a liquid — is the first phase change liquids go through as they cool; it's the opposite of evaporation. When your glasses fog up when you open the dishwasher, when you see dew on the grass in the morning, or when your cup of cold liquid "sweats" on a hot day, you're watching liquids condense. These events happen because your glasses, the ground, and your cup are colder than the environment they're in; they cause water molecules in the air to gather together and form a liquid.

Freezing is another way to change a molecule's state. The molecule's freezing point is the same as its melting point; it's just that the thermostat is moving in the opposite direction. Cooling a substance slows down the motion of its molecules until it becomes a solid.

Most substances go through the same progression of events to change states, but some elements go through the process of sublimation instead. *Sublimation* occurs when a substance goes directly from a solid state to a gaseous state with no liquid state in-between. One example is dry ice. Dry ice is solid carbon dioxide, and it's often used to create a smoke or fog effect in magic shows (and nightclubs). Dry ice turns into a colorless gas, but it creates a white cloud as it evaporates (the white cloud it forms is actually condensation of water vapor in the air because the dry ice is so cold). The reverse of sublimation is called *deposition,* where a gaseous substance becomes a solid without a liquid state in-between.

Compounds, mixtures, and reactions: When atoms and elements get together

Atoms are the building blocks of elements, which are pure substances made up of only one type of atom. Elements can join together in specific ratios, mix and mingle in different ratios, or react to each other to create different substances.

Compounds: Adding atoms together

Compounds are atoms that have joined by chemical bonds in a specific ratio. The water that comes out of your tap is a compound made of two elements (substances made of just one type of atom): hydrogen (represented by H in the periodic table) and oxygen (represented by O in the periodic table). These elements together make water if they're combined only in a very specific way: two hydrogen atoms for every one oxygen atom (that's why you see the compound written as H_2O). The little number 2 between the two elements tells you the compound has two hydrogen atoms; because there's no number after the O, you can assume that the compound has just one of them.

As you read a chemical formula, you have to deal with molecules and compounds in shorthand. The number of molecules is listed in front of the molecule, so you write "five molecules of helium" as "5He." You write the number of atoms in a molecule in subscript after the elemental symbol, so hydrogen with two atoms is H_2. Sometimes formulas have brackets, just like algebraic formulas do, to separate them when they're complex. Table 11-1 gives you examples of how to read chemical formulas. Use Figure 11-2 (the periodic table) earlier in the chapter to figure out which elements are in each compound.

The ASVAB may dish up a question or two that asks you to identify one (or more) of the components of a chemical formula. Though you don't have to memorize the symbols for each element, knowing how formulas work (and how to break them apart) can help boost your score. If you think of atoms like interlocking toy blocks that you can arrange into different structures (and make parts for an even bigger structure), you can visualize the letters and numbers inside brackets as parts that can be added to other molecules. Those parts are called *functional groups.* Like atoms, you indicate how many of these groups there are with the subscript number. $(NO_3)_3$ means that there are three NO_3 functional groups.

TABLE 11-1 Examples of Chemical Formulas

Formula	Shorthand	Number of Molecules	Number of Atoms	Name
$NaHCO_3$	Na = sodium	1 sodium	1 sodium	Baking soda
	H = hydrogen	1 hydrogen	1 hydrogen	
	C = carbon	1 carbon	1 carbon	
	O = oxygen	1 oxygen	3 oxygen	
NaCl	Na = sodium	1 sodium	1 sodium	Table salt
	Cl = chlorine	1 chlorine	1 chlorine	
$C_3H_5(NO_3)_3$	C = carbon	1 carbon	3 carbon	Nitroglycerin
	H = hydrogen	1 hydrogen	5 hydrogen	
	N = nitrogen	1 nitrogen	1 nitrogen	
	O = oxygen	1 oxygen	3 oxygen	
$AgNO_3$	Ag = silver	1 silver	1 silver	Silver nitrate
	N = nitrogen	1 nitrogen	1 nitrogen	
	O = oxygen	1 oxygen	3 oxygen	
$C_{10}H_{14}N_2$	C = carbon	1 carbon	10 carbon	Nicotine
	H = hydrogen	1 hydrogen	14 hydrogen	
	N = nitrogen	1 nitrogen	2 nitrogen	

Here's an example: I always add two (sometimes more) teaspoons of good, old-fashioned $C_{12}H_{22}O_{11}$ (that's sugar) to my coffee in the morning. Look at Figure 11-2 earlier in the chapter. Based on sugar's molecular formula, you can tell that it has 12 carbon atoms, 22 hydrogen atoms, and 11 oxygen atoms in each molecule. These three elements together, in this ratio only, make up sugar. If one is off, even by one atom, my coffee would taste a lot different (and may even be toxic). Acetone, which removes paint, serves as an ingredient in rubber cement, and does a bunch of other non-food-related tasks, is also made up of carbon, hydrogen, and oxygen. (In case you were wondering, acetone's chemical makeup is $(CH_3)_2O$, and it's nasty in coffee.)

Mixtures: Physical combinations of pure substances

In chemistry, a *mixture* is a physical combination of pure substances that don't have a constant composition. The composition of the mixture depends on who makes it. Bread tastes different when it comes from two different bakers because each uses a slightly different mixture even though they use all the same ingredients. In a mixture, though, each substance keeps its own chemical characteristics (the flour, oil, and water keep the same molecular structures from start to finish).

Chemical reactions

Boiling and freezing are changes in a substance's state (as I discuss earlier in the chapter), but a *chemical reaction* is a process that rearranges a substance's molecular structure. No matter what its physical state, water is still made up of H_2O. But if you compound it with another element, its atoms are redistributed to create a new substance. For example, when iron rusts, a chemical change occurs. The rust isn't the same molecule as the iron is.

In a normal chemical reaction, matter is neither created nor destroyed. That means the total mass of *reactants* (the elements that are changing) is the same as the total mass of *products* (the elements that have changed).

There are several types of chemical reactions, but the most common are these:

- **Combination:** *Combination reactions* occur when two or more reactants merge to form one product. One example is the way sodium and chlorine combine to create sodium chloride (that's table salt).
- **Decomposition:** *Decomposition reactions* are the opposite of combination reactions because a single compound breaks down into two or more simpler substances. This process happens when water decomposes into hydrogen and oxygen gases, for example.
- **Combustion:** *Combustion reactions* typically involve carbon and oxygen in the process known as burning. This type of reaction occurs in gas-powered cars, in open fires, and when some people try to cook.

Covering all the bases (and the acids, too)

Aqueous chemical compounds, substances, and mixtures (those that contain water) can be bases, acids, or neutral (neither an acid nor a base).

A *base* is a substance that gives up negatively charged hydroxyl ions when dissolved in water; they're often called *alkaline* substances. Liquid soap, ammonia, and baking soda are all bases. An *acid* gives up positively charged hydrogen ions when dissolved in water. Some examples of acids include vinegar, orange juice, and sulfuric acid.

Whether a solution is basic or acidic, it can be measured on a pH scale. The pH scale ranges from 0 to 14, with 0 being the most acidic (that's where you find battery acid) and 14 being the most basic (that's where liquid drain cleaner hangs out). Pure water falls right in the middle, at a very neutral 7. Figure 11-4 shows the pH scale with common household substances on it.

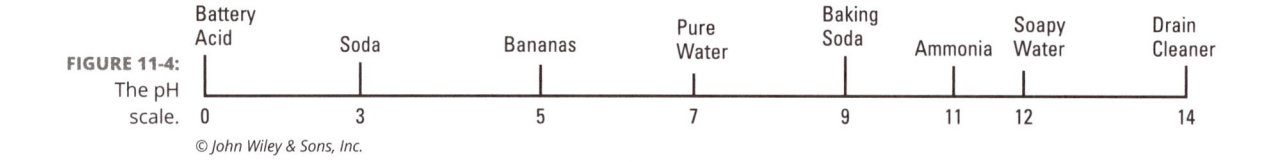

FIGURE 11-4: The pH scale.

Battery Acid	Soda	Bananas	Pure Water	Baking Soda	Ammonia	Soapy Water	Drain Cleaner
0	3	5	7	9	11	12	14

© John Wiley & Sons, Inc.

Each whole pH value below 7 — the most neutral number on the scale — is ten times more acidic than the value after it. That means something with a pH of 3 is 10 times more acidic than something with a pH of 4 and 100 times more acidic than something with a pH of 5.

TECHNICAL STUFF

pH stands for the Latin *potentia hydrogenii* — in English, potential hydrogen. The scale is based on the logarithm $pH = -\log(H+)$, where log is the base 10 logarithm and H+ is the hydrogen ion concentration measured in moles per liter.

Physics: It Matters (and It's Matter)

Physics is the branch of science that delves into matter and energy. It includes mechanics, heat, light, and other radiation. Physicists also study sound, magnetism, electricity, and the makeup and structure of atoms. You need a basic understanding of physics for both the General Science subtest and the Mechanical Comprehension subtest of the ASVAB. (You can brush up on what you need to know for Mechanical Comprehension in Chapter 15.)

New theories in physics don't always bring about new answers. In fact, more often than not, they bring up even more questions. In an attempt to answer them, physicists try to find relationships between what they already know and what's most likely to be true — and they often do so by using mathematical formulas.

Keeping track with SI units of measurement

Scientists around the world need a common language to share and explain their discoveries, so they use SI units of measurement I introduce in Chapter 10. Table 11-2 shows the base quantities, names, and abbreviations that physicists and other scientists use to communicate. (For easy conversion formulas, flip to Chapter 10.)

TABLE 11-2 Measurement, SI Base Quantities, and Abbreviations

Measurement	SI Base Quantity	Abbreviation
length	meter	m
mass	kilogram	kg
time	second	s
electric current	ampere	A
thermodynamic temperature	kelvin	K
amount of substance	mole	mol
luminous intensity	candela	cd

SI *derived units* are measurements you can get by using a system of equations. Table 11-3 shows the most common measurements, SI derived units, and the abbreviations and symbols that represent them.

Weight and mass

Weight and mass are two different things. Look at it this way: If you were on the moon, you'd weigh a lot less than you do here on Earth. Your body composition hasn't changed, so your mass would remain the same.

>> **Weight** is a measure of the force gravity exerts on an object or the force needed to support it. You're being pulled to the Earth at an accelerating rate of 9.8 meters per second squared, or m/s^2, but if you were on the moon, you'd be pulled to it at a rate of 1.62 m/s^2. You weigh less on the moon than you do on Earth.

>> **Mass** is a measure of an object's inertial property — the amount of matter it contains. An object's mass doesn't change, whether it's on the moon, in a compression device, or anywhere else.

TABLE 11-3 Measurements, SI Derived Units, and Symbols/Abbreviations

Measurement	SI Derived Unit	Symbol
area	square meter	m^2
volume	cubic meter	m^3
speed and velocity	meter per second	m/s
magnetic field strength	ampere per meter	A/m
luminance	candela per square meter	cd/m^2
force	newton	N
energy, work, and quantity of heat	joule	J
power	watt	W
electric resistance	ohm	f
electric charge and quantity of electricity	coulomb	C
electric potential difference and electromotive force	volt	V
frequency	hertz	Hz
pressure or stress	pascal	Pa

Newton's laws: The science of motion

Sir Isaac Newton, a brilliant English physicist and mathematician who lived in the late 17th and early 18th centuries, developed the principles of modern physics. He illustrated the laws of motion and made discoveries in mathematics and optics as well. He's even credited with developing essential theories of calculus. (It's safe to say he would've gotten a pretty high score on the ASVAB.)

Newton came up with three laws that describe motion and gravity, which I cover in the following sections.

REMEMBER As I explain in Chapter 10, the words *law* and *theory* don't mean the same things to scientists that they mean to the average person. Theories can evolve over time as new information becomes available, but they're pretty much accepted as true statements and explanations across the scientific community. Laws, on the other hand, are always true (that's why there are few laws and many theories), and they're often expressed in a simple statement.

Newton's first law of motion

Newton's first law of motion says that an object at rest will stay at rest, and an object in motion will stay in motion with the same speed and in the same direction, unless acted upon by an unbalanced force.

What that means is that without *friction* to slow down a moving object (and nothing to knock the object off its path), the object would keep going the same speed, on the same path. Newton's first law, which is sometimes called the *law of inertia*, basically means that objects tend to keep doing what they're doing unless something interrupts them. *Inertia* means a tendency to do nothing or to remain unchanged, and all matter resists changes in motion.

The key phrase in Newton's first law is *unbalanced force.* The first law of motion only works if forces are balanced — that is, if there's nothing to change the object's course. In that case, the object is in a state of *equilibrium* (the condition in which all forces balance) and won't accelerate, decelerate, or change course.

You've probably experienced the law of inertia yourself. When you're in the car with a hot cup of coffee and the driver hits the brakes, your coffee keeps moving in the same direction it's been moving the entire time you've been in the car, at the same speed (so you'd better have the lid on tight). The same is true for you; if you're in a crash and the car stops abruptly, you keep going in the same direction at the same speed (and right through the windshield, if you're not wearing a seat belt that acts as an unbalanced force to stop you).

Sometimes other forces, such as gravity, also act on objects. That's why when you throw a baseball from left field to first base, it follows an upward path but begins to drop by the time it (hopefully) reaches the first baseman, and why when you fire your M4 carbine at a 300-meter target, the bullet hits a little lower than it would've if you'd been firing at a 50-meter target.

Newton's second law of motion

Newton's second law of motion says that when dealing with an object for which all existing forces are not balanced, the acceleration of that object (as produced by the net force) is in the same direction as the net force and directly proportional to the magnitude of the net force, and is inversely proportional to the object's mass.

That's expressed by the mathematical formula acceleration = net force ÷ mass. If you're using this formula, you need to rely on these units of measurement: m/s², N, and kg. You can express Newton's second law of motion as $\vec{a} = \frac{\vec{F}}{m}$, where $\vec{a}$ represents acceleration, $\vec{F}$ represents net force, and *m* represents mass. The formula's equivalent form (to figure out force) is $\vec{F} = m\vec{a}$.

The greater an object's mass, the greater the force you need to overcome its inertia, which is described in Newton's first law of motion (see the preceding section).

Starting or stopping a moving 50-car train carrying lead is a lot harder than starting or stopping a toy car in motion. That's because the force necessary to overcome an object's inertia is inversely proportional to its mass. If you use the same force to push the toy car as you use to push the train, the toy car is going to accelerate a lot faster because it has less mass than the train does.

Newton's third law of motion

Newton's third law of motion says that for every action, there is an equal and opposite reaction. That means that when an object exerts a force on another object, the second object exerts an equal force in an opposite direction on the first object.

In every interaction between objects, a pair of forces is acting on the objects that are interacting. The forces on the first object equal the forces on the second object, but the directions of the forces are opposite. Forces always come in pairs, called *action-reaction force pairs.*

Birds can fly because of action-reaction force pairs. A bird's wings push air down, but because every action has an equal and opposite reaction, the air is pushing the bird's wings upward. (They're attached to the bird, so the whole bird stays airborne.) When your car rolls down the road, your wheels push the road backward. The road exerts the same force on your wheels (but in the opposite direction), which makes your car move forward.

Newton's law of universal gravitation

Newton also developed the law of universal gravitation, which says that all objects in the universe attract each other with an equal force that varies directly as a product of their masses, and inversely as a square of their distance from each other. This force is known as *gravity*.

The mathematical equation that Newton's law of universal gravitation relies on is expressed this way: $\vec{F}_g = \dfrac{G(m_1 m_2)}{r^2}$, where $\vec{F}$ represents the force of gravity between two objects, G represents the gravitational constant, m_1 and m_2 represent the mass of the first and second objects, and r represents the distance.

The sun and the Earth have a gravitational relationship. Because scientists know the law of universal gravitation, you know that if the Earth's mass was doubled, the force on Earth would double. If the sun's mass was doubled, the force on Earth would double. The force the sun exerts on the Earth is equal and opposite the force the Earth exerts on the sun, which brings in Newton's third law (see the preceding section).

Measuring work, force, energy, and power

Physicists define *work* as far more than "showing up at the right place at the right time in the right uniform" (you hear that phrase often in the military). To a physicist, a force performs *work* on an object when it causes the object to move. You can calculate the work performed on an object by multiplying the force by how much the object moves. The equation for work is $W = Fd$, where W represents work, F represents force, and d represents displacement. Units of work are measured in newton-meters (Nm) or joules (J) under the SI system, but under the U.S. system, they're measured in pounds.

Force is something that causes a change in an object's motion, such as a push or pull resulting from the object's interaction with another object. It can refer to gravity, pushing against something with your muscles, or smashing into something with a car; it's anything that takes away an object's inertia. Forces only exist as a result of an interaction between two objects, and they are typically measured in newtons (N).

TECHNICAL STUFF

The SI system is used in most of the world, but in the U.S., many common applications (and most engineering functions) use U.S. Standard Units. You may see either system on the ASVAB, which is designed to test the depth of your existing knowledge, but what you won't see is a mixture of the two systems in the same problem. Table 11-4 highlights some of the key differences between them.

TABLE 11-4 SI versus U.S. Standard Units

System	Mass	Acceleration	Force
SI	kilogram (kg)	meters/second/second (m/s^2)	newton (N)
U.S.	slug	feet/second/second (ft/sec^2)	pound-force (lbf)

EXAMPLE

Tech Sergeant Yost pushes a box of dental equipment across the dental clinic. He uses 60 newtons of force to move the box 2 meters away. How much work does Tech Sergeant Yost perform against the box?

(A) 120 joules

(B) 30 joules

(C) 15 joules

(D) 90 joules

Use the formula for work:

$W = Fd$

$W = 60 \text{ newtons} \cdot 2 \text{ meters}$

$W = 120 \text{ joules}$

Tech Sergeant Yost performed 120 joules of work on the box, Choice (A).

Energy, which is also measured in joules, is the capacity for doing work. It can exist in several forms, such as electrical, chemical, and thermal, but it's always either kinetic or potential. *Kinetic energy* is the energy an object possesses because of its motion, and *potential energy* is the energy an object stores due to its position or configuration. Potential energy turns into kinetic energy when an object begins moving.

When you shoot a rubber band at your brother and it's flying through the air, the rubber band has kinetic energy. Go back to the moment before you shot it, though — when you stretched the rubber band as far as it would go. When you began stretching it, it started to develop potential energy because of its position. As soon as you fired it, the potential energy turned into kinetic energy. If it has enough kinetic energy and your brother's arm is the force that stops it, it's going to sting!

Power is the rate of doing work or the rate of converting energy per unit of time. You can calculate it with the formula $P = \frac{w}{t}$, where P represents power, W represents work, and t represents time. Power is measured in watts, and one watt is defined as one joule per second. (If you don't know how much work was exerted when you're tackling an ASVAB problem, figure it out using the formula for work.)

Did you hear that? Understanding sound waves

Your favorite song, the bell ringing before class starts, and your mom reminding you to pick up your room all travel to your ears through *sound waves.* Sound waves are actually fast-moving waves of pressure that result in the vibrations of particles in the medium carrying them (most of the time, that's air). If you bang on a drum, you're causing the drum's tight surface to vibrate. In turn, that makes the air around the drum vibrate, sending energy out of the drum in all directions. When the vibrating air hits your eardrums, you perceive it as a sound; you're hearing energy making a journey. If that vibrating air hits a wall or another surface it can't go through, it bounces back in the form of an echo, which is technically called *sound reflection.*

TECHNICAL STUFF

Sound waves travel very quickly. At sea level, they speed through the air at about 760 miles per hour. When you hear about ultra-fast jets breaking the sound barrier, that means the jet is accelerating so quickly that it goes faster than the sound waves it's creating. The result is a *sonic boom* — a tremendous, explosion-like sound caused by the shock waves the jet makes.

Sound waves travel in ripples, like water (that's why you can hear around corners), and they spread out as they go. Sound is measured in *amplitude* and *wavelength*, as Figure 11-5 shows. The higher a sound's amplitude is, the more intense — and loud — it is. The higher a sound's wavelength (the number of sound waves it creates per second) is, the higher its pitch sounds. A violin makes more sound waves per second than a bass guitar does, so its pitch sounds higher. Wavelength and frequency are also related; the shorter the wavelength, the higher the frequency. Frequency is typically measured in hertz (Hz).

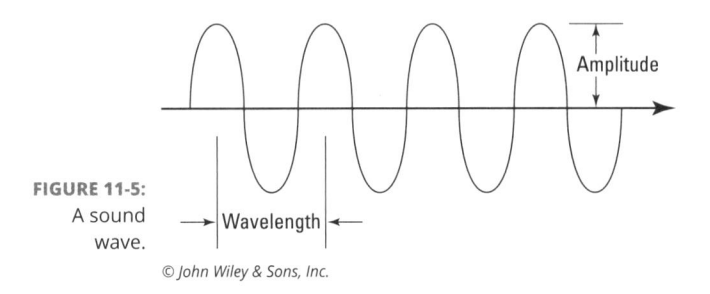

FIGURE 11-5: A sound wave.

© John Wiley & Sons, Inc.

The rainbow of frequencies on the electromagnetic spectrum

Visible light is only one part of the electromagnetic spectrum (shown in Figure 11-6), which covers all the wavelengths and frequencies of radiation. Radiation that produces long wavelengths and low frequencies falls on one side of the electromagnetic spectrum, while radiation that produces short wavelengths and high frequencies falls on the other.

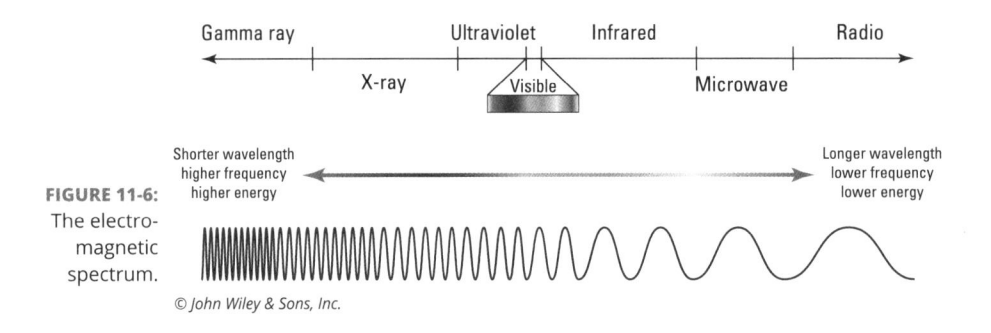

FIGURE 11-6: The electromagnetic spectrum.

© John Wiley & Sons, Inc.

On the electromagnetic spectrum, wavelengths are measured by the distance from the peak of one wave to the peak of the next wave. They're measured in kilometers (km), meters (m), centimeters (cm), millimeters (mm), and nanometers (nm). Frequencies are measured by how many waves occur per second, in hertz (Hz), kilohertz (kHz), megahertz (MHz), and gigahertz (GHz), with one Hz being one wave per second.

TECHNICAL STUFF

Your favorite FM radio station broadcasts radiation at about 100 MHz. A microwave oven generates a few GHz (one GHz equals 1 billion cycles per second), and X-ray machines create between 10^{18} and 10^{20} Hz.

The light you see falls near the middle of the electromagnetic spectrum. The frequency of a light wave determines the color it produces. The colors visible to the eye are the results of wavelengths between about 400 and 800 nanometers. Sunlight appears white because it emits over all visible frequencies.

238 PART 4 **Examining General Science Under a Microscope**

Light is a little bit like sound because it travels out from a specific source (see the preceding section); however, unlike sound, light can travel without a medium. Light waves can travel through empty space (a vacuum), and they move much faster than sound waves do.

The speed light travels is directly impacted by *refraction* and *reflection*. It travels faster through empty space (about 186,000 miles per second) and slower when it's passing through water, glass, or other mediums.

- » **Refraction** is the bending of light as it passes from one medium to another. Rainbows, the lenses of your glasses, and magnifying glasses are all possible because of refraction. Light refracts when it travels at an angle from one medium into another, such as from air to water. When the light slows down, it begins traveling at a different angle or in a different direction. The amount that light bends depends on its change in speed and the angle at which it hits the new medium. Rays of light that enter a *convex* lens, which curves outward, gather together at a focal point on the other side of the lens (like your eyeglasses or a magnifying glass). *Concave* lenses bend light away from a focal point and result in a smaller image for the person viewing it — like peepholes, binoculars, telescopes, and your car's mirrors.

- » **Reflection** occurs when light bounces off an object. If it bounces off a smooth, shiny surface (such as glass, water, shiny metal, or a mirror), the light reflects at the same angle it hits; that's called *specular reflection* and is what you see in the mirror or a smooth, mountain lake. When it reflects off a rough surface, you see *diffuse reflection*. Most of the things you see are due to diffuse reflection, which occurs when light hits your dog, your energy drink can, or this book. Light has reflected off each of those things and traveled in nearly all directions; the light that makes it to your eyes shines on your retina (in the back of your eyes), which passes a signal to your brain.

Heating things up with energy

Heat is the flow of energy from a warm object to a cooler object, and all matter contains heat energy (from volcanoes to ice cubes). Often called *thermal energy*, it's the result of atoms, molecules, and ions moving in solids, liquids, and gases. (Flip to Figure 11-3 earlier in the chapter for a quick look at the way particles are arranged when they're in different states.) At higher temperatures, particles have more energy and move faster than slower particles operating at lower temperatures do. When a higher-energy, higher-temperature particle hits a lower-energy, lower-temperature particle, the higher-energy particle transfers some of its energy to the lower-energy particle; that's the transfer of heat.

An ice cube and a glass of vodka both have heat energy. If you put the ice cube in the vodka, the vodka will transfer some of its heat energy into the ice cube. The ice will eventually melt, and the vodka and the water from the ice will be the same temperature. When this happens, the contents of the glass have reached a state of *thermal equilibrium*, a condition in which no heat is flowing between them anymore (see the following section for more information).

Faster-moving particles tend to "excite" particles near them. If a solid has enough heat, the movement causes the particles to break free from the bonds holding them together. The resulting change is what you know as *melting* — when matter changes from a solid to a liquid. If the heat keeps up, the particles can break their bonds even further and turn into a gas during the process of *evaporation*.

Heat energy can transfer in three ways: convection, conduction, and radiation.

- **Conduction** transfers thermal energy in solids. The moving particles in a warm solid can increase the thermal energy in particles of a cooler solid by directly transferring it, particle by particle. In solids, the particles are closer together (see Figure 11-3), and that makes them better conductors of heat than liquids or gases are. Some materials are really good at conducting heat, like metal (think about how hot a pan gets on the stove), so they're called *conductors*. Other materials, such as plastic, foam, and wood, aren't so good at conducting heat, so they're known as *insulators*.

- **Convection** transfers thermal energy through gases and liquids. The air heats up and gives particles thermal energy, and the particles move faster and farther apart while carrying the heat energy with them. If you're sitting in a warm room right now, thank convection.

- **Radiation** doesn't require particles to carry thermal energy. Instead, it uses infrared waves (see Figure 11-6 earlier in the chapter), which radiate out in all directions and travel at the speed of light until they hit something else. When the waves hit an object, the object can absorb or reflect the thermal energy they carry.

Fire uses all three methods of heat transfer. First, the substance that's burning uses conduction; the moving particles make other particles in nearby solids hot enough to catch (and stay) on fire. Convection heats the air above and around the fire, and you warm your hands near the flames because of radiant heat transfer.

The four laws of thermodynamics

The *zeroth law of thermodynamics* says that if two systems are in thermal equilibrium with a third system, then they are in thermal equilibrium with each other. *Thermal equilibrium* means that no heat transfers from one object to another because they're the same temperature.

TECHNICAL STUFF

The zeroth law of thermodynamics serves as the definition of temperature, but it wasn't created until after the first, second, and third laws of thermodynamics were. The first three laws were already well-known by the time this one came about, but it supersedes all of them. As a result, scientist Ralph H. Fowler — who was also a British soldier during World War I — proposed calling it the "zeroth" law.

All matter adheres to the zeroth law. It's the reason scientists can measure temperature (which they do in kelvins), and it makes the following three laws of thermodynamics possible:

- **The first law of thermodynamics:** The *first law of thermodynamics* is another version of the law of conservation of energy, which says that energy can be neither created nor destroyed. It can be transferred to other locations, though, and it can be converted to (and from) other forms of energy. However, the total quantity of energy in the universe always stays the same.

- **The second law of thermodynamics:** The *second law of thermodynamics* describes how energy affects matter, as well as the relationships between thermal energy (heat) and other types of energy. It says that the more energy is transferred or transformed, the more it's wasted. It also says that an isolated system has a tendency to degenerate into a more disordered state.

- **The third law of thermodynamics:** The *third law of thermodynamics* says that achieving a temperature of absolute zero is impossible. *Absolute zero* is the temperature matter would reach if it contained absolutely no heat energy.

Side effects: Feeling hot and cold

When substances get hot because their molecules are colliding fast, they expand. When things cool down, they shrink. Sometimes the change in size is so small that you don't notice it — but sometimes it's huge. One example of this change happens in burning houses. The air inside the house is hot, and its molecules are moving really quickly. The air expands so much that it creates tremendous pressure, and eventually, the windows explode outward.

Heat expansion is why mercury thermometers worked (back when people still used them, that is). Cold contraction is why a weather balloon looks emptier as it floats higher into the atmosphere.

The reason objects feel so hot or cold to the touch is because of the state their molecules are in. When you stick a metal spoon into a pot of boiling water, it excites the spoon's molecules — and remember, even in solids, the molecules are always moving. If you stick that same spoon in the freezer, you'll slow down its molecules so much that it will feel cold when you touch it. For example, you can test out how cold a metal light pole is by sticking your tongue on it during winter. (Wait! Bad idea. Please don't lick anything metal during winter. I just wanted to make sure you were still paying attention!)

Essentially, when you cool down an object, you're "freezing" the movement of its molecules.

You've heard that ice expands, and that's true. Although ice is frozen and its molecules aren't moving as much as they are in liquid form, its hydrogen bonds create a crystal lattice pattern (see Figure 11-3 earlier in this chapter for a peek at what a solid's molecules look like). In that pattern, each water molecule is held away from the molecules next to it at a distance equal to the length of its hydrogen bonds. Technically, cooling water shrinks until it starts to develop that crystal lattice pattern — then, because of the way the molecules arrange themselves, it expands.

Opposites attract: Magnetism and polarization

Hold two magnets up to each other. Sometimes they snap together, and other times they push against each other. This phenomenon occurs because magnets have two poles: north and south, just like the Earth. When you try to put two norths together, they repel each other; the same applies to two souths. But when you put a north and a south together, the old saying "opposites attract" is in full effect — the two magnets stick together.

Earth is magnetized and has a North Pole and a South Pole. Magnetic compasses work because their needles are magnetized, too. The point of the needle is the magnet's south pole, so it's automatically attracted to Earth's magnetic North Pole.

Physical Science Practice Questions

Physical science questions are sprinkled throughout the ASVAB's General Science subtest. Work your way through these 40 practice questions to see what areas need most of your attention if you're trying to ace this part of the test.

Easy physical science practice questions

1. Energy is measured in
   - (A) joules.
   - (B) newtons.
   - (C) calories.
   - (D) both Choice (A) and Choice (C).

2. Compasses work by
   - (A) measuring heat in the air.
   - (B) reacting to magnetic fields.
   - (C) repulsing wave currents.
   - (D) reacting to iron in the Earth's core.

3. Mass is a measure of
   - (A) how much matter an object contains.
   - (B) the force of gravity on an object.
   - (C) weight.
   - (D) the amount of force necessary to move an object.

4. Which of the following is not a state of matter?
   - (A) ether
   - (B) liquid
   - (C) gas
   - (D) solid

5. A chemical reaction
   - (A) can only be set off by adding negative ions.
   - (B) rearranges an element's molecular structure.
   - (C) requires fire or water.
   - (D) is always dangerous.

6. Which state of matter has a definite volume but no definite shape?
   - (A) solid
   - (B) liquid
   - (C) gas
   - (D) plasma

7. Which of the following is not a form of energy?
   - (A) thermal
   - (B) sound
   - (C) electric
   - (D) plastic

8. What term describes the amount of matter in an object?
   - (A) weight
   - (B) density
   - (C) volume
   - (D) mass

9. Which of the following is a chemical change?
   - (A) boiling water
   - (B) dissolving sugar in water
   - (C) rusting iron
   - (D) melting ice

10. What light phenomenon causes rainbows?
    - (A) reflection
    - (B) refraction
    - (C) diffraction
    - (D) polarization

Medium physical science practice questions

11. An element's atomic number indicates its number of
    - (A) neutrons.
    - (B) kelvins.
    - (C) protons.
    - (D) negatively charged ions.

12. The electromagnetic spectrum measures
    - (A) sound waves.
    - (B) only visible light.
    - (C) radiation.
    - (D) rainbows.

13. Compounds are elements that have
    - (A) mixed in various ratios.
    - (B) combined as liquids and solids.
    - (C) created toxic chemicals.
    - (D) joined together in specific ratios.

14. Which of the following is not true of gases?
    - (A) They have no definite volume.
    - (B) They have no definite shape.
    - (C) Gases cannot evenly fill a container.
    - (D) They are also called vapors.

15. The unit of frequency is
    - (A) hertz (Hz).
    - (B) newton (N).
    - (C) pascal (Pa).
    - (D) joule (j).

16. What is the SI unit of work?
    - (A) pound
    - (B) newton
    - (C) joule
    - (D) meter

17. Why do two magnets pull together when a north pole and south pole are close to each other?
    - (A) Like poles attract.
    - (B) There is a gravitational pull between them.
    - (C) Opposites attract.
    - (D) The Earth's magnetic field exerts force on them.

18. What is the primary process by which heat is transferred in solids?
    - (A) convection
    - (B) conduction
    - (C) radiation
    - (D) evaporation

19. Which of the following happens when a solid gains enough heat energy?
    - (A) It becomes denser.
    - (B) It changes color.
    - (C) It conducts electricity.
    - (D) It melts, changing from a solid to a liquid.

20. What is thermal equilibrium?
    - (A) the point where a subject changes from liquid to gas
    - (B) the condition where two objects are the same temperature and no heat flows between them
    - (C) the maximum temperature a substance can reach
    - (D) the temperature at which a substance burns

21. What determines an element's atomic number?
    - (A) the number of electrons
    - (B) the number of neutrons
    - (C) the number of protons
    - (D) the atomic weight

22. What element has an atomic number of 1?
    - (A) helium
    - (B) magnesium
    - (C) copper
    - (D) hydrogen

23. Which of Newton's laws says that every action has an equal and opposite reaction?

    (A) first law of motion
    (B) second law of motion
    (C) third law of motion
    (D) law of universal gravitation

24. What happens to a moving object when an unbalanced force acts upon it?

    (A) It changes speed, direction, or both.
    (B) It continues to move at the same speed and in the same direction.
    (C) It stops immediately.
    (D) It reverses direction.

25. Inertia is

    (A) a type of force.
    (B) a push something needs to start moving.
    (C) the pull of gravity on an object.
    (D) an object's tendency to resist changes in its movement.

26. What does the subscript in a chemical formula indicate?

    (A) the number of molecules in an atom
    (B) the number of compounds in a formula
    (C) the number of reactions of an element
    (D) the number of atoms of an element in a molecule

27. What determines whether matter is in a solid, liquid, or gas state in its usual condition?

    (A) particle size
    (B) kinetic energy
    (C) number of particles
    (D) particle color

28. When water is heated from a liquid to a gas,

    (A) the molecules move more slowly and get closer together.
    (B) the molecules stop moving and separate completely.
    (C) the molecules move more quickly and become more spread out.
    (D) the molecules become a different element.

29. What is the pH of pure water?

    (A) 0.
    (B) 7.
    (C) 14.
    (D) Water is not on the pH scale.

30. At what point does water stay at a constant temperature during the heating process?

    (A) as soon as it begins to heat up
    (B) when it reaches its freezing point
    (C) when it reaches its boiling point
    (D) after it becomes steam

Hard physical science practice questions

31. The formula you need to determine force is
    (A) $m = \vec{F}\vec{a}$.
    (B) $\vec{F} = m\vec{a}$.
    (C) $\vec{F} = mg$.
    (D) $\vec{a} = \dfrac{\vec{F}}{m^2}$.

32. The element with the lowest atomic number is
    (A) hydrogen.
    (B) helium.
    (C) lithium.
    (D) uranium.

33. What is the term for an element or molecule that results from a chemical reaction?
    (A) reactant
    (B) product
    (C) molecule
    (D) chemical

34. An object at rest
    (A) releases heat energy.
    (B) will stay at rest.
    (C) contains no potential energy.
    (D) cannot move with very slight force.

35. A substance with a pH of 3 is
    (A) more acidic than a substance with a pH of 10.
    (B) less acidic than a substance with a pH of 1.
    (C) a base.
    (D) none of the above.

36. How many atoms of hydrogen are in the chemical compound $H_2 Pr_5 I_{10}$?
    (A) 2
    (B) 7
    (C) 10
    (D) 17

37. What is the term for a change from a solid state directly to a gas state?
    (A) condensation
    (B) evaporation
    (C) sublimation
    (D) deposition

38. What type of energy is stored in the bonds of chemical compounds?
    (A) kinetic
    (B) thermal
    (C) chemical
    (D) nuclear

39. According to Newton's law of universal gravitation, what happens to the gravitational force between two objects if the distance between them is halved?
    (A) The force remains the same.
    (B) The force is halved.
    (C) The force is doubled.
    (D) The force is quadrupled.

40. How do you read H_2O as a chemical formula?
    (A) Two oxygen atoms for every hydrogen atom.
    (B) Two hydrogen atoms for every oxygen atom.
    (C) One hydrogen atom and two oxygen atoms.
    (D) One oxygen atom and one hydrogen atom.

Answers and Explanations

Use this answer key to score the physical science practice questions.

1. **D.** Energy is measured in joules (J) or calories (Cal). In case you were wondering, force is measured in newtons (N), which makes Choice (D) the one you should've picked.

2. **B.** A compass is a magnetized device that's attracted to the North Pole. Choice (B) is the correct answer.

3. **A.** Mass is a measurement of how much matter an object contains.

4. **A.** Matter can be a liquid, solid, or gas, which makes Choice (A) the only correct answer. The question asks which of the answer choices is *not* a state of matter. Ether is a class of chemicals.

5. **B.** Chemical reactions rearrange a substance's molecular structure. They don't require negative ions, or fire or water, so Choices (A) and (C) are wrong. They're not always dangerous, either, which rules out Choice (D).

6. **B.** Liquids have a definite volume, but they take the shape of their container. Solids have a definite shape and volume, whereas gases and plasma have neither a definite shape nor definite volume.

7. **D.** Plastic is a type of material (or a description of how a material deforms), but it is not a form of energy. Thermal is heat energy, sound is energy that travels through waves, and electric is energy caused by electrons' movement.

8. **D.** The amount of matter in an object is its mass, which stays the same whether the object is on Earth, floating in space, or compressed in a vacuum. (Weight is the force of gravity on an object, density is the mass per unit volume, and volume is the amount of space an object occupies.)

9. **C.** When iron rusts, its chemical composition changes. Boiling water, melting ice, and dissolving sugar in water are all physical changes that can be reversed and don't change the water's (or the sugar's) chemical composition.

10. **B.** When water droplets refract (bend) sunlight, a rainbow forms.

11. **C.** An element's atomic number indicates how many protons the element has and determines its place in the periodic table.

12. **C.** The electromagnetic spectrum measures radiation, from radio waves to gamma rays. It doesn't measure sound waves or only visible light, which makes Choices (A) and (B) wrong. Though rainbows do fall on the electromagnetic spectrum, they're only a tiny fraction of it (they're classified as visible light). Choice (C) is the correct answer. Be careful when you see an answer choice on the ASVAB that includes *only*, *always*, or *never*, because those answers are usually wrong.

13. **D.** Compounds are elements that have joined together by forming chemical bonds in specific ratios. Elements that are joined together in various ratios are considered mixtures, not compounds, so Choice (D) is the only correct answer.

14. **A.** Gases can, and do, evenly fill containers. The molecules in gases spread out after they're contained and don't pool at one end or another like those in a liquid do.

15. **A.** Hertz is the measure of frequency. A newton is a unit of force, a pascal is a unit of pressure, and a joule is a unit of energy.

16. **C.** A joule is the SI unit of work.

17. **C.** Opposites attract in magnetism (and in a few other areas of life). North and south poles attract each other, while like poles (north and north or south and south) repel each other. The Earth's gravity and magnetic field have nothing to do with magnets in this sense.

18. **B.** Conduction is the process where thermal energy is transferred from one particle to another in a solid through direct contact. If you were wondering, convection is the transfer of heat through fluids by particle movement, radiation is the transfer of energy through electromagnetic waves, and evaporation is the process of liquid turning into gas.

19. **D.** When a solid gains enough heat, its particles gain energy and become able to break free from their fixed positions — and that leads to the state change from solid to liquid that you see as melting.

20. **B.** Thermal equilibrium occurs when two objects are the same temperature and no heat flows between them.

21. **C.** The number of protons in the nucleus of an element's atoms determines its atomic number.

22. **D.** Hydrogen is the only element with one proton in its nucleus, which gives it an atomic number of 1. Helium's atomic number is 2, magnesium's is 12, and copper's is 29.

23. **C.** Newton's third law of motion says that for every action, there is an equal and opposite reaction.

24. **A.** An unbalanced force acting on a moving object causes the object to change speed, direction, or both.

25. **D.** Inertia is a resistance to change in motion; that means an object will resist changes to its state of rest or motion (whatever it's doing) unless an unbalanced force acts on it.

26. **D.** In a chemical formula, the subscript number indicates how many atoms of the preceding element are in the molecule. For example, in NO_2, the formula for nitrogen dioxide, the subscript 2 tells you that the molecule has two oxygen atoms.

27. **B.** The amount of kinetic energy (that is, motion energy) a particle has determines its state of matter. The size, number, and color of the particles don't have anything to do with whether something is a solid, liquid, or gas.

28. **C.** When you heat water in its liquid state, its molecules move more quickly and become more spread out — they turn into steam.

29. **B.** Pure water is neutral and falls right in the middle of the pH scale at 7.

30. **C.** When water reaches its boiling point, which is 100° Fahrenheit and 212° Celsius, its temperature stays the same. Above that point, it evaporates and becomes gas.

31. **B.** To determine how much force is exerted on an object, use the formula $\vec{F} = m\vec{a}$, where F represents force, *m* represents the object's mass, and *a* represents acceleration. Choice (B), which happens to be Newton's second law, is the right answer.

32. **A.** Hydrogen has an atomic number of 1. The atomic numbers for the other elements listed are 2 (helium), 3 (lithium), and 92 (uranium). The correct answer is Choice (A).

33. **B.** A *product* is a new element or molecule that results from a chemical reaction.

34. **B.** Newton's first law of motion says that an object at rest will stay at rest, and an object in motion will stay in motion with the same speed and in the same direction, unless acted upon by an unbalanced force.

35. **B.** The pH scale measures acids and bases. The lower a substance's pH is, the more acidic the substance is. The most acidic substances have a pH of 0; on the other end, the most basic substances have a pH of 14. Water has a pH of about 7.

36. **A.** The compound $H_2Pr_5I_{10}$ contains two hydrogen atoms. The small number in subscript immediately to the right of the H is what tells you how many atoms an element contains in a compound.

37. **C.** Sublimation is the process where a solid turns directly into a gas without becoming a liquid first.

38. **C.** Chemical energy is stored in the bonds of chemical compounds. Kinetic energy is the energy of motion, thermal is the energy of heat, and nuclear is stored in an atom's nucleus.

39. **D.** The force of gravity is inversely proportional to the square of the distance between the two objects. That means if the distance is halved, the gravitational force increases by a factor of four.

40. **B.** The chemical formula for water is H_2O, which says that for every oxygen atom, there are two hydrogen atoms.

IN THIS CHAPTER

» Rocking out with geology

» Storming through meteorology

» Digging into paleontology

» Spacing out among the stars

» Using language to solve science problems

Chapter 12
Earth and Space Sciences

Earth and space science — the two branches of science that deal with everything from the Earth's core to the farthest galaxies (and beyond) — are important if you want to ace the General Science subtest of the ASVAB. Whether you're going to shoot for the stars as a future astronaut in the Space Force or you want to be an Army meteorologist, this chapter is for you. The General Science subtest isn't used to calculate your Armed Forces Qualification Test (AFQT) score, which determines whether you're eligible to enlist in the military, but it does factor into several ASVAB line scores, such as General Maintenance (GM) and Skilled Technical (ST). Head to Chapter 2 to see which subtest scores feed into line scores so you know where to focus your study-time energy.

When you take the computerized version of the ASVAB, which most people do, you get 12 minutes to answer 15 General Science questions. If you're taking a General Science subtest with tryout questions, which I discuss in Chapter 1, you get 25 minutes to answer 30 questions. If you take the paper-and-pencil version, you have 11 minutes to answer 25 questions. Most new recruits find that they have time to spare after the General Science subtest, but if you're racing against the clock, use the tips for guessing I outline in Chapter 3.

If a high score on this subtest is on the horizon for you, but you still need more practice, check out *Geology For Dummies* by Alecia M. Spooner, *Weather For Dummies* by John D. Cox, *Archaeology For Dummies* by Nancy Marie White, and *Astronomy For Dummies* by Stephen P. Maran, PhD (all published by Wiley). You can also check out the free online flashcards that come with this book; just see the book's opening page for instructions on how to log in.

Staying Down to Earth with Geology

The study of the physical makeup of Earth is often called Earth science. *Geology* describes Earth's physical appearance and the processes that take place within it.

Peeling back the layers of the planet

Earth is like an onion in that it consists of several layers, which you can see in Figure 12-1. Scientists categorize Earth's layers by the elements and minerals found in each. The *crust* is Earth's surface, and there are two types: *continental,* which forms each of the continents and is about 12 miles thick, and *oceanic,* which lies beneath the oceans and is about 5 miles thick. The solid rock below the crust is the *mantle,* which accounts for about two-thirds of Earth's mass. The *core* is Earth's superheated, spinning metal center, and it has two parts: the inner core and the outer core. The *outer core* is about 1,800 miles (2,900 kilometers) below your feet, and the *inner core* is about 3,200 miles (5,200 kilometers) down.

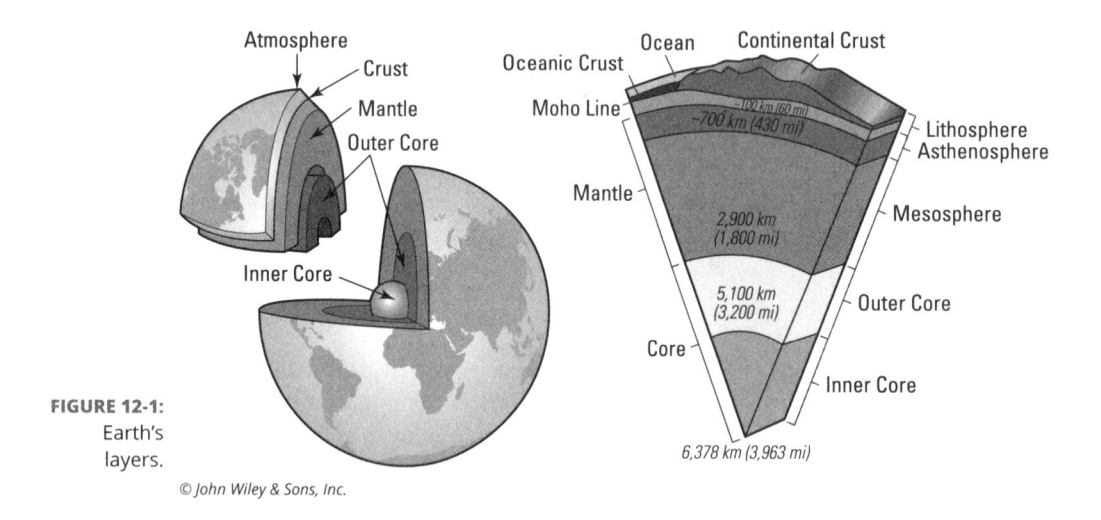

FIGURE 12-1: Earth's layers.

© John Wiley & Sons, Inc.

In 2023, *seismologists* — people who study earthquakes and seismic waves that travel through Earth — discovered that Earth's inner core may have its own core: the innermost inner core. In 2024, the Earth's core stopped spinning faster than the planet. It's now moving backward relative to the mantle in part of what scientists believe is a 70-year cycle.

Scientists haven't been able to sample the Earth's core, but based on experiments and interpretations, they believe the core is made from heavy metals, such as nickel and iron, and sulfur. Nobody can measure the inner or outer core's temperatures, but they're hot. *Geophysicists* — scientists who study Earth using gravity and magnetic, electrical, and seismic methods — estimate that the temperatures in Earth's core range between 8,000 degrees Fahrenheit and 10,000 degrees Fahrenheit. (For comparison, the sun's surface temperature is about 10,800 degrees Fahrenheit.)

Earth's outer core, which borders the mantle, is made of hot, liquid metal. It churns and sustains Earth's magnetic field. The inner core is even hotter, but it's not liquid. Even though the inner core's temperature is well above iron's melting point, the pressure is too great for the iron atoms to move into a liquid state.

Within the mantle, which is just outside the outer core, are rocks made of light elements and heavy elements. Scientists have classified the mantle into layers based on the composition of the elements in each and the way each responds to earthquakes. The layers of mantle are

> » **Mesosphere:** The *mesosphere* is located in the lower mantle, surrounding Earth's outer core. In the mesosphere, temperatures are high enough to melt rock, but a tremendous amount of pressure keeps all the materials solid.

- **Asthenosphere:** The *asthenosphere* is in the middle part of the mantle. The rocks there are solid, but they move like glaciers do. (It's called *plastic flow.*) The temperatures in the asthenosphere are still very high, which can lead to some melting.

- **Lithosphere:** The *lithosphere* is the uppermost part of Earth's mantle, and it's attached to the crust. The rocks in the lithosphere are solid, thick, and brittle, like the crust, but they're not officially part of the crust because they're made from different minerals than the crust is.

Sedimentary, metamorphic, and igneous rocks

Geologists classify rocks into three major categories: sedimentary, metamorphic, and igneous.

- **Sedimentary:** Formed by sediment (such as particles of sand, seashells, and other materials), *sedimentary* rocks "grow" in layers. Over a long period of time, sediment hardens — but it's still considered soft, as far as rocks go. This type of rock most often contains the fossils I discuss later in this chapter.

- **Metamorphic:** *Metamorphic* rocks form because of the heat and pressure below Earth's surface. These rocks sometimes have shiny crystals inside them and may form layers that look like ribbons, such as marble and gneiss.

- **Igneous:** *Magma,* the super-heated molten rock simmering below Earth's crust and above its mantle, collects in pockets called *magma chambers* beneath volcanoes that eventually erupt. (It's ultra-hot — between 1,000 degrees Fahrenheit and 3,000 degrees Fahrenheit.) When magma comes out through a volcano, it's lava. Cooled lava forms *igneous* rocks. Magma that cools quickly is shiny and glasslike; when it cools slowly, crystals can form. Obsidian and granite are types of igneous rock.

What's shakin'? A word on earthquakes

Earthquakes are usually, but not always, caused by rock underground breaking along a *fault* — the space between Earth's *tectonic plates.* Tectonic plates have rough edges that push against each other, but they don't move until the pressure causes one to break, slide past, or slide under the other. Pressure can build for hundreds of years, producing a huge earthquake when the plates finally move. This sudden release of energy causes seismic waves that make the ground shake. Figure 12-2 shows the three major types of faults in Earth's crust.

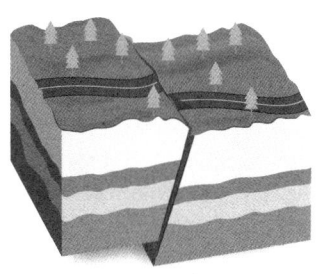

FIGURE 12-2: Types of faults.

Reverse fault   Normal fault   Strike-slip fault

© John Wiley & Sons, Inc.

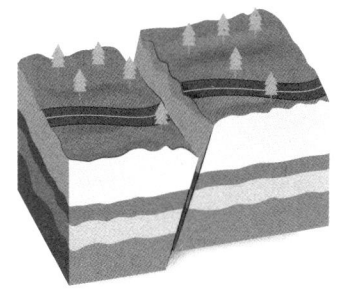

> ### HAPPY BIRTHDAY, PLANET EARTH
>
> Earth itself is about 4.54 billion years old, which scientists determined by studying the oldest mineral grains on Earth (tiny zirconium silicate crystals that are at least 4.3 billion years old), the moon, and Earth's other celestial neighbors, where there are no magma recycling rocks. Samples from the moon show it's between 4.4 and 4.5 billion years old, and samples of meteorites that fell to Earth from space are 4.5 billion years old. (The Earth is less than half the age of the Milky Way galaxy, whose last birthday brought it up to about 13.2 billion years old, and the rest of the universe, which is 13.8 billion years old.)

The *Richter magnitude scale* is a mathematical formula that scientists use to compare the size of earthquakes. Because it's based on a logarithm, each whole-number increase on the scale represents a quake ten times larger and releasing 31 times more energy than the next lowest whole number. Earthquakes can strike anywhere, at any time, but geologists have identified three zones where they usually occur: the Pacific Rim, the Alpide seismic belt (it extends from Java to Sumatra, running through the Himalayas and the Mediterranean), and the mid-Atlantic ridge, which is underwater. Scientists have never put an upper limit on the scale, but the largest earthquake ever recorded occurred about 100 miles off the coast of Chile on May 22, 1960. It registered as a magnitude 9.5 and caused an 80-foot tsunami, destroying cities all along the coast.

Sinking or Swimming: Oceanography

Oceanography, as you may have guessed, involves studying the ocean's physical and biological properties. You may be surprised to discover that Earth has only one global ocean, which covers nearly 71 percent of the planet and holds 96.5 percent of the planet's water. Scientists have divided the ocean it into five named oceans — the Atlantic, Pacific, Indian, Arctic, and Southern — to make keeping track of regions easier.

Oceanographers look at temperatures, rising and falling levels, sea creatures, ecosystems, chemical makeup, and the geologic frameworks that make the ocean, well, the ocean.

Because of its massive size, scientists have explored only about 5 percent of the global ocean, but it's the main driving force of Earth. It's often responsible for weather, regulates temperature, and supports all living organisms. It distributes heat around the planet after absorbing it near the equator, and it feeds into the rains that crops need. The ocean is also home to a tremendous amount of biodiversity (see Chapter 10 for more about why that's so important) and ensures that life on the third rock from the sun can continue.

Filling the ocean, one drop at a time

Earth didn't automatically come with an ocean. In fact, when the planet first formed, it was much hotter and looked much different than it does today. For the first 500 million years of its existence, Earth was bombarded by massive, crater-causing asteroids and comets that carried ice, which is abundant throughout the solar system. Earth was also a literal hotbed of volcanic activity. About 4.4 billion years ago, when Earth's surface cooled below water's boiling point, water vapor from the volcanoes, asteroids, and comets condensed, raining down and creating the first ocean.

This *primordial* ocean had a different chemical composition, geology, geography, and temperature than the seas have today. Back then, tremendous land masses called *supercontinents* emerged and broke apart, changing the Earth (and everything on it) forever thanks to the continuous movement of Earth's tectonic plates. See the earlier section "What's shakin'? A word on earthquakes" to discover how these movers and shakers impact the planet's surface.

TECHNICAL STUFF

Primeval seas — oceans in Earth's early history — were probably only a *little* salty. The modern global ocean has an average salinity of 35 parts per thousand. That means about 3.5 percent of its weight is composed of dissolved salts that mostly come from rocks on land. Here's how it happens: When rain falls, it contains some dissolved carbon dioxide from the air; that makes it slightly acidic. That slightly acidic rain erodes rock, and runoff from rivers and streams carries salts and minerals into the ocean.

Swirling around the currents

Ocean water moves constantly, and that movement affects nearly every process on Earth. *Currents* are continuous, directed movements that flow locally and globally. Wind, water density, tide, and coastal and sea floor features all contribute to the way currents move. Ocean currents in the Northern Hemisphere veer to the right, and those in the Southern Hemisphere veer to the left. Oceanographers divide ocean currents into the following two categories:

- **Surface currents:** *Surface ocean currents* are driven by global wind. The wind, which is fueled by solar energy, causes these currents to transfer heat from the *tropics* (the region on and around the equator) to the polar regions (the geographic North and South Poles). The *Gulf Stream,* a strong current that originates in the warm Caribbean and Gulf of Mexico, moves north, carrying about 150 times more water than the Amazon River does. It extends up the Atlantic coast of the United States and Canada, flowing all the way to Europe. The Gulf Stream loses heat on its way north; Florida has a warmer climate in winter than Maine or Alaska does. If not for the Gulf Stream's warm water, though, England would also have a much colder climate.

- **Deep currents:** *Deep ocean currents* result from different water temperatures and *salinity* (the amount of salt in the water). In cold areas, like the Norwegian Sea, ocean water loses heat to the atmosphere, and it becomes cold and dense. And when ocean water freezes, forming sea ice, it leaves salt behind. That makes the surrounding water become saltier and denser, which causes it to sink to the bottom. Surface water flows in to replace it, and the cycle repeats; the surface water becomes cold and saltier, and it sinks, too. The colder, saltier water moves south, traveling past the equator and down to Antarctica. The cold water returns to the surface thanks to winds that cause *upwelling* (which happens when wind pushes surface water away and cold water rises up to replace it) and to mixing with warmer water.

This whole system of deep ocean and surface currents is called the *global ocean conveyor belt*, and it circulates water all over Earth.

Making waves in the atmosphere

Because the global ocean makes up 71 percent of Earth's surface and holds about 97 percent of the planet's water, it absorbs most of the solar energy that reaches Earth. The waters at the *equator* — the invisible belt halfway between the North and South Poles — receive more of that energy than the rest of the planet does because the sun's rays hit Earth at about a 90-degree angle there. In other locations, it must travel at an angle (and through more atmosphere) before hitting Earth's surface.

TECHNICAL STUFF

Earth's atmosphere absorbs some of the sun's ultraviolet radiation, but at the equator, the light has to travel through less atmosphere. That's why the sun's UV rays are more intense there and you're likely to tan or burn faster in tropical regions closer to the equator.

The ocean stores solar radiation as heat. Warm water that's concentrated around the equator evaporates into the air, which increases temperature and humidity; that forms rain and storms, which are carried by trade winds. *Trade winds* are very predictable; they blow from the northeast in the Northern Hemisphere and the southeast in the Southern Hemisphere. The atmosphere prevents most of Earth's heat from escaping after the sun goes down. (Head to the later section "Outta This World: Checking the Atmosphere" for more on the atmosphere in general.)

The ocean stores about 91 percent of the excess heat energy trapped in Earth's climate system. Since the 1990s, the global ocean's temperature has increased significantly, causing more precipitation in wet areas and longer droughts in dry areas, stronger storms (including hurricanes), coral bleaching, melting glaciers and ice sheets, and even an increase in diseases for marine species.

Tugging on the moon with tides

Earth and the moon exert gravity on each other. The moon's gravitational pull causes the ocean to bulge out in two places: the side closest to the moon and the side farthest from it. The bulges create high tides, and low tides occur at the low points away from the bulges. Earth rotates, so its landmasses pass through the bulges and low points twice a day, which is why most shorelines experience high tides about every 12 hours with low tides on 12-hour schedules right between them.

Diving into basins, coasts, and estuaries

Scientists in the U.S. recognize five *ocean basins*, the Arctic, Atlantic, Indian, Pacific, and Southern. These basins are large, bowl-shaped depressions in Earth's surface that happen to be filled with water, and their features look a lot like what you see on land: mountains, plains, hills, valleys and trenches, and even volcanoes. The ocean is at its shallowest on *continental shelves* — the areas just off shorelines, which can stretch for miles or be very short. The deepest part of the ocean is the Mariana Trench, measuring nearly 7 miles deep.

Coasts, also called *shores*, are the areas where the land and oceans meet. They can include rocky shores, salt marshes, mangrove forests, and sandy beaches. The ocean's power changes shorelines every day through wave energy, sediment, storms, and erosion. *Estuaries*, also called *bays*, *lagoons*, and *sounds*, are where freshwater rivers and streams meet the sea. The salty ocean mixes with the fresh water to create *brackish* water. Chesapeake Bay is one example of an estuary; during the end of the last ice age, massive glaciers retreated. The Atlantic Ocean filled in the area around the Susquehanna River, drowning the river's mouth and creating brackish water as the two bodies mixed.

TECHNICAL STUFF

If you wanted to climb the tallest mountain on Earth, you wouldn't go to Mt. Everest. You'd start at the bottom of the Pacific's sea floor, where the base of Mauna Kea is. This volcanic mountain on Hawaii's Big Island is about 13,800 feet (about 2.6 miles) above sea level, but it starts 19,700 feet (roughly 3.7 miles) below the ocean's surface. Altogether, Mauna Kea measures 33,500 feet (a little under 6.4 miles) from base to summit.

Outta This World: Checking the Atmosphere

The atmosphere contains many layers of gases surrounding Earth's surface, and it's about 300 miles thick — although most of it is located within 10 miles of the surface. Starting with the layer closest to Earth and extending outward, Table 12-1 names those layers.

TABLE 12-1 Layers of Earth's Atmosphere

Layer Name	Location	Details
Troposphere	Extends between 6 and 12 miles above Earth and is higher at the equator than it is at the poles	This layer is where the jet stream (fast-flowing, narrow air currents) is located and where almost all weather changes occur.
Stratosphere	Extends about 30 miles	A major reported cause of ozone depletion is the presence of chlorofluorocarbons (CFCs) in Earth's stratosphere. CFCs undergo a series of chain reactions, which ultimately lead to the destruction of the ozone layer.
Mesosphere	Extends about 50 miles	Millions of meteors burn up daily in the mesosphere as a result of collisions with the gas particles contained there.
Ionosphere	Extends about 70 miles	This layer reflects most radio waves, making it important to communications. *Note:* Scientists disagree among themselves as to whether the ionosphere is a separate atmospheric layer or whether it's part of the thermosphere.
Thermosphere	Extends about 350 miles	The International Space Station has a stable orbit within the upper part of the thermosphere, between 208 and 285 miles up.
Exosphere	Extends about 6,200 miles	It's only from the exosphere that atmospheric gases, atoms, and molecules can escape into outer space. No boundary exists between the exosphere and space; therefore, *exosphere* is sometimes used synonymously with *outer space*.

Gases in the atmosphere

The entire atmosphere is made from a variety of gases — trace amounts of neon, helium, krypton (you can find that element on the periodic table in Chapter 11), methane, and hydrogen, as well as the following compositions:

- **Nitrogen:** 78 percent
- **Oxygen:** 21 percent
- **Argon:** 0.93 percent
- **Carbon dioxide:** 0.04 percent

Each of these gases has its own place in the atmosphere, and they need to stay in balance to keep things running smoothly down here on the surface. Methane, which is only supposed to be around in small amounts, is a major contributor to climate change. Scientists call it a "feedback loop" and say that methane hydrate being released from glacier deposits warms the atmosphere. The warming causes additional glacial melt, which releases even more methane, and the loop continues. All this methane is speeding up the warming of the planet. Carbon dioxide is on the rise, too, because there aren't enough plants and trees to keep up with human CO_2 output. (Chapter 10 has information on how plants pull CO_2 from the air.)

The magnetosphere: A polarizing force

Earth's *magnetosphere* is a globe of space around the planet that's controlled by the planet's *magnetic field*. It's not part of the atmosphere, but it's important because it deflects solar wind, which I discuss in "Where Few Have Gone Before: Astronomy" later in this chapter. Earth's magnetic field is invisible, but because Earth's core is made from iron and other hot, liquid metals that create electrical currents, it's there — and its protective forces come out of the Southern Hemisphere (where the magnetic South Pole is) and travel back into the planet in the Northern Hemisphere (where the magnetic North Pole is). Figure 12-3 shows how the magnetosphere works.

FIGURE 12-3: The magnetosphere.

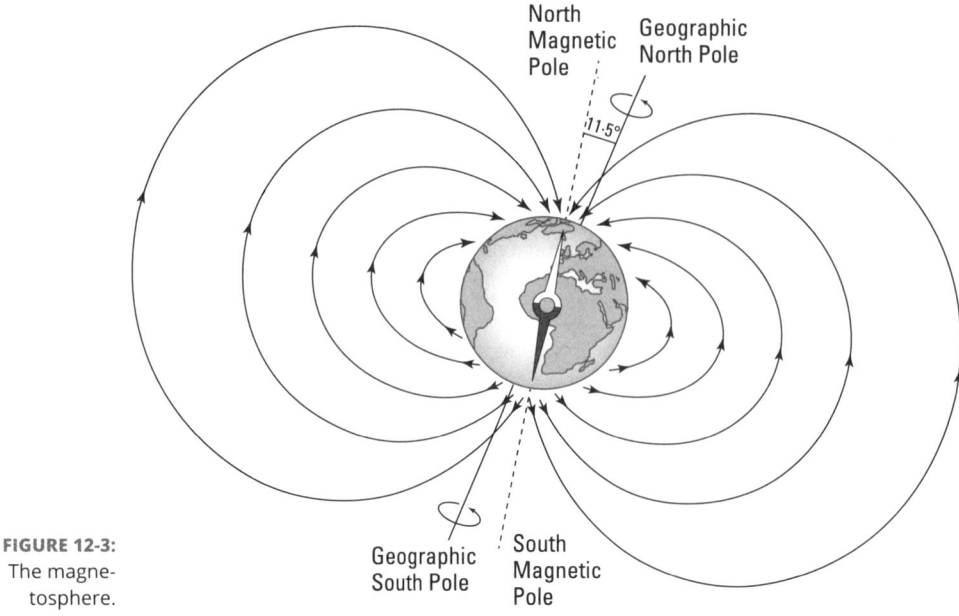

© John Wiley & Sons, Inc.

Warming up to cold fronts

Most weather events take place in the troposphere, where you're sitting right now. This layer of atmosphere begins on Earth's surface and extends between 6 and 12 miles up. Air is warmest near ground-level in the bottom of the troposphere, and it becomes colder at higher levels; that's why you can sometimes see snow on the peaks of big mountains in the summer and why jets leave white trails, called *contrails*, in the sky. The hot, humid exhaust from jets' engines mixes with the atmosphere, and the water vapor in the exhaust condenses or freezes.

When the sun shines, land and water absorb its warmth. Land warms up more quickly than large bodies of water do, so air over land is warmer than air over water during most of the day. At night, the air over land cools more quickly than air over water does.

Temperature affects *air density* (how closely packed the air molecules are). Cold air is denser than warm air. Because it's denser, cold air has high pressure, compared to warm air's low pressure. (A *barometer* measures atmospheric pressure.) Air moves from areas of high pressure to areas of low pressure, creating wind. The angle of the sun also affects air density (the sun shines directly over the equator but not the poles).

Air masses have certain characteristics depending on where they form:

>> If an air mass forms over land, it's dry, and if it forms over water, it's wet.

>> Air masses formed in Earth's northern and southern regions are cold, and those formed at the equator are warm.

When two different air masses meet, they don't mix. They form a boundary called a *front*. When cold air meets warm air, a *cold front* develops. The warm air may be pushed up to form clouds, causing heavy rain. When a warm air mass meets a cold air mass, a *warm front* develops. The warm air passes over the cold air, forming a different kind of cloud, which causes light rain.

We're not in Kansas anymore: Understanding what causes extreme weather events

The weather on Earth varies from day to day, but scientists agree that the world is falling victim to more adverse weather events than it used to because the planet is warming. Areas closer to the equator have fewer extremes than those between the equator and the poles do, but extreme weather events, such as tornadoes, hurricanes, tsunamis, blizzards, and dust storms, can occur at any time in any place. Since scientists began measuring temperature in the 1880s, the Earth's global average surface temperature has increased by 2 degrees, and though that doesn't seem like a big deal (what's a couple of degrees in either direction?), it's causing more severe heat waves, drought, and wildfires each year.

Natural weather cycles are the reason we experience many adverse weather events, but they're made more extreme because of Earth's temperature increase. As the oceans become warmer, they evaporate more. *Evapotranspiration,* the measure of the rate at which plants and the land release moisture into the air, has increased by about 10 percent since 2003. Water vapor, which is a greenhouse gas, amplifies the warming effect — so Earth is caught in a cycle that's affecting the whole planet's climate.

Keeping track of weather patterns

Meteorologists predict the weather with a number of tools, including weather balloons, radar systems, ocean buoys, sensors, satellites, and computer models that rely on past data. Often, the best meteorologists can do is make predictions about what is most likely to happen; too many unpredictable variables can come into play and sweep away a thunderstorm or usher in a tornado.

Climate scientists use the data that meteorologists collect to track weather over specific periods of time. These weather patterns are what make up Earth's *climate.* The National Oceanic and Atmospheric Administration (NOAA) and several international agencies look at the patterns of the past to watch for changes in atmospheric conditions and the relationships between the ocean, land, and sun. They look at air chemistry, temperatures, precipitation and cloud cover, and wind today and compare it with data from the past to create an accurate picture of what's happening on Earth. Climate scientists also study *paleoclimate* — prehistoric climate clues they obtain from natural records such as fossils, coral skeletons, sediment, and glaciers — to create longer-term models of the planet's climate patterns.

REMEMBER

Weather is different from climate. The term *weather* refers to daily atmospheric conditions, while *climate* refers to patterns in weather over time (usually 30 years or more). Weather fluctuates — sometimes it's 30 degrees Fahrenheit and sometimes it's 110 degrees Fahrenheit — and the term only refers to the weather you can see, feel, and remember in the recent past. Climate is an average pattern of weather across the whole Earth or in a specific region. For example, Alaska has a colder climate than Florida does, and Earth's overall climate is warmer now than it was a hundred years ago.

Classifying clouds

Clouds are made from small droplets of water or bits of ice that are spread out from each other. Rain (or snow) falls when the drops get too big and heavy to stay in the cloud. Clouds have three main types, and the ASVAB may ask you a question or two about their characteristics, which I detail in Table 12-2.

TABLE 12-2 Types of Clouds

Cloud Type	Description	What It Forecasts
Cirrus	Thin, wispy, high clouds that usually form between altitudes of 20,000 feet and 40,000 feet	Cirrus clouds generally indicate rain or snow in the near future, when they thicken and lower, becoming other types of clouds.
Cumulus	White, puffy pillows, often flat-bottomed with rounded tops that usually form at altitudes between 1,000 and 5,000 feet	Cumulus clouds are common during fair weather, but when they gather, they cause heavy rains.
Stratus	Broad, flat, and low-hanging (gray blanket) clouds that usually form below 2,000 feet but sometimes form as high as 4,000 feet	If close to the ground, stratus clouds may produce drizzle.

Additionally, the cloud name frequently includes a prefix or suffix to indicate which level of the atmosphere the cloud is in or whether it's producing *precipitation* (rain, sleet, snow, and the like):

» *Cirro-* is the prefix given to high clouds (base above 20,000 feet).

» *Alto-* is the prefix given to midlevel clouds (base between 6,000 and 20,000 feet).

» *Nimbo-* added to the beginning of a cloud name or *-nimbus* added to the end means the cloud is producing precipitation.

Therefore, a *cirrocumulus* cloud is a white, puffy, flat-bottomed, rounded-topped cloud at high altitude. *Altostratus* clouds are gray, broad, flat clouds at mid-altitude.

Weather can manifest in significant and potentially devasting storms. *Thunderstorms* form when air masses with different pressure collide, resulting in rain, lightning, wind, hail and tornadoes. *Tornadoes* are intense, rotating air columns that can feature wind speeds between 73 and 318 miles per hour. *Hurricanes* and *cyclones* are rotating, organized weather systems that originate over tropical and subtropical waters. These powerful storms can release as much energy as 10,000 nuclear weapons would — and people can't create or control them.

Figuring out temperature conversions

When you think of temperature, you may think of the Fahrenheit and Celsius scales, which measure temperatures in degrees. Scientists actually use three different scales to report temperature:

» **Fahrenheit (°F):** This scale is more common in the United States. On the Fahrenheit scale, water freezes at 32 degrees Fahrenheit and boils at 212 degrees Fahrenheit.

» **Celsius or Centigrade (°C):** This scale is the metric standard worldwide. On the Celsius scale, the freezing point for water is 0 degrees Celsius, and the boiling point for water is 100 degrees Celsius.

» **Kelvin (K):** Scientists have theorized that the coldest anything can get is –273.15 degrees Celsius. They believe that at this temperature, molecular motion would stop. That's pretty darn cold! This temperature, often called *absolute zero,* is assigned the number 0 on the Kelvin scale (with the units the same size as degrees on the Celsius scale). On this scale, the freezing point of water is 273.15 K, and the boiling point is 373.15 K.

The word *degrees* isn't used when stating temperature in kelvins. Scientists who work with thermodynamics, such as physicists and astronomers, measure temperature using kelvins. For instance, the surface temperature of planets is always stated in kelvins.

REMEMBER: An ASVAB question may ask you to convert temperatures from one scale to another, so here are some formulas to commit to memory (C stands for the temperature in degrees Celsius, and F is the temperature in degrees Fahrenheit):

- To convert from Celsius to Fahrenheit, use this formula:

  $$F = \frac{9}{5}C + 32$$

- To convert from Fahrenheit to Celsius, use the following formula:

  $$C = \frac{5}{9}(F - 32)$$

- To get temperatures in the Kelvin scale, add 273.15 degrees to the Celsius temperature:

  $$K = C + 273.15$$

  To go from kelvins to degrees Celsius, do the opposite: Subtract 273.15 from the Kelvin temperature. Then you can convert the Celsius temperature to Fahrenheit if you want to.

TIP: Here's a quick temperature conversion system that may be easier to remember. (*Note:* This process only works with Celsius and Fahrenheit.)

1. **Add 40 to the temperature you want to convert.**
2. **Multiply this sum by $\frac{5}{9}$ if converting from Fahrenheit to Celsius or $\frac{9}{5}$ if converting from Celsius to Fahrenheit.**
3. **Subtract the 40 you added at the beginning to yield the result.**

TIP: An easy way to remember whether to use $\frac{9}{5}$ or $\frac{5}{9}$ in the conversion is to associate the *f* in *Fahrenheit* with *Fraction* ($\frac{5}{9}$ is a proper fraction); similarly, $\frac{9}{5}$ can be *Converted* to a mixed number $\left(1\frac{4}{5}\right)$ — *c* is for *convert* and *Celsius*.

Paleontology: Can You Dig It?

Paleontologists — scientists who, in general, study fossil animals and plants — spend plenty of time working in a variety of subdisciplines, including these:

- **Invertebrate paleontology:** These paleontologists study invertebrate animal fossils, such as mollusks, brachiopods, and arthropods (like crabs, shrimp, and barnacles).

- **Vertebrate paleontology:** Is that a wooly mammoth or a tyrannosaurus rex? Vertebrate paleontologists can tell you. These scientists study vertebrate fossils, including fish and mammals.

- **Human paleontology:** Comparing anatomy between the apelike creatures that preceded humans and dating paleohuman (prehistoric) remains is a job for human paleontologists. This field is a little similar to the field of anthropology called paleoanthropology, which studies human culture, society, and biology.

- **Paleobotany:** These not-quite-garden-variety paleontologists deal with fossil plants to study their evolutionary history.

- **Micropaleontology:** Armed with microscopes and other tools, micropaleontologists study microscopic fossils from the ocean floor and all over land. Micropaleontology is the largest discipline within paleontology because the microorganisms these scientists study are so abundant.

- **Palynology:** Sifting through archaeological and geological deposits to study pollen grains and other spores is just another day at the office for a paleontologist who focuses on palynology.

- **Taphonomy:** Scientists who study taphonomy are looking at the process of how organisms decay and become fossils.

- **Ichnology:** Ichnology is a branch in several scientific disciplines (including biology and geology), but paleontologists who focus on it study fossil tracks, footprints, and trails.

- **Paleoecology:** Paleontologists who study paleoecology investigate the relationships between ancient organisms and their responses to changing environments.

Plants, germs, dinosaurs, and humans

No matter which area a paleontologist focuses on, they're looking at fossils, the fossil record, and data about how Earth and its inhabitants operated and evolved in the past. Sure, the scientists who dig up dinosaur bones get the most attention, but paleontologists all over the world are uncovering history's mysteries each day. Many paleontologists are also evolutionary biologists who study the origin, development, and evolution in species over time. The oldest fossils on Earth are more than 3.5 billion years old, so these scientists have plenty of time periods to choose from when they're evaluating these rock-like formations.

Studying the past with today's tools

Paleontologists use fossil remains and data from other sources to understand different aspects of extinct and living organisms. Using just one well-preserved fossil, a scientist might learn when an organism lived (and in what type of environment), what it consumed for food, and even how it died. Other fossils that contain whole fossilized specimens, such as amber, can hold the keys to a more complete picture of an organism's life cycle. Paleontologists look at the big picture, too, by evaluating sites where there are thousands of skeletons and fossils, to determine whether prehistoric animals traveled and lived in herds.

Table 12-3 shows Earth's many eras and why they cover specific time periods. Like the Linnaean taxonomic system I describe in Chapter 10, Earth's geologic eras are broken into large groups called *eons*, subgroups called *eras*, and very specific windows of history called *periods*.

Modern innovations allow paleontologists to learn more than ever about fossilized remains. Using neutron tomography, photogrammetry, microscopes, X-rays, lasers, MRIs, and CT scans, paleontologists can put data into computer models to create two- and three-dimensional visions of organisms to better understand them. These scientists also use techniques such as radiometric dating, stratigraphic dating, and index fossils to determine how old fossils are.

What fossils tell us

Fossils are like windows into the past. Some fossils are found in groups, which let paleontologists know that there were clusters of plants or animals living or traveling together. Others, like amber, trap and preserve ancient specimens (even air) that scientists can use to learn about prehistoric conditions. Fossils can also provide evidence of some organisms' evolution — that happens when paleontologists find fossils of extinct animals that are closely related to modern animals (including humans). Climatologists, anthropologists, and other scientists also use fossils to learn about changes in Earth's climate over time and cultures that existed in the past.

TABLE 12-3 **Earth's Geologic Eras**

Eon	Era	Period	What Occurred
Phanerozoic (540 million years ago–today)	Cenozoic	Quaternary (1.8 million years ago–today)	First humans, mammoths, mastodons, and saber-toothed cats lived
		Neogene (24 million years ago–1.8 million years ago)	Australopithecus appears; first sheep, cattle, modern whales, bears, mice, rats, apes, monkeys, dogs, and modern birds appear
		Paleogene (65 million years ago–24 million years ago)	First deer, cats, pigs, rhinos, elephants, horses, owls, hedgehogs, and rabbits evolve
	Mesozoic	Cretaceous (146 million years ago–65 million years ago)	First flowering plants, snakes, and crocodilians appear; mass extinction kills off dinosaurs
		Jurassic (208 million years ago–146 million years ago)	Dinosaurs roamed Earth; first birds appear
		Triassic (245 million years ago–208 million years ago)	First dinosaurs, mammals, frogs, turtles, and crocodyliforms appear
	Paleozoic	Permian (280 million years ago–245 million years ago)	Sail-back reptiles appear; amphibians are abundant; Pangea forms; ends with mass extinction
		Carboniferous (360 million years ago–280 million years ago)	First reptiles and winged insects appear
		Devonian (408 million years ago–360 million years ago)	First amphibians, sharks, bony fish, and spiders appear
		Silurian (438 million years ago–408 million years ago)	First insects and vascular plants appear on land
		Ordovician (505 million years ago–438 million years ago)	First land plants, corals, and nautiloids appear; ends with mass extinction
		Cambrian (540 million years ago–505 million years ago)	First shellfish, primitive fish, and mollusks appear
Proterozoic (2.5 billion years ago–540 million years ago)		Vendian (600 million years ago–540 million years ago)	First sponges and multicelled animals appear; Supercontinent Rodinia is formed
		Early Proterozoic (2.5 billion years ago–600 million years ago)	Oxygen builds up on Earth and the first life appears

Dating a caveman

If you visualize Earth's history as a 24-hour clock, modern humans didn't arrive until a little after 11:58 p.m. (that's 23:58 in military time, which you become very familiar with after you pass the ASVAB). Scientists can determine when the first apelike creatures appeared (which eventually evolved into humans over a 6-million-year period) based on where the fossils are found, the tools and other evidence found near or with the fossils, and what the fossils themselves contain. The earliest hominid (humanlike species) has been dated at 4.4 million years old, although other, older species have been identified and may eventually be classified as hominids.

Scientists use dozens of methods to determine the ages of fossils, but some of the most important are

- **Radiometric dating:** This technique involves observing the natural decay of radioactive elements.
- **Relative dating:** This technique involves evaluating the layers of sediments and rock in which the fossil was found; some layers and types of rock are older than others are, so scientists compare what they already know to what they find.
- **Paleomagnetism:** This method compares magnetic particles in sediment layers, which can be used for relative dating, to known worldwide shifts in the Earth's magnetic field.
- **Biochronology:** Animal fossils can often be dated by comparing them to other, well-dated species.

Where Few Have Gone Before: Astronomy

Earth's solar system is only a tiny part of its galaxy, the Milky Way. The Milky Way alone has a few hundred billion stars and planets. It's part of what astronomers call the *Local Group of Galaxies*, which are our neighbors in space. Beyond that, the Virgo Cluster is the closest group of galaxies (but it's about 54 million light-years away). There are tremendous *superclusters* (groups of many individual groups of galaxies) past that, and astronomers have even discovered *Great Walls* — light-years upon light-years of superclusters. Quite a bit of the universe is considered a cosmic void, though, with few detectable galaxies.

Because the space between most of the objects in the galaxy (and beyond) is so large, astronomers measure in light-years and astronomical units (AU). A *light-year* is a unit of astronomical distance equivalent to the distance that light travels in one year, which is nearly 6 trillion miles. One AU measures a distance of about 93 million miles, the average distance from Earth to the sun, which translates into about 8 *light-minutes*.

Taking a bite out of the Milky Way

The Milky Way galaxy (shown in Figure 12-4) doesn't have a rich, creamy center, but it does have a supermassive black hole called Sagittarius A, and all the stars, planets, asteroids, and other matter in the galaxy are spiraling around it.

Earth's solar system, which takes up only a fraction of the Milky Way galaxy, consists of the sun and a number of smaller bodies (such as planets, the planets' moons, and asteroids) that the sun's mass holds in orbit. The sun's mass creates gravity, and this gravity controls the movements of the smaller bodies.

Taking a quick glimpse at the sun

The sun is the largest and most important object in our solar system. It's a yellow dwarf star that contains 99.8 percent of the solar system's mass (quantity of matter). The sun provides most of the heat, light, and other energy that makes life possible. It's huge; the distance from the sun's center to its surface (the sun's radius) is about 109 times the radius of Earth. (To visualize this, hold a dime up to a jumbo beach ball.)

FIGURE 12-4: The Milky Way galaxy.

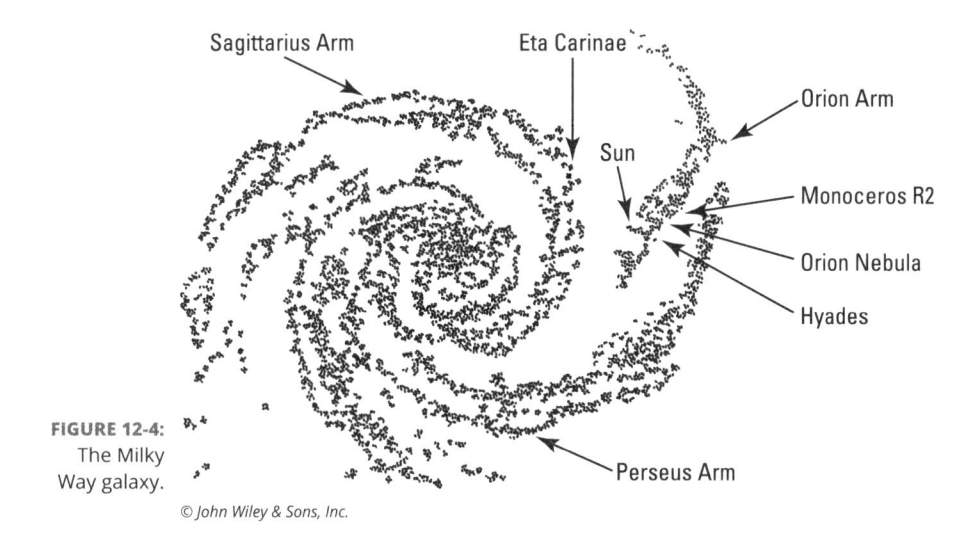

© John Wiley & Sons, Inc.

The sun's heat comes from its gravity and mass. All the matter is being pulled to the sun's core, where there's tremendous pressure — so much pressure that nuclear fusion takes place there, changing hydrogen to helium. Nuclear fusion produces tons of energy, released as light and heat over long periods of time.

The sun's outer layers are hot and stormy. Some of the streams of gas rising from the solar surface are even larger than Earth's diameter. The hot gases and electrically charged particles in those layers continually stream into space and often burst out in solar eruptions. This flow of gases and particles forms the *solar wind*, which bathes everything in the solar system.

TECHNICAL STUFF

At about 4.6 billion years old, the sun is nearly halfway through its life. When it runs out of nuclear fuel — its hydrogen — and the nuclear fusion turns off, it will begin to contract. The sun will become a red giant, shedding its outer layers in a massive push that will engulf Mercury, Venus, and Earth as it swells to about 150 times its present size. Gravity will reignite the sun's nuclear fusion process, but only for a short time; the sun will briefly become about 2,100 times brighter than it is now until it collapses again. Finally, it'll turn into a white dwarf and fizzle out.

Perusing the planets

A *planet* is a celestial body larger than an asteroid or comet, illuminated by light from a star that the planet revolves around (the planet doesn't emit its own light). The solar system consists of eight planets and five known dwarf planets. In order from closest to the sun to farthest from the sun, they are Mercury, Venus, Earth, Mars, Jupiter, Saturn, Uranus, and Neptune. (The five identified dwarf planets are Pluto, Ceres, Eris, Haumea, and Makemake, but NASA says the solar system may contain dozens that haven't been classified yet.)

Earth's orbit

Earth revolves around the sun in an oval-shaped pattern called an ellipse. Every $365\frac{1}{4}$ days, Earth completes its orbit around the sun and starts again. Earth rotates (spins) on its axis, completing a rotation every 24 hours. Because of Earth's tilt at a 23.5-degree angle, hours of daylight and darkness aren't equal, except for on two days a year. There are four important days during each revolution:

>> **Vernal equinox:** The first day of spring — the *vernal equinox* — is the day the sun crosses from south of the equator to north of it.

CHAPTER 12 **Earth and Space Sciences** 263

>> **Summer solstice:** *Summer solstice* is the day the sun reaches the farthest point north on the *ecliptic* (the path the sun takes each year).

>> **Autumnal equinox:** The sun crosses the equator toward the south and kicks off fall on the *autumnal equinox*.

>> **Winter solstice:** *Winter solstice* is the day the sun is as far south as possible on the ecliptic.

Planetary composition

The inner (first) four planets consist chiefly of iron and rock. They're known as the *terrestrial* (earthlike) planets because they're somewhat similar in size and composition. The outer planets, known as *Jovian* (Jupiter-like) planets, are giant worlds with thick, gaseous outer layers. Almost all their mass consists of hydrogen and helium, giving them compositions more like that of the sun than of Earth. Beneath their outer layers, the giant planets have no known solid surfaces. The pressure of their thick atmospheres turns their insides liquid, though they may have rocky cores.

Rings of dust, rock, and ice chunks encircle all the giant planets. Saturn's rings are the most familiar, but thin rings also surround Jupiter, Uranus, and Neptune.

To the Kuiper Belt and beyond

The Kuiper Belt, a region beyond Neptune and about 50 astronomical units from the sun, contains about 100,000 icy bodies, and it's where Pluto hangs out. Astronomers believe that the Kuiper Belt contains some remains from the earliest development of the solar system, and that it's the source of short-period comets. Beyond the Kuiper Belt, on the edges of the solar system, the Oort Cloud is an extended shell of icy objects that most likely produces long-period comets. (You can read more about short- and long-period comets in the later section "Watching for meteors, comets, and asteroids.")

Shooting for the moons

Moons (sometimes called *satellites*) orbit all the planets except Mercury and Venus because of each planet's gravitational pull. The moon you refer to as *the moon* revolves around Earth in the phases shown in Figure 12-5. It makes a complete revolution every $27\frac{1}{3}$ days and is slowly moving away from Earth at a rate of about 1.5 inches per year. When the moon moves into Earth's shadow, a *lunar eclipse* results; Earth is positioned between the sun and the moon. When Earth moves into the moon's shadow, a *solar eclipse* results; the moon is positioned between Earth and the sun.

IS PLUTO REALLY A PLANET?

In August 2006, the International Astronomical Union (IAU) established a new definition for the word *planet* that stripped Pluto of its designation as the ninth planet in our solar system, which it had held since its discovery in the 1930s. Pluto has so many unusual features that it was reclassified as a dwarf planet. For example, it travels around the sun in an elongated oval path much different from the nearly circular orbits of the other planets. And unlike the other outer planets, Pluto is small and solid and contains only $\frac{1}{500}$ of the mass of Earth.

According to the planet definition, the solar system consists of eight planets and five dwarf planets. The definition doesn't apply outside the solar system. The new definition was a controversial one; it has been variously criticized and supported by different astronomers.

FIGURE 12-5: Phases of the moon.

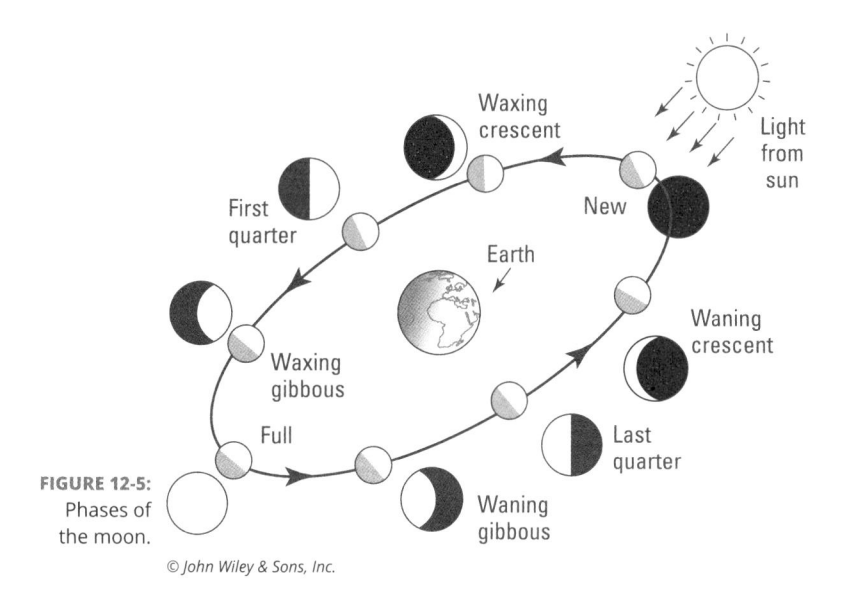

© John Wiley & Sons, Inc.

The inner planets have few moons. The giant planets probably have more small moons not yet discovered. See Table 12-4 for a lineup of the planets and their moon counts.

TABLE 12-4 The Number of Moons per Planet in Earth's Solar System

Planet	Number of Moons
Mercury	0
Venus	0
Earth	1
Mars	2
Jupiter	63
Saturn	61
Uranus	27
Neptune	13

TECHNICAL STUFF

Jupiter's four largest moons are known as the *Galilean satellites* because the Italian astronomer Galileo Galilei discovered them in 1610 with one of the first telescopes. The largest Galilean satellite — and the largest satellite in the solar system — is Ganymede, which is even bigger than Mercury and Pluto. The largest of Saturn's moons, Titan, has an atmosphere thicker than Earth's and a diameter larger than that of Mercury or Pluto. Pluto's largest moon, Charon, is more than half the size of Pluto.

Watching for meteors, comets, and asteroids

A *meteor* occurs when a rock from space (a *meteoroid*) hits Earth's atmosphere and glows as it heats up, resulting in a brief streak of light. It's often called a *shooting star*. When a meteoroid enters Earth's atmosphere, it usually burns up (and that's a good thing). If a meteoroid actually strikes Earth, it's called a *meteorite*.

> **MILITARY SPACE PROGRAMS AND THE U.S. SPACE FORCE**
>
> In 2003, the U.S. Army activated its 1st Space Brigade (Provisional) to develop and provide current and future global space, missile defense, and high-altitude capabilities to the United States and its allies. The Air Force Space Command and Naval Space Command are each much older than the Army's version, and today's recruits can join the Space Force. But don't count on participating in an intergalactic war anytime soon. Active-duty and reserve military members can apply for a position as an astronaut through NASA, and many astronauts come directly out of military service as pilots and support personnel.

Comets are snowballs composed mainly of ice and rock. When a comet approaches the sun, some of the ice in its nucleus (center) turns into gas. The gas shoots out of the sunlit side of the comet. The solar wind then carries the gas outward, forming it into a long tail. Astronomers divide comets into two main types:

» *Long-period comets,* which take 200 years or more to orbit the sun and originate in the Oort Cloud

» *Short-period comets,* which complete their orbits in fewer than 200 years and most likely originate in the Kuiper Belt

TECHNICAL STUFF

The most famous of all comets, Halley's Comet (also referred to as Comet Halley after Edmond Halley), is a comet that can be seen every 75 to 76 years, making it a short-period comet. Halley is the only short-period comet that is visible to the naked eye and will return within a human lifetime. Its many appearances over the centuries have had a notable effect on human history. Halley's Comet last appeared in the inner solar system in 1986 and will next appear in mid-2061.

Asteroids are sometimes called *minor planets* because they're small bodies that orbit the sun. Some have elliptical orbits that pass inside the orbit of Earth or even that of Mercury. Others travel on a circular path among the outer planets. Most asteroids circle the sun in a region called the *asteroid belt,* between the orbits of Mars and Jupiter. The belt contains more than 200 asteroids larger than 60 miles (100 kilometers) in diameter. Scientists estimate that more than 750,000 asteroids with diameters larger than $\frac{3}{5}$ mile (1 kilometer) exist in the belt. There are millions of smaller asteroids, and astronomers have even found several large asteroids with smaller asteroids orbiting them.

Getting Back to Your Latin Roots to Improve Your Test Score

TIP

Just when you thought vocabulary study was over, leave it to me to bring it up again. Many scientific words come from Latin or Greek. If you know the meaning of the Latin or Greek word, you can often figure out the meaning of the scientific word. Often, a Latin or Greek root word is used to create a longer, more specific word. (For common word roots, see Chapter 4.)

For example, the Latin root *homo* means human being, and the Greek root *homo* means same. *Homo sapiens* refers to members of the human species, but *homogeneous* means "of the same kind." If you were to run across the word *homologous* on the General Science subtest, you'd know that it has something to do with humans or with things that are the same.

Take a look at the following example question:

EXAMPLE

Which of the following instruments might an oceanographer be expected to use?

(A) aspirator
(B) hydrophone
(C) calorimeter
(D) centrifuge

Even if you don't have a clue about what any of these instruments do, if you know that hydro relates to water, you've significantly increased your chances of getting the right answer, Choice (B).

Earth and Space Science Practice Questions

Earth and space sciences are broad fields, so to do well on these questions on the ASVAB's General Science subtest, you need to have a firm grasp on the basics. See how well you do on the following 40 practice questions.

Easy Earth and space science practice questions

1. If the temperature in Fahrenheit is 212 degrees, the temperature in Celsius is
   (A) 0 degrees.
   (B) 32 degrees.
   (C) 100 degrees.
   (D) 106 degrees.

2. Earthquakes occur along
   (A) faults.
   (B) magma chambers.
   (C) the troposphere.
   (D) valleys.

3. Climate is
   (A) the weather conditions outside now.
   (B) patterns of weather over long periods of time.
   (C) not an area of scientific study.
   (D) a series of chemical reactions involving heat and cold.

4. What is the Earth's primary source of energy?
   (A) the moon
   (B) the sun
   (C) stars
   (D) geothermal heat

5. Which planet is known for its prominent ring system?
   (A) Mars
   (B) Jupiter
   (C) Saturn
   (D) Neptune

6. A scientist who studies space and the universe is a(n)
   (A) geologist.
   (B) biologist.
   (C) astronomer.
   (D) chemist.

7. What is the name of the galaxy that includes Earth?
   (A) Andromeda
   (B) Whirlpool
   (C) Triangulum
   (D) Milky Way

8. What causes the tides in Earth's oceans?
   (A) heat from the sun
   (B) the moon's gravitational pull
   (C) Earth's rotation
   (D) underwater earthquakes

9. Which planet is known as the Red Planet?
   (A) Mars
   (B) Venus
   (C) Jupiter
   (D) Mercury

10. Which is not a type of rock?
    (A) igneous
    (B) metamorphic
    (C) sedimentary
    (D) rudimentary

Medium Earth and space science practice questions

11. Dinosaurs existed during the
    - (A) Paleozoic era.
    - (B) Mesozoic era.
    - (C) Cenozoic era.
    - (D) Vendian period.

12. What element makes up most of Earth's atmosphere?
    - (A) water
    - (B) helium
    - (C) oxygen
    - (D) nitrogen

13. The process that takes place inside the sun's core is
    - (A) gravity.
    - (B) rotational pull.
    - (C) nuclear fusion.
    - (D) solar flares.

14. Which of the following is not a terrestrial planet?
    - (A) Earth
    - (B) Venus
    - (C) Saturn
    - (D) Mercury

15. Radiometric dating involves
    - (A) evaluating layers of sediment that contain fossils.
    - (B) comparing magnetic particles in sediment layers.
    - (C) observing the natural decay of radioactive elements in a fossil.
    - (D) comparing a newer fossil to an older fossil.

16. Why are regions of Earth unequal in daylight and darkness?
    - (A) because Earth rotates on a tilted axis
    - (B) because the sun changes direction halfway through the year
    - (C) because Earth's orbit is slower during different seasons
    - (D) because Earth's axis moves around during rotation

17. What is the term for the point on Earth's surface directly above an earthquake?
    - (A) hypocenter
    - (B) epicenter
    - (C) focal point
    - (D) seismocenter

18. Approximately how thick is Earth's continental crust?
    - (A) 5 miles
    - (B) 12 miles
    - (C) 1,800 miles
    - (D) 3,200 miles

19. What types of rocks are most likely to contain fossils?
    - (A) sedimentary
    - (B) metamorphic
    - (C) basaltic
    - (D) igneous

20. Approximately how hot is Earth's core?
    - (A) 1,000° F to 3,000° F
    - (B) 5,000° F to 15,000° F
    - (C) below 5,000° F
    - (D) over 15,000° F

21. What type of rock forms from slowly cooled magma?

(A) sedimentary
(B) metamorphic
(C) igneous
(D) marble

22. What percentage of Earth's surface is covered by the global ocean?

(A) 50%
(B) 72%
(C) 85%
(D) 97%

23. The ocean's primary role in Earth's climate system is to

(A) drive weather and regulate temperature.
(B) produce most of Earth's oxygen.
(C) absorb carbon dioxide.
(D) provide habitats for all living organisms.

24. The Earth's atmosphere is approximately

(A) 10 miles thick.
(B) 30 miles thick.
(C) 300 miles thick.
(D) 6,200 miles thick.

25. Most weather changes occur in Earth's

(A) troposphere.
(B) stratosphere.
(C) mesosphere.
(D) thermosphere.

26. What percentage of Earth's atmosphere is composed of nitrogen?

(A) 21%
(B) 0.93%
(C) 0.04%
(D) 78%

27. The magnetosphere

(A) is responsible for weather changes.
(B) reflects radio waves for communication.
(C) deflects solar wind.
(D) is the outermost layer of the atmosphere.

28. What happens when a cold front meets a warm air mass?

(A) The warm air is pushed up, forming clouds and potentially heavy rain.
(B) The cold air is pushed up, causing light rain.
(C) The two air masses mix, causing fog.
(D) The warm air passes over the cold air, causing snow.

29. What is the difference between climate and weather?

(A) Climate refers to daily atmospheric conditions, while weather refers to long-term patterns.
(B) Climate is an average pattern of weather across the Earth or a specific region, while weather refers to daily conditions.
(C) Climate can be measured only by satellite, while weather is measured by balloons.
(D) The sun's angle determines climate, while air pressure determines weather.

30. The dating technique that involves observing the natural decay of radioactive elements is

(A) radiometric dating.
(B) relative dating.
(C) paleomagnetism.
(D) biochronology.

Hard Earth and space science practice questions

31. Most weather events take place in Earth's
    (A) ionosphere.
    (B) stratosphere.
    (C) mesosphere.
    (D) troposphere.

32. Absolute zero is equivalent to
    (A) 0 degrees Kelvin.
    (B) 0 kelvins.
    (C) −273.15 degrees Kelvin.
    (D) −273.15 kelvins.

33. A comet's tail is visible when
    (A) the metal alloys react to the atmospheric change.
    (B) the ice and rock collide.
    (C) the comet is close enough to the sun.
    (D) the comet passes the Kuiper Belt.

34. Cooled lava forms
    (A) igneous rock.
    (B) sedimentary rock.
    (C) metamorphic rock.
    (D) shale.

35. What phenomenon occurs when Earth travels between the sun and the moon?
    (A) lunar eclipse
    (B) vernal equinox
    (C) solar eclipse
    (D) summer solstice

36. What are fast-flowing, narrow air currents located in Earth's atmosphere called?
    (A) density
    (B) air mass
    (C) jet streams
    (D) air chambers

37. The layer of earth directly above its outer core is the
    (A) crust.
    (B) mesosphere.
    (C) asthenosphere.
    (D) lithosphere.

38. Which prefix is given to midlevel clouds?
    (A) cirro-
    (B) alto-
    (C) strato-
    (D) nimbo-

39. If you want to convert a temperature from Celsius to Fahrenheit, which of the following steps is correct?
    (A) Divide by $\frac{5}{9}$ and subtract 32.
    (B) Multiply by $\frac{9}{5}$ and add 32.
    (C) Subtract 273.15 and divide by $\frac{5}{9}$.
    (D) Add 273.15 and multiply by $\frac{5}{9}$.

40. The first sheep, bears, apes, and modern birds appeared during the
    (A) Neogene period of the Cenozoic era.
    (B) Jurassic period of the Mesozoic era.
    (C) Devonian period of the Paleozoic era.
    (D) Vendian period of the Proterozoic era.

Answers and Explanations

Use this answer key to score the Earth and space science practice questions.

1. **C.** Measured in Celsius, the boiling point of water is 100 degrees. If you don't have this fact memorized, you can calculate it. To convert from Fahrenheit to Celsius, use the formula $C = \frac{5}{9}(F - 32)$. The correct answer is Choice (C).

2. **A.** Earthquakes occur along faults — the spaces between tectonic plates — as a result of pressure causing the plates to give way and move past each other.

3. **B.** Climate is a pattern of weather over long periods of time — typically 30 years or more. It's different from weather, which refers only to immediate conditions like rain, heat, and cold.

4. **B.** Earth's primary source of energy (unlike mine, which is coffee) is the sun. It provides the heat and light that sustain life and drive the climate and weather on this, the third rock from the sun.

5. **C.** Saturn is known for its extensive, bright ring system, which is made of ice particles, rocky debris, and dust.

6. **C.** Astronomers are scientists who study objects and matter outside Earth's atmosphere, such as stars, planets, comets, and galaxies far, far away.

7. **D.** The Milky Way is home to Earth, and it's known as a barred spiral galaxy because it features a central, bar-shaped structure composed of stars.

8. **B.** The moon's gravitational pull causes the tides in Earth's oceans; to a lesser extent, the sun's gravitational pull does, too.

9. **A.** Mars has a reddish appearance because its surface is covered in iron oxide (rust), so it's known as the Red Planet.

10. **D.** Igneous, metamorphic, and sedimentary are all types of rocks, but rudimentary isn't a rock at all. In fact, here's a bonus tip for the Word Knowledge subtest: *rudimentary* is an adjective that means involving or limited to basic principles.

11. **B.** Dinosaurs made their first and last appearances during the Mesozoic era, between 230 and 66 million years ago.

12. **D.** Earth's atmosphere is made primarily of nitrogen, which clocks in at about 78 percent.

13. **C.** Nuclear fusion, the result of the sun's mass and its gravity, takes place inside the sun's core.

14. **C.** Saturn is a Jovian planet, but the other three — Earth, Venus, and Mars — are terrestrial planets (as is Mercury.). The other Jovian planets are Jupiter, Uranus, and Neptune.

15. **C.** Radiometric dating is the process of observing the natural decay of radioactive elements. Scientists know how long it takes radioactive elements to decay and disappear entirely, so they can sometimes use radiometric dating to compare timelines with the radioactive elements inside a fossil.

16. **A.** Except for two days per year (known as the vernal and autumnal equinoxes), the hours of daylight and darkness are unequal because Earth spins on its axis on a tilt (think about your friends in Alaska). The tilt changes throughout the year, which gives us different seasons.

17. **B.** The epicenter is the point on Earth's surface located directly above the hypocenter, or focus, which is the point inside the Earth where an earthquake originates.

18. **B.** The continental crust, which forms the continents, is around 12 miles thick. For the record, oceanic crust is about 5 miles thick, and the depths of the outer and inner cores of the earth are 1,800 and 3,200 miles, respectively.

19. **A.** Sedimentary rocks form when sediment hardens. Sediment often includes particles of sand, seashells, and other materials, which means this type of rock is most likely to contain fossils.

20. **B.** Scientists believe that the temperature range in Earth's core is somewhere between 5,000° F and 15,000° F. For a little perspective, the surface of the sun is around 10,340° F. The hottest known star in the universe is WR 102, which is in the Sagittarius constellation; its surface temperature is 360,032° F.

21. **C.** Igneous rocks are formed form magma that cools slowly. When magma cools slowly, crystals can form, which is characteristic of many igneous rocks, like granite.

22. **B.** Earth's global ocean covers around 72 percent of the planet's surface. It's worth noting that 97 percent of the water on Earth is held in its oceans — but water doesn't cover that much of the surface.

23. **A.** The oceans drive weather and regulates temperature on Earth. While scientists estimate that the ocean provides over half of Earth's oxygen, the question specifically asks about the ocean's role in climate.

24. **C.** The Earth's atmosphere is about 300 miles thick, though most of it's located within 10 miles of the planet's surface.

25. **A.** Almost all weather changes occur in the troposphere. The troposphere touches the stratosphere, and the border between them is called the *tropopause*.

26. **D.** Nitrogen makes up 78 percent of Earth's atmosphere; 21 percent is oxygen, 0.93 percent is argon, and 0.04 percent is carbon dioxide.

27. **C.** Earth's magnetosphere deflects solar wind thanks to the planet's magnetic field. It's not responsible for weather changes (that's the troposphere), it doesn't reflect radio waves (that's the ionosphere), and it's not an atmospheric layer.

28. **A.** The warm air is pushed up, and when it meets the cold front, it forms clouds that can cause heavy rain.

29. **B.** Climate is an average pattern of weather across the Earth or a specific region, while weather refers to daily conditions you can observe right now.

30. **A.** Radiometric dating is a technique that involves observing the natural decay of radioactive elements to determine how old fossils are.

CHAPTER 12 **Earth and Space Sciences**

31. **D.** Nearly all weather events occur in Earth's troposphere, which is the atmospheric layer that extends between 6 and 12 miles above the surface.

32. **B.** Absolute zero is −273.15 degrees Celsius, which is equivalent to 0 kelvins. Temperatures stated in the Kelvin scale are measured by using units of kelvins, not degrees. The correct answer is Choice (B).

33. **C.** Comets are balls composed mainly of ice and rock. The comet's tail is formed when the ice turns into gas from the heat of the sun; therefore, the comet must be closer to the sun for the tail to be visible. The correct answer is Choice (C).

34. **A.** When lava cools, it forms igneous rock. Sedimentary rock is formed by layers of sediment, and metamorphic rock forms due to the pressure and heat below Earth's surface.

35. **A.** When Earth travels between the sun and the moon, it blocks the sun's rays from reaching the moon's surface, resulting in a lunar eclipse.

36. **C.** Jet streams are narrow air currents that flow in between the troposphere and the stratosphere.

37. **C.** The mesosphere is the layer of the mantle that surrounds Earth's outer core. The crust is the outermost layer, the asthenosphere is in the middle of the mantle, and the lithosphere is the uppermost part of the mantle attached to the crust.

38. **B.** Meteorologists use the prefix *alto-* to indicate midlevel clouds, which have bases between 6,000 and 20,000 feet. They use *cirro-* for high clouds.

39. **B.** To convert from Celsius to Fahrenheit, multiply by $\frac{5}{9}$ and then add 32.

40. **A.** The first sheep, bears, apes, modern birds, monkeys, and dogs first appeared during the Neogene period of the Cenozoic era.

5 The Whole Ball of Facts: Technical Skills

IN THIS PART . . .

Check out the basic automotive systems and various shop tools and fasteners that you may be asked about on the Auto & Shop Information subtests.

Practice identifying parts of simple machines and making calculations involving mechanical principles to prepare for the Mechanical Comprehension subtest.

Shock yourself with how much you already know about the principles of electricity and how these principles work in the real world as you prep for the Electronics Information subtest.

Discover what's required to ace the Assembling Objects subtest by looking at puzzle pieces and determining how they fit together.

Answer some practice questions at the end of each chapter to help you determine where you excel and where you could use some more review.

IN THIS CHAPTER

» Firing up your knowledge of automotive systems

» Giving your automotive vocabulary a tuneup

» Driving up your test score

Chapter 13
Auto Information

Ever wonder why automobile mechanics can charge so much money for labor to work on your car, even when the parts are cheap? Because if their jobs were easy, everyone would do them.

Fortunately, to do well on the Auto & Shop Information subtest(s) of the ASVAB, you don't have to get your hands greasy or chance hitting your thumb with a hammer. The questions on these subjects are pretty basic. Automotive questions usually ask about basic automotive systems and malfunctions.

REMEMBER The CAT-ASVAB presents Auto Information and Shop Information (which I cover in Chapter 14) as separate subtests but combines your results on them into one score (AS). The pencil-and-paper (P&P) version of the exam tests these topics in one subtest.

On the CAT-ASVAB, you have 7 minutes to answer 10 questions on Auto Information (18 minutes for 25 questions if you're taking a version of the test with tryout questions; see Chapter 1). If you happen to take the paper-and-pencil version, the Auto & Shop Information subtest consists of 25 questions you have to answer in 11 minutes (that's about 26.4 seconds for each question). About half of these 25 questions measure your basic knowledge of automotive principles, and half query you about shop tools and basic shop principles.

REMEMBER Each branch of the military uses the AS score to determine your qualifications for certain jobs only. It's not used in the calculation of your AFQT score. If you don't need to do well on these subjects to qualify for the kind of job you want, you may be better off studying for a different part of the ASVAB, but it's better to try to get the best possible score on every subtest. Doing so makes you a more desirable candidate and may open the door for more job opportunities if your first choice doesn't work out.

Checking under the Hood

The engines of planes, trains, and automobiles (and motorcycles, boats, and recreational vehicles) are complex machines that have undergone almost 150 years of evolution. Long before Henry Ford made headlines for mass-producing automobiles, Karl Benz received the first patent for a gas-fueled car (on January 29, 1886, in Germany, to be exact). Ford and Benz would probably be shocked to see what cars have become — and how fast they can go — compared to the horseless carriages of the 1800s.

The modern car is divided into several primary and secondary systems. I cover these systems in the next few sections.

Chassis and frame: Holding it all together

A vehicle's *chassis* keeps all its systems and components together. It accommodates the frame, gearbox, engine, axles, and every other system. Think of the chassis as a vehicle's skeleton, because without it, the vehicle is just a heap of parts sitting on the ground.

The frame is the main structure of the chassis, like the backbone. The frame supports the vehicle's body and all its mechanical components as well as the weight of passengers and cargo inside. It has a lot of other jobs, too: It deals with the torsional and vertical twisting caused by driving over uneven surfaces, torque from the engine and transmission, and tensile forces from starting, acceleration, and stopping.

TECHNICAL STUFF

Most modern cars and trucks feature *unibody* construction, which means the chassis (including the frame) and body are integrated into one piece. Older cars and most modern trucks feature *body-on-frame* construction, using two separate components for the body and frame.

The engine: Different strokes

How does an engine work? You turn the key or push the ignition button, and it starts, right? That's true, but there's more to it than that. Cars and other vehicles use an internal combustion engine, which burns a mixture of fuel and air. Gasoline and diesel are the most common fuels, but some vehicles use propane, natural gas, or alcohol. In the military, you'll most likely use a fuel called JP-8, which is kerosene-based.

Burning the fuel mixture makes it expand quickly — so quickly that it's an explosion. The energy from this explosion is transferred through several mechanical systems to make the vehicle move. Technically, what's happening is that the internal combustion engine is converting the air-fuel mixture's chemical energy into heat energy and then converting the heat energy into mechanical energy. (I explain energy in Chapter 11.)

Inside an internal combustion engine, this energy conversion happens over and over in a cycle. That's what makes the engine run. Most internal combustion engines use a *four-stroke cycle*, which means a piston in the engine must move four times to complete one cycle. The piston has two distinct positions: top dead center, or TDC, and bottom dead center, or BDC. Here are the four strokes that make up a cycle (Figure 13-1 illustrates a four-stroke engine):

1. **Intake stroke:** The intake valve opens as the connecting rod pulls the piston down from its TDC position, creating a vacuum that sucks the air-fuel mix into the cylinder. The piston goes to the BDC position. The intake valve closes, sealing the air-fuel mixture inside the combustion chamber portion of the cylinder.

2. **Compression stroke:** The connecting rod pushes the piston up, compressing the air-fuel mixture inside the combustion chamber. This compression builds up energy because it excites the molecules and generates heat. The flywheel helps compress the *charge* (the volume of compressed air-fuel mixture trapped inside the combustion chamber). The mixture ignites through a chemical reaction — combustion — when the piston is almost back at TDC and a

spark plug releases a spark. The spark heats the gases in the combustion chamber even more, which causes an explosion of energy.

3. **Combustion stroke:** The explosion forces the piston down. Because the intake and exhaust valves are still closed, the explosion pushes down on the connecting rod, turning the crankshaft; the crankshaft turns the flywheel, which keeps the engine going.

4. **Exhaust stroke:** The exhaust valve opens as the connecting rod moves the piston back up, pushing out the leftover gases from the explosion. At this point, their energy is spent. The valves are timed, of course, using push rods attached to the camshaft. Complete expulsion of the exhaust prepares the engine to repeat the intake stroke.

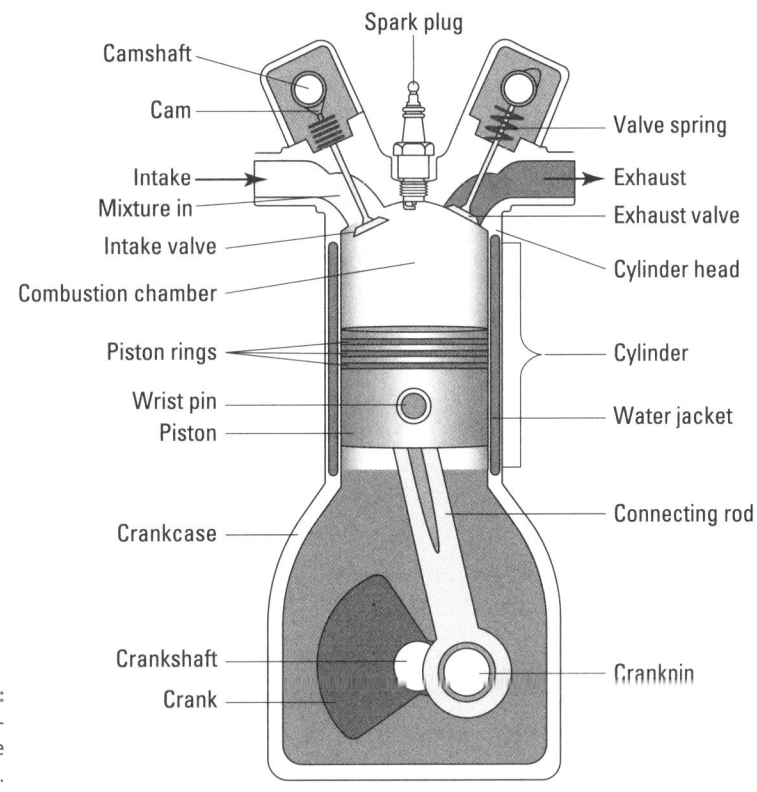

FIGURE 13-1: A four-stroke engine.

© John Wiley & Sons, Inc.

REMEMBER

Sometimes people refer to their engines as *four-cycle* engines. This isn't really true. It's a *four-stroke*, one-cycle engine. The intake stroke, compression stroke, combustion stroke, and exhaust stroke are one engine cycle. The crankshaft must rotate twice to complete an entire cycle. When the *tachometer* (an instrument measuring revolutions per minute [rpm]) on your dashboard shows 4,800 rpm, for example, that means the crankshaft is performing 4,800 rotations every minute (and that equals a total of 2,400 cycles).

In order for the cycle to happen at all, fuel must be properly mixed with air and transported within the cylinder at the right time. Various components perform this function. Depending on how old a car is, it may use a carburetor or fuel injectors:

» **Carburetors:** Carburetors are used on most older cars (those made before the early 1990s) to mix the fuel and air mechanically. As air moves quickly through the carburetor, it creates a vacuum, which draws more and more fuel into the mixture. While no major car manufacturers currently use carburetors, some manufacturers build motorcycles with them.

CHAPTER 13 **Auto Information** 279

- » **Fuel injectors:** Fuel injectors have replaced carburetors on newer cars to perform the air-fuel mixture function. (Fuel injectors have been around since the late 1950s, but they weren't widely introduced until the late 1980s and early 1990s.) The fuel injector acts as the fuel-dispensing nozzle. It injects liquid fuel directly into the engine's air stream. In almost all cases, this requires an external pump.

  All mass-produced cars today use an electronic fuel injection system, or EFI, which receives commands from the powertrain control module (PCM) computer. The PCM receives information from the sensors in the fuel, air, and exhaust system, and from that information it determines how much fuel the engine needs to operate at optimum levels.

A *throttle* is mechanically connected to the carburetor or electronically connected to the EFI computer. Advancing (opening) the throttle causes more fuel to be transferred to the carburetor or the fuel injectors. The accelerator (the gas pedal) is connected to the throttle by electrical connections and — in older vehicles — mechanical linkages. The harder you push on the gas pedal, the farther the throttle is advanced (opened). Thus, more fuel is transported to the carburetor or fuel injectors.

Whatever floats your boat: Considering common components of internal combustion engines

Most internal combustion engines have the same components within the engine block (the framework that holds it all together) to make a vehicle run:

- » **Pistons:** A *piston* is a cylindrical object with a solid crown at the top. One piston moves up and down in each cylinder.
- » **Piston rings:** *Piston rings* seal the piston to the cylinder. They prevent gases from leaking out. Similarly, oil rings stop engine oil from getting into the combustion chamber.
- » **Cylinders:** A *cylinder* houses a piston and other components. It's where the piston and the air-fuel mixture work together to transfer energy.
- » **Cylinder head:** A *cylinder head* is the part of the cylinder located above the piston. It's where you find the combustion chamber as well as the intake and exhaust valves and ports.
- » **Combustion chamber:** A *combustion chamber* is inside the cylinder head, right above the piston. The air-fuel mixture combusts inside the chamber.
- » **Intake valves:** An *intake valve* lets the air-fuel mix enter the combustion chamber. It seals after the mixture is inside.
- » **Exhaust valves:** The *exhaust valve* lets waste gases exit the combustion chamber after combustion.
- » **Crankshaft:** The crankshaft turns a piston's up-and-down motion into a rotary motion (like a crank).
- » **Camshaft:** A *camshaft* is what opens and closes the intake and exhaust valves. It turns at half the speed of the crankshaft.
- » **Wrist pins:** A *wrist pin* connects the piston to the connecting rod.
- » **Connecting rods:** A connecting rod connects each piston and wrist pin assembly to the crankshaft.

Running on all your cylinders

Most car engines have four, six, or eight cylinders, while motorcycles have between one and six. Engines with more cylinders can combust more fuel, which creates more movement to turn the crankshaft — and more power to move the vehicle. Engines with fewer cylinders tend to be more efficient, but they're usually less powerful than engines with more cylinders. Generally, you have to trade power for efficiency when you buy a vehicle with an internal combustion engine.

Usually, cylinders are arranged in-line, V-type, or horizontally opposed, which you can see in Figure 13-2.

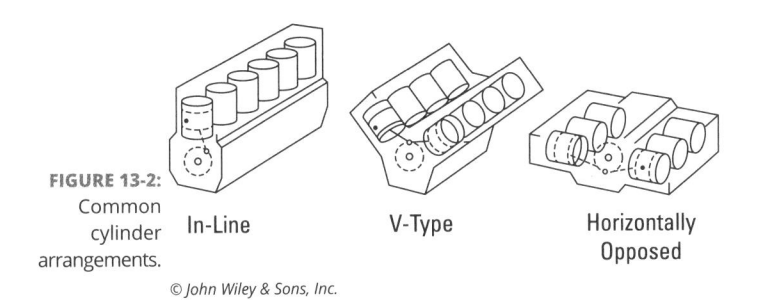

FIGURE 13-2: Common cylinder arrangements.

In-Line   V-Type   Horizontally Opposed

© John Wiley & Sons, Inc.

Diesel: Discovering the more powerful alternative

Diesel engines, also called *compression ignition engines*, are internal combustion engines, but they're a little simpler than standard gasoline engines. Many of the vehicles you'll use in the military are diesel-powered. Diesel engines don't rely on a spark to ignite the fuel. Instead, the engine injects fuel right into the combustion chamber of a cylinder, where the air is so compressed (and hot) that it ignites the fuel without a spark. Glow plugs assist in heating the air, but they don't produce an electrical spark.

MAKING THE GRADE: OCTANE RATINGS

Octane ratings measure gasoline's ability to resist *engine knock*, a rattling or pinging sound that results from premature ignition of the compressed air-fuel mixture in one or more cylinders. Most gas stations offer three octane grades: regular (usually 87 octane), midgrade (usually 89 octane), and premium (usually 91, 92, or 93). By federal law, the ratings must be posted on bright yellow stickers on each gasoline pump.

The octane rating correlates to how much the gasoline can be compressed before it ignites spontaneously. When gasoline ignites this way, instead of by the spark of a spark plug, the engine begins knocking. That's not a good thing because early ignition can cause engine damage over time.

But don't be fooled — that doesn't mean using higher octane gas is better. In most cases, using a higher octane gasoline than your owner's manual recommends offers absolutely no benefit. It won't make your car perform better, go faster, get better mileage, or run cleaner. The only time you may need to switch to a higher octane level is if your car engine knocks when you use the recommended fuel. This happens to a small percentage of cars. Buying higher octane gasoline can be a waste of money, too. Premium gas can cost at least 30 to 40 cents per gallon more than regular gas does. That can add up to hundreds of dollars a year in unnecessary spending.

How can you tell if you're using the right octane level? Read your owner's manual and listen to your car's engine. If it doesn't knock when you use the recommended octane, you're probably using the right grade of gasoline.

These engines are more powerful and more efficient with their fuel than gasoline-powered engines are (because they don't rely on throttling or a spark). This power is also available at lower RPMs, which can make diesel engines more efficient at heavy-duty work like towing. Most modern diesels produce less carbon dioxide than gas-powered engines, thanks to emissions control devices, but they still produce significant amounts of nitrogen oxide and nitrogen dioxide, as well as fine particulate matter that's harmful to human health.

Charging into the future with electric vehicles

Electric vehicles (EVs) are a lot like their gasoline- and diesel-powered counterparts, but they have one or more electric motors that take power from a large (and very heavy) battery. Some electric vehicles have a smaller electric motor at each wheel, which eliminates the need for a transmission, drive shaft, and axles, ultimately making them simpler than other types of engines. On-board computers control the amount of electricity sent to each motor for precise performance. Because they use electric motors, EVs have instant torque at their wheels and can reach high speeds very quickly.

The U.S. military intends to transition to a fully electric fleet of vehicles by 2050. EVs are quiet, have low heat signatures and plenty of torque, and are generally low maintenance with fewer moving parts, so the top brass see them as a way to gain advantage on the battlefield.

Mixing things up with hybrid vehicles

Hybrid vehicles use widely available gasoline or diesel fuel to help power electric motors. A small gasoline or diesel engine powers the vehicle *and* a generator; the generator provides electricity to the vehicle's electric motors. Sometimes the vehicle stores energy in a small battery bank, which allows it to run purely as an electric vehicle for a short time. Hybrids were originally designed for efficiency, and they're becoming increasingly popular — you'll even find them in some military applications.

Electrical and ignition systems: Starting up

Your car requires more than just gasoline to operate. It also needs a supply of electricity. In the old days, automotive electrical systems operated on 6 volts. Shortly after World War II, as electrical accessories became more prevalent in automobiles, 12 volts became the standard.

The battery powers an electrical motor that starts the engine when you turn the key or push the ignition button. This motor is called a *starter* (for obvious reasons). An *alternator* sends an electric current back to the battery, keeping it charged, and powers the electronics on your car when the engine is running.

The *ignition system* supplies a high-voltage current to the spark plugs to ignite the fuel mixture in the cylinders. (See the section "The engine: Different strokes" earlier in this chapter.) The system takes the 12-volt current from the battery, steps it up to about 20,000 volts, and then sends the current to the spark plugs.

In older cars and diesel engines, this increase of voltage is accomplished by means of a device called a *coil*, which uses electromagnetic induction to step up the voltage. The current then passes through an electrical/mechanical switching device called a *distributor*. A rotating shaft and a switch within the distributor, called *breaker points*, route the current through wires to the spark plugs. A *condenser* absorbs excess current and protects the breaker points from damage by the high-voltage surge. The distributor and other devices control the timing of the spark-plug discharges.

In the 1970s, the electronic ignition systems were introduced. In modern ignition systems, the distributor, coil, points, and condenser have been replaced by solid-state electronics controlled by a computer. A computer controls the ignition system and adjusts it to provide maximum efficiency in a variety of driving conditions.

Cooling systems: Preventing a meltdown

Engines need a built-in cooling system because of the high temperature at which fuel ignites, and because most vehicle engines only convert 20 to 30 percent of the chemical energy they create into work (with the remaining 70 to 80 percent being released as heat energy). Without a cooling system, the engine would melt, and you'd have to use your LPCs to get around (that's your *leather personnel carriers,* or combat boots).

Most modern internal combustion engines are liquid-cooled. A *water pump* pushes liquid coolant through *water jackets,* which surround the parts of the engine that reach the highest temperatures. The coolant picks up heat and carries it through the engine's *radiator,* where the heat disperses when the coolant is exposed to outside air.

The water in the system is usually mixed with coolant (antifreeze), which raises the boiling point of the water (which keeps the water from boiling away) and lowers its freezing point (which keeps the system from freezing up during cold weather).

Lubrication systems: Keeping the engine moving smoothly

When metal grinds against metal, it breaks down. The solution: engine oil. An *oil pump* circulates oil through the engine; oil flows through the crankshaft and connecting rods, lubricating as it goes. Oil does more than lubricate moving parts, though. When oil touches hot engine parts, like the pistons, it picks up the heat and transfers it elsewhere. It also acts as a sealer between things like the piston rings and cylinder walls. Motor oil is often mixed with additives that also snatch up contaminants and drop them off in the engine's oil filter. Even better, oil makes engines run more quietly (so your radio doesn't have to work as hard).

A standard lubrication system includes the following:

>> **Oil pump:** The *oil pump* pushes the motor oil through the engine. Usually, the camshaft controls the oil pump.

>> **Oil galleries:** *Oil galleries* are pathways that oil takes through the engine.

>> **Oil pan:** The *oil pan* is the reservoir where all the oil pools. It's at the bottom of the engine.

>> **Pickup tube and screen:** The *pickup tube* sends oil into the oil pump, and the *screen* filters out solid materials that could clog up the system.

>> **Oil filter:** The *oil filter* cleans out contaminants before the oil gets circulated back through the engine.

Exhaust systems: Where byproducts go to die

The byproducts of combustion and other engine functions have to go somewhere, and they have to be able to escape the engine freely. The exhaust system manages all of an engine's byproducts using these components:

- **Exhaust manifold:** The *manifold* connects to the exhaust ports on the cylinder head, where combustion takes place.

- **Catalytic converter:** The *catalytic converter* contains a honeycomb-like set of passageways or small ceramic beads coated with catalysts that create chemical reactions. These chemical reactions transform the most toxic compounds in exhaust to less-harmful compounds, like carbon dioxide and water.

- **Muffler:** The *muffler* provides a place for gases to expand (quietly) because it's made from sound-absorbing material.

- **Tailpipe:** The *tailpipe* is the exit door for exhaust.

When toxic fumes leave the exhaust ports, they gather in the exhaust manifold before making an unceremonious exit through steel exhaust pipes. The pipes take these gases to the catalytic converter (or two or three separate catalytic converters), where chemical reactions take place to neutralize them. When they're as neutral as they're going to get, the gases go to the muffler and out the tailpipe.

Emissions-control systems: Filtering out pollutants

Exhaust systems (see the preceding section) aren't the only systems that deal with emissions. Think of the engine as a giant cigarette and the emissions-control system as a filter. The exhaust from automobiles contains pollutants, including carbon monoxide. These pollutants are a result of the combustion process (or they're partially combusted or unburned fuel). To prevent these pollutants from poisoning the atmosphere, manufacturers place emissions-control systems on cars. These systems include the following:

- **Positive-crankcase ventilation:** An old method (still in use) that forces unspent or partially spent fuel back into the cylinder so the fuel can burn

- **Air-injection system:** System that forces air into the engine's exhaust system to reuse unburned or partially burned fuel before the fuel comes out the exhaust pipe

- **Catalytic converter:** Oxidizes hydrocarbons and carbon monoxide into water vapor and carbon dioxide (the same thing people exhale); doesn't control other types of pollutants such as nitrogen oxides

- **Exhaust-gas-recirculation system:** Helps control nitrogen-oxide emissions by forcing some of the gases back into the cylinders

Drive systems: Taking it for a spin

Having a working engine is all fine and dandy, but the power of the engine still has to be transferred to the wheels to make them move. This is the job of the *drive system*. Cars have *drivetrain* systems that run on axles. The *axle* is the shaft on which the wheels revolve. The *universal joint* allows the axle to move up and down without breaking the *drive shaft*. The drive shaft is the connecting component that carries torque and transmits rotation. Gears on the axle allow the vehicle to make turns. Axle shafts turn the wheels. The wheels on vehicles turn in three different ways:

- » **Rear-wheel drive:** The rear wheels push the car. The drive shaft extends from the transmission to the rear axle.
- » **Front-wheel drive:** The front wheels pull the car. The drive shaft extends from the transmission to the front axle.
- » **All-wheel drive (four-wheel drive):** All wheels push and pull the car at the same time. The drive shaft extends from the transmission to both axles.

TECHNICAL STUFF

Four-wheel drive vehicles typically have locking differentials (the handy mechanical components that allow powered wheels to turn at different speeds). The driver can choose to engage two wheels or all four. In all-wheel drive vehicles, which are common in SUVs, a computer controls braking and other functions to provide traction in slippery conditions.

The drive system also includes a *transmission.* The transmission changes the speed of the engine in relation to the speed of the rear wheels (in rear-wheel drive), the front wheels (in front-wheel drive), or all the wheels (in four-wheel or all-wheel drive). Vehicles have two types of transmissions: automatic or manual (stick shift).

The transmission consists of several gears that allow the driver to control the amount of torque used. When the terrain is difficult (for example, steep) the wheels need more *torque* (the force that produces rotation) in order to move. You need less torque when you're driving on slippery surfaces to help prevent your wheels from spinning. The transmission increases torque as needed. In an automatic transmission, the torque change is automatic thanks to a *torque converter.* In a manual transmission, the driver shifts the gears by compressing the *clutch,* which disconnects the engine from the drive shaft, and moving the *gear shift* inside the car by hand. Changing to a different gear (torque) requires temporarily disconnecting the engine. The clutch also allows the engine to run when the car isn't moving.

REMEMBER

People often refer to torque by assigning it a gear. Lower gears equal more engine power. For example, first gear produces the largest amount of torque; it's enough to get a heavy car moving when the car is at a dead stop. Automatic transmissions shift into higher gears (and drivers switch gears manually) when a vehicle is already rolling and doesn't need as much power to keep up its momentum.

Suspension and steering systems: Keeping it on the road

No matter how powerful an engine is, it's no use if you can't control the vehicle. The suspension system, steering system, and tires, with some help from on-board computers, tackle that big job.

The *suspension system* maximizes friction between the tires and the road surface by keeping the two in contact as much as possible, which gives a driver the ability to handle the car well. Without a suspension system, every little bump would transfer energy into the car's chassis — and riding in a car would be a lot more like riding in a jerking, jolting old horse carriage. (I discuss the chassis earlier in this chapter.) The springs and shock absorbers create a smoother ride as the vehicle rolls over bumps, potholes, and debris in the road.

Here's a rundown of the most important parts of a suspension system, which you can see in Figure 13-3:

- **Struts:** *Struts* support the weight of the vehicle and keep it from collapsing to the ground. Typically, a strut has an attached spring that helps the vehicle adapt to irregularities in the road.
- **Shock absorbers:** Also simply called *shocks,* these handy gadgets are part of the struts in modern cars. They consist of a piston inside a hydraulic fluid-filled, sealed tube. When the tire hits a bump (or anything else), it pushes up the piston inside the tube instead of jolting the vehicle's chassis.
- **Tires:** The tires are a vehicle's first — and hopefully only — contact with the road. The air inside the tires helps with stability and handling. The rubber creates traction caused by friction.
- **Springs:** Springs hold the chassis up and work with the shocks to let the wheels move up and down smoothly.
- **Steering knuckle:** The *steering knuckle* is the connection point between a tie rod and a wheel, and it's the point that controls where the wheel turns.
- **Control arms:** Also called *A-arms,* these long, metal pieces connect to the steering knuckle with ball joints and keep it vertical when the wheels move up and down. You find an upper and a lower arm on each steering knuckle.
- **Tie rods:** *Tie rods* transfer force from the steering linkage or steering rack to the steering knuckle, which causes a wheel to turn.

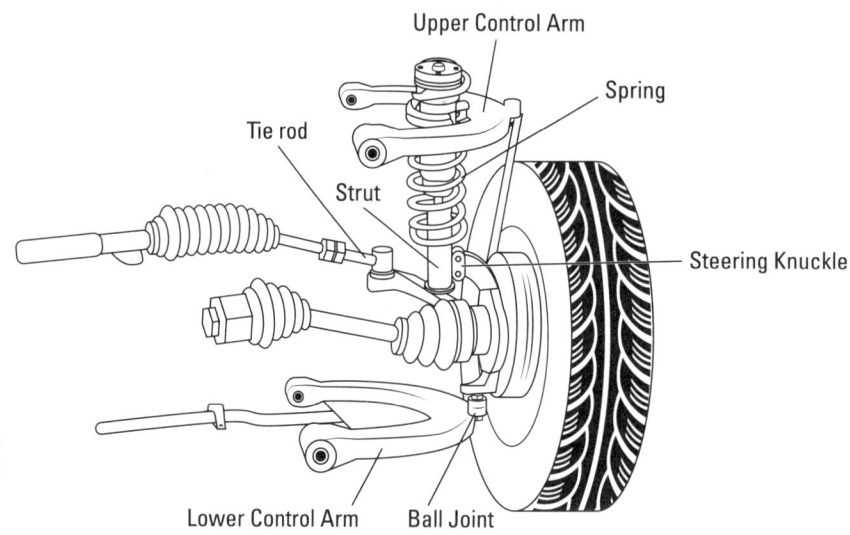

FIGURE 13-3: A basic suspension system.

© John Wiley & Sons, Inc.

A vehicle's steering system lets the driver control where the wheels go. A driver can use light force to steer a heavy car because most cars use one of two systems: rack-and-pinion or Pitman arm steering. Both of these types of steering are often power-assisted, which makes turning the steering wheel and getting a response from the vehicle's wheels easier.

THE MAGIC OF ABS

In the modern world of cars, most vehicles are equipped with an *antilock brake system* (ABS). The ABS is a four-wheel system (usually) that prevents the wheels from locking up. The system does this by automatically adjusting the brake pressure during an emergency stop. This enables the driver to maintain steering control and to stop in the shortest possible distance under most conditions.

The theory behind ABS is simple. If your car isn't equipped with ABS and you have to stop quickly, your wheels simply stop turning when you hit the brakes. If your tires don't have much traction on the road, your car may continue forward in a skid, even though the wheels are locked. You don't stop as quickly as you would with ABS, and you won't be able to steer. However, with ABS, your wheels are slowed to a stop as quickly as possible, without locking up, which gives you much better control during an emergency stop situation.

Brake system: Pulling out all the stops

When a vehicle is in motion, you apply brakes to stop the car from moving. Each wheel has a brake that applies friction to the wheel to stop its rotation. The friction takes motion energy and turns it into heat energy (which is why you shouldn't ride your brakes — they'll overheat and degrade).

All types of brake systems share several components. First, the *brake pedal* provides the connection between the driver and the braking mechanism. The *master cylinder* is just on the other side of the brake pedal, and its job is to push *brake fluid* through *brake lines* that operate the brake assemblies at the wheels. (That fluid comes from — and goes back to — the *fluid reservoir*, which sits on top of the master cylinder.) What happens next depends on the type of brakes:

» **Drum brakes:** In a drum brake, the lines are connected to a *hydraulic cylinder* on each wheel. This cylinder contains pistons that move outward and force two *brake shoes* against the metal drum that rotates with the wheel.

» **Disc brakes:** In a *disc-brake system,* the master cylinder forces a caliper containing a piston or pistons, with brake pads on each side, to squeeze against a rotor disc in each wheel, thus stopping your car by using fluid and pressure on both sides of the rotor.

TECHNICAL STUFF

Most modern cars use both drum brakes and disc brakes. Drum brakes are usually installed on the rear wheels, and disc brakes are generally installed on the front wheels. A drum brake system usually consists of a rotating drum with shoes that expand to rub the inside of a drum. This differs from the disc brake, which uses pads that pinch both sides of a rotating disc, effectively doubling the stopping power.

Cruising toward a Better Score

If you haven't picked up much automotive knowledge by this point in your life and want to do well on this part of the ASVAB, one thing you can do is get a car manual and take your car apart (hoping that you can get it back together again).

Or you can check out your local community college, which may be a more practical solution. Many community colleges offer basic automotive repair classes. You may also want to take a gander at the following books published by Wiley:

- *Auto Repair For Dummies* by Deanna Sclar
- *Car Hacks & Mods For Dummies* by David Vespremi

On this part of the exam, you usually either know the answer or you say, "Huh?" However, you can answer some questions you run into by using the common-sense approach. For example, say you run into a question on the ASVAB that reads something like the following:

The system responsible for cleaning toxic emissions from spent automobile fuel is the

(A) drivetrain.

(B) heating and cooling system.

(C) exhaust system.

(D) both Choice (B) and Choice (C).

Even if you haven't read up on the vehicle exhaust system, you probably know a car's exhaust is toxic. That means the common-sense answer would be Choice (C), which in this case is the correct answer.

Try another one:

Antifreeze mixed with water in an engine's coolant system will

(A) lower the boiling point of the water.

(B) lower the freezing point of the water.

(C) keep the boiling point of the water the same.

(D) raise the freezing point of the water.

In this case, the best answer would be Choice (B). It's an anti-freezing compound (hence the name), which means the temperature must be colder than normal (the normal freezing point of water is 32 degrees Fahrenheit and 0 degrees Celsius) for the coolant to freeze solid.

When all else fails, guessing is okay. If you guess, you have a 25 percent chance of guessing the right answer. If you leave the answer blank, you have a 0 percent chance. If you're taking the computerized version of the ASVAB, you don't have a choice, of course, because you must provide an answer before you're presented with the next question. For general guessing hints, check out Chapter 3.

Auto Information Practice Questions

If you like to tinker with cars and your idea of a fun weekend is to rebuild the engine, you should do well on this subtest without too much additional study. If your idea of fixing your car involves calling the mechanic down the street, a little extra study may be in order.

Easy Auto Information practice questions

1. A vehicle's underlying framework connecting its major components is its
   (A) chassis.
   (B) engine compartment.
   (C) wheel well.
   (D) frame.

2. Which of the following is NOT normally part of a routine automotive tuneup?
   (A) Replace the air filter.
   (B) Replace the spark plugs.
   (C) Replace the CV axles.
   (D) Check the fluids.

3. Antifreeze is used to
   (A) prevent the engine from overheating.
   (B) prevent water in the cooling system from freezing.
   (C) prevent damage to the engine block.
   (D) all of the above.

4. Why may you be hesitant to offer a jump start to another vehicle?
   (A) The battery terminals are not corroded.
   (B) One of the vehicles has a digital ignition system.
   (C) One of the vehicles makes a clicking sound when attempting to start.
   (D) The vehicle is really dirty.

5. What engine component keeps running power to a vehicle's electronics when the engine is running?
   (A) spark plugs
   (B) battery
   (C) alternator
   (D) rectifier

6. What part of a vehicle supports its weight?
   (A) shocks
   (B) struts
   (C) A-arms
   (D) crankcase

7. The instrument that measures revolutions per minute on a vehicle's dashboard is the
   (A) valve spring
   (B) speedometer
   (C) tachometer
   (D) compression management system

8. A compression ignition engine is also called a
   (A) diesel engine.
   (B) electric engine.
   (C) V-twin engine.
   (D) carbureted engine.

9. Most internal combustion engines are
   (A) air-cooled.
   (B) liquid-cooled.
   (C) oil-cooled.
   (D) distributor-cooled.

10. What part of an engine supplies a high-voltage current to spark plugs?
    (A) condenser system
    (B) fuel injector system
    (C) powertrain system
    (D) ignition system

11. What part of an engine houses a piston?
    (A) valves
    (B) cylinder
    (C) cylinder head
    (D) combustion chamber

12. Pressing a vehicle's accelerator
    (A) opens the throttle.
    (B) transports more fuel to the carburetor or fuel injectors.
    (C) causes the vehicle to move faster.
    (D) all of the above.

13. An antilock brake system prevents a vehicle's wheels from
    (A) moving.
    (B) turning.
    (C) locking.
    (D) steering.

14. The shaft on which wheels revolve is called the
    (A) axle.
    (B) driveshaft.
    (C) suspension.
    (D) shock.

15. What is most likely to occur if a spark plug's gap is too wide?
    (E) It could damage the motor.
    (F) It could misfire.
    (G) The car could swerve.
    (H) A fire could start in the engine.

Medium Auto Information practice questions

16. The component of a water-cooled engine that dissipates heat is the

    (A) radiator.
    (B) oil gallery.
    (C) water jacket.
    (D) manifold.

17. A carburetor has the same function as a/an

    (A) distributor.
    (B) fuel-injection system.
    (C) alternator.
    (D) exhaust system.

18. What is the primary purpose of an intake manifold?

    (A) to burn fuel
    (B) to distribute the air/fuel mixture
    (C) to ignite the spark plugs
    (D) to circulate coolant

19. The system that controls how much power goes to a vehicle's wheels is its

    (A) transmission.
    (B) fuel injector.
    (C) spark plug TDC.
    (D) spark plug BDC.

20. A catalytic converter

    (A) injects fuel into the combustion chamber.
    (B) converts chemical energy into mechanical energy.
    (C) runs the exhaust manifold.
    (D) reduces toxic emissions.

21. What is the stroke that creates a vacuum that sucks air-fuel mix into the cylinder?

    (A) intake stroke
    (B) compression stroke
    (C) combustion stroke
    (D) exhaust stroke

22. What are the main differences between carburetors and fuel injectors?

    (A) Carburetors are found only in new cars, and fuel injectors are found only in older cars.
    (B) Carburetors mix air and fuel mechanically, and fuel injectors use electronic systems to inject fuel.
    (C) Fuel injectors are used only in diesel engines.
    (D) Carburetors are more efficient than fuel injectors are.

23. A suspension system improves a vehicle's handling by

    (A) keeping the wheels in contact with the road and absorbing bumps.
    (B) ensuring the vehicle's engine produces maximum horsepower.
    (C) connecting to the driveshaft to make steering easier.
    (D) working better with certain types of tires.

24. Electric vehicles differ from gasoline-powered vehicles because they

    (A) use multiple internal combustion engines to generate power.
    (B) have instant torque at the wheels.
    (C) rely on gasoline and gasoline byproducts to power their electric motors.
    (D) require a transmission and drive shaft to transfer power to the wheels.

25. In a manual transmission vehicle, what is the clutch's role?

    (A) to increase the amount of fuel delivered to the engine
    (B) to assist in braking by reducing engine speed
    (C) to disconnect the engine from the drive shaft during gear changes
    (D) to control coolant's flow through the engine

26. An engine's exhaust manifold functions in the exhaust system by

(A) filtering exhaust gases and reducing emissions.

(B) cooling down exhaust gases.

(C) connecting the engine's exhaust ports, collecting gases from each cylinder.

(D) controlling the amount of fuel that enters the combustion chamber.

27. What does a timing belt do in an internal combustion engine?

(A) provides power to the alternator and water pump

(B) reduces engine noise

(C) increases fuel efficiency

(D) synchronizes the camshaft and crankshaft's rotation

28. In a vehicle's electrical system, the alternator

(A) stores electrical energy.

(B) converts battery energy into usable power.

(C) ensures spark plugs get the correct voltage.

(D) converts mechanical energy into electrical energy.

29. What happens during the compression stroke in a four-stroke engine?

(A) The air-fuel mixture is pressurized in the combustion chamber.

(B) Exhaust gases exit the cylinder.

(C) The spark plug ignites the air-fuel mixture.

(D) The piston moves down.

30. Piston rings

(A) prevent air from entering the combustion chamber and oil from leaking out.

(B) prevent oil from entering the combustion chamber and gases from leaking out.

(C) regulate the amount of fuel entering the cylinder.

(D) keep the crankshaft and camshaft lubricated.

Hard Auto Information practice questions

31. An engine's rotational energy is stored by using which mechanical device?

    (A) connecting rod
    (B) rear axle
    (C) flywheel
    (D) cylinder

32. A catalytic converter

    (A) charges the battery while the engine is running.
    (B) creates chemical reactions.
    (C) converts heat energy into power.
    (D) controls the drivetrain.

33. What assembly is pictured?

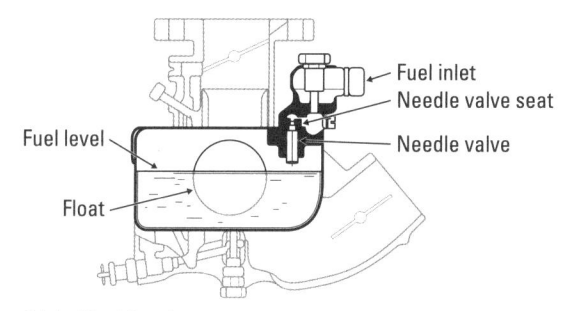

    © John Wiley & Sons, Inc.

    (A) exhaust
    (B) compressor
    (C) carburetor
    (D) radiator

34. Identify the vehicle part shown here.

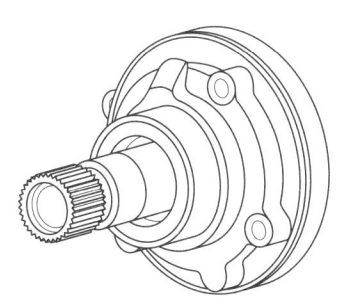

    © John Wiley & Sons, Inc.

    (A) water pump
    (B) fuel filter
    (C) oil pump
    (D) air compressor

35. What component in an internal combustion engine helps convert pistons' linear motion into rotational motion?

    (A) camshaft
    (B) alternator
    (C) crankshaft
    (D) timing belt

36. How does an exhaust gas recirculation system reduce emissions?

    (A) It filters carbon dioxide from the exhaust.
    (B) It recycles exhaust back into the combustion chamber.
    (C) It reduces the engine's temperature to prevent overheating.
    (D) It burns excess fuel in the exhaust system.

37. In a diesel engine, combustion occurs because

    (A) the fuel is preheated.
    (B) compressed air in the cylinder raises the temperature.
    (C) fuel is mixed with pure oxygen.
    (D) diesel fuel contains automatically igniting chemicals.

38. Glow plugs

    (A) ignite fuel by producing a spark.
    (B) regulate the flow of diesel fuel to the combustion chamber.
    (C) increase compression pressure.
    (D) preheat air in the combustion chamber.

CHAPTER 13 Auto Information   293

39. What does a positive crankcase ventilation system do?

- **(A)** allows unburned fuel and gases to recirculate into the cylinder
- **(B)** prevents the engine from overheating by releasing gases
- **(C)** expels exhaust gases from the combustion chamber at high speeds
- **(D)** controls the amount of fuel entering the compression chamber

40. The oil galleries in an internal combustion engine

- **(A)** store excess oil for future use.
- **(B)** allow oil to flow for lubrication and heat dissipation.
- **(C)** cool the pistons and cylinders by circulating oil directly through them.
- **(D)** increase the oil pump's pressure for better lubrication.

Answers and Explanations

Use this answer key to score the Auto Information practice questions.

1. **A.** The chassis is like the vehicle's skeleton, holding together and connecting all its major parts and systems, including the engine, transmission, wheels, suspension, and steering system.

2. **C.** A general automotive tuneup consists of checking or replacing the following: air and fuel filter, belts, spark plugs, battery, fluids, ignition timing, and tire pressure. You can also change the positive crankcase ventilation valve and change the points and condenser if you have an older vehicle. Replacing the CV (constant velocity) axles is something that happens when they become worn, which occurs after many routine replacements of plugs, filters, oil, and so on.

3. **D.** Antifreeze raises the boiling point of water and lowers the freezing point. This process keeps the water in the cooling system from overheating or freezing. Either condition can cause damage to the engine.

4. **B.** Capacitive discharge ignitions, like digital ignition systems, store charged energy for the spark in a capacitor within the vehicle, releasing it to the spark plug on demand. Because all the energy is stored in the capacitor for the vehicle to release the energy, using the battery doesn't help give or receive power and could result in an overload.

5. **C.** The alternator converts mechanical to electrical energy and uses it to operate the electronic accessories. It continues to circulate power through the vehicle and charge the battery while the vehicle is running.

6. **B.** Struts support a vehicle's weight. They contain a coil spring and shock absorbers, and they shift the weight of the car to its tires.

7. **C.** Tachometers measure the number of crankshaft revolutions per minute (rpm).

8. **A.** Diesel engines are also called compression engines. They don't rely on a spark to ignite fuel, but they do rely on glow plugs to heat the air in a cylinder's combustion chamber.

9. **B.** Most modern internal combustion engines are liquid-cooled; liquid coolant picks up heat and carries it through the radiator, where the heat disperses.

10. **D.** The ignition system takes current from the battery, steps it up, and sends it to the spark plugs.

11. **B.** Pistons live inside cylinders, where they move up and down.

12. **D.** An accelerator is connected to the throttle, and when you press it, you open the throttle. This allows more fuel to go to the carburetor or fuel injectors, resulting in the vehicle moving faster.

13. **C.** Like the name implies, an antilock brake system prevents a vehicle's wheels from locking when you apply the brake. It automatically adjusts brake pressure for you, helping prevent skids.

14. **A.** Wheels turn on an axle.

15. B. A spark plug that has too wide a gap may not fire at all, or it may misfire at high speeds.

16. A. Coolant (typically antifreeze mixed with water) runs through the radiator, which exposes it to outside air so heat energy can escape.

17. B. The alternator, exhaust system, and distributor all have very different purposes from the carburetor, which combines the fuel and air mixture and sends it to the engine, just as the fuel-injection system does.

18. B. The primary purpose of an *intake manifold* is to evenly distribute the air/fuel mixture to the cylinders in an internal combustion engine.

19. A. The transmission's job is to make sure the right amount of power gets to the vehicle's wheels so it can move at a certain speed. The transmission works because it contains a series of gears, and the lower the gear, the more power (but slower speed) it generates. First gear is the largest.

20. D. A catalytic converter creates chemical reactions that help neutralize toxins in a vehicle's exhaust.

21. A. During the intake stroke, the intake valve opens and the connecting rod pulls the piston down. This creates a vacuum that sucks air-fuel mix into the cylinder.

22. B. Carburetors rely on the mechanical vacuum created on an intake stroke to draw fuel into the air, while fuel injectors use electronics to spray fuel directly where it needs to be.

23. A. A vehicle's suspension system helps keep all the wheels (tires) in contact with the road and creates a springing motion when the vehicle runs over bumps.

24. B. Electric vehicles have instant torque at the wheels. Gasoline-powered cars require power to build up gradually as the engine revs up.

25. C. The clutch disconnects the engine from the drive shaft so you can change gears without damaging the transmission.

26. C. The exhaust manifold collects gases from each cylinder's exhaust port and then funnels them into the exhaust system.

27. D. The timing belt ensures the camshaft and crankshaft rotate in sync, which ensures that the valves open and close at the right times during combustion.

28. D. The alternator takes the mechanical energy that the engine's rotation generates and converts it into electrical energy. That energy can charge the car's battery and power all its electronics while the engine is running.

29. A. During the compression stroke, the piston moves up. This compresses the air-fuel mixture inside the combustion chamber, which prepares it for ignition.

30. B. Piston rings create a seal between the piston and cylinder wall to prevent oil from getting in and gases from getting out.

31. **C.** The flywheel accelerates a rotor to a high speed and uses rotational energy to maintain and store the energy to keep the engine speed constant as the flywheel and rotor work together. As for the other devices, the drive shaft turns the rear axle. The cylinder contains the piston that moves the connecting rod that's connected to the crankshaft, which turns the flywheel.

32. **B.** The catalytic converter creates chemical reactions that makes toxic gases less harmful.

33. **C.** A *carburetor* is an assembly used in an engine (mostly used in older cars and machines) that mixes fuel and air to an appropriate amount in order for the engine to run properly.

34. **C.** An *oil pump* is a small pump located in the crankcase that circulates the oil from the oil pan to the moving parts of the engine.

35. **C.** As the pistons move up and down (linearly) within the cylinders, the crankshaft rotates. That turns linear motion into rotational motion.

36. **B.** The exhaust gas recirculation system reduces nitrogen oxide emissions by recirculating some exhaust gases back into the combustion chamber, which lowers the combustion temperature.

37. **B.** In a diesel engine, the air inside the cylinder is highly compressed, and that raises its temperature. When the diesel fuel is injected, it ignites automatically because of the high temperature. No spark necessary!

38. **D.** Glow plugs preheat the air in the combustion chamber, especially when it's cold outside and the pressurized air may not be hot enough to ignite the fuel on its own.

39. **A.** The PCV system helps manage gases that escape the combustion chamber and build up in the engine's crankcase. It recirculates them back into the intake manifold, where they're burned in the combustion process, which reduces emissions and improves engine efficiency.

40. **B.** Oil galleries are passages that allow oil to flow and lubricate moving parts.

IN THIS CHAPTER

» **Identifying various types of tools**

» **Checking out the many uses of fasteners**

» **Nailing down a good test score**

Chapter 14
Shop Information

If you're afraid you'll end up hitting your thumb with a hammer studying to get a good score on the Auto & Shop Information subtest(s) of the ASVAB, don't worry. The shop questions generally just ask you to identify a tool or fastener, what you use it for, or how to choose the best tool for a job.

REMEMBER: The computerized exam (CAT-ASVAB) tests Shop Information and Auto Information (which I cover in Chapter 13) in separate subtests but combines your results on them into one score (AS). If you take the pencil-and-paper (P&P) test, you see these topics together in one subtest.

On the CAT-ASVAB, you have 7 minutes to answer 10 questions on Shop Information. If you're taking a computerized test that includes tryout questions, which I explain in Chapter 1, you'll have 18 minutes to answer 25 questions. The Auto & Shop Information subtest consists of 25 questions on the paper-and-pencil version. You get 11 minutes to answer those questions on the paper version of the test, and about half of the questions ask you about shop tools and basic shop principles. (The remaining questions are all about autos, so if you're iffy on engines, automotive tools, or anything else related to vehicles, flip to Chapter 13.)

REMEMBER: The AS score is a way for each branch of the military to gauge how qualified you are for certain jobs. It's not part of your AFQT score, which determines whether you're even eligible to join the military. Remember, though, that performing well on the entire battery of tests helps keep your options open.

Picking Up the Tools of the Trade

You've probably heard the phrase "Use the right tool for the job." The ASVAB folks also believe in using the right tool for the job, and many of the questions on the Shop Information portion of the exam ask you to identify the best tool for certain tasks.

Tools are easiest to understand when you classify them by their functions, so the following sections are divided by function.

Measuring tools

As any woodworking enthusiast will tell you, the golden rule of shop is to "measure twice and cut once." It's frustrating to cut a piece of material only to find it's just a little bit too short to fit in the place you intended or to have to make another cut to trim something down. You can check out some of the most common measuring tools in Figure 14-1.

Tape rules (tape measures), rigid steel rules, steel (or fiberglass) tape rules, and folding rules are all used to measure materials in the shop. *Micrometers* can measure down to thousandths of an inch, so you use them when you need to precisely measure the thickness of a flat object or the outside diameter of a cylinder. You use calipers in a similar way; *outside calipers* measure the external size of an object, and *inside calipers* measure the internal size. *Slide calipers* have a built-in rule.

Depth gauges measure the depth of holes. *Thickness gauges* measure the thickness of small gaps. *Thread gauges* measure the number of threads per inch in threaded fasteners. *Wire gauges* measure the thickness of wire.

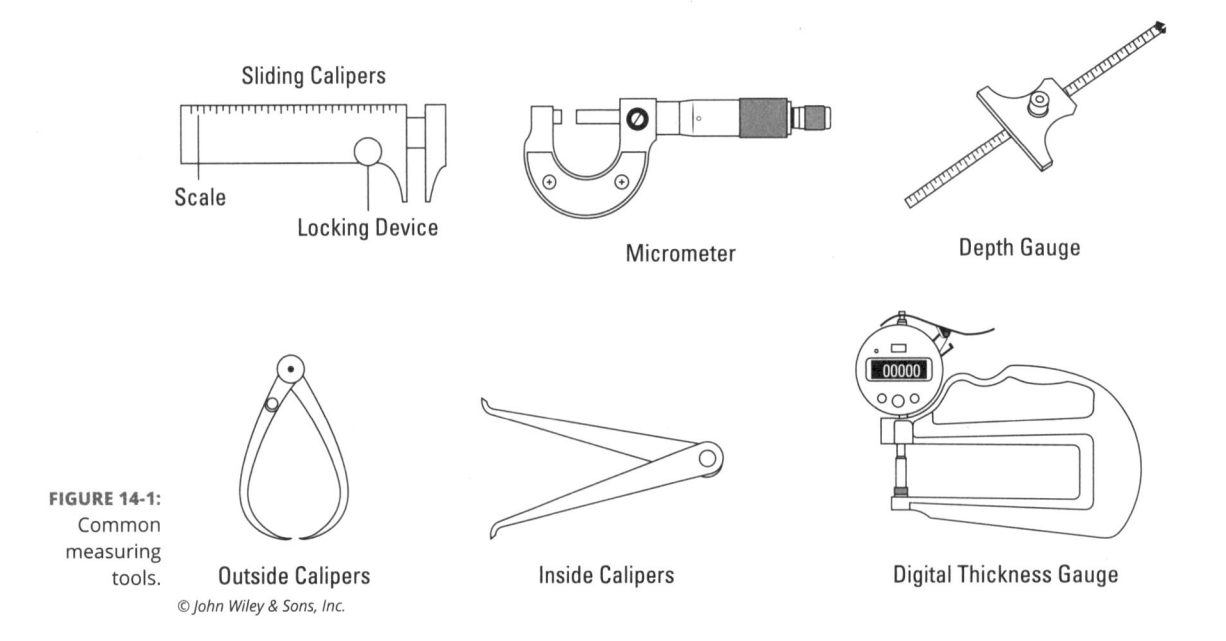

FIGURE 14-1: Common measuring tools.
© John Wiley & Sons, Inc.

Leveling and squaring tools

Levels show whether a horizontal surface is true. A torpedo level has one or more small tubes filled with a liquid (like alcohol) and an air bubble. If the level is placed on a surface and the bubble remains exactly in the center of the tube, the surface is level. When you need to measure trueness across a plane, like a tabletop, you use a bullseye level.

You use a *square* to check the trueness of an angle. Because most squares have a rule, you can also use them for measuring. Squares have two arms: a long one (the *blade*) and a short one (the *tongue*). The two arms meet at a right angle. You can set a square against any angle that's supposed to measure 90 degrees. If a gap exists between the square and the material, the material isn't true — that is, it's not at 90 degrees. A sliding T-bevel has an adjustable blade so you can check different angles.

A *plumb bob* is a heavy weight that's suspended from a line. It indicates vertical trueness. Check out Figure 14-2 to see different types of levels and squares.

FIGURE 14-2: Leveling and squaring tools.

© John Wiley & Sons, Inc.

Striking tools

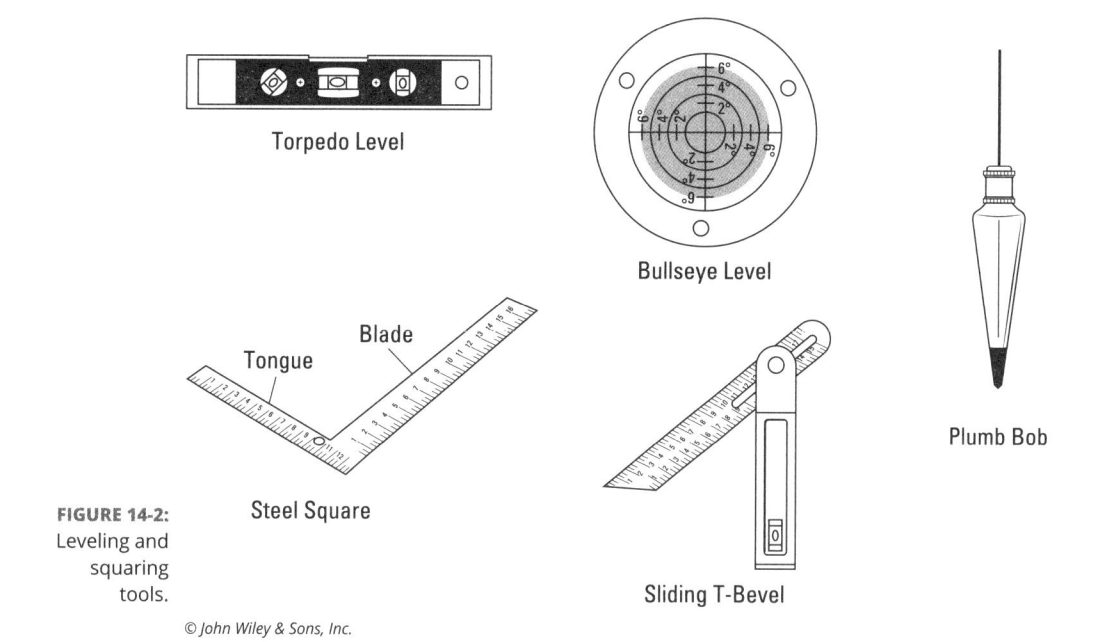

Striking tools apply driving force to an object. (Watch your fingers!) These tools include hammers, sledges, and mallets. Here's a brief explanation of all three:

- **Hammer:** A hammer is generally made of metal and consists of a handle, a head, a face (the part of the hammer that touches the nail or other fastener), a claw (to pull nails), and a wedge that attaches the head to the handle. The face of a hammer may be made of steel, brass, or lead.

- **Mallet:** A mallet is generally made of metal or plastic but may be made of wood or rubber. It's used to strike another tool or to strike a surface without damaging it. A mallet doesn't have a claw like its cousin, the hammer.

- **Sledge:** A sledge is generally made of metal. People use it to drive bolts and chisels and to break rock. Although a small sledge may be used with one hand, many are designed for two-hand use. A sledge doesn't have a claw, either.

Fastening tools

Fastening tools apply fasteners, such as screws, to objects. (For more info on fasteners, check out "Sticking Materials Together with Fasteners" later in this chapter.) Numerous tools make up the fastening category, which you can see in Figure 14-3:

- **Stapler:** A stapler is a fastening tool. Heavy-duty staplers can staple roofing felt to a roof, for instance.

- **Wrenches:** Wrenches turn nuts and bolts. The bolt or nut fits between the jaws of the wrench, and the wrench turns the bolt. Some wrenches have adjustable jaws. Not only can wrenches be used to turn nuts and bolts, but they may also be used to keep nuts and bolts stationary.
  - **Open-end wrenches:** These wrenches have open jaws.
  - **Box wrenches:** Box wrenches are closed. Some wrenches have open-end jaws on one end and a box wrench on the other.

CHAPTER 14 **Shop Information** 301

FIGURE 14-3: Fastening tools.
© John Wiley & Sons, Inc.

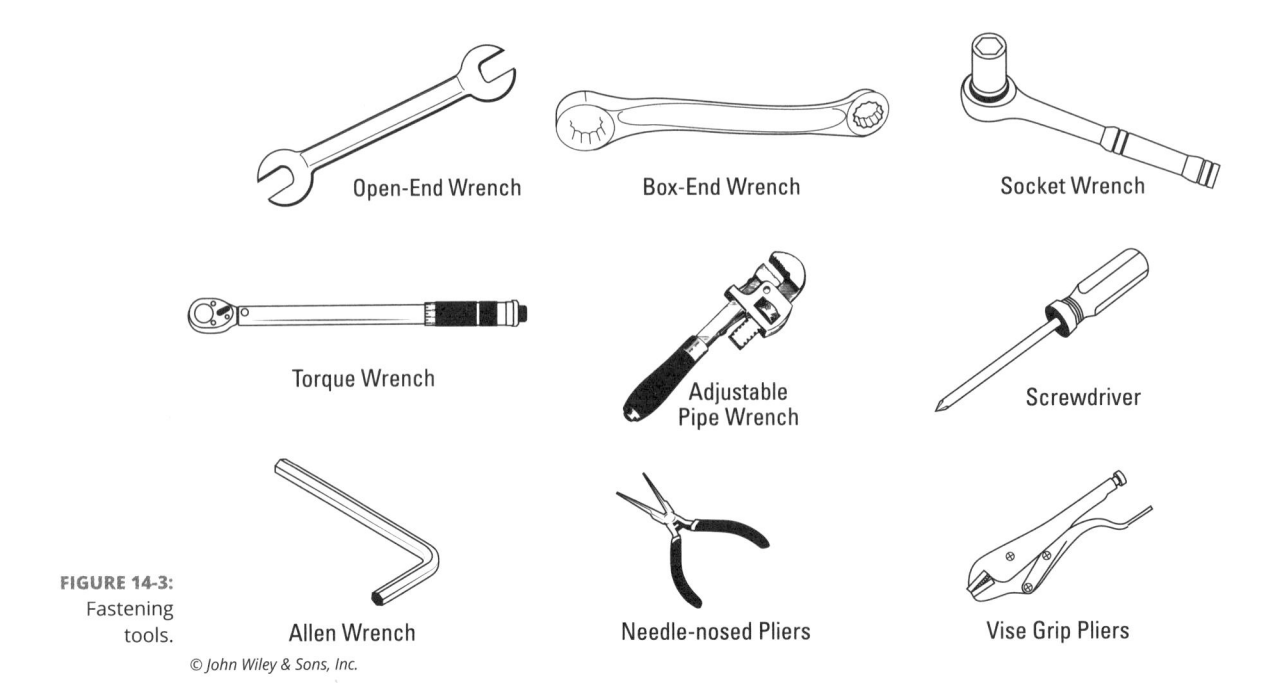

- **Socket wrenches:** Socket wrenches have box-type sockets of varying sizes that can be attached to a handle, which in turn can be attached to an extension.

  Note: Socket, box, and open-ended wrenches come in standard sizes — either in inches or in millimeters. They're not interchangeable. (Selecting the wrong socket wrench is how mechanics learn to use cuss words.)

- **Torque wrenches:** These wrenches apply measured leverage to a fastener. A torque wrench looks much like a socket wrench but has additional internal mechanisms designed to measure and limit the amount of torque (twisting force) being applied.

- **Pipe wrenches:** Pipe wrenches have serrated jaws and grip round objects.

» **Screwdrivers:** A screwdriver, in the shop world, turns screws. (In the civilian world, it's a pretty decent drink!) Some special screwdrivers have different tips to fit different types of screws:

- **Flathead screwdriver:** A flathead screwdriver has a flat tip at one end of the shank (the other end of the shank goes into a handle).

- **Phillips screwdriver:** Phillips screwdrivers have a tip that is shaped like a cross; this tip fits into a cross-shaped Phillips screw head.

- **Allen wrench:** An Allen wrench fits hexagonal screw heads. Nobody knows why this tool is called an Allen wrench instead of an Allen screwdriver; after all, it's used on hexagonal screws. It's sometimes also called a hex key.

  The Allen wrench, which was designed in 1910, gets its name from the Allen Manufacturing Company of Hartford, Connecticut.

- **Offset screwdriver:** Offset screwdrivers have the shank set at an angle to the blade to allow the tool to be used in cramped spaces. Offset screwdrivers can have a standard blade, Phillips blade, or any number of other blades.

» **Pliers:** Pliers can be used to fasten and unfasten fasteners, hold objects, and cut material. When you squeeze the handles, the jaws of the pliers come together.

- **Long-nosed or needle-nosed:** Long-nosed pliers, also called needle-nosed pliers, have tapered jaws that can hold small objects or fit into small spaces.

- **Curved-nose:** These pliers have curved jaws.
- **Slip-joint:** These pliers can be adjusted so the jaws open wider.
- **Wrench and vise-grip:** Wrench pliers and vise-grip pliers have serrated jaws that clamp onto and hold objects of all shapes. Vise-grip pliers are adjustable and can lock into a closed position.
- **Cutting:** These pliers are used to cut wire.

Soldering and welding tools

Soldering and welding are two methods of fastening materials together, but they're unlike the fastening methods I cover in the "Sticking Materials Together with Fasteners" section later in this chapter.

Soldering is a process that joins metals together by bonding a metal alloy (usually a combination of lead and tin) between two surfaces. Most soldering irons and soldering guns — the tools necessary for melting metal alloy — are electrically powered. Usually, you can solder two objects together with fairly low temperatures (less than 800 degrees Fahrenheit) because you are only melting the bonding alloy. The amount of lead in your solder determines how hot your iron or gun needs to be (more lead means a lower melting temperature).

Welding creates incredibly strong joints. Rather than melting a metal alloy to use like glue, welding involves melting the base metal of two surfaces you want to join — and it requires very high temperatures that depend on the types of metal you're joining. The two major types of welding are oxyacetylene welding and electric-arc welding. *Oxyacetylene welding* requires a torch fueled by oxygen and acetylene, which burns hot enough to melt steel and other iron-based metals. *Electric-arc* welding uses electricity to generate heat. Common forms of electric-arc welding are MIG, TIG, and stick welding.

Cutting tools

Cutting tools use sharp blades to cut through metal, wood, or other materials. Cutting tools have teeth. The number of teeth per inch (or points per inch) gives an indication of the type of work the saw can do. Because of the way points and teeth are counted, a saw always has one more point per inch than tooth per inch. A saw with fewer teeth is used for rough work, like cutting wood to size. A saw with more teeth cuts more finely and is used for more delicate work, like sawing joints and lightweight pieces of wood for molding in a house. Check out Table 14-1 for a breakdown of the different cutting tools that may be covered on the ASVAB.

Drilling, punching, and gouging tools

No, this section isn't about hand-to-hand combat training from basic training. Masters in the art of shop often make holes in the material they're working with in order to build that perfect birdhouse (or whatever they're working on). These holes can be made with a variety of tools, which I cover in the following sections. You can see some examples in Figure 14-4.

Drills and bits

Twist drills use *drill bits*, which are round pieces of steel shaped in a spiral, to create holes. Drill bits are attached to a drill (usually a power drill but sometimes a hand drill operated by manually turning a crank). The point of the drill bit is sharpened, and the shank is smooth and fits into the drill's adjustable chuck.

TABLE 14-1 Cutting Tools

Cutting Tool	Description/Function
Bolt cutters	Heavy-duty shears that produce enough force when the handles are closed to slice through metal bolts, chains, or rods
Circle snips	Used to cut curves
Coping saw	A type of handsaw that's used to cut curved lines or shapes
Crosscut saw	A type of handsaw that cuts against the grain of the wood; the shape of the teeth and the angle in which they're set are the main differences in this type of saw
Hacksaw	A type of handsaw that's used to cut metal; a hacksaw has an adjustable frame that holds thin blades of varying length in place; a handle is set in one end
Pipe cutters and tube cutters	Used to score and cut metal pipes and tubes
Ripsaw	A type of handsaw that cuts with the grain of the wood; the shape of the teeth and the angle in which they're set are the main differences in this type of saw
Snips and shears	Snips and shears have two cutting blades that scissor together when the handles close; the blades can be curved or straight

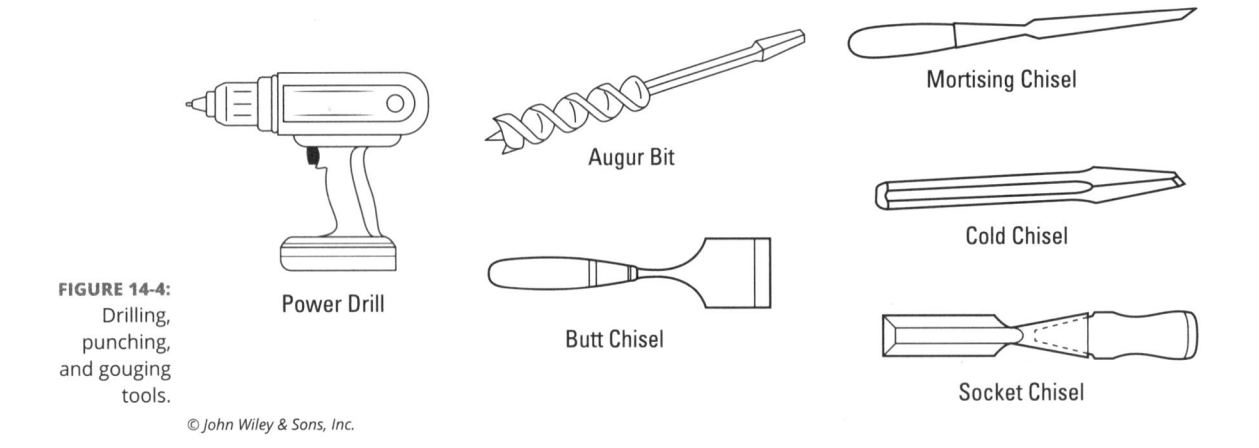

FIGURE 14-4: Drilling, punching, and gouging tools.

Power Drill, Augur Bit, Butt Chisel, Mortising Chisel, Cold Chisel, Socket Chisel

© John Wiley & Sons, Inc.

TECHNICAL STUFF

A *countersink* is a drill bit that enlarges just the surface of a hole so a screw head can be accommodated. A countersink allows the top of the fastener to be set flush with or below the material to which it's attached. Without a countersink, the fastener slightly protrudes from the material to which it's been attached.

Auger bits bore larger holes. They're shaped differently from drill bits. They have a long, deep spiral flute for easy chip removal. They're also much larger. Auger bits are most commonly used with a brace for drilling holes in wood. Their average length varies from 7 to 10 inches, but larger auger bits can be several feet long. Variants are even used to dig holes in the ground when attached to large machinery.

Punches

Punches have a sharp end that's placed against the material to be punctured; the other end is struck with a hammer. A center punch is used to mark where a drilled hole is to be placed; this keeps the drill bit in position and prevents the drill bit from wandering to another part of the material during the first few rotations.

WARNING: Using a Phillips screwdriver as a punch is bad form in the shop world because hitting the handle of a screwdriver with a hammer can damage it (and then you'll get talked about in serious shop circles).

Chisels

Chisels are made of steel and have a sharp cutting edge. They're used to chip or cut metal or wood:

- **Metal-cutting chisels:** Chisels that cut metal are usually struck with a hammer to make the cut. These chisels have different shapes depending on how they'll be used; *cold chisels* are flat, and they're used for cutting metals without using heating torches or forges, whereas *round chisels* make circular cuts.

- **Wood-cutting chisels:** Some wood chisels, called *socket chisels,* are struck with a mallet. Other wood chisels require only the pressure of your hands.

  Wood chisels also come in different shapes, depending on what they're used for. A *butt chisel* has a short blade and is used for in-close work. A *mortising chisel* has a narrow blade made for chiseling out the narrow mortises to create joints. A *framing chisel* has a heavy, strong blade meant for rough work.

WARNING: Because you use chisels with other tools and the pressure of your hands, there's a little bit of a risk involved with this tool. One slip, and these instruments can easily cut large chunks out of your skin, so be careful.

Finishing tools

Filing and finishing shop tools are used to sharpen the blades of other tools and to smooth the edges of cut objects. Files come in a range of coarseness, and the blades can cut in different patterns. Files also come in different shapes to finish different kinds of objects. Here are the different kinds of files:

- **Single-cut:** Single-cut files are used for finishing work and sharpening blades.
- **Double-cut:** Double-cut files are used for rough work.
- **Flat files and half-round:** These files are for general purposes.
- **Square and round:** These files fit square and round openings.

Planes are a type of finishing tool used to prepare wood for final finishing, to fit doors and trim, and to create flat surfaces for furniture. A plane body or frame has two handles: a handle to push with and a knob to guide with. A plane has four other parts: a blade or iron, a chip breaker, a lever cap, and a frog, which is used to hold the blade. *Bench planes* are used to smooth surfaces. Longer planes give a more uniform surface by shaving off a portion of the wood. A *planer* is a larger machine that takes the same concept and allows you to create a flat surface on a board by using several blades attached to a roller.

Clamping tools

A clamping tool is a device used to hold or fasten objects securely so they won't move while you're working on them. Several types of clamping tools are available for many different purposes:

» **Pliers:** Pliers (discussed in the "Fastening tools" section earlier in the chapter) can be used to hold objects while you're working on them.

» **Vises:** Vises hold material while it's being sawed, drilled, or glued. Here are some different types of vises:

- **Bench vise:** A bench vise has large, rough jaws that keep the material from slipping.
- **Pipe vise:** Pipe vises hold round material or pipes.
- **Hand screw vise:** A hand screw vise has two hard, wooden jaws connected by two long screws. The screws are tightened to bring the jaws of the hand screw vise together.

» **Clamps:** Clamps are used when a vise won't work. Vises generally attach to a workbench, while clamps generally connect only to the items being worked with. C-clamps consist of a cast-iron "C" frame and a screw that moves back and forth to open and shut the clamp. Bar clamps hold material together that can measure several feet wide.

Figure 14-5 shows you an example of a vise and a C-clamp.

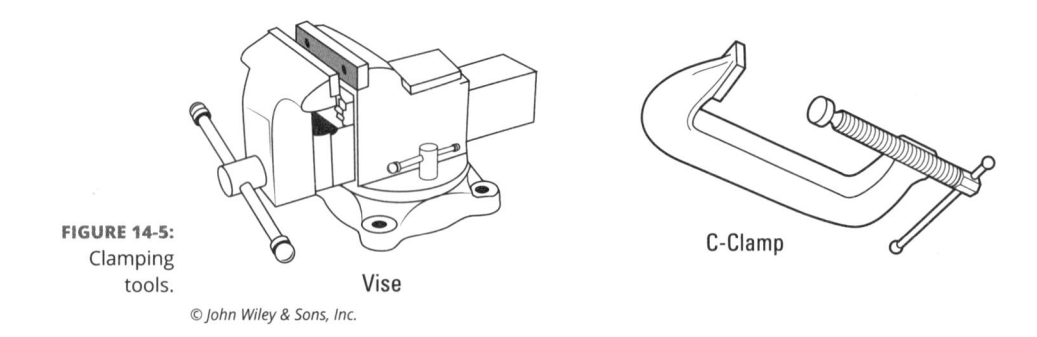

FIGURE 14-5: Clamping tools.

Vise   C-Clamp

© John Wiley & Sons, Inc.

Sticking Materials Together with Fasteners

Although wood and metal (and other materials) can be held together with glue, straps, duct tape, and other brilliant fastening methods, people usually fasten these types of materials with nails, screws, bolts, and rivets. These fasteners offer more strength and stability than the white glue that you used to fasten painted macaroni noodles onto construction paper in the first grade.

Nails

Nails are used to hold pieces of wood together. The nail head is flat, and the shank is usually round. Nails are preferable to screws for structures that need some flex, like the frame of a house, because nails bend more. Nail length is designated by the *penny system*, which is abbreviated with a *d*. A ten-penny nail is a 10d nail. Length and thickness generally correspond. The higher the penny size, the longer the nail. Nails that are larger than 20-penny are called *spikes* and are measured in inches.

TECHNICAL STUFF: The penny system is used in the United States. It originates from the price of 100 nails in the 15th century in England.

Other types of nails include the following:

- **Brads and finishing nails:** They have heads that are made to fit flush with or slightly below the surface of the wood.
- **Common nails:** These nails are the most commonly used nails. (How about that for a truly difficult vocab word?)
- **Double-headed nails:** These have two heads, one lower than the other, and a point on the other end. The nail is driven to the lower head but can be pulled out of the material because of the remaining higher head. These nails are used for temporary construction that will be taken apart.

Screws and bolts

Unlike nails, you can easily take screws and bolts out of the wood without causing additional damage to the wood (unless, of course, the threads are stripped). Figure 14-6 shows a few options. These fasteners also hold more tightly than nails, and the fit doesn't flex. Screws have flat heads, round heads, or oval heads; in addition to this classification, they also have standard heads (for flathead screwdrivers) or Phillips heads (with cross-shape slots). Screw sizes are based on length and the diameter of the unthreaded part of the screw.

Here's the lowdown on these types of fasteners:

- **Wood screws:** Wood screws are used to fasten wood. (Hmm, ingenious!)
- **Lag screws:** Lag screws have square- or hexagon-shaped heads and are used for large projects.
- **Bolts:** Bolts don't thread into wood. They have flat ends (as opposed to the pointed ends of screws). They're held in place by a nut (which is what actually screws into the threads) and washer. The body of the bolt may have few threads or many.
- **Machine screws:** Machine screws are used to fasten metal parts. Machine screws are sometimes used with nuts. They come in various lengths and widths and have a wide variety of heads.

FIGURE 14-6: Screws and bolts. Flathead Screw   Phillips Head Screw   Bolt
© John Wiley & Sons, Inc.

Nuts and washers

Nuts can be square, but more often they're hexagonal. *Cap nuts* are rounded and smooth; *stop nuts* prevent the screw or bolt from coming loose. *Wing nuts* have flanges on each side so they can be tightened by hand.

Washers prevent damage to the surface of a material by preventing the bolt head from digging into the material. They also help keep the bolt (or screw) in place. *Flat washers*, a simple ring of flat metal, are the most common type of washer. *Shake-proof washers* have teeth to prevent them from slipping, while *split lock washers* apply a small spring force that prevent the nut from vibrating off.

You can see many of these fasteners in Figure 14-7.

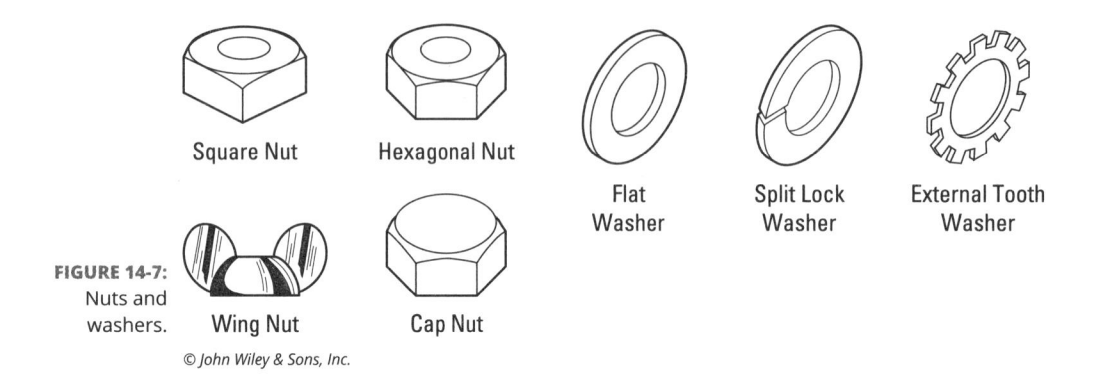

FIGURE 14-7: Nuts and washers.

Square Nut — Hexagonal Nut — Flat Washer — Split Lock Washer — External Tooth Washer — Wing Nut — Cap Nut

© John Wiley & Sons, Inc.

Rivets

Rivets are commonly used to fasten parts together, especially when welding would prevent the parts from being disassembled. You drive standard rivets by using a *bucking bar*. Rivets come in a wide variety of lengths, diameters, and head shapes. The rivet material should match the material being fastened. *Pop rivets* can be used when only one side of a joint is accessible.

Building a Better Score

If you want to do well on this subtest but you don't have a lot of experience in the woodshop yet, you can get a woodworking book and build some furniture for your mom. (Even if you mess it up, Mom always likes gifts from the heart.) Remember, too, that many community colleges offer basic shop classes.

On the Shop Information questions, you either know the answers or you don't — in most cases. Sometimes you can use your intuition to figure out the right answer. For example, you may find a question on the ASVAB that looks like this one:

EXAMPLE

When attaching two pieces of wood together, which of the following creates the most secure bond?

(A) wood screws

(B) nails

(C) wood glue

(D) both Choice (A) and Choice (C)

If you think about it, screws have threads, which are likely to "grab" wood more securely than a nail would. Glue would likely strengthen that bond even more. It's obvious that the common-sense answer would be Choice (D).

308   PART 5   **The Whole Ball of Facts: Technical Skills**

Try a variation of the same question:

EXAMPLE

The best fastening method to use when attaching pieces of wood together when time is of the essence would be

(A) screws.

(B) cutting mortise and tenon joints.

(C) wood glue.

(D) both Choice (A) and Choice (C).

In this case, the best answer would be Choice (A), because using a drill (or even a screwdriver) to put screws in wood is generally faster than making cuts in the wood or waiting for glue to dry.

REMEMBER

If you need to, you can guess on the ASVAB. The military doesn't expect every applicant to know every answer to every question, but it does expect every applicant to try to perform well on the test. (That's why too many incorrect answers at the end of a subtest on the CAT-ASVAB can incur a penalty; the military doesn't want you just clicking through willy-nilly.) Try to rule out obviously incorrect answers before you choose; that way, you'll maximize your chances of getting one right. For general guessing hints, check out Chapter 3.

Shop Information Practice Questions

Do you build birdhouses for leisure and speed through "name that tool" rounds on game shows? If so, you probably don't need a lot of practice for this part of the ASVAB. If you use those rounds as an opportunity to get a snack, on the other hand, you may want to check out the following sample questions to help you nail down some shop concepts.

1. A two-penny nail is
   - (A) thicker than a 10d nail.
   - (B) shorter than a 10d nail.
   - (C) the same thing as a 10d nail.
   - (D) harder than a 10d nail.

2. A hacksaw is used to cut
   - (A) with the grain of wood.
   - (B) against the grain of wood.
   - (C) round stock.
   - (D) metal.

3. To drive a cold chisel, the best object to use would be
   - (A) a hammer.
   - (B) a sledge.
   - (C) a mallet.
   - (D) a plane.

4. The best tool for cutting curves or shapes in wood is a
   - (A) ripsaw.
   - (B) crosscut saw.
   - (C) coping saw.
   - (D) pliant saw.

5. What is the next step after filling in a hole with plastic filler and letting it dry?
   - (A) Clean the area with a glass-cleaning solution.
   - (B) Sand the area with medium-grain sandpaper.
   - (C) Coat the area with a layer of primer.
   - (D) None of the above.

6. What type of joint is pictured?

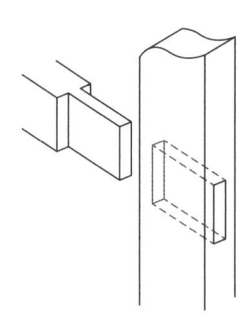

   © John Wiley & Sons, Inc.

   - (A) overlap joint
   - (B) butt joint
   - (C) dovetail joint
   - (D) mortise and tenon joint

7. Why is a cross-shaft lug wrench better than a single-shaft wrench?
   - (A) It gives more leverage.
   - (B) It holds lug nuts better.
   - (C) It fits better in storage because it's smaller.
   - (D) It doesn't scratch the lug nuts.

8. What is the strongest way to permanently join two pieces of metal?
   - (A) glue
   - (B) welding
   - (C) rivets
   - (D) soldering

9. What is the name of the tool shown here?

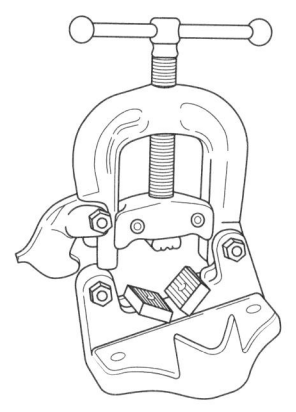

© John Wiley & Sons, Inc.

(A) bench vise
(B) pipe vise
(C) pipe cutter
(D) ripsaw

10. Without a key, what tool would you use to remove a padlock from a gate?

(A) bolt cutters
(B) a coping saw
(C) slip-joint pliers
(D) a cold chisel

Answers and Explanations

Use this answer key to score the Shop Information practice questions.

1. **B.** *Penny,* abbreviated *d* (for the ancient Roman *denarius* coin), indicates length; a 2d nail is shorter than a 10d nail.

2. **D.** The hacksaw has a blade specifically designed to cut metal, not wood.

3. **A.** A hammer has a smaller, harder striking surface than a mallet does. Mallets don't usually have metal striking surfaces, and a plane is a tool carpenters and woodworkers use to finish a wood surface.

4. **C.** *Coping saws* have thin blades with many teeth and are specifically designed to cut curves and shapes in wood.

5. **B.** After the filler dries completely, the next step is to sand the area to create a smooth surface for painting.

6. **D.** You use a *mortise and tenon joint* when you need it to withstand weight and movement, such as in a piece of furniture (for example, chairs).

7. **A.** A cross-shaft wrench (shaped like a cross) is better than the single-shaft wrench (one long handle) because you can push down and pull up at the same time, resulting in more leverage.

8. **B.** The answer is Choice (B), welding. Welding turns two pieces of metal into one by using extremely high temperatures. You can use glue on some metals, but its strength is inferior when compared to other methods, and soldering only melts an alloy between two pieces of metal (like an adhesive). Rivets, screws, and bolts are all temporary or semi-permanent methods of joining metal, but they're only as strong as the actual rivet, screw, or bolt.

9. **B.** *Pipe vises* hold round material or pipes.

10. **A.** *Bolt cutters* are heavy-duty shears that produce enough force to cut through the arms of a padlock.

> **IN THIS CHAPTER**
>
> » Weighing in on mass concepts
>
> » Using the forces of physics
>
> » Figuring out the principles of work
>
> » Manipulating machines to help you work
>
> » Jacking up your test score

Chapter 15
Mechanical Comprehension

When you need to clean your M-4 5.56 mm carbine, knowing how to take it apart and put it back together is going to come in handy. Of course, your drill sergeants in basic training will teach you (and ensure you get *plenty* of practice), but how easily you grasp such tasks depends greatly on your aptitude for understanding simple mechanical operations and *applied physics,* which relates to motion, force, and energy. That's the purpose of the Mechanical Comprehension (MC) subtest of the ASVAB.

The questions on this subtest measure your understanding of simple machines and mechanisms. Many of the questions on this subtest display a diagram, such as a series of connected gears, followed by a question, such as which direction a gear turns or how fast it revolves. The Mechanical Comprehension subtest is almost all about applied physics, so you may want to review some basic physics in Chapter 11 of this book. For even more study, check out *Physics I For Dummies* by Steven Holzner, PhD (Wiley). You can also access this book's free online flashcards; find instructions on how to get to them inside the front cover.

REMEMBER

Only some military jobs require a good score on this subtest. If you have no interest in taking apart a fighter aircraft or rebuilding a tank, you're better off reviewing for the Word Knowledge or Arithmetic Reasoning subtests, which make up part of the core exam (the AFQT; see Chapter 1) that you must do well on to even qualify for enlistment. Remember, though, it doesn't hurt to understand mechanical operations. You never know when you'll be offered an interesting job opportunity that requires a good score in this area.

To do well on this subtest, you also have to bone up on your mathematical skills. The Mechanical Comprehension subtest often asks you to make calculations based on formulas to explain mechanical principles. Don't panic; the formulas are easy to understand, but you do have to use math to come up with a final answer. See Part 3 for more information on math. In this chapter, you get the mathematical formulas for commonly asked questions on the ASVAB, so pay especially close attention to these little beauties. (If the information probably isn't on the ASVAB, I don't burden you with it here.)

The CAT-ASVAB (computerized test) has 15 Mechanical Comprehension questions that you're supposed to answer in 22 minutes. If you're taking a CAT-ASVAB with tryout questions, which I cover in Chapter 1, you get 42 minutes to answer 30 questions. For the paper version of the ASVAB, this subtest has 25 questions, and you have 19 minutes to answer them. That's enough time for a mechanically oriented individual to tackle this subtest and put a broken clock back together. Well, maybe not the whole clock.

A-mass-ing Knowledge on Matter, Weight, Density, and Relativity

A lot of people think that weight and mass are the same, and although they're not identical, they're similar. All matter has mass. An object's *mass* is a measure of how much matter it contains. *Weight* is a measure of the force that gravity exerts on the object (or the force necessary to support it). Essentially, weight is mass × gravity; weight is a force expressed by the relationship of multiplying an object's mass and gravity.

The simplest way to look at weight versus mass is to think about taking a trip to the moon. Your mass stays the same here on Earth and on the moon because mass is simply the amount of matter inside your body. But you weigh less on the moon than you do here because the moon's gravity is about a sixth as powerful as Earth's is. If you weigh 150 pounds here on Earth, you'd weigh about 25 pounds on the moon (or 380 pounds on Jupiter because it's a larger planet with more gravity). You can even figure out how much you'd weigh on other planets based on their gravity. Of course, that only makes a difference if you end up joining the Space Force.

Matter can vary in *density*, a measure of how much matter is inside an object (its mass) and how much space that matter takes up (its volume). Remember the old joke "Which weighs more: a ton of feathers or a ton of bricks?" They both weigh the same, but the two have different densities; a ton of feathers would probably take up a lot more space than a ton of bricks would.

An object made from a dense material, like iron, has less volume than the same object made from a less-dense material, like water. A one-gallon bag of iron doesn't just *feel* heavier than a one-gallon bag of water does; it *is* heavier because the iron is denser.

TIP Imagine an elevator in a high-rise building. The elevator starts with just one person in it, but as it moves between floors, it picks up more and more passengers. The space available inside the elevator never changes (that's its volume), but the density of the matter inside it (the people) does change. The people can be packed in like sardines, just like the atoms in a high-density object are.

"Energy equals mass times the speed of light squared" is the long way of saying the world's most famous equation: $E = mc^2$. Albert Einstein's theory of special relativity really says that mass and energy are the same physical entity, and that they can be changed into each other. According to the equation, m represents the mass of an object, c^2 represents the speed of light squared, and E represents that object's total energy (which I discuss later in the chapter). In a nutshell, the amount of mass in an object determines how much energy it has.

Understanding the Forces of the Universe

By applying *force* (a push or pull), you can open the door or close it, speed it up (slam it) or slow it down (catch it before it slams), or make it change direction (push it shut when the wind blows it open). In fact, all mechanical devices need force to move mass.

REMEMBER

In physics, applying force allows changes in the *velocity* (the speed and direction) of an object. A change (such as an increase) in velocity is known as *acceleration.* Here's the mathematical formula to determine force: Force = Mass × Acceleration.

TECHNICAL STUFF

Martial artists use this concept all the time. Although a larger fighter may have more size (mass), a smaller fighter can usually speed up more quickly (have more acceleration), possibly resulting in both fighters applying the same amount of force. This concept is why 110-pound martial artists can break boards and bricks just as well as 200-pound martial artists.

This section gives you the basics of force that you need to know for the ASVAB.

You hit me first! The basics of action and reaction

Sir Isaac Newton sure was one of the sharpest crayons in the box. His third law of motion states that for every action (force) in nature, there's an equal and opposite reaction. In other words, if object A exerts a force on object B, then object B also exerts an equal and opposite force on object A. Notice that the forces are exerted on the opposite object.

Take a look at Figure 15-1. As you sit in your chair, your body exerts a downward force on the chair, and the chair exerts an upward force on your body. There are two forces resulting from this interaction: a force on the chair and a force on your body. These two forces are called *action* and *reaction forces.*

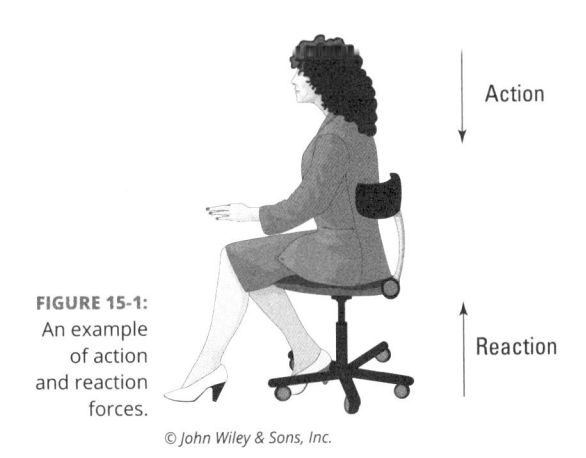

FIGURE 15-1:
An example of action and reaction forces.

© John Wiley & Sons, Inc.

This force can also be used to describe how a motorboat moves through the water. As the propellers turn, they push the water behind the boat (action). The water reacts by pushing the boat forward (reaction).

CHAPTER 15 **Mechanical Comprehension** 315

Equilibrium: Finding a balance

Forces are *vector* quantities. That means they have both a magnitude (size) and a direction associated with them. Forces applied in the same direction as other forces increase the total force, and forces that move in opposite directions reduce the total force. In general, an object can be acted on by several different forces at any one time.

REMEMBER A very basic concept when dealing with forces is the idea of *equilibrium* or balance. When two or more forces interact so that their combination cancels the other(s) out, a state of equilibrium occurs. In this state, the velocity of an object doesn't change. The forces are considered to be balanced if the rightward forces are balanced by the leftward forces and the upward forces are balanced by the downward forces.

If an object is at rest and is in a state of equilibrium, then it's at *static equilibrium*. *Static* means being stationary or at rest. For example, a glass of water sitting on a table is at static equilibrium. The table exerts an upward force on the glass to counteract the force of gravity.

Under pressure: Spreading out the force

REMEMBER *Pressure* is a measurement of force over an area. Pressure is usually measured in pounds per square inch (psi). The formula for deriving pressure is

$$\text{Pressure} = \frac{\text{Force (in pounds)}}{\text{Area (in square inches)}}$$

If 50 pounds of force is exerted on 10 square inches of surface, the amount of pressure is 5 pounds per square inch $(5 = 50 \div 10)$.

Consider this: If you're sleeping in bed, the amount of pressure being exerted per square inch is much less than when you're standing on your feet. The surface area of the bottoms of your feet (supporting all that weight) is much less than the surface area of all your body parts that touch the mattress.

TECHNICAL STUFF Ever wonder how a person can lie on a bed of nails? The answer involves elementary physics. The person's body rests evenly on hundreds of nails; therefore, no individual nail exerts a great amount of pressure against the skin. Have you ever seen someone stand on a bed of nails? That would be a lot more painful — and because there are fewer nails exerting pressure on a smaller surface area, they'd most likely puncture the feet.

A *barometer* is a gauge that measures atmospheric pressure. Normal atmospheric pressure is 14.7 psi. A change in air pressure means the weather is about to change. For more information on science and barometric pressure, see Chapters 10, 11, and 12.

Looking at kinds of forces

Here are some of the forces that act on objects:

- **Gravity** is the physical property that draws objects toward the center of Earth (and other objects that have mass), which is generally known as weight. Gravity generates a weight force when multiplied by an object's mass.
- **Applied force** is force a person or another object applies to an object through contact.
- **Tension** is transmitted through string, rope, cable, or wire when forces are acting on opposite ends.

> » **Friction** is resistance to the motion of two objects or surfaces that touch.
>
> » **Recoil** occurs when something regains its original form when an object exerting force on it is removed; it's also referred to as a *spring force*.
>
> » **Magnetism** is the property of attracting iron or steel.
>
> » **Static electricity** is the production of stationary electrical charges, often the result of friction.

In this section, I explain a few of these forces in detail.

Gravity: What goes up must come down

Isaac Newton didn't invent gravity, but the famous mathematician *was* the first to study it seriously. Robert Hooke, an English scientist and architect, proposed the idea in 1665. Hooke's idea provided a springboard for Newton's 1687 universal gravitation theory, which is now a scientific law. (Newton deliberately declined to credit Hooke, leading to a scientific spat that lasted until Hooke's death.)

REMEMBER

Newton's *law of universal gravitation* states that every object in the universe attracts every other object in the universe. Earth produces gravity, and so do the sun, other planets, your car, your house, and your body. The amount (force) of the attraction depends on the following:

> » **Mass:** The force of gravity depends on the mass of the object. If you're sitting in front of your television, you may be surprised to know that the television set is attracting you. However, because the mass of the TV is so small compared to the mass of Earth, you don't notice the physical "pull" toward the television set.
>
> Note that the force of gravity acting on an object is equal to the weight of the object. Of course, other planets have lesser or greater masses than Earth, so the weight of objects on those planets is different. (I discuss mass, and its relation to weight, in "A-mass-ing Knowledge on Matter, Weight, Density, and Relativity" earlier in this chapter.)
>
> » **Distance:** Newton's law also says that the greater the distance is between two objects, the less the objects attract each other. In other words, the farther away an object is from Earth (or any large body), the less it weighs. If you stand at the top of a high mountain, you'll weigh less than you will at sea level. Don't get too excited about this weight-loss technique, though. The difference is incredibly small. Gravitational pull isn't the next big diet craze. Sorry!
>
> For an object to really lose weight, it must be far away from Earth (or any other large body). When an object is far enough away from these bodies that it experiences practically no gravitational pull from them, it's said to experience weightlessness — just like the astronauts you see on TV.

Gravity pulls objects downward toward the center of Earth, so the old saying "what goes up must come down" is appropriate when discussing gravity. If you fire a bullet straight up into the air, it'll travel (overcoming the force of gravity) until it reaches its farthest or highest point, and then it'll fall. And during your marksmanship training in the military, you learn all about how gravity affects projectiles over distance.

When push comes to shove: Applied force

An *applied force* is any type of force that a person or another object exerts on something. If your drill sergeant tells you to mop the parking lot when it's raining, you'll run out there and apply force to the mop. You'll also apply force to the wringer in the mop bucket to get it to squeeze out the water. When one Humvee tows another, the towing vehicle applies force; likewise, when you throw a live grenade in basic training, your hand applies a force on the grenade, so you're looking at applied force in action.

CENTRIFUGAL FORCE: FALSE GRAVITY

An object traveling in a circle appears to experience a gravitational force. This isn't really gravity; instead, it's a concept known as *centrifugal force*. The amount of force depends on the mass of the object, the speed of rotation, and the distance from the center:

- The more massive the object, the greater the force.

- The greater the speed of the object, the greater the force. Faster rotating speed results in higher overall speed.

- The greater the distance from the center, the greater the force.

The centrifugal force, or effect, on an object is actually a fictitious outward force on an object moving along a curved path, which can be equal to the centripetal force on an object. *Centripetal force* points toward the center of an object's circular path, perpendicular to the direction of motion of an object.

If you're riding on a merry-go-round on the playground (whee!), you have to exert a constant force to keep from flying off. This feeling of being pushed outward isn't due to something actually pushing you in that direction but to your body's inertia trying to keep you moving in a straight line. (You can read more about inertia in the "Exerting force to make things happen" section in this chapter.) Because Newton's first law states that moving objects tend to want to travel in one direction, as the merry-go-round turns, your body wants to keep traveling in one direction (*tangent* to the circle, if you like math), so you feel you're being pushed outward.

Stretching out tension

Tension force is the force transmitted through a rope, string, or wire when force is applied to both ends. The force is the amount of tension directed along the rope, string, or wire and pulls equally on the objects at both ends. Tension force is usually measured in either pounds-force (lbf) or newtons (N); 4.45 newtons equal 1 pound-force. See Figure 15-2.

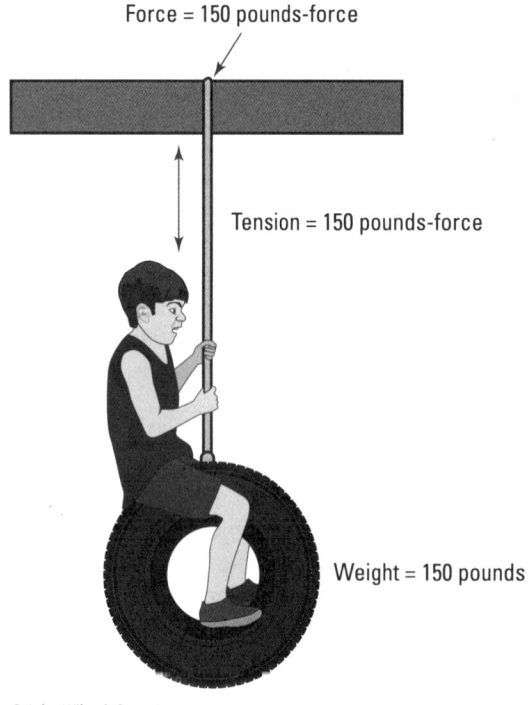

FIGURE 15-2: An example of tension force.

© John Wiley & Sons, Inc.

Friction: Resisting the urge to move

When one surface (such as a floor) resists the movement of another surface (the bottom of a box), the result is *frictional* resistance. (This friction isn't like resisting orders to cut the grass. That type of resistance may cause friction between you and your dad, but I'm talking about a different kind of resistance here.)

In order to perform work — that is, to get an object to move in the direction you're pushing or pulling — sometimes you have to overcome friction by applying more force. For example, when you're moving a box across a smooth, vinyl floor, little friction is produced, so the amount of force required to push the box comes from the box's weight and the very minor friction produced by the smooth floor. But when you're moving a box across a carpeted floor, more friction is produced, so you have to push harder to move the same box the same distance. (See the later section "You Call That Work?!" for more information on what's considered work in physics terms.)

Rolling friction (like the friction that occurs when you roll a wheel along the pavement) is always less than sliding friction (which occurs when you shove a box along the floor). If you put wheels on a box (or put the box on a wheeled tool, such as a dolly), it's much easier to push!

You can decrease friction by using a lubricant. Oil, grease, and similar materials reduce friction between two surfaces. So theoretically, if you oil the bottom of a box, it's easier to move! (Oiling the bottom of a box isn't recommended — for reasons involving the appearance of your floor and the contents of the box — but some oil on a dolly's wheel bearings would be a huge help.)

Elastic recoil: The trampoline of physics

Liquids and gases don't have a specific shape, but solid matter does. Solids are perfectly happy with the way they look and resist changes in shape. If you exert a force on a solid shape, it responds by exerting a force in the opposite direction. This force is called *elastic recoil*. It's also called a *spring force*. All material has a constant property (called a *spring constant*) that's directly proportional to the force it generates based on the distance it's deformed. The mathematical relationship is expressed as Spring Force = Spring Constant × Distance Displaced.

Take a look at Figure 15-3. The cat is standing on a board suspended on two blocks. While the board bends, the cat can feel the force of the board trying to regain its original shape. If the cat steps off the board, the board will recoil to its normal state.

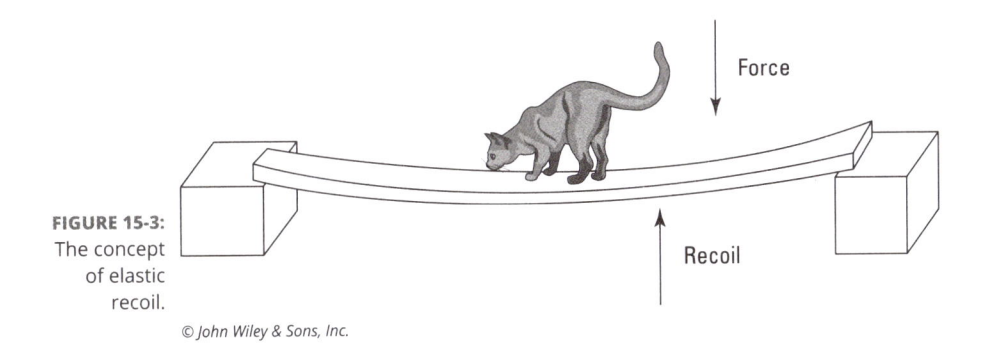

FIGURE 15-3: The concept of elastic recoil.

© John Wiley & Sons, Inc.

The law of attraction: Magnetism

Magnetism comes from the force (attract or repel) that magnets cause. The type of magnetism you're probably most familiar with is *ferromagnetism*, which involves iron; it's the strongest type.

All magnets have north and south poles, and opposite poles are attracted to each other. If you rub a piece of iron across a magnet, all the north-seeking poles in the iron line up in the same direction, and the force they generate creates a magnetic field. That magnetic field pulls or repels other objects, creating a type of force.

Every substance is made from atoms, and every atom has electrons that carry electric charges. These electrons spin and circle the atom's nucleus, which generates an electric current; as a result, each electron acts like a tiny magnet. Most substances have equal numbers of spinning electrons, and half spin in one direction while the other half spin in the other direction. That cancels out their magnetism, and it's why you can't use a refrigerator magnet to pick up a piece of paper or a shard of glass. But the refrigerator magnet is another story; it contains atoms where most of the electrons are spinning in the same direction.

Tapping into electrical forces

When you rub a balloon on your little brother's head and then touch the balloon to the wall, chances are that it'll stick. That's due to electrical force. This kind of force, called *static electricity,* is the buildup of electrical charges on the surface of a substance. Opposite electrical charges attract, so the charge on the balloon and the charge on the wall are literally pulling for each other.

Opening the window to drag forces

Drag forces slow down objects; the amount of drag depends on an object's shape and the substance it's moving through, such as air or water. If you've ever held your hand out of the car window horizontally, then rotated it vertically, you've experienced the increase in drag force that pushed your arm backward. Designers make cars and boats as streamlined as possible to reduce drag, making these vehicles as efficient as possible. (If your drill sergeant at Basic Combat Training calls you a "high-speed, low-drag" troop, it's a compliment — but don't respond with "Thanks!" Trust me on this one.)

You Call That Work?!

Mechanically speaking, *work* happens when a force (usually measured in pounds) moving over a measurable distance (usually measured in feet) overcomes a resistance. In the United States, the unit of measure for work is often called a *foot-pound.* (**Note:** The rest of the world uses the newton-meter, or joule.) One foot-pound of work occurs when a 1-pound weight is lifted to a height of 1 foot. You can represent this concept in equation form:

$$\text{Work} = \text{Force} \times \text{Distance}$$

Work is different from effort; work is the result of effort. You can think of *effort* as being force and of *work* as being what you produce with that force.

Contrasting the difference between potential and kinetic energy

Energy is the capacity to do work. Every object in the universe has energy, and it's either potential or kinetic. *Potential energy* is stored energy — energy that's not doing anything at the moment but that's in the object by virtue of its position in a field. If this book is resting in your hands right now, the book itself is holding potential energy. If you raise the book over your head, you're increasing its potential energy (thanks to the Earth's gravitational pull). When you accidentally drop it, all its potential energy becomes *kinetic energy,* or energy of motion. When the book hits the ground, its energy becomes potential again. (*Tip:* Don't drop the book if you're reading it as an e-book; replacing your tablet is going to be expensive.)

Potential energy can't be transferred between objects. The more massive an object is, the more potential and kinetic energy it has (so a bowling ball contains more energy than a basketball does). Both these forms of energy are measured in joules.

Exerting force to make things happen

"An object at rest stays at rest and an object in motion stays in motion with the same speed and in the same direction unless acted upon by an unbalanced force." That's Newton's first law of motion, and in plain English, it means that objects just keep on keepin' on until some outside force makes a change.

As I note in Chapter 11, an object's tendency to resist change in its state of motion is called *inertia.* All objects follow this law, even if they don't always look like it. Without gravity and physical obstacles, an object in motion would keep going in the same direction at the same speed forever.

Some objects resist changes more than others do, and it all comes down to mass. Mass is solely dependent on the inertia of an object, which means the more inertia an object has, the more mass it has. A more massive object, like a tactical military vehicle, has a greater tendency to resist changes in its state of motion than a smaller object, like a bowling ball, does. The earlier section "A-mass-ing Knowledge on Matter, Weight, Density, and Relativity" has more on mass.

Overcoming resistance

The resistance that the work overcomes isn't the same thing as the weight of the object. In other words, if you try to move a 1,200-pound piano, you'll probably notice a measurable difference between the amount of work it takes to shove it along the floor and the amount of work it takes to carry it up the stairs. But don't take my word for it — you can demonstrate this concept at home. First, find a 1,200-pound piano and push it across the floor. Next, put it on your back and carry it up the stairs. See the difference? (Really, don't put the piano on your back. I'm just trying to make a point here.)

When you move the piano across the floor, you're really working (pushing) against the frictional resistance (the force that's produced when two surfaces rub together) of the piano rather than its full weight. Under these circumstances, the frictional resistance of the piano offers less resistance than its full weight. There are times when an object's full weight is less than its frictional resistance. Consider trying to push a textbook across a deep-pile carpet. Picking the book up and carrying it is easier. (For more about friction, see the earlier section "Friction: Resisting the urge to move.")

Powering through work

Work, at least in terms of physics, is what happens when a force acts on an object over a length of displacement. The two main ingredients in work are force and displacement. You do work on your duffel bag when you drag it from the bus to the reception area on your first day in basic training. You do work on your groceries when you carry them in from the car. You do work on the barbell when you lift it over your head. In each of those scenarios, you apply force that causes displacement. In each of those scenarios, you apply force over some distance.

Power is the rate at which work is done. Mathematically speaking,

$$\text{Power} = \frac{\text{Work}}{\text{Time}}$$

In this formula, work is usually measured in joules, time is measured in seconds, and power is measured in watts.

In many machines, power is measured in *horsepower*, which you may be more familiar with than watts and joules. Using the same formula to calculate horsepower requires you to measure work in foot-pounds, time in minutes, and power in foot-pounds-per-minute. Horsepower is derived from the estimate that an average horse can do 33,000 foot-pounds of work in 1 minute (according to James Watt). Therefore, 1 horsepower = 33,000 foot-pounds per minute. One horsepower is also the same as 550 foot-pounds per second, which is equivalent to 745.7 watts.

Relying on Machines to Help You Work

Humans have used machines that help make work easier since early hominids (*Homo habilis*, to be specific) created crude wedges about 2 million years ago. The first wheel wasn't used on a chariot until about 3,200 BCE, but machines have steadily evolved to make humans more efficient.

In addition to increasing efficiency, machines are also used to help with work that couldn't be done otherwise. Think of the mechanisms and machines you use every day — from the simple (like the hinge that allows a door to move easily when you push it open) to the more complex (like the hydraulic lift that allows you to lift up a car to check its undercarriage). You could move most doors out of the way without hinges, but you couldn't lift a car over your head without some help.

REMEMBER

Machines give you the ability to magnify and change the direction and magnitude of forces. When a machine multiplies the force you use, it gives you a *mechanical advantage*. This concept can be stated as

$$\text{Mechanical Advantage} = \frac{\text{Resistance}}{\text{Effort}} = \frac{\text{Output Force}}{\text{Input Force}}$$

Some simple machines may give you a mechanical advantage of only 1 or 2. This means that they enable you to do one or two times the amount of work by expending the same effort. But those simple machines are still worth using! Often, even if a machine doesn't multiply your effort (or doesn't multiply your effort by much), it can at least spread your effort out and make it more effective.

Machines make work easier by providing some trade-off between the force applied and the distance over which it's applied. Keep reading to find out more on some basic types of machines.

Using levers to your advantage

You may not think of the seesaw at the neighborhood park as a machine, but it is. It's a lever. Levers are among the simplest machines used to help increase force.

All levers work by using a *fulcrum* (point of support) to reduce resistance and multiply the effect of effort. Resistance (such as a weight force from an object with mass) is exerted at one end of the lever (the *resistance arm*) and effort is exerted at the other (the *effort arm*). The effort arm moves the resistance arm. See Figure 15-4.

FIGURE 15-4: A simple lever.

© John Wiley & Sons, Inc.

REMEMBER

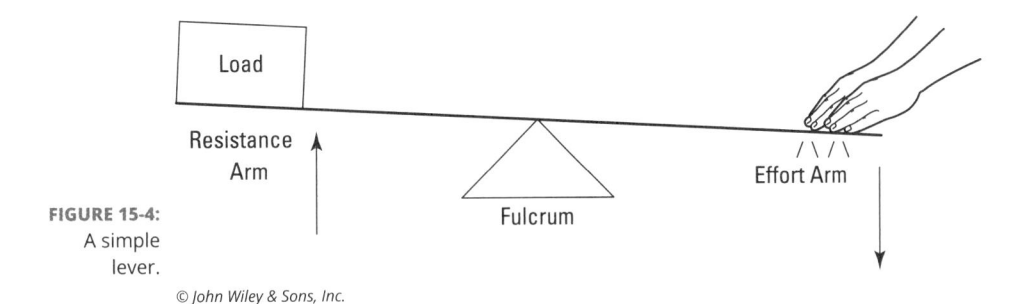

To determine how much a lever reduces the amount of effort needed to do work, use the following formula:

$$\frac{\text{Length of Effort Arm}}{\text{Length of Resistance Arm}} = \frac{\text{Resistance Force}}{\text{Effort Force}}$$

As you can see, the amount of effort needed to move the lever varies depending on how long the effort arm is and how long the resistance arm is. Keep in mind that a short resistance arm, although easier to move, can't move an object as far through space as a longer resistance arm can. Theoretically, you could lift a car off the ground with one hand if you had a half-mile-long lever — but why would you want to?

REMEMBER

The mechanical advantage of using a lever can be stated as

$$\text{Mechanical Advantage} = \frac{\text{Effort Arm}}{\text{Resistance Arm}}$$

If the effort arm is 6 inches and the resistance arm is 3 inches, the mechanical advantage is 2. If the effort arm is 6 feet and the resistance arm is 3 feet, the mechanical advantage is still 2.

Levers fall into classes: 1, 2, and 3. A *Class 1* lever's fulcrum is between the effort and load. Scissors, pliers, old-school seesaws, and the oars on a boat are examples of Class 1 levers, as is Figure 15-4. With a *Class 2* lever, the load is between the effort and the fulcrum; think wheelbarrows, crowbars, and nutcrackers. The fulcrum on a *Class 3* lever is beside the effort and opposite the load. Tweezers, staplers, and brooms are all Class 3 levers. Check out Figure 15-5 for examples of each class of lever.

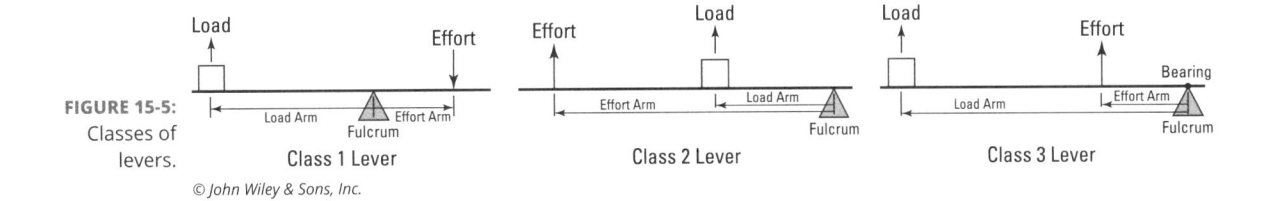

FIGURE 15-5: Classes of levers.

© John Wiley & Sons, Inc.

Ramping up the inclined plane

The *inclined plane*, also called a *ramp*, is another very simple machine that makes moving an object from one point to another easier. The ramp spreads your work out over a longer distance, so less force is needed to do the work.

For instance, suppose you have to lift a 50-pound barrel to a truck bed that's 3 feet off the ground. You'd have to use 50 pounds of force for 3 feet to move the barrel. But if you put a 6-foot ramp in place and pushed the barrel up the ramp, you'd only use half as much force to get the barrel in the truck (assuming there was no friction) because the mechanical advantage of such a ramp is 2.

REMEMBER The advantage of using a ramp can be expressed as

$$\frac{\text{Length of Ramp}}{\text{Height of Ramp}} = \frac{\text{Weight of Object Being Moved}}{\text{Force Required to Move Object}}$$

REMEMBER *Wedges* are a form of inclined plane and can multiply your effort in much the same way as a ramp can. Screws are also inclined planes, only in spiral form. Screw jacks, which you can use to lift your house up to build a new foundation, are a combination of a lever and an inclined plane.

Easing your effort: Pulleys and gears

Pulleys and gears are simple machines that can be used to change the magnitude (size) and direction of force. When you ride in an elevator, step onto an escalator, drive your car, or wind your watch, you're using pulleys and gears.

Block and tackle systems

When used in a *block and tackle* arrangement (see Figure 15-6), pulleys make lifting heavy objects easier. In block and tackle systems, pulleys can also be used to change the direction of your pull. If you tie a 200-pound crate to one end of a rope, run the rope through a pulley, and grab the other end of the rope, you can pull down on the rope to lift the crate up. Without a pulley, you could pull down on the crate all day, and it wouldn't go up. In this case, using a simple pulley, the force of your pull must equal the weight of the object being lifted. The regular pulley doesn't multiply your force, but it makes the process of lifting easier by allowing you to redirect the force.

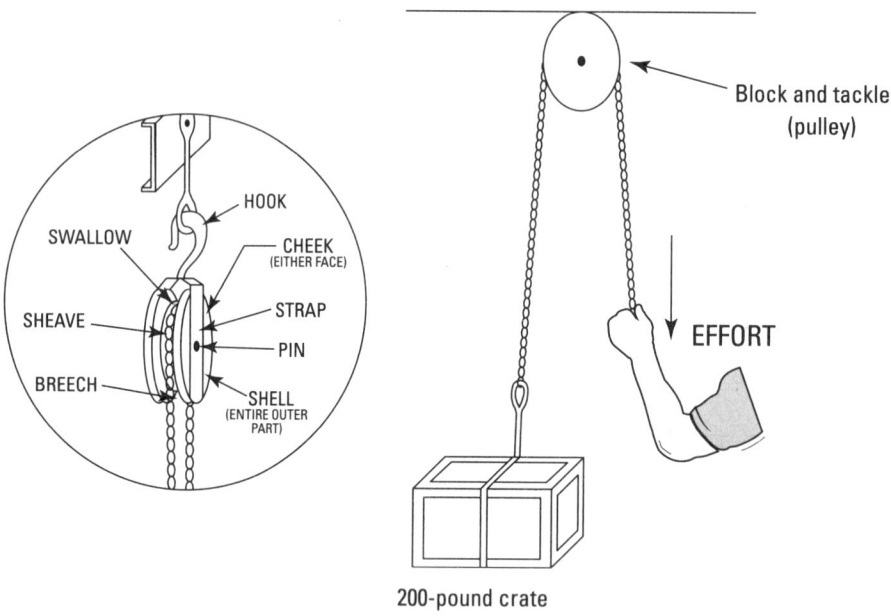

FIGURE 15-6: A pulley used in a block and tackle system.

© John Wiley & Sons, Inc.

Using a block and tackle system allows you to distribute your force more effectively. Instead of hoisting that entire 200-pound crate in one try, you can pull on a rope to lift it a few inches, pull on the rope some more to lift it a few more inches, and so on, provided you add a ratchet mechanism or trapped roller bearing. The block and tackle requires less force to lift the heavy crate, and the ratchet allows you to perform effort over short distances, creating smaller periods of work. This makes the work easier to perform.

A block and tackle system can also be used to reduce effort by magnifying force. To help understand how this works, look at Figure 15-7:

» Example 1 shows a 100-pound box secured to the ceiling by a single line. The weight supported by the line is equal to the weight of the box.

» In Example 2, the box is secured to the ceiling by using two lines. Each line is supporting one-half the weight of the box.

» In Example 3, a single line is threaded through a pulley. Although the line (as a whole) is supporting the entire weight of the box, each section of the line is supporting only one-half of the box's weight, just as in Example 2.

» In Example 4, a person is using this principle to lift the 100-pound box by applying only 50 pounds of force. In short, this block and tackle system provides the person with a mechanical advantage of 2. In receiving a mechanical advantage of force, the person must pull the rope farther than if they weren't using a pulley. In this example, the person would have to pull 2 feet of rope to raise the box 1 foot.

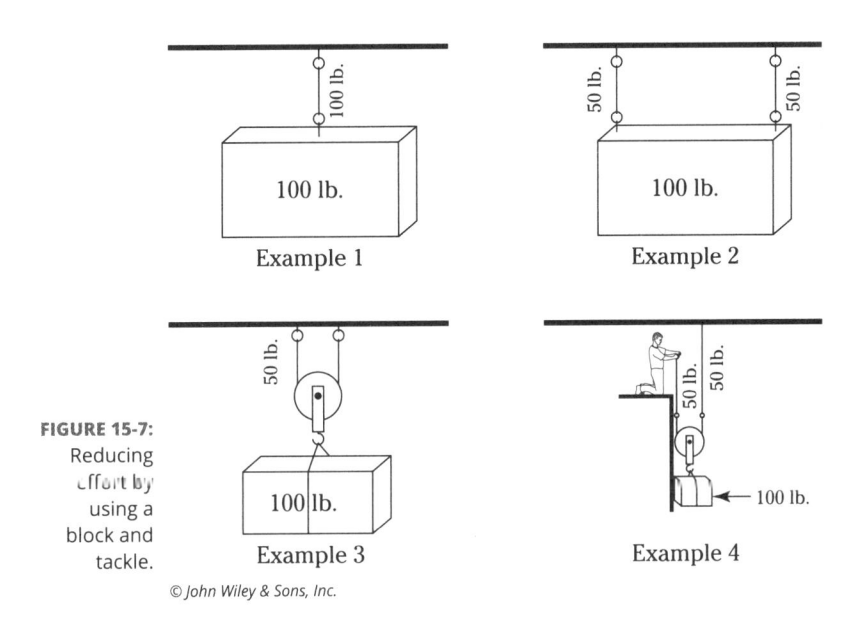

FIGURE 15-7: Reducing effort by using a block and tackle.

© John Wiley & Sons, Inc.

Additional pulleys can be added to a block and tackle arrangement to further increase the mechanical advantage. Figure 15-8 shows a couple of examples:

» Example 1 is a 2:1 pulley system in which two sections of rope produce a mechanical advantage of 2. Lifting a weight with this pulley arrangement requires only $\frac{1}{2}$ of the effort required to lift the weight directly. However, in order to lift the crate 1 foot, you have to pull 2 feet of rope. The fixed pulley in the upper-right side of the figure only redirects the tension force you need to pull up the weight.

» Example 2 illustrates a block and tackle system with six sections of rope. Using this arrangement provides you with a mechanical advantage of 6, but you have to pull the rope 6 feet for every foot you want to raise the box.

You notice in both examples that the mechanical advantage is determined by the number of rope sections only attached to the top of the box (and the pulley[s] fixed to the top of the box).

CHAPTER 15 **Mechanical Comprehension** 325

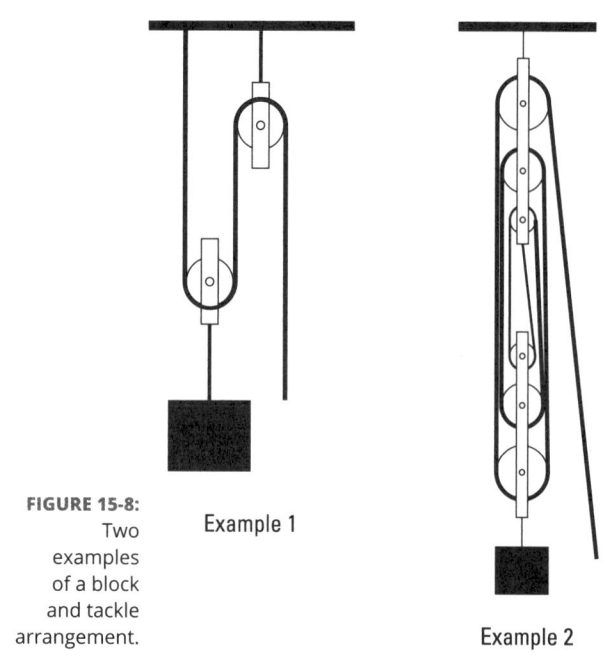

FIGURE 15-8: Two examples of a block and tackle arrangement.

Example 1

Example 2

© John Wiley & Sons, Inc.

Understanding how gears work

Machines often use gears to transmit motion from one place to another. An additional advantage of using gears is that they can be used to change direction, increase or decrease speed, or increase or decrease force.

REMEMBER Gears arranged in a series turn in the opposite direction of each other. If you have an even number of gears connected in a series, the first and last gear turn in opposite directions. If you have an odd number of gears aligned in a series, the first and last gear spin in the same direction. Look at Figure 15-9. Gear 1 is rotating counterclockwise, which causes Gear 2 to turn clockwise, resulting in Gear 3 spinning counterclockwise, with Gear 4 turning clockwise.

FIGURE 15-9: The motion of gears with an even number of gears aligned in a series.

© John Wiley & Sons, Inc.

REMEMBER The speed at which a gear rotates (in relation to the driving gear connected to it) depends on the number of teeth. In Figure 15-10, Gear 1 has six teeth, and Gear 2 has eight teeth. This relation of teeth can be expressed as a ratio of 6:8, which can be reduced to 3:4. That means Gear 1 has to rotate four times in order for Gear 2 to make three revolutions. Or expressed another way, for each rotation made by Gear 1, Gear 2 will make three-quarters of a revolution.

When gear shafts aren't parallel to one another, *bevel gears* can be used to connect shafts at different angles. The principles of gear rotation remain the same. Figure 15-11 shows an example of bevel gears designed to connect shafts having a 90-degree angle to the other. A car's differential, which takes a drive shaft rotating along the length of the car and sends power 90 degrees out to the rear tires, is an example of a bevel gear. A worm drive is another set of gears where the shafts aren't parallel; they need a worm screw to drive them, such as what's used in most car windows.

FIGURE 15-10: The ratio of teeth between two gears affects rotational speed.

6 teeth 8 teeth

Ratio = 3/4

© John Wiley & Sons, Inc.

FIGURE 15-11: Two bevel gears meet at a right angle.

90 Degrees

© John Wiley & Sons, Inc.

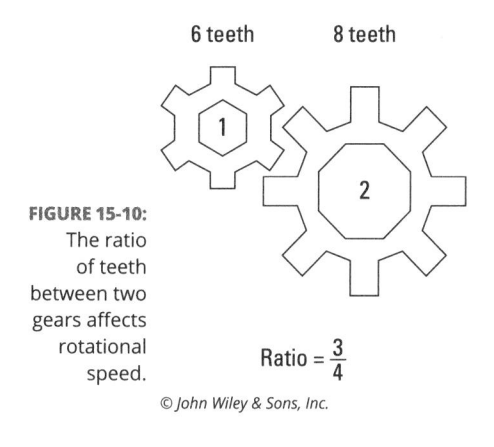

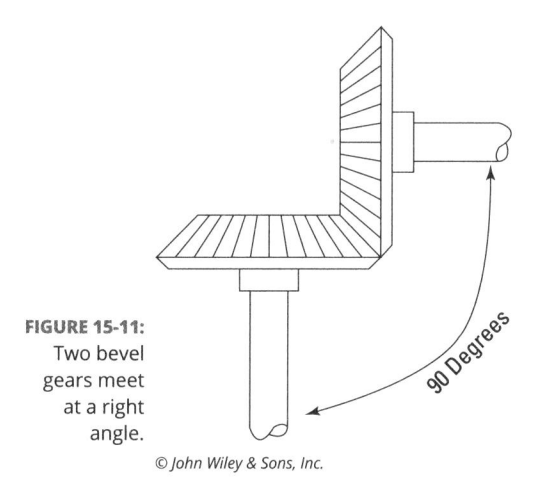

Pulley and belt arrangements

In addition to magnifying force as part of a block and tackle system, pulleys have another use. When connected by a system of belts, pulleys can drive other pulleys.

Like gears, pulleys are used to transmit motion from one location to another. However, the physical properties of pulleys are different from those of gears:

» **Turning direction:** Unless the driving belt is reversed (twisted), pulleys connected in series rotate in the same direction. Figure 15-12 illustrates this concept with two sets of pulleys. In the first set of pulleys, all the pulleys turn in the same direction (counterclockwise) as the driving pulley. However, in the second set of pulleys, the driving pulley and the lower pulley are rotating counterclockwise, but the right-hand pulley is rotating in a clockwise direction because the belt is twisted.

» **Speed of rotation:** Although the speed of gear rotation is determined by the number of teeth, how fast a pulley rotates depends on the diameter of the pulley in relation to the diameter of the pulley that's driving it. Have a look at Figure 15-13. Pulley A has a diameter of 1 inch, Pulley B has a diameter of 2 inches, and Pulley C measures 4 inches in diameter. The ratio among the three pulleys is 1:2:4. For every complete revolution made by Pulley A, Pulley B makes half of a revolution. Each time Pulley B makes a full revolution, Pulley C makes half of a revolution. Thus, for every full revolution of Pulley A, Pulley C makes a quarter of a revolution.

CHAPTER 15 **Mechanical Comprehension** 327

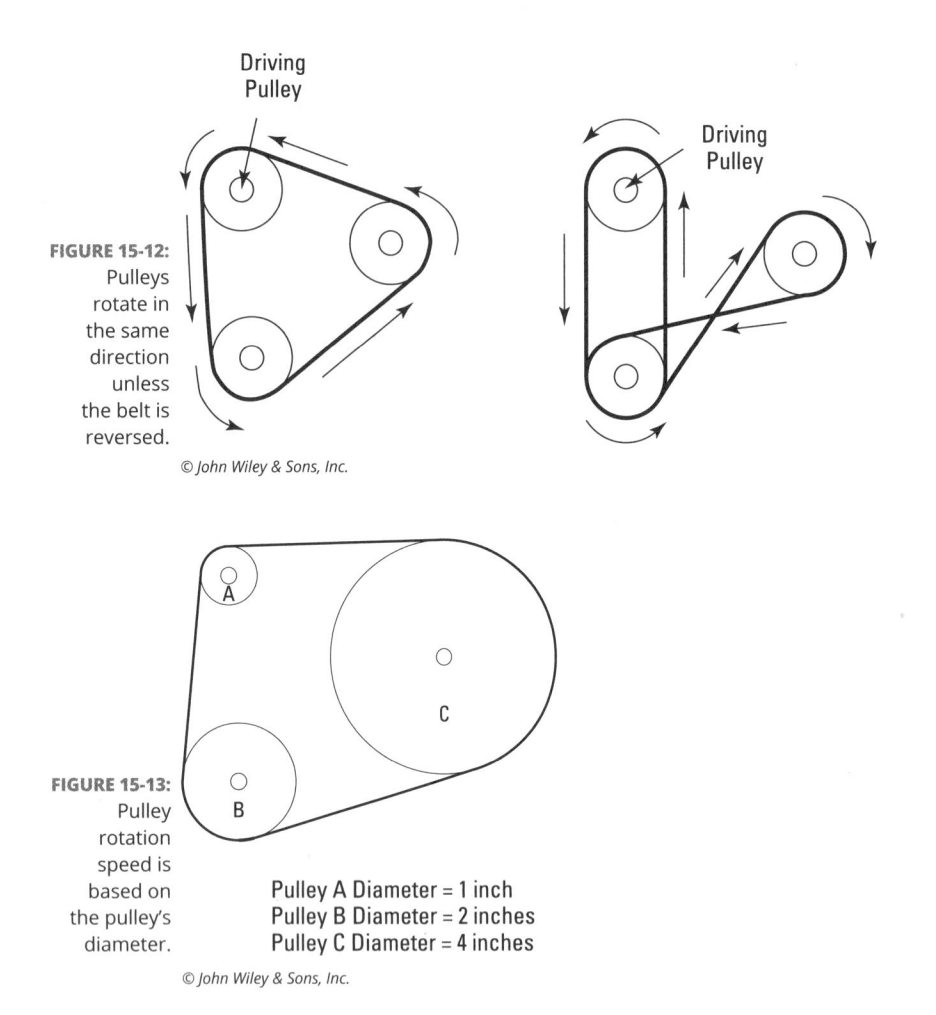

FIGURE 15-12: Pulleys rotate in the same direction unless the belt is reversed.

© John Wiley & Sons, Inc.

FIGURE 15-13: Pulley rotation speed is based on the pulley's diameter.

Pulley A Diameter = 1 inch
Pulley B Diameter = 2 inches
Pulley C Diameter = 4 inches

© John Wiley & Sons, Inc.

Multiplying your effort: Wheels and axles

The *wheel-and-axle* machine multiplies the effort you use, producing a greater force. When you steer a car by using a steering wheel (which is a wheel-and-axle device), a little effort exerted on the steering wheel turns the wheels of the car in the direction you desire. Turning your car wheels would be a lot more complicated if you didn't have the steering wheel.

In true wheel-and-axle machines, the wheel and the axle are fixed together and turn at the same time. This arrangement multiplies the amount of force you can exert by a considerable amount.

The relationship between the radius of the wheel and the radius of the area to which force is being applied determines the mechanical advantage you receive by using this piece of equipment. (Remember, the *radius* of a circle equals half the diameter; a straight line extending from the center of the circle to the edge is the radius of a circle.) A hand drill may apply 200 pounds of force for your 10 pounds of effort. (A hand drill uses a gear to convert the direction of the force.) See Figure 15-14.

Opening up the door to torque

Torque is a twisting or turning force that tends to cause rotation around an axis. Cars and other vehicles use torque to make their engines run (find out more about that in Chapter 13), but it's not just for drag racing. Torques are everywhere else in your life, too.

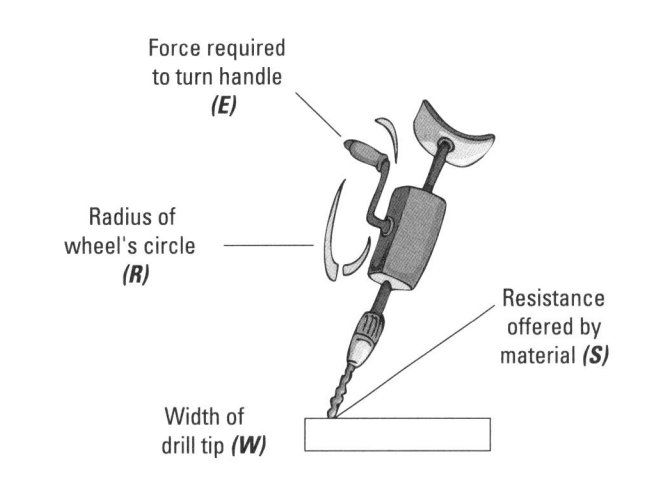

FIGURE 15-14:
A hand drill increases mechanical advantage.

Mechanical advantage of wheel and axle =

$$\frac{R}{\frac{1}{2}W} = \frac{S}{E}$$

Force required to turn handle **(E)**

Radius of wheel's circle **(R)**

Resistance offered by material **(S)**

Width of drill tip **(W)**

© John Wiley & Sons, Inc.

The simplest way to visualize torque is to open a door. Turning a doorknob and pushing a door open (and turning a key, for that matter) are examples of torque in action. Think of the door as the movement arm and its hinges as the axis. When you push on a door to open it, you push toward the edge that's not hinged to the wall because it's easier to open. (Try to open your front door by pushing on it about 6 inches from the hinges — it's a lot harder than you think.) When you're thinking proportionally, the wider the door is, the more easily you can open it from the side away from the hinges; it becomes harder as you move closer to the hinges. Torque is measured in newton-meters or pound-feet (see Chapter 11 for more SI units of measurement).

Torque can be static or dynamic. *Static torque* doesn't produce an angular acceleration — it's what happens if you push on a door marked "Pull," or pedal your bike at a constant speed without accelerating. *Dynamic torque* produces an angular acceleration, and it's what you see when a racecar takes off down the track.

Getting a grip on things with vises

Although many mechanisms are designed to transmit motion, some machines have the purpose of keeping things motionless. Vises are very useful because they can close around items and hold them with great force (much greater force than you could do by holding the item in your hands). Figure 15-15 shows an illustration of a standard shop vise.

HORSEPOWER: A MEASURABLE MARKETING TACTIC

Vehicle and other engines measure power output in *horsepower,* a term that comes from the 18th century. Steam power had been recently invented, and it was poised to send a lot of horses back to the stable. James Watt invented a new version of the steam engine and wanted to market it to buyers, but he had a big problem: He couldn't show people how valuable it was because he had no way to compare it to the amount of work output people were used to seeing from their hoofed helpers. Watt decided to watch mill horses who trod in circles all day, every day, to operate the gears that made mills run. He soon discovered that they usually walked a 24-foot-diameter circle about 144 times per hour, and each horse pulled with a force that he estimated to be 180 pounds. He calculated that one horsepower is equivalent to one horse doing 33,000 foot-pounds of work in one minute. Watt then used his unit of power to show off how much more work a steam engine could do than a horse, and the measurement stuck. It's now used for all kinds of engines, ranging from muscle cars and gas-powered leaf blowers to electric motors in washing machines.

FIGURE 15-15:
A standard shop vise.

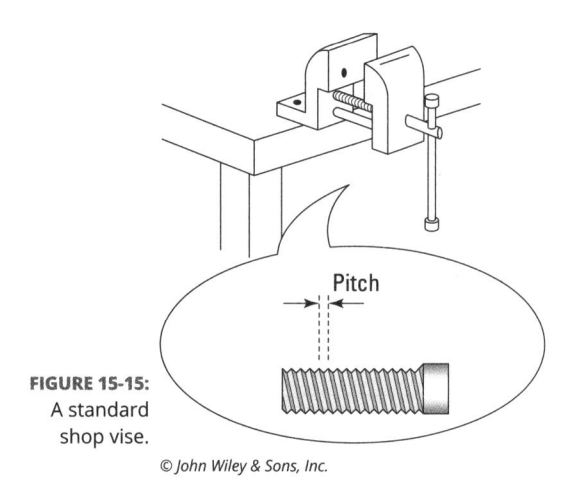

© John Wiley & Sons, Inc.

Rotating the handle on the vise causes a screw to turn, which either tightens or loosens the vise. A *screw* is a cylinder wrapped in a continuous spiral. The distance between the ridges of the spiral is called the *pitch* of the thread. The greater the pitch of the thread, the farther the jaws of the vice move for each revolution of the handle. However, there's a trade-off. Larger pitches require more force to rotate the handle than screws with smaller pitches do.

Magnifying your force with liquid: Hydraulic pressure

A *hydraulic jack* uses a nearly incompressible liquid, such as oil, to exert force in order to move an object (see Figure 15-16). As the handle moves, it applies pressure to the oil. Because the oil doesn't compress, the oil transmits whatever force is applied to it to the work cylinder with little or no loss in efficiency. The mechanical advantage is the ratio between the diameters of the two cylinders.

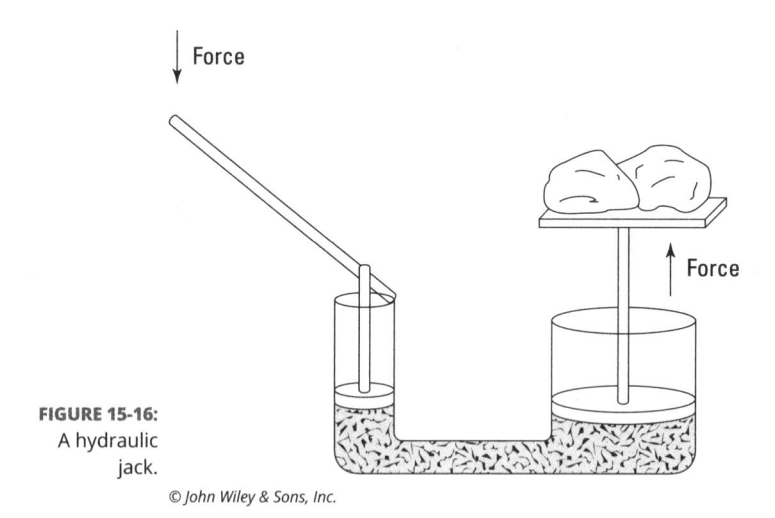

FIGURE 15-16:
A hydraulic jack.

© John Wiley & Sons, Inc.

In the figure, the small cylinder has a diameter of 1 inch and the large cylinder has a diameter of 4 inches. This difference in diameter results in a mechanical advantage of 4. If the rocks weigh a total of 100 pounds, only 25 pounds of force has to be applied to the piston in the small cylinder in order to lift the load. However, although the force required is reduced by a factor of 4, the smaller piston has to move 4 feet for every foot the piston in the larger cylinder moves.

Working Your Way to a Better Test Score

When you take the Mechanical Comprehension subtest, you may not know the correct answer to a question, or you may not know the mechanical principle involved. You may know the mechanical principle but not remember the formula you need to come up with the right answer. Never fear — you can still stumble through this test without totally crashing and burning.

Using your observations and common sense

Questions on this subtest often include illustrations. The ASVAB test-makers expect you to look at the illustrated device and guess how it operates. When you run across these types of questions, make sure you understand the illustration. Often, parts of the device are labeled. Make certain you read and understand these labels before you try to answer a question about the illustration.

Also, try to use a common-sense approach. You may see something like the following question:

Which of the following controls an automatic sump pump?

(A) mechanical switch

(B) manual switch

(C) pneumatic valve

(D) float

You may not know the answer to this question, but you can rule out Choice (B), manual switch, because the question asks you about an automatic sump pump, and anything manual isn't automatic. Eliminating one choice narrows your chances from one in four to one in three. Not a bad start, huh?

A *sump pump* is used to drain water from an area, and if you know that, you have an even better shot at getting this question right. Think about what type of device detects the presence of water, and you may guess correctly that Choice (D), float, is the right answer.

You can answer a lot of the questions correctly if you just think about what you've observed in the world around you. Remember, the Mechanical Comprehension subtest also tests your knowledge of physical principles of the world around you — questions you may expect to find on the General Science subtest. For example, a question may ask something like this:

If all the following objects are the same temperature, which one will feel coldest on a cool day?

(A) a wooden spoon

(B) a plastic spoon

(C) a metal spoon

(D) a fiberglass spoon

You don't need to know mechanical or scientific principles to know that a metal spoon will feel colder than the other spoons. So it makes sense to select Choice (C) as your answer, even if you can't explain the science behind this correct answer.

The nerve endings in your skin detect the difference between your inside body temperature and your outside skin temperature. Metal is an excellent conductor of heat, so heat readily flows from your hand into the metal. The heat is conducted rapidly away into the bulk of the metal, leaving your skin surface relatively cool. That's why metal feels cooler than other, less efficient conductors of heat, such as wood, plastic, or fiberglass.

Using the mathematics of mechanics

Mechanical principles are based on mathematical principles. Therefore, a screw making a complete revolution turns 360 degrees, because a mathematical principle states that 360 degrees are in a circle, a complete revolution. If you have to know the surface area of a floor to determine the pounds per square inch that a ton of tile would put on the floor, that's a mathematical principle, too (Area = Length × Width).

Suppose you run across this question:

A 3-inch-diameter flanged pipe with six holes is being fitted to a base with six holes. What's the maximum number of degrees the pipe must be rotated in order to line up the holes?

(A) 120 degrees

(B) 180 degrees

(C) 60 degrees

(D) 360 degrees

This isn't really a Mechanical Comprehension question at all — it's a math question. The only part that requires mechanical knowledge is knowing that the holes are spaced equally distant from one another on a flanged pipe. The answer is 360 degrees ÷ 6 = 60 degrees, Choice (C).

Guessing with a mechanical mind

Like most of the other subtests on the ASVAB, you can and should guess on the Mechanical Comprehension subtest when you don't know the answer (unless you're nearing the end of the CAT-ASVAB; too many incorrect answers at the end of a subtest give the impression you're just guessing and can bring on a penalty). Check out these tips to help you narrow the field:

» The amount of force needed to move an object with a mechanical advantage like a ramp or pulley system (not including friction resistance) is never greater than the weight of the object. Any answer that includes a force that's greater than the weight of the object being moved is probably wrong for this type of question.

» The correct answer is a mechanical answer. For example, if the question asks, "What's the purpose of lubricating oil in an engine?" the correct answer won't be "to make the parts look shiny." The answer may be "to reduce friction between moving parts."

» Any change in a mechanical operation almost always has pluses and minuses associated with it. So when a question proposes a change, the correct answer is probably the one that specifies the good, the bad, and the ugly. For instance, suppose the question says, "Enlarging the wheel on a hand drill will . . . ?" The correct answer is the one that says something like "increase the mechanical advantage and decrease the amount of effort needed to operate the drill."

For more general tips on guessing on the ASVAB, flip to Chapter 3.

Mechanical Comprehension Practice Questions

Mechanical Comprehension is all about figuring out how machines and mechanical mechanisms operate. A solid background in mechanical physics is a big advantage in scoring well in this area. Basic math skills are also a plus in this area. Test yourself with the next several questions.

1. The moisture that forms on the inside of a window on a cold day is called

   (A) condensation.
   (B) distillation.
   (C) evaporation.
   (D) tarnation.

2. If a 200-pound barrel must be lifted 4 feet to the bed of a box truck, an inclined plane will reduce the amount of effort required to move the barrel by half if the inclined plane is

   (A) 2 feet long.
   (B) 6 feet long.
   (C) 8 feet long.
   (D) 9 feet long.

3. While throwing a football, Dan exerts a forward force of 50 newtons on the ball and pushes it forward a distance of 1.2 meters. How much work does he do on the football?

   (A) 45 joules
   (B) 60 joules
   (C) 50 joules
   (D) 50.5 joules

4. A block and tackle is used to lift a truck engine with a weight of nearly 7,406 newtons. The input force required to lift this weight using the block and tackle is 308.6 newtons. What is the mechanical advantage of the block and tackle?

   (A) 23.99
   (B) 15
   (C) 25
   (D) 24.75

5. Which of the tanks will overfill?

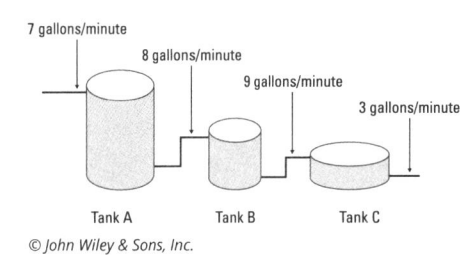

   © John Wiley & Sons, Inc.

   (A) Tank A
   (B) Tanks A and B
   (C) Tank C
   (D) Tanks B and C

6. Two people are carrying a 100-pound crate on a 2-x-8-x-12-foot board. To distribute the load evenly between the two people, the crate should be placed

   (A) 2 feet from the end of the board.
   (B) in the middle of the board.
   (C) 3 feet from the end of the board.
   (D) The load can't be evenly distributed.

7. Wheel A has a diameter of 9 feet. Wheel B has a diameter of 12 feet. If both wheels revolve at the same rate, Wheel B will cover a linear distance of 24 feet

   (A) at the same speed as Wheel A.
   (B) more slowly than Wheel A.
   (C) in half the time of Wheel A.
   (D) more quickly than Wheel A.

8. The shock absorber on a car is a very large spring. If Jonas's car hits a pothole with 600 pounds of force and the shock absorber compresses 3 inches, what is its spring constant in pounds per inch?

   (A) 200
   (B) 600
   (C) 20
   (D) 1,800

9. In the following figure, a 600-pound weight is placed on a 10-pound board that has been evenly balanced between two scales. How much does the left scale measure if the weight is $\frac{2}{3}$ closer to the left than to the right?

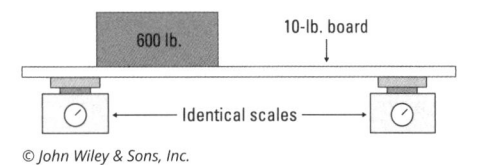

   (A) 400
   (B) 300
   (C) 405
   (D) 410

10. Daisy's single-speed bicycle has a front gear with 48 teeth and a rear gear with 12 teeth. If Daisy pedaled at 80 revolutions per minute (rpm), how fast would her rear wheel rotate?

    (A) 280 rpm
    (B) 320 rpm
    (C) 70 rpm
    (D) 128 rpm

11. Not including friction, a stationary single pulley gives a mechanical advantage of

    (A) 2.
    (B) 4.
    (C) 3.
    (D) 1.

12. Four gears are connected in a series. If Gear #1 is turning clockwise, Gear #4 will turn

    (A) clockwise.
    (B) counterclockwise.
    (C) more quickly than Gear #1.
    (D) more slowly than Gear #1.

13. James applies force at one end of a hydraulic jack. The area at the other end of the jack is five times the area where James is applying the force. How much larger is the exerted force than what James is applying?

    (A) twice as large
    (B) half as large
    (C) one-fifth as large
    (D) five times as large

14. Mr. Roth's children — Jake, Paul, and Jill — weigh 80, 60, and 50 pounds, respectively. They all sit on the same side of a seesaw together. Jake sits 3 feet from the fulcrum, Paul sits 5 feet from the fulcrum, and Jill sits 6 feet from the fulcrum. How far from the fulcrum must Mr. Roth sit on the other side to balance the seesaw if he weighs 200 pounds?

    (A) 4.2 feet
    (B) 5.5 feet
    (C) 5 feet
    (D) 4 feet

15. A rope is pulling a 320-pound box up an incline that's 16 feet long. If 80 pounds of force is used to move the box up the incline, how tall is the incline?

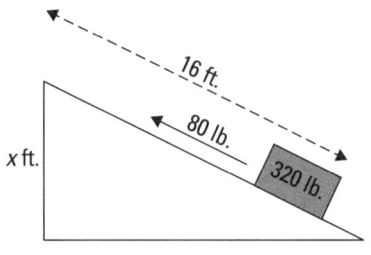

    (A) 6 feet
    (B) 10 feet
    (C) 4 feet
    (D) 8 feet

16. The sideways force one feels when a car turns sharply is often called

 (A) thrust force.

 (B) angle force.

 (C) centrifugal force.

 (D) positive force.

17. When two or more forces act to balance each other out, the condition is called

 (A) equilibrium.

 (B) static recoil.

 (C) gravitational balance.

 (D) concurrent forces.

18. Two balls of the same density, one large and one small, roll toward each other at the same speed. When they collide, what will happen to the larger ball?

 (A) It will be propelled backward.

 (B) It will jump over the smaller ball.

 (C) It will continue forward.

 (D) It will stop.

Answers and Explanations

Use this answer key to score the Mechanical Comprehension practice questions.

1. **A.** *Distillation* is the process of extracting or refining a substance using both boiling and condensation. *Evaporation* is the process of removing moisture from the surface of a liquid — the water molecules escape the surface and assume gas form. *Tarnation* is an interjection used to express anger. The correct answer is Choice (A), condensation.

2. **C.** The formula used for determining how an inclined plane reduces effort is Length of Ramp / Height of Ramp = Weight of the Object / Force, or $x \div 4 = 200 \div 100$. The amount of force needed to lift the object is equivalent to the object's weight, but the question wants to reduce that amount of force to half, so half of the object's weight is 100. Now do the math: $x \div 4 \times 4 = 2 \times 4$; $x = 8$. The correct answer is Choice (C).

3. **B.** Work is the amount of energy transferred by a force. To calculate how much work is done, use this formula (note that a newton-meter equals a joule):

$$\begin{aligned} \text{Work} &= \text{Force} \times \text{Distance} \\ &= (50 \text{ newtons})(1.2 \text{ meters}) \\ &= 60 \text{ joules} \end{aligned}$$

4. **A.** To find the mechanical advantage of the block and tackle, use the following formula:

$$\begin{aligned} MA &= \frac{\text{Output Force}}{\text{Input Force}} \\ &= \frac{7,406}{308.6} = 23.99 \end{aligned}$$

5. **C.** Tank C has an inflow greater than its outflow, so it will eventually overfill.

6. **B.** If the weight is placed closer to one person or the other, that person would carry more of the load, so the weight should be placed in the middle. Choice (B) is the correct answer.

7. **D.** Because Wheel A has a smaller circumference, it covers a shorter linear distance than Wheel B when turning at the same rate. Thus, Wheel B covers the distance of 24 feet faster than Wheel A. Choice (C) is inaccurate because the diameter of Wheel A isn't exactly half the diameter of Wheel B. If both wheels revolve at the same rate, then Wheel A turns 25 percent more slowly than Wheel B, because Wheel A's diameter is three-quarters of Wheel B's. Choice (D) is the correct answer.

8. **A.** The formula for force on a spring is $F = -kx$, with F representing force, k representing the spring constant, and x representing the displacement of the spring. The spring is compressed so the displacement, 3 inches, is negative. Just plug in the values from the question and solve:

$$\begin{aligned} 600 &= -k(-3) \\ 600 &= 3k \\ \frac{600}{3} &= \frac{3k}{3} \\ 200 &= k \end{aligned}$$

9. **C.** Two-thirds of the weight of the block (400 pounds) is supported by the left scale because the block is $\frac{2}{3}$ closer to the left than to the right. The board is evenly placed, so each scale supports $\frac{1}{2}$ of its weight (5 pounds). The total weight being supported by the left scale is 400 pounds + 5 pounds = 405 pounds.

10. **B.** Each full turn of the pedals turns the rear wheel 48 ÷ 12 = 4 revolutions. If the pedals were to turn at 80 rpm, the rear wheel would rotate at 4 × 80 rpm = 320 rpm.

11. **D.** A stationary single pulley allows you to change the direction of force but doesn't result in an increased mechanical advantage. The correct answer is Choice (D).

12. **B.** Gears connected in series turn in opposite directions of each other. Gears 1 and 3 rotate clockwise, and Gears 2 and 4 rotate counterclockwise. The size of gears is unknown, so there isn't enough information to determine whether Choice (C) or Choice (D) is correct. The correct answer is Choice (B).

13. **D.** A hydraulic jack uses an incompressible fluid, so the pressure has to be the same everywhere ($P_1 = P_2$). *Pressure* is force divided by area ($P = F/A$), so set up a proportion that represents the equal pressures:

$$P_1 = P_2$$
$$\frac{F_1}{A_1} = \frac{F_2}{A_2}$$

If the area at the output end of the jack is five times the area where James is applying the force, then the exerted force is five times the applied force:

$$\frac{F_1}{A_1} = \frac{5F_1}{5A_1}$$

Force is greater where the area is greater.

14. **A.** Let x = Mr. Roth's distance from the fulcrum.

$$200 \cdot x = (80 \cdot 3) + (60 \cdot 5) + (50 \cdot 6)$$
$$200x = 240 + 300 + 300$$
$$200x = 840$$
$$x = 4.2 \text{ feet}$$

15. **C.** First, determine the mechanical advantage of the ramp by using this formula:

$$MA = \frac{\text{Output Force}}{\text{Input Force}} = \frac{320}{80} = 4$$

The mechanical advantage of the ramp is also equal to the length of the ramp (16 feet) divided by the height of the ramp (x feet). Thus, the height of the ramp is 4 feet.

16. C. Although commonly referred to as centrifugal force, this property isn't actually a force at all but rather a property of inertia, one of Newton's laws of motion. As the car turns, your body is trying to continue traveling in a straight line. The correct answer is Choice (C).

17. A. When two or more forces interact so their combination cancels the other(s) out, there's a state of equilibrium. In this state, the velocity (speed and direction) of an object doesn't change. Choice (A) is the correct answer.

18. C. Because both balls are moving at the same speed, the ball with more mass (the larger one in this case, because both balls have the same density) will have more momentum. Upon impact, the heavier ball will slow down but continue in the same direction and knock the smaller, lighter ball backward.

IN THIS CHAPTER

» Understanding current, voltage, power, and more

» Comprehending electrical flow

» Deciphering circuit diagrams

» Amplifying your test score

Chapter 16
Electronics Information

When a guy I know was around 12 years old, he impressed his parents by taking apart an old television set and putting it back together. He impressed them right up to the point where he plugged it in and blew up the garage. But the world of electronics is a bit more complex than simply plugging something in and seeing whether it works. This kid (and his garage) learned this lesson the hard way, but six years later, when he took the ASVAB, he scored very well on the Electronics Information subtest. (Go figure!)

The Electronics Information subtest is designed to measure your knowledge of the principles of electricity and how these principles are applied in the real world. The questions are the same regardless of which military branch you intend to join. You may see questions about transistors, magnets, engines and motors, and radio and television.

You don't have to be an electronics whiz to score well on this subtest. If you're not familiar with this information and you want to pursue a military career that requires you to do well in this area, this chapter is calling your name. You also need to have some familiarity with basic mathematical and algebraic principles (see Chapters 6 and 7 for more information).

REMEMBER Not every military career requires a good score on this subtest. If the military feels that the Electronics Information subtest is important to your desired career, study intensively for this test. You can even take a course or two at the local community college if you don't have a strong enough background in this area.

You have 10 minutes to answer 15 questions on the computerized ASVAB or 21 minutes for 30 questions if you get tryout questions (more about those in Chapter 1). If you're taking the paper-and-pencil version of the test, you get 9 minutes to answer 20 questions. Although 9 or 10 minutes is sufficient time to answer the questions, it doesn't provide much time for anything else — if you don't know an answer, guess and go.

Uncovering the Secrets of Electricity

One day in 1752, Benjamin Franklin electrified the scientific community by tying a key to a kite and picking up an ambient electrical charge from a stormy sky. (You've probably heard the story, but what you haven't heard is that if lightning *had* struck the key, it would've killed Franklin — and in fact, it *did* kill a German physicist who tried to replicate the experiment the following year.) What that led to was an incredibly important discovery, though: that scientists could harness and store electrical energy from lightning.

Although electricity was just a hobby for Ben Franklin, he created many of the terms used today when people talk about electricity: battery, conductor, condenser, charge, discharge, uncharged, negative, minus, plus, electric shock, and electrician.

Electricity is a general term for the variety of phenomena resulting from the presence and flow of electric current. You can't see electricity running through a wire (but you can certainly feel it). You only know electricity is there when you flip on the light switch and the light turns on. Even though electricity appears to be pretty mysterious at first glance, scientists understand a great deal about its properties and how it works.

Electricity is measured in three ways:

- **Volts:** Volts measure the difference of potential between two points.
- **Amperes (amps):** Amps measure the number of electrons that move past a specific point in 1 second.
- **Ohms:** Ohms measure resistance, including anything that could limit the flow of electrons.

Here are some other electricity terms that are important for you to know for the ASVAB:

- **Current:** Electricity is like water — it flows. Electrical current occurs when electrons move from one place to another. The use of *conductors,* such as copper and water, allows the electrons to move freely. *Insulators,* such as rubber and wood, discourage the electric current.
- **Watt:** A watt measures *power,* the rate at which electrical energy is consumed or transformed into another type of energy, such as light or heat.
- **Watt-hour:** A *watt-hour* is the amount of energy used in 1 hour at a rate of 1 watt. Most electricity is measured in *kilowatt-hours,* which is how much energy you'd use if you ran a 1,000-watt (1-kilowatt) device for an hour. For example, 10 kilowatt-hours is enough energy to run a 10,000-watt speaker system for an hour-long outdoor concert, or it could run a 5,000-watt air conditioner for 2 hours or a 1,000-watt waffle iron for 10 hours. You find watt-hours by multiplying wattage by time (expressed in hours).
- **Kilowatt and kilowatt-hours:** One *kilowatt* (kW) equals 1,000 watts, and one *kilowatt-hour* (kWh) is one hour using electricity at a rate of 1,000 watts. Kilowatt-hours are what you see on your electricity bill; they're useful for measuring large amounts of electricity. For more on kWh, head to the later section "Measuring power."
- **Megawatt:** *Megawatts* (MW) are tremendous. One megawatt is equal to 1,000 kilowatts (and 1,000,000 watts). This unit measures things like power plants or how much electricity an entire city uses.
- **Gigawatt:** *Gigawatts* (GW) measure the capacity of large power plants (or multiple smaller power plants). One gigawatt is equal to 1,000 megawatts and 1 billion watts. (Rumor has it that 1.21 gigawatts can power a time machine.)

The following sections explain electricity in more detail.

Going subatomic

To understand electricity, you have to start with the basics: atoms. All matter is composed of atoms, the smallest particles that can be broken up without losing their original properties. (You know why you can't trust an atom? Because they make up everything.)

Atoms have a nucleus, just like a cell does. The nucleus is the central hub of the atom, and it's where you find two types of subatomic particles: protons and neutrons. Because *protons* have a positive charge and *neutrons* are neutrally charged, an atom's nucleus is positively charged. Protons and neutrons are packed together in a tiny, dense space, so the nucleus accounts for most of an atom's mass. Each proton and neutron has about 2,000 times more mass than a single electron does. (Check out Chapter 15 for a closer look at density and mass.) Outside the nucleus, in the electron shell, *electrons* (which have a negative charge) are constantly in motion. Atoms have different properties based on the number of basic particles they have and the way in which those basic particles are arranged.

A hydrogen atom (H) contains only one proton, one electron, and no neutrons. Look at the periodic table in Chapter 11. The first element you see is hydrogen, and it has an atomic number of 1. It's the simplest element in the periodic table. Helium, which contains two protons, has an atomic number of 2. Figure 16-1 shows a helium atom, with its pair of protons and electrons, plus two neutrons for good measure. An atom with two protons is helium, no matter what else is happening inside that atom. The same goes for any element and its respective number of protons.

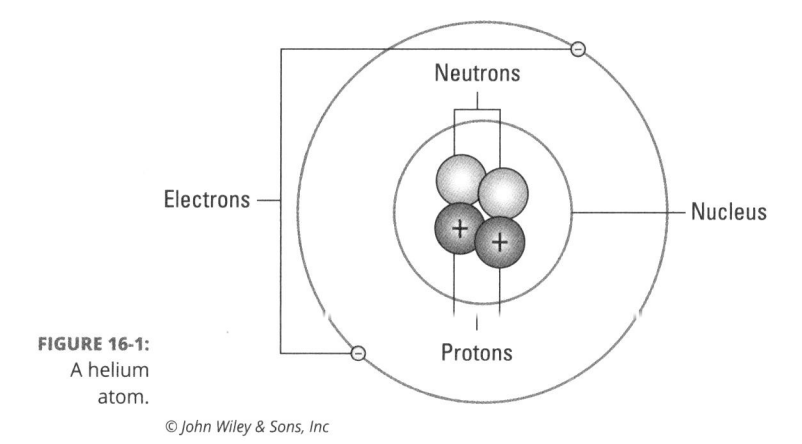

FIGURE 16-1: A helium atom.

© John Wiley & Sons, Inc

The number of neutrons in an atom doesn't count for much, at least in terms of the atomic number. Scientists count only the number of protons in an atom to determine its atomic number, but they add together both protons and neutrons when determining its average *atomic mass* (written on the bottom of each box in the periodic table within parentheses). Helium's atomic mass is 1.00797.

TECHNICAL STUFF

All the atoms on Earth (and in the rest of the universe) were created 13.7 billion years ago. Quarks came together to form protons and neutrons, and those protons and neutrons teamed up to form nuclei, but they weren't quite atoms yet. The universe took about 380,000 years to cool down enough for the nuclei to capture any electrons, which are necessary parts of atoms. When conditions were right, the first hydrogen and helium atoms (the simplest elements on the periodic table in Chapter 11) began to form. Even today, new atoms are created within hot, dense stars, and they launch into the universe when those stars eventually explode.

Earning the good conduct(or) medal

The number of electrons in the outer electron shell of an atom — called a *valence shell* — determines whether an element is a *conductor, semiconductor,* or *insulator.* Each runs this way:

- **Conductors** allow electrons to flow freely between different atoms. These valence shells have more empty spots than they have electrons.
- **Semiconductors** have half-full valence shells (or half-empty, depending on your attitude) and are neither good conductors nor good insulators.
- **Insulators** have pretty full valence shells (at least more than half), so electrons can't move much (or at all) between atoms. They're very poor conductors.

Electrons are negatively charged, and they attempt to shift from one atom to the next trying to get to a positive charge, such as the positive side of a battery. They're able to shift if the material is a conductor. But if the material is an insulator, the electrons are much, much less able to shift because of the insulating material's molecular structure. This flow is called *electrical current.*

Examining the current of the electrical river

Electrical current is the flow — or, more precisely, the rate of flow — of electrons in a conductor. Electrons carry an electrical charge that's expressed in *coulombs* (C). It's called a coulomb because a guy named Charles de Coulomb discovered it in the late 19th century, and the rules say that if you discover something, someone will stick your name on it.

If 1 coulomb (about 6,241,500,000,000,000,000 electrons) flows past a specified point in 1 second, that's a flow rate of 1 ampere (amp, abbreviated A). An *ampere* represents the movement (flow) of electrons, so electrical currents are measured in amps. Typically current is tiny, so small that it's measured in milliamperes; 1 *milliampere* is one-thousandth of an ampere. Current meters, called *ammeters,* measure the flow of current through a circuit. You can compare the flow of electrons to water coming from a garden hose; amps are equivalent to gallons-per-minute if you're washing your car in the driveway.

The amount of voltage (the difference in potential) and the resistance in a circuit determine the number of amperes along a wire — or whatever you're using to conduct the electricity from one place to another. More voltage (for instance, a higher-voltage battery) means that more amps flow in a wire (or conductor). You can read more about this relationship in the next section, which discusses Ohm's law.

Resistance: Putting the brakes on electrical flow

Current doesn't just flow in any properly working circuit unimpeded. Resistance pops up along the way. If the flow of electricity needs to be regulated, resistance is deliberately set up in a circuit so that electronics work properly. If the flow weren't regulated, the motors powering devices like can openers and microwave ovens would quickly overheat and melt. (But before that happened, hopefully a fuse would blow or a circuit breaker would trip, halting current flow and saving the equipment.) In a sense, even a wire, such as a filament in a light bulb, is a type of resistance and is a way to deliberately create circuit resistance.

Adding or removing resistance

Sometimes a circuit must be opened in order to add or remove resistance. In other words, the flow of the electricity must be interrupted in order to physically change the resistance. Using a *circuit breaker,* which is a device that automatically interrupts the electrical current, is an example of opening a circuit to control the current. When the circuit breaker *trips,* the electrical device can no longer operate.

Some devices use a *rheostat,* which can vary the resistance without opening the circuit — the device can continue to work even as the resistance is altered. If an application doesn't use all the electricity, the rheostat absorbs it. A dimmer switch on a light is an example of a rheostat. You increase the amount of resistance to dim the light and decrease the resistance to brighten the light.

Ohm's law: Relating resistance to current and voltage

The amount of resistance that interferes with the flow is measured in *ohms* (pronounced just like those yoga chants). The symbol for ohm is the Greek letter omega, which looks like an upside-down horseshoe: Ω. Resistance can be measured by dividing the voltage measured at any given point (the voltmeter reading) by the amount of current at the same point in a circuit (the ammeter reading). Or you can measure the resistance directly by an ohmmeter.

If you have a current flowing through a wire, three influences are present:

» The amount of voltage, measured in volts *(V)* or electromotive force *(EMF)*

» The resistance to the current, measured in ohms (Ω)

» The amount of current, measured in amperes and expressed as *I* or *i*

These three units are always present in a specific relationship to each other. If you know the value of any two of the influences, you can find the value of the third. (Yes, this requires more math. Sorry.)

Ohm's law, which was first stated by Georg Simon Ohm, reads, "The current in a circuit is directly proportional to the applied voltage and inversely proportional to the circuit resistance," but it's actually easier to understand in mathematical terms. When stating the relationship mathematically, abbreviations are used, where *i* is current, *v* is voltage, and *R* is resistance.

$$\text{Current (amperes)} = \frac{\text{Voltage (volts)}}{\text{Resistance (ohms)}}, \text{ or } I = \frac{V}{R}$$

This essentially means that current in a basic circuit is always dependent on the voltage and resistance in the circuit. If you use a higher-voltage battery (increase *V*), the resistance doesn't change, but current in the circuit increases. By the same token, if you leave the same battery in the circuit but increase the resistance (increase *R*), current decreases.

Here are two other ways to write the same formula, solved for voltage and resistance:

» Voltage = Current × Resistance, or $V = IR$

» Resistance = $\frac{\text{Voltage}}{\text{Current}}$, or $R = \frac{V}{I}$

Ohm's law works exactly the same, no matter which format you use.

Measuring voltage: Do you have the potential?

Voltage is the difference of the potential between two points in a circuit. (A *circuit* is just the path of an electrical current; you can read more about circuits in the later section "Getting around to circuits.") It's sometimes called the *voltage drop* or *difference of potential*. So, for instance, a 9-volt battery supplies 9 volts of electricity. To see what the voltage is anywhere in a circuit, you have to compare the voltage at that point to ground. *Ground* is any part of a circuit (or other object that has electricity running through it) that measures 0 volts, such as the case of your radio, the base of a lamp, or the chassis of your car. The negative terminal of a 9-volt battery is at ground potential, so the voltage from the negative terminal to ground measures 0 volts. The voltage from the positive terminal to either ground or the negative terminal of the battery measures 9 volts.

To measure voltage in a circuit, you use a *voltmeter* or a *multimeter*, which has several meters in one instrument. A voltmeter has two leads. To measure voltage, you place one lead somewhere in the circuit and one lead at another location in the circuit. The voltmeter tells you what the voltage is between those two points.

REMEMBER

A *cell* (a storage compartment for electricity in a battery) has a specific voltage. For example, in a particular battery, cells may be 1.5 volts. Therefore, you can figure out the number of cells that battery has by dividing the voltage of the battery by 1.5. Pretty handy stuff, huh?

Getting around to circuits

Although an earlier section suggests that electricity flows like water, it actually flows more like NASCAR. If you want to use its power, electricity must be sent along the path of a closed circle (a circuit), just like all those NASCAR speedsters roaring around the track. The drivers never actually get anywhere; they just keep driving in circles. Electrical charges are a lot like that.

However, electricity does flow like a river in one respect. Electricity follows every path available to it. Most electrons take the path of lowest resistance, but some still take a path of higher resistance. The conventional way in thinking about the electrical flow of current is based on the vacancies left by electrical particles "moving" from the positive (+) terminal to the negative (−) terminal of a battery. This concept is called *conventional current*. However, the military teaches current flow based on the actual flow of the electrons, and electrons, no matter how you look at them, flow from the negative terminal to the positive terminal (see Figure 16-2). This is referred to as *electron flow*.

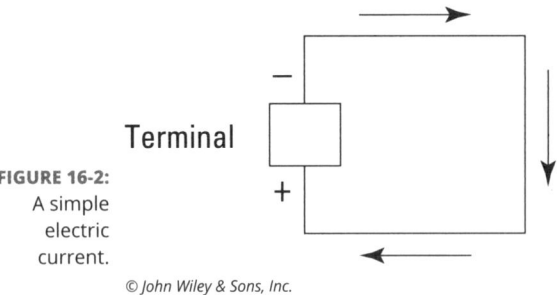

FIGURE 16-2: A simple electric current.

© John Wiley & Sons, Inc.

Electrical current can't flow without a circuit, and a working circuit must include three components:

>> A voltage source, such as a battery

>> A load, which is a source of resistance that converts electrical energy into another form of energy (like a light bulb)

>> Conductors, which are necessary to carry the current from Point A to Point B

Figure 16-2 shows the way current flows, but Figure 16-3 shows how electricity comes from a voltage source, powers something (like a light bulb), and returns to its original source. It also shows what happens if a circuit is opened, interrupting the flow of electricity. When you flip a light switch to its "Off" position, you open the light's circuit. The electricity can't flow to the light bulb anymore because there's an open gap in the wire. Electricity can't usually flow through air because air is an insulator (see "Earning the good conduct(or) medal" in this chapter), so the light turns off. When you flip the switch to the "On" position, the circuit closes and the electricity can flow uninterrupted, reaching the light bulb and turning it on.

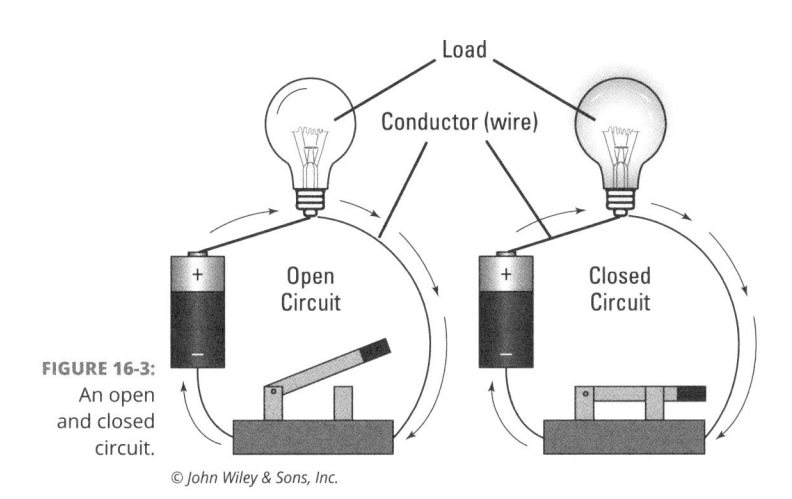

FIGURE 16-3: An open and closed circuit.

© John Wiley & Sons, Inc.

Circuit breakers and fuses

Circuit breakers are designed to break a circuit when too much energy is flowing through an electrical system. The circuit breaker panel in your house is a great example. If your washing machine is sucking too much power from the electrical outlet, putting too much of a load on your electrical system, the circuit breaker literally breaks the circuit to interrupt the flow before it can damage all the wiring in your house.

Fuses work the same way. *Fuses* are thin wires enclosed in a safe insulating material, and they're just part of a circuit. However, they're designed to burn up if the current heats up above a certain level. When the fuse disintegrates, the circuit is interrupted and can't carry any more electricity. Fuses work once only; you have to replace them if one is blown.

TECHNICAL STUFF

In some cases, current does flow through an insulator — if there's enough difference of potential (voltage). When lightning bridges an expanse of air from a cloud to ground (or a tree or a golfer), it's because a huge amount of voltage, on the order of 300 million volts, exists between the source of the lightning and ground.

When current flows, every electron carries its voltage all the way along the conductor. The electrons keep moving forward, pushing the ones in front of them while being pushed by the ones behind them. When even one electron stops, they all stop, and the current instantly becomes zero.

Types of circuits

Circuits come in three main types: series, parallel, and series-parallel.

Series circuits have only one path electrical current can take. A break anywhere in the circuit stops the whole operation. Figure 16-3 earlier in the chapter is a series circuit, but on official electrical diagrams, it's drawn like what you see in Figure 16-4. (What? I just really liked the light bulb's

CHAPTER 16 **Electronics Information** 345

visual effect.) The current flow in a series circuit is the same in every part of the circuit because it has nowhere else to go. If multiple loads are located along a series circuit, their resistances together create an overall sum. That means if R represents resistance, you can represent the loads this way: $R_{(total)} = R_1 + R_2 + R_3 + R_4$ (and so on). Voltage remains the same throughout the circuit based on Ohm's law. (You can read more about voltage in "Measuring voltage: Do you have the potential?" in this chapter.)

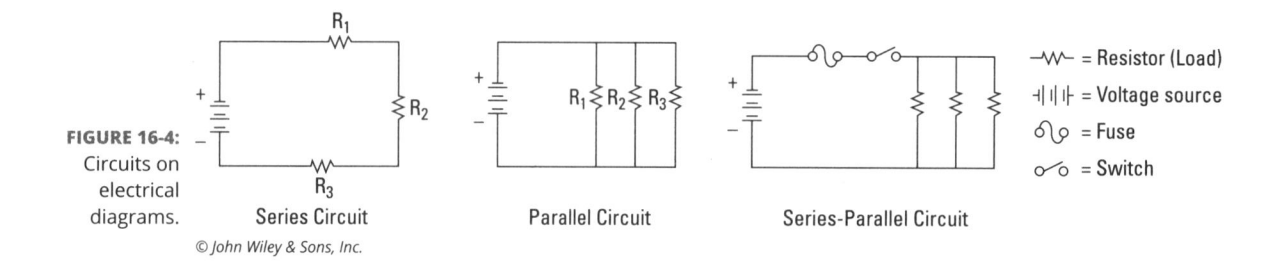

FIGURE 16-4: Circuits on electrical diagrams.
© John Wiley & Sons, Inc.

Parallel circuits are very common. In this type of circuit, every load is wired along its own path. If a break occurs in one path to one load, the current continues to flow to the other loads. The voltage in a parallel circuit remains the same throughout each parallel branch of the circuit, but the current flow can vary across each branch. The total current remains the same.

Adding a load in parallel decreases the total resistance of a current; that's because it provides an additional pathway for electrons to take. That's true even if the additional pathway provides more resistance than the first pathway. When you're working with a parallel circuit, you figure out the total resistance this way, where R represents each instance of resistance (each load): $\frac{1}{R_{(total)}} = \frac{1}{R_1} + \frac{1}{R_2} + \frac{1}{R_3} + \frac{1}{R_4}$ and so on.

Series–parallel circuits are the most common arrangement. Most houses are wired this way. These circuits are more complicated because they include more components, such as on/off switches and fuses. Despite their popularity, you aren't likely to have to calculate resistance for series–parallel circuits on the ASVAB; doing so requires you to use the right formula on each group of resistors until you can zero in on a single value.

HOLIDAY (LIGHT) BURNOUT

Holiday lights are an interesting way to look at series and parallel circuits. In some types of holiday lights, when one blue bulb burns out, all of the other blue bulbs go dark. That's because all the blue bulbs run along the same series circuit, and one burned-out or broken bulb interrupts the flow of electricity. However, the red, green, and white lights run on different series circuit paths. Although they're all connected to the same power source, the other colors stay illuminated because the power source isn't the problem; the series circuit containing blue lights is the problem. Sometimes holiday lights are several parallel circuits wired together. In cases like those, none of the other lights are affected when one bulb goes out, because current flows directly to each bulb from the source. If you buy strings of lights you can connect to each other, you create your own series-parallel circuit made from series and parallel circuits (and the technical specs of those are more complicated than anything you're likely to see on the ASVAB).

Note: Most modern holiday lights are wired with shunts, so if one of your blue bulbs goes out this year, it's not going to affect the rest of them. A *shunt* is a device that allows current to continue flowing through a circuit by creating a path of lower resistance. In holiday lights, shunts are small wires wrapped with an insulating substance; when a bulb gets too hot and burns out, it melts the insulating substance so the circuit can continue and your lights keep working.

When any wire accidentally crosses over another wire, causing the electricity to bypass the rest of the circuit and not follow its intended path, you get a *short circuit.* This issue is a circuit problem rather than a circuit type, but it's worth mentioning.

Most people are unlikely to see complex electrical problems that involve mathematical calculations on the ASVAB (if you do, it means you're blowing all the easy and medium questions out of the water with correct answers). The ASVAB tests your basic knowledge to see how trainable you are in each academic area; it's not judging you for not being an electronics expert. Just in case, check out this example about a simple parallel circuit.

EXAMPLE

Determine the total resistance in this series circuit.

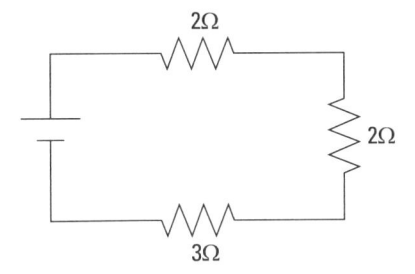

(A) 2Ω

(B) 4Ω

(C) 7Ω

(D) 5Ω

The formula for determining resistance in a series circuit is $R_{(total)} = R_1 + R_2 + R_3$, so the total resistance is 7Ω.

EXAMPLE

Determine the total resistance in this parallel circuit.

(A) 0.233Ω

(B) 0.35Ω

(C) 2.33Ω

(D) 4.29Ω

Remember that the formula for determining resistance in a parallel circuit is $\frac{1}{R_{(total)}} = \frac{1}{R_1} + \frac{1}{R_2} + \frac{1}{R_3}$. That means you have to formulate the problem this way: $\frac{1}{R_{(total)}} = \frac{1}{17} + \frac{1}{12} + \frac{1}{11}$. When you apply the mathematical principles in Chapter 6, you get a common denominator of 2,244. (Remember, you can't use a calculator on the ASVAB.) Your problem looks like this: $\frac{132}{2244} + \frac{187}{2244} + \frac{204}{2244} = \frac{523}{2244}$, or 0.233.

That decimal isn't your total resistance, though. The total resistance is in the denominator of the problem (the bottom part of the fraction). That means you need to find the inverse of the fraction. Because $\frac{1}{R_{total}} = \frac{0.233}{1}$, you need to find the inverse to calculate the total resistance: $R_{total} = \frac{1}{0.233}$, or approximately 4.29Ω.

The correct answer is Choice (D).

EXAMPLE

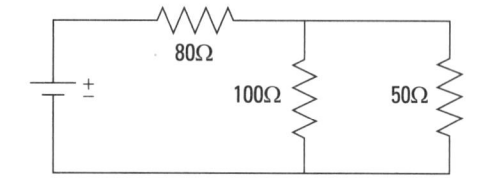

Determine the total resistance in this series-parallel circuit.

(A) 20Ω

(B) 70Ω

(C) 113.3Ω

(D) 230Ω

First find the resistance of the parallel combination using $\frac{1}{R_{(total)}} = \frac{1}{R_1} + \frac{1}{R_2}$, which is $\frac{1}{R_{(total)}} = \frac{1}{100} + \frac{1}{50}$, or 33.3Ω. You can redraw the circuit this way:

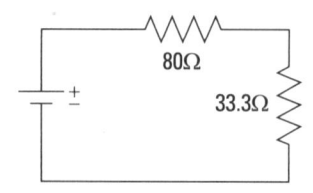

Because it's now a series circuit, add the two series resistances (80 and 33.3Ω) to determine that the total resistance is 113.3Ω, which is Choice (C).

Measuring power

Power is measured in *watts*. One watt is a very small amount of power. It would require nearly 750 watts to equal 1 horsepower. One kilowatt represents 1,000 watts.

A *kilowatt-hour* (kWh) — the amount of electricity a power plant generates or a customer uses — is equal to the energy of 1,000 watts working for one hour. Kilowatt-hours are determined by multiplying the number of kilowatts (kW) required by the number of hours of use. For example, if you use a 40-watt light bulb 5 hours a day, you've used 200 watt-hours, or 0.2 kilowatt-hours of electrical energy. The other way to find power (in watts) is by using this formula:

Power (watts) = Voltage (volts) × Current (amperes)

TECHNICAL STUFF

The term *watt* was named to honor James Watt, the inventor of the steam engine.

MAGNETIC, ELECTRIC: NO, NOT YOUR PERSONALITY

Certain magnetic effects always accompany an electric current, and these effects follow definite laws. In a wire, the *magnetic lines of force* (imaginary lines used to explain magnetic effects) are perpendicular to the conductor and parallel to each other.

But when you wrap a wire around a core and pass current through it, the wire forms a coil. As the lines of force around the core take on a different shape, the field around each turn of wire links with the fields from the other turns of wire around it. The combined influence of all the turns of wire produces a two-pole magnetic field, very much like the magnetic field of a simple bar magnet — one end of the coil is a north pole; the other end is a south pole.

The strength of the magnetic field depends on several factors. Here are the main ones:

- **Number of turns:** If you increase the number of turns, you increase the field strength.
- **Closeness of the turns:** The closer the turns, the stronger the field.
- **Amount of current:** If you increase current, you increase field strength.
- **Material in the core:** Most coils are classified as either air or soft iron, based on their cores. *Air coils* are usually wrapped around a piece of cardboard; *soft-iron coils* are wrapped around a piece of iron. Soft iron offers a better path for magnetic lines of force because its high permeability offers less reluctance to magnetic flux, resulting in more lines of force. (Think of *magnetic flux* as a measurement of magnetic strength located on a two-dimensional surface. A good example of magnetic flux would be the magnetic strength of one side of a magnet.) The more lines of force, the stronger the magnetic field.

Passing a suspended loop of conductive material (wire) through a magnetic field creates *electromagnetic induction,* which is the basic principle behind the electric generator. When the conductor is standing still, current doesn't flow through it. But when the loop starts to rotate clockwise through the lines of force of the magnets, the lines of force induce free electrons to move through the wire.

Producing electrical effects

Electric currents can produce different effects. These effects are packaged and sold commercially. The following is a description of effects produced by current and some of their commercial applications:

- **Chemical effect:** Current produces this effect when it passes through a chemical compound and breaks up that compound. Also called *electrolytic decomposition,* this phenomenon is used in *electroplating,* a process used to cover objects with a very thin coating of metal. This effect is used to make less expensive jewelry.

- **Heat effect:** Conducting electricity causes wires to become heated. Heat develops because the current must overcome the resistance of the wire. This heat energy can be quite obvious or hardly noticeable to touch, depending on the size of the wire and the amount of current. You've used this effect to cook dinner if you have an electric stove.

- **Magnetic effect:** When a wire is introduced into a magnetic field, electricity flows through the wire and creates a magnetic field that repels a magnet. This effect is used to create energy through *electromagnetic induction,* the basic principle behind the electric generator. If the wire is wrapped around an iron core and a current is sent through the wire, the iron becomes magnetized. (See the nearby sidebar for more on the magnetic effect.) Huge electromagnets help sort out metal at recycling plants.

>> **Physiological effect:** Current produces this effect when it passes through your bicep (or any of your muscles, for that matter) and causes the muscle to contract. This effect is used in medicine.

Switching Things Up with Alternating and Direct Current

A current doesn't always flow in one direction. A *direct current* (DC) does — it only and always flows in one direction. An *alternating current* (AC), however, constantly changes direction in a regular pattern. Higher voltages are easier to obtain with alternating current, and transferring high voltage down a power line is ultimately cheaper than transferring low voltage, so most electricity comes in the form of AC.

>> **Direct current** often comes from a battery. It's what your phone, kids' toys, and flashlights use when you're not charging them in a wall.

>> **Alternating current** comes directly into your home from the power company. It can change direction and voltage from higher to lower current when it encounters a transformer (not Bumblebee or Optimus Prime — the electrical kind).

>> **AC/DC** is a combination of the two. Your laptop uses it, a wall-plug phone charger uses it, and some vehicles use it. AC comes in through the outlet, and the box (the rectifier) between the outlet and the part that plugs into your device transforms it to DC.

The following sections cover some important points about alternating and direct current.

Figuring out frequency

The number of times an alternating current changes direction per second is known as its *frequency*. *Hertz* (Hz) is the unit of measurement for frequency. One hertz (Hz) equals one complete cycle per second. In other words, the current makes two complete alternations of direction.

The AC in your house probably completes 60 alternating cycles per second. Therefore, the AC in your house has a frequency of 60 Hz. Most electronic devices operate at higher frequencies; therefore, frequencies may be measured in kilohertz (kHz, 1,000 hertz), megahertz (MHz, 1 million hertz), or even gigahertz (GHz, 1 billion hertz).

GROUNDING YOURSELF WITH BASIC ELECTRICAL SAFETY

Grounding is an important aspect of working with electricity. In practice, it gives excess electricity a place to go without harming anyone in the process: the ground. Any wiring system can fail, so some systems — most notably, homes — include a series of grounding wires that run parallel to "hot" and "neutral" wires. That way, if a rat gnaws through a live wire that's carrying current, the grounding wires can capture the stray current and send it where it belongs (usually a grounding rod driven deep into the ground outside) so it doesn't shock someone or start a fire.

TECHNICAL STUFF: AM radio stations often broadcast in the 530–1,700 kHz range. Television stations may broadcast at as low as 7 to as high as 1,002 MHz. Traditional radar operates in the 1–40 GHz range.

Impedance: Join the resistance!

Resistance interferes with the flow of current in a circuit. But the flow of current is also impeded by two properties of alternating currents:

- **Capacitive reactance (capacitance):** *Capacitive reactance* is a measure of a capacitor's opposition to alternating current, and it's measured in ohms. Capacitance is the storage of energy that occurs in a nonconductor, and it's measured in farads *(F)*. This property resists any change in voltage in a circuit.

- **Inductive reactance (inductance):** *Inductive reactance,* also measured in ohms, is the resistance to a change in the flow of current. Inductance is the property that causes current to increase or decrease even more based on changes in current induced in a circuit. This inductance creates an electromotive force and is measured in henrys (H).

REMEMBER: These two types of reactance combine to impede the flow of current. Impedance can become incredibly complex, but in its simplest form, it can be expressed as the ratio of electromotive force to the current:

$$\text{Impedance} = \frac{\text{Electromotive force}}{\text{Current}}$$

Electronic devices often require a specific capacitive or inductive reactance to work. *Capacitors* and *inductors* are devices used in circuits to provide the type of reactance needed. Capacitors are rated in microfarads (μF), and inductors are rated in millihenries (mH). For an in-depth look at impedance and other information that professional electricians use, check out *Electronics For Dummies* by Cathleen Shamieh (Wiley).

TIP: You can relate impedance to Ohm's law in reference to AC circuits. Simply substitute resistance in Ohm's law with impedance and voltage with electromotive force.

> ### SORTING OUT CAPACITORS AND INDUCTORS
>
> Capacitors store or hold a charge of electrons. In an AC circuit, because AC voltage goes positive and negative in each cycle, the capacitor is constantly charging and discharging. The rate of the charging and discharging acts as opposition to the changing AC voltage — as a resistive effect called *capacitive reactance*.
>
> *Inductors* are coils of wire that make use of the properties of a magnetic field. The property specifically desired is the flow of current through the wire. With full current, the magnetic field is at its maximum. However, if you take away the current, the field doesn't disappear immediately. It decays gradually, and the decay continues to push electrons in the path they were going. But in an AC circuit, the current constantly reverses. The rate of changing current flow and the resulting collapse and regeneration of the magnetic field in the coil act as opposition to changing AC current — a resistive effect called *inductive reactance*.

CHAPTER 16 **Electronics Information**

Rectifying the situation: Going direct

Certain electronic circuits are engineered to change alternating current to direct current. The process of making the change is called *rectification*, and the circuits that perform the rectification are called *rectifiers*.

Rectifiers contain *semiconductor diodes*, a component made of a material with conductivity somewhere between that of a conductor and an insulator. *Diodes* conduct electricity in only one direction. Rectification also often requires inductors and capacitors (see the preceding section).

Rectification helps appliances run at cooler temperatures and allows them to run at variable speeds. Devices typically need direct current to run properly. The process of rectification changes the incoming AC to DC. Manufacturers often use diodes, which used to be housed in big, glass vacuum tubes, to rectify current in many appliances and electronic devices.

Turning up the transistor radio

A transistor is a *semiconductor* (an object that conducts electricity poorly at low temperatures) that controls the flow of electricity in a circuit. It's usually made of germanium or silicon. This electrical device can amplify a signal, which is why it's used in transistor radios. Transistors have many properties:

- Unlike rectifier diodes (see the preceding section), a transistor doesn't require a vacuum to operate.
- Transistors are small, require little power, and last a long time.
- A transistor contains at least three terminals:
  - The *emitter* is the voltage output.
  - The *base* acts like a gate, and the voltage at the base controls the flow of current through the transistor (and therefore the voltage).
  - The *collector* is the voltage input.

Picture It: Decoding Electrical Circuit Codes

Electronic circuits can be combined to create *complex systems*, such as those required to operate a stereo system. *Block diagrams* are used to show the various combined circuits that form a complex system.

Many of the questions on the Electronics Information subtest require you to identify an electronic component symbol and know what that component does in an electronic circuit. Figure 16-5 shows the most common component symbols. The figure's items are grouped based on similarity of functions. For example, cells, batteries, DC power supplies, and AC power supplies all have similar functions (they supply power to the circuit).

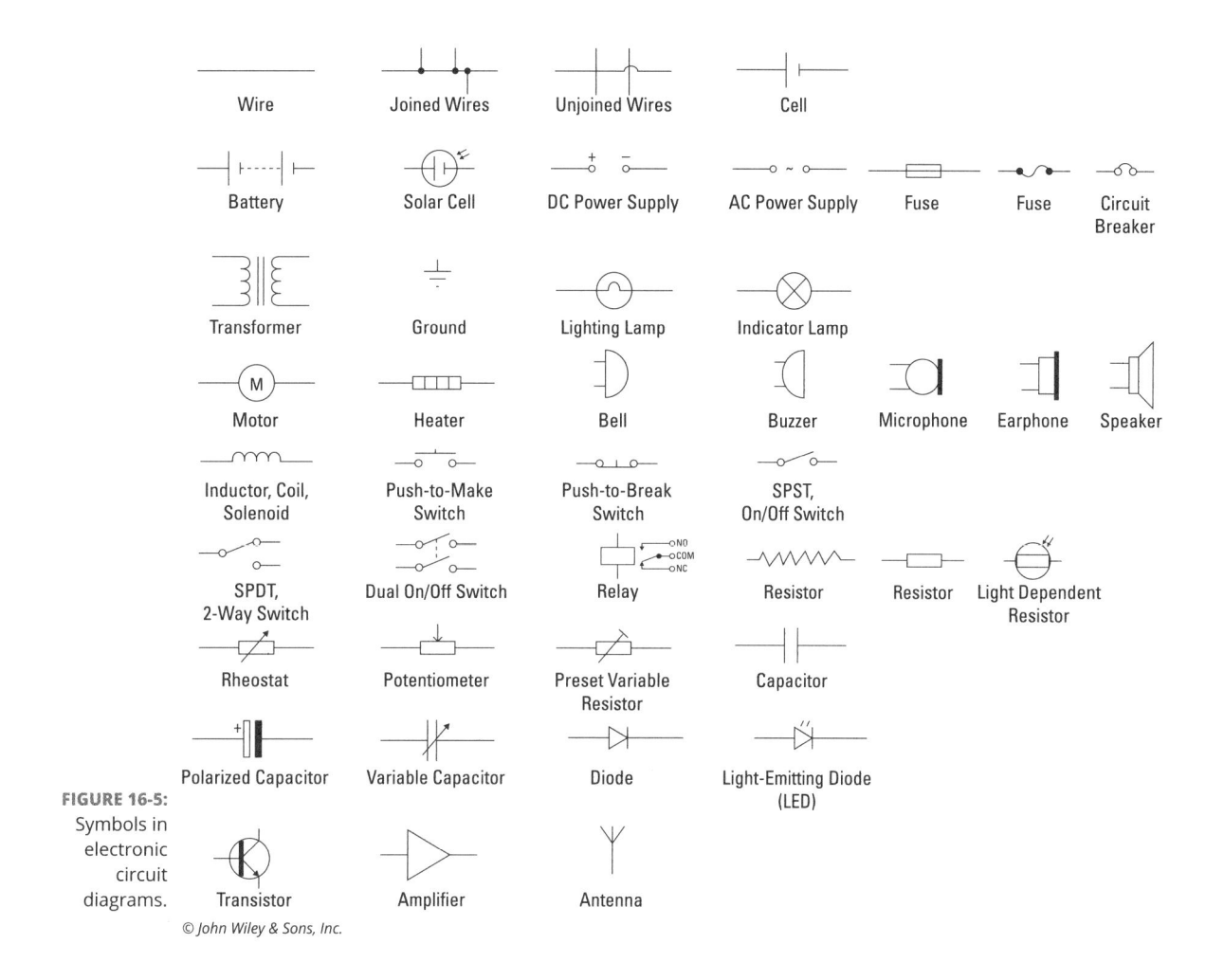

FIGURE 16-5: Symbols in electronic circuit diagrams.

© John Wiley & Sons, Inc.

So what do all these electronic doodads do when connected in a circuit? I cover each item in the following list:

- **Wires:** Wires are used to pass current from one part of the component to another. Wires that are connected to each other are indicated by a dark circle and are called *joined wires*. Sometimes in complex circuit diagrams, it's necessary to draw wires crossing even though they aren't connected. In this case, the dark circle is omitted, or a hump symbol is drawn to make it clear the wires aren't connected — these are called *unjoined wires*.

- **Cell:** A cell supplies electrical current. Some call this a battery, but technically a battery is more than one cell. The large terminal (on the left side of the cell image in Figure 16-5) is positive.

- **Battery:** A battery is two or more cells. The large terminal is positive.

- **DC power supply:** A DC power supply provides direct current. Direct current always flows in one direction.

- **AC power supply:** An AC power supply provides alternating current. Alternating current constantly changes direction at a specific frequency.

- **Fuse:** A fuse is a safety device that *blows* (melts) if the current flowing through it exceeds a specified value. Read more about fuses in the earlier section "Circuit breakers and fuses."

CHAPTER 16 **Electronics Information** 353

- **Transformer:** A transformer consists of two coils of wire linked by an iron core. Transformers are used to step up (increase) and step down (decrease) AC voltages. No electrical connection exists between the coils. Energy is transferred between the coils by the magnetic field in the core.
- **Ground:** A ground is a connection to the Earth.
- **Transducer:** A transducer is a device that converts energy from one form to another. Here are various types of transducers:
  - **Lighting lamp:** Converts electrical energy to light, such as in a light bulb or automobile headlight
  - **Indicator lamp:** Converts electrical energy to light for such uses as a warning light on a car's dashboard
  - **Motor:** Converts electrical energy to kinetic energy (motion)
  - **Heater:** Converts electrical energy to heat
  - **Bells and buzzers:** Convert electrical energy to sound
  - **Microphone:** Converts sound to electrical energy
  - **Earphones and speakers:** Convert electrical energy to sound
- **Inductor:** An *inductor* is a coil of wire that creates a magnetic field when current passes through it.
- **Switch:** Here are several types of switches:
  - **Push switch:** A push switch allows current to flow only when the button is pressed, such as in a doorbell.
  - **Push-to-break switch:** With this switch, the circuit is normally closed (the device is on); the circuit is open (device is off) only when the button is pressed.
  - **On/off switch:** An on/off switch allows current to flow only when it's in the closed (on) position.
  - **Two-way switch:** A two-way switch directs the flow of current to one of two routes, according to its position.
  - **Dual on/off switch:** This type is often used to switch main electricity because it can isolate both the live and neutral connections.
  - **Relay (relay switch):** A relay is an electrically operated switch that may operate multiple switches at one time. Typically a small current flowing through a coil sets up a magnetic field, which causes the lever(s) to move, effectively changing the (relay) switch's position(s). As an example, a 5-volt signal from your dashboard turns on your 12-volt headlights through a relay.
- **Resistor (nonvariable):** There are two different versions of the basic resistor symbol. Resistors restrict the flow of electric current. Resistors are rated in ohms and have a color code on them to indicate their value, tolerance, and sometimes quality. The band code is as follows:
  - Black is 0.
  - Brown is 1.
  - Red is 2.
  - Orange is 3.
  - Yellow is 4.

- Green is 5.
- Blue is 6.
- Violet is 7.
- Gray is 8.
- White is 9.

The first and second bands on the resistor are the first two digits in the resistor's value. The next band indicates the multiplier (number of zeros after the first two numbers). So if the first band is red, the second is yellow, and the third band is orange, the resistor's value is 24,000 ohms. A gold or silver band after the first bands indicates tolerance, and a quality band may follow the tolerance band.

>> **Variable resistor:** Variable resistors also restrict the flow of electric current. There are several symbols in use in circuit diagrams for standard variable and preset variable resistors. Types of variable resistors include the following:

- **Rheostat:** A type of variable resistor with two contacts, usually used to control current; examples of controlling current would be adjusting lamp brightness or adjusting motor speed
- **Potentiometer:** A type of variable resistor with three contacts that's used to control voltage
- **Preset variable resistor:** A device that operates with a small screwdriver or similar tool; it's designed to be set when the circuit is made and then left without further adjustment

>> **Capacitor:** Capacitors store electric charge. They're used with resistors in timing circuits because it takes time for a capacitor to fill with charge. They're also used in filter circuits because capacitors easily pass AC (changing voltage) signals but they block DC (constant voltage) signals. Two types of capacitors include the following:

- Polarized capacitors must be connected the correct way in circuit.
- Variable capacitors are used most often in radio tuning circuits.

>> **Diode:** Diodes allow electricity to flow in only one direction. The arrow of the circuit symbol shows the direction in which the current can flow. Diodes are the electrical version of a valve, and early diodes were actually called *valves*. Light-emitting diodes (LEDs) emit light when an electric current passes through them. Specialized diodes, called *Zener diodes*, do allow current in the opposite direction after a threshold is met.

>> **Transistor:** Transistors amplify current. For example, they can be used to amplify the small output current from a logic chip so it can operate a lamp, relay, or other high-current device.

>> **Amplifier:** An amplifier isn't actually an electronic component but instead is a complex circuit. The block diagram symbol shows where an amplifier circuit would be connected. Amplifier circuits are used to magnify power, current, or voltage.

>> **Antenna:** An antenna is a device designed to receive and/or transmit radio signals.

Circuit diagrams show how electronic components are connected together. These diagrams show the connections as clearly as possible with all wires drawn neatly as straight lines. The actual layout of the components is usually quite different from the circuit diagram, however. Circuit diagrams are useful when testing a circuit and for understanding how it works. Figure 16-6 shows a diagram of an adjustable timer circuit. See how many components you can identify.

FIGURE 16-6: An adjustable timer circuit.

© John Wiley & Sons, Inc.

Coming in Hot: Wire Color Codes Used in the U.S.

In the United States, electrical wires follow color standards. The process started after the 1940s, so older wiring systems don't necessarily follow the same standards, and different types of wires have different color codes. In electrical terms, *phase* refers to the distribution of a load. A single-phase wire has three wires within the insulation (two hot, or live, wires and one neutral wire). A Phase 2 wire has two live wires, each providing the same voltage but with different peaks and dips in voltage, and one or two neutral wires. A Phase 3 wire contains three hot wires (and sometimes a neutral wire), with each phase AC signal being 120 electrical degrees apart.

WARNING All electrical wires can carry a current, so no matter how they're labeled, treat them as if they could shock you.

AC wires that travel between the last protective device (such as a circuit breaker) and the load on branch circuits carrying 120, 208, or 240 volts are

- » **Black** for Phase 1
- » **Red** for Phase 2
- » **Blue** for Phase 3
- » **White** if they're neutral
- » **Green, green with a yellow stripe, or bare wire** if they're ground wires
- » **Orange** if the wiring system has one phase at a higher voltage than the others

AC wires in 277- or 480-volt systems are

- » **Brown** for Phase 1
- » **Orange** for Phase 2
- » **Yellow** for Phase 3
- » **Gray** if they are neutral
- » **Green, green with a yellow stripe, or bare wire** if they're ground wires

DC wires are different (such as those you use as jumper cables on your car battery). Those are red for positive, black for negative, and white or gray for ground.

Consider black and brown wires to be live (that is, carrying a current) at all times. They transfer power to switches and outlets. Red wires are secondary live wires, and you can use them in *switch legs* (connections that link a switch to an electrical load). Blue and yellow wires carry a current through a conduit. Neutral wires in white or gray connect a conductive piece of metal that attracts electric current so it can be distributed everywhere it needs to go. (And for the record, they may carry a current even though they're called "neutral.") Finally, green wires are the failsafe; they give electricity a place to escape into the ground if it has nowhere else to go. These wires can be live if the system has a fault somewhere.

Eyeing Some Electronics Information Test Tips

When it comes to the electronics test, don't feel like you have to know as much as Ben Franklin to get a passing score. Just use your common sense. If a question asks, "What's the safest way to run an extension cord to a reading light?" the answer "across the middle of the floor" is probably going to be wrong.

You can also figure out quite a few answers if you remember these units of measure:

- **Current:** Amperes (or amps)
- **Voltage:** Volts
- **Resistance:** Ohms
- **Power:** Watts
- **Energy:** Watt-hours

Memorizing simple principles

If you commit the following principles to memory, you'll have an easier time succeeding on the Electronics Information subtest:

- Ohm's law: $Current = \frac{Voltage}{Resistance}$.
- Power (watts) = Voltage (volts) × Current (amperes), or $P = VI$.
- Current flows from a negative pole to a positive pole.
- A closed circuit must exist for electricity to flow. (Think NASCAR.)
- Alternating current (AC) changes direction constantly at a constant rate. The number of times a current completes two alternations of direction per second is known as its *frequency;* the unit of measurement for frequency is the hertz (Hz).
- Electronic devices operate at very high frequencies.
- Electronic devices often require a specific capacitive or inductive reactance to work. Capacitors and inductors are devices used in circuits to provide the type of reactance needed.
- Devices that change alternating current to direct current are called *rectifiers.*
- A *transistor* can amplify a signal.

Playing the guessing game

The Electronics Information subtest is the type of test where you either know the answer or you don't. But if you don't know the answer, you should still guess (just be cautious about guessing on the CAT-ASVAB; if you click random answers quickly at the end of the subtest, you may be penalized). Remember, you don't have a lot of time to ponder the answer choices. Guess and move on. To increase your chances of guessing correctly, you can often eliminate an incorrect answer.

Sometimes one answer is obviously wrong, or one answer is more obviously right than another. The electronics answer is usually the right answer. Therefore, an answer that has to do with how much something costs or how pretty it looks is probably wrong.

Not all questions are specifically electronics questions. You may be asked something like "A milliradian measures what quantity?" Think about how you've seen that prefix used before, such as in the word millimeter. A millimeter, you may remember, is one-thousandth of a meter. And like other SI units of measurement, a *milliradian* is one-thousandth of a radian. For additional guessing help, flip to Chapter 3.

Electronics Information Practice Questions

The questions in this section measure your knowledge of basic electronics principles.

If you need a good score on this subtest to get your military dream job or you want to rebuild that old television set without sacrificing your garage, you may want to check out *Electronics For Dummies* by Cathleen Shamieh (Wiley) for additional help.

1. What does the abbreviation DC stand for?

    (A) duplicate charge
    (B) direct charge
    (C) direct current
    (D) diode current

2. Which of the following is the ohm symbol?

    (A) Σ
    (B) Δ
    (C) Φ
    (D) Ω

3. Which of the following has the least resistance?

    (A) iron
    (B) rubber
    (C) copper
    (D) wood

4. What conclusion can you draw based on the following diagram of a flashbulb circuit?

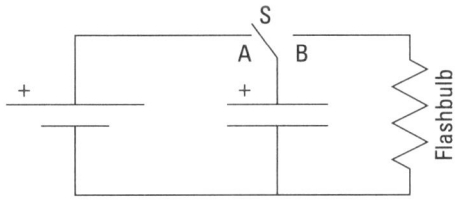

    © John Wiley & Sons, Inc.

    (A) There is no power to the circuit.
    (B) The flashbulb is turned off.
    (C) Only one battery is working.
    (D) The flashbulb is in parallel.

5. What increases or decreases the voltage in a system without the need for an electrical connection?

    (A) terminal
    (B) trigger
    (C) transmitter
    (D) transformer

6. A device used to amplify a signal is called a

    (A) diode.
    (B) transformer.
    (C) rectifier.
    (D) transistor.

7. What process changes incoming alternating current (AC) to direct current (DC)?

    (A) magnetic effect
    (B) rectification
    (C) transformation
    (D) impedance

8. The amount of electrical power is measured in units called

    (A) volts.
    (B) amperes.
    (C) watts.
    (D) ohms.

9. What does the arrow over the resistor symbol represent?

    © John Wiley & Sons, Inc.

    (A) indicator
    (B) direct current
    (C) variable
    (D) live

10. Components designed to store electrical charge are called

(A) capacitors.
(B) transformers.
(C) resistors.
(D) transistors.

11. In what direction does current go in electron flow notation?

(A) from negative to positive
(B) from positive to negative
(C) any direction
(D) horizontally

12. In an electronic circuit diagram, the symbol used to show wires connecting is a/an

(A) X symbol.
(B) dot.
(C) dark square.
(D) T symbol.

13. What occurs when a wire is wrapped around an iron core and a current is sent through the wire?

(A) chemical effect
(B) heat effect
(C) magnetic effect
(D) physiological effect

14. What is the term for magnetic effects that are perpendicular to the conductor and parallel to each other?

(A) north pole
(B) semiconductor
(C) lines of force
(D) electroplating

15. What symbol is not shown in the following circuit diagram?

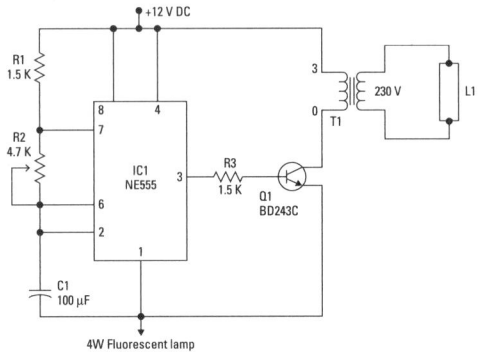

© John Wiley & Sons, Inc.

(A) transformer
(B) fuse
(C) resistor
(D) transistor

16. What is commonly used in a circuit in which the flow of electricity needs to be regulated for the device to run properly?

(A) resistance
(B) transformer
(C) diodes
(D) batteries

17. What color wire from the following choices is not considered a "hot" wire?

(A) red
(B) black
(C) gray
(D) blue

18. What does the following symbol represent?

© John Wiley & Sons, Inc.

(A) fuse
(B) ground
(C) outlet
(D) resistor

Answers and Explanations

Use this answer key to score the Electronics Information practice questions.

1. **C.** DC stands for *direct current.* I made up the other choices. The correct answer is Choice (C).

2. **D.** Remember, the upside-down horseshoe (the Greek letter omega) is the symbol for ohm, the measure of electrical resistance. The correct answer is Choice (D).

3. **C.** Copper is the best conductor of electricity of those listed here. Therefore, it offers the least resistance to an electric current. The correct answer is Choice (C).

4. **B.** When the switch is in contact with point A (as shown), the charges are being stored. When the switch moves to point B, the flashbulb turns on.

5. **D.** A transformer is an inductor with two or more windings, a *terminal* is a device that connects electrical circuits together, a *trigger* initiates a circuit action, and a *transmitter* is a device used to achieve transmission. *Windings* are magnetic wires that are coated with enamel and wrapped around the core of a transformer. The primary winding is driven by transistors, and the secondary winding is driven by the core's magnetic field, produced by the primary winding. Choice (D) is the correct answer.

6. **D.** A *diode* is a semiconductor that conducts electricity in one direction only; a *transformer* is a device that changes voltage (either "transforming" low voltage to high voltage or high voltage to low voltage); a *rectifier* is a circuit that changes alternating current to direct current. Choice (D) is the correct answer.

7. **B.** Rectification occurs in certain electronic circuits that need to change incoming AC to DC in order to run properly.

8. **C.** A *watt* measures the amount of power, the rate at which energy is produced or used. The correct answer is Choice (C).

9. **C.** A *variable resistor* is a potentiometer with two connecting wires instead of three; it allows for finer control over the current by changing the amount of resistance.

10. **A.** *Capacitors* store electric charge. They're used with resistors in timing circuits because it takes time for a capacitor to store voltage (to become charged). The correct answer is Choice (A).

11. **A.** In conventional flow notation, the motion of charge is shown according to the (technically incorrect) labels of + and −, with the electric charge moving from positive to negative. But in electron flow notation, the actual motion of electrons in the circuit is followed. Negative electrons are always searching for positive charges, so current flows from a negative pole to a positive pole.

12. **B.** Wires connected to each other are indicated by a darkened circle. The correct answer is Choice (B).

13. **C.** When a wire is wrapped around an iron core and a current is sent through the wire, the iron becomes magnetized.

14. C. In a wire, magnetic lines of force are perpendicular to the conductor and parallel to each other.

15. B.

© John Wiley & Sons, Inc.

This symbol represents a fuse; the circuit doesn't contain a fuse.

16. A. Resistance is set up in a circuit to regulate the electricity so the device isn't destroyed by electrical heat.

17. C. Red, black, and blue wires are always "hot" and should never be tampered with unless the power is off. The gray wire is a neutral, Earth-connected wire.

18. B. The symbol represents ground. Grounding an electrical circuit provides a safe place to discharge electricity.

IN THIS CHAPTER

» Checking out a newer ASVAB subtest

» Connecting the dots and putting the pieces together

» Getting your test score into shape

Chapter 17
Assembling Objects

Although much of the ASVAB measures academic knowledge at the high school level, Assembling Objects is a subtest that probably doesn't resemble any of your high school classes (unless your high school offered a course called Jigsaw Puzzles 101).

The Assembling Objects subtest is designed to measure your ability to look at pieces of an object and determine how those pieces should fit together (technically called *visualizing spatial relationships*). Spatial skills, which help people figure out maps and interpret technical drawings, are important to everyday living as well as for performing well in school and on the job. Demand for workers with good spatial skills, including interpretation of graphs, maps, architectural drawings, and X-rays, is growing.

The Assembling Objects subtest of the CAT-ASVAB consists of 15 graphical problems that you have to solve in 18 minutes, unless you're taking a version of the test with tryout questions (which I describe in Chapter 1). In that case, you have 38 minutes to answer 30 questions. The paper version of the ASVAB has 25 questions for you to solve in 15 minutes. That gives you a little less than a minute for each question, which is plenty of time to finish if you're good at jigsaw puzzles.

Getting the Picture about Assembling Objects

The Assembling Objects subtest is relatively new to the ASVAB. It was added when the ASVAB was revised in 2005, when the Numerical Operations and Coding Speed subtests were deleted. First it was added only to the computerized version of the ASVAB, and then it was added to the paper enlistment version about a year later. If you're taking the high school version of the ASVAB, you won't see this subtest.

REMEMBER

At the time of this writing, only the Navy uses the score from the Assembling Objects subtest for job qualification purposes. Additionally, only a few ratings (what the Navy calls *jobs*) require a score in this area.

But even though the other branches don't currently use the results of this subtest at all, they may in the future. That means if you want to get a different job down the line, having a good score in your records for this subtest may make your path easier. (Otherwise, you may have to dig this book out of storage and retake the test.) So going over this chapter, even if you think you don't need it, is a good idea so you don't have to worry about it later.

Two Types of Questions for the Price of One

The Assembling Objects subtest has two types of questions, both of which consist of five separate drawings. In the first drawing, you see a picture with various disassembled parts, followed by four drawings that show the parts assembled or connected. Your task is to choose the drawing that shows what the parts may actually look like after they're assembled or connected properly.

REMEMBER

Both types of Assembling Objects problems require you to perform mental rotation — a process through which you predict what an array of objects would look like if they were rotated or turned by some number of degrees.

Putting tab A into slot B: Connectors

The first type of problem presents you with simple geometric figures such as stars, cloud shapes, letter shapes, circles, and triangles. In the first drawing, you can see shapes and lines labeled with dots and the letters A and B. These letters and dots indicate points of attachment.

The next four drawings show possible solutions of what the shapes would look like if connected at designated points by the line. The shapes may be reoriented or rotated from what you observe in the first drawing. The correct solution shows the line connected correctly to reflect the points shown in the first drawing.

Look at Figure 17-1 and see whether you can solve it. In the first drawing, you see a star and a sort of lopsided *T*. There's a small dot on the short appendage of the *T*, labeled A, and a dot on one of the points of the star, labeled B.

FIGURE 17-1:
Identifying points and shapes.

© John Wiley & Sons, Inc.

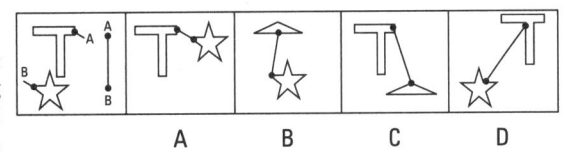

In Figure 17-1, Choice (A) is the correct solution. Choices (B) and (C) include shapes that aren't included in the first drawing, so they're obviously incorrect. Although Choice (D) has the correct shapes, they aren't connected at the same points depicted in the first drawing.

Okay, that sounds simple, doesn't it? Don't worry; it gets more complicated (sorry to burst your bubble). Figure 17-2 shows the same problem but with a different twist.

FIGURE 17-2:
Rotated shapes make the problem harder.

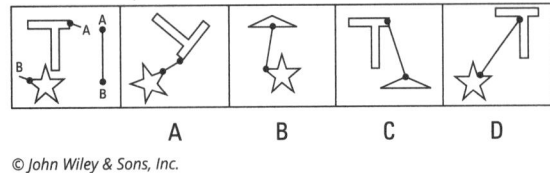

© John Wiley & Sons, Inc.

Choice (A) is the correct solution for the problem in Figure 17-2. In this case, the two shapes have been repositioned and rotated.

On the flip side: Avoiding mirrors

Mirroring (or flipping or reflecting) isn't the same as rotation, as Figure 17-3 illustrates. The shape in Box B isn't the same as the shape in Box A. It's a mirror image. No matter how you rotate the shape in Box A, it will never look like the shape in Box B. Think of it this way: You can turn a jigsaw puzzle piece upside down (so the picture side is facing the table), and it may fit, but that's not the proper method of putting the puzzle together. (It wouldn't look very pretty, either.) The Assembling Objects subtest is the same way. The possible solutions may include shapes that are reflections of a shape shown in the first drawing, but they'll never be the correct solution.

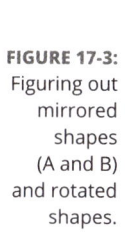

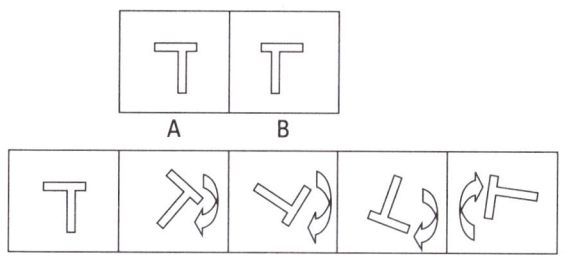

FIGURE 17-3: Figuring out mirrored shapes (A and B) and rotated shapes.

© John Wiley & Sons, Inc.

Crossing over the right places

If a shape in the first drawing shows a line that goes through any part of the shape, the correct solution must also reflect the same line-shape relationship. Check out Figure 17-4. In the first drawing, Point B is in the center of the star. But note the line intersects the star at one of its indentations and not one of its points. That means the correct solution must show the same intersection.

FIGURE 17-4: Line-shape relationships.

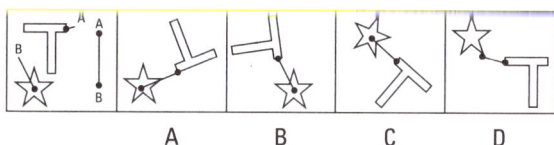

© John Wiley & Sons, Inc.

In this example, Choice (B) is the correct solution. At first glance, Choice (C) looks like it could be correct. Can you spot the reason it's *not* the correct solution? The lopsided *T* shape in the image is a reflection of the shape shown in the first drawing.

Putting it all together

Try a couple more, just to get into shape. Look at Figure 17-5.

FIGURE 17-5: Another example of spatial relationships.

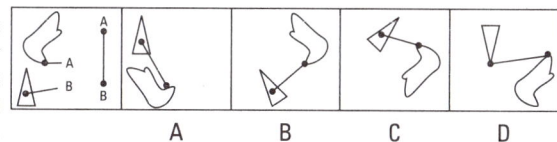

© John Wiley & Sons, Inc.

CHAPTER 17 **Assembling Objects**   365

In Figure 17-5, did you select Choice (C) as the correct answer? If so, good job! Choice (A) is incorrect because the line intersects the triangle at the wrong point and the connection point A is misplaced. Choice (B) is incorrect because the weird shape is actually a mirror image of the shape shown in the first drawing. Choice (D) is incorrect because the points don't correlate to the points depicted in the first drawing.

Now try Figure 17-6. The first drawing includes a shape that kind of looks like a Y and a shape that looks like the letter C.

FIGURE 17-6: More shapes to test your spatial skills.

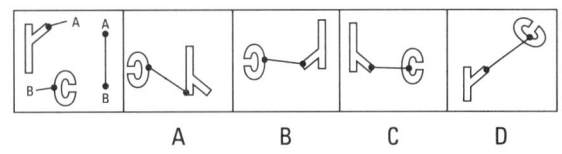

© John Wiley & Sons, Inc.

The correct answer for the problem shown in Figure 17-6 is Choice (B). Choice (A) is incorrect because the Y shape is a mirror image of the shape shown in the first drawing, and the connection points don't correspond to the first drawing's points. Choice (C) is incorrect because the Y shape is a mirror image of the shape shown in the first drawing. Choice (D) is incorrect because the Y shape is a different shape (the stem is much shorter) than the shape shown in the first drawing and because the connection dot on the C shape is in the wrong location.

Solving the jigsaw puzzle: Shapes

Many people may find the second type of Assembling Objects problem easier than the connection problems. This type of problem is very much like a jigsaw puzzle, except it doesn't result in a picture of the Statue of Liberty or a map of the United States. Also, these problems have far fewer pieces than that 1,000-piece puzzle your grandma kept wanting you to help her with. The difficulty lies in the fact that you can't use your hands to twist the pieces around on the table in order to see how they fit. You have to rotate and move the pieces mentally.

In Figure 17-7, the solution is pretty straightforward.

FIGURE 17-7: A simple jigsaw example.

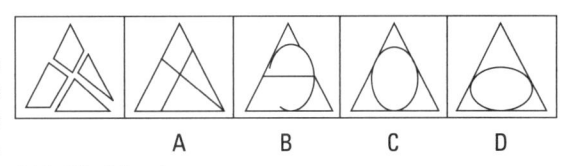

© John Wiley & Sons, Inc.

By mentally sliding the shapes in the first drawing together, it's easy to see that they fit together to form the picture shown in Choice (A). Now look at Figure 17-8.

FIGURE 17-8: Putting pieces together with rotation.

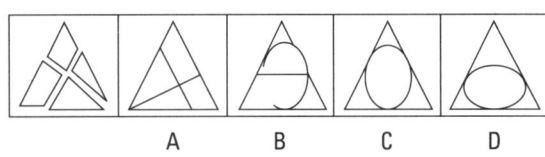

© John Wiley & Sons, Inc.

Choice (A) is the correct answer. The figure shown in Choice (A) is the same as the figure depicted in Choice (A) of Figure 17-7, except it's been rotated.

The previous two figures were warm-up exercises — the questions on the ASVAB are harder. Check out Figure 17-9 for a better representation of the types of questions on the ASVAB.

FIGURE 17-9: A harder example of spatial rotation.

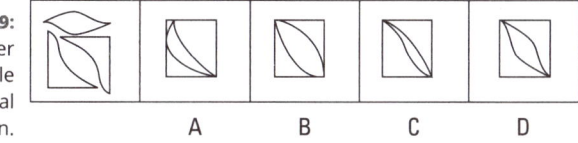

© John Wiley & Sons, Inc.

Pay attention to the curve of the leaf shape inside the square. It's not bowed out as in Choice (B) — the edges have more of a wave shape. Choice (C) has that shape but too thin. If you selected Choice (D) as the correct solution, give yourself a pat on the back. Examining spatial relationships can help locate the correct answer with ease. Try a couple more examples to see if you've gotten the hang of it. Check out Figure 17-10.

In Figure 17-10, Choice (B) is the correct answer. Mentally rotate and relocate the pieces in the first picture until you can see how they fit together to form the shape in Choice (B). In the puzzle, three pieces have both a curved edge and a single straight edge. Practice eliminating choices that lack these characteristics. Choice (A) lacks these shapes, so you can discount it right away. Notice the curved pieces are all different sizes. Visualize fitting these pieces of the puzzle in your mind and compare the sizes and differences. Now try Figure 17-11.

FIGURE 17-10: Practice mentally rotating and relocating pieces of puzzles.

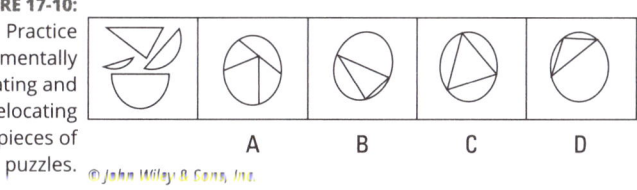

© John Wiley & Sons, Inc.

In Figure 17-11, Choice (A) is the correct answer. If you didn't get this one quite right, don't worry. You can hone your skills with the practice questions at the end of this chapter.

FIGURE 17-11: Putting the pieces of the puzzle together with your mental spatial skills.

© John Wiley & Sons, Inc.

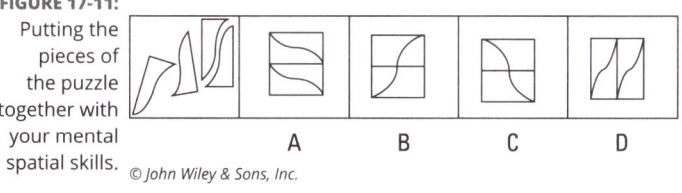

Tips for the Assembling Objects Subtest

In the following sections, I offer some tips for improving your score on the Assembling Objects subtest. I suggest strategies for eliminating wrong answers during the test, and I name some ways you can improve your spatial skills in general (which may come in handy the next time you have to read a map, too).

Comparing one piece or point at a time

TIP On the Assembling Objects subtest, you can sometimes improve your odds of getting the answer right if you select just one shape from the first drawing and then quickly look at each of the choices to see whether that shape is represented there but in a different orientation. This process can help you quickly eliminate answer choices that are obviously wrong.

On connection-type problems, note the position of the dot on one of the shapes in the first drawing and then quickly scan the possible answers, eliminating any choice that depicts the dot in a different location or that shows the line passing through the shape at a different point than that shown in the first drawing.

REMEMBER Remember to be aware of mirror images — shapes that are reflected (instead of rotated) from the image shown in the first drawing. The sneaky test-makers often make use of such mirror representations to see whether they can trick your eyes.

Visualizing success: Practicing spatial skills ahead of time

TIP Researchers at the University of Chicago have determined that your basic foundation for spatial skills is established at a very early age, perhaps as young as age 4 or 5. But don't worry. That doesn't mean all is lost if your parents never got you that model rocket kit you wanted. The same research has concluded that you can still improve spatial skills by engaging in activities that are spatially oriented. Some of those activities include the following:

» **Practicing reading maps:** Map reading can help you develop the ability to gauge scales of size and direction between related objects (roads, rivers, towns, cities, and so on).

» **Putting together jigsaw puzzles:** This way is an obvious form of practice for improving your spatial perceptions.

» **Playing puzzle games online:** Many online puzzle games exercise the skill of identifying spatial relationships and visual similarities.

» **Playing graphical computer games:** Computer games may help to improve your spatial skills. A study conducted in the United Kingdom showed that children who played computer games consistently scored higher on spatial aptitude tests than children who didn't play the games.

» **Sketching:** Look at an object or a picture and attempt to sketch it as viewed from a different view. This exercise can help to improve your ability to mentally visualize angles.

Assembling Objects Practice Questions

Assembling Objects questions measure your spatial skills. There are two types of questions: connecting questions and putting-pieces-together questions. In connection questions, your task is to choose the answer that shows the shapes properly connected together at the designated points. In the jigsaw puzzle–type questions, you must choose the answer that best shows what the shapes in the first drawing would look like if assembled together.

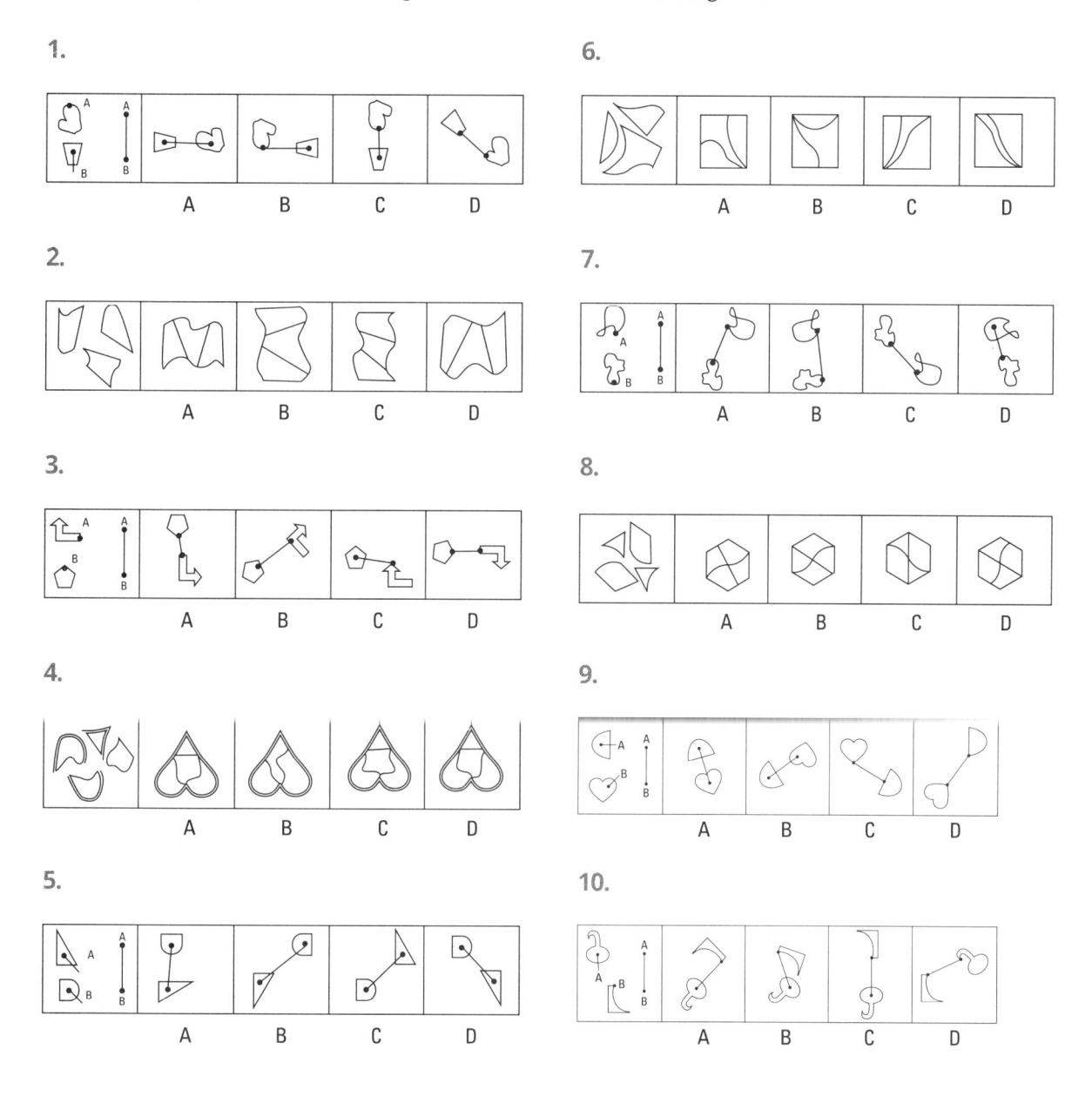

1.

2.

3.

4.

5.

6.

7.

8.

9.

10.

11.

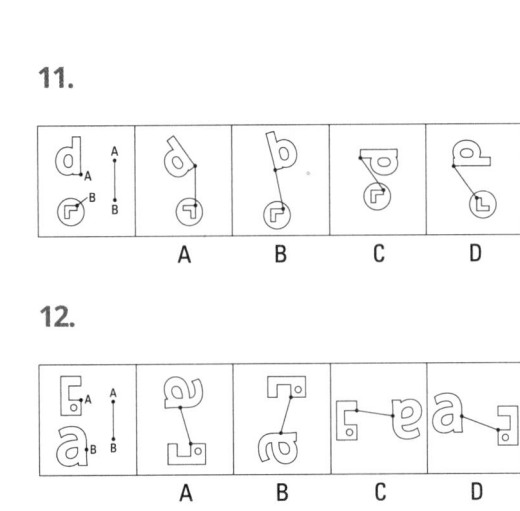

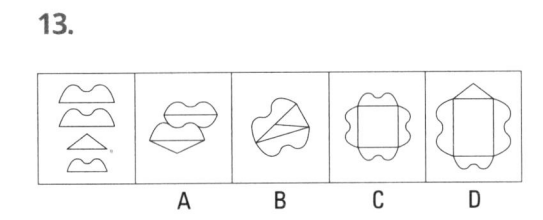

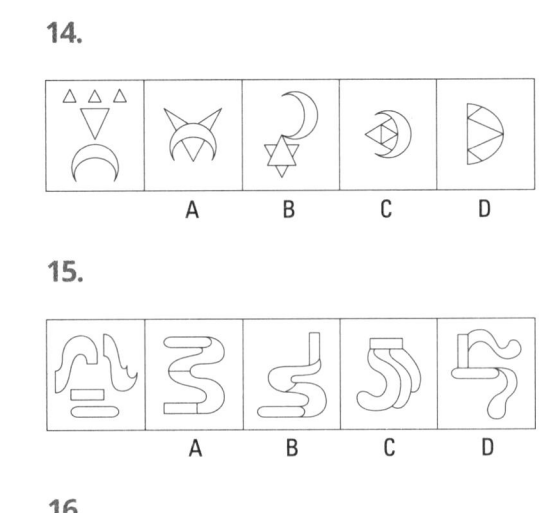

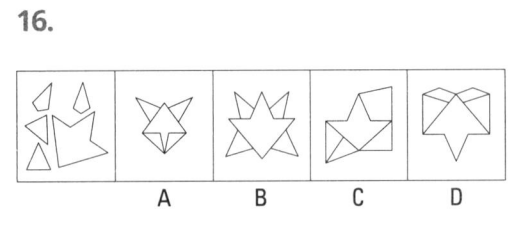

12.

13.

14.

15.

16.

A B C D

Answers and Explanations

Use this answer key to score the Assembling Objects practice questions.

1. **B.** Note that the bottom figure in the first drawing has a line that intersects the short side of the trapezoid shape, so Choices (C) and (D) are wrong. Connection point A is at the tip of the mitten shape, so Choice (A) is wrong as well. The correct answer is Choice (B).

2. **C.** Mentally rotate and reposition the shapes in the first drawing until you can see how they fit together to form the shape shown in Choice (C) — the correct answer. In the first drawing, notice that the shape at the upper right resembles a shark fin — it has two sharp points, and the third point is curved. Choice (C) is the only image that contains this shape (it's at the bottom).

3. **D.** If you selected Choice (A), you were fooled. The arrow shape shown in Choice (A) is a mirror of the shape depicted in the first drawing. The correct answer is Choice (D).

4. **A.** Mentally rotate and reposition the shapes in the first drawing until you can see how they fit together to form the shape shown in Choice (A) — the correct answer. If you had trouble with this one, notice that the piece in the center of the upside-down heart should have a corner that dips a bit on the left. Choice (C) has the dip in the center, and Choice (D) has it on the right, so these answers are wrong. Choice (B) has only three pieces.

5. **D.** Note that both shapes in the first drawing have lines that intersect the shapes at designated points. If you selected Choice (B), your eyes were fooled by mirror images. The correct answer is Choice (D).

6. **B.** Mentally rotate and reposition the shapes in the first drawing until you can see how they fit together to form the shape shown in Choice (B) — the correct answer. Here, you can take a mental snapshot of the largest shape and look for it in the answers — Choice (B) is the only choice that has it. Verify that this is the right answer by recognizing that Choice (B) is also the only answer that contains a segment of a circle, at the top.

7. **A.** Don't be fooled by the mirror shape in Choice (B), because the correct answer is Choice (A).

8. **C.** Mentally rotate and reposition the shapes in the first drawing until you can see how they fit together to form the shape shown in Choice (C), which is the correct answer. Here, you may note that the first drawing contains two shapes that resemble triangles with one side curved inward. Choice (C) is the only image that contains those shapes.

9. **B.** Take note of the point of intersection in the heart in the question; then match it up with the correct answer, Choice (B).

10. **A.** Awkward shapes plus mirrored images make this one a little tricky, but when you look at the points and the positions of the images, you can see that Choice (A) is right.

11. **D.** Choice (D) is the only answer that shows the right intersection between the circle and L-shaped object.

12. **A.** Keeping your eye on the points of assembly and staying clear of any mirrored images, you can see that Choice (A) is connected appropriately.

13. D. The rectangle in the middle of Choices (C) and (D) is a negative space. You can tell Choice (D) is correct by sizing up the proportions of the three curvy shapes and the triangle.

14. B. Counting out the shapes and identifying the right proportions help you see Choice (B) as your shining star.

15. A. Awkward shapes can make it difficult to mentally piece together multiple objects with the correct proportions. Don't be distracted by the shapes. Notice the proportions and lines in relation to one another. Make sure each element in the question appears in your answer.

16. B. Unusual shapes can be awkward to dissect, but Choice (B) reflects the correct assembly. It has the right number of shapes in the right proportions.

6 Practice ASVAB Exams

IN THIS PART . . .

Discover your areas of strength and weakness by taking a full-length ASVAB practice test or two (or three).

Sharpen your strategies for math, vocabulary, and reading passage questions by taking two practice AFQTs.

Determine where you went wrong (or right) by reading through answer explanations for practice test questions.

Chapter 18
Practice Exam 1

This sample test features nine subtests, just like the paper-and-pencil ASVAB. As you may have guessed, the sample tests in this book are paper-based tests. When you take the actual ASVAB, it may be a computer-based or paper-based exam. The computer version has mostly the same subtests as the paper version, but it separates Auto Information and Shop Information, follows a different time format, and has a different number of questions.

Another difference with the computer-based test is that you can't skip a question and go back to it, and you can't change an answer after you enter it into the computer. You can find out about the computer-based test in greater detail in Chapter 3.

To get the most out of this sample test, take it under the same conditions as the real ASVAB:

> » Allow yourself about 3 hours to take the entire exam, and take the whole thing at one time.
>
> » Find a quiet place where you won't be interrupted.
>
> » Bring a timer that you can set for various lengths of time, some scratch paper (you get two pieces during the exam, but you can get more; just ask for it as needed), and a pencil.
>
> » At the start of each subtest, set your timer for the specified period. Don't go on to the next section until the timer has gone off, and don't go back to a previous section. If you finish early, check your work for that section only.
>
> » Use the answer sheet that's provided.
>
> » Don't take a break during any subtest. You can take a short 1- or 2-minute break between subtests if you need it.

After you complete the entire sample test, check your answers against the answers and explanations in Chapter 19.

Your primary goal with this sample test is to determine your strengths and weaknesses. If you miss only one question on the Word Knowledge subtest but you miss 15 on Arithmetic Reasoning, you know where to spend your study time. If you're not going to pursue a career that requires a score on a particular subtest or the type of knowledge a subtest covers, don't worry about your score there.

Answer Sheet for Practice Exam 1

Subtest 1: General Science

1. Ⓐ Ⓑ Ⓒ Ⓓ
2. Ⓐ Ⓑ Ⓒ Ⓓ
3. Ⓐ Ⓑ Ⓒ Ⓓ
4. Ⓐ Ⓑ Ⓒ Ⓓ
5. Ⓐ Ⓑ Ⓒ Ⓓ
6. Ⓐ Ⓑ Ⓒ Ⓓ
7. Ⓐ Ⓑ Ⓒ Ⓓ
8. Ⓐ Ⓑ Ⓒ Ⓓ
9. Ⓐ Ⓑ Ⓒ Ⓓ
10. Ⓐ Ⓑ Ⓒ Ⓓ
11. Ⓐ Ⓑ Ⓒ Ⓓ
12. Ⓐ Ⓑ Ⓒ Ⓓ
13. Ⓐ Ⓑ Ⓒ Ⓓ
14. Ⓐ Ⓑ Ⓒ Ⓓ
15. Ⓐ Ⓑ Ⓒ Ⓓ
16. Ⓐ Ⓑ Ⓒ Ⓓ
17. Ⓐ Ⓑ Ⓒ Ⓓ
18. Ⓐ Ⓑ Ⓒ Ⓓ
19. Ⓐ Ⓑ Ⓒ Ⓓ
20. Ⓐ Ⓑ Ⓒ Ⓓ
21. Ⓐ Ⓑ Ⓒ Ⓓ
22. Ⓐ Ⓑ Ⓒ Ⓓ
23. Ⓐ Ⓑ Ⓒ Ⓓ
24. Ⓐ Ⓑ Ⓒ Ⓓ
25. Ⓐ Ⓑ Ⓒ Ⓓ

Subtest 2: Arithmetic Reasoning

1. Ⓐ Ⓑ Ⓒ Ⓓ
2. Ⓐ Ⓑ Ⓒ Ⓓ
3. Ⓐ Ⓑ Ⓒ Ⓓ
4. Ⓐ Ⓑ Ⓒ Ⓓ
5. Ⓐ Ⓑ Ⓒ Ⓓ
6. Ⓐ Ⓑ Ⓒ Ⓓ
7. Ⓐ Ⓑ Ⓒ Ⓓ
8. Ⓐ Ⓑ Ⓒ Ⓓ
9. Ⓐ Ⓑ Ⓒ Ⓓ
10. Ⓐ Ⓑ Ⓒ Ⓓ
11. Ⓐ Ⓑ Ⓒ Ⓓ
12. Ⓐ Ⓑ Ⓒ Ⓓ
13. Ⓐ Ⓑ Ⓒ Ⓓ
14. Ⓐ Ⓑ Ⓒ Ⓓ
15. Ⓐ Ⓑ Ⓒ Ⓓ
16. Ⓐ Ⓑ Ⓒ Ⓓ
17. Ⓐ Ⓑ Ⓒ Ⓓ
18. Ⓐ Ⓑ Ⓒ Ⓓ
19. Ⓐ Ⓑ Ⓒ Ⓓ
20. Ⓐ Ⓑ Ⓒ Ⓓ
21. Ⓐ Ⓑ Ⓒ Ⓓ
22. Ⓐ Ⓑ Ⓒ Ⓓ
23. Ⓐ Ⓑ Ⓒ Ⓓ
24. Ⓐ Ⓑ Ⓒ Ⓓ
25. Ⓐ Ⓑ Ⓒ Ⓓ
26. Ⓐ Ⓑ Ⓒ Ⓓ
27. Ⓐ Ⓑ Ⓒ Ⓓ
28. Ⓐ Ⓑ Ⓒ Ⓓ
29. Ⓐ Ⓑ Ⓒ Ⓓ
30. Ⓐ Ⓑ Ⓒ Ⓓ

Subtest 3: Word Knowledge

1. Ⓐ Ⓑ Ⓒ Ⓓ
2. Ⓐ Ⓑ Ⓒ Ⓓ
3. Ⓐ Ⓑ Ⓒ Ⓓ
4. Ⓐ Ⓑ Ⓒ Ⓓ
5. Ⓐ Ⓑ Ⓒ Ⓓ
6. Ⓐ Ⓑ Ⓒ Ⓓ
7. Ⓐ Ⓑ Ⓒ Ⓓ
8. Ⓐ Ⓑ Ⓒ Ⓓ
9. Ⓐ Ⓑ Ⓒ Ⓓ
10. Ⓐ Ⓑ Ⓒ Ⓓ
11. Ⓐ Ⓑ Ⓒ Ⓓ
12. Ⓐ Ⓑ Ⓒ Ⓓ
13. Ⓐ Ⓑ Ⓒ Ⓓ
14. Ⓐ Ⓑ Ⓒ Ⓓ
15. Ⓐ Ⓑ Ⓒ Ⓓ
16. Ⓐ Ⓑ Ⓒ Ⓓ
17. Ⓐ Ⓑ Ⓒ Ⓓ
18. Ⓐ Ⓑ Ⓒ Ⓓ
19. Ⓐ Ⓑ Ⓒ Ⓓ
20. Ⓐ Ⓑ Ⓒ Ⓓ
21. Ⓐ Ⓑ Ⓒ Ⓓ
22. Ⓐ Ⓑ Ⓒ Ⓓ
23. Ⓐ Ⓑ Ⓒ Ⓓ
24. Ⓐ Ⓑ Ⓒ Ⓓ
25. Ⓐ Ⓑ Ⓒ Ⓓ
26. Ⓐ Ⓑ Ⓒ Ⓓ
27. Ⓐ Ⓑ Ⓒ Ⓓ
28. Ⓐ Ⓑ Ⓒ Ⓓ
29. Ⓐ Ⓑ Ⓒ Ⓓ
30. Ⓐ Ⓑ Ⓒ Ⓓ
31. Ⓐ Ⓑ Ⓒ Ⓓ
32. Ⓐ Ⓑ Ⓒ Ⓓ
33. Ⓐ Ⓑ Ⓒ Ⓓ
34. Ⓐ Ⓑ Ⓒ Ⓓ
35. Ⓐ Ⓑ Ⓒ Ⓓ

Subtest 4: Paragraph Comprehension

1. Ⓐ Ⓑ Ⓒ Ⓓ
2. Ⓐ Ⓑ Ⓒ Ⓓ
3. Ⓐ Ⓑ Ⓒ Ⓓ
4. Ⓐ Ⓑ Ⓒ Ⓓ
5. Ⓐ Ⓑ Ⓒ Ⓓ
6. Ⓐ Ⓑ Ⓒ Ⓓ
7. Ⓐ Ⓑ Ⓒ Ⓓ
8. Ⓐ Ⓑ Ⓒ Ⓓ
9. Ⓐ Ⓑ Ⓒ Ⓓ
10. Ⓐ Ⓑ Ⓒ Ⓓ
11. Ⓐ Ⓑ Ⓒ Ⓓ
12. Ⓐ Ⓑ Ⓒ Ⓓ
13. Ⓐ Ⓑ Ⓒ Ⓓ
14. Ⓐ Ⓑ Ⓒ Ⓓ
15. Ⓐ Ⓑ Ⓒ Ⓓ

Subtest 5: Mathematics Knowledge

1. Ⓐ Ⓑ Ⓒ Ⓓ
2. Ⓐ Ⓑ Ⓒ Ⓓ
3. Ⓐ Ⓑ Ⓒ Ⓓ
4. Ⓐ Ⓑ Ⓒ Ⓓ
5. Ⓐ Ⓑ Ⓒ Ⓓ
6. Ⓐ Ⓑ Ⓒ Ⓓ
7. Ⓐ Ⓑ Ⓒ Ⓓ
8. Ⓐ Ⓑ Ⓒ Ⓓ
9. Ⓐ Ⓑ Ⓒ Ⓓ
10. Ⓐ Ⓑ Ⓒ Ⓓ
11. Ⓐ Ⓑ Ⓒ Ⓓ
12. Ⓐ Ⓑ Ⓒ Ⓓ
13. Ⓐ Ⓑ Ⓒ Ⓓ
14. Ⓐ Ⓑ Ⓒ Ⓓ
15. Ⓐ Ⓑ Ⓒ Ⓓ
16. Ⓐ Ⓑ Ⓒ Ⓓ
17. Ⓐ Ⓑ Ⓒ Ⓓ
18. Ⓐ Ⓑ Ⓒ Ⓓ
19. Ⓐ Ⓑ Ⓒ Ⓓ
20. Ⓐ Ⓑ Ⓒ Ⓓ
21. Ⓐ Ⓑ Ⓒ Ⓓ
22. Ⓐ Ⓑ Ⓒ Ⓓ
23. Ⓐ Ⓑ Ⓒ Ⓓ
24. Ⓐ Ⓑ Ⓒ Ⓓ
25. Ⓐ Ⓑ Ⓒ Ⓓ

Subtest 6: Electronics Information

1. Ⓐ Ⓑ Ⓒ Ⓓ
2. Ⓐ Ⓑ Ⓒ Ⓓ
3. Ⓐ Ⓑ Ⓒ Ⓓ
4. Ⓐ Ⓑ Ⓒ Ⓓ
5. Ⓐ Ⓑ Ⓒ Ⓓ
6. Ⓐ Ⓑ Ⓒ Ⓓ
7. Ⓐ Ⓑ Ⓒ Ⓓ
8. Ⓐ Ⓑ Ⓒ Ⓓ
9. Ⓐ Ⓑ Ⓒ Ⓓ
10. Ⓐ Ⓑ Ⓒ Ⓓ
11. Ⓐ Ⓑ Ⓒ Ⓓ
12. Ⓐ Ⓑ Ⓒ Ⓓ
13. Ⓐ Ⓑ Ⓒ Ⓓ
14. Ⓐ Ⓑ Ⓒ Ⓓ
15. Ⓐ Ⓑ Ⓒ Ⓓ
16. Ⓐ Ⓑ Ⓒ Ⓓ
17. Ⓐ Ⓑ Ⓒ Ⓓ
18. Ⓐ Ⓑ Ⓒ Ⓓ
19. Ⓐ Ⓑ Ⓒ Ⓓ
20. Ⓐ Ⓑ Ⓒ Ⓓ

Subtest 7: Auto & Shop Information

1. Ⓐ Ⓑ Ⓒ Ⓓ
2. Ⓐ Ⓑ Ⓒ Ⓓ
3. Ⓐ Ⓑ Ⓒ Ⓓ
4. Ⓐ Ⓑ Ⓒ Ⓓ
5. Ⓐ Ⓑ Ⓒ Ⓓ
6. Ⓐ Ⓑ Ⓒ Ⓓ
7. Ⓐ Ⓑ Ⓒ Ⓓ
8. Ⓐ Ⓑ Ⓒ Ⓓ
9. Ⓐ Ⓑ Ⓒ Ⓓ
10. Ⓐ Ⓑ Ⓒ Ⓓ
11. Ⓐ Ⓑ Ⓒ Ⓓ
12. Ⓐ Ⓑ Ⓒ Ⓓ
13. Ⓐ Ⓑ Ⓒ Ⓓ
14. Ⓐ Ⓑ Ⓒ Ⓓ
15. Ⓐ Ⓑ Ⓒ Ⓓ
16. Ⓐ Ⓑ Ⓒ Ⓓ
17. Ⓐ Ⓑ Ⓒ Ⓓ
18. Ⓐ Ⓑ Ⓒ Ⓓ
19. Ⓐ Ⓑ Ⓒ Ⓓ
20. Ⓐ Ⓑ Ⓒ Ⓓ
21. Ⓐ Ⓑ Ⓒ Ⓓ
22. Ⓐ Ⓑ Ⓒ Ⓓ
23. Ⓐ Ⓑ Ⓒ Ⓓ
24. Ⓐ Ⓑ Ⓒ Ⓓ
25. Ⓐ Ⓑ Ⓒ Ⓓ

Subtest 8: Mechanical Comprehension

1. Ⓐ Ⓑ Ⓒ Ⓓ
2. Ⓐ Ⓑ Ⓒ Ⓓ
3. Ⓐ Ⓑ Ⓒ Ⓓ
4. Ⓐ Ⓑ Ⓒ Ⓓ
5. Ⓐ Ⓑ Ⓒ Ⓓ
6. Ⓐ Ⓑ Ⓒ Ⓓ
7. Ⓐ Ⓑ Ⓒ Ⓓ
8. Ⓐ Ⓑ Ⓒ Ⓓ
9. Ⓐ Ⓑ Ⓒ Ⓓ
10. Ⓐ Ⓑ Ⓒ Ⓓ
11. Ⓐ Ⓑ Ⓒ Ⓓ
12. Ⓐ Ⓑ Ⓒ Ⓓ
13. Ⓐ Ⓑ Ⓒ Ⓓ
14. Ⓐ Ⓑ Ⓒ Ⓓ
15. Ⓐ Ⓑ Ⓒ Ⓓ
16. Ⓐ Ⓑ Ⓒ Ⓓ
17. Ⓐ Ⓑ Ⓒ Ⓓ
18. Ⓐ Ⓑ Ⓒ Ⓓ
19. Ⓐ Ⓑ Ⓒ Ⓓ
20. Ⓐ Ⓑ Ⓒ Ⓓ
21. Ⓐ Ⓑ Ⓒ Ⓓ
22. Ⓐ Ⓑ Ⓒ Ⓓ
23. Ⓐ Ⓑ Ⓒ Ⓓ
24. Ⓐ Ⓑ Ⓒ Ⓓ
25. Ⓐ Ⓑ Ⓒ Ⓓ

Subtest 9: Assembling Objects

1. Ⓐ Ⓑ Ⓒ Ⓓ
2. Ⓐ Ⓑ Ⓒ Ⓓ
3. Ⓐ Ⓑ Ⓒ Ⓓ
4. Ⓐ Ⓑ Ⓒ Ⓓ
5. Ⓐ Ⓑ Ⓒ Ⓓ
6. Ⓐ Ⓑ Ⓒ Ⓓ
7. Ⓐ Ⓑ Ⓒ Ⓓ
8. Ⓐ Ⓑ Ⓒ Ⓓ
9. Ⓐ Ⓑ Ⓒ Ⓓ
10. Ⓐ Ⓑ Ⓒ Ⓓ
11. Ⓐ Ⓑ Ⓒ Ⓓ
12. Ⓐ Ⓑ Ⓒ Ⓓ
13. Ⓐ Ⓑ Ⓒ Ⓓ
14. Ⓐ Ⓑ Ⓒ Ⓓ
15. Ⓐ Ⓑ Ⓒ Ⓓ
16. Ⓐ Ⓑ Ⓒ Ⓓ
17. Ⓐ Ⓑ Ⓒ Ⓓ
18. Ⓐ Ⓑ Ⓒ Ⓓ
19. Ⓐ Ⓑ Ⓒ Ⓓ
20. Ⓐ Ⓑ Ⓒ Ⓓ
21. Ⓐ Ⓑ Ⓒ Ⓓ
22. Ⓐ Ⓑ Ⓒ Ⓓ
23. Ⓐ Ⓑ Ⓒ Ⓓ
24. Ⓐ Ⓑ Ⓒ Ⓓ
25. Ⓐ Ⓑ Ⓒ Ⓓ

Subtest 1: General Science

TIME: 11 minutes for 25 questions

DIRECTIONS: This subtest tests your knowledge of general science principles usually covered in high school classes. Pick the best answer for each question and then mark the space on your answer sheet that corresponds to the letter indicating your choice.

1. Which planet is named after the Greek god who personified the sky?
   - (A) Earth
   - (B) Mars
   - (C) Pluto
   - (D) Uranus

2. An animal that eats only meat is called a(n)
   - (A) omnivore.
   - (B) herbivore.
   - (C) carnivore.
   - (D) voracious.

3. The chemical process in which electrons are removed from a molecule is called
   - (A) respiration.
   - (B) recreation.
   - (C) oxidation.
   - (D) metabolism.

4. What is a single unit of quanta called?
   - (A) quantum
   - (B) quantumonium
   - (C) quantus
   - (D) quanfactorial

5. In a vacuum, light waves travel at a rate of about
   - (A) 186,000 miles per hour.
   - (B) 186,000 miles per minute.
   - (C) 18,600 miles per hour.
   - (D) 186,000 miles per second.

6. The largest planet in the solar system is
   - (A) Earth.
   - (B) Mars.
   - (C) Saturn.
   - (D) Jupiter.

7. The intestines are part of the
   - (A) circulatory system.
   - (B) nervous system.
   - (C) respiratory system.
   - (D) digestive system.

8. Joints that hold bones firmly together are called
   - (A) hinge joints.
   - (B) ball and socket joints.
   - (C) fixed joints.
   - (D) pivot joints.

9. Of the levels listed, the top or broadest level of the classification system for living organisms is called the
   - (A) class.
   - (B) phylum.
   - (C) kingdom.
   - (D) genus.

10. Which planet is the brightest object in the sky, aside from the sun and moon?
    - (A) Saturn
    - (B) Pluto
    - (C) Venus
    - (D) Mercury

11. The human heart includes
    - (A) 2 chambers.
    - (B) 3 chambers.
    - (C) 4 chambers.
    - (D) 5 chambers.

12. White blood cells
    - (A) produce antibodies.
    - (B) fight infections.
    - (C) carry oxygen and carbon dioxide.
    - (D) Both A and B.

GO ON TO NEXT PAGE

13. A measureable amount of protein can be found in all of the following foods EXCEPT
    (A) eggs.
    (B) meat.
    (C) peas.
    (D) apples.

14. What is the most abundant element, by mass, in Earth's crust?
    (A) carbon
    (B) oxygen
    (C) gold
    (D) salt

15. Osmosis is
    (A) diffusion of a solvent.
    (B) transfer of oxygen.
    (C) low blood sugar.
    (D) protein.

16. A meter consists of
    (A) 10 centimeters.
    (B) 100 millimeters.
    (C) 100 centimeters.
    (D) 10 millimeters.

17. One light-year is
    (A) the distance traveled by light in one year.
    (B) the brightness of light at 30,000 miles.
    (C) 17 standard Earth years.
    (D) the distance Earth must travel around the sun.

18. Electrons are particles that are
    (A) positively charged.
    (B) neutral.
    (C) able to move freely.
    (D) negatively charged.

19. The asteroid belt is located
    (A) around Mercury.
    (B) between Mars and Jupiter.
    (C) inside the orbit of Venus.
    (D) There is no such thing as an asteroid belt.

20. The atomic number of an atom is determined by
    (A) the size of its nucleus.
    (B) the number of protons.
    (C) the number of electrons.
    (D) its location in the periodic table.

21. The "control center" of a cell is called the
    (A) nucleus.
    (B) compound.
    (C) mitochondria.
    (D) atom.

22. How many planets in the solar system have rings?
    (A) one
    (B) two
    (C) three
    (D) four

23. The temperature at which a substance's solid and liquid states exist in equilibrium is its
    (A) melting point.
    (B) boiling point.
    (C) anti-freezing point.
    (D) concentration point.

24. The atmosphere of Mars is composed mostly of
    (A) oxygen.
    (B) carbon dioxide.
    (C) helium.
    (D) Mars has no atmosphere.

25. Not counting the sun, the closest star to Earth is
    (A) Rigel.
    (B) Proxima Centauri.
    (C) Antares.
    (D) Betelgeuse.

DO NOT TURN THE PAGE UNTIL TOLD TO DO SO STOP **DO NOT RETURN TO A PREVIOUS TEST**

Subtest 2: Arithmetic Reasoning

TIME: 36 minutes for 30 questions

DIRECTIONS: This test contains questions about arithmetic. Each question is followed by four possible answers. Decide which answer is correct and then mark the space on your answer sheet that has the same number and letter as your choice. Use scratch paper for any figuring you want to do. A calculator is not allowed.

1. If a car is towed 12 miles to the repair shop and the tow charge is $3.50 per mile, how much does the tow cost?
   (A) $12.00
   (B) $3.50
   (C) $42.00
   (D) $100.00

2. The sum of two numbers is 70. One number is 8 more than the other. What's the smaller number?
   (A) 31
   (B) 33
   (C) 35
   (D) 36

3. A sales manager buys antacid in bottles by the gross. If they go through 3 bottles of antacid every day, how long will the gross last?
   (A) 144 days
   (B) 3 days
   (C) 20 days
   (D) 48 days

4. Jenny's test grades are 93, 89, 96, and 98. If she wishes to raise her average to 95, what does she need to score on her next test?
   (A) 100
   (B) 99
   (C) 97
   (D) 95

5. A server earns an average tip of 12% of the cost of the food they serve. If they serve $375 worth of food in one evening, how much money in tips will they earn on average?
   (A) $37
   (B) $45
   (C) $42
   (D) $420

6. How many square feet of carpeting are needed to carpet a 12-foot-x-12-foot room?
   (A) 24
   (B) 120
   (C) 48
   (D) 144

7. Carpet stain protector costs $0.65 per square yard to apply. How much will it cost to apply the protector to a 16-foot-x-18-foot carpet?
   (A) $187.20
   (B) $62.40
   (C) $20.80
   (D) $96.00

8. A printing plant that produces baseball cards has a monthly overhead of $6,000. It costs 18 cents to print each card, and the cards sell for 30 cents each. How many cards must the printing plant sell each month in order to make a profit?
   (A) 30,000
   (B) 40,000
   (C) 50,000
   (D) 60,000

9. Joe received an hourly wage of $8.15. His boss gave him a 7% raise. How much does Joe make per hour now?

   (A) $0.57
   (B) $8.90
   (C) $8.72
   (D) $13.85

10. Alice leaves her house, driving east at 45 miles per hour (mph). Thirty minutes later, her husband, Dave, notices she forgot her cellphone and sets off after her. How fast must Dave travel in order to catch up with Alice 3 hours after she leaves?

    (A) 49 mph
    (B) 50.5 mph
    (C) 52.5 mph
    (D) 54 mph

11. A baker made 20 pies. A Boy Scout troop buys one-fourth of the pies, a preschool teacher buys one-third of the pies, and a caterer buys one-sixth of the pies. How many pies does the baker have left?

    (A) $\frac{3}{4}$
    (B) 15
    (C) 12
    (D) 5

12. Miriam bought five cases of motor oil on sale. A case of motor oil normally costs $24.00, but she was able to purchase the oil for $22.50 a case. How much money did Miriam save on her entire purchase?

    (A) $7.50
    (B) $1.50
    (C) $8.00
    (D) $22.50

13. A security guard walks the equivalent of six city blocks when they make a circuit around the building. If they walk at a pace of eight city blocks every 30 minutes, how long will it take them to complete a circuit around the building, assuming they don't run into any thieves?

    (A) 20.00 minutes
    (B) 3.75 minutes
    (C) 22.50 minutes
    (D) 7.5 minutes

14. The population of Grand Island, Nebraska, grew by 600,000 people between 1995 and 2005, one-fifth more than the town council predicted. The town council originally predicted the city's population would grow by

    (A) 400,000
    (B) 500,000
    (C) 300,000
    (D) 100,000

15. Joan is taking an admissions examination. If she has to get at least 40 of the 60 questions right to pass, what percent of the questions does she need to answer correctly?

    (A) 30%
    (B) 40%
    (C) $66\frac{1}{3}\%$
    (D) $66\frac{2}{3}\%$

16. A teacher deposits $3,000 in a retirement fund. If they don't add any more money to the fund, which earns an annual interest rate of 6%, how much money will they have in 1 year?

    (A) $180
    (B) $3,006
    (C) $3,180
    (D) $6,000

17. The high school track measures one-quarter of a mile around. How many laps would you have to run in order to run three and a half miles?

(A) 12
(B) 14
(C) 16
(D) 18

18. Karl is driving in Austria, where the speed limit is posted in kilometers per hour. The car's speedometer shows that he's traveling at a rate of 75 kilometers per hour. Karl knows that a kilometer is about $\frac{5}{8}$ of a mile. Approximately how many miles per hour is Karl traveling?

(A) 47
(B) 120
(C) 50
(D) 53

19. A carpenter earns $12.30 an hour for a 40-hour week. Their overtime pay is $1\frac{1}{2}$ times their base pay. If they put in a 46-hour week, how much is their weekly pay?

(A) $602.70
(B) $492.00
(C) $565.80
(D) $110.70

20. An office building has 30 employees and provides 42 square feet of work space per employee. If five more employees are hired, how much less work space will each employee have?

(A) 6 square feet
(B) 7 square feet
(C) 7.5 square feet
(D) 36 square feet

21. Stan bought a monster truck for $2,000 down and payments of $450 a month for five years. What's the total cost of the monster truck?

(A) $4,250
(B) $29,000
(C) $27,000
(D) $34,400

22. Darla spent $120.37 on groceries in January, $108.45 in February, and $114.86 in March. What was the average monthly cost of Darla's groceries?

(A) $343.68
(B) $110.45
(C) $114.86
(D) $114.56

23. Keith is driving from Reno to Kansas City to meet his girlfriend. The distance between the two cities is 1,650 miles. If Keith can average 50 miles per hour, how many hours will it take him to complete his trip?

(A) 8 hours
(B) 30 hours
(C) 33 hours
(D) 82 hours

24. Michael needs 55 gallons of paint to paint an apartment building. He would like to purchase the paint for the least amount of money possible. Which of the following should he buy?

(A) two 25-gallon buckets at $550 each
(B) eleven 5-gallon buckets at $108 each
(C) six 10-gallon buckets at $215 each
(D) fifty-five 1-gallon buckets at $23 each

25. As a member of FEMA, you're required to set up a contingency plan to supply meals to residents of a town devastated by a tornado. A breakfast ration weighs 12 ounces, and the lunch and dinner rations weigh 18 ounces each. Assuming a food truck can carry 3 tons and that each resident will receive 3 meals per day, how many residents can you feed from one truck during a 10-day period?

(A) 150 residents
(B) 200 residents
(C) 250 residents
(D) 300 residents

26. A train headed south for Wichita left the station at the same time a train headed north for Des Moines left the same station. The train headed for Wichita traveled at 55 miles per hour. The train headed for Des Moines traveled at 70 miles per hour. How many miles apart are the trains at the end of 3 hours?

(A) 210 miles
(B) 165 miles
(C) 125 miles
(D) 375 miles

27. A carpenter needs to cut four sections, each 3 feet, 8 inches long, from a piece of molding. If the board is only sold by the foot, what's the shortest length of board the carpenter can buy?

(A) 15 feet
(B) 14 feet
(C) 16 feet
(D) 12 feet

28. Kiya had only one coupon for 10% off one frozen turkey breast. The turkey breasts cost $8.50 each, and Kiya wanted to buy two. How much did she pay?

(A) $16.15
(B) $17.00
(C) $15.30
(D) $7.65

29. A recruiter travels 1,100 miles during a 40-hour workweek. If they spend $\frac{2}{5}$ of their time traveling, how many hours do they spend traveling?

(A) 22
(B) $5\frac{1}{2}$
(C) 16
(D) 8

30. Your car uses gasoline at the rate of 21 miles per gallon. If gasoline costs $2.82 per gallon and you drive for 7 hours at a speed of 48 miles per hour, how much will you pay for gasoline for the trip?

(A) $38.18
(B) $45.12
(C) $47.73
(D) $59.27

Subtest 3: Word Knowledge

TIME: 11 minutes for 35 questions

DIRECTIONS: This test is about the meanings of words. Each question has a word underlined. You may be asked to decide which one of the four words in the choices most nearly means the same thing as the underlined word or which one of the four words means the opposite. If the underlined word is used in a sentence, decide which of the four choices most nearly means the same thing as the underlined word, as used in the context of the sentence. Mark the corresponding space on your answer sheet.

1. Tim promised to meet us at the apex.
   - (A) top
   - (B) bottom
   - (C) canyon
   - (D) river

2. Assimilate most nearly means
   - (A) absorb.
   - (B) react.
   - (C) pretend.
   - (D) lie.

3. Brittle most nearly means
   - (A) soft.
   - (B) fragile.
   - (C) study.
   - (D) hard.

4. Datum most nearly means
   - (A) fiscal year date.
   - (B) congruence.
   - (C) fact.
   - (D) positive result.

5. The exchange student was proficient in French, German, and English.
   - (A) poor
   - (B) knowledgeable
   - (C) adept
   - (D) exacting

6. The judge imposed a severe penalty due to Tom's actions.
   - (A) scheduled
   - (B) made an example of
   - (C) levied
   - (D) questioned

7. Mary went to the store and bought peanuts galore.
   - (A) abundant
   - (B) salty
   - (C) on sale
   - (D) roasted

8. I ran headlong into the fight.
   - (A) headfirst
   - (B) reluctantly
   - (C) happily
   - (D) recklessly

9. Frugal most nearly means
   - (A) quiet.
   - (B) amazing.
   - (C) delayed.
   - (D) economical.

10. The word most opposite in meaning to stimulate is
    - (A) support.
    - (B) arrest.
    - (C) travel.
    - (D) dislike.

GO ON TO NEXT PAGE

11. Illicit most nearly means
    (A) historical.
    (B) unlawful.
    (C) storied.
    (D) willfully.

12. Vacate most nearly means
    (A) crawl.
    (B) impel.
    (C) exhume.
    (D) leave.

13. The sergeant gave their reasoned opinion.
    (A) irate
    (B) logical
    (C) impressive
    (D) uninformed

14. Tacit most nearly means
    (A) loud.
    (B) understood.
    (C) commendable.
    (D) transparent.

15. The brass was not burnished.
    (A) yellow
    (B) dull
    (C) expensive
    (D) polished

16. The commodity was sold.
    (A) product
    (B) stock
    (C) idea
    (D) table

17. Your motives were contrived.
    (A) premeditated
    (B) emotional
    (C) obscure
    (D) amusing

18. Supplicate most nearly means
    (A) to make superior.
    (B) to be unnecessary.
    (C) to beg.
    (D) to be expansive.

19. The word most opposite in meaning to hypocrisy is
    (A) honesty.
    (B) happy.
    (C) angry.
    (D) threatening.

20. Bob found the peaches to be extremely succulent.
    (A) large
    (B) tasteless
    (C) old
    (D) juicy

21. The Army soldiers were ordered to immediate garrison duty.
    (A) field
    (B) combat
    (C) latrine
    (D) fort

22. Furtherance most nearly means
    (A) advancement.
    (B) finance.
    (C) practicality.
    (D) destruction.

23. Domicile most nearly means
    (A) office.
    (B) shopping.
    (C) home.
    (D) vacation.

24. Abrogate most nearly means
    (A) recover.
    (B) aid.
    (C) foreclose.
    (D) abolish.

25. Compensation most nearly means
    (A) religion.
    (B) commission.
    (C) boathouse.
    (D) shower.

26. They gave a brusque account of the events.
    (A) passionate
    (B) lengthy
    (C) uncensored
    (D) abrupt

27. The vote resulted in the demise of the proposed new law.
    (A) passage
    (B) death
    (C) postponement
    (D) abatement

28. We commemorated our veterans during the ceremony.
    (A) denied
    (B) remembered
    (C) thanked
    (D) took pictures of

29. Bore most nearly means
    (A) deepen.
    (B) hide.
    (C) dig.
    (D) jump.

30. That custom still prevails.
    (A) angers
    (B) persists
    (C) surprises
    (D) excites

31. Defray most nearly means
    (A) invade.
    (B) obstruct.
    (C) pay.
    (D) reverse.

32. Chasm most nearly means
    (A) abyss.
    (B) sky.
    (C) mountain.
    (D) valley.

33. Fundamental most nearly means
    (A) radical.
    (B) religious.
    (C) basic.
    (D) excessive.

34. Susceptible most nearly means
    (A) travel.
    (B) resistant.
    (C) limited.
    (D) vulnerable.

35. Emblem most nearly means
    (A) symbol.
    (B) picture.
    (C) statue.
    (D) religion.

Subtest 4: Paragraph Comprehension

TIME: 13 minutes for 15 questions

DIRECTIONS: This test contains items that measure your ability to understand what you read. This section includes one or more paragraphs of reading material followed by incomplete statements or questions. Read the paragraph and select the choice that best completes the statement or answers the question. Mark your choice on your answer sheet, using the correct letter with each question number.

An important stage of personal time management is to take control of appointments. Determined by external obligation, appointments constitute interaction with other people and an agreed-on interface between your activities and those of others. Start with a simple appointment diary. List all appointments, including regular and recurring ones. Now, be ruthless and eliminate the unnecessary. There may be committees where you can't productively contribute or where a subordinate may be able to participate. Eliminate the waste of your time.

1. Effectively managing your appointments allows you to
   (A) spend more time with your subordinates.
   (B) delegate responsibility to subordinates.
   (C) make more efficient use of your time.
   (D) attend only the most important meetings.

The U.S. Congress consists of 100 senators and 435 representatives. Two senators are elected from each state. The number of representatives from each state is based on population, although each state has at least one representative. Senators serve six-year terms, and representatives serve two-year terms.

2. According to this passage,
   (A) there are equal numbers of senators and representatives.
   (B) the number of representatives from each state is decided by a lottery.
   (C) it's possible for a state to have no representatives.
   (D) senators and representatives have different term lengths.

Indo-European languages consist of those languages spoken by most of Europe and in those parts of the world that Europeans have colonized since the 16th century (such as the United States). Indo-European languages are also spoken in India, Iran, parts of western Afghanistan, and in some areas of Asia.

3. The author of this passage would agree that
   (A) Indo-European languages are spoken in areas all over the world.
   (B) Indo-European languages include all the languages spoken in the world.
   (C) only Europeans speak Indo-European languages.
   (D) Indo-European language speakers can easily understand one another.

In privatization, the government relies on the private sector to provide a service. However, the government divests itself of the entire process, including all assets. With privatized functions, the government may specify quality, quantity, and timeliness requirements, but it has no control over the operations of the activity. Also, the government may not be the only customer. Whomever the government chooses to provide the services would likely provide the same services to others.

4. This paragraph best supports the statement that
   (A) the government must closely supervise privatized functions.
   (B) privatized functions consist of a mixture of government employees, military personnel, and private contractors.
   (C) privatized functions are those institutions that provide services only to a government agency.
   (D) privatized functions provide essential services to the government.

The success or failure of a conference lies largely with its leader. A leader's zest and enthusiasm must be real, apparent, and contagious. The leader is responsible for getting the ball rolling and making the attendees feel as if the meeting is theirs and its success depends on their participation. A good, thorough introduction helps establish the right climate.

5. A good title to this paragraph would be
   (A) "Lead by Example."
   (B) "The Importance of Proper Introductions."
   (C) "Leading a Successful Conference."
   (D) "Conference Participation Basics."

Cloud seeding is accomplished by dropping particles of dry ice (solid carbon dioxide) from a plane onto super-cooled clouds. This process encourages condensation of water droplets in the clouds, which usually, but not always, results in rain or snow.

6. From this passage, it's reasonable to assume that
   (A) cloud seeding could be used to end a drought.
   (B) cloud seeding is prohibitively expensive.
   (C) cloud seeding is rarely used.
   (D) cloud seeding can be accomplished by using regular ice.

To write or not to write — that is the question. If assigned a writing task, there's no option. However, if someone is looking for a specific answer, find out if they need a short answer or a detailed one. Can the requirement be met with a telephone call, email, or short note, or is something more necessary? A former CEO of a major corporation once commented that he had looked at 13,000 pieces of paper in a 5-day period. Think how much easier and more economical it would be if people would use the telephone, send an email, or write a short note.

7. The main point of this passage is that
   (A) written records are important because they provide detailed documentation.
   (B) more businesspeople should invest time and energy improving their writing skills.
   (C) writing may not be the best way to communicate information.
   (D) it's pointless for businesspeople to spend time improving their writing skills.

The transistor, a small, solid-state device that can amplify sound, was invented in 1947. At first, it was too expensive and too difficult to produce to be used in cheap, mass-market products. By 1954, though, these cost and production problems had been overcome, and the first transistor radio was put on the market.

8. According to this passage,
   (A) there was no market for transistors before 1954.
   (B) when transistors could be produced cheaply and easily, the transistor radio was put on the market.
   (C) transistors were invented in 1947 by order of the Department of Defense.
   (D) transistors are still expensive to produce.

I returned from the City about three o'clock on that May afternoon pretty well disgusted with life. I had been three months in the Old Country and was fed up with it. If people had told me a year ago that I would've been feeling like that I should've laughed at them; but there was the fact. The weather made me liverish, the talk of the ordinary Englishman made me sick, I couldn't get enough exercise, and the amusements of London seemed as flat as soda water that had been standing in the sun.

9. The author is speaking of his travels in
   (A) Spain.
   (B) Great Britain.
   (C) Germany.
   (D) Scotland.

Surveys show that the average child under the age of 18 watches four hours of television per day. Although some of the programming may be educational, most isn't. Spending this much time watching television interferes with a child's ability to pursue other interests, such as reading, participating in sports, and playing with friends.

10. The author of this passage would agree that

(A) television viewing should be restricted.

(B) parents who let their children watch this much television are neglectful.

(C) reading, participating in sports, playing with friends, and watching television should all be given equal time.

(D) adults over 18 can watch as much television as they want.

Questions 11 and 12 are based on the following passage.

High school and college graduates attempting to find jobs should participate in mock job interviews. These mock interviews help students prepare for the types of questions they'll be asked, make them more comfortable with common interview formats, and help them critique their performance before facing a real interviewer. Because they're such a valuable aid, schools should organize mock job interviews for all their graduating students.

11. The above passage states that mock job interviews

(A) frighten students.

(B) should be offered to the best students.

(C) help prepare students for real job interviews.

(D) should be organized by students.

12. From the above passage, it is reasonable to assume that

(A) mock interviews can increase a student's confidence when they go into a real job interview.

(B) mock interviews are expensive to organize.

(C) few students are interested in mock interviews.

(D) students don't need job interview preparation.

Questions 13 through 15 are based on the following passage.

Due process, the guarantee of fairness in the administration of justice, is part of the 5th Amendment to the U.S. Constitution. The 14th Amendment further requires states to abide by due process. After this amendment was enacted, the U.S. Supreme Court struck down many state laws that infringed on the civil rights guaranteed to citizens in the Bill of Rights.

13. According to the above passage, due process

(A) is an outdated concept.

(B) guarantees fairness in the justice system.

(C) never became part of the U.S. Constitution.

(D) is the process by which winning lottery tickets are selected.

14. According to the above passage, it's reasonable to assume that the 5th Amendment

(A) is about taxes.

(B) guarantees due process in all criminal and civil cases.

(C) guarantees due process in federal law.

(D) should never have become part of the Bill of Rights.

15. The author of the above passage would agree that

(A) without the passage of the 14th Amendment, many laws restricting civil rights would still exist in various states.

(B) the Supreme Court overstepped its jurisdiction when it struck down laws infringing on citizens' civil rights.

(C) the Supreme Court had every right to strike down state laws before the passage of the 14th Amendment.

(D) the 14th Amendment was opposed by all states.

Subtest 5: Mathematics Knowledge

TIME: 24 minutes for 25 questions

DIRECTIONS: This section tests your ability to solve general mathematical problems. Select the correct answer from the choices given, and then mark the corresponding space on your answer sheet. Use scratch paper to do any figuring.

1. If $x = 8$, what's the value of y in the equation $y = (x^2 \div 4) - 2$?
   - (A) 14
   - (B) 16
   - (C) 18
   - (D) 20

2. The cube of 5 is
   - (A) 125
   - (B) 25
   - (C) 15
   - (D) 50

3. $2.5 \times 3^3 =$
   - (A) 22.5
   - (B) 75.0
   - (C) 67.5
   - (D) 675.0

4. The fourth root of 16 is
   - (A) 4
   - (B) 1
   - (C) 3
   - (D) 2

5. What's the equation of a line that passes through points (0, −1) and (2, 3)?
   - (A) $y = 2x - 1$
   - (B) $y = 2x + 1$
   - (C) $x = 2y - 1$
   - (D) $x = 2y + 1$

6. $(12 \text{ yards} + 14 \text{ feet}) \div 5 =$
   - (A) 12 feet
   - (B) $5\frac{1}{5}$ feet
   - (C) 10 feet
   - (D) $2\frac{1}{2}$ feet

7. $x^3 \cdot x^4 =$
   - (A) x^{12}
   - (B) $2x^7$
   - (C) $2x^{12}$
   - (D) x^7

8. $(x + 4)(x + 2) =$
   - (A) $x^2 + 6x + 6$
   - (B) $x^2 + 8x + 8$
   - (C) $x^2 + 8x + 6$
   - (D) $x^2 + 6x + 8$

9. $1.5 \times 10^3 =$
   - (A) 45
   - (B) 150
   - (C) 1,500
   - (D) 15

10. Which of the following is a prime number?
    - (A) 27
    - (B) 11
    - (C) 8
    - (D) 4

GO ON TO NEXT PAGE

11. What's the mode of the following series of numbers? 4 4 8 8 8 10 10 12 12

(A) 9
(B) 8
(C) 11
(D) 10

12. If $a = 4$, then $a^3 \div a =$

(A) 4
(B) 12
(C) 64
(D) 16

13. Solve: 5!

(A) 25
(B) 125
(C) 120
(D) 15

14. $(900 \times 2) \div 6 =$

(A) 30
(B) 300
(C) 150
(D) 3,000

15. If $x = 2$, then $xx(x) =$

(A) 8
(B) $2xx$
(C) 4
(D) 6

16. If $(5+1)(6 \div 3)(8-5) = (3+3)x$, then $x =$

(A) 12
(B) 3
(C) 4
(D) 6

17. $\sqrt{49} \times \sqrt{64} =$

(A) 56
(B) 15
(C) 42
(D) 3,136

18. Which of the following fractions is the largest?

(A) $\frac{2}{5}$
(B) $\frac{3}{8}$
(C) $\frac{7}{10}$
(D) $\frac{13}{16}$

19. If $2 + x \geq 4$, then $x \geq$

(A) 6
(B) 2
(C) 4
(D) $\frac{1}{2}$

20. If a circle has a radius of 12 feet, what's its circumference most nearly?

(A) 24 feet
(B) 72 feet
(C) 75 feet
(D) 36 feet

21. An aquarium measures 16 inches long x 8 inches deep x 18 inches high. What's its volume?

(A) 2,304 cubic inches
(B) 128 cubic inches
(C) 42 cubic inches
(D) 288 cubic inches

22. Triangle ABC is a(n)

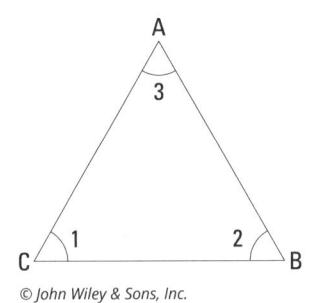

(A) right triangle.
(B) obtuse triangle.
(C) equilateral triangle.
(D) isosceles triangle.

23. The sum of the measures of the angles of a trapezoid is

   (A) 360 degrees.
   (B) 540 degrees.
   (C) 180 degrees.
   (D) 720 degrees.

24. Angles 1 and 2 are

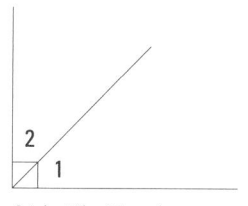

   © John Wiley & Sons, Inc.

   (A) supplementary.
   (B) complementary.
   (C) both obtuse.
   (D) both right angles.

25. Convert 24% to a fraction.

   (A) $\frac{6}{25}$
   (B) $\frac{1}{25}$
   (C) $\frac{6}{24}$
   (D) $\frac{1}{24}$

Subtest 6: Electronics Information

TIME: 9 minutes for 20 questions

DIRECTIONS: This test contains questions to challenge your knowledge of electrical, radio, and electronics information. Select the correct response from the choices given and then mark the corresponding space on your answer sheet.

1. Ohm's law states
   - (A) Voltage = Current × Resistance
   - (B) Amperes = Current × Resistance
   - (C) Voltage = Resistance ÷ Amperes
   - (D) Ohms = Current ÷ Voltage

2. A resistor's first three color bands are brown, black, and red. What is its value?
   - (A) 1,000 ohms
   - (B) 500 ohms
   - (C) 500 volts
   - (D) 50 volts

3. In the U.S., all metal equipment, electrical or not, connected to a swimming pool must be
   - (A) freestanding.
   - (B) bonded together.
   - (C) certified.
   - (D) none of the above.

4. Voltage can also be expressed as
   - (A) watts.
   - (B) amps.
   - (C) current.
   - (D) electrical potential difference.

5. Newer cellphones contain a removable memory card, which is often called a
   - (A) SIM card.
   - (B) DIM chip.
   - (C) PIN card.
   - (D) PIN chip.

6. Made from a variety of materials, such as carbon, this inhibits the flow of current.
   - (A) resistor
   - (B) diode
   - (C) transformer
   - (D) generator

7. This is a type of semiconductor that only allows current to flow in one direction. It is usually used to rectify AC signals (conversion to DC).
   - (A) capacitor
   - (B) inductor
   - (C) diode
   - (D) transformer

8. Radar can operate at frequencies as high as
   - (A) 100,000 Hz.
   - (B) 100,000 kHz.
   - (C) 100,000 MHz.
   - (D) 500,000 MHz.

9. What do AC and DC stand for in the electrical field?
   - (A) amplified capacity and differential capacity
   - (B) alternating current and direct current
   - (C) accelerated climate and deduced climate
   - (D) none of the above

10. Changing AC to DC is called what?
    - (A) capacitance
    - (B) impedance
    - (C) rectification
    - (D) induction

11. A 5,000 BTU air conditioner can efficiently cool up to 150 square feet, or a 10-foot-x-15-foot room. What does BTU stand for?
    (A) basic thermal unit
    (B) basic temperature unit
    (C) British thermal unit
    (D) none of the above

12. Which is the most correct definition of current?
    (A) the measure of electrical pressure
    (B) the amount of electricity used in a heater
    (C) the electricity used in heating a kilo of water
    (D) the presence of electron flow

13. A device that transforms energy from one form to another is called
    (A) a capacitor.
    (B) a transducer.
    (C) a transformer.
    (D) magic.

14. Which one of the following is an active element?
    (A) 15 kΩ resistor
    (B) 10 mH inductor
    (C) 25 pF capacitor
    (D) 10 V power supply

15. A light bulb is 60 watts. Operated at 120 volts, how much current does it draw?
    (A) 0.5 amperes
    (B) 5.0 amperes
    (C) 50.0 amperes
    (D) 7,200 amperes

16. A number-12 wire, compared to a number-6 wire,
    (A) is longer.
    (B) is shorter.
    (C) is smaller in diameter.
    (D) is larger in diameter.

17. A fuse with a higher-than-required rating used in an electrical circuit
    (A) improves safety.
    (B) increases maintenance.
    (C) may not work properly.
    (D) is less expensive.

18. Neutral wire is always
    (A) whitish or natural.
    (B) black.
    (C) green with stripes.
    (D) blue.

19. To measure electrical power, you would use a(n)
    (A) ammeter.
    (B) ohmmeter.
    (C) voltmeter.
    (D) wattmeter.

20. What will happen if you operate an incandescent light bulb at less than its rated voltage?
    (A) The bulb will burn brighter and last longer.
    (B) The bulb will burn dimmer and last longer.
    (C) The bulb will burn brighter but won't last as long.
    (D) The bulb will burn dimmer but won't last as long.

DO NOT TURN THE PAGE UNTIL TOLD TO DO SO **STOP** **DO NOT RETURN TO A PREVIOUS TEST**

Subtest 7: Auto & Shop Information

TIME: 11 minutes for 25 questions

DIRECTIONS: This test is about automobiles, shop practices, and the use of tools. Pick the best answer for each question and then mark the corresponding space on your answer sheet.

1. Overheating the engine can cause all of the following problems EXCEPT
    - (A) burned engine bearings.
    - (B) enlarged pistons.
    - (C) melted engine parts.
    - (D) improved fuel efficiency.

2. The device that converts an automobile's mechanical energy to electrical energy is called the
    - (A) converter.
    - (B) alternator.
    - (C) battery.
    - (D) brakes.

3. A primary advantage of the electronic ignition system over conventional ignition systems is that
    - (A) the electronic ignition system is less expensive to repair.
    - (B) the electronic ignition system requires a lower voltage to provide a higher voltage for spark.
    - (C) the electronic ignition system allows for use of a lower octane fuel.
    - (D) all of the above.

4. The primary purpose of piston rings is to
    - (A) seal the combustion chamber and allow the pistons to move freely.
    - (B) connect the piston to the crankshaft.
    - (C) allow fuel to enter the piston cylinder.
    - (D) provide lubrication to the piston cylinder.

5. The crankshaft typically connects to a
    - (A) flywheel.
    - (B) fuel pump.
    - (C) muffler.
    - (D) battery.

6. What component allows the left and right wheels to turn at different speeds when cornering?
    - (A) differential
    - (B) camshaft
    - (C) valve rotator
    - (D) battery

7. If a car's ignition system, lights, and radio don't work, the part that's probably malfunctioned is the
    - (A) cylinder block.
    - (B) water pump.
    - (C) carburetor.
    - (D) battery.

8. A good tool to cut intricate shapes in wood would be a
    - (A) ripsaw.
    - (B) hacksaw.
    - (C) coping saw.
    - (D) pocket knife.

9. A two-stroke engine will normally be found on
    - (A) small cars.
    - (B) large diesel trucks.
    - (C) trucks, vans, and some cars.
    - (D) snowmobiles, chainsaws, and some motorcycles.

10. A belt sander would best be used to
    (A) cut wood.
    (B) finish wood.
    (C) shape wood.
    (D) keep your pants up.

11. A car equipped with limited-slip differential
    (A) can be readily put into all-wheel (four-wheel) drive.
    (B) won't lock up when the brakes are applied steadily.
    (C) transfers the most driving force to the wheel with the greatest amount of traction.
    (D) is rated for off-road driving.

12. Big block engines generally have
    (A) more than 5.9 L of displacement.
    (B) better gas mileage than small block engines.
    (C) less than 6 L of displacement.
    (D) air conditioning.

13. A good tool for spreading and/or shaping mortar would be a
    (A) cement shaper.
    (B) hammer.
    (C) trowel.
    (D) broom.

14. Plumb bobs are used to
    (A) clean pipes.
    (B) check vertical reference.
    (C) fix the toilet.
    (D) carve stones.

15. Rebar is used to
    (A) measure the depth of concrete.
    (B) reinforce concrete.
    (C) stir concrete.
    (D) smooth concrete.

16. Annular ring, clout, and spring head are types of
    (A) hammers.
    (B) saws.
    (C) nails.
    (D) screwdrivers.

17. A ripsaw cuts
    (A) against the grain of the wood.
    (B) with the grain of the wood.
    (C) most materials, including metal.
    (D) only plastic.

18. A cam belt is also known as a
    (A) piston.
    (B) timing belt.
    (C) transmission belt.
    (D) lug nut.

19. To check for horizontal trueness, the best tool to use is a
    (A) steel tape rule.
    (B) plumb bob.
    (C) level.
    (D) sliding T-bevel.

20. A bucking bar is used to
    (A) pull nails.
    (B) pry wood apart.
    (C) form rivet bucktails.
    (D) drive screws.

21. Washers that have teeth all around the circumference to prevent them from slipping are called
    (A) shake-proof washers.
    (B) jaw washers.
    (C) flat washers.
    (D) split lock washers.

22. The tool below measures

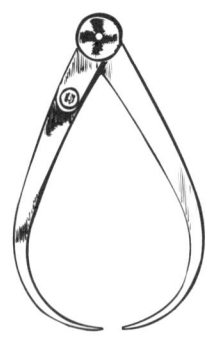

© John Wiley & Sons, Inc.

(A) an inside curve.
(B) an outside curve.
(C) the depth of a hole.
(D) the thickness of wire.

23. The object below is a type of

© John Wiley & Sons, Inc.

(A) nut.
(B) washer.
(C) screw.
(D) bolt.

24. The tool below is used to

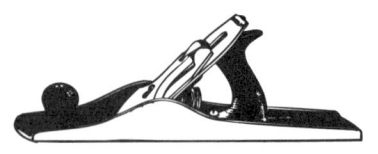

© John Wiley & Sons, Inc.

(A) finish concrete.
(B) spread joint compound.
(C) smooth wallpaper.
(D) dress wood.

25. The chisel used to cut metal is

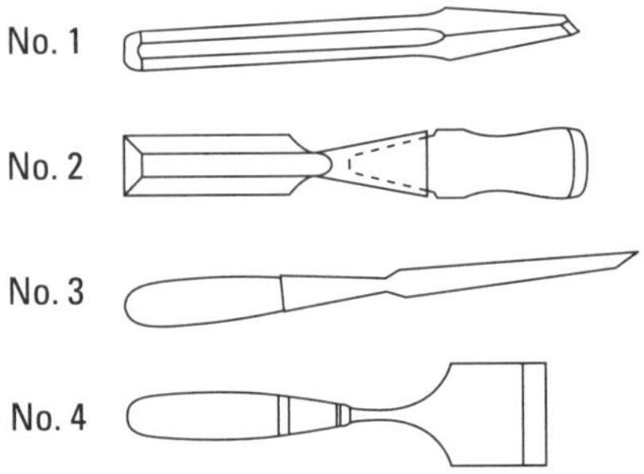

No. 1
No. 2
No. 3
No. 4

© John Wiley & Sons, Inc.

(A) No. 1
(B) No. 2
(C) No. 3
(D) No. 4

Subtest 8: Mechanical Comprehension

TIME: 19 minutes for 25 questions

DIRECTIONS: This test is about mechanical principles. Many of the questions use drawings to illustrate specific principles. Choose the correct answer and mark the corresponding space on the answer sheet.

1. An induction clutch works by
   - (A) magnetism.
   - (B) pneumatics.
   - (C) hydraulics.
   - (D) friction.

2. If a first-class lever with a resistance arm measuring 2 feet and an effort arm measuring 8 feet are being used, what's the mechanical advantage?
   - (A) 2
   - (B) 4
   - (C) 6
   - (D) 1

3. The bottoms of four boxes are shown below. The boxes all have the same volume. If postal regulations state that the sides of a box must meet a minimum height, which box is most likely to be too short to go through the mail?

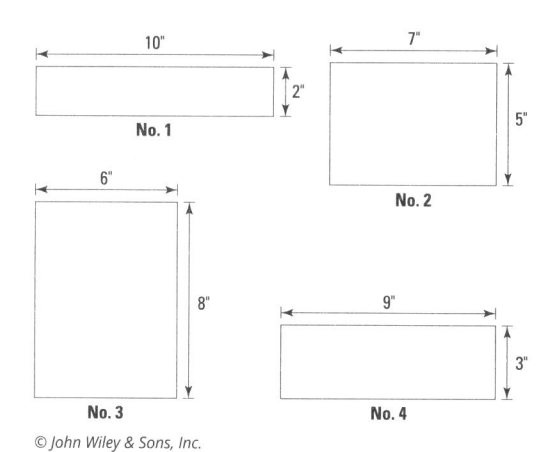

   © John Wiley & Sons, Inc.

   - (A) No. 1
   - (B) No. 2
   - (C) No. 3
   - (D) No. 4

4. Looking at the figure below where Anvil A and B have the same mass, when Anvil B lands on the seesaw, Anvil A will

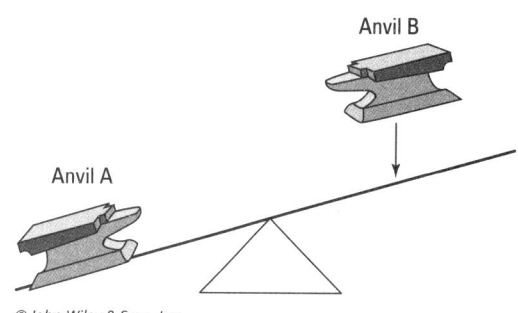

   © John Wiley & Sons, Inc.

   - (A) remain stationary.
   - (B) hit the ground hard.
   - (C) rise in the air quickly.
   - (D) enter the stratosphere.

5. Air pressure at sea level is about 15 psi. What's the amount of force exerted on the top of your head, given a surface area of 24 square inches?
   - (A) 360 pounds
   - (B) 625 pounds
   - (C) $\frac{5}{8}$ pound
   - (D) 180 pounds

6. The force produced when a boxer's hand hits a heavy bag and "bounces" off it is called
   - (A) response time.
   - (B) bounce.
   - (C) recoil.
   - (D) gravity.

CHAPTER 18 Practice Exam 1

7. In the figure below, if Gear 1 has 25 teeth and Gear 2 has 15 teeth, how many revolutions does Gear 2 make for every 10 revolutions Gear 1 makes?

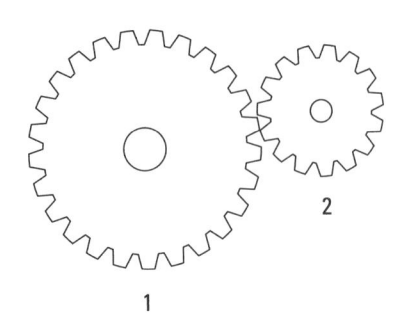

© John Wiley & Sons, Inc.

(A) about $16\frac{2}{3}$
(B) 12
(C) about $\frac{1}{3}$ more
(D) about 20

8. A cubic foot of water weighs about 62.5 pounds. If an aquarium is 18 feet long, 10 feet deep, and 12 feet wide, what's the approximate pressure in pounds per square inch (psi) on the bottom of the tank?

(A) 2 psi
(B) 4 psi
(C) 5 psi
(D) 7 psi

9. Springs used in machines are usually made of

(A) plastic.
(B) bronze.
(C) nylon fiber.
(D) steel.

10. A clutch is a type of

(A) universal joint.
(B) coupling.
(C) gear differential.
(D) cam follower.

11. When Cam A completes one revolution, the lever will touch the contact point

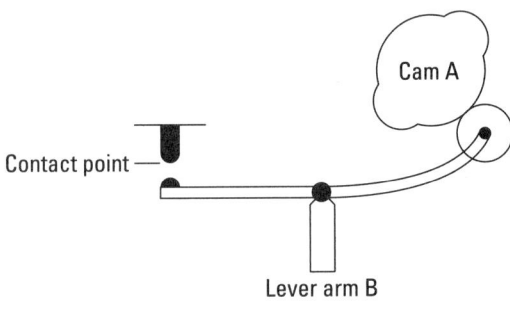

© John Wiley & Sons, Inc.

(A) once.
(B) never.
(C) four times.
(D) twice.

12. A single moveable block-and-fall is called a

(A) fixed pulley.
(B) gun tackle.
(C) runner.
(D) sheave.

13. In the figure below, if the fulcrum supporting the lever is moved closer to the anvil, the anvil will be

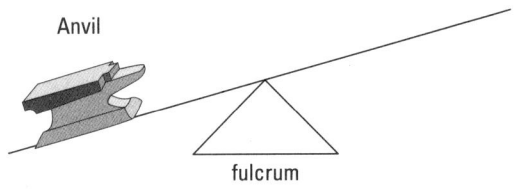

© John Wiley & Sons, Inc.

(A) easier to lift and will move higher.
(B) harder to lift but will move higher.
(C) easier to lift but will not move as high.
(D) harder to lift and will not move as high.

14. The mechanical advantage of the block-and-tackle arrangement shown below is

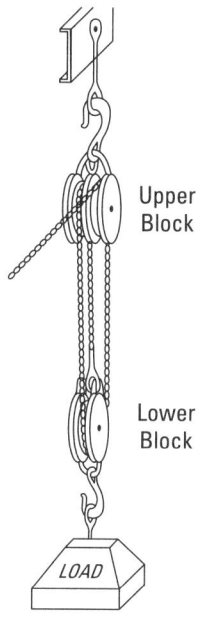

(A) 2
(B) 3
(C) 6
(D) 1

15. In the figure below, if the cogs move up the track at the same rate of speed, Cog A will

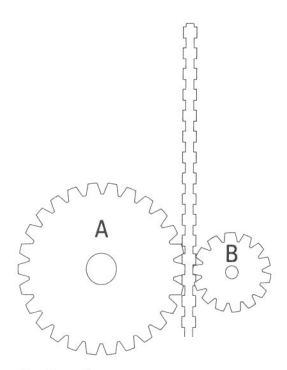

(A) reach the top at the same time as Cog B.
(B) reach the top after Cog B.
(C) reach the top before Cog B.
(D) have greater difficulty staying on track.

16. If a house key, a wooden spoon, a plastic hanger, and a wool jacket are all the same temperature on a cool day, which one feels the coldest?

(A) key
(B) spoon
(C) hanger
(D) jacket

17. In the figure below, assume the valves are all closed. To fill the tank but prevent it from filling entirely, which valves should be open?

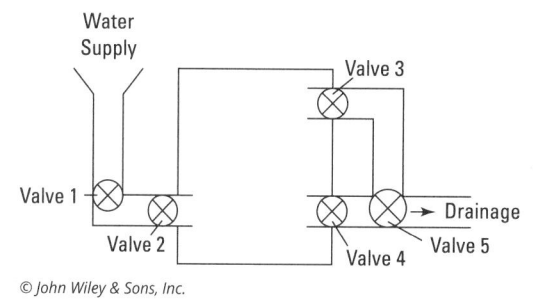

(A) 1 and 2 only
(B) 1, 2, and 3 only
(C) 1, 2, and 4 only
(D) 1, 2, 3, and 5 only

18. If Gear A is turned to the left,

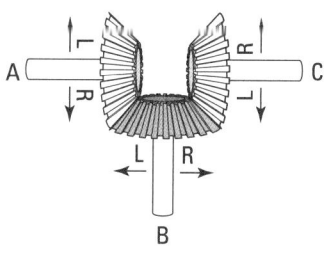

(A) Gear B turns to the right and Gear C turns to the left.
(B) Gear B turns to the left and Gear C turns to the left.
(C) Gear B turns to the right and Gear C turns to the right.
(D) Gear B turns to the left and Gear C turns to the right.

19. If Gear 1 moves in a clockwise direction, which other gears also turn clockwise?

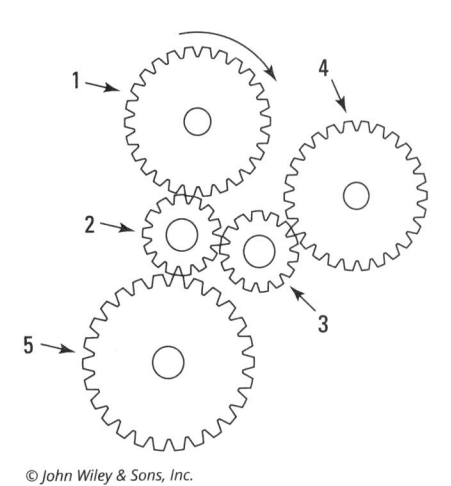

(A) 3 and 5
(B) 3, 4, and 5
(C) 2 and 5
(D) 3 and 4

20. The pressure gauge in the figure below shows a reading of

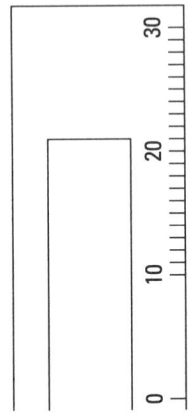

(A) 15.0
(B) 19.5
(C) 21.0
(D) 23.0

21. A way to determine the amount of power being used is to

(A) multiply the amount of work done by the time it takes.
(B) multiply the distance covered by the time it takes to move a load.
(C) divide the amount of work done by 550 pounds per second.
(D) divide the amount of work done by the amount of time it takes.

22. A wood tool, a silver tool, and a steel tool are placed in boiling water for cleaning. Which tool will get hot most quickly?

(A) steel
(B) wood
(C) silver
(D) All three are equally hot.

23. A whip is being used in the figure shown. How much effort is the boy who's lifting the 50-pound anvil using? Disregard friction, wind resistance, and the weight of the pulley and the rope.

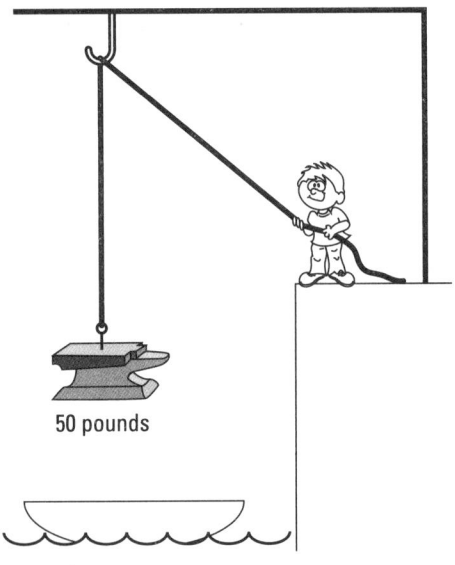

(A) 50-pound effort
(B) 100-pound effort
(C) 25-pound effort
(D) 10-pound effort

24. In the figure below, at what point was the ball traveling most slowly?

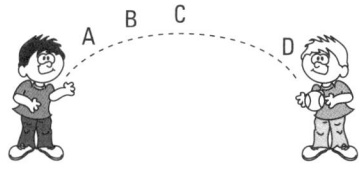

© John Wiley & Sons, Inc.

(A) A
(B) B
(C) C
(D) D

25. In the figure below, which angle is braced most solidly?

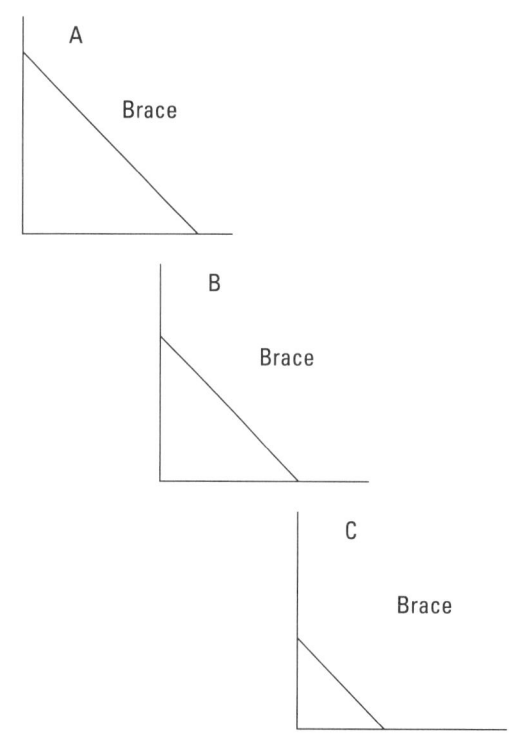

© John Wiley & Sons, Inc.

(A) A
(B) B
(C) C
(D) All are braced equally solidly.

Subtest 9: Assembling Objects

TIME: 15 minutes for 25 questions

DIRECTIONS: The Assembling Objects subtest consists of questions that measure your ability to mentally picture items in two dimensions. Each question is comprised of five separate drawings. The problem is presented in the first drawing, and the remaining four drawings are possible solutions. Determine which of the choices best solves the problem shown in the first picture and then mark the corresponding choice on your answer sheet.

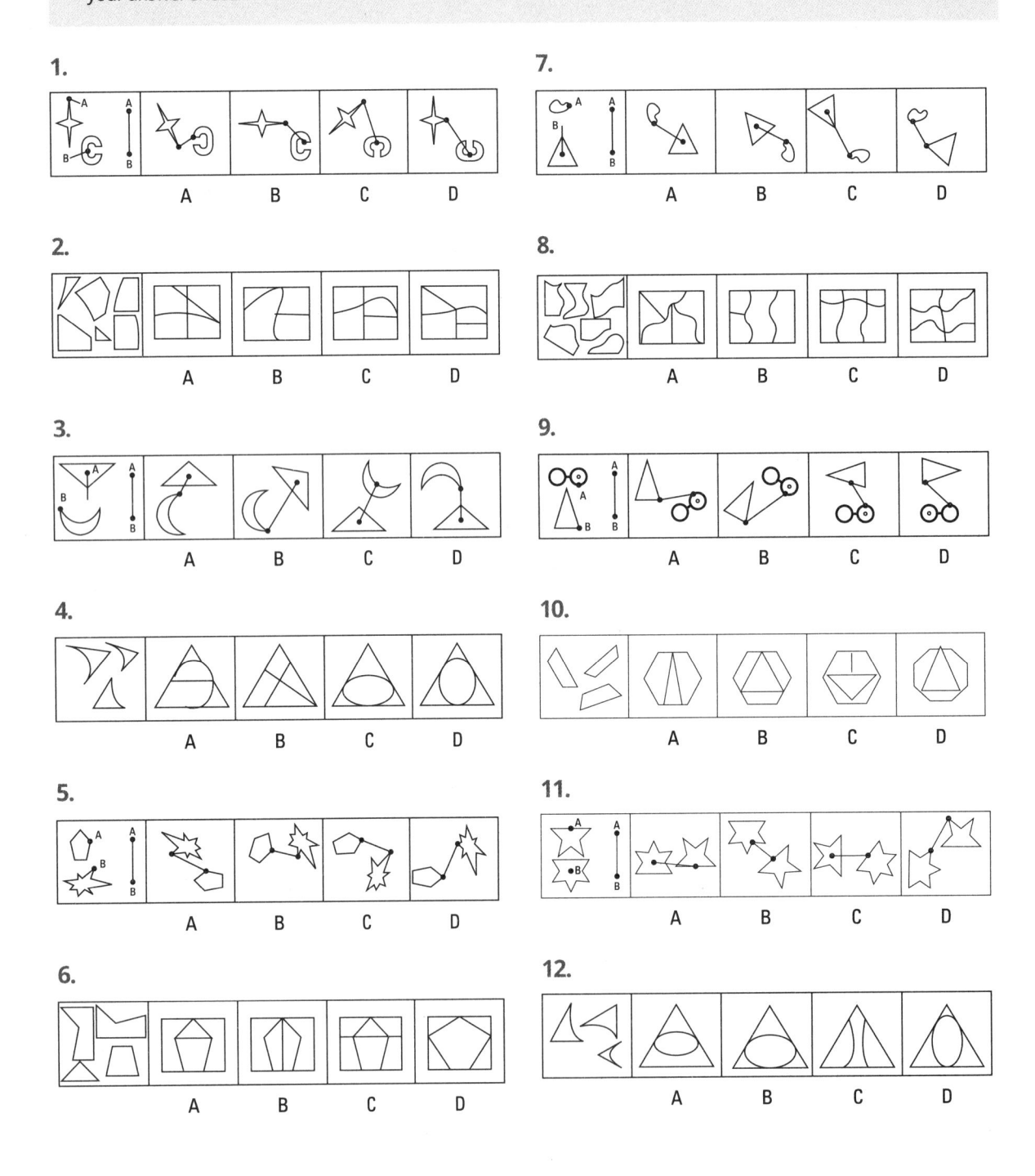

1.
2.
3.
4.
5.
6.
7.
8.
9.
10.
11.
12.

404 PART 6 Practice ASVAB Exams

13.
14.
15.
16.
17.
18.
19.
20.
21.
22.
23.
24.
25.

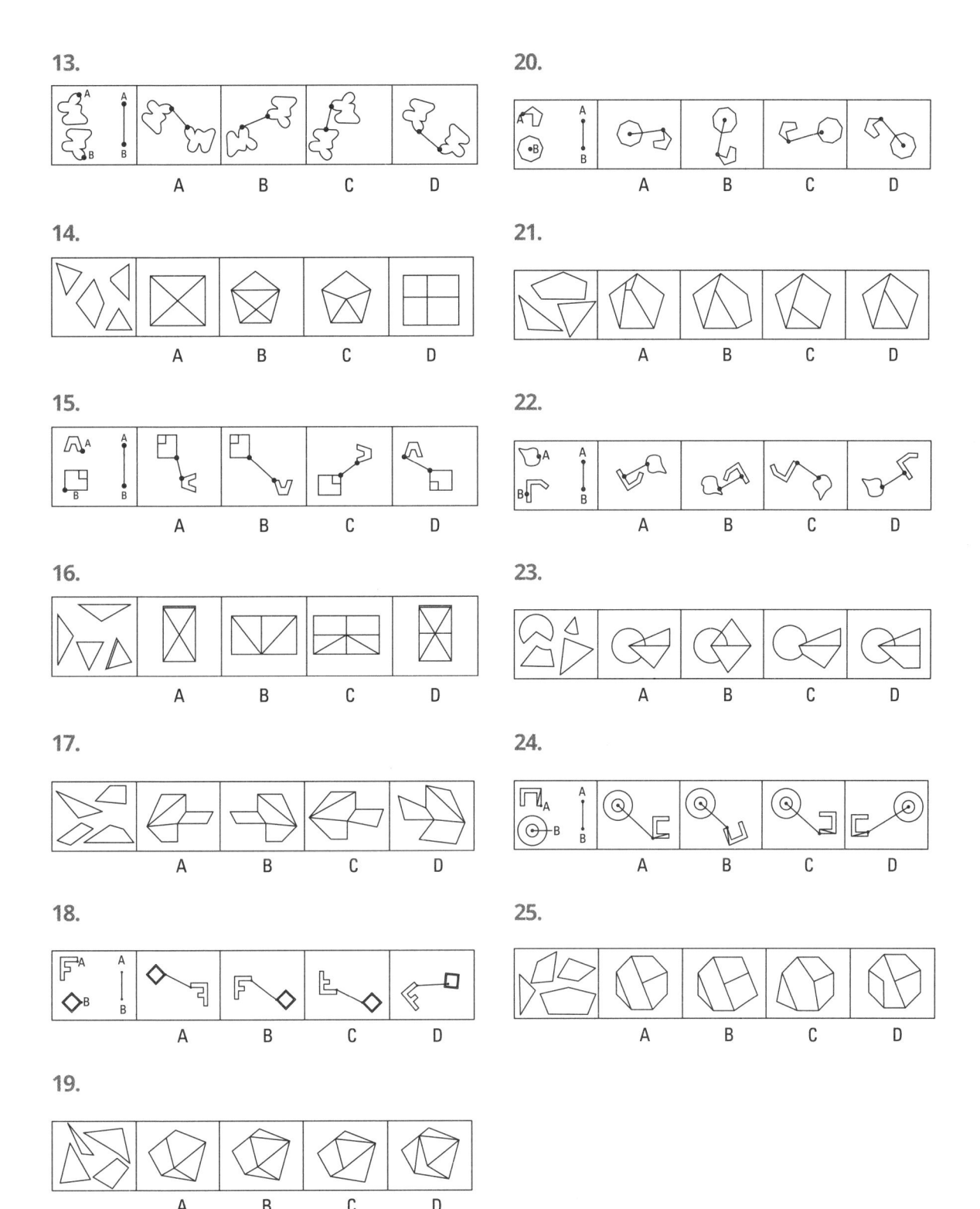

DO NOT TURN THE PAGE UNTIL TOLD TO DO SO STOP **DO NOT RETURN TO A PREVIOUS TEST**

CHAPTER 18 Practice Exam 1   405

Chapter 19
Practice Exam 1: Answers and Explanations

With the first practice test out of the way, you're probably anxious to see how well you did. Use the answer keys in this chapter to score yourself on each of the nine subtests. Remember, your scores on this practice exam don't equate to scores on the actual ASVAB. That's because on the enlistment ASVAB, you get more points for answering harder questions correctly than you do for easier questions. The test is scored by comparing your raw score to other people's scores, which produces a scaled score, so missing 20 out of 225 questions doesn't mean that your score is 205. The practice exam, however, is a valuable tool for determining which subject areas you need to brush up on. (Turn to Chapter 1 to find out how the ASVAB is scored.)

Subtest 1: General Science Answers

The General Science subtest tests your knowledge of science facts. If you missed a few questions, reread the questions and try to figure out where you went wrong. If you missed more than a few questions, review Chapters 10, 11, and 12.

TIP General Science is a broad field, but some of the following books may help you: *Chemistry For Dummies* by John T. Moore, *Biology For Dummies* by Donna Rae Siegfried, *Astronomy For Dummies* by Stephen P. Maran, *Weather For Dummies* by John D. Cox, and *Physics I For Dummies* by Steven Holzner, all published by Wiley. You can find additional practice questions in Chapters 10, 11, and 12.

1. **D.** The planet Uranus was named for the Greek god Uranus, who personified the sky.

2. **C.** From the Latin, *carne* means flesh and *vorare* means to devour — hence the word *carnivore*, a meat-eater. Choice (C) is correct.

3. **C.** In the chemical process of *oxidation*, an atom loses electrons in its *valence shell* (the outermost shell of electrons). Oxidation is usually paired with *reduction*, in which another atom or molecule gains those electrons. Together, reduction and oxidation form a *redox* reaction.

4. **A.** The plural of *quantum* is *quanta*.

5. **D.** Light waves travel at 299,792 kilometers (or approximately 186,000 miles) per second. That's why light from the sun takes about 8.3 minutes to reach Earth.

6. **D.** Jupiter is the largest planet in our solar system.

7. **D.** Both the large and small intestines are part of the digestive system.

8. **C.** Joints that hold bones firmly together are called *fixed joints*.

9. **C.** The levels of classification of living creatures from broadest to narrowest are kingdom, phylum, class, order, family, genus, and species.

10. **C.** Venus is the brightest planet and is sometimes called the *morning* or *evening star*.

11. **C.** The left and right ventricles, with the left and right atria, make up the four heart chambers in a human.

12. **D.** White blood cells produce antibodies and fight infection, making Choice (D) correct.

13. **D.** Eggs, meat, and peas all contain protein. A negligible amount of protein occurs in apples.

14. **B.** Oxygen makes up about 46.6 percent of the Earth's crust. Silicon is the next-most abundant, coming in at 27.7 percent.

15. **A.** *Osmosis* is a passive process in which water or another solvent moves through a partially permeable membrane. If the solution on one side of the membrane has a high concentration of solute and the other has a lower concentration of solute, the water moves through the membrane toward the highly concentrated side until the concentrations are equal.

16. **C.** A centimeter is one-hundredth of a meter; therefore, you find 100 centimeters in a meter.

17. **A.** The distance light travels in one year is one *light-year*.

18. **D.** *Electrons* are the negatively charged parts of an atom.

19. **B.** The asteroid belt is located between the planets Mars and Jupiter.

20. **B.** The number of protons in an atom's nucleus determines the atomic number of an atom.

21. **A.** A cell's nucleus contains its nuclear genome. It's sometimes called the control center.

22. **D.** Jupiter, Saturn, Neptune, and Uranus are the four planets with rings.

23. **A.** The melting point of a substance is a state of equilibrium between its solid and liquid states. The melting point is equal to the freezing point.

24. **B.** Mars's atmosphere is comprised mainly of carbon dioxide.

25. **B.** Proxima Centauri C (or Alpha Centauri C) is the closest star to the Earth (after our sun).

Subtest 2: Arithmetic Reasoning Answers

Arithmetic Reasoning is one of the four ASVAB subtests that make up your Armed Forces Qualification Test (AFQT) score, which determines whether you qualify to join the service branch of your choice. If you missed more than five or six questions, dig out that old high school math textbook and wrap your brain around some math problems. The chapters in Part 3 may also help you out.

Some books that may help you score better on the Arithmetic Reasoning subtest include *Basic Math & Pre-Algebra For Dummies* by Mark Zegarelli, *Algebra I For Dummies* and *Algebra II For Dummies* by Mary Jane Sterling, and *Geometry For Dummies* by Mark Ryan, as well as the related workbooks. You can also check out Mark Zegarelli's *SAT Math For Dummies* and *ACT Math For Dummies* for some math test practice. (All these books are published by Wiley.)

1. **C.** Multiply 12 miles by $3.50 per mile: $12 \times \$3.50 = \$42.00$.

2. **A.** Let x equal the smaller number and $x + 8$ equal the larger number. Because the sum of the two numbers is 70, you can express this mathematically as $x + x + 8 = 70$. Now all you have to do is solve for x. Combine the like terms: $2x + 8 = 70$. Then subtract 8 from both sides of the equation: $2x + 8 - 8 = 70 - 8$, or $2x = 62$. Divide both sides of the equation by 2, and you find that x is equal to 31.

3. **D.** 144 bottles are in a gross, and $144 \div 3$ (bottles per day) = 48 days.

4. **B.** To determine Jenny's average, add the test scores and divide the sum by the number of tests she took. You want to know what she needs on the next test to achieve an average of 95, so let x equal the unknown score. Set up the equation as $(93 + 89 + 96 + 98 + x) \div 5 = 95$. Combine the like terms: $(376 + x) \div 5 = 95$. Multiplying both sides by 5 results in $376 + x = 475$, so $x = 99$.

   Choice (A) is very close to the correct answer, but it isn't the best answer. If Jenny's next test score is 100, her average would be raised to 95.2.

5. **D.** Multiply the total amount spent on food, $375, by 12% (or 0.12) to determine the amount of tips: $\$375 \times 0.12 = \$45$.

6. **D.** You determine square footage by multiplying length by width: $12 \times 12 = 144$.

7. **C.** First determine the number of square feet of carpet you want to protect: 16 ft. $\times$ 18 ft. = 288 ft.^{2} The carpet stain protector is priced by the square yard, so divide 288 by 9 to convert square feet to square yards (because 1 yd.^{2} = 3 ft. $\times$ 3 ft. = 9 ft.^{2}): 288 ft.$^2 \div$ 9 ft.^{2}/yd. = 32 yd.^{2}

   Multiply the number of square yards by the cost of protection per square yard, $0.65, to get the correct answer: 32 yd.$^2 \times \$0.65$/yd.^{2} = \$20.80.

8. **C.** Let x equal the number of cards printed and sold each month. Each card costs $0.18 to print and sells for $0.30. Therefore, the cost is equal to $6{,}000 + 0.18x$, and revenue is equal to $0.30x$. You're looking for the point where revenue is greater than the cost (revenue > cost). The inequality is $0.30x > 6{,}000 + 0.18x$.

Now solve for *x*. Subtract 0.18*x* from both sides of the inequality and then divide both sides by 0.12:

$$0.12x > 6{,}000$$
$$x > 50{,}000$$

The printing plant would have to print and sell at least 50,000 cards per month to make a profit.

9. **C.** Joe gets a 7% raise. To calculate the new wage, start off by multiplying $8.15 × 0.07 = $0.57. Then add that number (the amount of Joe's raise) to his original hourly wage. Joe's new hourly wage is $8.15 + $0.57 = $8.72.

10. **C.** To find distance, you multiply speed by time. First find how far Alice travels before Dave catches up with her. By the time Dave leaves, Alice has already been traveling for half an hour. Three hours later, she would've been traveling for $3\frac{1}{2}$ hours at 45 mph, or 157.5 miles: 3.5 hr. × 45 mph = 157.5 mi. Dave has three hours to cover this distance. Now find his speed. To travel 157.5 miles in 3 hours, Dave would have to travel at 52.5 mph: 157.5 mi. ÷ 3 hr. = 52.5 mph.

11. **D.** To find the amount of pie purchased (which, by the way, does not give you the final answer), you have to add the fractions. But first the fractions need to have a common denominator. The denominators (4, 3, and 6) all divide evenly into 12, so use 12 as the common denominator.

    To convert the fractions to the least common denominator of 12, do the following:

    $$\frac{1}{4} \times \frac{3}{3} = \frac{3}{12}$$
    $$\frac{1}{3} \times \frac{4}{4} = \frac{4}{12}$$
    $$\frac{1}{6} \times \frac{2}{2} = \frac{2}{12}$$

    Now you can add the fractions together:

    $$\frac{3}{12} + \frac{4}{12} + \frac{2}{12} = \frac{3+4+2}{12} = \frac{9}{12}$$

    Nine-twelfths of 20 pies is the same thing as $\frac{3}{4}$, or 75%, of the 20 pies. That equals 15 pies. But that's not what the question asks. One more step: Subtract the pies sold (15) from the original 20, leaving 5 pies, which makes Choice (D) correct.

12. **A.** Subtract the sale price from the regular price to find how much she saved on each case: $24.00 − $22.50 = $1.50. Multiply the answer by the total number of cases to get your final answer: $1.50 × 5 = $7.50.

13. **C.** Divide 30 by 8 to determine how long the security guard takes to walk one city block: 30 ÷ 8 = 3.75 minutes. Then multiply 3.75 by 6, the number of blocks it takes to complete the circuit. The answer is 22.50 minutes.

14. **B.** Let *x* equal the original number of how much Grand Island would grow. An additional $\frac{1}{5}$ would make the population growth $\frac{6}{5}$, or 120%, of *x*. You can express the equation as $1.2x = 600{,}000$. To solve for *x*, divide both sides of the equation by 1.2, which gives you $x = 500{,}000$.

15. **D.** Divide the number of questions she has to get right (40) by the total number of questions (60) to reach $66\frac{2}{3}\%$.

16. **C.** The interest formula says that interest equals principal times rate times time, or $I = Prt$. To determine the amount of interest earned, multiply the principal ($3,000) by the interest rate (6%) and the number of years interest accrues (1 year): $\$3,000 \times 0.06 \times 1 = \$180$. Add the interest earned to the principal to show how much total money the teacher would have: $\$180 + \$3,000 = \$3,180$.

17. **B.** Recognize that if the track is a quarter mile long, then 1 mile equals four laps. Therefore, multiply 4 times 3.5 miles; the answer is 14 laps.

18. **A.** One kilometer is approximately $\frac{5}{8}$ of 1 mile, so you can multiply $75 \times \frac{5}{8}$: $75 \times 5 = 375$, and $375 \div 8 =$ about 46.8. Therefore, Karl was traveling at 47 miles per hour.

19. **A.** You need to add the carpenter's base pay and overtime pay to find their total pay for the week. First find their base pay per week: $\$12.30/\text{hr.} \times 40 \text{ hr.} = \$492$. Then find their overtime rate per hour, which is $1\frac{1}{2}$ times their base pay: $\$12.30/\text{hr.} \times 1.5 = \$18.45$. Multiply this rate by the number of hours of overtime to find the overtime pay: $\$18.45/\text{hr.} \times 6 \text{ hr.} = \$110.70$. Finally, add the base pay and overtime pay to find the total pay for the week: $\$492.00 + \$110.70 = \$602.70$.

20. **A.** The office has 1,260 square feet of space (multiply 42 square feet by 30 employees). With 35 employees, each employee will have 36 square feet of work space $(1,260 \div 35)$, which is 6 square feet less than the amount was originally.

21. **B.** The total cost is the down payment plus 5 years' worth of monthly payments. Five years contain 60 months, so multiply $\$450$ (monthly payment) $\times 60 = \$27,000$ (total payments). Then add $\$27,0000$ (total payments) $+ \$2,000$ (down payment) $= \$29,000$ (total cost).

22. **D.** Add the three monthly amounts to determine the total amount Darla spent on groceries: $\$120.37 + \$108.45 + \$114.86 = \$343.68$. Divide the total by 3 to determine the average monthly cost: $\$114.56$.

23. **C.** Distance equals speed times time, so divide the total distance by Keith's average speed to find how long the trip took: $1,650 \text{ mi.} \div 50 \text{ mph} = 33 \text{ hr.}$

24. **B.** Choice (A) doesn't provide enough paint (2×25 gal. = 50 gal.), so it's wrong. Now determine the cost of each of the other options:

    Choice (B): $11 \times \$108 = \$1,188$
    Choice (C): $6 \times \$215 = \$1,290$
    Choice (D): $55 \times \$23 = \$1,265$

    The lowest price is $\$1,188$, Choice (B).

25. **B.** First find how many ounces of rations each truck can hold. One ton is 2,000 pounds, so one truck can carry three times that, or 6,000 pounds. There are 16 ounces in a pound, so one truck can carry 96,000 ounces: $6,000 \text{ lb.} \times 16 \text{ oz.} = 96,000 \text{ oz.}$

    Then figure out how many daily rations are in a truckload. The total daily ration for each resident is 12 ounces + 18 ounces + 18 ounces, or 48 ounces. You can express the number of daily rations supplied as 96,000 oz. ÷ 48 oz./daily ration = 2,000 daily rations. These rations need to last 10 days. Dividing 2,000 by 10 days results in 200 residents who can be fed by one truck during this 10-day period.

26. **D.** The train headed for Wichita traveled 55 miles/hour × 3 hours = 165 total miles. The train headed for Des Moines traveled 70 miles/hour × 3 hours = 210 total miles. Adding the distances together gives you the number of miles apart the two trains are after three hours: 210 + 165 = 375. Another option: You can add the two rates of speed (55 + 70) and multiply the sum by 3 hours (125 × 3 hours = 375).

27. **A.** Convert the mixed number to inches: 3 feet, 8 inches equals 44 inches (12 in./ft. × 3 ft. = 36 in., and 36 in. + 8 in. = 44 in.). Each section needs to be 44 inches long, and you need four sections. So 44 in. × 4 = 176 in. The total amount of molding needed is 176 inches. To find the amount of molding needed in feet, convert 176 inches into feet by dividing 176 inches by 12 inches.

    You get $14\frac{2}{3}$ feet, so the shortest board length necessary is 15 feet.

28. **A.** One turkey breast costs $8.50 minus 10% of $8.50 (which is $0.85), or $8.50 − $0.85 = $7.65. The other turkey breast is full price, so add the two costs: $7.65 + $8.50 = $16.15.

29. **C.** Don't let the number of miles traveled confuse you. You don't use them to solve the problem. Finding $\frac{2}{5}$ of a 40-hour workweek is the same thing as multiplying 40 times 2, which is 80, and then dividing 80 by 5, which equals 16 hours the recruiter travels weekly.

30. **B.** Your first step is to determine the number of miles traveled. Multiply the rate of travel by the time: 48 × 7 = 336 mi. The amount of gas used is the total miles driven divided by the number of miles per gallon: 336 ÷ 21 = 16 gal. used. At the price of $2.82 per gallon, you spent $45.12 for gas: $2.82 × 16 = $45.12.

Subtest 3: Word Knowledge Answers

The Word Knowledge subtest is nothing more than a vocabulary test. However, it's very important because it's another one of the four subtests used to make up your AFQT score. If you find you need to improve your vocabulary, see Chapter 4.

TIP

See Chapter 4 for more practice questions.

1. **A.** *Apex* is a noun that means the top or highest part of something, especially when it forms a point.

2. **A.** *Assimilate* is a verb that means to take in and understand or to cause something to resemble another thing.

3. **B.** *Brittle* is an adjective that means hard but liable to break easily.

4. **C.** *Datum* is a noun that refers to a piece of information.

5. **C.** *Proficient* is an adjective that means competent or skilled in doing (or using) something.

6. **C.** *Impose* is a verb that means to force acceptance of something unwelcome or unfamiliar.

7. **A.** *Galore* is an adjective that means in abundance.

8. **D.** *Headlong* is an adverb and an adjective, and it means with the head foremost or in a reckless rush.

9. **D.** *Frugal* is an adjective that means sparing or economical, particularly as it relates to money or food.

10. **B.** *Stimulate* is a verb that means to raise levels of physiological or nervous activity within the body or another biological system. It also means to encourage interest or activity in someone or something or to encourage development of increased activity in a state or process. Therefore, the opposite is to arrest, or stop.

11. **B.** *Illicit* is an adjective that means forbidden by law, rules, or customs.

12. **D.** *Vacate* is a verb that means to leave a place that was previously occupied.

13. **B.** *Reasoned* is an adjective that means underpinned by logic or sense.

14. **B.** *Tacit* is an adjective that means understood or implied.

15. **D.** *Burnish* is a verb that means to polish something by rubbing.

16. **A.** *Commodity* is a noun that means a raw material or agricultural product that can be bought or sold; it can also refer to a useful or valuable thing.

17. **A.** *Contrived* is an adjective that means deliberately created instead of arising naturally or spontaneously.

18. **C.** *Supplicate* is a verb that means to ask or beg for something humbly or earnestly.

19. **A.** *Hypocrisy* is a noun that means the practice of claiming standards or beliefs without actually conforming to them. The word most opposite in meaning is *honesty*.

20. **D.** *Succulent* is an adjective that refers to food being juicy, tender, and delicious.

21. **D.** *Garrison* is a noun that refers to troops stationed in a fortress or town to defend it.

22. **A.** *Furtherance* is a noun that refers to the advancement of an interest or scheme.

23. **C.** *Domicile* is a noun that means a permanent home or a place in which someone lives and has a substantial connection with; it often refers to countries (particularly as it relates to U.S. laws), but not always.

24. **D.** *Abrogate* is a verb that means to repeal or do away with.

25. **B.** *Compensation* is a noun that refers to something awarded to someone as reimbursement for loss, injury, or suffering. It can also refer to the money an employer gives to an employee as a salary or wages.

26. **D.** *Brusque* is an adjective that means abrupt or offhand in speech or manner.

27. **B.** *Demise* is a noun that means someone's or something's death.

28. **B.** *Commemorate* is a verb that means to recall and show respect for someone or something; it also means to celebrate or serve as a memorial to something.

29. **C.** *Bore* is a verb that means to make a hole in something or to make one's way through something.

30. **B.** *Prevail* is a verb that means to be victorious, to be widespread, or to be current.

31. **C.** *Defray* is a verb that means to provide money to pay a cost or expense.

32. **A.** *Chasm* is a noun that refers to a deep fissure in the earth, rock, or another surface; it can also refer to a vast difference between two things.

33. **C.** *Fundamental* is an adjective that means forming a needed base or core; it also refers to a central or main rule or principle on which something is based.

34. **D.** *Susceptible* is an adjective that means likely to be influenced or harmed by something.

35. **A.** *Emblem* is a noun that means a device or symbolic object that's used as a badge or something that serves as a symbolic representation of a characteristic or concept.

Subtest 4: Paragraph Comprehension Answers

Like Word Knowledge, your Paragraph Comprehension score goes toward your AFQT score, so pay special attention if you've missed more than a couple of these answers — you need some study time (see Chapter 5). Remember that rereading the paragraph several times to make sure you have the right answer is perfectly fine. You can find additional practice questions in Chapter 5.

1. **C.** Effective appointment management eliminates the waste of your time, as the last sentence of the passage explains.

2. **D.** The passage gives the numbers of senators and representatives, so Choice (A) is incorrect. The passage states that each state's population determines the number of representatives a state has, so Choice (B) is incorrect. As the passage states, each state has at least one representative, so Choice (C) is incorrect.

3. **A.** Many languages are excluded from the Indo-European language group, so Choice (B) is incorrect. Indians, Iranians, Asians, and Afghans aren't Europeans, so Choice (C) is incorrect. The passage gives no evidence to support Choice (D), which isn't true.

4. **D.** Privatized functions operate independently of the government, making Choices (A) and (B) incorrect. The passage states that privatized functions may sell goods and services to other customers as well as the government, so Choice (C) is also incorrect. Choice (D) is the correct answer, because privatized functions do perform essential services to government agencies.

5. **C.** Choice (A) — "Lead by Example" — is a good philosophy but isn't pertinent to the main point of the passage. Choices (B) and (D) are subpoints, which support the main point of the passage: how to lead a successful conference, Choice (C).

6. **A.** You can assume that causing rain or snow would end a drought, Choice (A). Nothing in the passage has to do with expense, so Choice (B) is incorrect. The passage says nothing about how frequently the process is used, so Choice (C) is incorrect. The passage specifies that dry ice (solid carbon dioxide) is used; regular ice (solid water) is a different substance, so Choice (D) is wrong.

7. **C.** Choices (A) and (B) may be true in certain situations, but they're not the point of this particular paragraph. The passage doesn't say anything about working to improve writing skills being a waste of time, so Choice (D) is incorrect. The main point of the paragraph is that writing may not be the most efficient way of communicating, depending on the situation.

8. **B.** Products with transistors weren't widely sold before 1954 because of the expense and difficulty of production, not because markets didn't exist, so Choice (A) is incorrect. Choice (C) has the right date, but the passage doesn't say who invented the transistor, so it's wrong as well. Choice (D) is wrong because the passage states that the problem of transistors being expensive to produce was solved in 1954. The last sentence notes that the first transistor radio went on the market after cost and production problems were overcome, so Choice (B) is the right answer.

9. **B.** The words *London* and *Englishman* make it clear that the author is speaking of his travels in England, which is part of Great Britain.

10. **A.** The author makes no reference to parents in the passage, so Choice (B) is incorrect. The author doesn't imply anything about all these interests requiring equal time, so Choice (C) is incorrect. The passage is about children under 18; you can't draw a conclusion about what the author thinks people over 18 should do, so Choice (D) is incorrect.

11. **C.** The passage doesn't say anything about mock job interviews being frightening, so Choice (A) is wrong. The passage says that mock job interviews should be available to all students, so Choice (B) is wrong. The passage says that schools, not students, should organize mock interviews, so Choice (D) is incorrect.

12. **A.** Choices (B), (C), and (D) are the opposite of what the paragraph states and implies.

13. **B.** Nothing in the paragraph supports Choice (A), which is incorrect. When an amendment is passed, it becomes part of the Constitution, so Choice (C) is incorrect. The passage doesn't support Choice (D), because the passage doesn't mention anything related to lottery tickets. The passage defines *due process* as "the guarantee of fairness in the administration of justice," so Choice (B) is correct.

14. **C.** Because the 14th Amendment guarantees due process in states' laws, the 5th Amendment must guarantee due process only in federal law, which makes Choice (C) right. Nothing in the passage implies that the 5th Amendment is about taxes, so Choice (A) is wrong. Because the passage states that the 14th Amendment had to be enacted to require states to abide by due process, Choice (B) is incorrect. Choice (D) is neither stated nor implied in the passage.

15. **A.** Because the Supreme Court struck down many state laws after the 14th Amendment was enacted, it's probably true that these laws would still exist if there'd been no 14th Amendment. The passage doesn't support Choices (B), (C), or (D).

Subtest 5: Mathematics Knowledge Answers

This subtest is also used to calculate your AFQT score, so it's important. If you miss more than four or five, consider brushing up on your basic math skills. Chapters 6, 7, and 8 can help with this.

> The following books may also be of some help: *Algebra I For Dummies* and *Algebra II For Dummies* by Mary Jane Sterling, *Geometry For Dummies* and *Calculus For Dummies* by Mark Ryan, and *SAT Math For Dummies* by Mark Zegarelli (all books published by Wiley).

1. **A.** Substitute 8 for *x* in the equation and then solve for *y*:

   $$y = (x^2 \div 4) - 2$$
   $$= (8^2 \div 4) - 2$$
   $$= (64 \div 4) - 2$$
   $$= 16 - 2$$
   $$= 14$$

2. **A.** The cube of 5 is 5^3, which is $5 \times 5 \times 5 = 125$.

3. **C.** Because of the order of operations, you need to find 3^3 first and then multiply by 2.5:

   $$2.5 \times 3^3 = 2.5(3 \times 3 \times 3)$$
   $$= 2.5 \times 27$$
   $$= 67.5$$

4. **D.** Because $2^4 = 16$, the fourth root of 16 is 2.

5. **A.** To get the equation of the line, you need to know the line's slope and *y*-intercept. The slope of the line is equal to the change in *y* values divided by the change in *x* values. The change in *y* values is $3 - (-1) = 4$. The change in *x* values is $2 - 0 = 2$. Thus, the slope is $\frac{4}{2} = 2$. The line passes through the point (0, 1), so to find the intercept, substitute 0 for *x* and −1 for *y* in the equation $y = 2x + b$:

   $$-1 = 2(0) + b$$
   $$b = -1$$

   Therefore, $b = -1$, so the full equation is $y = 2x - 1$.

6. **C.** Do what's in parentheses first. You need consistent units of measurement, so convert 12 yards to feet; then add 14 feet:

   $$(12 \text{ yards} \times 3 \text{ feet/yard}) + 14 \text{ feet}$$
   $$= 36 \text{ feet} + 14 \text{ feet}$$
   $$= 50 \text{ feet}$$

   The original problem asks for $(12 \text{ yards} + 14 \text{ feet}) \div 5$, so divide by 5 as instructed: $50 \text{ feet} \div 5 = 10 \text{ feet}$.

7. **D.** If two powers have the same base, you multiply them by keeping the base the same and adding the powers together: $x^3 \cdot x^4 = x^{3+4} = x^7$.

8. **D.** To find $(x+4)(x+2)$, you need to multiply every term in the first set of parentheses by every term in the second set and then add the results. The acronym FOIL (First, Outer, Inner, Last) can help you keep track of which terms you're multiplying:

   - **First:** Multiply the first variable in the first set of parentheses by the first variable in the second set of parentheses: $x(x) = x^2$.

- **Outer:** Next, multiply the first variable in the first set of parentheses by the second number in the second set of parentheses: $x(2) = 2x$. So far, the results are $x^2 + 2x$.
- **Inner:** Now multiply the second number in the first set of parentheses by the first variable in the second set of parentheses: $4(x) = 4x$.
- **Last:** Next, multiply the second number in the first set of parentheses by the second number in the second set of parentheses: $4(2) = 8$.

The solution is $x^2 + 2x + 4x + 8$. Combining the like terms results in $x^2 + 6x + 8$.

9. **C.** You need to do powers (exponents) first, so find 10^3 and then multiply by 1.5:

$$1.5 \times 10^3 = 1.5 \times (10 \times 10 \times 10)$$
$$= 1.5 \times 1,000$$
$$= 1,500$$

10. **B.** A *prime number* is a number that can be divided evenly by itself or by 1 but not by any other number. Choices (A), (C), and (D) can all be divided evenly by other numbers.

11. **B.** The *mode* of a series of numbers is the number that appears in the series the most frequently. In this case, it's 8.

12. **D.** Substitute 4 for all *a*'s in the problem and then solve, doing the powers first:

$$4^3 \div 4 = (4 \times 4 \times 4) \div 4$$
$$= 64 \div 4$$
$$= 16$$

13. **C.** The factorial (!) of a number is the number multiplied by the next-smallest whole number, then by the next smallest whole number, and so on down to 1:

$$5! = 5 \times 4 \times 3 \times 2 \times 1 = 120$$

14. **B.** Use the order of operations and do what's in parentheses first:

$$(900 \times 2) \div 6 = 1,800 \div 6 = 300$$

15. **A.** Substitute 2 for all *x*'s in the problem and then simplify, starting with the powers:

$$2 \times 2(2) = 4(2) = 8$$

16. **D.** The problem asks you to solve $(5+1)(6 \div 3)(8-5) = (3+3)x$ for *x*. First find the values in parentheses:

$$(6)(2)(3) = 36$$

Therefore, the whole equation becomes $36 = (3+3)x$, which simplifies to $36 = 6x$. Solve for *x*:

$$36 \div 6 = 6x \div 6$$
$$6 = x$$

To check your answer, substitute 6 for *x*.

17. **A.** The square root of 49 is 7; the square root of 64 is 8. And $7 \times 8 = 56$.

18. **D.** Find a common denominator for the fractions. In this case, 80 works for all the fractions. Convert all the fractions using the following method:

$$\frac{2}{5} \times \frac{16}{16} = \frac{32}{80}$$
$$\frac{3}{8} \times \frac{10}{10} = \frac{30}{80}$$
$$\frac{7}{10} \times \frac{8}{8} = \frac{56}{80}$$
$$\frac{13}{16} \times \frac{5}{5} = \frac{65}{80}$$

Comparing the fractions, you can see that $\frac{65}{80}$ (or $\frac{13}{16}$) is the largest fraction.

19. **B.** Solve as you would solve for any unknown:

$$2 + x \geq 4$$
$$2 + x - 2 \geq 4 - 2$$

Therefore, $x \geq 2$. To check your answer, substitute 2 for x: $2 + 2 \geq 4$. That's true, so the answer is correct.

20. **C.** Circumference equals $\pi \times$ diameter, and diameter is equal to two times the radius (or mathematically, $C = \pi d$ and $d = 2r$). For this problem, $C = \pi \times 24$. If you round π to 3.14, the answer is about 75.36, or about 75 feet.

21. **A.** Volume equals length $\times$ width $\times$ height $(V = lwh)$, so plug in the numbers and solve: $16 \times 8 \times 18 = 2{,}304$ in.^{3}

22. **C.** In an equilateral triangle, all sides are equal and all angles are equal.

23. **A.** All quadrilaterals (four-sided figures) have angles that total 360 degrees.

24. **B.** If the sum of two angles equals 90 degrees, they're called *complementary angles*.

25. **A.** $24\% = \frac{24}{100}$. You further reduce this fraction to $\frac{6}{25}$ by dividing the numerator and denominator by 4.

Subtest 6: Electronics Information Answers

The Electronics Information subtest is particularly important if you want to obtain a job that requires a solid score in this area. If so, you shouldn't miss more than five questions in this practice exam. If you do, you may want to review Chapter 16.

TIP If you need even more study, check out *Electronics For Dummies,* by Cathleen Shamieh (Wiley) or consider enrolling in a quick course at a community college.

1. **A.** Ohm's law states that Voltage $(V$ or $E) =$ Current $(I) \times$ Resistance (R). All other answers are incorrect expressions of this law.

2. **A.** You read a resistor's color bands from left to right. The first band denotes the first digit, the second band denotes the second digit, and the third band denotes the subsequent number of zeros. In this example, brown is one, black is zero, and red means there are two additional zeros.

3. **B.** Heaters, pumps, stairs, diving boards, railings, and rebar, among other things, must be bonded together by a minimum #8 wire for safety purposes.

4. **D.** *Voltage* is commonly used as a short name for electrical potential difference, and it is measured in volts.

5. **A.** SIM stands for *Subscriber Identity Module.* The card contains information such as your phone number, your billing information, and your address book. The card makes it easier to switch from one cellphone to another.

6. **A.** A resistor is so named because it resists (or inhibits) the flow of current.

7. **C.** A diode has two terminals, the anode and the cathode, which is why it's called a *di*ode. It restricts current flow to only one direction.

8. **C.** Radar can operate as high as 100,000 MHz (megahertz).

9. **B.** *Current* is the flow of charged particles. The difference between alternating current (AC) and direct current (DC) is that the electrons in an AC circuit regularly reverse their direction. In a DC circuit, electrons always flow in the same direction.

10. **C.** Changing AC to DC is a process called *rectification.*

11. **C.** A British thermal unit (BTU) is a measure of heat energy.

12. **D.** *Current* is the presence of electron flow.

13. **B.** *Transducers,* which transform or convert energy, can be switches, strain gauges, temperature sensors, or inductive switches. A transformer is an inductor that increases or decreases voltage.

14. **D.** *Active elements* are electronic devices that can create energy (such as voltage supplies and current supplies). *Passive elements* are electronic devices that cannot create energy.

15. **A.** Power = Current × Voltage or, written another way, Current = Power ÷ Voltage. Plug in the numbers and do the math: 60 watts ÷ 120 volts = 0.5 amperes.

16. **C.** The larger the number, the smaller the diameter of the wire.

17. **C.** Because fuses are designed to prevent current overload at a specific level, a fuse with a high rating may allow a higher current to flow through a circuit not designed to work at that higher current, possibly causing damage to the circuit.

18. **A.** Neutral wire is always whitish or natural colored.

19. **D.** Electrical power is measured in watts, so you use a wattmeter. An ammeter measures amps (current). An ohmmeter measures ohms (resistance). A voltmeter measures volts (voltage).

20. **B.** The bulb will burn dimmer because its full potential isn't used; it'll last longer for the same reason.

Subtest 7: Auto & Shop Information Answers

The Auto & Shop Information subtest is fairly straightforward. You either know the information or you don't. Not knowing the info may not matter to you as long as the career you want doesn't require a subtest score in this area. But if you do need to do well on this subtest and you've missed more than five answers, review the material in Chapters 13 and 14.

Reviewing *Auto Repair For Dummies* by Deanna Sclar (Wiley) may also help you score better on this subtest. *Home Improvement All-in-One For Dummies* by Roy Barnhart, James Carey, Morris Carey, Gene Hamilton, Katie Hamilton, Donald R. Prestly, and Jeff Strong (Wiley) can help you get a better handle on basic tools and their uses. You may even want to take a class at a nearby community college or at least hang out at the garage and help some mechanics for a couple of weeks.

1. **D.** Overheating can melt engine parts, enlarge pistons, and burn engine bearings.

2. **B.** Alternators convert mechanical energy (rotary motion) into electrical energy (output current).

3. **B.** Electronic ignition systems use lower input voltages to get higher output voltages (for spark).

4. **A.** Piston rings are seals that keep the exploding gases in the combustion chamber.

5. **A.** The crankshaft is connected to the flywheel, which causes it to rotate, operating the pistons.

6. **A.** A differential lets wheels turn at different rates. When one tire is spinning, the other can have traction.

7. **D.** The ignition system starts a car. If there doesn't seem to be any electricity, check the battery.

8. **C.** You use a coping saw to make intricate cuts in wood.

9. **D.** Snowmobiles, chainsaws, lawn mowers, and some motorcycles need only two-stroke engines.

10. **B.** You often use a belt sander is often used to finish wood because doing so is faster than hand sanding for large areas.

11. **C.** A limited-slip-differential transfers the most driving force to the wheel with greatest traction.

12. **A.** Big block engines generally have greater than 5.9-liter displacement.

13. **C.** A trowel would be a good tool for spreading and/or shaping mortar.

14. **B.** You use a plumb bob to check vertical reference using a pointed weight on a line.

15. **B.** Rebar is an iron bar that is embedded in cement to reinforce it.

16. **C.** Annular ring, clout, and spring head are all types of nails.

17. **B.** A ripsaw cuts wood with the grain, called *ripping*, because it's easier than cutting against the grain.

18. **B.** A cam belt, also known as a *timing belt*, connects the crankshaft to the camshaft.

19. **C.** You use a level to check for horizontal trueness.

20. **C.** A bucking bar is used to form rivet bucktails.

21. **A.** Washers that have teeth all around the circumference are called shake-proof washers.

22. **D.** The tool shown is an outside caliper, and it measures the thickness of wire and other objects.

23. **A.** The object pictured is a nut.

24. **D.** The tool is a plane, and you use it to dress (prepare, smooth, and shave) wood.

25. **A.** Commonly called a cold chisel, this tool cuts through metal screws, bolts, nails, and other metals.

Subtest 8: Mechanical Comprehension Answers

The Mechanical Comprehension subtest is important only if you want to pursue a military career that requires a good score on this subtest. Otherwise, spend your time studying more important areas of the ASVAB. If you're considering a military job that requires a high mechanical aptitude and you missed more than four or five questions on this subtest, give Chapter 15 another once over.

1. **A.** An induction clutch is a magnetic clutch. When a conductor (wire) is wrapped around a core and electricity is passed through the wire, it sets up a magnetic field. The same wire also acts as an inductor, which produces inductance, during AC current flow. It's similar to resistance in a resistor in that it "resists" current flow, but the value of inductance is based on the value of the inductor (written as L) and the frequency of the AC current. Therefore, an induction clutch uses magnetism to operate.

2. **B.** You can calculate mechanical advantage as Length of Effort Arm ÷ Length of Resistance Arm. Simply plug in the numbers: $MA = 8 \div 2 = 4$.

3. **C.** The box with the largest area on the bottom will have the shortest sides. If Length × Width × Height = Volume and all the boxes have equal volume, then the sides must be shortest on the box with the largest area on the bottom. Calculate the area of each box bottom:

   No. 1 = 20 square inches
   No. 2 = 35 square inches
   No. 3 = 48 square inches
   No. 4 = 27 square inches

   No. 3, which has the largest area, will have the shortest sides.

4. **C.** Anvil B's landing on the seesaw will propel Anvil A into the air.

5. **A.** Pressure equals force divided by area in square inches ($P = F \div A$). You can also state this formula as $F = A \times P$. Substitute the known quantities: $F = 15 \times 24 = 360$ pounds.

6. **C.** *Recoil* occurs when an object producing a force is kicked back.

7. **A.** To determine the answer, multiply the number of teeth Gear 1 has (*D*) and the number of revolutions it makes (*R*). Divide that number by the number of teeth Gear 2 has (*d*) to determine the number of revolutions Gear 2 makes (*r*). Because the gears are proportional, this formula shows you the ratio of teeth to revolutions.

$$r = \frac{DR}{d}$$
$$= \frac{25 \times 10}{15}$$
$$= \frac{250}{15} = \frac{50}{3} = 16\frac{2}{3}$$

That means Gear 2 (the smaller gear) makes $16\frac{2}{3}$ revolutions for every 10 revolutions that Gear 1 (the larger gear) makes.

8. **B.** You can determine the pressure of all that water by multiplying the volume of the aquarium by the weight of the water. Volume = *lwh*. The bottom of the tank is 18 feet long by 12 feet wide by 10 feet high for a total volume of 2,160 cubic feet: $18 \times 12 \times 10 = 2,160$ ft.^{3} A cubic foot of water weighs approximately 62.5 pounds, so multiply the volume of water by 62.5: $2,160 \times 62.5 = 135,000$.

That gives an approximate pressure on the bottom of the tank of about 135,000 pounds over the entire surface area. The surface area of the bottom of the tank is length × width. Convert feet to inches and then find the area: $A = (18 \text{ ft.} \times 12 \text{ in./ft.}) \times (12 \text{ ft.} \times 12 \text{ in./ft.}) = 216 \text{ in.} \times 144 \text{ in.} = 31,104 \text{ in.}^2$

Dividing the pressure of 135,000 by the number of square inches of surface area gives an approximate psi of 4.

9. **D.** Machine springs are usually made of steel, although sometimes they're made of brass or other metal alloys.

10. **B.** Clutches connect and disconnect parts, so they're a type of coupling.

11. **D.** When the high point of the cam connects with the lever arm, the lever arm will touch the contact point. Two high points on the cam mean the lever arm will touch the contact point twice with each revolution of the cam.

12. **C.** A single moveable block-and-fall is called a runner. A runner provides a way to get mechanical advantage by threading a rope through a pulley attached to the load, anchoring one end to a stationary point, and you pulling on the other end of the rope, hoisting the load.

13. **C.** If the fulcrum is moved closer to the anvil, the length of the effort arm of the lever will be increased, making the anvil easier to raise, but the height to which the anvil can be raised will be reduced.

14. **B.** In this block-and-tackle arrangement, there are three segments coming off the load, which gives this arrangement a mechanical advantage of 3.

15. **C.** The larger cog (Cog A) covers a greater linear distance in a given period of time, so Cog A reaches the top first.

16. A. The key will feel coldest because metal is a better conductor than the other materials.

17. D. All but Valve 4 should be open. Opening Valves 1 and 2 allows water to enter the tank. Opening Valves 3 and 5 prevents water from filling the tank entirely. Opening Valve 4 allows water to leave the tank.

18. A. Gears with their teeth together in mesh turn in opposite directions. Gear A turns Gear B in the opposite direction (right), and Gear B turns Gear C in the opposite direction (left).

19. A. Gears with their teeth together in mesh turn in opposite directions. Gear 1 turns clockwise. Gear 2, in mesh with Gear 1, turns counterclockwise. Gear 3, in mesh with Gear 2, turns clockwise. Gear 4, in mesh with Gear 3, turns counterclockwise. Gear 5, in mesh with Gear 2, turns clockwise.

20. C. The gauge shows a reading of 21.

21. D. The formula for determining power is Power = Work ÷ Time.

22. C. Silver is the best conductor, so it will become hotter faster than the other objects because heat transfers faster into materials with greater conductivity than with those with lower conductivity.

23. A. Stationary pulleys (often called whips) give no mechanical advantage, so effort equals the weight of the crate, or 50 pounds.

24. C. At the height of the arc, the ball has no upward momentum, so it goes the slowest at that point (it has zero upward movement at its highest point).

25. A. The brace on Angle A covers more area of the angle, so it's more solidly braced.

Subtest 9: Assembling Objects Answers

For more information about the Assembling Objects subtest and additional practice questions, see Chapter 17.

TIP

Try to envision the shapes matching each figure before you select an answer. If the right answer doesn't just pop out at you, use strategy to help you rule out incorrect choices.

1. C. Connect Point A on the star and Point A on the line. Rotate the star-shaped figure about 45 degrees and connect Point B on the line to Point B on the shape, rotating the shape 90 degrees.

2. A. Count the number of shapes in the original image (there are seven). Only one answer choice includes the seven shapes in the original figure. In this case, Choices (B), (C), and (D) just don't have enough shapes — and that makes it easy to get this question correct.

3. D. Point B in the original image is on the end of the crescent, which means you can automatically rule out Choice (C), in which the point is in the center of the figure. Choices (A) and (B) are also incorrect, because in the original figure, the line goes directly through the point of the triangle. The only answer that reflects that intersection is Choice (D).

4. **D.** There are three shapes in the original puzzlelike diagram, so you can automatically rule out Choices (A) and (B) — they each have four. If you rotate the shapes depicted in the question, you'll see that there are two sections that are larger than the remaining one. The only reasonable answer is Choice (D), because it shows an oval inside a triangle with more space in two corners than there is in the remaining corner.

5. **A.** Rotate the pentagon to the left so Point A is on the top. Flip the other shape almost 180 degrees so Point B is on the bottom. Connect the two shapes with the line's corresponding points, and you'll have Choice (A) on your hands.

   If you're unsure, you can always rule out answers that you know aren't correct. In this case, you can tell Choice (B) is wrong because Point B is in the wrong place; it doesn't match the original diagram. Choice (C) is incorrect because neither of the points are in the correct places, and Choice (D) is wrong for the same reasons.

6. **A.** Reconfigure the shapes in the original figure so that the two largest are side-by-side and symmetrical, with the uppermost points touching. The remaining two shapes fit right inside, like a puzzle. (On this question, you can immediately rule out *all* the other choices because the shapes don't match the original figure; Choices (C) and (D) even depict too many shapes to be contenders.)

7. **C.** On Assembling Objects questions, pay attention to the original figures. In this question, the line in Shape B starts in the center of the triangle and travels through one of the triangle's points. The only answer choice that depicts Figure B in the correct way is Choice (C), so you can ignore all the other choices.

8. **D.** Start by counting the number of shapes in the original diagram — there are six. Remember that counting shapes doesn't always work to rule out incorrect answers, but you can tell (in this problem, at least) that Choice (B) is incorrect because it depicts only four shapes. If you can't picture the correct answer in your mind, go through the rest of the choices to eliminate those that are clearly wrong. Choice (A) can't be correct, because it depicts two triangle-like shapes that aren't in the original diagram. Choice (C) can't be correct, because the shapes it depicts aren't even similar to those depicted in the question, which leaves Choice (D) as the only possible correct answer.

9. **B.** Choice (B) is correct because Point A on the circle and Point B on the triangle match the original diagram, as does the length of the line. Choice (A) can't be right, because Figure A is flipped and the line connecting the two figures is too short, and Choice (C) shows Point B on the wrong place on the triangle. Choice (D) is wrong, too, because Point A is on the wrong circle.

10. **B.** The shapes in the original diagram are all very similar (and this is one case where counting the number of shapes won't work). The shapes in Choices (A), (C), and (D) don't match those in the original diagram, leaving Choice (B). If you rearrange the three trapezoids in your mind by connecting the points on the longest side of each, you'll see Choice (B) take shape.

11. **A.** Point A is on the long, flat side of the first shape (the one with four points), whereas Point B is just about in the center of the second shape (the one with five points). When you look at the answer choices, you'll see that Choices (B) and (D) both depict the points in the wrong places, so those choices are automatically wrong. Choice (C) looks like it has the points in the correct places, but not so fast — they're attached to the wrong shapes.

12. **D.** Compare the shapes in the question with the shapes in the answer choices. You can see that Choice (A) is incorrect because the shapes don't match; so is Choice (C). The shapes in the question include three figures that are very similar, but two are large and one is small. Choice (B) can't be correct, then, because two of the shapes are small and one is large, creating an oval tucked into the bottom of a triangle. Choice (D) is the right answer, because it takes two larger shapes and one smaller shape to create an upright oval inside a triangle.

13. **D.** Both of the figures in the original diagram are the same; they're just mirror images of each other. Choice (D) is correct because it's the only figure that shows them as mirror images of each other with the points in the correct places.

14. **C.** You can put Choice (A) in the recycle bin right away — it depicts four triangles put together. The same is true for Choice (D), except it depicts a square and three rectangles. Choice (B) shows five triangles, which can't be correct, either (the original diagram shows four shapes, and only three of them are triangles). Choice (C) is the only one that can possibly be correct.

15. **B.** The first thing you should do on a problem like this one is check out where the points are located on the shapes in the original diagram. On this question, you can rule out Choices (A), (C), and (D) because the points are in the wrong places.

16. **A.** One of the figures in the original diagram is a triangle with a line running parallel to one side. Choices (B) and (C) don't show any such shape, so those are out the window. Choice (D) has too many triangles (there are six, but the original figure depicts only four), leaving Choice (A) as the correct answer.

17. **B.** Choices (C) and (D) are incorrect because they each feature shapes that aren't depicted in the original diagram. Choice (A) is also incorrect; although it's a mirror image of the correct answer, Choice (B), it requires you to flip the shapes rather than rotate them.

18. **B.** Look closely at where the points are in the original diagram — particularly Point B, which is on the corner of the square. You know that Choice (D) isn't the answer, because it shows Point B inside the square. Choices (A) and (C) are wrong, too, because they require you to flip the *F* shape, whereas Choice (B) doesn't even require you to rotate it.

19. **C.** Choice (C) is the only choice in which each of the shapes corresponds with a shape in the original diagram.

20. **A.** The only answer choice that doesn't require you to invert a shape and doesn't feature a point in the wrong place on one of the shapes is Choice (A). Choice (B) requires you to flip the shape with Point A on it, and so does Choice (D). Choice (C) has the point on the wrong place inside the hexagon.

21. **B.** Choice (A) depicts four shapes (the smallest of which isn't in the original diagram), so you can rule that one out immediately. Choices (C) and (D) don't use any five-sided shapes, but there's one in the original diagram. Choice (B) is the only figure that uses replicas of the three shapes in the original illustration.

22. **D.** Point B is clearly marked in the original illustration, but in Choices (A), (B), and (C), it's in all the wrong places; that leaves you with Choice (D) as the correct answer.

23. A. Look closely at Choice (C) — it has a part missing, so you know it can't be correct. Choice (A) is the only one that makes use of all the shapes depicted in the original diagram; Choices (B) and (D) use shapes that aren't in the question.

24. C. Point A is located on the lower-right corner of the original figure in the question, so you can ignore Choices (A), (B), and (D) because they don't match.

25. C. Check each shape to see which answer choices it appears in before you try to put together this puzzle. The only answer choice that features the right shapes in the right proportions (those that match the original illustration) is Choice (C). All the other answers have odd shapes that don't match.

Chapter 20
Practice Exam 2

I've designed the second practice test so you can see how much you've improved. This exam is exactly like the first one from Chapter 18, except (of course) the questions are different. I hope you used the results from the first practice exam to pinpoint your weak areas and then spent some time hitting the books and recharging your thinking cap.

TIP

To get the most out of this practice exam, take it like you'd take the real ASVAB under the same conditions:

>> Allow yourself about 3 hours to take the entire exam, and take the whole thing at one time.

>> Find a quiet place where nothing will interrupt you.

>> Bring a timer that you can set for various lengths of time, some scratch paper, and a pencil.

>> At the start of each subtest, set your timer for the specified period of time. Don't go on to the next section until the timer has gone off, and don't go back to a previous section. If you finish early, check your work for that section only.

>> Use the answer sheet that's provided.

>> Keep testing until you've gone through all the subtests. You don't get any breaks in between subtests during the real thing.

After you complete the entire sample test, check your answers against the answer explanations and key in Chapter 21.

Answer Sheet for Practice Exam 2

Subtest 1: General Science

1. Ⓐ Ⓑ Ⓒ Ⓓ
2. Ⓐ Ⓑ Ⓒ Ⓓ
3. Ⓐ Ⓑ Ⓒ Ⓓ
4. Ⓐ Ⓑ Ⓒ Ⓓ
5. Ⓐ Ⓑ Ⓒ Ⓓ
6. Ⓐ Ⓑ Ⓒ Ⓓ
7. Ⓐ Ⓑ Ⓒ Ⓓ
8. Ⓐ Ⓑ Ⓒ Ⓓ
9. Ⓐ Ⓑ Ⓒ Ⓓ
10. Ⓐ Ⓑ Ⓒ Ⓓ
11. Ⓐ Ⓑ Ⓒ Ⓓ
12. Ⓐ Ⓑ Ⓒ Ⓓ
13. Ⓐ Ⓑ Ⓒ Ⓓ
14. Ⓐ Ⓑ Ⓒ Ⓓ
15. Ⓐ Ⓑ Ⓒ Ⓓ
16. Ⓐ Ⓑ Ⓒ Ⓓ
17. Ⓐ Ⓑ Ⓒ Ⓓ
18. Ⓐ Ⓑ Ⓒ Ⓓ
19. Ⓐ Ⓑ Ⓒ Ⓓ
20. Ⓐ Ⓑ Ⓒ Ⓓ
21. Ⓐ Ⓑ Ⓒ Ⓓ
22. Ⓐ Ⓑ Ⓒ Ⓓ
23. Ⓐ Ⓑ Ⓒ Ⓓ
24. Ⓐ Ⓑ Ⓒ Ⓓ
25. Ⓐ Ⓑ Ⓒ Ⓓ

Subtest 2: Arithmetic Reasoning

1. Ⓐ Ⓑ Ⓒ Ⓓ
2. Ⓐ Ⓑ Ⓒ Ⓓ
3. Ⓐ Ⓑ Ⓒ Ⓓ
4. Ⓐ Ⓑ Ⓒ Ⓓ
5. Ⓐ Ⓑ Ⓒ Ⓓ
6. Ⓐ Ⓑ Ⓒ Ⓓ
7. Ⓐ Ⓑ Ⓒ Ⓓ
8. Ⓐ Ⓑ Ⓒ Ⓓ
9. Ⓐ Ⓑ Ⓒ Ⓓ
10. Ⓐ Ⓑ Ⓒ Ⓓ
11. Ⓐ Ⓑ Ⓒ Ⓓ
12. Ⓐ Ⓑ Ⓒ Ⓓ
13. Ⓐ Ⓑ Ⓒ Ⓓ
14. Ⓐ Ⓑ Ⓒ Ⓓ
15. Ⓐ Ⓑ Ⓒ Ⓓ
16. Ⓐ Ⓑ Ⓒ Ⓓ
17. Ⓐ Ⓑ Ⓒ Ⓓ
18. Ⓐ Ⓑ Ⓒ Ⓓ
19. Ⓐ Ⓑ Ⓒ Ⓓ
20. Ⓐ Ⓑ Ⓒ Ⓓ
21. Ⓐ Ⓑ Ⓒ Ⓓ
22. Ⓐ Ⓑ Ⓒ Ⓓ
23. Ⓐ Ⓑ Ⓒ Ⓓ
24. Ⓐ Ⓑ Ⓒ Ⓓ
25. Ⓐ Ⓑ Ⓒ Ⓓ
26. Ⓐ Ⓑ Ⓒ Ⓓ
27. Ⓐ Ⓑ Ⓒ Ⓓ
28. Ⓐ Ⓑ Ⓒ Ⓓ
29. Ⓐ Ⓑ Ⓒ Ⓓ
30. Ⓐ Ⓑ Ⓒ Ⓓ

Subtest 3: Word Knowledge

1. Ⓐ Ⓑ Ⓒ Ⓓ
2. Ⓐ Ⓑ Ⓒ Ⓓ
3. Ⓐ Ⓑ Ⓒ Ⓓ
4. Ⓐ Ⓑ Ⓒ Ⓓ
5. Ⓐ Ⓑ Ⓒ Ⓓ
6. Ⓐ Ⓑ Ⓒ Ⓓ
7. Ⓐ Ⓑ Ⓒ Ⓓ
8. Ⓐ Ⓑ Ⓒ Ⓓ
9. Ⓐ Ⓑ Ⓒ Ⓓ
10. Ⓐ Ⓑ Ⓒ Ⓓ
11. Ⓐ Ⓑ Ⓒ Ⓓ
12. Ⓐ Ⓑ Ⓒ Ⓓ
13. Ⓐ Ⓑ Ⓒ Ⓓ
14. Ⓐ Ⓑ Ⓒ Ⓓ
15. Ⓐ Ⓑ Ⓒ Ⓓ
16. Ⓐ Ⓑ Ⓒ Ⓓ
17. Ⓐ Ⓑ Ⓒ Ⓓ
18. Ⓐ Ⓑ Ⓒ Ⓓ
19. Ⓐ Ⓑ Ⓒ Ⓓ
20. Ⓐ Ⓑ Ⓒ Ⓓ
21. Ⓐ Ⓑ Ⓒ Ⓓ
22. Ⓐ Ⓑ Ⓒ Ⓓ
23. Ⓐ Ⓑ Ⓒ Ⓓ
24. Ⓐ Ⓑ Ⓒ Ⓓ
25. Ⓐ Ⓑ Ⓒ Ⓓ
26. Ⓐ Ⓑ Ⓒ Ⓓ
27. Ⓐ Ⓑ Ⓒ Ⓓ
28. Ⓐ Ⓑ Ⓒ Ⓓ
29. Ⓐ Ⓑ Ⓒ Ⓓ
30. Ⓐ Ⓑ Ⓒ Ⓓ
31. Ⓐ Ⓑ Ⓒ Ⓓ
32. Ⓐ Ⓑ Ⓒ Ⓓ
33. Ⓐ Ⓑ Ⓒ Ⓓ
34. Ⓐ Ⓑ Ⓒ Ⓓ
35. Ⓐ Ⓑ Ⓒ Ⓓ

Subtest 4: Paragraph Comprehension

1. Ⓐ Ⓑ Ⓒ Ⓓ
2. Ⓐ Ⓑ Ⓒ Ⓓ
3. Ⓐ Ⓑ Ⓒ Ⓓ
4. Ⓐ Ⓑ Ⓒ Ⓓ
5. Ⓐ Ⓑ Ⓒ Ⓓ
6. Ⓐ Ⓑ Ⓒ Ⓓ
7. Ⓐ Ⓑ Ⓒ Ⓓ
8. Ⓐ Ⓑ Ⓒ Ⓓ
9. Ⓐ Ⓑ Ⓒ Ⓓ
10. Ⓐ Ⓑ Ⓒ Ⓓ
11. Ⓐ Ⓑ Ⓒ Ⓓ
12. Ⓐ Ⓑ Ⓒ Ⓓ
13. Ⓐ Ⓑ Ⓒ Ⓓ
14. Ⓐ Ⓑ Ⓒ Ⓓ
15. Ⓐ Ⓑ Ⓒ Ⓓ

Subtest 5: Mathematics Knowledge

1. Ⓐ Ⓑ Ⓒ Ⓓ
2. Ⓐ Ⓑ Ⓒ Ⓓ
3. Ⓐ Ⓑ Ⓒ Ⓓ
4. Ⓐ Ⓑ Ⓒ Ⓓ
5. Ⓐ Ⓑ Ⓒ Ⓓ
6. Ⓐ Ⓑ Ⓒ Ⓓ
7. Ⓐ Ⓑ Ⓒ Ⓓ
8. Ⓐ Ⓑ Ⓒ Ⓓ
9. Ⓐ Ⓑ Ⓒ Ⓓ
10. Ⓐ Ⓑ Ⓒ Ⓓ
11. Ⓐ Ⓑ Ⓒ Ⓓ
12. Ⓐ Ⓑ Ⓒ Ⓓ
13. Ⓐ Ⓑ Ⓒ Ⓓ
14. Ⓐ Ⓑ Ⓒ Ⓓ
15. Ⓐ Ⓑ Ⓒ Ⓓ
16. Ⓐ Ⓑ Ⓒ Ⓓ
17. Ⓐ Ⓑ Ⓒ Ⓓ
18. Ⓐ Ⓑ Ⓒ Ⓓ
19. Ⓐ Ⓑ Ⓒ Ⓓ
20. Ⓐ Ⓑ Ⓒ Ⓓ
21. Ⓐ Ⓑ Ⓒ Ⓓ
22. Ⓐ Ⓑ Ⓒ Ⓓ
23. Ⓐ Ⓑ Ⓒ Ⓓ
24. Ⓐ Ⓑ Ⓒ Ⓓ
25. Ⓐ Ⓑ Ⓒ Ⓓ

Subtest 6: Electronics Information

1. Ⓐ Ⓑ Ⓒ Ⓓ
2. Ⓐ Ⓑ Ⓒ Ⓓ
3. Ⓐ Ⓑ Ⓒ Ⓓ
4. Ⓐ Ⓑ Ⓒ Ⓓ
5. Ⓐ Ⓑ Ⓒ Ⓓ
6. Ⓐ Ⓑ Ⓒ Ⓓ
7. Ⓐ Ⓑ Ⓒ Ⓓ
8. Ⓐ Ⓑ Ⓒ Ⓓ
9. Ⓐ Ⓑ Ⓒ Ⓓ
10. Ⓐ Ⓑ Ⓒ Ⓓ
11. Ⓐ Ⓑ Ⓒ Ⓓ
12. Ⓐ Ⓑ Ⓒ Ⓓ
13. Ⓐ Ⓑ Ⓒ Ⓓ
14. Ⓐ Ⓑ Ⓒ Ⓓ
15. Ⓐ Ⓑ Ⓒ Ⓓ
16. Ⓐ Ⓑ Ⓒ Ⓓ
17. Ⓐ Ⓑ Ⓒ Ⓓ
18. Ⓐ Ⓑ Ⓒ Ⓓ
19. Ⓐ Ⓑ Ⓒ Ⓓ
20. Ⓐ Ⓑ Ⓒ Ⓓ

Subtest 7: Auto & Shop Information

1. Ⓐ Ⓑ Ⓒ Ⓓ
2. Ⓐ Ⓑ Ⓒ Ⓓ
3. Ⓐ Ⓑ Ⓒ Ⓓ
4. Ⓐ Ⓑ Ⓒ Ⓓ
5. Ⓐ Ⓑ Ⓒ Ⓓ
6. Ⓐ Ⓑ Ⓒ Ⓓ
7. Ⓐ Ⓑ Ⓒ Ⓓ
8. Ⓐ Ⓑ Ⓒ Ⓓ
9. Ⓐ Ⓑ Ⓒ Ⓓ
10. Ⓐ Ⓑ Ⓒ Ⓓ
11. Ⓐ Ⓑ Ⓒ Ⓓ
12. Ⓐ Ⓑ Ⓒ Ⓓ
13. Ⓐ Ⓑ Ⓒ Ⓓ
14. Ⓐ Ⓑ Ⓒ Ⓓ
15. Ⓐ Ⓑ Ⓒ Ⓓ
16. Ⓐ Ⓑ Ⓒ Ⓓ
17. Ⓐ Ⓑ Ⓒ Ⓓ
18. Ⓐ Ⓑ Ⓒ Ⓓ
19. Ⓐ Ⓑ Ⓒ Ⓓ
20. Ⓐ Ⓑ Ⓒ Ⓓ
21. Ⓐ Ⓑ Ⓒ Ⓓ
22. Ⓐ Ⓑ Ⓒ Ⓓ
23. Ⓐ Ⓑ Ⓒ Ⓓ
24. Ⓐ Ⓑ Ⓒ Ⓓ
25. Ⓐ Ⓑ Ⓒ Ⓓ

Subtest 8: Mechanical Comprehension

1. Ⓐ Ⓑ Ⓒ Ⓓ
2. Ⓐ Ⓑ Ⓒ Ⓓ
3. Ⓐ Ⓑ Ⓒ Ⓓ
4. Ⓐ Ⓑ Ⓒ Ⓓ
5. Ⓐ Ⓑ Ⓒ Ⓓ
6. Ⓐ Ⓑ Ⓒ Ⓓ
7. Ⓐ Ⓑ Ⓒ Ⓓ
8. Ⓐ Ⓑ Ⓒ Ⓓ
9. Ⓐ Ⓑ Ⓒ Ⓓ
10. Ⓐ Ⓑ Ⓒ Ⓓ
11. Ⓐ Ⓑ Ⓒ Ⓓ
12. Ⓐ Ⓑ Ⓒ Ⓓ
13. Ⓐ Ⓑ Ⓒ Ⓓ
14. Ⓐ Ⓑ Ⓒ Ⓓ
15. Ⓐ Ⓑ Ⓒ Ⓓ
16. Ⓐ Ⓑ Ⓒ Ⓓ
17. Ⓐ Ⓑ Ⓒ Ⓓ
18. Ⓐ Ⓑ Ⓒ Ⓓ
19. Ⓐ Ⓑ Ⓒ Ⓓ
20. Ⓐ Ⓑ Ⓒ Ⓓ
21. Ⓐ Ⓑ Ⓒ Ⓓ
22. Ⓐ Ⓑ Ⓒ Ⓓ
23. Ⓐ Ⓑ Ⓒ Ⓓ
24. Ⓐ Ⓑ Ⓒ Ⓓ
25. Ⓐ Ⓑ Ⓒ Ⓓ

Subtest 9: Assembling Objects

1. Ⓐ Ⓑ Ⓒ Ⓓ
2. Ⓐ Ⓑ Ⓒ Ⓓ
3. Ⓐ Ⓑ Ⓒ Ⓓ
4. Ⓐ Ⓑ Ⓒ Ⓓ
5. Ⓐ Ⓑ Ⓒ Ⓓ
6. Ⓐ Ⓑ Ⓒ Ⓓ
7. Ⓐ Ⓑ Ⓒ Ⓓ
8. Ⓐ Ⓑ Ⓒ Ⓓ
9. Ⓐ Ⓑ Ⓒ Ⓓ
10. Ⓐ Ⓑ Ⓒ Ⓓ
11. Ⓐ Ⓑ Ⓒ Ⓓ
12. Ⓐ Ⓑ Ⓒ Ⓓ
13. Ⓐ Ⓑ Ⓒ Ⓓ
14. Ⓐ Ⓑ Ⓒ Ⓓ
15. Ⓐ Ⓑ Ⓒ Ⓓ
16. Ⓐ Ⓑ Ⓒ Ⓓ
17. Ⓐ Ⓑ Ⓒ Ⓓ
18. Ⓐ Ⓑ Ⓒ Ⓓ
19. Ⓐ Ⓑ Ⓒ Ⓓ
20. Ⓐ Ⓑ Ⓒ Ⓓ
21. Ⓐ Ⓑ Ⓒ Ⓓ
22. Ⓐ Ⓑ Ⓒ Ⓓ
23. Ⓐ Ⓑ Ⓒ Ⓓ
24. Ⓐ Ⓑ Ⓒ Ⓓ
25. Ⓐ Ⓑ Ⓒ Ⓓ

Subtest 1: General Science

TIME: 11 minutes for 25 questions

DIRECTIONS: This exam tests your knowledge of general science principles usually covered in high school classes. Pick the best answer for each question and then mark the space on your answer sheet that corresponds to the question number and the letter indicating your choice.

1. What is the change in body form that some insects undergo from birth to maturity?
   - (A) transformation
   - (B) metamorphosis
   - (C) trinity
   - (D) transmutation

2. An earthquake that measures 4 on the Richter scale would be how many times stronger than an earthquake that measured 2?
   - (A) 2 times stronger
   - (B) 4 times stronger
   - (C) 10 times stronger
   - (D) 100 times stronger

3. Muscles attach to bone with
   - (A) nonconnective tissue.
   - (B) ligaments.
   - (C) tendons.
   - (D) rubber bands.

4. The male part of a flower is called
   - (A) the stamen.
   - (B) the pistil.
   - (C) the throttle.
   - (D) stubborn.

5. Blood leaving the lungs is
   - (A) hydrogenated.
   - (B) coagulated.
   - (C) watery.
   - (D) oxygenated.

6. Of these, which river is the longest?
   - (A) Mississippi
   - (B) Nile
   - (C) Colorado
   - (D) Congo

7. The branch of science that studies matter and energy is called
   - (A) chemistry.
   - (B) physics.
   - (C) oceanography.
   - (D) trigonometry.

8. Which type of cloud's name comes from the Latin word meaning "rain"?
   - (A) nimbus
   - (B) cirrus
   - (C) strato
   - (D) alto

9. Deoxyribonucleic acid is better known as
   - (A) antacid.
   - (B) carbohydrates.
   - (C) triglyceride.
   - (D) DNA.

10. The instrument used to measure wind speed is
    - (A) barometer.
    - (B) anemometer.
    - (C) altimeter.
    - (D) fanometer.

11. Electric charges can be
    - (A) positive or negative.
    - (B) positive or neutral.
    - (C) negative or neutral.
    - (D) neutral only.

12. Which planet in the solar system has the most moons?
    - (A) Neptune
    - (B) Saturn
    - (C) Jupiter
    - (D) Uranus

CHAPTER 20 Practice Exam 2

13. The law of universal gravitation was discovered by
    (A) Albert Einstein.
    (B) Isaac Newton.
    (C) Alexander Graham Bell.
    (D) Rod Powers.

14. Which U.S. space program is responsible for putting 12 men on the moon?
    (A) Gemini
    (B) Titan
    (C) Voyager
    (D) Apollo

15. Animals that eat both plants and animals are called
    (A) herbivores.
    (B) carnivores.
    (C) omnivores.
    (D) ambidextrous.

16. Unlike most other fish, sharks have no
    (A) gills.
    (B) bones.
    (C) liver.
    (D) heart.

17. What human organ is responsible for detoxification of blood?
    (A) liver
    (B) kidneys
    (C) intestines
    (D) stomach

18. Kinetic energy is the energy that
    (A) is produced by sound waves.
    (B) an object potentially has.
    (C) is possessed by a moving object.
    (D) results from the attraction of two magnets.

19. The terrestrial planets consist of
    (A) Jupiter, Saturn, Uranus, and Neptune.
    (B) Pluto and Neptune.
    (C) Mercury, Venus, Earth, and Mars.
    (D) any planet.

20. An example of a mineral is
    (A) calcium.
    (B) vitamin C.
    (C) granite.
    (D) almonds.

21. Which animal has the heaviest brain?
    (A) human
    (B) elephant
    (C) rhinoceros
    (D) sperm whale

22. The sun is what type of star?
    (A) O type
    (B) G type
    (C) F type
    (D) M type

23. Molecules are created when
    (A) matter is created.
    (B) matter is destroyed.
    (C) atoms combine together.
    (D) atoms are separated.

24. An example of an embryonic plant would be a
    (A) tree.
    (B) rose.
    (C) seed.
    (D) cabbage.

25. The vernal equinox is
    (A) the first day of winter.
    (B) near the equator.
    (C) the first day of spring.
    (D) a lunar eclipse.

Subtest 2: Arithmetic Reasoning

TIME: 36 minutes for 30 questions

DIRECTIONS: The questions in the arithmetic test are each followed by four possible answers. Decide which answer is correct and then mark the space on your answer sheet that has the same number and letter as your choice. Use scratch paper for any figuring you need to do. Calculators are not allowed.

1. If you roll two six-sided dice, what's the probability of not rolling a five on either die?
   - (A) $\frac{1}{36}$
   - (B) $\frac{1}{6}$
   - (C) $\frac{4}{36}$
   - (D) $\frac{25}{36}$

2. Jack loaned Bob $1,500 at an annual interest rate of 7%. If Bob makes no payments, how much will he owe Jack after one year?
   - (A) $105
   - (B) $1,500
   - (C) $1,605
   - (D) $1,507

3. A 2-ton truck is taxed at a rate of $0.12 per pound. How much is the total tax bill?
   - (A) $480
   - (B) $240
   - (C) $120
   - (D) $600

4. If $ab = 10$ and $a^2 + b^2 = 30$, solve for y in the equation $y = (a+b)^2$.
   - (A) 40
   - (B) 45
   - (C) 50
   - (D) 55

5. A half-pint of cream is what part of a gallon?
   - (A) $\frac{1}{8}$
   - (B) $\frac{1}{4}$
   - (C) $\frac{1}{16}$
   - (D) $\frac{1}{6}$

6. The cost of a protein bar increased from $2.50 to $2.80. The percent increase to the $2.80 rate was how much?
   - (A) 16%
   - (B) 10%
   - (C) 15%
   - (D) 12%

7. An aircraft flies over Boondock Air Force Base at 10:20 a.m. At 10:32 a.m., the aircraft passes over Sea Side Naval Air Station, 120 miles away. How fast is the aircraft traveling?
   - (A) 400 mph
   - (B) 500 mph
   - (C) 600 mph
   - (D) 700 mph

8. Last year, Margot grew 50 bushels of corn in her backyard. This year, the yield has increased 8%. How many bushels of corn did Margot grow this year?
   - (A) 56
   - (B) 52
   - (C) 60
   - (D) 54

9. Junior has saved money in his piggy bank over the winter. He wants to buy a $30 computer game. If he has 14 one-dollar bills, 16 half dollars, 12 quarters, 8 dimes, 25 nickels, and 10 pennies, how much more does he need to borrow from Dad to buy the game?
   - (A) $27.15
   - (B) $2.85
   - (C) $2.95
   - (D) $1.85

CHAPTER 20 Practice Exam 2   433

10. Debbie receives a weekly salary of $80, plus a 5% commission on any sales. During the week, she has $800 in total sales. What's the ratio of her commission to her salary?

    (A) 2:1
    (B) 1:2
    (C) 3:1
    (D) 1:3

11. How many 1-quart cans can be filled from 25 gallons of paint?

    (A) 50
    (B) 75
    (C) 100
    (D) 80

12. If a crew of four people can paint the barn in three days, how long will it take a crew of two people?

    (A) 4 days
    (B) $1\frac{1}{2}$ days
    (C) 8 days
    (D) 6 days

13. Brian works for five hours and is paid $24. Christina works for three hours and is paid $10.95. How much more per hour does Brian make than Christina?

    (A) $1.15
    (B) $1.25
    (C) $1.35
    (D) $1.37

14. Margaret is getting married and must be ready by 11:15 a.m. If it's now 8:30 a.m., how much time does she have to get ready?

    (A) $1\frac{1}{2}$ hours
    (B) $2\frac{1}{2}$ hours
    (C) $2\frac{3}{4}$ hours
    (D) $2\frac{1}{3}$ hours

15. An accounting-firm employee is asked to shred 900 documents. If they can shred documents at a rate of 7 per minute, the number of documents remaining after $1\frac{1}{2}$ hours of shredding is

    (A) 630
    (B) 90
    (C) 270
    (D) 810

16. A home stereo depreciates by 20% each year. What's the value of a stereo, purchased new for $1,200, after two years?

    (A) $768
    (B) $693
    (C) $827
    (D) $654

17. Janet's old pickup truck can only reach a speed of 45 miles per hour. If she drives at top speed, how long will it take her to reach a city 135 miles away?

    (A) 3 hours
    (B) 2 hours
    (C) 4 hours
    (D) $2\frac{1}{2}$ hours

18. A blouse normally costs $18.50. How much money is saved if the blouse is purchased at a 20% discount?

    (A) $1.85
    (B) $14.80
    (C) $4.50
    (D) $3.70

19. A clerk's weekly salary of $320 is increased to $360. The percent increase is

    (A) $10\frac{1}{2}$%
    (B) 11%
    (C) $12\frac{1}{2}$%
    (D) 12%

20. Go-Cart One and Go-Cart Two are on a 360-foot circular track. There is a camera at the center of the track for each go-cart. Camera One is following Go-Cart One, and Camera Two is following Go-Cart Two. If the angle between the two cameras is 40 degrees, how far apart are the two go-carts?

- (A) 30 feet
- (B) 40 feet
- (C) 50 feet
- (D) 60 feet

21. Dinner at a nice restaurant costs $35.98. If Joan gave the cashier $40.00, how much change should she get back?

- (A) $5.02
- (B) $4.02
- (C) $3.92
- (D) $1.02

22. A balloonist circumnavigated the globe in 13 days, 12 hours, 16 minutes, and 13 seconds. A plane circumnavigated the globe in 4 days, 10 hours, 15 minutes, and 7 seconds. How much longer did it take for the balloon to go around the world?

- (A) 12 days, 7 hours, 11 minutes, and 35 seconds
- (B) 9 days, 2 hours, 1 minute, and 6 seconds
- (C) 8 days, 14 hours, 16 minutes, and 6 seconds
- (D) 9 days, 7 hours, 3 minutes, and 20 seconds

23. Darlene bought 12 boxes of cookies for $48.00. What was the cost of each box of cookies?

- (A) $4.00
- (B) $0.48
- (C) $0.40
- (D) $4.80

24. A tuneup increases a car's fuel efficiency by 5%. If a car averaged 20 miles per gallon before the tuneup, how many miles per gallon will it average after the tuneup?

- (A) 25
- (B) 22
- (C) $20\frac{1}{2}$
- (D) 21

25. A lumberjack wishes to drive a spike through the center of a tree with a circumference of 43.96 feet. What's the minimum length of the spike needed to go completely through the tree, passing through the center?

- (A) 14 feet
- (B) 15 feet
- (C) 16 feet
- (D) 17 feet

26. A bin of hard candy holds $10\frac{1}{2}$ pounds. How many $\frac{3}{4}$-pound boxes of candy can be filled from the bin?

- (A) 30 boxes
- (B) $15\frac{1}{4}$ boxes
- (C) $7\frac{7}{8}$ boxes
- (D) 14 boxes

27. A patio measures 12 feet by 14 feet. How many 8-inch-square paving stones are needed to pave the patio?

- (A) 21
- (B) 252
- (C) 378
- (D) 168

28. A computer programmer is making $25,000 per year, and 28% of their salary is withheld for federal and state deductions. How much is the computer programmer's net pay?

- (A) $20,000
- (B) $7,000
- (C) $18,750
- (D) $18,000

29. Pam cuts a pie in half in a straight line. She then cuts a line from the center to the edge, creating a 55-degree angle. What's the supplement of that angle?

(A) 55 degrees
(B) 125 degrees
(C) 70 degrees
(D) 35 degrees

30. A stack of lumber is 6 feet high. If each piece of lumber is 4 inches thick, how many pieces of lumber are in the stack?

(A) 72
(B) 12
(C) 18
(D) 10

Subtest 3: Word Knowledge

TIME: 11 minutes for 35 questions

DIRECTIONS: This test's questions cover the meanings of words. Each question has an underlined word. You may be asked to decide which one of the four words in the choices most nearly means the same thing as the underlined word or which one of the four words means the opposite. If the underlined word is used in a sentence, decide which of the four choices most nearly means the same thing as the underlined word as used in the context of the sentence. Mark the corresponding space on your answer sheet.

1. Abeyance most nearly means
   - (A) trustworthiness.
   - (B) passion.
   - (C) suspension.
   - (D) business.

2. It was a sturdy table.
   - (A) well-built
   - (B) ugly
   - (C) thick
   - (D) small

3. Bullock most nearly means
   - (A) ox.
   - (B) inattentive.
   - (C) lazy.
   - (D) panther.

4. Brevity is the soul of wit.
   - (A) beauty
   - (B) intelligence
   - (C) clarity
   - (D) humor

5. Paradigm most nearly means
   - (A) twenty cents.
   - (B) model.
   - (C) heaven.
   - (D) basis.

6. My manger facilitated my promotion.
   - (A) hindered
   - (B) helped
   - (C) disliked
   - (D) ignored

7. Quiescence most nearly means
   - (A) kill.
   - (B) preserve.
   - (C) small.
   - (D) quiet.

8. The spectator enjoyed the game.
   - (A) competitor
   - (B) observer
   - (C) referee
   - (D) organizer

9. Joy reclined against the far wall.
   - (A) sat
   - (B) leaned
   - (C) jumped
   - (D) paraded

10. The teacher cited some examples.
    - (A) memorized
    - (B) finished
    - (C) quoted
    - (D) examined

11. Surround most nearly means
    - (A) line.
    - (B) benefit.
    - (C) encircle.
    - (D) speaker.

12. Illustrious most nearly means
    - (A) illustrated.
    - (B) famous.
    - (C) foolish.
    - (D) intelligent.

13. Inhabitant most nearly means
    (A) invalid.
    (B) nun.
    (C) seeker.
    (D) dweller.

14. Tim had a penchant for engaging in subterfuge.
    (A) religion
    (B) intrigue
    (C) gambling
    (D) danger

15. Megan found the adults' costumes to be ghastly.
    (A) hideous
    (B) cute
    (C) large
    (D) comfortable

16. Rigid most nearly means
    (A) strong.
    (B) weak.
    (C) pliable.
    (D) inflexible.

17. Billy yearned to join the fraternal organization.
    (A) brotherly
    (B) large
    (C) fun
    (D) special

18. Deplore most nearly means
    (A) accept.
    (B) insult.
    (C) disapprove.
    (D) salute.

19. Meager most nearly means
    (A) space.
    (B) sparse.
    (C) brief.
    (D) thirsty.

20. Weal most nearly means
    (A) happiness.
    (B) blow.
    (C) scream.
    (D) tire.

21. To be guileless, I think your hair looks ugly.
    (A) helpful
    (B) kind
    (C) frank
    (D) serious

22. The customs agent confiscated the goods.
    (A) bought
    (B) noticed
    (C) seized
    (D) stole

23. Dubious most nearly means
    (A) long.
    (B) beautiful.
    (C) articulate.
    (D) doubtful.

24. Illusion most nearly means
    (A) mirage.
    (B) distant.
    (C) sight.
    (D) perspective.

25. Becky developed a sudden craving for ice cream.
    (A) disgust
    (B) passion
    (C) hatred
    (D) desire

26. Enmity most nearly means
    (A) enemy.
    (B) hostility.
    (C) anger.
    (D) childish.

27. Arbor most nearly means
    (A) native.
    (B) tree.
    (C) travel.
    (D) delirious.

28. They terminated the contract.
    (A) bought
    (B) extended
    (C) sold
    (D) ended

29. Tim always considered Chuck to be a big buffoon.
    (A) clown
    (B) help
    (C) liar
    (D) pain

30. Null most nearly means
    (A) zero.
    (B) dull.
    (C) unskilled.
    (D) rapid.

31. Tom had to provide proof to the judge that he was not indigent.
    (A) guilty
    (B) rich
    (C) poor
    (D) ugly

32. Impertinent most nearly means
    (A) fun.
    (B) boring.
    (C) rude.
    (D) impatient.

33. Lustrous most nearly means
    (A) expensive.
    (B) lazy.
    (C) cold.
    (D) polished.

34. Pardon most nearly means
    (A) courtesy.
    (B) excuse.
    (C) believe.
    (D) respect.

35. Veracious most nearly means
    (A) fast.
    (B) slow.
    (C) equal.
    (D) truthful.

Subtest 4: Paragraph Comprehension

TIME: 13 minutes for 15 questions

DIRECTIONS: This test measures your ability to understand what you read. This section includes one or more paragraphs of reading material followed by incomplete statements or questions. Read the paragraph and select the choice that best completes the statement or answers the question.

Questions 1 and 2 are based on the following passage.

There is not a single town of any size within a distance of forty miles, yet already the rural population of this county is quite large. The whole country, within a wide circuit north, south, east, and west, partakes of the same general character; mountain ridges, half tilled, half wood, screening cultivated valleys, sprinkled with farms and hamlets, among which some pretty stream generally winds its way. The waters in our immediate neighborhood all flow to the southward, though only a few miles to the north of our village, the brooks are found running in an opposite course, this valley lying just within the borders of the dividing ridge. The river itself, though farther south it becomes one of the great streams of the country, cannot boast of much breadth so near its source, and running quietly among the meadows, half screened by the groves and thickets, scarcely shows in the general view.

1. According to this passage,
   (A) the author lives in a large city.
   (B) the author lives in the country.
   (C) the author lives on the seashore.
   (D) the author lives on Mars.

2. According to this passage, the brooks are running in which direction within the author's neighborhood?
   (A) north
   (B) south
   (C) east
   (D) west

The Panama Canal is a ship canal that cuts through the Isthmus of Panama, connecting the Atlantic and Pacific oceans. Although several foreign companies tried to build the canal throughout the 19th century, none were successful. After the U.S. helped Panama revolt against Colombia, the U.S. was given rights to the land the canal occupied. The U.S. government finished the canal in 1914.

3. According to this passage,
   (A) Panama and Colombia fought a war over the Panama Canal.
   (B) the U.S. was given rights to the canal land.
   (C) foreign companies built the canal before the U.S. stepped in.
   (D) Panama built the canal in 1914.

Extreme care must be exercised to ensure proper handling and cleaning of soiled U.S. flags. A torn flag may be professionally mended, but a badly torn or tattered flag should be destroyed. When the flag is in such a condition that it's no longer a fitting emblem for display, destroy it in a dignified manner, preferably by burning.

4. According to this passage, torn flags should be
   (A) mended.
   (B) burned.
   (C) destroyed.
   (D) all of the above.

Medieval guilds were similar to modern-day labor unions. These groups of merchants or craftspeople set rules regarding economic activity in order to protect themselves. Some guilds held considerable economic power, but even small guilds protected members. Guilds also served a social purpose.

5. According to this passage, guilds
   (A) had only one purpose.
   (B) had little in common with modern labor unions.
   (C) exploited workers.
   (D) held considerable economic power.

After a series of well-publicized failures by various inventors, Orville and Wilbur Wright succeeded in flying and controlling a heavier-than-air craft on December 17, 1903. The War Department, stung by its investment in a failed effort by Samuel Langley and compounded by the Wrights' own secretiveness, initially rejected the brothers' overtures toward the government to buy the aircraft. Prevailing sentiments held that the immediate future still belonged to the balloon. In August 1908, the two brothers delivered the first Army aircraft to the U.S. Government. That the U.S. Government managed to purchase an airplane was a minor miracle. For more than four years after the Wright brothers' successful flight at Kitty Hawk, North Carolina, the government refused to accept the fact that man had flown in a heavier-than-air machine.

6. Which of the following statements is not supported by the above passage?
   (A) The U.S. Government felt that balloons were more practical than airplanes.
   (B) The Wright brothers' own secretiveness contributed to their problems in getting the government interested in their aircraft.
   (C) The historic flight took place on the East Coast.
   (D) It took more than six years for the Wright brothers to interest the U.S. Government in their airplane.

If anyone should be inclined to overrate the state of our present knowledge of mental life, all that would be needed to force him to assume a modest attitude would be to remind him of the function of memory. No psychologic theory has yet been able to account for the connection between the fundamental phenomena of remembering and forgetting; indeed, even the complete analysis of that which one can actually observe has as yet scarcely been grasped. Today forgetting has perhaps grown more puzzling than remembering, especially since we have learned from the study of dreams and pathologic states that even what for a long time we believed forgotten may suddenly return to consciousness.

7. The primary subject of this paragraph is
   (A) bowling.
   (B) puzzles.
   (C) memory.
   (D) government service.

Troy weight is based on a pound of 12 ounces and an ounce of 480 grains. Common, or avoirdupois, weight is based on a pound having 16 ounces and an ounce having 437.5 grains. A common pound has 7,000 grains while a troy pound has 5,760.

8. According to this passage,
   (A) in common weight, an ounce is less than 438 grains.
   (B) a troy pound and a common pound are the same weight.
   (C) common weight and avoirdupois weight are different measures.
   (D) a troy ounce equals 437.5 grains.

Good leaders get involved in their subordinates' careers. People merely obey arbitrary commands and orders, but they respond quickly and usually give extra effort for leaders who genuinely care for them. An often neglected leadership principle in today's environment of technology and specialization is knowing the workers and showing sincere interest in their problems, career development, and welfare. Leadership is reflected in the degree of efficiency, productivity, morale, and motivation demonstrated by subordinates. Leadership involvement is the key ingredient to maximizing worker performance.

9. A key leadership principle that's often ignored is
   (A) leading by example.
   (B) showing sincere interest in the problems of the workers.
   (C) ensuring workers have access to the most modern technology.
   (D) maximizing worker performance.

Leukemia is a blood disease in which white blood cells in the blood or bone marrow reproduce rapidly, interfering with the body's ability to produce red blood cells. Red blood cells are needed to perform vital bodily functions.

10. According to this passage,

  (A) white blood cells perform no vital function in the body.
  (B) no treatment for leukemia exists.
  (C) leukemia makes it hard for the body to produce red blood cells.
  (D) white blood cells are found only in the blood.

Questions 11 and 12 are based on the following passage.

Any discussion of distinctive military capabilities would be incomplete without looking at their relationship to the Joint Service vision of the future. JV 2020 guides all the Services into the next century with its vision of future war fighting. JV 2020 sets forth four overarching operational concepts: dominant maneuver, precision engagement, focused logistics, and full-dimensional protection. Each of these operational concepts reinforces the others. The aggregate of these four concepts, along with their interaction with information superiority and innovation, allows joint forces to dominate the full range of military operations from humanitarian assistance through peace operations to the highest intensity conflict.

11. According to the passage above, which of the following is not an operational concept?

  (A) dominant maneuver
  (B) focused logistics
  (C) high intensity conflict
  (D) precision engagement

12. The document discussed in the above passage is primarily about

  (A) military operations of the past.
  (B) present military operations.
  (C) military operations in the future.
  (D) training for future military operations.

Questions 13 through 15 are based on the following passage.

Genetics is a branch of science dealing with heredity. The field is concerned with how genes operate and the way genes are transmitted to offspring. Subdivisions in the field include cytogenetics, which is the study of the cellular basis of inheritance; microbial genetics, the study of inheritance in microbes; molecular genetics, the study of the biochemical foundation of inheritance; and human genetics, the study of how people inherit traits that are medically and socially important. Genetic counselors are primarily concerned with human genetics. They advise couples and families on the chances of their offspring having specific genetic defects.

13. In the passage above, cytogenetics is defined as

  (A) the study of the psychological impact of genetics.
  (B) the study of the cellular foundation of inheritance.
  (C) the study of molecular genetics.
  (D) the study of human genetics.

14. According to the passage, genetics

  (A) concerns how genes operate and how they're passed along.
  (B) is a field of study populated by quacks, fakes, and frauds.
  (C) is a field of study only concerned with human genetics.
  (D) is a new field of study.

15. According to the passage, it's reasonable to assume that genetic counseling

  (A) is restricted to the very rich.
  (B) is used to diagnose diseases.
  (C) can be used by parents to learn if their offspring are likely to inherit a disease one of the parents has.
  (D) can be used by parents to prevent their offspring from inheriting a specific genetic defect.

Subtest 5: Mathematics Knowledge

TIME: 24 minutes for 25 questions

DIRECTIONS: This test is a test of your ability to solve general mathematical problems. Select the correct answer from the choices given and then mark the corresponding space on your answer sheet. Use scratch paper to do any figuring.

1. $x^2(x^4) =$
   - (A) x^6
   - (B) x^8
   - (C) $2x^6$
   - (D) $2x^8$

2. If a rectangle has a perimeter of 36 feet and is 4 feet wide, what's its area?
   - (A) 56 square feet
   - (B) 128 square feet
   - (C) 112 square feet
   - (D) 16 square feet

3. The cube root of 64 is
   - (A) 3
   - (B) 9
   - (C) 2
   - (D) 4

4. Convert 314,000 to scientific notation.
   - (A) 3.14×10^5
   - (B) 3.14×10^{-5}
   - (C) 314×10
   - (D) 31.4×100

5. The reciprocal of $\frac{1}{6}$ is
   - (A) 1
   - (B) 3
   - (C) 6
   - (D) $\frac{1}{3}$

6. If $0.05 \div x = 1$, then $x =$
   - (A) 0.05
   - (B) 0.5
   - (C) 50.0
   - (D) 5.0

7. Factor $x^2 - 6x + 9$.
   - (A) $(x+6)(x+6)$
   - (B) $(x-6)(x+6)$
   - (C) $(x-3)^2$
   - (D) $(x+3)^2$

8. $(3 \times 2)(7-2)(6+2) = (6 \times 4)x$. What's the value of x?
   - (A) -5
   - (B) 5
   - (C) 10
   - (D) 1

9. Solve for x: $2x - 6 = x + 5$.
   - (A) 3
   - (B) 11
   - (C) 7
   - (D) 5

10. If $I = Prt$, and $P = \$1{,}000$, $r = 7\%$, and $t = 1$, what does I equal?
    - (A) $35
    - (B) $1,000
    - (C) $700
    - (D) $70

11. Solve for x in the equation $(x-7)^2 - 4 = (x+1)^2$.
    - (A) $2\frac{1}{2}$
    - (B) $2\frac{3}{4}$
    - (C) $4\frac{1}{2}$
    - (D) $4\frac{3}{4}$

12. A circle has a radius of 5 inches. What's its approximate area?

(A) 78.5 inches
(B) 70.0 inches
(C) 314.0 inches
(D) 25.0 inches

13. Solve the following inequality: $\frac{2}{3}(6x-9)+4 > 5x+1$.

(A) $x > 6$
(B) $x < 6$
(C) $x > -3$
(D) $x < -3$

14. A tube has a radius of 3 inches and a height of 5 inches. What's its approximate volume?

(A) 34 cubic inches
(B) 141 cubic inches
(C) 565 cubic inches
(D) 45 cubic inches

15. Triangle ABC (shown below) is a(n)

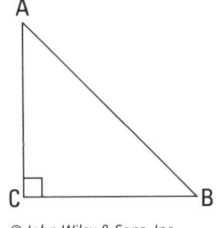

© John Wiley & Sons, Inc.

(A) right triangle.
(B) equilateral triangle.
(C) scalene triangle.
(D) isosceles triangle.

16. The following figure is what type of quadrilateral?

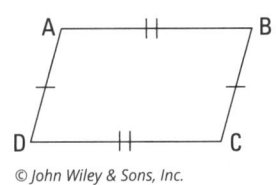

© John Wiley & Sons, Inc.

(A) square
(B) rhombus
(C) trapezoid
(D) parallelogram

17. The angle shown below is a(n)

© John Wiley & Sons, Inc.

(A) complementary angle.
(B) supplementary angle.
(C) acute angle.
(D) obtuse angle.

18. Solve for x: $-x^2 - x + 30 = 0$.

(A) 4, −8
(B) −6, 5
(C) −4, 5
(D) 6, −3

19. A square box has a volume of 64 cubic inches. What's the perimeter of one of its faces?

(A) 8 inches
(B) 16 inches
(C) 64 inches
(D) 32 inches

20. A cube has a volume of 27 cubic inches. What's its surface area?

   (A) 9 square inches
   (B) 6 square inches
   (C) 54 square inches
   (D) 4.5 square inches

21. $\left(x^3\right)^3 =$

   (A) $3x^3$
   (B) x^6
   (C) x^9
   (D) $2x^6$

22. $4! =$

   (A) 16
   (B) 40
   (C) 0
   (D) 24

23. If $a^3 + b^3 = a^3 + x^3$, then $b =$

   (A) $b^3 - a^3$
   (B) x
   (C) $a^3 - b^3$
   (D) a

24. What's the sum of the integers from 1 to 300?

   (A) 38,243
   (B) 45,150
   (C) 49,923
   (D) 52,024

25. $\left(y^2\right)^3 + y^2 =$

   (A) y^7
   (B) $y^6 + y^2$
   (C) $y^8 + y^2$
   (D) $3y^2$

Subtest 6: Electronics Information

TIME: 9 minutes for 20 questions

DIRECTIONS: This part tests your knowledge of electrical, radio, and electronics information. Select the correct response from the choices given and then mark the corresponding space on your answer sheet.

1. What is used to measure current that is going through a circuit?
   - (A) multimeter
   - (B) amp gauge
   - (C) currentometer
   - (D) tri-gauge

2. Which of the following isn't a component of a DC motor?
   - (A) rotor bars
   - (B) armature
   - (C) field poles
   - (D) yoke

3. The television broadcast standard in the United States is
   - (A) NTSC.
   - (B) RGB.
   - (C) SECAM.
   - (D) RTSC.

4. In a closed electrical circuit,
   - (A) one terminal is always positive, and one terminal is always negative.
   - (B) both terminals can be positive.
   - (C) both terminals can be negative.
   - (D) terminals are neither positive nor negative.

5. Electrical current is counted in what measurement?
   - (A) hertz
   - (B) voltage
   - (C) amps
   - (D) ohms

6. The following symbol is a/an

   © John Wiley & Sons, Inc.

   - (A) resistor.
   - (B) fuse.
   - (C) capacitor.
   - (D) inductor.

7. In the United States, what is the specification for an electrical outlet in a bathroom near a sink?
   - (A) If within 6 feet of a sink, an outlet must have a childproof cover.
   - (B) If within 2 feet of a sink, an outlet must not be GFCI protected.
   - (C) If within 6 feet of a sink, an outlet must be GFCI protected.
   - (D) If within 2 feet of a sink, an outlet must also be within reach of the bathtub.

8. The following symbol is a/an

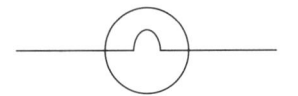

   © John Wiley & Sons, Inc.

   - (A) lamp.
   - (B) fuse.
   - (C) inductor.
   - (D) bell.

9. When a circuit breaker trips, in what position will you find the operating handle?
   - (A) on position
   - (B) off position
   - (C) halfway between on and off
   - (D) three-fourths of the way between the on position and the off position

10. Which wire is smallest?
    (A) 00 AWG
    (B) 4 AWG
    (C) 10 AWG
    (D) 12 AWG

11. Which of the following is the best conductor of electricity?
    (A) plastic
    (B) wood
    (C) aluminum
    (D) copper

12. How many paths of electrical flow can be found in a series circuit?
    (A) one
    (B) two
    (C) two or more
    (D) It can't be determined from the information given.

13. A microwave is rated at 1,200 watts. At 120 volts, how much current does it draw?
    (A) 1 amp
    (B) 10 amps
    (C) 100 amps
    (D) 1,440 amps

14. Electricians use the term *low potential* to refer to
    (A) electrical circuits with a low potential for overload.
    (B) building codes that reduce the risk of fire.
    (C) the likelihood of getting a raise this year.
    (D) 600 watts or less.

15. Which of the following isn't a conductor of electricity?
    (A) water
    (B) graphite
    (C) gold
    (D) glass

16. The ground wire is always
    (A) green.
    (B) black.
    (C) whitish.
    (D) blue.

17. What does AM mean?
    (A) amp metrics
    (B) alien mothers
    (C) amplitude modulation
    (D) anode matrix

18. Silver is a better conductor than copper. But copper is more often used because of
    (A) the cost of silver.
    (B) the brittleness of copper.
    (C) the low melting point of silver.
    (D) the tendency of silver to tarnish.

19. Electronic circuits that produce high frequencies are called
    (A) amplifiers.
    (B) regulators.
    (C) transformers.
    (D) oscillators.

20. If you plug an appliance designed for AC into a DC power source, the appliance
    (A) will operate normally.
    (B) will produce excessive heat.
    (C) won't operate.
    (D) will explode into tiny pieces.

Subtest 7: Auto & Shop Information

TIME: 11 minutes for 25 questions

DIRECTIONS: This test is about automobiles, shop practices, and the use of tools. Pick the best answer for each question and then mark the corresponding space on your answer sheet.

1. If a car uses too much oil, which of the following parts may be worn?
   - (A) camshaft
   - (B) connecting rods
   - (C) fuel pump
   - (D) piston rings

2. Clean air filters are important because
   - (A) dirty filters can cause a decrease in fuel mileage.
   - (B) they remove pollutants, which can decrease engine performance.
   - (C) they keep the oil from becoming contaminated.
   - (D) Both A and B.

3. The alternator
   - (A) starts the engine.
   - (B) supplies regulated power to the battery.
   - (C) connects the ignition system to the engine.
   - (D) can be used as an alternative to motor oil.

4. In which automotive system would you find a "wishbone"?
   - (A) suspension
   - (B) engine
   - (C) exhaust
   - (D) oil pan

5. If the electrolyte solution in a battery is too low, you should add
   - (A) sulfuric acid.
   - (B) antifreeze.
   - (C) distilled water.
   - (D) gasoline.

6. What area of your car should be flushed periodically to maintain optimum performance?
   - (A) exhaust system
   - (B) brake system
   - (C) cooling system
   - (D) ignition system

7. The primary purpose of a carburetor is to
   - (A) maintain engine timing.
   - (B) regulate oil pressure.
   - (C) mix fuel and air.
   - (D) monitor tire pressure.

8. Car restorers often seek NOS parts. What does NOS stand for?
   - (A) Near Original Specifications
   - (B) NASCAR Operating Standards
   - (C) New Old Stock
   - (D) none of the above

9. To make spark plugs work effectively, the coil and breaker

   (A) provide a gap between the electrodes.
   (B) ignite the spark.
   (C) transfer the electricity to the correct spark plug.
   (D) create a very high electrical voltage.

10. Schrader valves can be found in your car's

    (A) tires.
    (B) engine.
    (C) transmission.
    (D) electronic ignition.

11. A bent frame causes

    (A) improper tracking.
    (B) auto accidents.
    (C) poor visibility
    (D) excessive rust.

12. In the tire designation 205/55 R 15 92 H, what does the "H" signify?

    (A) tread type
    (B) tire height
    (C) maximum sustained speed
    (D) turning radius

13. When the tightness of screws and/or bolts is important, it's best to use

    (A) a screwdriver.
    (B) a torque wrench.
    (C) tin snips.
    (D) a coping saw.

14. Hammer faces are commonly made of each of the following materials EXCEPT

    (A) steel.
    (B) brass.
    (C) glass.
    (D) lead.

15. Hammers, mallets, and sledges are all striking tools, but mallets and sledges don't have

    (A) claws.
    (B) metal parts.
    (C) as much durability.
    (D) heads.

16. Round objects can be measured most exactly using a

    (A) rigid steel rule.
    (B) folding rule.
    (C) set of calipers.
    (D) depth gauge.

17. The best chisel to use when making a circular cut in metal is a

    (A) masonry chisel.
    (B) socket chisel.
    (C) butt chisel.
    (D) round chisel.

18. A Stillson wrench is a type of

    (A) strap wrench.
    (B) hammer.
    (C) plumb bob.
    (D) pipe wrench.

19. Painting on a surface with too much moisture

    (A) causes no problems.
    (B) causes bubbling.
    (C) requires an extra coat of paint.
    (D) takes longer.

20. A tool used to control the location and/or motion of another tool is called a

    (A) control tool.
    (B) jig.
    (C) nail.
    (D) static rectifier.

21. An 8-point saw

(A) has 7 teeth per inch.

(B) weighs 8 ounces.

(C) can saw 8 kinds of material.

(D) is 8 inches long.

22. Concrete is made by mixing

(A) cement.

(B) cement and water.

(C) liquid cement and chemical additives.

(D) mineral aggregate, a binder, and water.

23. Which of the following tools isn't used to cut metal?

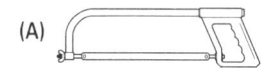

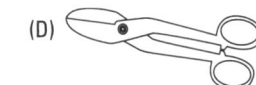

(A)   (C)

(B)   (D)

24. The following tool is used to

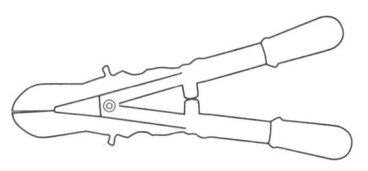

© John Wiley & Sons, Inc.

(A) cut tile.

(B) cut wire.

(C) turn screws.

(D) cut bolts.

25. The following tool is a(n)

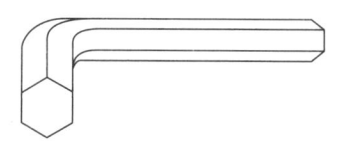

© John Wiley & Sons, Inc.

(A) Phillips screwdriver.

(B) Allen wrench.

(C) socket wrench.

(D) offset screwdriver.

Subtest 8: Mechanical Comprehension

TIME: 19 minutes for 25 questions

DIRECTIONS: This test is about mechanical principles. Many of the questions use drawings to illustrate specific principles. Choose the correct answer and mark the corresponding space on the answer sheet.

1. A simple fixed pulley gives a mechanical advantage of
   - (A) 2
   - (B) 3
   - (C) 1
   - (D) unknown

2. The baskets are balanced on the arm in the figure below. If cherries are removed from Basket B, then to rebalance the arm,

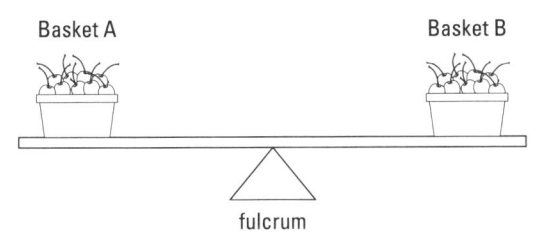

   © John Wiley & Sons, Inc.

   - (A) the fulcrum will have to be moved to the right.
   - (B) Basket B will have to be moved to the right.
   - (C) Basket A will have to be moved to the left.
   - (D) Basket A will have to be moved to the right.

3. If both Wheel A and Wheel B revolve at the same rate in the figure below, Wheel A will cover a linear distance of 12 feet

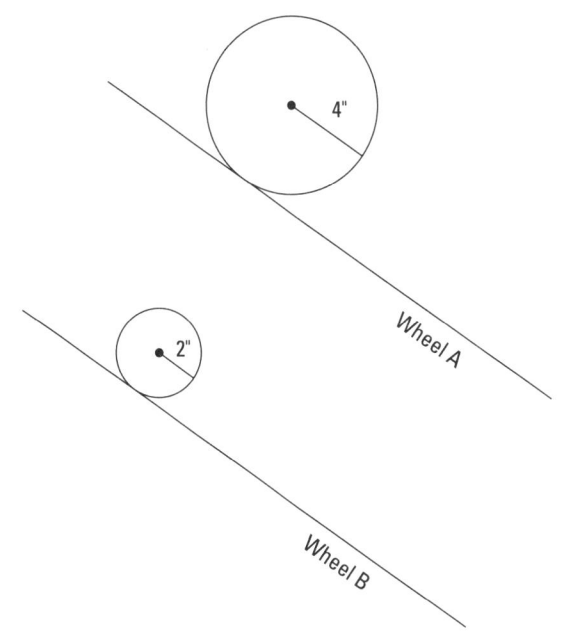

   © John Wiley & Sons, Inc.

   - (A) faster than Wheel B.
   - (B) slower than Wheel B.
   - (C) in about the same time as Wheel B.
   - (D) half as quickly as Wheel B.

CHAPTER 20 Practice Exam 2

4. If a force of 200 pounds is exerted over an area of 10 square inches, what's the psi?

(A) 10
(B) 15
(C) 20
(D) 200

5. In the following figure, if you move Anvil A toward the middle of the seesaw, Anvil B will

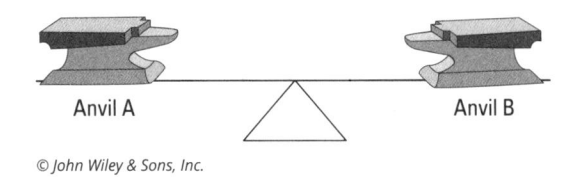

© John Wiley & Sons, Inc.

(A) remain stationary.
(B) move toward the ground.
(C) rise in the air.
(D) lose weight.

6. If a ramp measures 6 feet in length and 3 feet in height, an object weighing 200 pounds requires how much effort to move using the ramp?

(A) 200 pounds
(B) 100 pounds
(C) 50 pounds
(D) 300 pounds

7. A micrometer is used to measure

(A) small changes in temperature.
(B) changes in psi.
(C) thicknesses to a few thousandths of an inch.
(D) objects invisible to the unaided eye.

8. If the weight is removed from Side B of the seesaw, what happens to the weight on Side A?

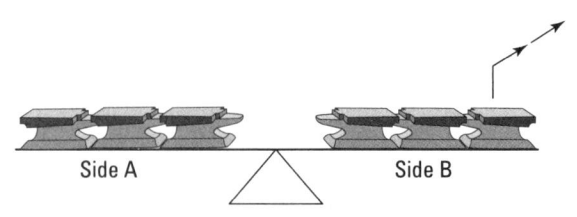

© John Wiley & Sons, Inc.

(A) The weight will never move from Side B.
(B) The weight on Side A will move up in the air.
(C) The weight on Side A will move toward the ground.
(D) Nothing will happen.

9. The force produced when two objects rub against each other is called

(A) gravity.
(B) recoil.
(C) magnetism.
(D) friction.

10. Normally, atmospheric pressure is approximately

(A) 14.7 psi
(B) 23.2 psi
(C) 7.0 psi
(D) 10.1 psi

11. For Gear A and Gear B to mesh properly in the following figure,

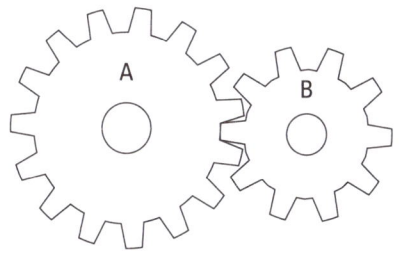

    (A) they must be the same size.
    (B) they must turn at different rates.
    (C) they must both turn in the same direction.
    (D) their teeth must be of equal size.

12. Torsion springs
    (A) produce a direct pull.
    (B) exert no pull.
    (C) produce a twisting action.
    (D) coil but do not uncoil.

13. To move a 400-pound crate from the floor of a warehouse to the bed of a truck 4 feet off the ground, the most efficient device to use is a
    (A) lever.
    (B) inclined plane.
    (C) fixed pulley.
    (D) jackscrew.

14. Water in an engine can cause damage in winter weather because
    (A) it can vaporize.
    (B) water expands when it freezes.
    (C) ice is heavier than water.
    (D) cold water creates more steam than warm water.

15. The weight of the load is being carried on the backs of the two anvils shown in the figure. Which anvil is carrying the most weight?

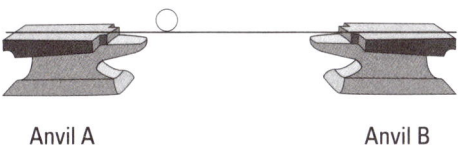

    (A) Anvil A
    (B) Anvil B
    (C) Both are carrying an equal amount of weight.
    (D) It can't be determined without more information.

16. When the block-and-tackle arrangement shown in the figure is used to lift a load, all the following parts remain stationary except

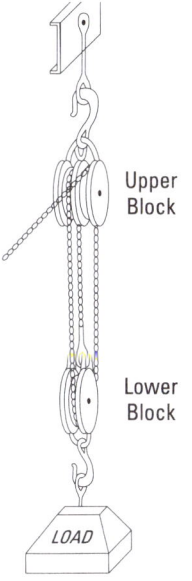

    (A) the upper hook.
    (B) the upper block.
    (C) the lower block.
    (D) All the parts move.

17. In the following figure, what effort (E) must be applied to lift the anvil?

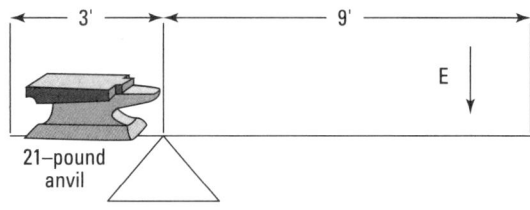

(A) 7.0 pounds
(B) 9.0 pounds
(C) 21.0 pounds
(D) 10.5 pounds

18. In the figure below, for each complete revolution the cam makes, how many times will the valve open?

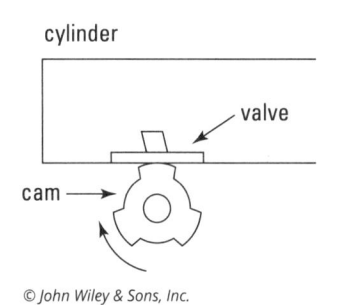

(A) 1
(B) 6
(C) 3
(D) 2

19. In the following figure, assume the valves are all open. Which valves need to be closed for the tank to fill up completely?

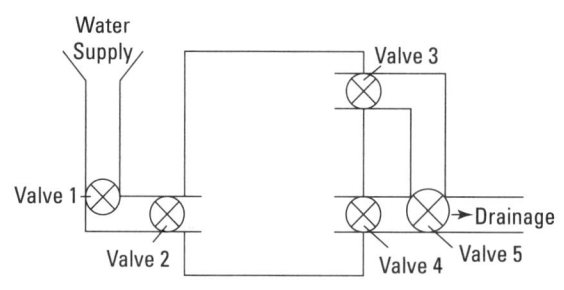

(A) 3 and 4 only
(B) 3, 4, and 5
(C) 2, 3, and 4
(D) 4 only

20. If Gear A turns left in the figure below, Gear B

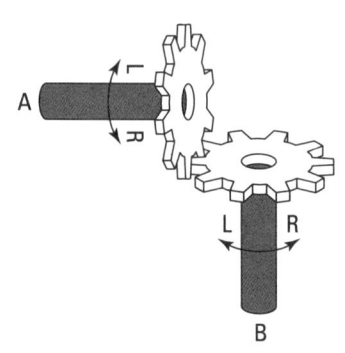

(A) won't turn.
(B) turns left.
(C) turns right.
(D) It can't be determined.

454 PART 6 Practice ASVAB Exams

21. If Gear 1 makes 10 complete clockwise revolutions per minute in the figure below, then

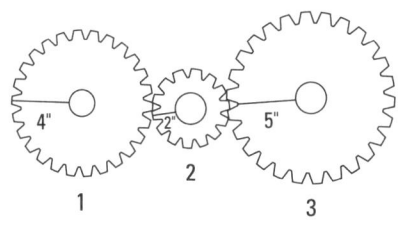

(A) Gear 2 makes 10 complete clockwise revolutions per minute.

(B) Gear 2 makes 20 complete counterclockwise revolutions per minute.

(C) Gear 2 makes 5 complete counterclockwise revolutions per minute.

(D) Gear 3 keeps Gear 2 from making any revolutions.

22. For the fuel to travel from Reservoir A to Reservoir B, passing through Filters C and D on the way, which valves must be open?

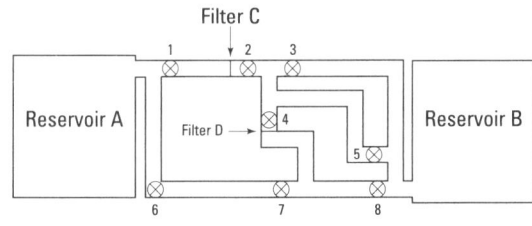

(A) 1, 2, 4, and 8
(B) 1, 2, and 3
(C) 6, 7, and 8
(D) 4, 6, and 7

23. A yellow flame on a gas furnace indicates that

(A) everything is fine.
(B) the fuel-air mixture is too rich.
(C) the fuel-air mixture is too lean.
(D) the gas pressure is too low.

24. If a water tank on a toilet keeps overflowing, the problem is probably a

(A) defective float.
(B) clogged pipe.
(C) crimped chain.
(D) improper seal.

25. In the figure below, the board holds the anvil. The board is placed on two identical scales. Each scale reads

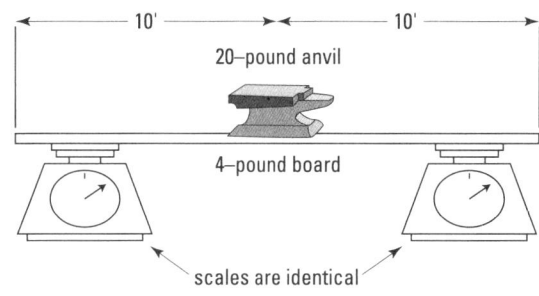

(A) 24
(B) 10
(C) 12
(D) 40

Subtest 9: Assembling Objects

TIME: 15 minutes for 25 questions

DIRECTIONS: The Assembling Objects subtest consists of questions that measure your ability to mentally picture items in two dimensions. Each question is comprised of five separate drawings. The problem is presented in the first drawing and the remaining four drawings are possible solutions. Determine which of the choices best solves the problem shown in the first picture; then mark the corresponding choice on your answer sheet.

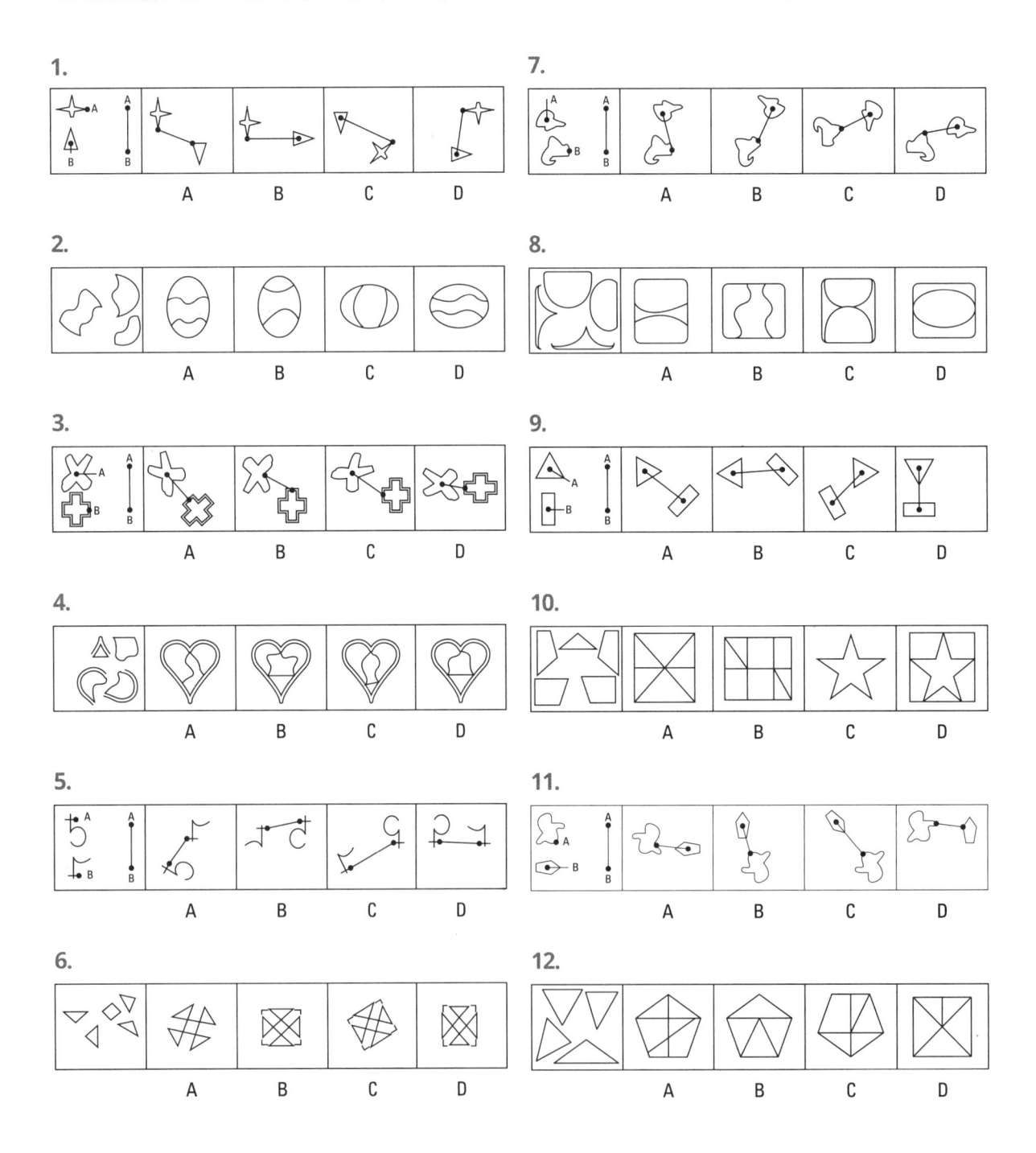

1. A   B   C   D

2. A   B   C   D

3. A   B   C   D

4. A   B   C   D

5. A   B   C   D

6. A   B   C   D

7. A   B   C   D

8. A   B   C   D

9. A   B   C   D

10. A   B   C   D

11. A   B   C   D

12. A   B   C   D

13.
14.
15.
16.
17.
18.
19.
20.
21.
22.
23.
24.
25.

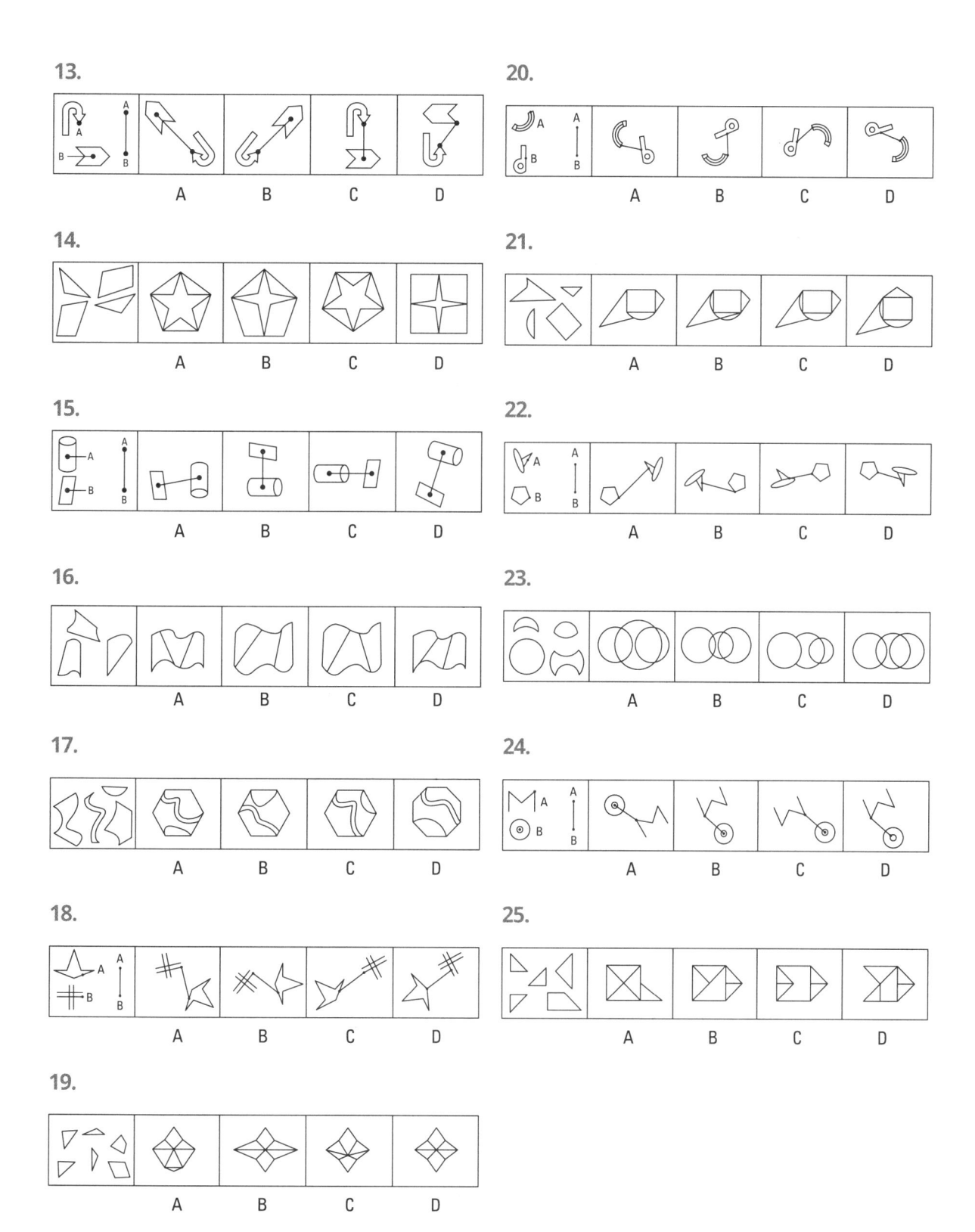

CHAPTER 20 Practice Exam 2

Chapter 21
Practice Exam 2: Answers and Explanations

Here are the answers and explanations for the practice exam in Chapter 20. Read over each question from Chapter 20 as you check your answers. Doing so reminds you what the question is about and serves as a helpful review. If you look at each question and the possible answers, you can also identify some of the traps that you may run across on the ASVAB.

You don't have to be an algebra ace to determine whether you're making progress through your review efforts. Simply compare the number of wrong answers you got on Practice Exam 1 (Chapter 18) against the number of wrong answers you got on this test. If you put the work in, you'll probably find that you made fewer errors on Practice Exam 2.

By the time you've scored Practice Exam 2, you should have a good idea of your strengths and weaknesses. If some subjects or subtests still give you problems, keep studying — just follow the cross-references for some tips and additional practice questions. If you find you need in-depth study, check out the beginning of each subtest's chapter, where I name some books on various subjects covered in the subtests.

REMEMBER: The ASVAB is technically scored by comparing your raw score to the scores of other people, which produces a scaled score. Turn to Chapter 2 to find out how the ASVAB is scored.

Subtest 1: General Science Answers

The answers to the questions on the General Science subtest are fairly straightforward — you either know the answer or you don't. This can be a hard subject to study for because General Science includes the entire scope of scientific disciplines. The good news is you may not even have to score well on this subtest; it depends on the job you're interested in. You can find additional science practice questions in Chapters 10, 11, and 12.

1. **B.** *Metamorphosis* is the change an insect's body undergoes.

2. **D.** Each increase of 1 in magnitude means a quake is 10 times stronger. Therefore, an earthquake that registers as a 4 on the Richter scale is 100 times stronger than one that rates a 2.

3. **C.** Muscles connect to bone with connective tissue called *tendons.*

4. **A.** The *stamen* in a flower is the male part.

5. **D.** The lungs oxygenate the incoming blood.

6. **B.** At more than 4,100 miles, the Nile River is the longest of the rivers listed. Whether it's the longest in the world, as long thought, is now up for debate. In 2007, a group of scientists claimed to have found a new starting point for the Amazon River, which would give the Amazon about a 65-mile lead over the Nile.

7. **B.** Physics is the study of matter and its motion, energy, and force.

8. **A.** Any meteorologist will tell you that *nimbus* clouds mean rain.

9. **D.** Deoxyribonucleic acid — the stuff that genes are made of — is the full term for DNA.

10. **B.** *Anemos* is the Greek word for wind. An anemometer measures wind speed.

11. **A.** Electrical charges can be positive or negative, so Choice (A) is correct.

12. **C.** Jupiter is the planet with the most moons in the solar system, with a total of 63 (and possibly more to be categorized in the future).

13. **B.** Isaac Newton discovered the law of gravity.

14. **D.** The Apollo space program has put 12 men on the moon, with *Apollo* 11 being the first mission.

15. **C.** *Omni* is an English prefix for "all." Omnivores eat plants and animals.

16. **B.** Sharks have only cartilage (in place of bones).

17. **A.** The function of the liver is to remove toxins from the blood.

18. **C.** *Kinetic* comes from the Greek word *kinesis,* meaning to move.

19. **C.** Terrestrial planets are made up of materials other than just gases.

20. **A.** Calcium is a mineral found in dairy, green vegetables, and other foods.

21. **D.** The brain of a sperm whale is the largest and heaviest in the Animal kingdom.

22. **B.** Stars are classified by makeup, heat produced, and so on. Earth's sun is a G type star.

23. **C.** As an example, H_2O is two atoms of hydrogen combined with one oxygen atom.

24. **C.** A seed is a plant embryo enclosed in a casing.

25. **C.** *Vernal* means spring. *Equinox* means a point in time when day and night are of equal length. This equality occurs twice a year. The correct answer is the first day of spring.

Subtest 2: Arithmetic Reasoning Answers

This subtest is one of the most important because it makes up a portion of your AFQT score, the score that determines your overall mental qualifications to enlist in the military.

If you think you need more in-depth study, review Part 3 or see whether you can find some high school–level math textbooks at your local library.

1. **D.** For each die, the probability of rolling a 5 is 1 out of 6 (that is, $\frac{1}{6}$), so the probability of not rolling a 5 is $1 - \frac{1}{6}$, or $\frac{5}{6}$. With two dice, the probability of not rolling a 5 is $\frac{5}{6} \times \frac{5}{6}$, or $\frac{25}{36}$.

2. **C.** Multiply $1,500 by 7%, or 0.07, and get $105. Then add $105 to $1,500 to find the answer, $1,605.

   Sometimes you can actually save time by not working the problem. In this problem, simply recognizing that the answer has to be more than $1,500 makes it obvious that Choices (A) and (B) are wrong. It also should be obvious that 7% of $1,500 has to be more than $7, so Choice (D) is also wrong. That only leaves the correct answer, Choice (C).

3. **A.** Two tons = 4,000 pounds; $4,000 \times \$0.12 = \$480$.

4. **C.** Expanding the equation $y = (a+b)^2$ results in $y = a^2 + b^2 + 2ab + b^2 = a^2 + b^2 + 2ab$. You are given that $a^2 + b^2 = 30$ and $ab = 10$. When you substitute these values into the equation, you get $y = 30 + 2(10)$. Simplifying, $y = 50$.

5. **C.** There are 2 pints in a quart, and 4 quarts make up a gallon; therefore, a gallon contains $2 \times 4 = 8$ pints, or 16 half-pints. One half-pint equals $\frac{1}{16}$ of a gallon.

6. **D.** First subtract the old cost from the new cost: $\$2.80 - \$2.50 = \$0.30$. Then divide the difference by the old cost to find the percent change: $\$0.30 \div \$2.50 = 0.12 = 12\%$.

7. **C.** The aircraft travels 120 miles in 12 minutes, which is $\frac{1}{5}$ of an hour. Therefore, in $\frac{5}{5}$ (or 1 hour), it would travel 5×120, or 600 miles. The aircraft is traveling 600 miles per hour.

8. **D.** Multiply 50 bushels by 8% to find the yield increase in bushels: $50 \times 0.08 = 4$. Add 4 bushels (the amount of the increase) to 50 bushels (the original yield) to determine that an 8% increase equals 54 bushels.

9. **B.** Convert the change to dollars and cents, then add:

   $$\begin{aligned}
   14 \text{ dollars} &= \$14.00 \\
   16 \text{ half dollars} &= \$8.00 \\
   12 \text{ quarters} &= \$3.00 \\
   8 \text{ dimes} &= \$0.80 \\
   25 \text{ nickels} &= \$1.25 \\
   \underline{10 \text{ pennies}} &= \underline{\$0.10} \\
   &= \$27.15
   \end{aligned}$$

   Subtract the total from $30.00 to determine how much money Junior must borrow: $\$30.00 - \$27.15 = \$2.85$.

10. **B.** Her commission for the week was $40 (because $0.05 \times 800 = 40$). The ratio of her commission to her salary is 40:80, which can be reduced to 1:2.

11. **C.** A gallon consists of 4 quarts, and $4 \times 25 = 100$.

12. **D.** Four members is twice as many as two members. Multiply the number of days it would take four people to paint by 2 (that is, $3 \times 2 = 6$) to determine how long it would take two people to do the same task.

13. **A.** Brian's hourly wage is $24 \div 5 = \$4.80$. Christina's hourly wage is $10.95 \div 3 = \$3.65$. The difference is $\$4.80 - \$3.65 = \$1.15$.

14. **B.** The amount of time from 8:30 a.m. to 11:15 a.m. is 2 hours, 45 minutes. From 8:30 a.m. until 10:30 a.m. is 2 hours. From 10:30 until 11:15 is 45 minutes, or $\frac{3}{4}$ of an hour, for a total of $2\frac{3}{4}$ hours.

15. **C.** At a rate of 7 documents per minute, the employee can shred 630 documents in 90 minutes. How do you come up with that number? Multiply 7 by 90 (the number of minutes in 1½ hours). Subtract 630 from 900 total documents to determine that after $1\frac{1}{2}$ hours of shredding, 270 documents remain.

16. **A.** If the stereo depreciates 20%, the value of the stereo then becomes 80% of its original value. After depreciation, the value of the stereo the first year is \$960 $(0.08 \times 1{,}200)$. The value of the stereo after the second year is \$768 (0.08×960). \$768 is Choice (A).

17. **A.** Divide the distance (135 miles) by the speed (45 miles per hour) to determine that Janet will take 3 hours to reach the city.

18. **D.** Multiply the price of the blouse by the amount of the discount: $\$18.50 \times 0.20 = \$3.70$.

19. **C.** Subtract the original salary from the new salary to get the difference in salary: $\$360 - \$320 = \$40$. Then divide the difference in salary (\$40) by the original salary (\$320) to determine the percent increase: $40 \div 320 = 0.125 = 12.5\%$.

20. **B.** A circle is 360 degrees, so 40 degrees is $\frac{1}{9}$ of a circle $(360° \div 40° = 9)$. To get the answer, multiply the circumference of the track by $\frac{1}{9}$: $\left(360 \text{ ft.} \times \frac{1}{9} = 40 \text{ ft.}\right)$.

21. **B.** Subtract \$35.98 from \$40.00 to get \$4.02.

22. **B.** Subtract the time of the plane from the time of the balloon to determine how much longer it took the balloonist:

$$\begin{array}{r} 13 \text{ days}, 12 \text{ hours}, 16 \text{ minutes}, 13 \text{ minutes} \\ -\,4 \text{ days}, 10 \text{ hours}, 15 \text{ minutes}, \ 7 \text{ minutes} \\ \hline 9 \text{ days}, \ 2 \text{ hours}, \ 1 \text{ minute}, \ \ 6 \text{ minutes} \end{array}$$

23. **A.** Divide the total cost by the number of boxes purchased to determine the cost per box: $\$48 \div 12 = \$4$.

24. **D.** Multiply 20×0.05 to determine how many more miles per gallon the car will get. The answer is 1. Then add the number of additional miles per gallon the car will get to the original number of miles per gallon the car gets to reach the new average: $1 + 20 = 21$.

25. **A.** The minimum length of the spike is equal to the diameter of the tree. To find the diameter of the tree, use the formula, $C = \pi d$, where $C = 43.96$ and $\pi \approx 3.14$: $43.96 \approx 3.14 \times d$; $d \approx 43.96 \div 3.14$; $d \approx 14$.

26. **D.** Divide 10½ by ¾. You can perform this operation by multiplying $10\frac{1}{2}$ by the reciprocal of $\frac{3}{4}$: $10\frac{1}{2} \times \frac{4}{3} = \frac{21}{2} \times \frac{4}{3} = \frac{84}{6}$. Divide 84 by 6, and the answer is 14.

27. **C.** First figure out how many stones will be needed along the 12-foot side of the patio and then how many stones will be needed along the 14-foot side of the patio. Then multiply those two numbers together to get the total number of stones required. Here's the math: Convert 12 feet to inches: 12 ft. × 12 in./ft. = 144 inches. The paving stones are 8 inches square, so divide 144 inches by 8 inches (144 ÷ 8), which gives you 18 stones.

    Do the same math for the 14-foot length: 14 ft. × 12 in./ft. = 168 in., and 168 ÷ 8 = 21. Therefore, 21 stones are needed on the 14-foot side.

    Now multiply the stones: 18 stones × 21 stones = 378 stones, which is Choice (C).

28. **D.** Calculate the amount of the deduction by multiplying the programmer's salary by the percent deducted: $25,000 × 28% = $25,000 × 0.28 = $7,000. Subtract that product from the salary to determine the net pay: $25,000 − $7,000 = $18,000.

29. **B.** When the sum of two angles is 180 degrees, the angles are said to be supplementary to each other. To find the supplement, subtract 55 from 180: 180 − 55 = 125.

30. **C.** Multiply the height of the stack in feet by 12 to determine the height of the stack in inches: 6 × 12 = 72 inches. Divide that number by 4 inches, the thickness of each board, to determine the number of pieces of lumber in the stack: 72 ÷ 4 = 18.

Subtest 3: Word Knowledge Answers

Keep in mind that your score on the Word Knowledge subtest counts toward your AFQT score (see Chapter 1), so make sure you're getting comfortable with this portion of the test.

If your score on the Word Knowledge subtest has improved since you took the first test, congratulations! If not, don't be too surprised. Improving your score on this subtest in a short period of time is difficult, but it can be done. Review the information from Chapter 4 and set aside time each day (maybe several times a day, depending on how soon you plan on taking the ASVAB) to memorize words, roots, prefixes, and suffixes. Make sure you sink your dictionary into the additional practice questions at the end of Chapter 4, too.

1. **C.** *Abeyance* is a noun that means a state of temporary disuse or suspension.

2. **A.** *Sturdy* is an adjective used to describe something that's strongly and solidly built.

3. **A.** *Bullock* is a noun that's used as a term for a young bull or steer.

4. **C.** *Brevity* is a noun that means the concise, exact use of words, whether in writing or speech. It can also mean shortness of time.

5. **B.** *Paradigm* is a noun that refers to a typical example or pattern of something; it can also mean a model.

6. **B.** *Facilitated* is the past tense of the verb *facilitate*, which means to make something easy or easier.

7. **D.** *Quiescence* is a noun that refers to a state of inactivity.

8. **B.** *Spectator* is a noun that refers to a person who watches something.

9. **B.** *Reclined* is the past tense of the verb *recline*, which means to lean or lie back in a relaxed position with the back supported.

10. **C.** *Cited* is the past tense of the verb *cite*, which means to quote something as evidence or to justify an argument or statement.

11. **C.** *Surround* is a verb that means to be all around something.

12. **B.** *Illustrious* is an adjective that means well-known, admired for past achievements, and respected.

13. **D.** *Inhabitant* is a noun that refers to a person or animal that lives in or occupies a place.

14. **B.** *Subterfuge* is a noun that means deceit used in order to achieve a goal.

15. **A.** *Ghastly* is an adjective that refers to something that causes great horror or fear.

16. **D.** *Rigid* is an adjective that means unable to bend or inflexible.

17. **A.** *Fraternal* is an adjective that means of or like a brother (or brothers).

18. **C.** *Deplore* is a verb that means to feel or express strong disapproval of something.

19. **B.** *Meager* is an adjective that means lacking in quantity or quality.

20. **A.** *Weal* is a noun that means well-being, happiness, or prosperity. Don't let Choice (B) throw you off; another definition of *weal* is a red, swollen mark left behind after a blow or pressure.

21. **C.** *Guileless* is an adjective that means innocent and without deception.

22. **C.** *Confiscate* is a verb that means to take or seize someone's property with authority.

23. **D.** *Dubious* is an adjective that means hesitating, doubting, or not to be relied upon.

24. **A.** *Illusion* is a noun that refers to something that is, or is likely to be, wrongly interpreted or perceived by the senses.

25. **D.** *Craving* is a noun that means a powerful desire for something.

26. **B.** *Enmity* is a noun that refers to feeling or being opposed or hostile to someone or something.

27. **B.** *Arbor* is a noun that means tree. It can also refer to the leafy, shady area that tree branches or shrubs create.

28. **D.** *Terminated* is the past tense of the verb *terminate*, which means to bring to an end.

29. **A.** *Buffoon* is a noun that means a ridiculous but amusing person.

30. **A.** *Null* is an adjective that means having or associated with the value zero; it also refers to something that has no legal or binding force or to something that is invalid.

31. **C.** *Indigent* is an adjective that means poor or needy. It's also a noun that refers to a needy person.

32. **C.** *Impertinent* is an adjective that means rude or not showing proper respect.

33. **D.** *Lustrous* is an adjective that means shining or glossy.

34. **B.** *Pardon* is a verb that means to forgive or excuse someone or something. It's also a noun that refers to the action of forgiving (or being forgiven) for something.

35. **D.** *Veracious* is an adjective that means speaking or representing the truth.

Subtest 4: Paragraph Comprehension Answers

Like Word Knowledge, the Paragraph Comprehension subtest also counts toward your AFQT score. If you're missing more answers than you should, review the info in Chapter 5 and concentrate on improving your analytical reading skills. For example, when you're reading a news story online, ask yourself what the main point of an article is. Or when you finish a news story, set the paper down and try to remember what the president said about the budget deficit. Think of this technique as a workout for your mind.

1. **B.** The author is describing a quaint country setting.

2. **B.** The passage states that the brooks in the village run south, so the answer is Choice (B). A few miles north, the brooks run in an opposite direction (north).

3. **B.** The passage states that Panama revolted against Colombia, not that they fought over the canal, so Choice (A) is incorrect. The passage states that the foreign companies were unsuccessful in building the canal, so Choice (C) is incorrect. The United States, not Panama, built the canal, so Choice (D) is wrong. In the next to last sentence, the passage states that the U.S. was given rights to the land the canal occupied, making Choice (B) the correct answer.

4. **D.** According to the passage, a torn U.S. flag can be professionally mended, but a severely torn flag should be destroyed. The preferred method of destruction is by burning.

5. **D.** The passage states that guilds had economic and social purposes, so Choice (A) is incorrect. The passage states that guilds were similar to labor unions, so Choice (B) is incorrect. The passage states that guilds protected merchants and craftspeople; it says nothing about exploiting workers, so Choice (C) is incorrect. The third sentence states that some guilds held considerable economic power, but even small guilds protected members, making Choice (D) the correct answer.

6. **D.** According to the passage, it took more than 4 years for the government to believe that anyone had flown a heavier-than-air craft. The historic flight was in December 1903, and the Wright brothers delivered the first aircraft to the government in August 1908, 4.5 years later. The passage supports all the other statements.

7. **C.** Freud comments on the characteristics of memory throughout the entire passage.

8. **A.** The passage describes how troy and common weights are different, so Choice (B) is incorrect. Common and avoirdupois are the same system, so Choice (C) is incorrect. A troy ounce is 480 grains, so Choice (D) is incorrect. Choice (A) is the correct answer because the second sentence states that a common ounce is 437.5 grains, which is just shy of 438 grains.

9. **B.** The passage doesn't address leading by example or use of technology by workers, so Choices (A) and (C) are incorrect. Maximizing worker performance is a result of leadership involvement, not a principle of leadership, making Choice (D) incorrect. The correct answer, showing interest in workers' problems, is in the third sentence of the passage.

10. **C.** The passage doesn't support Choices (A) or (B). The passage states that white blood cells are found in blood and bone marrow, so Choice (D) is wrong. The correct answer, Choice (C), can be found in the first sentence. The passage states that leukemia interferes with "the body's ability to produce red blood cells."

11. **C.** High intensity conflict is listed as a type of military operation (in the last sentence), not one of the four operational concepts.

12. **C.** The JV 2020 guides all the military services with its vision of future war fighting. Although Choice (D) is close, the passage doesn't specifically reference military training.

13. **B.** Cytogenetics is the study of the cellular basis of inheritance; the text doesn't support Choices (A), (C), or (D).

14. **A.** Nothing in the passage supports Choices (B) or (D). Although human genetics is an important subfield of genetics, nothing in the passage suggests that it's the only concern of geneticists. Microbial genetics, as the passage mentions, is a subfield in genetics that has nothing to do with humans, so Choice (C) is incorrect. Choice (A) is the correct answer — the second sentence mentions genes and their transmission to offspring.

15. **C.** Nothing in the passage supports Choices (A), (B), or (D). Choice (C) is the correct answer because the last sentence in the passage states, "[Genetic counselors] advise couples and families on the chances of their offspring having specific genetic defects." Note it does not state that genetic counselors use genetics to *prevent* offspring from inheriting defects, which is what Choice (D) states, making Choice (D) an incorrect answer.

Subtest 5: Mathematics Knowledge Answers

Although the military doesn't expect you to be the next Einstein, a solid grasp of mathematics is important because math skills make up half of your AFQT score. If you're still struggling on this subtest, it's time to hit the books. (Actually, as much as you may feel like it, I don't recommend that you literally hit the books — just study them.) See Chapters 6, 7, and 8 for some more fun practice questions.

1. **A.** If two exponents have the same base, you can multiply them by keeping the base and adding the exponents together: $x^2(x^4) = x^{2+4} = x^6$.

2. **A.** To find area, multiply length times width ($A = lw$). You have the width, so you need to find the length. For a rectangle, $P = 2l + 2w$, so plug in the values you know and

solve for *l*. To determine the length, subtract two times the width from the perimeter: $36 - 2(4) = 36 - 8 = 28$. Divide the answer by 2 to determine the length of one side: $28 \div 2 = 14$. Then multiply length times width to determine the area: $A = 14 \times 4 = 56$.

3. **D.** The cube of 4 is $4 \times 4 \times 4 = 64$, so 4 is the cube root of 64.

4. **A.** To convert this number to scientific notation, move the decimal point to the left until it's to the immediate right of the first number, while counting the number of moves. In this case, you move it five places. The result is then multiplied by 10 raised to the power of the number of places the decimal point was moved. The exponent is positive here because the original number, 314,000, is larger than 3.14. Choice (B), 3.14×10^{-5}, is equal to 0.0000314, so it's incorrect.

5. **B.** A reciprocal is the number by which a number can be multiplied to produce 1. The reciprocal $\frac{1}{6}$ is 6, because $\frac{1}{6} \times 6 = 1$.

6. **A.** You start with $0.05 \div x = 1$. Multiply both sides of the equation by *x*: $0.05 = 1x$ or $x = 0.05$. Check by substituting 0.05 for *x* in the original equation.

7. **C.** $x^2 - 6x + 9 = (x-3)(x-3) = (x-3)^2$.

8. **C.** You start with $(3 \times 2)(7-2)(6+2) = (6 \times 4)x$. Solve the left side of the equation first. $(6)(5)(8) = (30)(8) = 240$. Therefore, $240 = (6 \times 4)x$, which equals $420 = 24x$. Now isolate *x* by dividing both sides of the equation by 24: $240 \div 24 = 24x \div 24$, or $10 = x$. Check your answer by substituting 10 for *x* in the original equation.

9. **B.** Isolate *x* on one side of the equation. Subtract *x* from both sides of the equation and then add 6 to both sides:

$$2x - 6 = x + 5$$
$$x - 6 = 5$$
$$x = 11$$

Check by substituting 11 for *x* in the original equation.

10. **D.** Solve for *I*. $I = (1,000)(7\%)(1)$, or $I = (1,000)(0.07)(1) = 70$.

11. **B.** Multiply out what's in parentheses. Then simplify and solve for *x*:

$$(x-7)^2 - 4 = (x+1)^2$$
$$(x-7)(x-7) - 4 = (x+1)(x+1)$$
$$x^2 - 14x + 49 - 4 = x^2 + 2x + 1$$
$$x^2 - 14x + 45 = x^2 + 2x + 1$$
$$-14x + 45 = 2x + 1$$
$$44 = 16x$$
$$2\frac{3}{4} = x$$

12. **A.** The area of a circle is $A = \pi r^2$, so $A = \pi 5^2$. The number π is approximately 3.14, so 3.14×25 means *A* is approximately 78.5 square inches.

13. **D.** Distribute the $\frac{2}{3}$, simplify, and solve for x. Note that when you divide by a negative number, you have to switch the direction of the inequality sign.

$$\frac{2}{3}(6x-9)+4 > 5x+1$$
$$4x-6+4 > 5x+1$$
$$4x-2 > 5x+1$$
$$-x > 3$$
$$x < -3$$

14. **B.** For cylinders, Volume = $\pi r^2 h$. In this problem, $V = \pi(3)^2(5)$. Assume π is approximately 3.14. V is approximately equal to $(3.14)(9)(5)$, or 141 cubic inches.

15. **A.** A right triangle has one right angle (one 90-degree angle).

16. **D.** Parallelograms have opposite sides of equal length.

17. **D.** Angles measuring more than 90 degrees are obtuse angles.

18. **B.** This is a quadratic equation, which you solve by factoring. First factor out the −1; then factor the quadratic expression and solve for x:

$$-x^2 - x + 30 = 0$$
$$-(x^2 + x - 30) = 0$$
$$-(x+6)(x-5) = 0$$
$$x = -6, 5$$

19. **B.** Volume equals length times width times height $(V = lwh)$. In this case, $V = 64$, so one edge of the box is 4 inches long (because 4 is the cube root of 64: $64 = 4 \times 4 \times 4$). Find the perimeter by adding the four sides together: $4 + 4 + 4 + 4 = 16$.

20. **C.** You calculate volume by multiplying length times width times height $(V = lwh)$. Because the edges are equal on a cube, each edge is 3 inches (because $3 \times 3 \times 3 = 27$). The area of one face of the cube is $3 \times 3 = 9$ square inches, and because a cube has 6 sides, you multiply 9×6 to find the surface area of the cube, 54 square inches.

21. **C.** $(x^3)^3$ is the same as $(x^3)(x^3)(x^3)$. If two exponents have the same base, you multiply them by keeping the base and adding the exponents together: $(x^3)(x^3)(x^3) = x^{3+3+3} = x^9$.

22. **D.** $4!$ (4 factorial) $= 4 \times 3 \times 2 \times 1 = 24$.

23. **B.** You start with $a^3 + b^3 = a^3 + x^3$. To solve, subtract a^3 from both sides of the equation and then take the cube root:

$$a^3 + b^3 = a^3 + x^3$$
$$b^3 = x^3$$
$$\sqrt[3]{b^3} = \sqrt[3]{x^3}$$
$$b = x$$

24. **B.** The formula to find the sum of a finite arithmetic sequence is $S = \frac{n}{2}(a+b)$, where n is the number of terms, a is the first term in the sequence, and b is the last term in the sequence. In this case, there are 300 terms (*n*), and the first term is 1 and the final term is 300.

$$S = \frac{n}{2}(a+b)$$
$$= \frac{300}{2}(1+300)$$
$$= 150(301)$$
$$= 45{,}150$$

25. **B.** $\left(y^2\right)^3$ is the same as $\left(y^2\right)\left(y^2\right)\left(y^2\right)$. Multiply exponents with the same base by keeping the base and adding the exponents: $\left(y^2\right)\left(y^2\right)\left(y^2\right) = y^{2+2+2} = y^6$. The second $\left(y^2\right)$ in the equation cannot be added into the first term because now they are not like terms, so the answer is Choice (B), $y^6 + y^2$.

Subtest 6: Electronics Information Answers

If you're having difficulty defining the difference between AC and DC, you may want to spend some additional time studying basic electronic information. Reviewing Chapter 16 can help. You can also wrap your wires around the practice questions in that chapter as well.

On the other hand, you may not be interested in a military job that requires a decent score on this subtest, in which case, try not to worry too much. Your main goal is to score well in all areas of the ASVAB. The better you do on each subtest, the more desirable you become as a candidate for all the available jobs.

1. **A.** A multimeter includes several pieces of test equipment, including an ammeter, which measures inline current.

2. **A.** Rotor bars are only on AC induction motors, not DC motors.

3. **A.** NTSC stands for National Television System Committee and, although it's gradually being replaced by ATSC (Advanced Television Systems Committee), NTSC is currently the broadcast standard in the U.S. Choice (B) is incorrect because RGB stands for red, green, and blue — the colors of light used to create an image. Although most televisions use this standard, it is not a broadcast standard. Choice (C) is incorrect because SECAM (*Séquentielcouleur avec mémoire,* or sequential color with memory) is a standard used in other countries. Choice (D) is RTSC, which stands for Raytheon Technical Services Company and is therefore not the correct answer.

4. **A.** In a closed circuit, one terminal is always positive, and the other is always negative.

5. **C.** Amperes (or amps) are the unit of measure of electric current. Hertz is the unit of measurement of frequency, not current. Current equals voltage divided by resistance. Resistance is measured in ohms. Therefore, neither voltage nor ohms can be the unit of measure for current.

6. **B.** The symbol is a fuse. Fuses are designed to *blow* (melt) if the current flowing through them exceeds a specified value.

7. **C.** This is code prescribed by the NEC (National Electric Code). Outlets within 6 feet of a sink need to be GFCI protected for safety reasons.

8. **A.** The symbol is a lamp. A *lamp* is a transducer that converts electrical energy to light.

9. **C.** Conventional circuit breaker handles have three positions: on, off, and trip. When tripped, the handle moves between the on and off positions. To reset the breaker, move the handle to the off position and then to the on position.

10. **D.** The smaller the wire, the larger the number.

11. **D.** Plastic does not conduct, and wood is a poor conductor. Aluminum is a good conductor but not better than copper.

12. **A.** A series circuit has only one path, so if you break the circuit's path at any point, electricity stops flowing. An example of a series circuit is a string of Christmas lights that no longer works if a single bulb burns out.

13. **B.** I (current) = Power (watts) ÷ Effort (volts). In this case, $I = 1{,}200 \div 120 = 10$ amperes.

14. **D.** *Potential* equals voltage; *low potential* is anything less than 600 watts.

15. **D.** Glass is an insulator. Other insulators include plastics, paper, and rubber.

16. **A.** Ground wires are always green.

17. **C.** Amplitude modulation (AM) was the first type of audio modulation to be used in radio. It works well with high frequency (HF) and Morse code.

18. **A.** Silver is a better conductor, but it's more brittle than copper and more expensive.

19. **D.** Oscillators produce high frequencies. An *amplifier* changes the amplitude of a signal. A *regulator* is a circuit that maintains a constant voltage. A *transformer* is a device that changes (transforms) the voltage at its input side to a different voltage on its output side.

20. **B.** When DC is applied to an AC appliance, the amount of resistance is less, so more current flows through the wire and heat builds up.

Subtest 7: Auto & Shop Information Answers

You need to do well on this subtest to qualify for certain military jobs. If you care about those jobs and you're missing more than a few questions on this subtest, it's time for more extreme measures — like taking your mother's car apart and putting it back together (or going back over Chapters 13 and 14).

1. **D.** Using too much oil is a symptom of piston ring wear.

2. **D.** Clean air filters allow your engine to breathe. Air filters remove airborne pollutants from the engine, such as microscopic dirt that can damage cylinder walls, pistons, and piston rings. They also filter out smoke, fumes, and odors. A dirty filter can decrease engine performance and cause a decrease in fuel mileage.

3. **B.** The alternator recharges (or supplies power to) the battery.

4. **A.** You can find a wishbone in a car's suspension.

5. **C.** For a non-sealed battery, if the electrolyte solution is too low, you need to add distilled water.

6. **C.** For optimum performance, you should flush an automobile's cooling system periodically.

7. **C.** In a combustion engine that has a carburetor, the purpose of the carburetor is to mix fuel and air.

8. **C.** In the world of automobile restorers, NOS stands for New Old Stock.

9. **D.** To fire, spark plugs need a very high electrical voltage, supplied by the coil and breaker.

10. **A.** The valve you use when filling your car's tires with air is a type of Schrader valve.

11. **A.** A bent frame causes improper tracking, which means that the right angle between the centerline and axles is not maintained.

12. **C.** The *H* signifies the maximum sustained speed at which the vehicle is stable.

13. **B.** When specific tightness of screws and/or bolts is required, use a torque wrench.

14. **C.** Hammer faces aren't made of glass.

15. **A.** Mallets and sledge hammers don't have claws.

16. **C.** A set of calipers is the most accurate widely used tool to measure round objects.

17. **D.** You use a round chisel to make circular cuts in metal.

18. **D.** A Stillson wrench is a type of a pipe wrench.

19. **B.** Paint will bubble if the surface you're painting has too much moisture in it.

20. **B.** A *jig* is a tool you use to control the location and/or motion of another tool.

21. **A.** Saws have one fewer tooth than they have points per inch.

22. **D.** A mineral aggregate (such as sand, gravel, or crushed stone), a binder such as natural or synthetic cement, and water make concrete. The mix sometimes contains chemical additives as well.

23. **B.** Choice (B) is an image of a hand saw (carpentry saw), which you wouldn't use to cut metal.

24. **D.** The image is of a bolt cutter.

25. **B.** The image is of an Allen wrench.

Subtest 8: Mechanical Comprehension Answers

If you need to do well on the Mechanical Comprehension subtest (as in you're hoping for a military career that requires a score for this subtest) but you're still missing more answers than you should be, ask yourself whether your math skills need work. Go back to Chapters 6, 7, and 8 if they do. Many of the formulas you need to know for this subtest require an understanding of arithmetic and basic algebra. If the math isn't the problem, revisit Chapter 15 for more practice with Mechanical Comprehension principles.

TIP

Usually, improving your arithmetic and basic algebra skills will improve your score on the Mechanical Comprehension subtest. Improving your knowledge of physics is also beneficial. Take a look at Chapter 11.

1. **C.** A simple fixed pulley gives no mechanical advantage, although it does make work easier by directing the applied force. The mechanical advantage is 1.

2. **D.** Moving Basket A to the right counterbalances the loss of cherries from Basket B.

3. **A.** Wheel B has to make more revolutions to cover the same ground as Wheel A, so it covers the distance more slowly.

4. **C.** You can calculate psi as Pressure = Force ÷ Area. In this problem, $P = 200 \div 10 = 20$.

5. **B.** If you move Anvil A toward the center, Anvil B will move toward the ground.

6. **B.** The formula to determine mechanical advantage of an inclined plane is Length of Ramp ÷ Height of Ramp = Weight of Object ÷ Effort. Plugging in the numbers gives you

$$\frac{6}{3} = \frac{200}{E}$$
$$6E = 600$$
$$E = 100$$

7. **C.** Micrometers measure very small but not microscopic objects.

8. **C.** Reducing the weight on Side B will cause Side A to move toward the ground.

9. **D.** Objects rubbing together produce friction.

10. **A.** Normal atmospheric pressure (the average atmospheric pressure at sea level) is 14.7 psi.

11. **D.** Gears of unequal size can mesh properly as long as their teeth are of equal size.

12. **C.** Torsion springs coil or uncoil and produce a twisting action, not a direct pull; in other words, torsion springs apply torque.

13. **B.** To move a heavy object a few feet in height, the inclined plane is the most efficient device (of those listed) to use. *Note:* The mechanical advantage of an inclined plane is equal to the slope of the plane divided by the height. The longer the slope is (compared to the height), the greater the mechanical advantage will be.

14. **B.** Water expands when it freezes, possibly damaging engine components.

15. **A.** The load is closer to Anvil A, so it's carrying the greater portion of the weight.

16. **C.** All the listed parts remain stationary except the lower block.

17. **A.** Apply the leverage formula: Length of Effort Arm ÷ Length of Resistance Arm = Resistance Force ÷ Effort Force:

    $$\frac{9}{3} = \frac{21}{E}$$
    $$3 = \frac{21}{E}$$
    $$3E = 21$$
    $$E = 7$$

18. **C.** The valve will open each time a high point of the cam hits it. The cam has three high points, so the valve will open three times per revolution.

19. **A.** Closing only Valves 3 and 4 keeps the water from leaving the tank.

20. **C.** Gears in mesh always turn in opposite directions.

21. **B.** If Gear 1 turns at 10 rpm, then Gear 2, which is half the size, turns twice as fast, at a rate of 20 rpm.

22. **A.** Opening Valves 1, 2, 4, and 8 allows the fuel to travel through the filters. Opening Valves 1, 2, and 3 doesn't allow the fuel to travel through Filter D. Opening Valves 6, 7, and 8 doesn't allow the fuel to travel through the filters. Opening Valves 4, 6, and 7 doesn't allow fuel to travel to Reservoir B.

23. **B.** A yellow flame indicates too much fuel or not enough air. More air should be allowed to enter and mix with the gas. Thus, the fuel-air mixture is too rich.

24. **A.** The float measures the water level in the tank. If the tank overflows, the float is probably defective.

25. **C.** The 20-pound anvil and the 4-pound board weigh 24 pounds total or, divided by 2, 12 pounds per scale.

Subtest 9: Assembling Objects Answers

So far, only the Navy has elected to use scores from the Assembling Objects subtest and only for a few jobs. If you're planning to join the Navy and you're interested in a Navy career that requires a score on this subtest, review Chapter 17 for help on improving your score.

TIP: Sometimes the fastest (and most accurate) way to choose the right answer on Assembling Objects questions is to eliminate choices that can't be right. You can always strategically determine the correct answer if it's not obvious right away.

1. **B.** Pay attention to where the points are in the original diagram. Point A is located on one of the three spikes in the uppermost figure, and Point B is located near the center of the triangle with a line extending at a 90-degree angle from its shortest side. You can rule out Choices (A), (C), and (D) because of the line coming from Point B.

2. **A.** Match each possible answer with the figures in the original diagram. Choices (B), (C), and (D) don't depict the original figures.

3. **C.** Point A is attached to a line that leaves the X-shaped figure on what's depicted as the right side. Rotate the X-shaped figure about 45 degrees and rotate the figure containing Point B 180 degrees, and you'll have Choice (C). Choices (A) and (D) can't be right; Point A's line comes out of the figure at the wrong angle. Choice (B) is incorrect because it shows Point A directly on the shape.

4. **D.** Each of the answer choices you're given in this problem is in the shape of a double-lined heart, so look at the shape inside the heart. The only one that matches that extra shape is Choice (D).

5. **C.** You can immediately rule out Choices (B) and (D) because the figure containing Point A is inverted in both of them. (Assembling Objects questions feature two-dimensional figures, not three-dimensional figures!) Choice (A) is wrong because the figure containing Point B has the point on the wrong side, which leaves you with Choice (C), a rotated and connected version of the original figures.

6. **A.** Choices (B), (C), and (D) are essentially the same, but the lines that enclose each figure are missing from the original image. That leaves you one choice: Choice (A).

7. **B.** Check out the locations of Point A and Point B. Point A comes out of the first amoeba (they look like amoebas, don't they?) through its rounded top. Point B is attached to the second one in a specific spot, too. The only choice that features accurate depictions of the points is Choice (B).

8. **C.** You need to make sure the pieces of this figure fit together properly, like the pieces of a puzzle. The easiest way may be to count the shapes (there are four) in the original diagram and compare them to each of the answer choices. Choices (A), (B), and (D) each only show three puzzle pieces. The only one that shows all four (and happens to be the correct answer) is Choice (C).

9. **D.** If you start by paying attention to the points and the lines that are attached to them, you'll see that Point A's line comes right out of the point of the triangle. You can fast-forward through all the other answers and skip to Choice (D), which is the only one that depicts the line coming from the triangle in the correct place.

10. **D.** Do some detective work and compare the shapes in the original diagram with those in the answer choices. Choice (A) shows six shapes, and only one of the shapes depicted matches with one in the original diagram. Choice (B) shows eight shapes, and none of them match the original shapes. Choice (C) doesn't match any of them, which leaves you with only one possible answer: Choice (D).

11. **C.** Look at where the points lie on each of the original figures, and pay attention to where the lines exit the figures, too. You can rule out Choices (A), (B), and (D) immediately because the points are in the wrong places on each figure.

12. **B.** Match up the shapes in the original figure and those in each answer choice. Choice (A) depicts a few shapes that don't appear in the original diagram, and so does Choice (C). Choice (D) doesn't add up to what you'd get by rearranging the original figures, but Choice (B) does.

13. **A.** Each figure in the answer choices depicts Point A in the correct place, but if you look closely, you'll see that the figure Point A is on is inverted in Choices (B) and (D). You can rule out the final incorrect choice by noting where the line from Point B extends from the shape — it's right through the middle of the angle, which means Choice (C) is wrong. The only possible answer is Choice (A).

14. **B.** Glance at the question, and then look at each answer choice. All the answer choices require the shapes to be identical in size and shape, but that's not the case with the original figures. For example, in Choice (A), you'd need to have five equally sized triangles to make the figure work, and Choice (C) is the same; it's simply rotated. Choice (D) also requires you to have four identical shapes, leaving Choice (B) as the correct answer.

15. **D.** Choices (A), (B), and (C) are wrong, although you'll have to look closely to determine why. Choice (A) is wrong because of the angle at which each line extends from each figure and because the figure that contains Point B is inverted. Choice (B) is incorrect because the figure with Point A in its center is inverted rather than simply rotated, and Choice (C) is wrong because the line coming from Point A comes from the top of the cylinder, not out of its side.

16. **D.** This question simply asks you to match the original shapes with those in the answer choices. Compare each and you'll see that the only figure that contains each of the shapes is Choice (D).

17. **C.** Put a big mental X over Choice (B), because it's obviously wrong (look at the thinnest wavy shape inside the figure, and you'll see that it doesn't match the one in the diagram). That means Choice (D) is wrong, too. Where did the largest shape in Choice (A) come from? It's not in the original diagram, which means you'd be wrong if you picked that one. But you'd be right if you picked Choice (C), because all the shapes in that figure match those in the original figure.

18. **B.** You'll have to wrap your brain around rotating versus inverting for this problem. Choice (D) is clearly wrong because Point A is in the wrong place, so just focus on Choices (A), (B), and (C). Point B is on the right side of the original figure, which looks like an intersection; it's on the southeast side, if that helps you visualize it. Tilt your head if you have to; you'll see that Choice (A) can't be correct because in that figure, Point B is on the northwest side of the intersection. Choice (C) shows the point in the northwest quadrant, too, which means only Choice (B) is correct.

19. **C.** This puzzle question is tough, so the best way to solve it is by matching the shapes in each answer choice with those in the original diagram. Start with the kite on the upper right of the original figure (sometimes it's easiest to start with shapes that are clearly out of place among the rest). The only figure it appears in is Choice (C). For the record, you could also base your decision on the two thin triangles in the original depiction; they also appear only in Choice (C).

20. **C.** Point A on the rainbow (you don't see a rainbow?) lies on the end of the center line in the figure, so forget about Choices (B) and (D). Now look at the lowercase *d*. In Choice (A), you're looking at a lowercase *b*, and you know that Assembling Objects questions want you to rotate, *not invert*, figures; that means the correct answer is Choice (C).

21. **A.** The crafty test-question writers who work on the ASVAB will throw plenty of these puzzle problems your way, so use the tried-and-true matching strategy. The only figure among the answer choices that depicts the four-sided, angular shape you see in the original diagram is Choice (A).

22. D. The pentagon in this figure isn't going to help you; whether you invert it, twist it, or turn it, Point B will always be in the right place. The other figure — the one containing Point A — is what will lead you to the right answer. Choice (C) is a no-go (that's military slang for "failure") because the point is in the wrong place. Choices (A) and (B) are also wrong, because the figure containing Point A is inverted, not rotated.

23. C. If you look at each of the answer choices, you'll see that there's an odd shape in each; it's one that resembles an apple core, and it occurs in the middle of each diagram, where the circles overlap. Compare the similar shape in the original diagram with each of the answer choices, and you'll see that it appears only in Choice (C).

24. B. Choices (A), (B), and (D) can't be right because of where Point A lies on the M-shaped figure, so eliminate those from the pool right away. The only one left is Choice (B), which shows Point A in the correct spot on the figure.

25. D. The odd figure out among the triangles is the trapezoid, so look through the answer choices to find it. The only one that contains it is Choice (D), which is the correct answer.

Chapter 22
Practice Exam 3

I suggest you take the third practice exam at least a week (or more, if you're following the study timeline outlined in Chapter 3) before you're scheduled to take the real ASVAB. Use it to refresh your memory of the material or to increase your knowledge on any of the subtests that you have to do better on than you've been doing.

REMEMBER: Don't forget to use the test-taking strategies and the guessing tips in each of the subtest chapters earlier in this book. Chapter 3 provides additional information on how to improve your score just by using smart test-taking strategies.

This sample test features nine subtests and follows the same format as the actual paper-and-pencil ASVAB. To get the most out of this sample test, take it under the same conditions as the real ASVAB:

- Allow yourself about 3 hours to take the entire exam, and take the whole thing at one time.
- Find a quiet place where you won't be interrupted.
- Bring a timer that you can set for various lengths of time, some scratch paper, and a pencil.
- At the start of each subtest, set your timer for the specified period of time. Don't go on to the next section until the timer has gone off, and don't go back to a previous section. If you finish early, check your work for that section only.
- Use the answer sheet that's provided.
- Don't take a break during any subtest. You can take a short 1- or 2-minute break between subtests if you need it.

After you complete the entire test, check your answers against the answer keys and explanations in Chapter 23. Then compare the results to your results on Practice Exams 1 and 2. You should see some improvement.

Answer Sheet for Practice Exam 3

Subtest 1: General Science

1. Ⓐ Ⓑ Ⓒ Ⓓ
2. Ⓐ Ⓑ Ⓒ Ⓓ
3. Ⓐ Ⓑ Ⓒ Ⓓ
4. Ⓐ Ⓑ Ⓒ Ⓓ
5. Ⓐ Ⓑ Ⓒ Ⓓ
6. Ⓐ Ⓑ Ⓒ Ⓓ
7. Ⓐ Ⓑ Ⓒ Ⓓ
8. Ⓐ Ⓑ Ⓒ Ⓓ
9. Ⓐ Ⓑ Ⓒ Ⓓ
10. Ⓐ Ⓑ Ⓒ Ⓓ
11. Ⓐ Ⓑ Ⓒ Ⓓ
12. Ⓐ Ⓑ Ⓒ Ⓓ
13. Ⓐ Ⓑ Ⓒ Ⓓ
14. Ⓐ Ⓑ Ⓒ Ⓓ
15. Ⓐ Ⓑ Ⓒ Ⓓ
16. Ⓐ Ⓑ Ⓒ Ⓓ
17. Ⓐ Ⓑ Ⓒ Ⓓ
18. Ⓐ Ⓑ Ⓒ Ⓓ
19. Ⓐ Ⓑ Ⓒ Ⓓ
20. Ⓐ Ⓑ Ⓒ Ⓓ
21. Ⓐ Ⓑ Ⓒ Ⓓ
22. Ⓐ Ⓑ Ⓒ Ⓓ
23. Ⓐ Ⓑ Ⓒ Ⓓ
24. Ⓐ Ⓑ Ⓒ Ⓓ
25. Ⓐ Ⓑ Ⓒ Ⓓ

Subtest 2: Arithmetic Reasoning

1. Ⓐ Ⓑ Ⓒ Ⓓ
2. Ⓐ Ⓑ Ⓒ Ⓓ
3. Ⓐ Ⓑ Ⓒ Ⓓ
4. Ⓐ Ⓑ Ⓒ Ⓓ
5. Ⓐ Ⓑ Ⓒ Ⓓ
6. Ⓐ Ⓑ Ⓒ Ⓓ
7. Ⓐ Ⓑ Ⓒ Ⓓ
8. Ⓐ Ⓑ Ⓒ Ⓓ
9. Ⓐ Ⓑ Ⓒ Ⓓ
10. Ⓐ Ⓑ Ⓒ Ⓓ
11. Ⓐ Ⓑ Ⓒ Ⓓ
12. Ⓐ Ⓑ Ⓒ Ⓓ
13. Ⓐ Ⓑ Ⓒ Ⓓ
14. Ⓐ Ⓑ Ⓒ Ⓓ
15. Ⓐ Ⓑ Ⓒ Ⓓ
16. Ⓐ Ⓑ Ⓒ Ⓓ
17. Ⓐ Ⓑ Ⓒ Ⓓ
18. Ⓐ Ⓑ Ⓒ Ⓓ
19. Ⓐ Ⓑ Ⓒ Ⓓ
20. Ⓐ Ⓑ Ⓒ Ⓓ
21. Ⓐ Ⓑ Ⓒ Ⓓ
22. Ⓐ Ⓑ Ⓒ Ⓓ
23. Ⓐ Ⓑ Ⓒ Ⓓ
24. Ⓐ Ⓑ Ⓒ Ⓓ
25. Ⓐ Ⓑ Ⓒ Ⓓ
26. Ⓐ Ⓑ Ⓒ Ⓓ
27. Ⓐ Ⓑ Ⓒ Ⓓ
28. Ⓐ Ⓑ Ⓒ Ⓓ
29. Ⓐ Ⓑ Ⓒ Ⓓ
30. Ⓐ Ⓑ Ⓒ Ⓓ

Subtest 3: Word Knowledge

1. Ⓐ Ⓑ Ⓒ Ⓓ
2. Ⓐ Ⓑ Ⓒ Ⓓ
3. Ⓐ Ⓑ Ⓒ Ⓓ
4. Ⓐ Ⓑ Ⓒ Ⓓ
5. Ⓐ Ⓑ Ⓒ Ⓓ
6. Ⓐ Ⓑ Ⓒ Ⓓ
7. Ⓐ Ⓑ Ⓒ Ⓓ
8. Ⓐ Ⓑ Ⓒ Ⓓ
9. Ⓐ Ⓑ Ⓒ Ⓓ
10. Ⓐ Ⓑ Ⓒ Ⓓ
11. Ⓐ Ⓑ Ⓒ Ⓓ
12. Ⓐ Ⓑ Ⓒ Ⓓ
13. Ⓐ Ⓑ Ⓒ Ⓓ
14. Ⓐ Ⓑ Ⓒ Ⓓ
15. Ⓐ Ⓑ Ⓒ Ⓓ
16. Ⓐ Ⓑ Ⓒ Ⓓ
17. Ⓐ Ⓑ Ⓒ Ⓓ
18. Ⓐ Ⓑ Ⓒ Ⓓ
19. Ⓐ Ⓑ Ⓒ Ⓓ
20. Ⓐ Ⓑ Ⓒ Ⓓ
21. Ⓐ Ⓑ Ⓒ Ⓓ
22. Ⓐ Ⓑ Ⓒ Ⓓ
23. Ⓐ Ⓑ Ⓒ Ⓓ
24. Ⓐ Ⓑ Ⓒ Ⓓ
25. Ⓐ Ⓑ Ⓒ Ⓓ
26. Ⓐ Ⓑ Ⓒ Ⓓ
27. Ⓐ Ⓑ Ⓒ Ⓓ
28. Ⓐ Ⓑ Ⓒ Ⓓ
29. Ⓐ Ⓑ Ⓒ Ⓓ
30. Ⓐ Ⓑ Ⓒ Ⓓ
31. Ⓐ Ⓑ Ⓒ Ⓓ
32. Ⓐ Ⓑ Ⓒ Ⓓ
33. Ⓐ Ⓑ Ⓒ Ⓓ
34. Ⓐ Ⓑ Ⓒ Ⓓ
35. Ⓐ Ⓑ Ⓒ Ⓓ

Subtest 4: Paragraph Comprehension

1. Ⓐ Ⓑ Ⓒ Ⓓ
2. Ⓐ Ⓑ Ⓒ Ⓓ
3. Ⓐ Ⓑ Ⓒ Ⓓ
4. Ⓐ Ⓑ Ⓒ Ⓓ
5. Ⓐ Ⓑ Ⓒ Ⓓ
6. Ⓐ Ⓑ Ⓒ Ⓓ
7. Ⓐ Ⓑ Ⓒ Ⓓ
8. Ⓐ Ⓑ Ⓒ Ⓓ
9. Ⓐ Ⓑ Ⓒ Ⓓ
10. Ⓐ Ⓑ Ⓒ Ⓓ
11. Ⓐ Ⓑ Ⓒ Ⓓ
12. Ⓐ Ⓑ Ⓒ Ⓓ
13. Ⓐ Ⓑ Ⓒ Ⓓ
14. Ⓐ Ⓑ Ⓒ Ⓓ
15. Ⓐ Ⓑ Ⓒ Ⓓ

Subtest 5: Mathematics Knowledge

1. Ⓐ Ⓑ Ⓒ Ⓓ
2. Ⓐ Ⓑ Ⓒ Ⓓ
3. Ⓐ Ⓑ Ⓒ Ⓓ
4. Ⓐ Ⓑ Ⓒ Ⓓ
5. Ⓐ Ⓑ Ⓒ Ⓓ
6. Ⓐ Ⓑ Ⓒ Ⓓ
7. Ⓐ Ⓑ Ⓒ Ⓓ
8. Ⓐ Ⓑ Ⓒ Ⓓ
9. Ⓐ Ⓑ Ⓒ Ⓓ
10. Ⓐ Ⓑ Ⓒ Ⓓ
11. Ⓐ Ⓑ Ⓒ Ⓓ
12. Ⓐ Ⓑ Ⓒ Ⓓ
13. Ⓐ Ⓑ Ⓒ Ⓓ
14. Ⓐ Ⓑ Ⓒ Ⓓ
15. Ⓐ Ⓑ Ⓒ Ⓓ
16. Ⓐ Ⓑ Ⓒ Ⓓ
17. Ⓐ Ⓑ Ⓒ Ⓓ
18. Ⓐ Ⓑ Ⓒ Ⓓ
19. Ⓐ Ⓑ Ⓒ Ⓓ
20. Ⓐ Ⓑ Ⓒ Ⓓ
21. Ⓐ Ⓑ Ⓒ Ⓓ
22. Ⓐ Ⓑ Ⓒ Ⓓ
23. Ⓐ Ⓑ Ⓒ Ⓓ
24. Ⓐ Ⓑ Ⓒ Ⓓ
25. Ⓐ Ⓑ Ⓒ Ⓓ

Subtest 6: Electronics Information

1. Ⓐ Ⓑ Ⓒ Ⓓ
2. Ⓐ Ⓑ Ⓒ Ⓓ
3. Ⓐ Ⓑ Ⓒ Ⓓ
4. Ⓐ Ⓑ Ⓒ Ⓓ
5. Ⓐ Ⓑ Ⓒ Ⓓ
6. Ⓐ Ⓑ Ⓒ Ⓓ
7. Ⓐ Ⓑ Ⓒ Ⓓ
8. Ⓐ Ⓑ Ⓒ Ⓓ
9. Ⓐ Ⓑ Ⓒ Ⓓ
10. Ⓐ Ⓑ Ⓒ Ⓓ
11. Ⓐ Ⓑ Ⓒ Ⓓ
12. Ⓐ Ⓑ Ⓒ Ⓓ
13. Ⓐ Ⓑ Ⓒ Ⓓ
14. Ⓐ Ⓑ Ⓒ Ⓓ
15. Ⓐ Ⓑ Ⓒ Ⓓ
16. Ⓐ Ⓑ Ⓒ Ⓓ
17. Ⓐ Ⓑ Ⓒ Ⓓ
18. Ⓐ Ⓑ Ⓒ Ⓓ
19. Ⓐ Ⓑ Ⓒ Ⓓ
20. Ⓐ Ⓑ Ⓒ Ⓓ

Subtest 7: Auto & Shop Information

1. Ⓐ Ⓑ Ⓒ Ⓓ   6. Ⓐ Ⓑ Ⓒ Ⓓ   11. Ⓐ Ⓑ Ⓒ Ⓓ   16. Ⓐ Ⓑ Ⓒ Ⓓ   21. Ⓐ Ⓑ Ⓒ Ⓓ
2. Ⓐ Ⓑ Ⓒ Ⓓ   7. Ⓐ Ⓑ Ⓒ Ⓓ   12. Ⓐ Ⓑ Ⓒ Ⓓ   17. Ⓐ Ⓑ Ⓒ Ⓓ   22. Ⓐ Ⓑ Ⓒ Ⓓ
3. Ⓐ Ⓑ Ⓒ Ⓓ   8. Ⓐ Ⓑ Ⓒ Ⓓ   13. Ⓐ Ⓑ Ⓒ Ⓓ   18. Ⓐ Ⓑ Ⓒ Ⓓ   23. Ⓐ Ⓑ Ⓒ Ⓓ
4. Ⓐ Ⓑ Ⓒ Ⓓ   9. Ⓐ Ⓑ Ⓒ Ⓓ   14. Ⓐ Ⓑ Ⓒ Ⓓ   19. Ⓐ Ⓑ Ⓒ Ⓓ   24. Ⓐ Ⓑ Ⓒ Ⓓ
5. Ⓐ Ⓑ Ⓒ Ⓓ   10. Ⓐ Ⓑ Ⓒ Ⓓ   15. Ⓐ Ⓑ Ⓒ Ⓓ   20. Ⓐ Ⓑ Ⓒ Ⓓ   25. Ⓐ Ⓑ Ⓒ Ⓓ

Subtest 8: Mechanical Comprehension

1. Ⓐ Ⓑ Ⓒ Ⓓ   6. Ⓐ Ⓑ Ⓒ Ⓓ   11. Ⓐ Ⓑ Ⓒ Ⓓ   16. Ⓐ Ⓑ Ⓒ Ⓓ   21. Ⓐ Ⓑ Ⓒ Ⓓ
2. Ⓐ Ⓑ Ⓒ Ⓓ   7. Ⓐ Ⓑ Ⓒ Ⓓ   12. Ⓐ Ⓑ Ⓒ Ⓓ   17. Ⓐ Ⓑ Ⓒ Ⓓ   22. Ⓐ Ⓑ Ⓒ Ⓓ
3. Ⓐ Ⓑ Ⓒ Ⓓ   8. Ⓐ Ⓑ Ⓒ Ⓓ   13. Ⓐ Ⓑ Ⓒ Ⓓ   18. Ⓐ Ⓑ Ⓒ Ⓓ   23. Ⓐ Ⓑ Ⓒ Ⓓ
4. Ⓐ Ⓑ Ⓒ Ⓓ   9. Ⓐ Ⓑ Ⓒ Ⓓ   14. Ⓐ Ⓑ Ⓒ Ⓓ   19. Ⓐ Ⓑ Ⓒ Ⓓ   24. Ⓐ Ⓑ Ⓒ Ⓓ
5. Ⓐ Ⓑ Ⓒ Ⓓ   10. Ⓐ Ⓑ Ⓒ Ⓓ   15. Ⓐ Ⓑ Ⓒ Ⓓ   20. Ⓐ Ⓑ Ⓒ Ⓓ   25. Ⓐ Ⓑ Ⓒ Ⓓ

Subtest 9: Assembling Objects

1. Ⓐ Ⓑ Ⓒ Ⓓ   6. Ⓐ Ⓑ Ⓒ Ⓓ   11. Ⓐ Ⓑ Ⓒ Ⓓ   16. Ⓐ Ⓑ Ⓒ Ⓓ   21. Ⓐ Ⓑ Ⓒ Ⓓ
2. Ⓐ Ⓑ Ⓒ Ⓓ   7. Ⓐ Ⓑ Ⓒ Ⓓ   12. Ⓐ Ⓑ Ⓒ Ⓓ   17. Ⓐ Ⓑ Ⓒ Ⓓ   22. Ⓐ Ⓑ Ⓒ Ⓓ
3. Ⓐ Ⓑ Ⓒ Ⓓ   8. Ⓐ Ⓑ Ⓒ Ⓓ   13. Ⓐ Ⓑ Ⓒ Ⓓ   18. Ⓐ Ⓑ Ⓒ Ⓓ   23. Ⓐ Ⓑ Ⓒ Ⓓ
4. Ⓐ Ⓑ Ⓒ Ⓓ   9. Ⓐ Ⓑ Ⓒ Ⓓ   14. Ⓐ Ⓑ Ⓒ Ⓓ   19. Ⓐ Ⓑ Ⓒ Ⓓ   24. Ⓐ Ⓑ Ⓒ Ⓓ
5. Ⓐ Ⓑ Ⓒ Ⓓ   10. Ⓐ Ⓑ Ⓒ Ⓓ   15. Ⓐ Ⓑ Ⓒ Ⓓ   20. Ⓐ Ⓑ Ⓒ Ⓓ   25. Ⓐ Ⓑ Ⓒ Ⓓ

Subtest 1: General Science

TIME: 11 minutes for 25 questions

DIRECTIONS: This test challenges your knowledge of general science principles usually covered in high school classes. Pick the best answer for each question and then mark the space on your answer sheet that corresponds to the question number and the letter indicating your choice.

1. The moon completes a revolution around Earth approximately every
   - (A) 28 days.
   - (B) 365 days.
   - (C) 24 hours.
   - (D) 7 days.

2. Carcinogens are chemicals that cause
   - (A) high blood pressure.
   - (B) gene mutations.
   - (C) blood clots.
   - (D) diabetes.

3. A paramecium is
   - (A) a one-celled organism.
   - (B) algae.
   - (C) bacteria.
   - (D) a many-celled organism.

4. What substance is essential for the function of the thyroid gland?
   - (A) potassium chloride
   - (B) hemoglobin
   - (C) calcium
   - (D) iodine

5. The brainstem controls
   - (A) vision.
   - (B) voluntary muscle movements.
   - (C) your sense of balance.
   - (D) some involuntary activities.

6. Which element is the most abundant one in the atmosphere?
   - (A) oxygen
   - (B) nitrogen
   - (C) helium
   - (D) hydrogen

7. Minerals are necessary for
   - (A) respiration.
   - (B) eliminating waste.
   - (C) preventing night blindness.
   - (D) metabolic function.

8. What's the only metallic element found as a liquid at room temperature?
   - (A) bromine
   - (B) tellurium
   - (C) mercury
   - (D) silver

9. Which of the following isn't a type of telescope?
   - (A) reflecting
   - (B) convexing
   - (C) refracting
   - (D) catadioptric

10. A dekagram
    - (A) is larger than a kilogram.
    - (B) is smaller than a kilogram.
    - (C) is the same as a kilogram.
    - (D) doesn't exist.

GO ON TO NEXT PAGE

11. The aurora borealis can be seen only in the
    (A) winter.
    (B) summer.
    (C) Southern Hemisphere.
    (D) Northern Hemisphere.

12. The three important properties of sound waves are
    (A) wavelength, speed, and crest.
    (B) speed, frequency, and reflection.
    (C) wavelength, frequency, and vibration.
    (D) wavelength, frequency, and speed.

13. Between which two planets can most of the asteroids in the solar system be found?
    (A) Mars and Jupiter
    (B) Saturn and Jupiter
    (C) Earth and Mars
    (D) Mercury and Venus

14. At room temperature, an element can be a
    (A) gas.
    (B) liquid or gas.
    (C) gas or solid.
    (D) liquid, gas, or solid.

15. The elements hydrogen and helium comprise what percentage of almost all matter in the universe?
    (A) 75%
    (B) 82%
    (C) 90%
    (D) 98%

16. Compounds are created when
    (A) atoms of two or more like elements are combined.
    (B) atoms of two or more different elements are combined.
    (C) two or more molecules are combined.
    (D) a molecule decomposes.

17. What theory suggests the universe will come to an end when its ever-increasing rate of expansion causes all matter to fly apart?
    (A) The Big Rip
    (B) The Big Bang
    (C) The Big Crunch
    (D) The Big Easy

18. A watt-hour measures
    (A) the amount of work performed or generated.
    (B) the number of electrons moving past a specific point.
    (C) resistance.
    (D) voltage.

19. Which of the following planets, known as *gas giants,* have no rings?
    (A) Neptune
    (B) Jupiter
    (C) Uranus
    (D) They all have rings.

20. Gas particles move
    (A) more slowly than liquid particles.
    (B) more slowly than solid particles.
    (C) more quickly than liquid particles.
    (D) at the same rate as all other particles.

21. Absolute zero is
    (A) 0 degrees Fahrenheit.
    (B) 0 degrees Celsius.
    (C) −273 degrees Celsius.
    (D) −32 degrees Fahrenheit.

22. Radiology is employed when doing which of the following?
    (A) using a Magnetic Resonance Imaging machine
    (B) using a blood pressure cuff
    (C) blood typing
    (D) breathing

23. Which of the following statements is not true?

    (A) The human female chin is usually more rounded or pointed than the human male chin.
    (B) The human female pelvis is usually narrower than the human male pelvis.
    (C) The human male skull is usually larger than the human female skull.
    (D) The human male skull has a larger brow ridge than the human female skull.

24. A lunar eclipse occurs when

    (A) Earth moves into the moon's shadow.
    (B) the sun blocks the moon from view.
    (C) Earth moves into the sun's shadow.
    (D) the moon moves into Earth's shadow.

25. What chemical can be used to detect blood, even if it's been wiped from a surface?

    (A) luminol
    (B) cyanide
    (C) ninhydrin
    (D) alcohol

Subtest 2: Arithmetic Reasoning

TIME: 36 minutes for 30 questions

DIRECTIONS: This test is about arithmetic. Each question is followed by four possible answers. Decide which answer is correct and then mark the space on your answer sheet that has the same number and letter as your choice. Calculators are not permitted. Use scratch paper for any figuring you need to do.

1. A baker sells a dozen donuts for $3.99. The cost to make three donuts is $0.45. How much is the total profit on 5 dozen donuts?
   - (A) $17.70
   - (B) $13.20
   - (C) $2.19
   - (D) $10.95

2. Your piggy bank contains $19.75 in dimes and quarters. There are 100 coins in all. How many dimes are there?
   - (A) 25
   - (B) 30
   - (C) 35
   - (D) 40

3. A bricklayer charges $8 per square foot to lay a patio. How much would it cost for the bricklayer to lay a 12-foot-by-16-foot patio?
   - (A) $960
   - (B) $192
   - (C) $224
   - (D) $1,536

4. Terry earns three times more per hour than Tim. Tim earns $2 more per hour than Angie. As a group, they earn $43 per hour. What's Angie's hourly wage?
   - (A) $7.00
   - (B) $8.00
   - (C) $9.00
   - (D) $10.00

5. If four people can run eight machines, how many machines can two people run?
   - (A) 2
   - (B) 4
   - (C) 1
   - (D) 3

6. The price of daily admission at an amusement park is $36. The park sells an unlimited season pass for $240. How many trips would you need to make with the season pass in order for it to cost less than paying the daily admission rate?
   - (A) 6
   - (B) 7
   - (C) 8
   - (D) 9

7. A plumber needs four lengths of pipe, each 3 feet, 6 inches long. Pipes are sold by the foot. How many feet does the plumber need to buy?
   - (A) 15
   - (B) 16
   - (C) 14
   - (D) 12

8. The product of two consecutive odd numbers is 399. What are the numbers?
   - (A) 17 and 19
   - (B) 19 and 21
   - (C) 21 and 23
   - (D) 25 and 27

9. A personal trainer earns a 65% commission on training sales. If they sell $530 worth of training, how much commission do they make?
   - (A) $874.50
   - (B) $34.45
   - (C) $344.50
   - (D) $185.50

10. A rectangle is 1 inch longer than it is wide. Its diagonal is 5 inches. What's the width of the rectangle?
    - (A) 2 inches
    - (B) 3 inches
    - (C) 4 inches
    - (D) 5 inches

11. A treasure map is drawn to a scale of 2 inches equals 3 miles. On the map, the distance between Point A and X-marks-the-spot is $9\frac{1}{2}$ inches. How many actual miles does this represent?

    (A) $20\frac{1}{2}$ miles

    (B) $14\frac{1}{4}$ miles

    (C) $6\frac{1}{3}$ miles

    (D) 19 miles

12. A painter has painted a picture on a piece of canvas that measures 10 by 14 inches. To accommodate a frame, they have left an unpainted margin of 1 inch all the way around. What part of the canvas has been painted?

    (A) 96%

    (B) 91%

    (C) 65%

    (D) 69%

13. A dog trainer is building a rectangular dog run that measures 9 by 16 feet. If they want to fence the perimeter of the run, how many feet of chain link fence will they need?

    (A) 144 feet

    (B) 25 feet

    (C) 32 feet

    (D) 50 feet

14. A rectangle is $1\frac{1}{2}$ times as long as it is wide. The perimeter of the rectangle is 100 inches. What's the length of the rectangle?

    (A) 20 inches

    (B) 30 inches

    (C) 40 inches

    (D) 45 inches

15. Miguel passed seven of his history quizzes and failed three. The fraction of quizzes he passed is correctly expressed as

    (A) $\frac{7}{3}$

    (B) $\frac{3}{7}$

    (C) $\frac{7}{10}$

    (D) $\frac{3}{5}$

16. A 3-yard-long ribbon was used to trim four dresses. Each dress used the same amount of ribbon. How much ribbon was used for each dress?

    (A) 1 yard

    (B) $\frac{2}{3}$ yard

    (C) $\frac{1}{2}$ yard

    (D) $\frac{3}{4}$ yard

17. Kelly bought a painting at an antiques sale for $500, and the following day she was able to sell it for an additional $30. What percentage of the sale price was her profit?

    (A) 5%

    (B) 6%

    (C) 7%

    (D) 4%

18. A bin of bolts at the hardware store contains 7 dozen bolts when full. The stock clerk is supposed to reorder bolts when the bin is $\frac{1}{6}$ full. How many bolts are in the bin when it's time to reorder?

    (A) 14 bolts

    (B) 1 bolt

    (C) 84 bolts

    (D) 12 bolts

19. Two bicyclists head toward each other from the opposite ends of Main Street, which is 6 miles long. The first biker started at 2:05 going 12 mph. The second biker began peddling 4 minutes later at a rate of 14 mph. What time will they meet?

    (A) 2:13

    (B) 2:24

    (C) 2:21

    (D) 2:34

20. A recipe calls for 8 ounces of black beans or red beans. The cheapest option to buy and use would be

    (A) two 4-ounce cans of black beans at $0.79 each.

    (B) one 8-ounce can of red beans at $1.49.

    (C) two 3-ounce cans of black beans at $0.59 each.

    (D) three 3-ounce cans of red beans at $0.65 each.

21. A street vendor sells $25.70 worth of pretzels on Friday, $32.30 on Saturday, and $31.80 on Sunday. They spend a fourth of the money over the weekend. How much money do they have left?

    (A) $89.80
    (B) $22.45
    (C) $44.90
    (D) $67.35

22. A recruit has $30.00. They saw some camouflage socks for $3.95 a pair. How many pairs of socks can they buy?

    (A) 9
    (B) 7
    (C) 6
    (D) 4

23. A crate containing a puppy weighs 60 pounds, 5 ounces. The puppy weighs 43 pounds, 7 ounces. How much does the crate alone weigh?

    (A) 16 pounds, 8 ounces
    (B) 16 pounds, 2 ounces
    (C) 17 pounds
    (D) 16 pounds, 14 ounces

24. In a manufacturing plant that produces new computers, a 0.15 probability exists that a computer will be defective. If five computers are manufactured, what's the probability that all of them will be defective?

    (A) 7.6
    (B) 0.60
    (C) 0.00042
    (D) 0.000076

25. A house contains one 12-foot-x-14-foot bedroom, one 12-foot-x-10-foot bedroom, and one 8-foot-x-12-foot bedroom. What's the total amount of carpeting needed to carpet all three bedrooms?

    (A) 383 square yards
    (B) 128 square yards
    (C) 88 square yards
    (D) 43 square yards

26. Rafael can type 9 pages an hour. How long will it take him to type 126 pages?

    (A) 14 hours
    (B) 9 hours
    (C) 7 hours
    (D) 16 hours

27. In a 60-minute gym class, 48 students want to play volleyball, but only 12 can play at a time. For each player to get the same amount of playing time, how many minutes should each person play?

    (A) $1\frac{1}{2}$ minutes
    (B) 6 minutes
    (C) 30 minutes
    (D) 15 minutes

28. The public library charges $2.00 for the first day a borrowed DVD is overdue and $1.25 for each day after that. If a person paid $8.25 in late fees, how many days was the DVD overdue?

    (A) 7 days
    (B) 6 days
    (C) 4 days
    (D) 5 days

29. A half-cup of pudding has 150 calories. The same amount of broccoli has 60 calories. How much broccoli can a person eat to equal the same number of calories in the $\frac{1}{2}$ cup of pudding?

    (A) 2 cups
    (B) $2\frac{1}{2}$ cups
    (C) $1\frac{1}{2}$ cups
    (D) $1\frac{1}{4}$ cups

30. The neighbor's dog barks at a raccoon every 15 minutes at night. If it first barks at 10 p.m., when you're trying to fall asleep, how many times will it have barked by 2 a.m., when you give up trying to sleep and decide to read a book instead?

    (A) 16 times
    (B) 132 times
    (C) 17 times
    (D) 15 times

Subtest 3: Word Knowledge

TIME: 11 minutes for 35 questions

DIRECTIONS: This test is about the meanings of words. Each question has an underlined word. You may be asked to decide which one of the four words in the choices most nearly means the same thing as the underlined word or which one of the four words means the opposite. If the underlined word is used in a sentence, decide which of the four choices most nearly means the same thing as the underlined word as used in the context of the sentence. Mark the corresponding space on your answer sheet.

1. Lackadaisical most nearly means
   - (A) flowerless.
   - (B) listless.
   - (C) promiscuous.
   - (D) suitable.

2. The fruit was edible.
   - (A) waxy
   - (B) expensive
   - (C) foreign
   - (D) digestible

3. Universities and colleges should be designed to cater to the philomaths.
   - (A) athletes
   - (B) scholars
   - (C) teachers
   - (D) faculty

4. Pretense most nearly means
   - (A) politeness.
   - (B) dishonesty.
   - (C) stress.
   - (D) appearance.

5. At an early age Jane showed a proclivity for music and dancing.
   - (A) predisposition
   - (B) interest
   - (C) dislike
   - (D) fever

6. The conversation was incoherent.
   - (A) eloquent
   - (B) succinct
   - (C) unintelligible
   - (D) amusing

7. The week following Joe DiMaggio's death was filled with often mawkish eulogies.
   - (A) long
   - (B) sentimental
   - (C) boring
   - (D) detailed

8. They established proof.
   - (A) offered
   - (B) invented
   - (C) demanded
   - (D) demonstrated

9. Ephemeral most nearly means
   - (A) short-lived.
   - (B) mythical.
   - (C) dead.
   - (D) exceptional.

10. Avocation most nearly means
    - (A) hobby.
    - (B) occupation.
    - (C) vacation.
    - (D) education.

11. Kvetch most nearly means
    - (A) assert.
    - (B) yell.
    - (C) complain.
    - (D) argue.

12. Their eyesight was acute.
    - (A) sharp
    - (B) poor
    - (C) unusual
    - (D) tested

13. Inamorata most nearly means
    (A) boyfriend.
    (B) mistress.
    (C) best friend.
    (D) acquaintance.

14. Their thoughts on the matter were inconsequential.
    (A) profound
    (B) disturbing
    (C) irrelevant
    (D) confused

15. Debouch most nearly means
    (A) emerge.
    (B) fight.
    (C) relax.
    (D) capture.

16. They were an amateur astronomer.
    (A) veteran
    (B) novice
    (C) interested
    (D) pleased

17. I had no idea how to react to my ludic boyfriend.
    (A) playful
    (B) cheating
    (C) crazy
    (D) lazy

18. The rose was crimson.
    (A) blooming
    (B) colorful
    (C) fragrant
    (D) red

19. The word most opposite in meaning to benison is
    (A) theft.
    (B) replaceable.
    (C) curse.
    (D) heavy.

20. They were exempt from gym class.
    (A) banned
    (B) excused
    (C) tired
    (D) refreshed

21. The eldritch light of the desert can play tricks on your eyes.
    (A) bright
    (B) wavering
    (C) strange
    (D) yellow

22. Defective most nearly means
    (A) flawed.
    (B) noticeable.
    (C) rare.
    (D) durable.

23. Allot most nearly means
    (A) plow.
    (B) assign.
    (C) property.
    (D) test.

24. The doctor gave the patient a cursory examination.
    (A) in-depth
    (B) painful
    (C) unnecessary
    (D) superficial

25. Arcanum most nearly means
    (A) rare.
    (B) secret.
    (C) tangible.
    (D) false.

26. Their answer was terse.
    (A) defensive
    (B) angry
    (C) lengthy
    (D) brief

27. The dulcet songs of the band got the attention of the audience.
    (A) harmonious
    (B) love
    (C) jazzy
    (D) loud

28. They were arrested on a misdemeanor charge.
    (A) theft
    (B) serious
    (C) petty crime
    (D) bogus

29. Embonpoint most nearly means
    (A) plumpness.
    (B) height.
    (C) quickness.
    (D) cold.

30. They concocted a story about me.
    (A) told
    (B) rehearsed
    (C) invented
    (D) remembered

31. I spent my days searching fruitlessly for that chimera, my true self.
    (A) personality
    (B) enigma
    (C) talent
    (D) monster

32. Their former home was in Colorado.
    (A) previous
    (B) current
    (C) second
    (D) abandoned

33. Mulct most nearly means
    (A) complain.
    (B) play.
    (C) work.
    (D) fleece.

34. My voice is strident.
    (A) soft
    (B) melodious
    (C) harsh
    (D) baritone

35. Raffish most nearly means
    (A) clean.
    (B) serene.
    (C) tawdry.
    (D) expensive.

Subtest 4: Paragraph Comprehension

TIME: 13 minutes for 15 questions

DIRECTIONS: This test measures your ability to understand what you read. This section includes paragraphs of reading material followed by incomplete statements or questions. Read each paragraph and select the choice that best completes the statement or answers the question. Mark your choice on your answer sheet by using the correct letter with each question number.

Because leadership is charged with bringing new ideas, methods, or solutions into use, innovation is inextricably connected with the process of being an effective leader. Innovation means change, and change requires leadership. Leaders must be the chief transformation officers in their organizations and learn everything there is to know about the change before it even takes place. Furthermore, they must learn how to deal with the emotions that result from the chaos and fear associated with change.

1. According to the passage,
    - (A) leaders should resist making changes that subordinates are likely to resist.
    - (B) innovation and change are distinctly different processes.
    - (C) it's not necessary for the leader to know everything about a change before it's implemented.
    - (D) change is often associated with panic and disorder.

Cougars are the most wide-ranging big cats in North America, inhabiting a wide variety of environments. A cougar, also called a puma or a mountain lion, lives about 18 years in the wild, can jump 20 feet (in distance) at a time, and can range 50 miles when on the prowl for food.

2. According to this passage,
    - (A) a cougar isn't the same thing as a mountain lion.
    - (B) cougars are an endangered species.
    - (C) cougars live in many areas of North America.
    - (D) cougars live only a few years in the wild.

A helping relationship refers to interactions in which the counselor makes a determined effort to contribute in a positive way to the counselee's improvement. In counseling, the counselor establishes a helping relationship by drawing on practices that help the counselee live more in harmony with themselves and others and with a greater self-understanding. The relationship develops because the counselee needs assistance, instruction, or understanding.

3. Which of the following statements is not supported by the passage?
    - (A) Successful counseling requires developing a relationship.
    - (B) Most counselees initially reject advice given by the counselor.
    - (C) Counseling helps a counselee develop a greater understanding of themself.
    - (D) Counseling relationships are developed by relying on helpful practices.

Many small cities and towns rely on volunteer fire departments to put out fires. A professional fire department, however, has more training, more expertise, and more experience in fighting fires and investigating their causes. In many cases, it's worthwhile for even very small towns to hire professional firefighters.

4. According to this passage, it's reasonable to assume that
    - (A) volunteer firefighters have less training, expertise, and experience than professional firefighters.
    - (B) volunteer firefighters have the skills and resources to investigate the causes of fires.
    - (C) professional firefighters don't know what causes fires.
    - (D) a professional fire department is cost-prohibitive for small towns.

The idea being an alarming one, he scrambled out of bed and groped his way to the window. He was obliged to rub the frost off with the sleeve of his dressing-gown before he could see anything and could see very little then. All he could make out was that it was still very foggy and extremely cold and that there was no noise of people running to and fro and making a great stir, as there unquestionably would've been if night had beaten off bright day, and taken possession of the world.

5. This story takes place
   (A) in Ireland.
   (B) on a calm summer evening.
   (C) on a winter night.
   (D) both A and C.

Epidemiology is the study of what causes diseases, injuries, and other physiological damage to humans and why such problems occur. Epidemiologists examine where and when disease outbreaks occur. By using statistics and other scientific methods, epidemiologists determine what factors affect the frequency and severity of disease patterns. The primary goal of epidemiology is to control or prevent outbreaks of disease — other goals are subordinate.

6. What would be the best title for this passage?
   (A) "Epidemiology: The Study of Disease Patterns"
   (B) "Goals for the Future of Epidemiology"
   (C) "Using Statistical Methods in Epidemiology"
   (D) "Employment Outlook for Epidemiologists"

Buddhism is a religion that must be viewed from many angles. Its original form, as preached by Gautama in India and developed in the early years succeeding and as embodied in the sacred literature of early Buddhism, isn't representative of the actual Buddhism of any land today.

7. According to this passage,
   (A) most Buddhists live in India.
   (B) Buddhist teachings have changed over the years.
   (C) Buddhism draws its teachings from early Christianity.
   (D) Buddhist temples can be found in any land of the world.

Questions 8 and 9 are based on the following passage.

Many criminal-law statutes permit more severe punishment of a person convicted of a crime if they intended to harm another person. For example, voluntary manslaughter carries a heavier penalty than involuntary manslaughter in most states. Planned crimes are also punished more severely than spur-of-the-moment crimes.

The problem is that juries find it difficult to know what the intent of a person was at the time they committed a crime. Many defendants will deny that they intended to harm the other person and claim that any harm that occurred was "accidental." The law asks too much of juries when it expects them to determine what a person was thinking. Juries should only be asked to weigh objective evidence.

8. The author of this passage would agree that
   (A) laws should not punish people based on intention.
   (B) juries aren't intelligent enough to weigh evidence.
   (C) more laws should distinguish between crimes committed with intent and crimes committed on the spur of the moment.
   (D) lawyers will lie about anything.

9. According to this passage,
   (A) most states don't distinguish between voluntary and involuntary manslaughter.
   (B) punishing people more severely for voluntary manslaughter is unconstitutional.
   (C) it's difficult for juries to determine a defendant's intentions at the time a crime was committed.
   (D) prosecutors can, through careful questioning, show a defendant's intention at the time a crime was committed.

Questions 10 through 12 are based on the following passage.

Ergonomics is the science of designing and arranging workspaces so that people and objects interact efficiently and safely. Lack of attention to ergonomics causes thousands of workers to suffer repetitive stress injury, eye fatigue, muscle soreness, and many other medical problems each year.

Adequate lighting, well-designed chairs, and clutter-free work areas contribute to effective ergonomic design. The opportunity to take short breaks every hour or two, especially for desk-bound workers, is also helpful. It's also important for workers to avoid performing the same movements over and over for hours at a time. Variety in the type of work being done can decrease the chance of injury.

10. According to this passage,
    (A) ergonomics can cause injuries.
    (B) ergonomics is about designing and arranging workspaces efficiently and safely.
    (C) ergonomics is expensive and time-consuming.
    (D) few people experience problems due to poor ergonomics.

11. According to this passage,
    (A) adequate lighting and well-designed chairs, although important, have nothing to do with ergonomics.
    (B) repetition in the type of work people do helps them accomplish their tasks safely and efficiently.
    (C) short breaks aren't important for desk-bound employees because they do little heavy labor.
    (D) ergonomic design also includes keeping work areas well-lit and clutter-free.

12. According to this passage, it's reasonable to assume that
    (A) employers should invest in ergonomic design to protect workers.
    (B) lack of ergonomic design isn't dangerous.
    (C) labor unions have opposed ergonomic design.
    (D) poor design is responsible for most employee accidents.

Questions 13 through 15 are based on the following passage.

Electricity is the most inefficient and costly way to heat a home. One kilowatt-hour of electricity creates about 3,400 British thermal units (BTUs). (BTUs are a standard heat measurement.) The price of electricity per kilowatt-hour is between $0.10 and $0.25 or between $29.35 and $73.13 per million BTUs.

In contrast, fuel oil, which produces 140,000 BTUs per gallon, costs about $8.33 to $13.89 per million BTUs. Natural gas, which produces 100,000 BTUs per therm, can be purchased for $5.00 to $22.50 per million BTUs. Oak firewood, which produces 26,000,000 BTUs per cord, costs $5.77 to $13.46 per million BTUs.

Choosing the right heating method for your home, based on the cost of fuel, may be more expensive at installation but will be cheaper in the long run.

13. According to the passage, a BTU
    (A) is an unusual method of measuring heat.
    (B) stands for "British thermal unit."
    (C) is the abbreviation for a "big thermal unit."
    (D) can heat a 9-x-12 room.

14. According to the passage,
    (A) heating with fuel oil is always cheaper than other methods.
    (B) oak firewood produces fewer BTUs per dollar than the other types of fuel.
    (C) natural gas costs more than all other fuels except oak firewood.
    (D) electricity is always the most expensive way to heat a house.

15. The title of this passage should be
    (A) "Choosing the Right Heating Method"
    (B) "Heating Methods for Houses"
    (C) "Know Your BTUs"
    (D) "Price List for Fuel"

Subtest 5: Mathematics Knowledge

TIME: 24 minutes for 25 questions

DIRECTIONS: This section tests your ability to solve general mathematical problems. Select the correct answer from the choices given and then mark the corresponding space on your answer sheet. Use scratch paper to do any figuring.

1. If $y = 6$, then $2y \times y =$
   - (A) 12
   - (B) 72
   - (C) 18
   - (D) 242

2. If $0.05x = 1$, then x equals
   - (A) $\frac{1}{20}$
   - (B) 20
   - (C) 10
   - (D) 5

3. Simplify: $\sqrt{25x^2}$
   - (A) x
   - (B) x^2
   - (C) $5x$
   - (D) $-5x^2$

4. Factor: $9x^3 + 18x^2 - x - 2$
   - (A) $(9x^2 - 1)(x + 2)$
   - (B) $(9x^2 + 1)(x - 2)$
   - (C) $(9x^2 + 2)(x - 1)$
   - (D) $(9x^2 - 2)(x + 1)$

5. Solve for x: $5x + 7 = 6(x - 2) - 4(2x - 3)$
   - (A) 1
   - (B) −1
   - (C) 2
   - (D) −2

6. Simplify: $x(x^2) =$
   - (A) x^2
   - (B) $2x$
   - (C) $2x^2$
   - (D) x^3

7. Simplify: $\sqrt{(5+x)^2} =$
   - (A) $5 - x$
   - (B) $5 + x$
   - (C) $\sqrt{5} - \sqrt{x}$
   - (D) $\sqrt{5} + \sqrt{x}$

8. $(3 \times 3)(5 - 3)(6 + 2) = x^2$. What's the value of x?
   - (A) 6
   - (B) 12
   - (C) 144
   - (D) 64

9. If $-5x = 25$, x equals
   - (A) −5
   - (B) 5
   - (C) 10
   - (D) 0

10. A circle measures 12 feet in diameter. What's its area to the nearest foot?
    - (A) 452
    - (B) 24
    - (C) 113
    - (D) 48

11. A square box has 6-inch sides. What's its volume?
    - (A) 18 cubic inches
    - (B) 216 cubic inches
    - (C) 12 cubic inches
    - (D) 36 cubic inches

GO ON TO NEXT PAGE

12. A circle has a diameter of 10 inches. What's its approximate area?

(A) $\pi(10)^2$
(B) $\pi(25)$
(C) $\pi(5)$
(D) $\pi(10)^2(10)$

13. A cylinder has a diameter of 12 inches and a height of 10 inches. What's its approximate volume?

(A) 4,521 cubic inches
(B) 120 cubic inches
(C) 1,130 cubic inches
(D) 1,440 cubic inches

14. Triangle *ABC* is a(n)

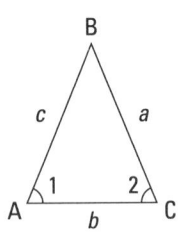

© John Wiley & Sons, Inc.

(A) equilateral triangle.
(B) right triangle.
(C) scalene triangle.
(D) isosceles triangle.

15. The interior angles of the following quadrilateral

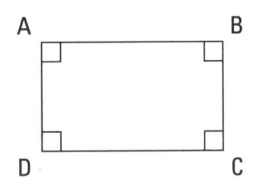

© John Wiley & Sons, Inc.

(A) are all right angles.
(B) each equals 45 degrees.
(C) are all unequal.
(D) total 180 degrees.

16. In the following figure, the sum of Angles 1 and 2 equals

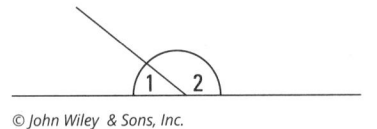

© John Wiley & Sons, Inc.

(A) 180 degrees.
(B) 90 degrees.
(C) 45 degrees.
(D) 360 degrees.

17. Solve for *x*: $3(2x-5)-2(4x+1)=-5(x+3)-2$.

(A) 0
(B) 1
(C) 2
(D) 3

18. A cube has a volume of 64 cubic inches. What's the length of one side of the cube?

(A) 4 inches
(B) 16 inches
(C) 8 inches
(D) 32 inches

19. Simplify: $(x^3)^2 =$

(A) x^5
(B) x^6
(C) x^9
(D) $2x^3$

20. If *r* inches of rain fall in one minute, how many inches fall in *h* hours?

(A) $rh \div 60$
(B) $60 - h$
(C) rh
(D) $60rh$

21. If $x = y$, then $6 + 4(x - y) =$

(A) $6xy + 4$
(B) $6 + 4xy$
(C) $10x - 10y$
(D) 6

494 PART 6 Practice ASVAB Exams

22. $\sqrt{820}$ is a number between

(A) 20 and 30.
(B) 10 and 20.
(C) 80 and 90.
(D) 40 and 50.

23. Simplify: $(x+2)(x+2) =$

(A) $x^2 + 2x + 4$
(B) $x^2 + 4x + 4$
(C) $x^2 + 4x + 2$
(D) $x^2 + 2x + 0$

24. Evaluate the expression $6a - 3x - 2y$ if $a = -3$, $x = -7$, and $y = 4$.

(A) -5
(B) -40
(C) 31
(D) 40

25. Simplify: $(x+4)(3x+5) =$

(A) $3x^2 + 9x + 20$
(B) $3x^2 + 17x + 15$
(C) $3x^2 + 17x + 20$
(D) $3x^2 + 9x + 15$

Subtest 6: Electronics Information

TIME: 9 minutes for 20 questions

DIRECTIONS: This section tests your knowledge of electrical, radio, and electronics information. Select the correct response from the choices given and then mark the corresponding space on your answer sheet.

1. What effect does a speaker wire's gauge have on speaker sound quality?
   - (A) Higher gauge wires are thicker with better sound quality.
   - (B) Lower gauge wires are thicker with better sound quality.
   - (C) Lower gauge wires are thicker with lesser sound quality.
   - (D) Higher gauge wires are thicker with lesser sound quality.

2. What's the primary advantage of a quad-band cellphone over a dual-band cellphone?
   - (A) transmission strength
   - (B) coverage area
   - (C) reception strength
   - (D) smaller phone size

3. When working with electricity, you should assume that all electrical equipment is alive unless you know for certain otherwise. This prevents
   - (A) damage to circuits.
   - (B) personal injury.
   - (C) unnecessary labor.
   - (D) overheating the equipment.

4. The heat effect of current occurs
   - (A) when the pressure of the current in the wire breaks up impurities in the wire, creating heat.
   - (B) when the current in the wire decays electrons, causing them to move more quickly, creating heat.
   - (C) when the current overcomes resistance in the wire, creating heat.
   - (D) The heat effect of current is only theoretical; it has never been proven to exist.

5. What special type of diode is commonly used to regulate voltage?
   - (A) capacitor
   - (B) transistor
   - (C) Zener
   - (D) LED

6. This symbol means

   © John Wiley & Sons, Inc.

   - (A) ohm.
   - (B) ampere.
   - (C) high voltage.
   - (D) wattage.

7. Electromotive force is another way of saying
   - (A) frequency.
   - (B) watts.
   - (C) cycles per second.
   - (D) voltage.

8. A primary advantage of using a Li-Ion battery instead of a NiMH battery in your cellphone is
   - (A) Li-Ion batteries are lighter.
   - (B) Li-Ion batteries last longer.
   - (C) Li-Ion batteries don't interfere with signal quality.
   - (D) none of the above.

9. Transistors contain at least three terminals called the
   - (A) base, emitter, and collector.
   - (B) base, positive terminal, and negative terminal.
   - (C) emitter, amplifier, and collector.
   - (D) base and two gates.

10. To control a light fixture from two different wall switches, you should use
    (A) a single-pole switch and a four-way switch.
    (B) two three-way switches.
    (C) two four-way switches.
    (D) two single-pole switches.

11. A transistor is also called a(n)
    (A) rectifier.
    (B) cathode.
    (C) amplifier.
    (D) semiconductor.

12. This symbol means

    © John Wiley & Sons, Inc.

    (A) ground.
    (B) resistor.
    (C) diode.
    (D) battery.

13. To decrease capacitance, capacitors
    (A) should have less voltage applied to them.
    (B) should be connected in parallel.
    (C) should be connected in series.
    (D) should be eliminated.

14. A resistor marked 2.5K ohms has the value of
    (A) 2.5 ohms.
    (B) 250 watts.
    (C) 2,500 ohms.
    (D) 25,000 ohms.

15. A 9-volt battery contains
    (A) 1 cell.
    (B) 6 cells.
    (C) 9 cells.
    (D) 3 cells.

16. The hot wire is always
    (A) purple.
    (B) green.
    (C) whitish.
    (D) black.

17. How wide is the full AT motherboard?
    (A) 11 inches
    (B) 11.5 inches
    (C) 12 inches
    (D) 12.5 inches

18. The following symbol represents a(n)

    © John Wiley & Sons, Inc.

    (A) relay.
    (B) on-off switch.
    (C) push switch.
    (D) connected wire.

19. If a 120-volt current is protected by a 25-amp circuit breaker, what's the largest number of watts an appliance can safely use?
    (A) 1,200 watts
    (B) 1,800 watts
    (C) 3,000 watts
    (D) 3,600 watts

20. The following symbol represents a

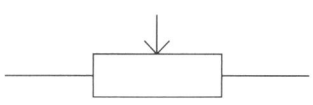

    © John Wiley & Sons, Inc.

    (A) rheostat.
    (B) capacitor.
    (C) relay.
    (D) potentiometer.

Subtest 7: Auto & Shop Information

TIME: 11 minutes for 25 questions

DIRECTIONS: This test contains questions about automobiles, shop practices, and the use of tools. Pick the best answer for each question and then mark the corresponding space on your answer sheet.

1. A symptom of worn piston rings is
   - (A) a knocking and pinging sound when driving.
   - (B) soft and spongy acceleration.
   - (C) the smell of exhaust in the car.
   - (D) an engine using excessive amounts of oil.

2. What term refers to the rebuilding of an engine to precise factory specifications?
   - (A) blueprinting
   - (B) speccing
   - (C) gold rebuild
   - (D) silver rebuild

3. The number of cranks a crankshaft has on a V-8 engine is
   - (A) 6.
   - (B) 4.
   - (C) 3.
   - (D) 8.

4. When an engine runs on after the ignition key is turned off, it's called
   - (A) dieseling.
   - (B) sputtering.
   - (C) ignition recharge.
   - (D) ignition malfunction.

5. If a radiator fails, the engine
   - (A) will idle roughly.
   - (B) may burn fuel less efficiently.
   - (C) works hard to maintain speed.
   - (D) can quickly overheat.

6. On modern automobile engines, what's the purpose of the intake manifold?
   - (A) It regulates airflow to the cooling system.
   - (B) It provides airflow to the air-conditioner and heater.
   - (C) It distributes air evenly between each cylinder.
   - (D) It regulates fuel pump pressure.

7. Brake systems work by
   - (A) applying friction to the wheels to stop their rotation.
   - (B) reversing power to the wheels.
   - (C) applying pressure to the axle.
   - (D) interrupting power to the transmission.

8. Which of the following isn't a component of the cooling system?
   - (A) heater core
   - (B) radiator
   - (C) thermostat
   - (D) hydrator

9. A catalytic converter
   - (A) combines the fuel-air mixture.
   - (B) reduces dangerous exhaust emissions.
   - (C) converts the up-and-down motion of the pistons to rotary motion.
   - (D) charges the battery when the engine is in operation.

10. If the steering wheel vibrates at high speeds, the most likely problem is
    - (A) front end alignment.
    - (B) front tire balance.
    - (C) cracked steering column.
    - (D) overinflated tires.

11. During the compression stroke on a four-cycle engine,
    (A) the intake valve opens to fill the cylinder with fuel.
    (B) the burning fuel mixture forces the piston to the bottom of the cylinder.
    (C) the intake valve closes, and the piston moves to the top of the cylinder.
    (D) the exhaust valve releases the burned gas.

12. On older cars with carburetors, the air filter can be found
    (A) on top of the engine.
    (B) under the engine.
    (C) behind the engine.
    (D) on the left or right side of the engine.

13. Glazing is the process of
    (A) cutting glass to size.
    (B) using putty to hold glass to a window frame.
    (C) polishing glass before using.
    (D) removing glass from a window.

14. A wrench with fixed, open jaws is called a(n)
    (A) adjustable wrench.
    (B) Allen wrench.
    (C) socket wrench.
    (D) open-end wrench.

15. All hammers have a
    (A) head, face, and handle.
    (B) head, toe, and handle.
    (C) head and foot.
    (D) head and claw.

16. To determine the number of threads per inch on a fastener, use a
    (A) depth gauge.
    (B) thread gauge.
    (C) thickness gauge.
    (D) wire gauge.

17. To chip or cut wood in close, the best tool is a
    (A) screwdriver.
    (B) butt chisel.
    (C) framing chisel.
    (D) paring chisel.

18. Machine screws
    (A) are made by machines.
    (B) can be used interchangeably with wood screws.
    (C) have uniform threads from top to bottom.
    (D) are machined to fine tolerances.

19. Double-headed nails are used
    (A) to reinforce a joint.
    (B) on temporary construction.
    (C) to make frames for furniture.
    (D) when a larger striking surface is needed.

20. To thin oil-based paint, use
    (A) turpentine.
    (B) baby oil.
    (C) benzene.
    (D) varnish.

21. When finishing a piece of wood, it's best to sand
    (A) diagonal to the grain.
    (B) against the grain.
    (C) with the grain.
    (D) in small circles.

22. To transfer an angle, the best tool to use is a
    (A) square.
    (B) caliper.
    (C) level.
    (D) sliding T-bevel.

23. The following tool is a(n)

© John Wiley & Sons, Inc.

- **(A)** pipe wrench.
- **(B)** socket wrench.
- **(C)** adjustable crescent wrench.
- **(D)** box-end wrench.

24. Which of the following screw heads requires a Phillips screwdriver?

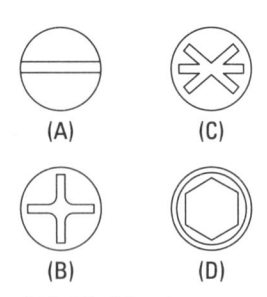

© John Wiley & Sons, Inc.

25. The following tool is used to

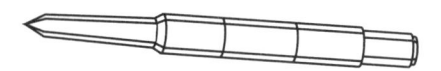

© John Wiley & Sons, Inc.

- **(A)** punch holes.
- **(B)** drive nails.
- **(C)** measure thickness.
- **(D)** set nails.

Subtest 8: Mechanical Comprehension

TIME: 19 minutes for 25 questions

DIRECTIONS: This test is about mechanical principles. Many of the questions use drawings to illustrate specific principles. Choose the correct answer and mark the corresponding space on the answer sheet.

1. Helical gears have
   - (A) straight teeth.
   - (B) slanted teeth.
   - (C) teeth of unequal size.
   - (D) no advantage over spur gears.

2. In the following figure, which pillar supports the greater load of the anvil?

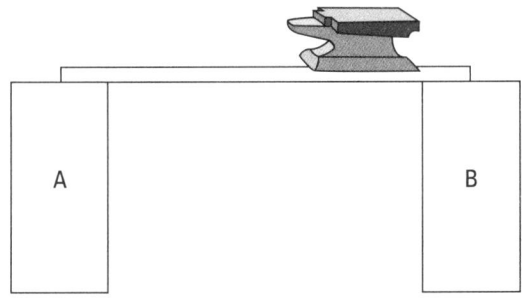

   © John Wiley & Sons, Inc.

   - (A) Pillar A
   - (B) Pillar B
   - (C) Both pillars support the anvil equally.
   - (D) It's impossible to determine from the information given.

3. Wheel A has a diameter of 10 feet. Wheel B has a diameter of 8 feet. If both wheels revolve at the same rate, Wheel B will cover a linear distance of 16 feet
   - (A) at the same time as Wheel A.
   - (B) more slowly than Wheel A.
   - (C) in twice the time as Wheel A.
   - (D) faster than Wheel A.

4. What effort must be used to lift a 30-pound anvil (see the following figure) using a first-class lever? (Don't include the weight of the lever in your calculations.)

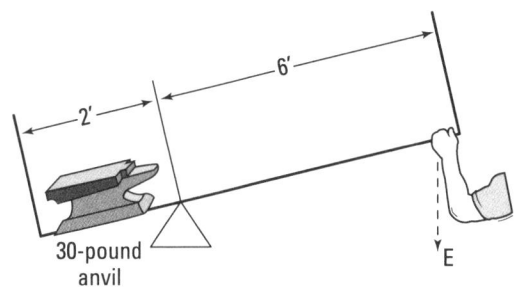

   © John Wiley & Sons, Inc.

   - (A) 10 pounds
   - (B) 15 pounds
   - (C) 50 pounds
   - (D) 5 pounds

5. What mechanical advantage does the block-and-tackle arrangement in the following figure give?

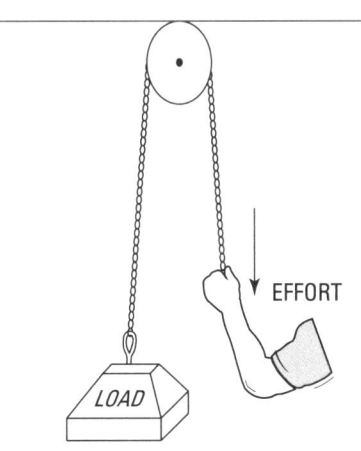

   © John Wiley & Sons, Inc.

   - (A) 1
   - (B) 3
   - (C) 2
   - (D) 4

6. If a ramp is 8 feet long and 4 feet high, how much effort is required to move a 400-pound object up the ramp?
   (A) 35 pounds
   (B) 150 pounds
   (C) 800 pounds
   (D) 200 pounds

7. 33,000 foot-pounds of work done in one minute is called
   (A) a job for an enlisted soldier.
   (B) 1 horsepower.
   (C) 330 psi.
   (D) meaningful force.

8. A 130-pound person is wearing shoes with heels that measure 1-inch square. If the person is standing on one heel, what psi does the heel exert as it rests on the ground? (Disregard atmospheric pressure in your calculations.)
   (A) 130
   (B) 65
   (C) 260
   (D) 11

9. Clothes from the dryer stick together because of
   (A) gravity.
   (B) magnetism.
   (C) friction.
   (D) static electricity.

10. An aneroid barometer measures
    (A) atmospheric pressure.
    (B) water pressure.
    (C) hydraulic-fluid pressure.
    (D) the ambient temperature.

11. If Gear A is revolving in a clockwise manner, as in the following figure, Gear B

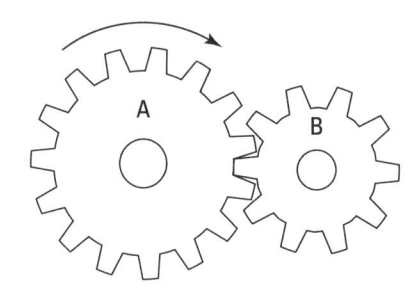

    © John Wiley & Sons, Inc.

    (A) remains stationary.
    (B) revolves in a clockwise manner.
    (C) revolves in a counterclockwise manner.
    (D) turns more slowly than Gear A.

12. Springs are used for all of the following purposes EXCEPT
    (A) to store energy for part of a mechanical cycle.
    (B) to force a mechanical component to maintain contact with another component.
    (C) to reduce shock or impact.
    (D) to increase the weight of a mechanism.

13. The floats in Tubes A and B measure specific gravity. Which tube contains the liquid with the higher specific gravity?

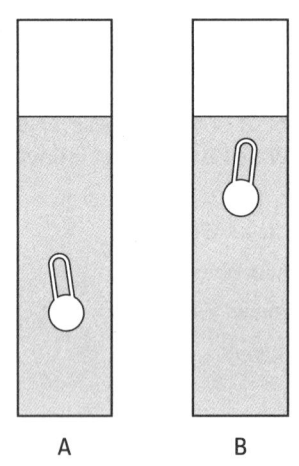

    © John Wiley & Sons, Inc.

    (A) Tube A
    (B) Tube B
    (C) It can't be determined.
    (D) Both Tube A and Tube B have the same specific gravity.

14. Universal joints are used to

(A) connect ball bearings.

(B) fix two shafts so they don't pivot or rotate.

(C) connect shafts in a U-shape.

(D) couple two shafts set at different angles.

15. The try-cock in the following schematic measures

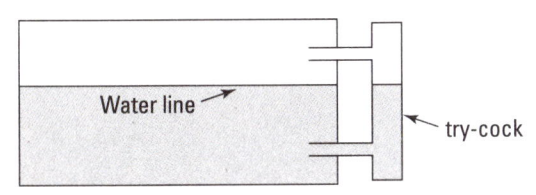

(A) temperature of water.

(B) pressure of water.

(C) pressure of steam buildup.

(D) level of water.

16. The steel plate below is held in place by different machine screws, each indicated by different symbols. How many different types of machine screws have been used?

(A) 6

(B) 15

(C) 5

(D) 9

17. The amount of force (F) needed to balance the lever in the following figure is most nearly

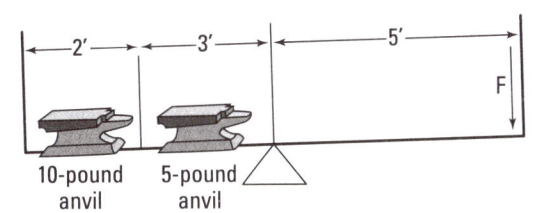

(A) 15 pounds.

(B) 13 pounds.

(C) 7.5 pounds.

(D) 20 pounds.

18. With one complete revolution of the cable winch shown below, the load will move

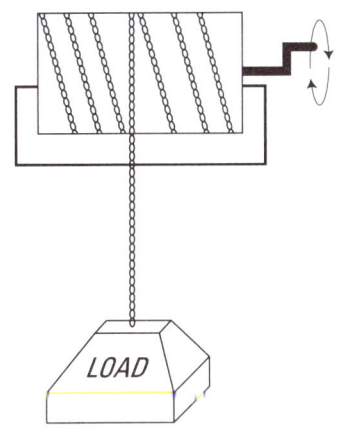

(A) 12 inches.

(B) 6 inches.

(C) 24 inches.

(D) 36 inches.

19. In the following figure, assume the valves are all closed. Which valves need to be open to fill the tank entirely?

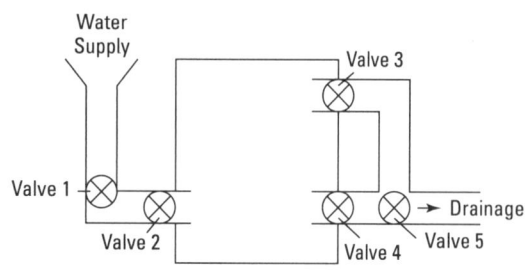

(A) 1 and 2 only
(B) 1 only
(C) 1, 2, and 3
(D) 2 only

20. If Gear 1 in the following figure makes 10 complete clockwise revolutions per minute, then

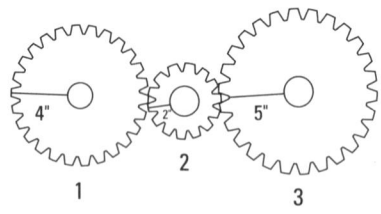

(A) Gear 2 makes 2 clockwise revolutions per minute.
(B) Gear 3 makes 8 clockwise revolutions per minute.
(C) Gear 3 makes 30 clockwise revolutions per minute.
(D) Gear 3 makes 9 counterclockwise revolutions per minute.

21. A gear and pinion have a ratio of 1 to 4. If the gear makes 200 revolutions per minute, the speed of the pinion is

(A) 50 rpm.
(B) 800 rpm.
(C) 400 rpm.
(D) 200 rpm.

22. The gas gauge in an automobile relies on what mechanical device to measure the amount of gas in the tank?

(A) ball and cock
(B) automatic valve
(C) float
(D) mechanical switch

23. Using a runner gives you a mechanical advantage of

(A) 4.
(B) 2.
(C) 3.
(D) 1.

24. For the valve shown in the figure below to open once each second, the cam must revolve at a rate of

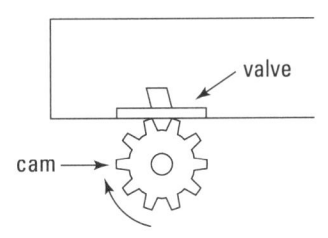

© John Wiley & Sons, Inc.

(A) 6 rpm.
(B) 10 rpm.
(C) 15 rpm.
(D) 3 rpm.

25. The following figure represents a water tank. Which of the following statements is not true?

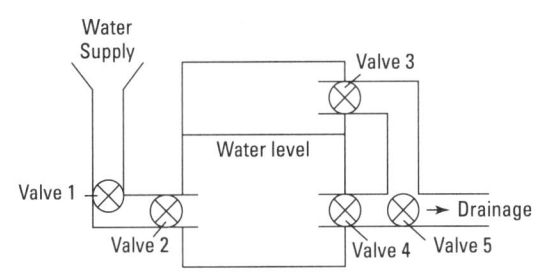

© John Wiley & Sons, Inc.

(A) If Valves 1 and 2 are open and Valves 3, 4, and 5 are closed, the tank will eventually overflow.

(B) If all valves are open, the water will remain at a constant level as long as the rate of intake is equal to the rate of discharge.

(C) Water in the tank will rise if Valves 1 and 2 are open and Valves 3 and 4 are closed.

(D) The tank will empty entirely if Valves 1 and 2 are closed and Valves 4 and 5 are open.

Subtest 9: Assembling Objects

TIME: 15 minutes for 25 questions

DIRECTIONS: The Assembling Objects subtest consists of questions that measure your ability to mentally picture items in two dimensions. Each question is comprised of five separate drawings. The problem is presented in the first drawing and the remaining four drawings are possible solutions. Determine which of the choices best solves the problem shown in the first picture, and then mark the corresponding choice on your answer sheet.

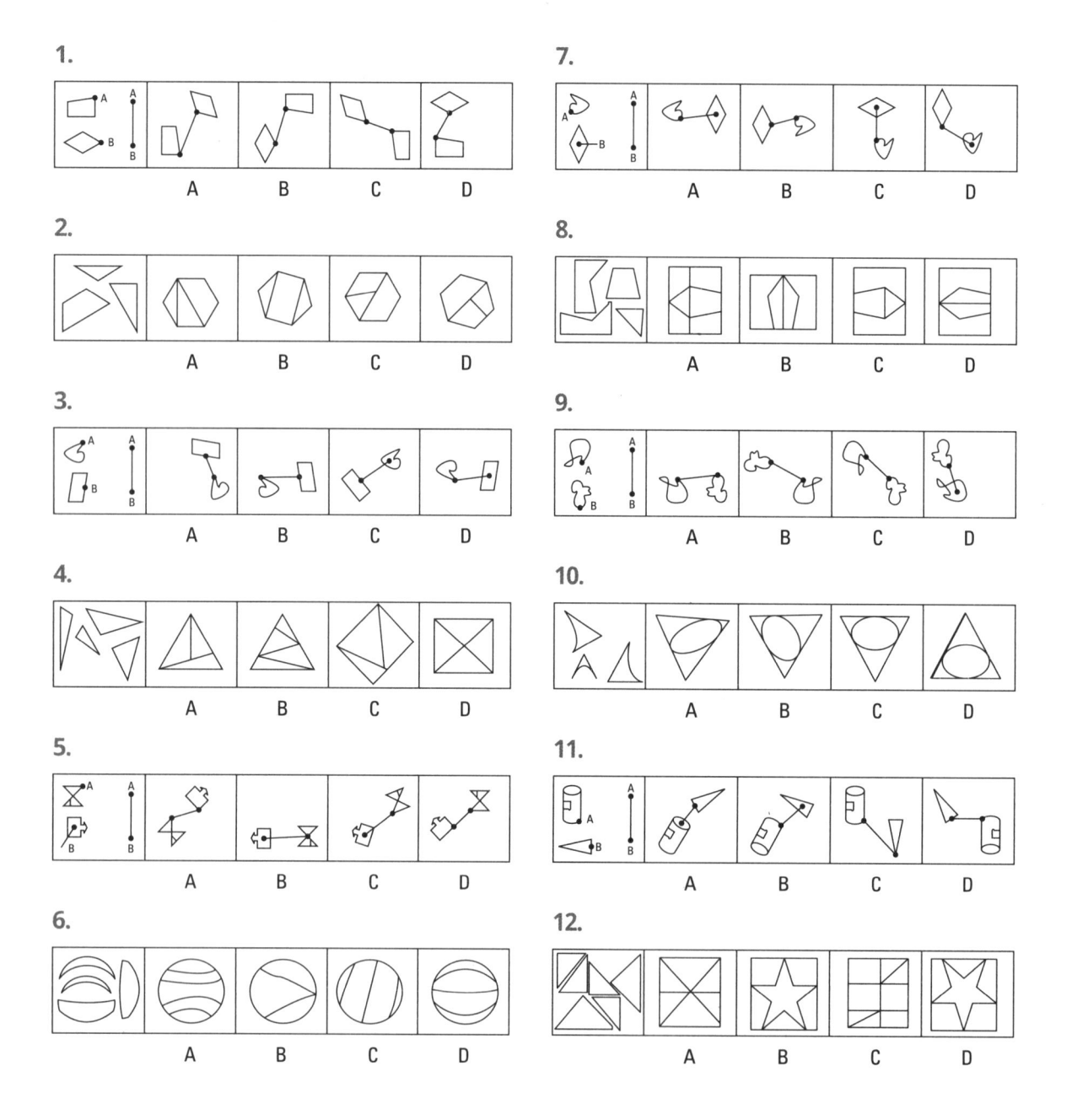

13.
14.
15.
16.
17.
18.
19.
20.
21.
22.
23.
24.
25.

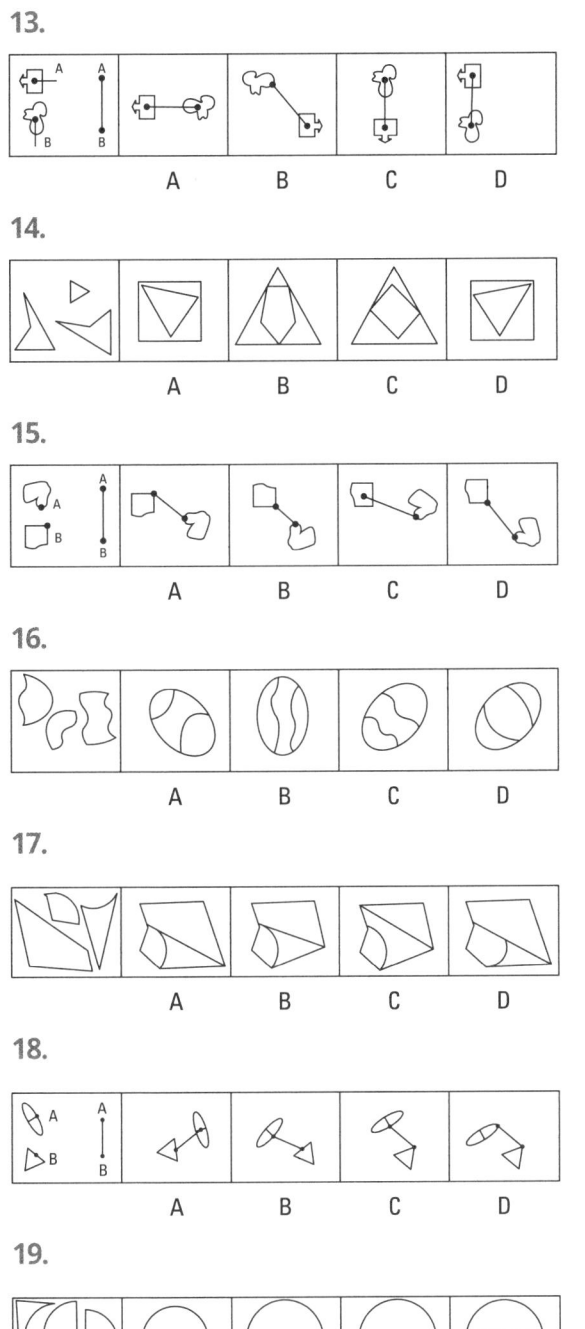

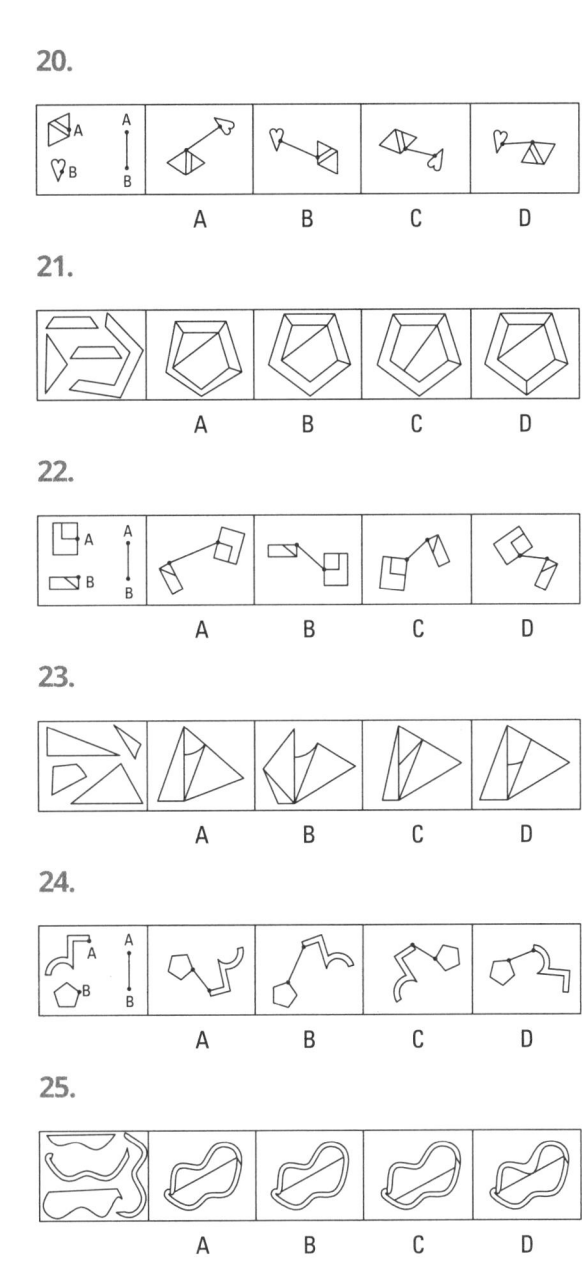

DO NOT TURN THE PAGE UNTIL TOLD TO DO SO STOP **DO NOT RETURN TO A PREVIOUS TEST**

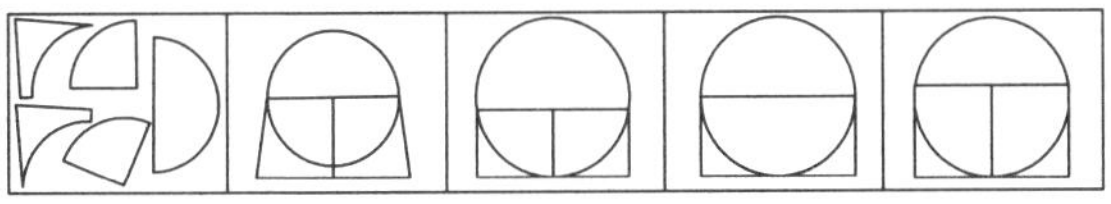

CHAPTER 22 Practice Exam 3 507

Chapter 23

Practice Exam 3: Answers and Explanations

Read over each question from Chapter 22 as you check the answer key. I hope you did well on this practice exam. If you find you need to study more for any subtest, follow the cross-references. (And for in-depth study, check out some of the book recommendations in Chapter 19.)

Subtest 1: General Science Answers

If you're still having problems figuring out the difference between an isotope and an ion, remember you may not have to do well on this subtest. It depends on the military career you're interested in. If this subtest is important to your military career aspirations, consider putting in some extra study. You can find additional information and practice questions in Chapters 10, 11, and 12.

1. **A.** The moon orbits the Earth approximately every 27.3 days. The closest answer is Choice (A).

2. **B.** *Carcinogens* cause gene mutations and can cause cancer.

3. **A.** A *paramecium* is a slipper-shaped one-celled organism.

4. **D.** Iodine is necessary for the thyroid gland to function.

5. **D.** The brainstem controls some involuntary muscle activities.

6. **B.** The element most abundant in the atmosphere is nitrogen (about 78%), followed by oxygen (about 21%).

7. **D.** Minerals are essential for various bodily functions, including the metabolic processes that turn food into energy.

8. **C.** Mercury, found in older-style thermometers, is the only metal that is in its liquid state at room temperature. Bromine is liquid at room temperature, but it's not a metallic element (be careful to read every word of the questions you see on the ASVAB).

9. **B.** Reflecting, refracting, and catadioptric are all types of telescopes, so Choice (B) is correct.

10. **B.** A dekagram is 10 grams, and a kilogram is 1,000 grams, so a dekagram is smaller than a kilogram.

11. **D.** The aurora borealis can be seen only in the Northern Hemisphere — hence the nickname Northern Lights.

12. **D.** Characteristics of sound waves include wavelength, frequency, velocity (speed), and amplitude. *Crests* are the high points of longitudinal waves, like the up-and-down waves in a string. Reflection (echoing) is a behavior of sound waves, but it isn't considered a wave property.

13. **A.** Most asteroids in our solar system are in a belt between Mars and Jupiter.

14. **D.** Substances can be liquid (for example, water), gas (for example, oxygen), or solid (for example, iron) at room temperature.

15. **D.** About 98% of all matter in the universe is composed of hydrogen and helium.

16. **B.** When unlike atoms combine, the result is a *compound* (for example, iron and oxygen become iron oxide). If atoms of the same element come together (such as if two hydrogen atoms combine), they form elemental molecules, which aren't considered compounds.

17. **A.** The Big Bang is the most widely accepted scientific theory on the origin of the universe. The Big Rip is a theory regarding the end.

18. **A.** A watt-hour measures the amount of work performed or generated, such as in household appliances.

19. **D.** All the gas giants (planets) listed have rings.

20. **C.** Gas particles move more quickly than liquid particles, which move more quickly than solid particles, which makes Choice (C) correct.

21. **C.** *Absolute zero* is 0 kelvin, which is the same measure as −273.15 degrees Celsius.

22. **A.** Magnetic Resonance Imaging (MRI) machines employ radiology (dealing with radiation) to produce images.

23. **B.** The human female pelvis is usually wider than the male pelvis. (The question asks which choice isn't true, and paying attention to detail can make the difference in getting a question right or wrong on the ASVAB.)

24. **D.** A *lunar eclipse* occurs when the moon passes behind the Earth, so the moon is in the shadow of the Earth.

25. **A.** Luminol is used to detect minute traces of blood. Cyanide, ninhydrin, and alcohol can't do that.

Subtest 2: Arithmetic Reasoning Answers

You have to do well on this subtest to qualify for military enlistment — your score from the Arithmetic Reasoning subtest counts toward your AFQT score. If you're still doing poorly on this test, you may want to postpone taking the ASVAB until you have more study time under your belt (and perhaps take a math class or two). You may also want to review Part 3 of this book.

1. **D.** Multiply $0.45 (the cost of making three donuts) by 4 to find the cost of making a dozen donuts: $0.45 × 4 = $1.80. Then subtract the cost of making one dozen donuts from the selling price of one dozen donuts to get the profit on one dozen donuts: $3.99 − $1.80 = $2.19.

    Because the baker sold five dozen donuts, multiply the profit on one dozen donuts times 5 to determine the profit on five dozen donuts: $2.19 × 5 = $10.95.

2. **C.** Let x equal the number of dimes. Then $100 - x$ represents the number of quarters. You have $0.10x$ in dimes and $0.25(100 - x)$ in quarters, so set up your equation and solve for x:

    $$0.10x + 0.25(100 - x) = 19.75$$
    $$0.10x + 25 - 0.25x = 19.75$$
    $$-0.15x = -5.25$$
    $$x = 35$$

3. **D.** First determine the square footage of the patio: 12 feet × 16 feet = 192 square feet. Then multiply this number by the cost per square foot to determine what the bricklayer charges: 192 × $8 = $1,536.

4. **A.** Let x equal Angie's hourly wage; $x + 2$ would then represent Tim's hourly wage, and $3(x + 2)$ would represent Terry's hourly wage. Set up your equation and solve for x:

    $$x + (x + 2) + 3(x + 2) = 43$$
    $$x + x + 2 + 3x + 6 = 43$$
    $$5x + 8 = 43$$
    $$5x = 35$$
    $$x = 7$$

5. **B.** Two people is half as many as four people. Multiply the number of machines four people can run by $\frac{1}{2}$ to determine how many machines two people can run: $8 \times \frac{1}{2} = 4$.

6. **B.** Let x equal the number of daily tickets you would purchase; $36x$ equals the daily ticket cost:

    $$240 < 36x$$
    $$\frac{240}{36} < x$$
    $$6\frac{2}{3} < x$$

    You would need to use the ticket more than $6\frac{2}{3}$ times (or 7 times) for it to be cheaper to use the season ticket.

7. **C.** You can convert the lengths of the pipes from feet and inches to inches and then divide the total inches needed by 12 to get the total number of feet of pipe needed. However, the easiest and fastest way to do this problem is to realize that 3 feet, 6 inches is 3.5 feet. Multiply the number of pipes needed by 3.5 feet to get the number of feet of pipe needed.

    $$4 \times 3.5 = 14$$

8. **B.** The fastest way to solve this is to simply multiply some possible pairs of consecutive odd numbers. Since $20 \times 20 = 400$, try the odd numbers closest to that: $19 \times 21 = 399$. However, you can also solve this with algebra. Let x equal the first number and $x + 2$ equal the second number:

$$x(x+2) = 399$$
$$x^2 + 2x = 399$$

This is a quadratic equation that you can solve by setting it equal to zero and factoring.

$$x^2 + 2x - 399 = 0$$
$$(x - 19) + (x + 21) = 0$$
$$x - 19 = 0 \quad \text{or} \quad x + 21 = 0$$
$$x = 19 \qquad\qquad x = -21$$
$$x + 2 = 21 \qquad x + 2 = -19$$

Two solutions are possible: 19 and 21, and −21 and −19. Because the latter pair isn't one of the answer choices, the first pair is the correct answer.

9. **C.** Multiply the trainer's total sales by the percent commission to find the commission: $\$530 \times 0.65 = \$344.50$. You could also start with an estimate: $500 \times 0.7 = 350$. Choice (C) is the only value that's close.

10. **B.** The formula for the length of the diagonal of a rectangle is $d^2 = l^2 + w^2$ (this is the Pythagorean theorem, where l and w are the sides of a right triangle and d is the hypotenuse). In this case, $d = 5$ and $l = w + 1$. Substituting the known values into the formula results in $5^2 = (w + 1)^2 + w^2$.

$$5^2 = (w+1)(w+1) + w^2$$
$$25 = w^2 + 2w + 1 + w^2$$
$$25 = 2w^2 + 2w + 1$$

This equation is a quadratic equation, which you can solve by setting it equal to zero and factoring.

$$0 = 2w^2 + 2w - 24$$
$$\tfrac{1}{2}(0) = \tfrac{1}{2}(2w^2 + 2w - 24)$$
$$0 = w^2 + w - 12$$
$$0 = (w-3)(w+4)$$
$$w - 3 = 0 \quad \text{or} \quad w + 4 = 0$$
$$w = 3 \qquad\qquad w = -4 \text{ (not a possible solution)}$$

11. **B.** If 2 inches = 3 miles, then 1 inch equals 1.5 miles: $3 \div 2 = 1.5$. Multiply 1.5 miles × 9.5 inches to determine the actual distance: $1.5 \times 9.5 = 14.25$, or $14\tfrac{1}{4}$ miles.

12. **D.** The area of the entire piece of canvas = 10 inches × 14 inches = 140 square inches. The portion painted on equals 8 inches × 12 inches = 96 square inches. (This is determined by subtracting 2 inches — 1 inch on each side — from the length of each side to account for the margins.) Divide 96 by 140 to determine that about 68.5% of the canvas is covered with paint. You can round up to 69%.

13. **D.** Calculate perimeter by adding the lengths of all four sides of a quadrilateral: $9 + 9 + 16 + 16 = 50$ feet.

14. B. The formula for the perimeter of a rectangle is $P = 2l + 2w$. In this case, $P = 100$ and $l = 1.5w$. Set up your equation and solve for w:

$$100 = 2(1.5w) + 2w$$
$$100 = 3w + 2w$$
$$100 = 5w$$
$$w = 20$$

The width of the rectangle is 20 inches. Because the length is $1\frac{1}{2}$ times the width, $1.5 \times 20 = 30$.

15. C. The total number of quizzes is 10. If he passed seven of them, the fraction would be expressed as $\frac{7}{10}$.

16. D. Divide the amount of ribbon (in yards) used by the number of dresses to determine how much ribbon (in yards) was used in each dress: $3 \div 4 = \frac{3}{4}$. Three-quarters of a yard of ribbon was used to make each dress.

17. B. Divide $30 by $530 ($500 + $30) to determine the percentage of the sale price that the profit comprised: $30 \div 530 = 0.056 = 6\%$.

18. A. First find how many bolts a full bin contains: $7 \times 12 = 84$ bolts. Then multiply the total number of bolts in a full bin by $\frac{1}{6}$ to find how many bolts are in the bin when it's $\frac{1}{6}$ full: $84 \times \frac{1}{6} = \frac{84}{6} = 14$ bolts.

Tip: A shortcut is to find $\frac{1}{6}$ of a dozen first and then multiply by 7, the number of dozens. That is, $12 \times \frac{1}{6} = 2$ bolts, and $2 \times 7 = 14$ bolts. You can do this because multiplication is commutative — you can multiply the numbers in any order.

19. C. The first bike got a $\frac{4}{5}$-mile head start $\left(12 \text{ mph} \times \frac{4}{60} \text{ hr.} = \frac{48}{60} = \frac{4}{5} \text{ mi.}\right)$. Therefore, by the time the second bike leaves, there are $5\frac{1}{5}$ miles between them $\left(6 - \frac{4}{5}\right)$. Their combined rate of travel is $12 + 14 = 26$ mph. Let t = the number of hours the second bike travels.

$$26t = 5\frac{1}{5}$$
$$26t = \frac{26}{5}$$
$$t = \frac{26}{5} \div \frac{26}{1}$$
$$t = \frac{26}{5} \times \frac{1}{26}$$
$$t = \frac{1}{5}$$

One-fifth of an hour equals $60 \div 5 = 12$ minutes. The second bike left at 2:09, so both bikes will meet at 2:21.

20. B. Choice (B) is the cheapest option that gives you enough beans. Calculate each answer option and compare:

- **Choice (A):** $2 \times \$0.79 = \$1.58$
- **Choice (B):** $\$1.49$
- **Choice (C):** Two 3-ounce cans give you less than 8 ounces, so this answer can't be correct.
- **Choice (D):** $3 \times \$0.65 = \$1.95$

21. **D.** Add the sales amounts together: $25.70 + $32.30 + $31.80 = $89.80. Then multiply the total sales by $\frac{3}{4}$ to determine how much money the vendor has left: $89.80 × 0.75 = $67.35.

22. **B.** Divide $30.00 by $3.95. The whole number is the number of pairs of socks the recruit could buy: $30.00 ÷ $3.95 = 7.59, or 7 pairs of socks. In cases like this, you could also start with an estimate: 30 ÷ 4 ≈ 7, which is the only one that comes close to Choice (B).

23. **D.** Subtract 43 pounds, 7 ounces (the weight of the puppy) from 60 pounds, 5 ounces (the weight of the crate). Converting an additional pound of the crate to ounces makes the subtraction possible. Sixteen ounces make a pound, so 60 pounds, 5 ounces is the same as 59 pounds, 21 ounces. Do the subtraction:

    $$\begin{array}{r} 59 \text{ pounds, } 21 \text{ ounces} \\ -43 \text{ pounds, } 7 \text{ ounces} \\ \hline 16 \text{ pounds, } 14 \text{ ounces} \end{array}$$

24. **D.** The probability that all five computers will be defective is $0.15 \times 0.15 \times 0.15 \times 0.15 \times 0.15 = 0.0000759$ (round up to 0.000076). If you start with an estimate, like $(0.1)^5 = 0.00001$, you'll see that only Choice (D) is close to that value.

25. **D.** Find the area of each bedroom and add them together: $12 \times 14 = 168$; $12 \times 10 = 120$; $8 \times 12 = 96$; and $168 + 120 + 96 = 384$ square feet. Then, because 9 square feet make up a square yard, divide the total area in square feet by 9 to determine the number of square yards needed: $384 ÷ 9 = 42.6$ square yards. You can round up to 43 square yards.

26. **A.** Divide the total number of pages to be typed by the number of pages Rafael can type per hour to find the number of hours it will take him to type the pages: 126 pages ÷ 9 pages per hour = 14 hours.

27. **D.** Divide the group of 48 students by the number of students who can play at the same time: 48 ÷ 12 = 4. This means four groups of students have to share the 60 minutes: 60 minutes ÷ 4 = 15 minutes. Thus, each student plays for 15 minutes.

28. **B.** Subtract the first day's late charge from the total: $8.25 − $2.00 = $6.25. Then divide that amount by $1.25 to determine the number of additional days the movie was overdue: $6.25 ÷ $1.25 = 5. Add those 5 days to the first day the movie was late to find that the movie was 6 days overdue.

29. **D.** Divide the number of calories in the pudding by the number of calories in the broccoli: 150 ÷ 60 = 2.5. The calorie-counter can eat 2.5 times the amount of broccoli as they can eat pudding for the same number of calories. Multiply 2.5 by 0.5 cup (the amount of pudding that contains 150 calories) to find how many cups of broccoli this person can eat for 150 calories:

    $$2.5 \times 0.5 = 1.25 = 1\frac{1}{4} \text{ cups}$$

30. **C.** The dog is barking every 15 minutes, or 4 times per hour. The time between 10 p.m. and 2 a.m. is 4 hours. Multiply the total number of hours in the time period by 4 barks per hour. Then add 1 because the dog barked at the beginning of the period also: $(4 \times 4) + 1 = 16 + 1 = 17$.

Subtest 3: Word Knowledge Answers

The Word Knowledge subtest is another one of the "big four" that counts toward your AFQT score. If you're not seeing the improvement in your scores that you need to see, work with a partner who can quiz you on vocabulary. Review your vocabulary words intensely, even several times a day, to ensure your success on this subtest. See Chapter 4 for more help on improving your word knowledge. You also have a chance to practice this subtest topic in the practice AFQTs in Chapters 24 and 26.

1. **B.** *Lackadaisical* is an adjective that means carelessly lazy or lacking enthusiasm and determination.

2. **D.** *Edible* is an adjective that means fit to be eaten.

3. **B.** *Philomath* is a noun that refers to a person who enjoys learning new things.

4. **B.** *Pretense* is a noun that means an attempt to make something that isn't true appear to be true. (It's related to the word *pretend*.)

5. **A.** *Proclivity* is a noun that means a tendency to choose or do something regularly; it's an inclination or predisposition toward something.

6. **C.** *Incoherent* is an adjective that describes spoken or written language as being expressed in a confusing, unclear way.

7. **B.** *Mawkish* is an adjective that means sentimental in a feeble or sickly way.

8. **D.** *Established* is an adjective that means having been in existence for a long time, recognized, and accepted.

9. **A.** *Ephemeral* is an adjective that means lasting for a very short time.

10. **A.** *Avocation* is a noun that means a minor occupation or a hobby.

11. **C.** *Kvetch* is a verb that means to complain; it's also a noun used to refer to a person who complains a lot.

12. **A.** *Acute* is an adjective that means having or showing a perceptive understanding or insight; it also means shrewd.

13. **B.** *Inamorata* is a noun that means a person's female lover. (Not surprisingly, *inamorato* is a noun that means a person's male lover.)

14. **C.** *Inconsequential* is an adjective that means unimportant or not significant.

15. **A.** *Debouch* is a verb that means to emerge from a narrow or confined space into an open area. (Don't confuse *debouch* with *debauch*, which means to corrupt something.)

16. **B.** *Amateur* is a noun that refers to a person who engages in something on an unpaid basis. It's also an adjective that means engaging or engaged in something without payment or nonprofessionally.

17. **A.** *Ludic* is an adjective that means showing spontaneous playfulness.

18. **D.** *Crimson* is an adjective that means of a rich, deep red color that leans toward purple on the color spectrum.

19. **C.** *Benison* is a noun that means a blessing, so the opposite is a curse.

20. **B.** *Exempt* is an adjective that means free from an obligation imposed by others.

21. **C.** *Eldritch* is an adjective that means weird and sinister, or ghostly.

22. **A.** *Defective* is an adjective that means imperfect or faulty.

23. **B.** *Allot* is a verb that means to give something to someone as a share or task.

24. **D.** *Cursory* is an adjective that means hasty and therefore not detailed or thorough.

25. **B.** *Arcanum* is a noun that refers to a deep secret or mystery.

26. **D.** *Terse* is an adjective that means abrupt or sparing in the use of words.

27. **A.** *Dulcet* is an adjective that usually refers to sound and means sweet and soothing.

28. **C.** *Misdemeanor* is a noun that means a minor wrongdoing.

29. **A.** *Embonpoint* is a noun that refers to the plump, fleshy part of a person's body.

30. **C.** *Concocted* is the past tense of the verb *concoct*, which means to make something by putting together various ingredients. It also refers to creating or devising a story or plan.

31. **D.** *Chimera* is a noun that means a thing that is hoped or wished for but is illusory or impossible to achieve.

32. **A.** *Former* is an adjective that means having previously filled a role or been a particular thing.

33. **D.** *Mulct* is a verb that means to extract money from someone by fining or taxing.

34. **C.** *Strident* is an adjective that means harsh and loud. It also means presenting a certain point of view in an unpleasant and excessive way.

35. **C.** *Raffish* is an adjective that means unconventional and slightly disreputable, especially in an attractive way.

Subtest 4: Paragraph Comprehension Answers

Because the military uses the Paragraph Comprehension subtest to determine whether you even qualify for enlistment (it counts toward your AFQT score), you need to do well here. If you're still struggling, remember to take your time when you read the passages. And after you read each question, you can quickly reread the passage just to make sure you're on the money. The information is in the paragraph; you just have to concentrate to pull it out. Turn to Chapter 5 if you still need additional help to pull off a good score on this subtest. Additional opportunities to practice taking this subtest are in Chapters 24 and 26.

1. **D.** The last sentence in the passage states that chaos and fear are associated with change, making Choice (D) the correct choice. The passage states that leaders must learn to deal with negative emotions connected with change, making Choice (A) incorrect. The second sentence makes it clear that innovation means change, so Choice (B) is incorrect. The third sentence clearly states that leaders must learn everything there is to know about the change, making Choice (C) the wrong choice.

2. **C.** The first sentence says cougars are wide-ranging big cats in North America, making Choice (C) correct. The passage states that pumas, mountain lions, and cougars are the same thing, so Choice (A) is incorrect. Nothing in the passage supports Choice (B), which says cougars are endangered. The passage states that cougars live about 18 years in the wild, so Choice (D) is incorrect.

3. **B.** The counseling process works because the counselee feels the need for assistance, instruction, or understanding. Therefore, Choice (B) — counselees initially reject the advice of their counselors — isn't supported by the passage. The other three choices are all supported by the content of the paragraph.

4. **A.** The second sentence says that professional fire departments have more training, expertise, and experience. Therefore, the reader can infer that volunteer departments have less training, expertise, and experience than professionals. The passage says that professionals, not volunteers, have the skills needed to investigate fires, so Choice (B) is incorrect. The passage states that professional firefighters have more experience investigating the causes of fires, so Choice (C) is incorrect. The passage states that hiring professional firefighters is worthwhile, so Choice (D) is incorrect.

5. **C.** The passage doesn't state the locale of the story, so Choices (A) and (D) are incorrect. The references to extreme cold and lack of light make Choice (B) an incorrect answer. In sentence three, the author says it was still very foggy and extremely cold, so Choice (C) is the answer.

6. **A.** The main point of the passage is to define epidemiology, as evidenced by the opening sentence. Epidemiology is the study of what causes diseases. Choices (B), (C), and (D) aren't the main points of the passage.

7. **B.** The only statement that's supported by the passage is Choice (B), which says Buddhist teachings have changed. In fact, this sentence is the primary theme of the passage. The other choices aren't supported by information contained in the paragraph.

8. **A.** Choice (B), which questions jurors' intelligence, isn't supported by the passage. Choice (C), which asks for more laws that take intent into consideration, is the opposite of what the author argues. The text doesn't support Choice (D), which calls lawyers liars. The first line of the passage states that statutes permit more severe punishment of a person convicted of a crime if they intended to harm another person. The last sentence says juries should only be asked to weigh objective evidence, so the author would no doubt agree that laws should not punish people based on intention, Choice (A).

9. **C.** The passage says that most states punish voluntary manslaughter more severely than involuntary manslaughter, so Choice (A) is incorrect. The argument that punishing people more severely for voluntary manslaughter is unconstitutional isn't made in the passage, so Choice (B) is incorrect. The passage doesn't support Choice (D), which says prosecutors can establish intent. The first sentence of the second paragraph states that juries find it difficult to know what the intent of a person was at the time they committed a crime, so Choice (C) is correct.

10. **B.** Lack of attention to ergonomics, not ergonomics itself, can cause injury, so Choice (A) is incorrect. The passage doesn't support Choice (C), which discusses cost and time. The passage states that many people suffer injuries when sufficient attention isn't paid to ergonomics, so Choice (D) is incorrect. The first says, "Ergonomics is the science of designing and arranging workspaces so that people and objects interact efficiently and safely," so Choice (B) is correct.

11. **D.** The passage states that adequate lighting and well-designed chairs are part of ergonomic design, so Choice (A) is incorrect. The passage states that repetitious work can cause injury, so Choice (B) is incorrect. The passage states that desk-bound workers should take breaks, so Choice (C) is incorrect. The first sentence in the second paragraph states that adequate lighting, well-designed chairs, and clutter-free work areas contribute to effective ergonomic design, so Choice (D) is correct.

12. **A.** The passage makes it clear that lack of ergonomic design is dangerous, so Choice (B) is incorrect. Nothing in the passage supports Choice (C), which brings up labor unions. Although the passage claims that lack of ergonomic design causes injury, nothing in the passage supports Choice (D). The passage's second sentence says that lack of attention to ergonomics causes thousands of workers to suffer repetitive stress injury, eye fatigue, muscle soreness, and many other medical problems, so it's reasonable to assume that employers should invest in ergonomic design to protect workers, which makes Choice (A) correct.

13. **B.** The passage says that BTUs are the standard measure of heat, so Choice (A) is incorrect. BTU stands for British thermal unit, so Choice (C) is incorrect. Nothing in the passage supports Choice (D), which names room dimensions.

14. **D.** The passage shows that fuel oil can be more expensive than other heating methods, so Choice (A) is incorrect. Oak firewood is sometimes less expensive than other types of fuel, so Choice (B) is incorrect. Natural gas can sometimes cost less than firewood, so Choice (C) is incorrect. The first sentence states that electricity is always the most inefficient and costly way to heat a home, which makes Choice (D) correct.

15. **A.** The main point of this passage deals with choosing the right fuel based on price; only Choice (A) summarizes this point. Choices (B), (C), and (D) are less important points. The final sentence makes Choice (A) correct.

Subtest 5: Mathematics Knowledge Answers

The Mathematics Knowledge subtest is used to determine whether you qualify for enlistment, so you need to do well. If you're still missing too many questions, you may need to take more drastic measures, such as enrolling in a basic algebra class at a local community college. If your scores are improving, keep hitting the books and testing yourself up until the day of the ASVAB. Turn to Chapters 6, 7, and 8 for more information. The practice AFQTs in Chapters 24 and 26 also give you a chance to gauge your progress.

1. **B.** Substitute 6 for y in the equation: $2(6) \times 6 = 12 \times 6 = 72$.

2. **B.** Divide both sides of the equation by 0.05 to solve for x: $0.05x \div 0.05 = 1 \div 0.05$, or $x = 20$. To check your answer, substitute 20 for x in the original equation.

3. **C.** The radical symbol represents the nonnegative square root, so $\sqrt{25x^2} = \sqrt{(5x)^2} = 5x$.

4. **A.** $9x^3 + 18x^2 - x - 2 = 9x^2(x+2) - 1(x+2) = (9x^2 - 1)(x+2)$. The fully factored answer is $(3x+1)(3x-1)(x+2)$, but that's not what the question asks. Make sure you look for the answer to the question. Another method: Try multiplying the pieces. All the answer choices feature $9x^2 \times x = 9x^3$, and the constant is always -2. Only Choice (A) multiplies to have a positive $18x^2$.

5. **B.** Solve for *x*:

    $$5x + 7 = 6(x - 2) - 4(2x - 3)$$
    $$5x + 7 = 6x - 12 - 8x + 12$$
    $$5x + 7 = -2x$$
    $$7x + 7 = 0$$
    $$7x = -7$$
    $$x = -1$$

6. **D.** If two powers have the same base, they can be multiplied by keeping the base and adding the exponents together. In this case, x is the same as x^1: $x \cdot x^2 = x^{1+2} = x^3$.

7. **B.** This is so easy that it may tempt you to think that the correct answer is too obvious. The square root of $(5 + x)^2$ is simply $5 + x$.

8. **B.** You start with $(3 \times 3)(5 - 3)(6 + 2) = x^2$. First solve the left side of the equation: $(9)(2)(8) = 144$. So $x^2 = 144$. Find the square root of each side: $x = 12$.

9. **A.** You start with $-5x = 25$. Isolate *x* by dividing each side of the equation by -5: $x = -5$.

10. **C.** The area of a circle equals π times the radius squared. The radius is half the diameter, which is 12 in this problem. Plug in the known values: $A = \pi r^2$; $A = \pi 6^2 = 36\pi$. If π is approximately 3.14, the area of the circle is approximately 3.14×36, or 113 square feet.

11. **B.** Volume equals length $\times$ width $\times$ height $(V = lwh)$: $6 \times 6 \times 6 = 36 \times 6 = 216$ cubic inches.

12. **B.** The area of a circle is $A = \pi r^2$. Radius is half the diameter, so the radius is 5. In this problem, $A = \pi 5^2 = 25\pi$.

13. **C.** For cylinders, Volume $= \pi r^2(h)$. Because the radius is half the diameter, you can calculate the problem this way: $V = \pi(6^2)10 = \pi(36)10$. If π is approximately 3.14, then $3.14 \times 36 \times 10 = 1{,}130$ cubic inches.

14. **D.** In an isosceles triangle, sides *a* and *c* are equal, and angles 1 and 2 are equal.

15. **A.** Rectangles have four equal angles, and all angles are right angles.

16. **A.** The sum of the measures of supplementary angles always equal 180 degrees.

17. **A.** Solve for *x*:

    $$3(2x - 5) - 2(4x + 1) = -5(x + 3) - 2$$
    $$6x - 15 - 8x - 2 = -5x - 15 - 2$$
    $$-2x - 17 = -5x - 17$$
    $$3x - 17 = -17$$
    $$3x = 0$$
    $$x = 0$$

18. **A.** Volume equals length × width × height ($V = lwh$). Finding the cube root of 64 shows that each edge measures 4 inches ($4 \times 4 \times 4 = 64$).

19. **B.** $(x^3)^2$ is the same as $(x^3)(x^3)$. To multiply exponents with the same base, keep the base and add the exponents: $(x^3)(x^3) = x^{3+3} = x^6$.

20. **D.** To find out how much rain falls in an hour, multiply the amount that falls in one minute by 60, because 60 minutes make up an hour. In *h* hours, the amount of rain is 60*rh*.

21. **D.** Because $x = y$, you can plug in *x* for each *y* in the problem. Therefore, $6 + 4(x - x) = 6 + 4(0) = 6 + 0 = 6$.

22. **A.** The problem asks for the square root of 820. You know that $20^2 = 400$ and $30^2 = 900$, so the range of 20 to 30 is correct.

23. **B.** The problem asks you to find $(x + 2)(x + 2)$. Using the FOIL method (First, Outer, Inner, Last), systematically multiply each term in the first set of parentheses by each term in the second set of parentheses:

    - **Multiply the First terms:** $x(x) = x^2$.
    - **Multiply the Outer terms:** $x(2) = 2x$.
    - **Multiply the Inner terms:** $2(x) = 2x$.
    - **Multiply the Last terms:** $2 \times 2 = 4$.

    Now add all the products together, and you get $x^2 + 2x + 2x + 4$. Add like terms to get the final answer of $x^2 + 4x + 4$.

24. **A.** Replace the unknowns with the numbers given: $(6)(-3) - 3(-7) - 2(4) = -18 + 21 - 8 = -5$.

25. **C.** The problem asks you to find $(x + 4)(3x + 5)$. Use the FOIL method:

    - **Multiply the First terms:** $x(3x) = 3x^2$.
    - **Multiply the Outer terms:** $x(5) = 5x$.
    - **Multiply the Inner terms:** $4(3x) = 12x$.
    - **Multiply the Last terms:** $4(5) = 20$.

    Now add all the products together, and you get $3x^2 + 5x + 12x + 20$. Add like terms to get the final answer, $3x^2 + 17x + 20$.

Subtest 6: Electronics Information Answers

If you need to do well on the Electronics Information subtest to qualify for a certain military career and you're still missing questions, review Chapter 16 and spend some time memorizing key electronics concepts, including the mathematical formulas (like Power = Voltage × Current) that help you solve all kinds of electronics problems.

1. **B.** Unless a specific gauge is specified by the speaker manufacturer, you should always choose lower gauges for better sound quality.

2. **B.** There are four frequency bands used throughout the world. A quad-band cellphone would be able to access any of these frequency bands.

3. **B.** The greatest concern when dealing with electricity is personal injury.

4. **C.** *Heat effect* occurs when electrical current must overcome the resistance of the wire. Heat effect can be quite obvious or very subtle.

5. **C.** Like other diodes, Zener diodes allow current in only one direction, except if the voltage across it is greater than a threshold voltage (called *breakdown voltage*), at which point current also flows through the Zener diode in the opposite direction. This action allows the Zener diode to regulate voltage.

6. **A.** The symbol stands for *ohm*.

7. **D.** *Electromotive force* is the difference of potential, so the term is another way of saying *voltage*.

8. **A.** Lithium-Ion (Li-Ion) batteries are much lighter than nickel metal hydride (NiMH) batteries.

9. **A.** The three terminals a transistor must have are the base, emitter, and collector.

10. **B.** To control a light fixture from two different positions, use two three-way switches.

11. **C.** *Amplifier* is another name for *transistor*.

12. **A.** The symbol means *ground*.

13. **C.** Capacitance is the ability to hold an electrical charge. Connecting capacitors in series reduces the capacitance.

14. **C.** 2.5K ohms is 2,500 ohms. K = 1 kilo, or 1,000.

15. **B.** A cell is equal to about 1.5 volts, so $9 \div 1.5 = 6$.

16. **D.** Primary live wires are black.

17. **C.** A motherboard is the physical arrangement in a computer that contains the computer's basic circuitry and components. Motherboards come in various sizes and component arrangements referred to as form factors to fit standard case sizes, components required, and so on. AT is a standard form factor that has a width of 12 inches and a length of 13.8 inches.

18. **B.** An on-off switch allows current to flow only when it's in the closed (on) position.

19. **C.** Determine the wattage that could cause the circuit breaker to trip with this formula: Watts = Volts × Amps, or $120 \times 25 = 3,000$ watts.

20. **D.** A *potentiometer* is a type of variable resister with three contacts that's used to control voltage.

Subtest 7: Auto & Shop Information Answers

If you have your heart set on fixing Jeeps and tanks or doing other related military jobs and you're still struggling on this test, review Chapters 13 and 14 and go through the practice questions at the end of those chapters.

1. **D.** The function of piston rings is to keep oil in the cylinders. When the rings are worn, more oil is used.

2. **A.** An engine is said to be *blueprinted* when the builder has double-checked all tolerances and used custom specifications for the vehicle to ensure manufacturer's rated power (or greater) is achieved.

3. **B.** A V-8 engine's crankshaft has 4 cranks (crankpins), one for each pair of the 2 pistons in a V configuration. The piston's push rods connect to the camshaft at the crankpin or journal. This is true for the more common crossplane crankshaft as well as the flatplane crankshaft for a V-8.

4. **A.** Dieseling occurs when an engine continues to run due to fuel in the cylinders after the compression stroke.

5. **D.** A radiator is part of the cooling system, and if any part of that system fails, an engine can quickly overheat, Choice (D).

6. **C.** The intake manifold distributes air evenly between each of an engine's cylinders.

7. **A.** Calipers cause brake pads to press on the wheels, slowing the rotation and slowing or stopping the car.

8. **D.** The heater core, radiator, and thermostat are all part of the cooling system.

9. **B.** A *catalytic converter* is part of the emissions control system; it reduces dangerous exhaust emissions.

10. **B.** If the steering wheel vibrates, the front wheels may need balancing, or you may have a bent rim.

11. **C.** In a cylinder, the intake valve closes and the piston moves to the top during the compression stroke.

12. **A.** On older cars, you can find the air filter on top of the carburetor, on the top of the engine.

13. **B.** *Glazing* is a process used when replacing a pane of glass in a window frame.

14. **D.** A wrench with fixed open jaws, usually listed in a standard or metric size, is called an *open-end wrench*.

15. **A.** All hammers (such as ball peen, mallet, and so on) have a handle and a head with a face.

16. **B.** You use a thread gauge when determining the threads per inch on a threaded fastener.

17. **B.** You use a butt chisel (which has a short blade) to chip or cut wood in close quarters.

18. **C.** Machine screws have uniform threads that maintain the exact same diameter over the entire length of the fastener, unlike other screws with tapered threads.

19. **B.** Double-headed (or duplex-headed) nails are easier to remove and are used in temporary construction.

20. **A.** You can thin oil-based paint by using turpentine.

21. **C.** To make a smoother finish, sand wood with the grain.

22. **D.** To transfer an angle, you use a sliding T-bevel.

23. **C.** The tool shown is an adjustable crescent wrench.

24. **B.** Choice (B) shows a screw that requires a Phillips (also called Phillips-head) screwdriver.

25. **A.** The tool shown in the figure is used to punch holes.

Subtest 8: Mechanical Comprehension Answers

If you need to do well on the Mechanical Comprehension subtest, don't forget to apply your math skills to the concepts. (A little extra physics study wouldn't hurt, either.) But simply using your common sense can help you quite a bit, too. For example, you may not know exactly why a metal spoon feels colder than a wooden spoon when they're at the same temperature, but at least you know that it feels colder. And knowing that may help you answer a question correctly. Check out Chapter 15 for more information on the Mechanical Comprehension test and Chapter 11 for more in-depth discussion of physics.

1. **B.** The teeth of helical gears are slanted.

2. **B.** The anvil is closer to Pillar B, so Pillar B bears more weight.

3. **B.** Wheel B is smaller. It has to make more revolutions than Wheel A to cover the same amount of distance, so it will take longer.

4. **A.** E stands for *effort needed*. Here's how to set up the equation: 30 (weight of the anvil) $\times$ 2 (length of resistance arm) $= x(6)$ (length of effort arm). Do a little multiplication, and you get $60 = 6x$. To isolate x, divide each side by 6: $10 = x$.

5. **A.** A fixed, simple pulley gives no mechanical advantage, so its mechanical advantage number is 1.

6. **D.** The formula to determine the mechanical advantage of an inclined plane is Length of Ramp ÷ Height of Ramp = Weight of Object ÷ Effort:

$$\frac{8}{4} = \frac{400}{E}$$
$$8E = 400(4)$$
$$8E = 1,600$$
$$E = 200$$

7. **B.** One horsepower equals 33,000 foot-pounds per minute.

8. **A.** Pressure = Force ÷ Area. *Psi* stands for *pounds per square inch,* so you don't have to change the units of measurement. Just plug in your numbers: $P = 130 \text{ lb.} \div 1 \text{ in.}^2 = 130$ psi.

9. **D.** *Static electricity* is the buildup of electrical charge on surfaces, which causes materials to "stick" together this way.

10. **A.** An aneroid barometer measures atmospheric pressure.

11. **C.** Meshed gears always turn in opposite directions.

12. **D.** Springs are used for all the listed purposes except to add weight.

13. **B.** *Specific gravity* is a comparison between the density of a liquid and the density of water. The liquid with the higher specific gravity will have a float that rises higher.

14. **D.** Universal joints are used to connect shafts that aren't in the same plane.

15. **D.** Try-cocks are valves that measure water level. Water seeks a level throughout a system, so in the schematic, the try-cock correctly indicates the water level.

16. **A.** There are six different symbols, so six different types of machine screws were used.

17. **B.** To determine the amount of force the anvils exert, first multiply the length of the resistance arm (as it applies to the anvil) by the weight of each anvil and add the products together. The 10-pound anvil is supported by the entire weight of the resistance arm, so $5 \times 10 = 50$. The 5-pound anvil is being supported by 3 feet of the resistance arm, so $3 \times 5 = 15$. Add 'em up: $50 + 15 = 65$. This number is equal to the length of the resistance arm times effort (force), or $65 = 5F$. To isolate F, divide both sides by 5: $13 = F$.

18. **C.** One revolution of the winch will move the weight 24 inches, the circumference of the winch drum.

19. **A.** Valves 1 and 2 need to be open to fill the tank.

20. **B.** The number of revolutions a gear makes is inversely proportional to its difference in size from the gear that's turning it. Gear 1 makes 10 clockwise revolutions per minute. Gear 2 is half the size of Gear 1, so to determine the number of revolutions it makes, multiply the number of revolutions Gear 1 makes by the inverse (reciprocal) of $\frac{1}{2}$, which is $\frac{2}{1}$ (or just 2): $10 \times 2 = 20$. Therefore, Gear 2 makes 20 counterclockwise revolutions per minute. Gear 3 is 2.5 times (or $\frac{5}{2}$ times) the size of Gear 2. To determine the number of revolutions Gear 3 makes, multiply the inverse of $\frac{5}{2}$ the number of revolutions Gear 2 makes: $\frac{2}{5} \times 20 = \frac{40}{5} = 8$ revolutions per minute.

21. **B.** The pinion turns four times as often as the gear: $4 \times 200 = 800$ rpm.

22. **C.** A float indicates the level of liquid in a container.

23. **B.** Using a runner (a single, moveable pulley) gives a mechanical advantage of 2.

24. **A.** Because 60 seconds comprise a minute, the valve must open 60 times per minute. The cam will open the valve 10 times per revolution, and $60 \div 10 = 6$. The cam must make 6 revolutions per minute to raise the valve 60 times per minute.

25. **D.** Because Valve 4 is above the bottom of the tank, some water will remain in the tank below the level of the valve, so the tank will never be completely empty.

Subtest 9: Assembling Objects Answers

At present, only the Navy uses the scores from this subtest. If you plan to sail the Seven Seas and you want one of the few Navy jobs that requires you to put parts A and B together, you may want to go over the practice subtests again. For additional practice questions, see Chapter 17.

TIP

Try to rearrange the original figure in your head so it matches an answer choice. If the right answer isn't readily apparent, rule out incorrect choices before you decide on one.

1. **C.** As with many Assembling Objects questions, this one requires you to pay attention to where the points are located on each figure. You can immediately rule out Choices (A), (B), and (D) because Point B is in the wrong place on each of them.

2. **A.** You know Choice (B) is wrong because it depicts four shapes, and there are only three in the original diagram. Choice (C) is incorrect because it depicts two four-sided shapes, and there's only one four-sided shape in the question. Choice (D) is also wrong because it doesn't even contain the triangles the original diagram shows you, leaving only Choice (A) as the correct answer.

3. **A.** The first answer to rule out is Choice (C) because it depicts Point A in the center of the figure rather than on its point. Choice (D) can go, too, because Point B is in the wrong place. Finally, you can eliminate Choice (B) because it requires you to invert the figure that contains Point A. Choice (A) is the only figure that rotates the original figures and has the points in the right places.

4. **B.** Choices (A) and (C) aren't contenders in this question because they depict only three triangles, whereas the original figure shows four. Choice (D) is wrong because all the triangles are the same size with the same dimensions, so Choice (B) must be correct.

5. **C.** Make a mental note of where Point A lies on its figure in the original diagram; it's opposite the small triangle in the lower-left corner. That tells you Choices (B) and (D) are wrong. Now note where Point B lies and where its line leaves its figure. Choice (A) is incorrect because the Point B is outside the figure, not inside it (as it is in the original diagram).

6. **D.** Counting shapes tells you that Choice (A) is incorrect (it shows five shapes rather than four) and that Choice (B) is incorrect (it shows only three shapes, and one of them resembles a triangle). Choice (C) can't be right, either, because there are no figures in the original diagram that have parallel sides.

7. **C.** It's obvious that Choices (B) and (D) are incorrect because Point B lies on the outside of the diamond rather than inside it. Choice (A) is incorrect for two reasons: The angle of the line exiting the diamond is wrong, and it inverts the shape that Point A lies on instead of simply rotating it.

8. **C.** Pick a shape that stands out in the original diagram, such as the triangle. The triangle doesn't appear anywhere in Choice (B) or (D), so those are out. Choice (A) shows the two largest shapes as four shapes stuck together. The only answer choice that matches the exact shapes from the original diagram is Choice (C).

9. **B.** Start with the figure that includes Point A. Point A is in the wrong place in Choice (D), so even if you guess between the remaining answers, you have a better chance of getting this question right. Look at the original figure containing Point B next, which is depicted incorrectly in Choice (C). (Your chances have improved to 50-50!) Rotate the figure containing Point A; it's the opposite of what's depicted in Choice (A). You now have a 100 percent chance of answering this question correctly by choosing Choice (B).

10. **A.** The two larger figures in the problem appear to be the same size, so you can rule out Choices (B), (C), and (D), because each of those shows two smaller figures of the same size. The only answer choice that uses two large figures and one small one is Choice (A).

11. **D.** The points are dead giveaways on this question. Check out Point A, and you'll see that in Choice (A), it's in the wrong place. Point B is in the wrong place in Choices (B) and (C), which leaves you with the right answer: Choice (D).

12. **A.** Rule out Choices (B), (C), and (D) because they include shapes that aren't in the original diagram, which includes only triangles. Choice (A) is the only figure that uses two triangles that are larger than the remaining four.

13. **C.** Point A and its line leave the box at what appears to be a right angle, so you can rule out Choices (B) and (D) right off the bat. Without rotating the shape, you can see that the correct answer is Choice (C), but if you do rotate it, you'll see that Choice (A) is incorrect because it requires you to flip, not rotate, that figure.

14. **B.** Choices (A) and (D) are the same, so if one's right, the other is, too. That's not possible on the ASVAB, so eliminate those two from your choices. Besides, their shapes don't match those in the original diagram. Now compare the shapes in Choices (B) and (C), and you'll find out that those depicted in Choice (C) don't match those in the original diagram, either; that makes Choice (B) correct.

15. **D.** Ignore Choice (C) because it shows Point B in the center of the shape (the original diagram shows the point on a corner). In Choice (B), the figure containing Point B is inverted rather than rotated, so that can't be correct. Now look at the figure that contains Point A, which is inverted in Choice (A) but not in Choice (D). That means Choice (D) is the one you should choose.

16. **C.** Compare the shapes in this puzzle problem. The shapes in Choices (A), (B), and (D) don't match those in the original diagram, so Choice (C) is the clear winner.

17. **A.** Choice (C) depicts a triangle, and there's no triangle in the original diagram, so it's incorrect. Choice (D) depicts another shape that doesn't appear in the original image. Choices (A) and (B) are close, but if you look at the dimensions of the largest shape, you'll see that Choice (A) is the correct answer.

18. **B.** Forget Choices (A) and (D), because Point A's location doesn't match the original image in either. You can ignore Choice (C) because Point B is in the wrong place, too. Your last remaining choice, Choice (B), is the right answer.

19. **A.** By now, you probably know the best strategy for puzzle questions (find an odd shape and look for it in each answer choice). In this case, it's the pair of corner pieces that appear on the left side of the diagram. The only pieces that match those two show up in Choice (A), and you can be sure because each one features a pointed end and an end with a straight edge — it's almost as if the point were cut off.

20. **C.** Point A lies on the outer edge of the diamond-shaped figure where the shorter line meets the edge. The only answer choice that depicts that accurately is Choice (C). Don't let Choice (B) throw you off; it contains an inverted version of the shape containing Point A, and on the ASVAB, you'll rotate but never invert.

21. **B.** Choice (C) doesn't feature a triangle at all, but there's one in the original diagram, so scratch that one off your list of possibilities. Choice (D) shows four separate pieces making up the pentagon's perimeter, but the original figure gives you only three; that one's out, too. Choice (A)'s borders have the wrong dimensions (particularly the largest border piece), so the only possible answer is Choice (B).

22. **D.** Choice (C) is automatically wrong because Point A isn't in the same place as it is in the original diagram. Choices (A) and (B) show the figure containing Point B as a mirror image of the original (it's inverted), so neither of those can be correct. That leaves you with Choice (D), which depicts the original figures slightly rotated and connected.

23. **D.** Start comparing puzzle pieces to see what matches. Choice (A)'s largest triangle isn't a match for the original figure's largest triangle, so it's incorrect. Choice (B) features an odd shape (the third one in from the left) that doesn't appear in the original, so that's also incorrect. Choice (C) shows two thin triangles, and neither of them appears in the original diagram. However, Choice (D) has everything the original diagram has, so it's the right answer.

24. **A.** The pentagon isn't going to give you any help on this question (neither the one in the figure nor the official Pentagon in Arlington, Virginia), so you'll have to look at Point A and its figure to find the right answer here. Point A is on the lower corner of the straight edge, which doesn't match up with Choice (C) or (D). Look closely at Choice (B), and you'll see that the figure is inverted, which leaves you with Choice (A) as the correct answer.

25. **C.** The double-lined outer edge in Choice (B) is a continuous shape, which isn't possible given the original image, so rule that one out right away. Choice (A) depicts shapes inside the border with dimensions that don't match the original diagram, and if you look even more closely, you'll see that the interior shape on the bottom of the figure isn't a match at all. Choice (D) has two curved shapes on the upper part of the figure, but that's not possible with the original figures. Choice (C) has all the right ingredients, and in this case, it's the winning recipe.

Chapter 24
AFQT Practice Exam 1

If you're wondering what in the world this exam is doing in a book on the ASVAB, don't be confused. The *Armed Forces Qualification Test*, or AFQT, is part of the ASVAB — in a way, it's a test within a test. Your scaled AFQT score is derived from four subtests of the ASVAB, and it determines your overall mental qualification to join the service branch of your choice. Each branch of military service has set its own minimum AFQT score in order to qualify for enlistment. The four subtests that can make or break your chances of joining the military are Arithmetic Reasoning (AR), Word Knowledge (WK), Paragraph Comprehension (PC), and Mathematics Knowledge (MK).

Because I like you (and because you were kind enough to buy this book), I've included a couple of extra chances for you to evaluate your communication and math skills before you head over to the MEPS (Military Entrance Processing Station), your school, or the local National Guard Armory for the real deal.

After you complete the entire practice test, check your answers in Chapter 25. If you decide you want even more practice on the AFQT, head to Chapter 26.

REMEMBER Your goal here is to determine where you may still need to spend some more time studying. If you miss only one question on the Word Knowledge subtest but you miss 15 on Arithmetic Reasoning, you may want to dedicate some extra study time to further develop your math skills before you take the actual ASVAB.

Answer Sheet for AFQT Practice Exam 1

Subtest 1: Arithmetic Reasoning

1. Ⓐ Ⓑ Ⓒ Ⓓ
2. Ⓐ Ⓑ Ⓒ Ⓓ
3. Ⓐ Ⓑ Ⓒ Ⓓ
4. Ⓐ Ⓑ Ⓒ Ⓓ
5. Ⓐ Ⓑ Ⓒ Ⓓ
6. Ⓐ Ⓑ Ⓒ Ⓓ
7. Ⓐ Ⓑ Ⓒ Ⓓ
8. Ⓐ Ⓑ Ⓒ Ⓓ
9. Ⓐ Ⓑ Ⓒ Ⓓ
10. Ⓐ Ⓑ Ⓒ Ⓓ
11. Ⓐ Ⓑ Ⓒ Ⓓ
12. Ⓐ Ⓑ Ⓒ Ⓓ
13. Ⓐ Ⓑ Ⓒ Ⓓ
14. Ⓐ Ⓑ Ⓒ Ⓓ
15. Ⓐ Ⓑ Ⓒ Ⓓ
16. Ⓐ Ⓑ Ⓒ Ⓓ
17. Ⓐ Ⓑ Ⓒ Ⓓ
18. Ⓐ Ⓑ Ⓒ Ⓓ
19. Ⓐ Ⓑ Ⓒ Ⓓ
20. Ⓐ Ⓑ Ⓒ Ⓓ
21. Ⓐ Ⓑ Ⓒ Ⓓ
22. Ⓐ Ⓑ Ⓒ Ⓓ
23. Ⓐ Ⓑ Ⓒ Ⓓ
24. Ⓐ Ⓑ Ⓒ Ⓓ
25. Ⓐ Ⓑ Ⓒ Ⓓ
26. Ⓐ Ⓑ Ⓒ Ⓓ
27. Ⓐ Ⓑ Ⓒ Ⓓ
28. Ⓐ Ⓑ Ⓒ Ⓓ
29. Ⓐ Ⓑ Ⓒ Ⓓ
30. Ⓐ Ⓑ Ⓒ Ⓓ

Subtest 2: Word Knowledge

1. Ⓐ Ⓑ Ⓒ Ⓓ
2. Ⓐ Ⓑ Ⓒ Ⓓ
3. Ⓐ Ⓑ Ⓒ Ⓓ
4. Ⓐ Ⓑ Ⓒ Ⓓ
5. Ⓐ Ⓑ Ⓒ Ⓓ
6. Ⓐ Ⓑ Ⓒ Ⓓ
7. Ⓐ Ⓑ Ⓒ Ⓓ
8. Ⓐ Ⓑ Ⓒ Ⓓ
9. Ⓐ Ⓑ Ⓒ Ⓓ
10. Ⓐ Ⓑ Ⓒ Ⓓ
11. Ⓐ Ⓑ Ⓒ Ⓓ
12. Ⓐ Ⓑ Ⓒ Ⓓ
13. Ⓐ Ⓑ Ⓒ Ⓓ
14. Ⓐ Ⓑ Ⓒ Ⓓ
15. Ⓐ Ⓑ Ⓒ Ⓓ
16. Ⓐ Ⓑ Ⓒ Ⓓ
17. Ⓐ Ⓑ Ⓒ Ⓓ
18. Ⓐ Ⓑ Ⓒ Ⓓ
19. Ⓐ Ⓑ Ⓒ Ⓓ
20. Ⓐ Ⓑ Ⓒ Ⓓ
21. Ⓐ Ⓑ Ⓒ Ⓓ
22. Ⓐ Ⓑ Ⓒ Ⓓ
23. Ⓐ Ⓑ Ⓒ Ⓓ
24. Ⓐ Ⓑ Ⓒ Ⓓ
25. Ⓐ Ⓑ Ⓒ Ⓓ
26. Ⓐ Ⓑ Ⓒ Ⓓ
27. Ⓐ Ⓑ Ⓒ Ⓓ
28. Ⓐ Ⓑ Ⓒ Ⓓ
29. Ⓐ Ⓑ Ⓒ Ⓓ
30. Ⓐ Ⓑ Ⓒ Ⓓ
31. Ⓐ Ⓑ Ⓒ Ⓓ
32. Ⓐ Ⓑ Ⓒ Ⓓ
33. Ⓐ Ⓑ Ⓒ Ⓓ
34. Ⓐ Ⓑ Ⓒ Ⓓ
35. Ⓐ Ⓑ Ⓒ Ⓓ

Subtest 3: Paragraph Comprehension

1. Ⓐ Ⓑ Ⓒ Ⓓ
2. Ⓐ Ⓑ Ⓒ Ⓓ
3. Ⓐ Ⓑ Ⓒ Ⓓ
4. Ⓐ Ⓑ Ⓒ Ⓓ
5. Ⓐ Ⓑ Ⓒ Ⓓ
6. Ⓐ Ⓑ Ⓒ Ⓓ
7. Ⓐ Ⓑ Ⓒ Ⓓ
8. Ⓐ Ⓑ Ⓒ Ⓓ
9. Ⓐ Ⓑ Ⓒ Ⓓ
10. Ⓐ Ⓑ Ⓒ Ⓓ
11. Ⓐ Ⓑ Ⓒ Ⓓ
12. Ⓐ Ⓑ Ⓒ Ⓓ
13. Ⓐ Ⓑ Ⓒ Ⓓ
14. Ⓐ Ⓑ Ⓒ Ⓓ
15. Ⓐ Ⓑ Ⓒ Ⓓ

Subtest 4: Mathematics Knowledge

1. Ⓐ Ⓑ Ⓒ Ⓓ
2. Ⓐ Ⓑ Ⓒ Ⓓ
3. Ⓐ Ⓑ Ⓒ Ⓓ
4. Ⓐ Ⓑ Ⓒ Ⓓ
5. Ⓐ Ⓑ Ⓒ Ⓓ
6. Ⓐ Ⓑ Ⓒ Ⓓ
7. Ⓐ Ⓑ Ⓒ Ⓓ
8. Ⓐ Ⓑ Ⓒ Ⓓ
9. Ⓐ Ⓑ Ⓒ Ⓓ
10. Ⓐ Ⓑ Ⓒ Ⓓ
11. Ⓐ Ⓑ Ⓒ Ⓓ
12. Ⓐ Ⓑ Ⓒ Ⓓ
13. Ⓐ Ⓑ Ⓒ Ⓓ
14. Ⓐ Ⓑ Ⓒ Ⓓ
15. Ⓐ Ⓑ Ⓒ Ⓓ
16. Ⓐ Ⓑ Ⓒ Ⓓ
17. Ⓐ Ⓑ Ⓒ Ⓓ
18. Ⓐ Ⓑ Ⓒ Ⓓ
19. Ⓐ Ⓑ Ⓒ Ⓓ
20. Ⓐ Ⓑ Ⓒ Ⓓ
21. Ⓐ Ⓑ Ⓒ Ⓓ
22. Ⓐ Ⓑ Ⓒ Ⓓ
23. Ⓐ Ⓑ Ⓒ Ⓓ
24. Ⓐ Ⓑ Ⓒ Ⓓ
25. Ⓐ Ⓑ Ⓒ Ⓓ

Subtest 1: Arithmetic Reasoning

TIME: 36 minutes for 30 questions

DIRECTIONS: This test contains questions about arithmetic. Each question is followed by four possible answers. Decide which answer is correct and then mark the space on your answer sheet that has the same number and letter as your choice. Use scratch paper for any figuring you need to do. Calculators are not allowed.

1. If Salvatore is capable of cutting the hair of 35 people per day and he works 7 days per week, how many haircuts could he give during the months of April, May, and June?

   (A) 3,185
   (B) 3,150
   (C) 2,545
   (D) 2,555

2. If you type 45 words per minute, how many words can you type in 12 minutes?

   (A) 490
   (B) 540
   (C) 605
   (D) 615

3. Tom is flying a kite at the end of a 500-foot string. His friend Kathy is standing directly under the kite 300 feet away from Tom. How high is the kite flying?

   (A) 300 feet
   (B) 350 feet
   (C) 400 feet
   (D) 450 feet

4. Amy wants to fence in a yard using 400 feet of fencing. If she wants the yard to be 30 feet wide, what will its length be?

   (A) 170 feet
   (B) 175 feet
   (C) 180 feet
   (D) 185 feet

5. A three-digit code must be used to access a computer file. The first digit must be an A or a B. The second digit must be a number between 0 and 9. The final digit is a single letter from the alphabet from A to Z. How many possible access codes can there be?

   (A) 38
   (B) 468
   (C) 520
   (D) 640

6. The sun is 93 million miles from Earth, and light travels at a rate of 186,000 miles per second. How long does it take for light from the sun to reach Earth?

   (A) 5 minutes
   (B) $6\frac{1}{2}$ minutes
   (C) 7 minutes
   (D) $8\frac{1}{3}$ minutes

7. A tanning-bed pass for unlimited tanning costs $53 per month this year, but it was only $50 per month last year. What was the percentage of increase?

   (A) 5%
   (B) 5.5%
   (C) 6%
   (D) 6.5%

8. Eleven plus forty-one is divided by a number. If the result is thirteen, what's the number?

   (A) 2
   (B) 4
   (C) 6
   (D) 8

9. Mark received an hourly wage of $9.25. His boss gave him a 4% raise. How much does Mark make per hour now?

   (A) $9.29
   (B) $9.62
   (C) $9.89
   (D) $9.99

10. How many pounds of nails costing $7 per pound must be mixed with 6 pounds of nails costing $3 per pound to yield a mixture costing $4 per pound?

    (A) 2 pounds
    (B) 2.5 pounds
    (C) 3 pounds
    (D) 3.5 pounds

11. Theodore has 24 baseball cards. He sells $\frac{1}{4}$ of his cards to Tom and $\frac{1}{3}$ of his cards to Larry, and his mom accidently throws away $\frac{1}{6}$ of his cards. How many baseball cards does Theodore have left?

    (A) 2
    (B) 18
    (C) 12
    (D) 6

12. Theresa bought five karaoke CDs on sale. A karaoke CD normally costs $24, but she was able to purchase the CDs for $22.50 each. How much money did Theresa save on her entire purchase?

    (A) $7.50
    (B) $1.50
    (C) $8.00
    (D) $22.50

13. On a trip to the beach, you travel 200 miles in 300 minutes. How fast did you travel?

    (A) 30 mph
    (B) 40 mph
    (C) 50 mph
    (D) 60 mph

14. Twenty-one students, or 60% of the class, passed the final exam. How many students are in the class?

    (A) 45
    (B) 40
    (C) 35
    (D) 30

15. Joan invests $4,000 in an account that earns 3% simple interest. How much will Joan have in the account in 10 years?

    (A) $4,500
    (B) $4,800
    (C) $5,200
    (D) $5,400

16. A rectangle has a perimeter of 36 inches. Its length is 3 inches greater than twice the width. What's the rectangle's length?

    (A) 5 inches
    (B) 13 inches
    (C) 18 inches
    (D) 20 inches

17. A backyard is 50 feet by 100 feet. What's its area?

    (A) 150 square feet
    (B) 300 square feet
    (C) 500 square feet
    (D) 5,000 square feet

18. Eric is driving a car in which the speedometer displays speed in kilometers per hour (kph). He notes that his car is traveling at a rate of 75 kph, when he passes a speed limit sign stating the limit is 40 miles per hour (mph). He knows that a kilometer is about $\frac{5}{8}$ of a mile. If a police officer stops him at this point, how many miles per hour over the limit will the ticket read?

    (A) 5
    (B) 7
    (C) 9
    (D) 11

19. Three apples and twice as many pears add up to one-half the number of grapes in a fruit basket. How many grapes are in the basket?

   (A) 8
   (B) 18
   (C) 28
   (D) 38

20. Apples are on sale for "Buy 2 pounds, get 1 pound free." How many pounds must Janet purchase to get 2 pounds free?

   (A) 2 pounds
   (B) 4 pounds
   (C) 6 apples
   (D) 3 pounds

21. If four pipes of equal length measure 44 feet when they're connected together, how long is each pipe?

   (A) 11 feet
   (B) 4 feet
   (C) 22 feet
   (D) 9 feet

22. A German shepherd and an Alaskan malamute are both headed toward the same fire hydrant. The German shepherd is 120 feet away from the hydrant, and the Alaskan malamute is 75 feet away from the hydrant. How much closer to the hydrant is the Alaskan malamute?

   (A) 45 feet
   (B) 25 feet
   (C) 75 feet
   (D) 195 feet

23. A recruit reporting to boot camp took a bus from their home to the military processing center in another city. The trip took 14 hours. If they left at 6 a.m., what time did they arrive at the processing center?

   (A) 7 p.m.
   (B) 12 a.m.
   (C) 8 p.m.
   (D) 9 p.m.

24. A pair of farmers sold 3 pints of strawberries for $1.98 each, 5 pints of raspberries for $2.49 each, and a bushel of peaches for $5.50 at their roadside stand. How much money did the farmers make?

   (A) $9.97
   (B) $23.89
   (C) $18.39
   (D) $18.91

25. A librarian wants to shelve 532 books. If four books fit on a 1-foot length of shelving, how many feet of shelving do they need to shelve all the books?

   (A) 13
   (B) 45
   (C) 33
   (D) 133

26. A student buys a science textbook for $18.00, a math textbook for $14.50, and a dictionary for $9.95. What's the total cost of the books?

   (A) $27.95
   (B) $42.45
   (C) $41.95
   (D) $38.50

27. Debra works an 8-hour shift on Friday. How many minutes does she work on Friday?

   (A) 480 minutes
   (B) 800 minutes
   (C) 240 minutes
   (D) 400 minutes

28. Six people can run three machines in the factory. How many machines can 18 people run?

   (A) 7
   (B) 9
   (C) 6
   (D) 8

29. On a map drawn to scale, $\frac{1}{2}$ inch equals 1 mile. What length on the map equals 5 miles?

(A) 2.5 inches
(B) 5.0 inches
(C) 10.0 inches
(D) 1.5 inches

30. A man bought a pair of jeans for $23.00, a shirt for $14.95, and two ties for $7.98 each. What was the total cost of his clothing?

(A) $53.91
(B) $45.93
(C) $51.99
(D) $54.50

Subtest 2: Word Knowledge

TIME: 11 minutes for 35 questions

DIRECTIONS: This test has questions about the meanings of words. Each question has an underlined word. You need to decide which one of the four words in the choices most nearly means the same thing as the underlined word and then mark the corresponding space on your answer sheet.

1. The abhorrent smell from the lake overpowered the picnickers gathered on the shore.
   - (A) strong
   - (B) pleasant
   - (C) offensive
   - (D) tantalizing

2. Belie most nearly means
   - (A) pleasure.
   - (B) rule.
   - (C) pretend.
   - (D) misrepresent.

3. The water was calm that day with detritus slowly moving in the small eddies.
   - (A) fish
   - (B) lily pads
   - (C) plants
   - (D) debris

4. The prime minister was always cautious about leaving their redoubt in Belgrade.
   - (A) city
   - (B) stronghold
   - (C) house
   - (D) country

5. Mike was afraid he might be ostracized for stepping out of line.
   - (A) banished
   - (B) scolded
   - (C) assaulted
   - (D) arrested

6. The hotel was specifically designed for the wayworn traveler.
   - (A) lost
   - (B) weary
   - (C) demanding
   - (D) happy

7. The park has no showers and no potable water.
   - (A) usable
   - (B) clear
   - (C) drinkable
   - (D) tasty

8. Decamp most nearly means
   - (A) to backpack.
   - (B) to leave.
   - (C) to doubt.
   - (D) to act with abandon.

9. Glorious most nearly means
   - (A) splendid.
   - (B) particular.
   - (C) delayed.
   - (D) contentious.

10. Duplicity most nearly means
    - (A) hyperactivity.
    - (B) godlike.
    - (C) deception.
    - (D) criticalness.

11. Mallet most nearly means
    - (A) sermon.
    - (B) participate.
    - (C) hammer.
    - (D) fish.

12. Hosiery most nearly means
    - (A) dangerous.
    - (B) illegal.
    - (C) stocking.
    - (D) automatic.

13. Hale most nearly means
    (A) old.
    (B) healthy.
    (C) customary.
    (D) uninformed.

14. Magnitude most nearly means
    (A) importance.
    (B) peculiar.
    (C) alone.
    (D) tantamount.

15. My brother's vapid presentation earned him a C in the class.
    (A) difficult
    (B) plagiarized
    (C) dull
    (D) polished

16. Percival was unpopular at the meeting because he imparted so much extraneous data.
    (A) extensive
    (B) unwelcome
    (C) superfluous
    (D) radical

17. Chelsea was often solicitous of her father's feelings.
    (A) careful
    (B) ignorant
    (C) forgetful
    (D) abusive

18. I could never get over those liquid blue, limpid eyes.
    (A) bright
    (B) clear
    (C) attentive
    (D) dull

19. The goal of the treaty is to develop international amity and reciprocal trade.
    (A) agreement
    (B) friendship
    (C) standards
    (D) understanding

20. I often bragged about the bravery of my favorite cohort.
    (A) person
    (B) teacher
    (C) companion
    (D) employee

21. Speechless most nearly means
    (A) well-spoken.
    (B) silent.
    (C) restless.
    (D) talkative.

22. Indigenous most nearly means
    (A) poor.
    (B) rich.
    (C) immigrant.
    (D) native.

23. Illusive most nearly means
    (A) insignificant.
    (B) deceptive.
    (C) useful.
    (D) hidden.

24. Hesitate most nearly means
    (A) slam.
    (B) slow to act.
    (C) foreclose.
    (D) end.

25. Gravity most nearly means
    (A) planet.
    (B) relationship.
    (C) earn.
    (D) seriousness.

26. Fondle most nearly means
    (A) stir.
    (B) handle.
    (C) ogle.
    (D) radiate.

27. <u>Fete</u> most nearly means
    (A) festival.
    (B) criticize.
    (C) approve.
    (D) eat.

28. <u>Encore</u> most nearly means
    (A) play.
    (B) applause.
    (C) repetition.
    (D) excite.

29. <u>Diverse</u> most nearly means
    (A) various.
    (B) hidden.
    (C) nestled.
    (D) pastime.

30. <u>Detest</u> most nearly means
    (A) anger.
    (B) hate.
    (C) surprise.
    (D) excite.

31. Mike was known as a smart aleck, able to deliver <u>acerbic</u> one-liners with no effort.
    (A) funny
    (B) cheap
    (C) sharp
    (D) poetic

32. It took a great degree of <u>inexorable</u> force to break into the cavern.
    (A) strong
    (B) unyielding
    (C) acute
    (D) powerful

33. Attendants were stationed at intervals, with the obvious intent to <u>hector</u> those who moved too slowly.
    (A) hurry
    (B) harass
    (C) encourage
    (D) note

34. Reggie was as <u>gauche</u> in this group of polite company as he always had been.
    (A) funny
    (B) entertaining
    (C) tactless
    (D) embarrassed

35. <u>Confident</u> most nearly means
    (A) assured.
    (B) positive.
    (C) intelligent.
    (D) educated.

Subtest 3: Paragraph Comprehension

TIME: 13 minutes for 15 questions

DIRECTIONS: This test contains items that measure your ability to understand what you read. This section includes one or more paragraphs of reading material followed by incomplete statements or questions. Read the paragraph and select the choice that best completes the statement or answers the question. Mark your choice on your answer sheet by using the correct letter with each question number.

On June 22, 1944, President Franklin Delano Roosevelt signed into law one of the most significant pieces of legislation ever produced by the United States government: The Servicemembers' Readjustment Act of 1944, commonly known as the GI Bill of Rights. By the time the original GI Bill ended in July 1956, 7.8 million World War II veterans had participated in an education or training program, and 2.4 million veterans had home loans backed by the Veterans Administration (VA).

1. The GI Bill provided

    (A) free housing, training, and education.

    (B) medical coverage, education, and assistance to veterans.

    (C) home loan guarantees, training, and education for many former military members.

    (D) a means to exempt veterans from Social Security taxes.

You can put up to $3,000 a year into an individual retirement account (IRA) on a tax-deductible basis if your spouse isn't covered by a retirement plan at work or as long as your combined income isn't too high. You also can put the same amount tax-deferred into an IRA for a nonworking spouse if you file your income tax return jointly.

2. The maximum amount that a married couple could possibly save in a tax-deferred IRA during a year is

    (A) $3,000.

    (B) $6,000.

    (C) $9,000.

    (D) The question can't be answered based on the information contained in the passage.

Presidential appointments are an ongoing effort. Some of a president's appointments require Senate confirmation. These appointments are for positions throughout the federal government, for the Cabinet and subcabinet, for members of regulatory commissions, for ambassadorships, for judgeships, and for members of numerous advisory boards.

3. Which of the following statements is not true?

    (A) All presidential appointments require Senate confirmation.

    (B) A position on a regulatory commission is an example of a presidential appointment.

    (C) Presidential appointments happen throughout the president's term in office.

    (D) All of the above statements are true.

A link between advertising and alcohol consumption is intuitively compelling but hasn't been consistently supported by research. Because alcohol advertising is pervasive, econometric studies may not be sensitive to change or assess in a range where change actually makes a difference. In dealing with advertising, partial bans aren't likely to be effective, and total bans aren't practical. Advertising bans in one medium also are weakened by substitution of increased advertising in alternative media and/or other promotions.

4. The author of this passage believes that

   (A) advertisement of alcoholic beverages should be illegal.
   (B) partial bans on alcohol advertising could be effective in some cases.
   (C) bans on alcohol advertising aren't likely to work.
   (D) clear links have been established between alcohol consumption and advertising.

The etymology of the word or name *Alabama* has evoked much discussion among philological researchers. It was the name of a noted southern Indian tribe whose habitat when first known to Europeans was in what is now central Alabama. One of the major waterways in the state was named for this group and from this river, in turn, the name of the state was derived. According to some investigations, the tribal name Alabama must be sought in the Choctaw tongue, because it isn't uncommon for tribes to accept a name given them by a neighboring tribe.

5. The state of Alabama was named after

   (A) a Choctaw Indian tribe.
   (B) European settlers.
   (C) a river.
   (D) an Indian chief.

Each of the 94 federal judicial districts handles bankruptcy matters, and in almost all districts, bankruptcy cases are filed in the bankruptcy court. Bankruptcy cases can't be filed in state court. Bankruptcy laws help people who can no longer pay their creditors get a fresh start by liquidating their assets to pay their debts or by creating a repayment plan. Bankruptcy laws also protect troubled businesses and provide for orderly distributions to business creditors through reorganization or liquidation.

6. Which of the following statements is not supported by the passage?

   (A) Bankruptcy must be filed in a federal court.
   (B) Bankruptcy is designed to help individuals and protect businesses.
   (C) Businesses can be reorganized or liquidated through bankruptcy.
   (D) Bankruptcy must be filed in the bankruptcy court.

Questions 7 and 8 are based on the following passage.

The U.S. Department of Justice has prepared a report about hate crimes in the United States between 1997 and 1999. In 60% of hate crime incidents, the most serious offense was a violent crime, most commonly intimidation or simple assault. The majority of incidents motivated by race, ethnicity, sexual orientation, or disability involved a violent offense, while two-thirds of incidents motivated by religion involved a property offense, most commonly vandalism. Younger offenders were responsible for most hate crimes. Thirty-one percent of violent offenders and 46% of property offenders were under age 18.

7. Most property offense hate crimes were motivated by

   (A) religion.
   (B) race.
   (C) sexual orientation.
   (D) abortion.

8. The majority of hate crimes during this period can be classified as

   (A) property offenses.
   (B) violent crimes.
   (C) assault.
   (D) intimidation.

Linewatch operations are conducted near international boundaries and coastlines in areas of Border Patrol jurisdiction to prevent the illegal entry and smuggling of aliens into the United States and to intercept those who do enter illegally before they can escape from border areas. Sign cutting is the detection and the interpretation of any disturbances in natural terrain conditions that indicate the presence or passage of people, animals, or vehicles.

9. The activity that's designed to detect changes in the natural environment, which may indicate passage of undocumented aliens, is called

   (A) linewatching.
   (B) sign cutting.
   (C) Border Patrol Operations.
   (D) Terrain Observation.

Wales was in ancient times divided into three parts nearly equal, consideration having been paid, in this division, more to the value than to the just quantity or proportion of territory. They were Venedotia, now called North Wales; Demetia, or South Wales, which in British is called Deheubarth, that is, the southern part; and Powys, the middle or eastern district. Roderic the Great, or Rhodri Mawr, who was king over all Wales, was the cause of this division. He had three sons, Mervin, Anarawt, and Cadell, amongst whom he partitioned the whole principality.

10. Wales was divided into divisions because

   (A) natural boundaries such as rivers and mountains made the division necessary.
   (B) Wales was too large for the king to oversee personally.
   (C) the King of Wales wanted his sons to rule.
   (D) all of the above.

Questions 11 and 12 are based on the following passage.

The fierce and warlike tribe, called the Huns, who'd driven the Goths to seek new homes, came from Asia into Southeastern Europe and took possession of a large territory lying north of the River Danube. During the first half of the fifth century, the Huns had a famous king named Attila. He was only 21 years old when he became their king. But although he was young, he was very brave and ambitious, and he wanted to be a great and powerful king. As soon as his army was ready, he marched with it into countries, which belonged to Rome. He defeated the Romans in several great battles and captured many of their cities. The Roman Emperor Theodosius had to ask for terms of peace. Attila agreed that there should be peace, but soon afterwards he found out that Theodosius had formed a plot to murder him. He was so enraged at this that he again began war. He plundered and burned cities wherever he went, and at last the emperor had to give him a large sum of money and a portion of the country south of the Danube.

11. A good title for the above paragraph would be

   (A) "The Burning of Rome"
   (B) "Emperor Theodosius"
   (C) "Attila the Hun"
   (D) "Rome For Dummies"

12. After terms of peace were offered, Attila resumed the war against Rome because

   (A) he discovered the emperor wanted to assassinate him.
   (B) he wanted to further expand his kingdom.
   (C) the emperor of Rome offered too little money in the peace terms.
   (D) Danube, his second-in-charge, advised him not to accept the peace terms.

Questions 13 through 15 are based on the following passage.

In the military, as in all professions, the issue of competence is directly relevant to professional integrity. Because human life, national security, and expenditures from the national treasury are so frequently at issue when the military acts, the obligation to be competent isn't merely prudential. That obligation is a moral one, and culpable incompetence here is clearly a violation of professional integrity. Part of the social aspect of professional integrity involves the joint responsibility for conduct and competence shared by all members of the profession. Only fellow professionals are capable of evaluating competence in some instances; hence, fellow professionals must accept the responsibility of upholding the standards of the profession. Fellow military members can spot derelictions of duty, failures of leadership, failures of competence, and the venalities of conduct that interfere with the goals of the military mission. Often, the obligations of professional integrity may be pitted against personal loyalties or friendships; and, where the stakes for society are so high, professional integrity should win out.

13. One word that best describes the primary theme of this passage would be
    (A) proficiency.
    (B) equality.
    (C) evaluations.
    (D) relationships.

14. Professional competence is
    (A) a moral obligation.
    (B) directly relevant to professional integrity.
    (C) essential because military operations impact human life, national security, and use of taxpayer funds.
    (D) all of the above.

15. The author of the passage would agree that
    (A) friendship must often take a back seat to professional integrity.
    (B) only fellow professionals should evaluate competence.
    (C) professional competence is a direct result of effective training programs.
    (D) all of the above.

Subtest 4: Mathematics Knowledge

TIME: 24 minutes for 25 questions

DIRECTIONS: This section is a test of your ability to solve general mathematical problems. Select the correct answer from the choices given and then mark the corresponding space on your answer sheet. Use scratch paper to do any figuring. Calculators are not allowed.

1. Solve for x: $5x - 2x = 7x + 2x - 24$
   - (A) 2
   - (B) −2
   - (C) 4
   - (D) −4

2. The cube of 6 is
   - (A) 125
   - (B) 225
   - (C) 216
   - (D) 238

3. In the graph $3x + 7y = 21$, at what point is the x-axis intersected?
   - (A) $(7, 0)$
   - (B) $(0, 7)$
   - (C) $(0, 4)$
   - (D) $(4, 0)$

4. $x + y = 6$ and $x - y = 4$. Find the value of x.
   - (A) 3
   - (B) 5
   - (C) 7
   - (D) 8

5. Solve for y: $4(y + 3) + 7 = 3$
   - (A) 2
   - (B) −2
   - (C) 4
   - (D) −4

6. $(12 \text{ yards} + 14 \text{ feet}) \div 2 =$
   - (A) 25 feet
   - (B) 12 feet
   - (C) 50 feet
   - (D) 8 feet

7. $x^3(x^3) =$
   - (A) x^9
   - (B) $2x^9$
   - (C) $2x^6$
   - (D) x^6

8. $4\frac{1}{5} + 1\frac{2}{5} + 3\frac{3}{10} =$
   - (A) $6\frac{1}{5}$
   - (B) $8\frac{9}{10}$
   - (C) $5\frac{1}{2}$
   - (D) $7\frac{1}{5}$

9. $1.5 \times 10^2 =$
   - (A) 45
   - (B) 150
   - (C) 1,500
   - (D) 15

10. The average of 54, 61, 70, and 75 is
    - (A) 50
    - (B) 52
    - (C) 55
    - (D) 65

11. 2 feet, 4 inches + 4 feet, 8 inches =
    - (A) 6 feet, 8 inches
    - (B) 7 feet
    - (C) 7 feet, 2 inches
    - (D) 8 feet

12. If $x = 4$, then $x^4 \div x =$
    - (A) 12
    - (B) 36
    - (C) 64
    - (D) 72

13. Solve for x: $5 - 3x \geq 14 + 6x$
    - (A) $x \geq -1$
    - (B) $x \leq -1$
    - (C) $x > -1$
    - (D) $x < -1$

14. $(900 \times 3) \div 6 =$
    - (A) 45
    - (B) 450
    - (C) 55
    - (D) 550

15. If $x = 2$, then $x^x(x^x) =$
    - (A) 16
    - (B) $2x^x$
    - (C) 8
    - (D) 24

16. Solve for x: $x^2 - 2x - 15 = 0$
    - (A) 4, −2
    - (B) 3, −3
    - (C) 5, −3
    - (D) −1, 1

17. $\sqrt{49} \div \sqrt{64} =$
    - (A) $\frac{1}{4}$
    - (B) $\frac{1}{2}$
    - (C) $\frac{1}{3}$
    - (D) $\frac{7}{8}$

18. If $5y^2 = 80$, then y is
    - (A) a positive number.
    - (B) a negative number.
    - (C) either a positive or negative number.
    - (D) an imaginary number.

19. If $2 + x \geq 15$, what's the value of x?
    - (A) $x < 13$
    - (B) $x > 13$
    - (C) $x \geq 13$
    - (D) $x \leq 13$

20. If a circle has a radius of 15 feet, which is the best estimate of its circumference?
    - (A) 24 feet
    - (B) 72 feet
    - (C) 94 feet
    - (D) 36 feet

21. What's the volume of a box measuring 12 inches long by 8 inches deep by 10 inches high?
    - (A) 960 cubic inches
    - (B) 128 cubic inches
    - (C) 42 cubic inches
    - (D) 288 cubic inches

22. The following figure is a(n)

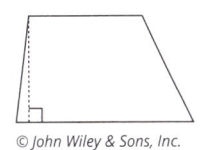

    © John Wiley & Sons, Inc.

    - (A) parallelogram.
    - (B) obtuse triangle.
    - (C) trapezoid.
    - (D) rectangle.

23. The sum of the measures of the interior angles of a parallelogram is
    - (A) 360 degrees.
    - (B) 540 degrees.
    - (C) 180 degrees.
    - (D) 720 degrees.

24. What is the prime factorization of 100?
    - (A) 2×50
    - (B) $2^2 \times 5^2$
    - (C) 4×25
    - (D) 25^2

25. $\sqrt{-9}$ is an example of a(n)
    - (A) real number.
    - (B) imaginary number.
    - (C) irrational number.
    - (D) rational number.

Chapter 25
AFQT Practice Exam 1: Answers and Explanations

Use this answer key to score the Practice AFQT Exam in Chapter 24. Note that the actual AFQT is scored by comparing your raw score to other people's scores, which produces a scaled score. Turn to Chapter 1 to find out how the AFQT score is derived from the Arithmetic Reasoning, Word Knowledge, Paragraph Comprehension, and Mathematics Knowledge subtests. Keep in mind that these four subtests determine whether you can even get into the military. If you find you're still struggling in any of these subtest areas, you may want to concentrate some additional study effort before knocking on your recruiter's door to say, "I'm ready!"

Subtest 1: Arithmetic Reasoning Answers

Mathematical word problems can be tough for some people. You have to zero in on relevant facts, turn those facts into a mathematical formula, and reach the correct solution. Yikes! No wonder there are so many math books on the market. If you still need work on this subtest, I recommend reviewing the chapters in Part 3. Running through the additional practice questions at the ends of those chapters may also help.

1. **A.** There are 30 days in April, 31 days in May, and 30 days in June for a total of 91 days. Multiply the number of days by the number of haircuts per day: $91 \times 35 = 3,185$.

2. **B.** Multiply the number of words you can type per minute (45) by the number of minutes you'll be typing (12): $45 \times 12 = 540$.

3. C. Visualize a right triangle, where the kite string represents the hypotenuse and the line between Tom and Kathy represents one of the legs. The Pythagorean theorem states that if you know the length of two sides of a right triangle, you can determine the length of the third side using the formula $a^2 + b^2 = c^2$. In this case, $300^2 + b^2 = 500^2$. Solve for b:

$$90,000 + b^2 = 250,000$$
$$b^2 = 250,000 - 90,000$$
$$b^2 = 160,000$$
$$b = \sqrt{160,000}$$
$$b = 400$$

4. A. The formula used to determine the perimeter of a rectangle is $P = 2(l + w)$. The width is 30, and the perimeter is 400. Plug in the numbers and solve for l:

$$400 = 2(l + 30)$$
$$400 = 2l + 60$$
$$340 = 2l$$
$$l = 170$$

5. C. There are two possibilities for the first digit (A or B), 10 possibilities for the second digit (0 to 9), and 26 possibilities for the third digit. Using the multiplication principle, $2 \times 10 \times 26 = 520$ possible access codes.

6. D. The distance formula is distance equals rate times time, or $d = rt$. Substitute the known values: $93,000,000 = 186,000t$. Therefore, $t = 500$ seconds. Divide 500 by 60 to convert to minutes: 500 seconds ÷ 60 seconds/minute = $8\frac{1}{3}$ minutes.

7. C. The difference in the price is $3, so divide the difference by the original price: $\$3 \div \$50 = 0.06$, or 6%.

8. B. Let x = the unknown number. Set up the equation as $\frac{11+41}{x} = 13$. Then solve for x:

$$\frac{11+41}{x} = 13$$
$$\frac{52}{x} = 13$$
$$52 = 13x$$
$$x = 4$$

9. B. Mark received a 4% raise, so to calculate the new wage, start off by finding the raise: $\$9.25 \times 0.04 = \$0.37$. Then add that number (the amount of Mark's raise) to his original hourly wage. Mark's new hourly wage is $\$9.25 + \$0.37 = \$9.62$.

10. A. Let x = the weight of nails costing $7 per pound. The total cost of the mixture (M) equals the sum of the cost for each type of nail, or $M = A + B$, where $A = 7x$, $B = 3(6)$, and $M = 4(6 + x)$. Substitute the known values into the equation and solve for x:

$$4(6 + x) = 7x + 18$$
$$24 + 4x = 7x + 18$$
$$24 - 18 = 7x - 4x$$
$$6 = 3x$$
$$x = 2$$

11. D. You need to add the fractions, so convert the different denominators to a common denominator — 4, 3, and 6 all divide evenly into 12, so use 12 as the common denominator.
$\frac{1}{4} \times \frac{3}{3} = \frac{3}{12}$ $\frac{1}{3} \times \frac{4}{4} = \frac{4}{12}$ $\frac{1}{6} \times \frac{2}{2} = \frac{2}{12}$
To add the fractions, first add the new numerators together: $3+4+2=9$. Place the added numerator over the new denominator, 12, and you can see that $\frac{9}{12}$ of the cards have been sold or lost. You can reduce $\frac{9}{12}$ to $\frac{3}{4}$, so $\frac{1}{4}$ of the cards remain. $\frac{1}{4}$ of 24 is $\frac{1}{4} \times 24 = 6$, so 6 cards remain.

12. A. Subtract the sale price from the regular price: $24.00 - $22.50 = $1.50. Multiply the difference by the number of CDs to find out how much Theresa saved altogether: $1.50 \times 5 = $7.50.

13. B. First convert the 300 minutes to hours by dividing by 60 (300 minutes ÷ 60 minutes/hour = 5 hours). Use the distance formula ($d = rt$) and substitute the known values: $200 = 5r$; $r = 40$ mph.

14. C. Let x = the number of people in the class; 60% of $x = 21$, so $0.60x = 21$, and $x = 35$.

15. C. Use the interest formula ($I = Prt$) to determine the amount of interest earned, where the principal (P) is 4,000, the rate (r) is 0.03 (3%), and the time (t) is 10. $I = 4,000(0.03)(10)$, or $I = $1,200. Add the interest earned to the original amount invested: $4,000 + $1,200 = $5,200.

16. B. A rectangle's perimeter is determined by the formula $P = 2(l+w)$. The length of this rectangle is $3 + 2w$. Substituting the known values into the formula results in

$36 = 2(w + 3 + 2w)$
$36 = 2(3w + 3)$
$18 = 3w + 3$
$15 = 3w$
$w = 5$

The length is $3 + 2w$, so $l = 3 + 2(5) = 13$.

17. D. The area of a rectangle is the length times the width of the rectangle, or $A = lw$: $50 \times 100 = 5,000$ square feet.

18. B. A kilometer is $\frac{5}{8}$ of a mile, so multiply $75 \times \frac{5}{8} = \frac{375}{8}$. Divide 375 by 8 to determine that Eric was traveling at about 47 miles per hour, 7 mph over the 40 mph posted limit.

19. B. Let x = the number of grapes; 3 apples and 6 pears (twice the number of apples) equals $\frac{1}{2}$ of x, or

$3 + 6 = \frac{1}{2}x$
$9 = \frac{1}{2}x$
$2(9) = x$
$x = 18$

20. B. If Janet must purchase 2 pounds of apples to get 1 free pound, then to get 2 free pounds, she would need to purchase twice as many apples, or 4 pounds of apples.

21. **A.** All pipes are equal in length, so divide the total length, 44 feet, by the total number of pipes, 4. The answer, 11, is the length of each individual pipe. You can check this answer by multiplying: $4 \times 11 = 44$.

22. **A.** Subtract the Alaskan malamute's distance from the German shepherd's distance $(120 - 75 = 45)$ to determine how much closer the Alaskan malamute is to the hydrant.

23. **C.** Simply add 14 hours to 6 a.m. to reach 8 p.m. Twelve hours from 6 a.m. is 6 p.m., and two hours after that brings you to 8 p.m.

24. **B.** Multiply 3 pints of strawberries at $1.98 ($3 \times \$1.98 = \$5.94$), 5 pints of raspberries at $2.49 ($5 \times \$2.49 = \$12.45$), and 1 bushel of peaches at $5.50 ($1 \times \$5.50 = \$5.50$). Add the products together to determine the amount of cash the farmers earned: $\$5.94 + \$12.45 + \$5.50 = \$23.89$. You can also start with an estimate by rounding the prices and multiplying, like this: $(3 \times 2) + (5 \times 2.5) + 5.5 = 6 + 12.5 + 5.5 = 24$. Choice (B) is the only value close to the estimate.

25. **D.** Divide 532 by 4 to determine how many feet of shelving the librarian will need: 532 books $\div$ 4 books/foot = 133 feet.

26. **A.** Simply add the cost of all the books: $\$18.00 + \$14.50 + \$9.95 = \$42.45$.

27. **A.** 8 hours $\times$ 60 minutes/hour = 480 minutes.

28. **B.** Eighteen people can run three times the number of machines 6 people can run, because $18 = 3 \times 6$ (divide 18 by 6). Six people can run 3 machines, so multiply 3×3 machines = 9 machines. Therefore, 18 people can run 9 machines.

29. **A.** Multiply the scale measurement for 1 mile $\left(\frac{1}{2}\text{ inch per mile}\right)$ by 5 miles: $\frac{1}{2} \times 5 = \frac{1}{2} \times \frac{5}{1} = \frac{5}{2}$. Divide 5 by 2, and you get 2.5 inches.

30. **A.** Simply add the cost of all the items: $\$23.00 + \$14.95 + \$7.98 + \$7.98 = \$53.91$. To save time, you can also round up the cost of each item to the next-highest dollar amount and add the rounded numbers. Your answer ($54) is a little higher than Choice (A), which makes it the right answer.

Subtest 2: Word Knowledge Answers

I hope you did well on this subtest. (I was crossing my fingers the whole time!) If not, you may want to take another gander at Chapter 4.

1. **C.** *Abhorrent* is an adjective that means repugnant or inspiring disgust and loathing.

2. **D.** *Belie* is a verb that means to fail to give a true impression of something. It also means to disguise, contradict, or betray.

3. **D.** *Detritus* is a noun that refers to waste or debris.

4. **B.** *Redoubt* is a noun that refers to a temporary or supplementary fortification that usually doesn't have flanking defenses.

5. **A.** *Ostracized* is the past tense of the verb *ostracize*, which means to exclude someone from a group or society.

6. **B.** *Wayworn* is an adjective that means weary from traveling.

7. **C.** *Potable* is an adjective that means safe to drink. (In basic training, you'll see huge water tanks spray-painted with "Potable Water," so that's where you'll go to rehydrate.)

8. **B.** *Decamp* is a verb that means to depart secretly or suddenly, especially to relocate to another area.

9. **A.** *Glorious* is an adjective that means having exceptional beauty that evokes feelings of admiration. It also means having, bringing, or worthy of fame or admiration.

10. **C.** *Duplicity* is a noun that means deceitfulness.

11. **C.** *Mallet* is a noun that refers to a hammer with a large head.

12. **C.** *Hosiery* is a noun that refers to stockings, pantyhose, and socks collectively.

13. **B.** *Hale* is an adjective that means strong and healthy (when referring to a person).

14. **A.** *Magnitude* is a noun that refers to the great size or extent of something; it also means great importance or consequence.

15. **C.** *Vapid* is an adjective that means offering nothing stimulating or challenging.

16. **C.** *Extraneous* is an adjective that means unrelated or irrelevant to the current subject, and one of its synonyms is *superfluous* (which means unnecessary, especially when something is in abundance).

17. **A.** *Solicitous* is an adjective that means showing interest or concern.

18. **B.** *Limpid* is an adjective that means clear and unclouded.

19. **B.** *Amity* is a noun that refers to a friendly relationship.

20. **C.** *Cohort* is a noun that means a group of people banded together as a group or treated as a group.

21. **B.** *Speechless* is an adjective that means temporarily unable to speak, refraining from speech, or lacking the ability to speak.

22. **D.** *Indigenous* is an adjective that means native or originating or occurring naturally in a certain place.

23. **B.** *Illusive* is an adjective that means deceptive (like an illusion). Don't confuse *illusive* with *elusive*, which means difficult to find, catch, or achieve.

24. **B.** *Hesitate* is a verb that means to pause before doing or saying something or to be reluctant to do something.

25. **D.** *Gravity* is a noun that refers to extreme or alarming importance or seriousness. (It's also what keeps you from floating into space, which is pretty serious *and* important.)

26. **B.** *Fondle* is a verb that means to stroke or caress lovingly or erotically.

27. **A.** *Fete* is a noun that refers to a celebration or festival. It can also be a verb that means to honor or entertain someone lavishly.

28. **C.** *Encore* is a noun that means a repeated or additional performance of something.

29. **A.** *Diverse* is an adjective that means showing a substantial amount of variety. It also means very different.

30. **B.** *Detest* is a verb that means to dislike intensely.

31. **C.** *Acerbic* is an adjective that means sharp and forthright, especially when referring to a comment or a style of speaking.

32. **B.** *Inexorable* is an adjective that means impossible to prevent or stop. It also means unyielding or unalterable.

33. **B.** *Hector* is a verb that means to talk to someone in a bullying way.

34. **C.** *Gauche* is an adjective that means lacking grace, unsophisticated, and socially awkward.

35. **A.** *Confident* is an adjective that means feeling or showing confidence in oneself. It also means self-assured.

Subtest 3: Paragraph Comprehension Answers

If you still need to boost your score, engage in some more reading practice. Improving your vocabulary can also help improve your reading comprehension skills. See Chapter 5 for some tips.

1. **C.** According to the passage, millions of veterans received home loan guarantees, education, and training, making Choice (C) the correct answer. Be careful here, because Choice (A) is tempting, but nothing in the passage indicates that the housing, education, and training were totally free.

2. **B.** The paragraph states that the maximum amount one can place into a tax-deferred IRA is $3,000, plus an additional $3,000 if the spouse isn't employed. The question asks about a couple, so add $3,000 + $3,000 to get $6,000.

3. **A.** Although many presidential appointments require Senate confirmation, not all do. The passage mentions only some appointments, so Choice (A) is an incorrect statement.

4. **C.** The author specifically states that partial bans on alcohol advertising aren't likely to be effective and that total bans wouldn't be practical.

5. **C.** According to the passage, a river was named after the Alabama Indian tribe, and the state derived its name from this river.

6. **D.** The question here is looking for the incorrect (unsupported) statement. The first sentence states that bankruptcy is usually (not always) filed in bankruptcy court, making Choice (D) an incorrect statement.

7. **A.** The second sentence states that most violent crimes were motivated by such factors as race and sexual orientation, and most property crimes were motivated by religion. The question refers to property crimes, so Choice (A) is the right answer.

8. **B.** Sixty percent of all hate crimes during the period were violent crimes. Assault and intimidation are examples of violent crimes.

9. **B.** The last sentence in the passage describes the sign cutting operation.

10. **C.** The rationale for the division is explained in the final sentence, which mentions the king's sons. The passage makes no reference to the size of Wales or the natural boundaries.

11. **C.** The primary subject of this paragraph is Attila, who was king of the Huns.

12. **A.** Attila agreed to peace but soon after discovered that the Roman emperor had launched a plot to kill him.

13. **A.** The primary theme of the passage is stated in the first sentence. *Proficiency* is closest in meaning to the word *competence*, which is the primary theme of the passage.

14. **D.** The passage directly supports all the statements.

15. **A.** The author specifically states that when pitted against friendship, professional integrity should win out. The author explains that only fellow professionals can evaluate other professionals in some (not all) cases, making Choice (B) incorrect. Choice (C) isn't supported by information in the passage.

Subtest 4: Mathematics Knowledge Answers

If you didn't do as well as you'd hoped on the Mathematics Knowledge subtest, review Chapters 6, 7, and 8.

1. **C.**

$$5x - 2x = 7x + 2x - 24$$
$$3x = 9x - 24$$
$$-6x = -24$$
$$6x = 24$$
$$x = 4$$

2. **C.** The cube of 6 is $6^3 = 6 \times 6 \times 6 = 216$.

3. **A.** The equation $3x + 7y = 21$ is the equation for a line, and a line intersects the x-axis at the point where the y-coordinate is 0 ($y = 0$). Substitute 0 for y in the equation to find the value for x at the intersection point:

$$3x + 7y = 21$$
$$3x + 7(0) = 21$$
$$3x = 21$$
$$x = 7$$

The point's coordinates are (7, 0).

4. **B.** This problem gives you a system of equations — two equations with two variables. You can find x by solving one of the equations for y and plugging that value into the other equation. First, $x + y = 6$, so $y = 6 - x$. Substitute this known value for y in the second equation and solve for x:

$$x - y = 4$$
$$x - (6 - x) = 4$$
$$x - 6 + x = 4$$
$$2x - 6 = 4$$
$$2x = 10$$
$$x = 5$$

5. **D.**

$$4(y + 3) + 7 = 3$$
$$4y + 12 + 7 = 3$$
$$4y + 19 = 3$$
$$4y = -16$$
$$y = -4$$

6. **A.** Convert 12 yards, 14 feet to feet:

$$(12 \text{ yards} \times 3 \text{ feet/yard}) + 14 \text{ feet}$$
$$= 36 \text{ feet} + 14 \text{ feet}$$
$$= 50 \text{ feet}$$

Divide by 2 as instructed: 50 feet ÷ 2 = 25 feet.

7. **D.** If two powers have the same base, the numbers can be multiplied by keeping the base the same and adding the powers (exponents) together: $x^3(x^3) = x^{3+3} = x^6$.

8. **B.** Convert to the lowest common denominator (which is 10), and then add: $4\frac{1}{5} + 1\frac{2}{5} + 3\frac{3}{10} = 4\frac{2}{10} + 1\frac{4}{10} + 3\frac{3}{10} = 8\frac{9}{10}$.

9. **B.** Following the order of operations, you have to find the power (10^2) before multiplying: $1.5 \times 10^2 = 1.5 \times (10 \times 10) = 1.5 \times 100 = 150$.

10. **D.** Add the numbers and then divide by the number of terms to find the mean. The sum is $54 + 61 + 70 + 75 = 260$. You have four numbers, and $260 \div 4 = 65$.

11. **B.** 2 feet + 4 feet = 6 feet, and 4 inches + 8 inches = 12 inches (the equivalent to 1 foot). Therefore, you have a total of 7 feet.

12. **C.** Your first reaction may be to substitute 4 for each x and then do the math. But you can save yourself some work (and time) by first dividing x^4 by x, which is x^3. Then substitute 4 for each x, and you find that the equation is now $4 \times 4 \times 4$. Then multiply: 4×4 is 16, and 16×4 is 64, which is your final answer.

13. **B.** As you solve this inequality, remember that when you multiply or divide an inequality by a negative number, you need to reverse the direction of the inequality sign:

$$5 - 3x \geq 14 + 6x$$
$$5 - 3x - 6x \geq 14$$
$$-9x \geq 14 - 5$$
$$-9x \geq 9$$
$$x \leq -1$$

14. **B.** $(900 \times 3) \div 6 = 2{,}700 \div 6 = 450$.

15. **A.** Substitute 2 for all the x's: $x^x(x^x) = 2^2 \times 2^2 = 4 \times 4 = 16$.

16. **C.** This is a quadratic equation that you can solve by factoring and setting each factor equal to zero:

$$x^2 - 2x - 15 = 0$$
$$(x-5)(x+3) = 0$$
$$x - 5 = 0 \quad \text{or} \quad x + 3 = 0$$
$$x = 5 \qquad\qquad x = -3$$

17. **D.** Find the square roots before dividing. The square root of 49 is 7, and the square root of 64 is 8. Now divide: $7 \div 8 = \frac{7}{8}$.

18. **C.** The square root of a positive number can be either positive or negative. For instance, the square root of 16 is ± 4, because 4^2 and $(-4)^2$ both give you the positive number 16.

19. **C.** Solving this inequality doesn't require multiplying or dividing by a negative number, so the inequality sign remains the same: $2 + x \geq 15$; $x \geq 13$.

20. **C.** Circumference equals π times diameter, and diameter is equal to two times the radius. In other words, $C = \pi d$, and $d = 2r$. Thus, $C = \pi(2)(15) = \pi 30$. If you round π to 3.14, the answer is 94.2, or about 94 feet.

21. **A.** Volume equals length times width times height ($V = lwh$). Plug in the numbers and solve: $V = 12 \times 8 \times 10 = 960$ cubic inches.

22. **C.** In a trapezoid, two of four sides are parallel to each other.

23. **A.** All quadrilaterals have angles that total 360 degrees.

24. **B.** A *prime number* only has 1 and itself as factors. You can find the prime factors of 100 by factoring until you can't factor any value further:

$$100 = 4 \times 25 = 2 \times 2 \times 5 \times 5 = 2^2 \times 5^2$$

25. **B.** The square root of a negative number doesn't exist as far as real numbers are concerned. In mathematics, this is called an imaginary number, and imaginary numbers are represented by the letter i where $i^2 = -1$. In this example, $\sqrt{-9} = \sqrt{-1}\sqrt{9} = i\sqrt{9}$.

Chapter 26
AFQT Practice Exam 2

The Armed Forces Qualification Test (AFQT) consists of four of the subtests on the Armed Services Vocational Aptitude Battery (ASVAB). The four subtests used to determine your AFQT score are Arithmetic Reasoning, Word Knowledge, Paragraph Comprehension, and Mathematics Knowledge.

The AFQT score is very important. Although all the ASVAB subtests are used to determine which military jobs you qualify for, the AFQT score determines whether you're even eligible to join the military. All the military service branches have established minimum AFQT scores, according to their needs (see Chapter 2 for more information).

The AFQT is not a stand-alone test (it's part of the ASVAB), but in this chapter, I present the subtests applicable to the AFQT in the same order in which you'll encounter them when you take the actual ASVAB.

After you complete the entire practice test, check your answers against the answer key in Chapter 27.

REMEMBER

The test is scored by comparing your raw score to the scores of other people, which produces a scaled score. So just because you missed a total of 20 questions doesn't mean that your score is 80. (That would be too simple.) Turn to Chapter 1 to find out how the AFQT score is derived from these four subtests.

Your goal in taking this practice test is to determine which areas you may still need to study. If you miss only one question on the Word Knowledge subtest but 15 questions on Arithmetic Reasoning, you probably want to devote some extra study time to developing your math skills before you take the ASVAB.

Answer Sheet for AFQT Practice Exam 2

Subtest 1: Arithmetic Reasoning

1. Ⓐ Ⓑ Ⓒ Ⓓ
2. Ⓐ Ⓑ Ⓒ Ⓓ
3. Ⓐ Ⓑ Ⓒ Ⓓ
4. Ⓐ Ⓑ Ⓒ Ⓓ
5. Ⓐ Ⓑ Ⓒ Ⓓ
6. Ⓐ Ⓑ Ⓒ Ⓓ
7. Ⓐ Ⓑ Ⓒ Ⓓ
8. Ⓐ Ⓑ Ⓒ Ⓓ
9. Ⓐ Ⓑ Ⓒ Ⓓ
10. Ⓐ Ⓑ Ⓒ Ⓓ
11. Ⓐ Ⓑ Ⓒ Ⓓ
12. Ⓐ Ⓑ Ⓒ Ⓓ
13. Ⓐ Ⓑ Ⓒ Ⓓ
14. Ⓐ Ⓑ Ⓒ Ⓓ
15. Ⓐ Ⓑ Ⓒ Ⓓ
16. Ⓐ Ⓑ Ⓒ Ⓓ
17. Ⓐ Ⓑ Ⓒ Ⓓ
18. Ⓐ Ⓑ Ⓒ Ⓓ
19. Ⓐ Ⓑ Ⓒ Ⓓ
20. Ⓐ Ⓑ Ⓒ Ⓓ
21. Ⓐ Ⓑ Ⓒ Ⓓ
22. Ⓐ Ⓑ Ⓒ Ⓓ
23. Ⓐ Ⓑ Ⓒ Ⓓ
24. Ⓐ Ⓑ Ⓒ Ⓓ
25. Ⓐ Ⓑ Ⓒ Ⓓ
26. Ⓐ Ⓑ Ⓒ Ⓓ
27. Ⓐ Ⓑ Ⓒ Ⓓ
28. Ⓐ Ⓑ Ⓒ Ⓓ
29. Ⓐ Ⓑ Ⓒ Ⓓ
30. Ⓐ Ⓑ Ⓒ Ⓓ

Subtest 2: Word Knowledge

1. Ⓐ Ⓑ Ⓒ Ⓓ
2. Ⓐ Ⓑ Ⓒ Ⓓ
3. Ⓐ Ⓑ Ⓒ Ⓓ
4. Ⓐ Ⓑ Ⓒ Ⓓ
5. Ⓐ Ⓑ Ⓒ Ⓓ
6. Ⓐ Ⓑ Ⓒ Ⓓ
7. Ⓐ Ⓑ Ⓒ Ⓓ
8. Ⓐ Ⓑ Ⓒ Ⓓ
9. Ⓐ Ⓑ Ⓒ Ⓓ
10. Ⓐ Ⓑ Ⓒ Ⓓ
11. Ⓐ Ⓑ Ⓒ Ⓓ
12. Ⓐ Ⓑ Ⓒ Ⓓ
13. Ⓐ Ⓑ Ⓒ Ⓓ
14. Ⓐ Ⓑ Ⓒ Ⓓ
15. Ⓐ Ⓑ Ⓒ Ⓓ
16. Ⓐ Ⓑ Ⓒ Ⓓ
17. Ⓐ Ⓑ Ⓒ Ⓓ
18. Ⓐ Ⓑ Ⓒ Ⓓ
19. Ⓐ Ⓑ Ⓒ Ⓓ
20. Ⓐ Ⓑ Ⓒ Ⓓ
21. Ⓐ Ⓑ Ⓒ Ⓓ
22. Ⓐ Ⓑ Ⓒ Ⓓ
23. Ⓐ Ⓑ Ⓒ Ⓓ
24. Ⓐ Ⓑ Ⓒ Ⓓ
25. Ⓐ Ⓑ Ⓒ Ⓓ
26. Ⓐ Ⓑ Ⓒ Ⓓ
27. Ⓐ Ⓑ Ⓒ Ⓓ
28. Ⓐ Ⓑ Ⓒ Ⓓ
29. Ⓐ Ⓑ Ⓒ Ⓓ
30. Ⓐ Ⓑ Ⓒ Ⓓ
31. Ⓐ Ⓑ Ⓒ Ⓓ
32. Ⓐ Ⓑ Ⓒ Ⓓ
33. Ⓐ Ⓑ Ⓒ Ⓓ
34. Ⓐ Ⓑ Ⓒ Ⓓ
35. Ⓐ Ⓑ Ⓒ Ⓓ

Subtest 3: Paragraph Comprehension

1. Ⓐ Ⓑ Ⓒ Ⓓ
2. Ⓐ Ⓑ Ⓒ Ⓓ
3. Ⓐ Ⓑ Ⓒ Ⓓ
4. Ⓐ Ⓑ Ⓒ Ⓓ
5. Ⓐ Ⓑ Ⓒ Ⓓ
6. Ⓐ Ⓑ Ⓒ Ⓓ
7. Ⓐ Ⓑ Ⓒ Ⓓ
8. Ⓐ Ⓑ Ⓒ Ⓓ
9. Ⓐ Ⓑ Ⓒ Ⓓ
10. Ⓐ Ⓑ Ⓒ Ⓓ
11. Ⓐ Ⓑ Ⓒ Ⓓ
12. Ⓐ Ⓑ Ⓒ Ⓓ
13. Ⓐ Ⓑ Ⓒ Ⓓ
14. Ⓐ Ⓑ Ⓒ Ⓓ
15. Ⓐ Ⓑ Ⓒ Ⓓ

Subtest 4: Mathematics Knowledge

1. Ⓐ Ⓑ Ⓒ Ⓓ
2. Ⓐ Ⓑ Ⓒ Ⓓ
3. Ⓐ Ⓑ Ⓒ Ⓓ
4. Ⓐ Ⓑ Ⓒ Ⓓ
5. Ⓐ Ⓑ Ⓒ Ⓓ
6. Ⓐ Ⓑ Ⓒ Ⓓ
7. Ⓐ Ⓑ Ⓒ Ⓓ
8. Ⓐ Ⓑ Ⓒ Ⓓ
9. Ⓐ Ⓑ Ⓒ Ⓓ
10. Ⓐ Ⓑ Ⓒ Ⓓ
11. Ⓐ Ⓑ Ⓒ Ⓓ
12. Ⓐ Ⓑ Ⓒ Ⓓ
13. Ⓐ Ⓑ Ⓒ Ⓓ
14. Ⓐ Ⓑ Ⓒ Ⓓ
15. Ⓐ Ⓑ Ⓒ Ⓓ
16. Ⓐ Ⓑ Ⓒ Ⓓ
17. Ⓐ Ⓑ Ⓒ Ⓓ
18. Ⓐ Ⓑ Ⓒ Ⓓ
19. Ⓐ Ⓑ Ⓒ Ⓓ
20. Ⓐ Ⓑ Ⓒ Ⓓ
21. Ⓐ Ⓑ Ⓒ Ⓓ
22. Ⓐ Ⓑ Ⓒ Ⓓ
23. Ⓐ Ⓑ Ⓒ Ⓓ
24. Ⓐ Ⓑ Ⓒ Ⓓ
25. Ⓐ Ⓑ Ⓒ Ⓓ

Subtest 1: Arithmetic Reasoning

TIME: 36 minutes for 30 questions

DIRECTIONS: This test contains questions about arithmetic. Each question is followed by four possible answers. Decide which answer is correct and then mark the space on your answer sheet that has the same number and letter as your choice. Use scratch paper for any figuring you need to do. Calculators are not allowed.

1. Mike has $5.25 in quarters and dimes. He has exactly 15 dimes. How many quarters does he have?

    (A) 6
    (B) 12
    (C) 15
    (D) 21

2. Kelly used to pay $500 a month for rent. Now she pays $525 a month for rent. By what percent did her rent increase?

    (A) 0.5 percent
    (B) 5 percent
    (C) 10 percent
    (D) 12.5 percent

3. A bag has 8 pennies, 5 dimes, and 7 nickels. A coin is randomly chosen from the bag. What is the probability that the coin chosen is a dime?

    (A) $\frac{1}{20}$
    (B) $\frac{1}{4}$
    (C) $\frac{1}{3}$
    (D) $\frac{3}{10}$

4. There are 2 pints in 1 quart and 4 quarts in a gallon. How many pints are in 2 gallons?

    (A) 32 pints
    (B) 16 pints
    (C) 8 pints
    (D) 4 pints

5. Paul invests $2,000 in an account that pays 4 percent annual interest. How much will he earn in interest in one year?

    (A) $160
    (B) $80
    (C) $120
    (D) $800

6. One mile is equal to 5,280 feet. Sergeant Jeffries walked 1.2 miles. What distance (in feet) did the sergeant walk?

    (A) 7,392 ft.
    (B) 1,056 ft.
    (C) 5,780 ft.
    (D) 6,336 ft.

7. A total of 200 people attended a conference. Use the chart to determine how many attendees were women.

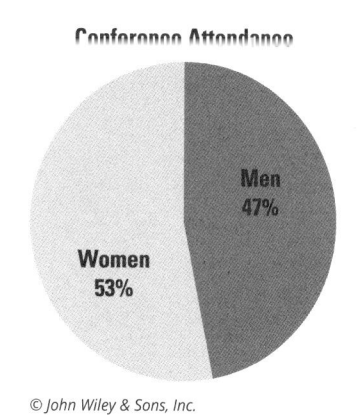

    Conference Attendance

    Men 47%
    Women 53%

    © John Wiley & Sons, Inc.

    (A) 94
    (B) 212
    (C) 53
    (D) 106

8. Suppose you have $88 in your checking account. You use your debit card to pay $22 for a sweater and $8 for lunch, and then you deposit a $38 check. What is the balance in your account?

   (A) $58
   (B) $96
   (C) $20
   (D) $156

9. There are 24 right-handed students in a class of 30. A student is chosen from the class at random. What is the probability that the student is left-handed?

   (A) $\frac{1}{2}$
   (B) $\frac{1}{5}$
   (C) $\frac{4}{5}$
   (D) $\frac{1}{4}$

10. At a laundromat, it costs $1.75 to wash each load of laundry and $1.50 to dry each load of laundry. How much will you pay to wash and dry four loads of laundry?

    (A) $2.25
    (B) $20.00
    (C) $20.25
    (D) $13.00

11. Delia has been walking at a constant speed of 2.5 miles per hour for 12 minutes. How many miles has she walked?

    (A) 0.2 mile
    (B) 0.5 mile
    (C) 2 miles
    (D) 4.8 miles

12. A rectangular deck is 6 meters long and 8 meters wide. What is the distance from one corner of the deck to the opposite corner?

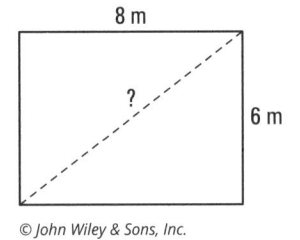

    © John Wiley & Sons, Inc.

    (A) 10 m
    (B) 12 m
    (C) 14 m
    (D) 15 m

13. Tom is going to hang three framed pictures side by side on a wall. How many different ways can he arrange the pictures?

    (A) 9
    (B) 5
    (C) 6
    (D) 27

14. A cleaning company charges by the square foot. The company charged $600 to clean 4,800 square feet of space. How much would the company charge to clean 12,000 square feet of space?

    (A) $950
    (B) $1,200
    (C) $1,400
    (D) $1,500

15. Kendra earns $12 an hour. Her employer pays 1.5 times her normal pay rate for overtime. Last week, she worked 40 hours plus 4 hours overtime. How much did she earn last week?

    (A) $552
    (B) $528
    (C) $1,400
    (D) $480

16. A hot tub is 75 percent full with 600 gallons of water. How many gallons of water are in the hot tub when it's half full?

    (A) 200 gallons
    (B) 400 gallons
    (C) 800 gallons
    (D) 300 gallons

17. Angela has 15 coins (quarters and dimes) in the cash register. The total value of the quarters and dimes is $2.55. How many dimes are in the cash register?

    (A) 8 dimes
    (B) 7 dimes
    (C) 3 dimes
    (D) 10 dimes

18. A rectangular tabletop measures 48 inches long by 36 inches wide. A square game board that is 18 inches on each side is on the tabletop. Which amount of the tabletop's area is not covered by the game board?

    (A) 1,710 in.²
    (B) 1,404 in.²
    (C) 1,656 in.²
    (D) 96 in.²

19. A map of Texas has a scale of 1 cm = 11 km. The actual distance between Dallas and San Antonio is about 440 km. How far apart are the cities on the map?

    (A) 11 cm
    (B) 44 cm
    (C) 40 cm
    (D) 22 cm

20. Jake is four years older than Kenneth. Alicia is two years younger than Kenneth. The sum of Jake's, Kenneth's, and Alicia's ages is 38. What is Kenneth's age?

    (A) 9
    (B) 15
    (C) 12
    (D) 10

21. Mrs. Jacobs is making a large circular rug with a radius of 10 feet. Every square foot of material used to make the rug costs her $0.50. Approximately how much will the material for the entire rug cost?

    (A) $157
    (B) $167
    (C) $628
    (D) $314

22. John's quiz scores in science class are 8, 6, 10, 7, 9, and 5. What is John's average quiz score?

    (A) 6
    (B) 8
    (C) 7.5
    (D) 8.5

23. Robert charges a flat fee of $15 plus $20 per half-hour to repair computers. He started one job at 8:45 a.m. and worked until he finished. The total charge for that job was $75. What time did he finish the job?

    (A) 12:15 p.m.
    (B) 11:45 a.m.
    (C) 10:15 a.m.
    (D) 9:30 a.m.

24. The measure of angle P is 44°. Angle Q is 12° less than half the measure of the supplement of angle P. What is the measure of angle Q?

    (A) 136°
    (B) 80°
    (C) 124°
    (D) 56°

25. Rose and Carla play on the same basketball team. During the last game, Rose scored $\frac{3}{5}$ of the team's points. Carla scored 16 percent of the team's points. What percentage of the team's points were not scored by either Rose or Carla?

    (A) 76 percent
    (B) 66 percent
    (C) 24 percent
    (D) 34 percent

26. John and Garret are running in a marathon. John runs at a steady rate of 3.5 miles per hour, and Garret runs at a steady rate of 4.25 miles per hour. How far apart will they be 2 hours after the race starts?

   (A) 0.75 mile
   (B) 2.5 miles
   (C) 1.5 miles
   (D) 2.25 miles

27. Jim can repair a heating unit in 2 hours. Kyle can repair the same unit in 3 hours. How long will they take to repair the unit if they work together?

   (A) 1 hour and 10 minutes
   (B) 1 hour and 12 minutes
   (C) 48 minutes
   (D) 50 minutes

28. A square has an area of 121 cm². What is the perimeter?

   (A) 121 cm
   (B) 22 cm
   (C) 33 cm
   (D) 44 cm

29. How many gallons of water should you add to 4 gallons of a juice that is 20 percent water so the final mixture is 50 percent water?

   (A) 2.2 gallons
   (B) 2 gallons
   (C) 2.4 gallons
   (D) 1.4 gallons

30. David is at a car dealership trying to decide between buying a truck or a sedan. The truck is available in three colors, and the sedan is available in four colors. Each vehicle also has both a 2-wheel-drive and a 4-wheel-drive option in all available colors. How many different choices does he have?

   (A) 48
   (B) 14
   (C) 12
   (D) 6

Subtest 2: Word Knowledge

TIME: 11 minutes for 35 questions

DIRECTIONS: This test has questions about the meanings of words. Each question has an underlined word. You need to decide which one of the four words in the choices most nearly means the same or opposite thing as the underlined word and then mark the corresponding space on your answer sheet.

1. Kindle most nearly means
   - (A) devise.
   - (B) ignite.
   - (C) boil.
   - (D) expire.

2. The word most opposite in meaning to burnout is
   - (A) successful.
   - (B) ruined.
   - (C) enthusiasm.
   - (D) fatigue.

3. Blatant most nearly means
   - (A) obvious.
   - (B) overdrawn.
   - (C) certain.
   - (D) hidden.

4. Hasten most nearly means
   - (A) delay.
   - (B) anxious.
   - (C) rush.
   - (D) stabilize.

5. Objective most nearly means
   - (A) massive.
   - (B) favored.
   - (C) neutral.
   - (D) dependent.

6. Good luck convincing a headstrong teen that they're wrong.
   - (A) cruel
   - (B) stubborn
   - (C) friendly
   - (D) unaffected

7. The thought of dissecting the frog made me cringe in disgust.
   - (A) recoil
   - (B) volunteer
   - (C) wail
   - (D) rally

8. Despite her wild past, Bobbi prefers to live a more domestic lifestyle these days.
   - (A) native
   - (B) homebound
   - (C) foreign
   - (D) elaborate

9. Grandma always taught us to be frugal and grateful for what we had.
   - (A) careless
   - (B) excessive
   - (C) cheap
   - (D) thrifty

10. I wanted to curtail the date because of Bob's cat obsession.
    - (A) develop
    - (B) shorten
    - (C) postpone
    - (D) continue

11. The captain received many accolades for bravery during the battle.
    - (A) honors
    - (B) criticisms
    - (C) presents
    - (D) promotions

12. Covert most nearly means
    (A) tiresome.
    (B) popular.
    (C) secret.
    (D) unruly.

13. Abhor most nearly means
    (A) commence.
    (B) embrace.
    (C) remove.
    (D) dislike.

14. The mandate to report at exactly 9 a.m. the next day was written on my boss's personal stationery.
    (A) invitation
    (B) greeting
    (C) command
    (D) permission

15. The word most opposite in meaning to assortment is
    (A) variety.
    (B) difference.
    (C) mixture.
    (D) consistency.

16. Credible most nearly means
    (A) cynical.
    (B) rehearsed.
    (C) genuine.
    (D) vague.

17. Reprieve most nearly means
    (A) on hold.
    (B) complete.
    (C) final.
    (D) justice.

18. Tedious most nearly means
    (A) fresh.
    (B) dreary.
    (C) difficult.
    (D) annoying.

19. Jackson's music was so loud he was oblivious to the honking car behind him.
    (A) cognizant
    (B) superfluous
    (C) ignorant
    (D) perceptive

20. The coach knew how to bolster the team's morale in the final moments.
    (A) recruit
    (B) demean
    (C) allude
    (D) encourage

21. The word most opposite in meaning to abstract is
    (A) exclusive.
    (B) realistic.
    (C) imaginative.
    (D) far-fetched.

22. The rain hampered the runner's ability to break the record.
    (A) facilitated
    (B) eased
    (C) forced
    (D) hindered

23. Cower most nearly means
    (A) attack.
    (B) celebrate.
    (C) cringe.
    (D) sublime.

24. Tangent most nearly means
    (A) detour.
    (B) wavering.
    (C) focus.
    (D) perfect.

25. Nullify most nearly means
    (A) suggest.
    (B) cancel.
    (C) perform.
    (D) promote.

26. Tangible most nearly means
    (A) theoretical.
    (B) fragile.
    (C) possessive.
    (D) physical.

27. Absolution most nearly means
    (A) condemnation.
    (B) owing a debt.
    (C) assurance.
    (D) forgiveness.

28. Abrogate most nearly means
    (A) materialize.
    (B) terminate.
    (C) embark.
    (D) constitute.

29. I wanted to temper the dinner conversation so Grandpa wouldn't walk out.
    (A) ignore
    (B) irritate
    (C) soothe
    (D) anger

30. Plethora most nearly means
    (A) scarcity.
    (B) infection.
    (C) unique.
    (D) abundance.

31. Mary was tentative about buying the more expensive car.
    (A) unhappy
    (B) optimistic
    (C) hesitant
    (D) certain

32. The word most opposite in meaning to retaliation is
    (A) vengeance.
    (B) forgiveness.
    (C) recognition.
    (D) payback.

33. Jennifer tried to admonish me about asking Mr. Michelson questions because of his long-winded nature.
    (A) encourage
    (B) punish
    (C) spurn
    (D) warn

34. The memo was more like a diatribe of all the things Kathy hated about work.
    (A) novel
    (B) tirade
    (C) compliment
    (D) dispute

35. The word most opposite in meaning to memento is
    (A) rubbish.
    (B) souvenir.
    (C) jewel.
    (D) prize.

Subtest 3: Paragraph Comprehension

TIME: 13 minutes for 15 questions

DIRECTIONS: This test contains items that measure your ability to understand what you read. This section includes one or more paragraphs of reading material followed by incomplete statements or questions. Read the paragraph and select the choice that best completes the statement or answers the question. Mark your choice on your answer sheet by using the correct letter with each question number.

Terry always wanted to move back to Chicago, the city of her birth, because of fond childhood memories. After convincing her husband, Jim, to leave sunny California, her dream was coming true. They moved in the fall, just in time to catch the leaves changing. However, the worst winter in the city's history was too much for their beach bum mentality, and Terry soon regretted her decision. Her dream wasn't the same as reality, and she realized you can't always go back.

1. Why does Terry feel like "you can't always go back"?

(A) Chicago is too far.
(B) She is no longer a child.
(C) California had changed her.
(D) Winter was her favorite season.

Questions 2 and 3 refer to the following passage.

A new study shows that since the 1970s, the number of households with pets has almost tripled. Yet despite this increased pet ownership, the number of animals euthanized at shelters each year is still between 2.5 and 3 million. In fact, according to the Humane Society of the United States, in 2012, only 30 percent of the 62 percent of households with pets got the animals from shelters or rescue organizations. Furthermore, many of the euthanized animals are healthy, and 25 percent of the dogs euthanized are purebred. There is still a lot of work to do to spread the word about rescue pets to ensure healthy animals don't meet this fate.

2. What is the main point of the passage?

(A) Americans have more pets than ever before.
(B) More households should adopt rescue animals.
(C) More cats are adopted than dogs.
(D) Shelters house only sick or hurt dogs.

3. Of the households that had pets in 2012, how many of them got their pets from a shelter or rescue organization?

(A) 62 percent
(B) 25 percent
(C) 3 percent
(D) 30 percent

Christo and Jeanne-Claude were an artistic couple known for their elaborate and grandiose projects. Their projects involved giant sheets of nylon wrapped or hanging in an unlikely environment. They achieved notoriety for their artistic installations, such as Valley Curtain, which displayed a 200,200-square-foot curtain hanging between two Colorado mountains. Although their unconventional penchant for wrapping monuments and buildings wasn't understood by everyone, no one can dispute that their work was respected nonetheless.

4. In this passage, penchant means

(A) inclination.
(B) disinterest.
(C) incompetence.
(D) experience.

Despite having used her new shoes for only three months during her frequent marathon training, Tara was having pains in her feet while running. All the articles she read said that running shoes should last at least six months if used an average of two to three times a week. Tara decided she had bought the wrong shoes.

5. Based on the passage, what other reason could Tara's shoes be worn out sooner than six months?

   (A) She runs with bad form.
   (B) The shoes are cheap.
   (C) She runs more than average.
   (D) She damaged her shoes on rough terrain.

Robert De Niro may never have won his first Academy Award if he had gotten the role he wanted as Michael Corleone in *The Godfather*. In 1975, he received his first nomination and win for his role as young Vito Corleone in *The Godfather: Part II*. By 2013, he'd scored six more nominations (including another win in 1981).

6. According to the passage, how many Academy Awards has Robert De Niro been nominated for?

   (A) 3
   (B) 6
   (C) 7
   (D) 0

Questions 7 and 8 refer to the following passage.

Tiffany often wished her family lived closer to another airport. It seemed like her flights were always either canceled or delayed due to weather. In fact, she missed Christmas one year because of a blizzard, and her flight home from her grandma's birthday celebration was postponed for five hours because of a thunderstorm. But she couldn't do anything about it. The region just had terrible weather sometimes.

7. What is the main point of the passage?

   (A) Tiffany doesn't like visiting her family.
   (B) The region's weather is unpredictable.
   (C) Tiffany's local airport is terrible.
   (D) Tiffany has bad luck.

8. In this passage, postponed means

   (A) ruined.
   (B) over.
   (C) expedited.
   (D) delayed.

Historical battle reenactments date back to the Middle Ages, when actors would perform scenes from Ancient Rome to entertain a public audience. The most famous reenactments, of course, are those pertaining to the American Civil War, which became popular during the war's centennial celebration in 1961. Almost 50,000 people gathered to commemorate the beginning of the Civil War, which started on April 12, 1861. These days, anywhere from 500 to 20,000 people will congregate to reenact a famous battle from the war. Both the Confederate and Union armies are equally represented.

9. How many years does a centennial celebration recognize?

   (A) 20,000
   (B) 100
   (C) 500
   (D) 1,861

Questions 10 and 11 refer to the following passage.

When you're driving in snow, a few bits of knowledge can be the difference between a safe trip and an accident. Never slam on the brakes in the snow. Tapping the brakes helps you slow down without skidding. If you are skidding, turn into the direction of the skid, not away from it. This approach will help you gain control of the vehicle.

10. The author wrote this passage to

   (A) convince the reader to drive in the snow.
   (B) provide driving tips for snowy conditions.
   (C) make sure your brakes are tuned.
   (D) scare the reader about driving in the snow.

11. Driving safely in snowy conditions means

(A) understanding the results of your actions.

(B) avoiding braking.

(C) avoiding busy roads.

(D) relinquishing control.

The crowd at the store was growing quickly. Children reached for their favorite-colored backpack. Notebooks flew off the shelves, and pencils of different shapes and sizes were running low in stock. Back-to-school shopping had definitely begun.

12. What is the author telling the reader in the passage?

(A) that school supplies are scarce

(B) that the store isn't prepared

(C) that parents spend too much money on supplies

(D) that the beginning of school is approaching

Questions 13 and 14 refer to the following passage.

The 70-year career of Frank Lloyd Wright is one of the most remarkable and renowned in the architecture world. He designed 1,141 buildings, and 532 of those designs were actually developed. The 409 that remain are considered individual works of art. His name is as famous as Bruce Springsteen's in modern-day society.

13. How many buildings were constructed from Frank Lloyd Wright's designs?

(A) 532

(B) 1,141

(C) 70

(D) 409

14. In this passage, renowned means

(A) common.

(B) popular.

(C) misunderstood.

(D) famous.

Sailors don't like to share the water with motorboaters because of the massive wake left by the high-speed boats. The waves disrupt the easy flow of the sailboats, causing them to twist and turn in the wind. The sentiment between sailors and speedboaters is similar to that between skiers and snowboarders.

15. How do skiers feel about snowboarders?

(A) They think snowboarders are a great addition to the slopes.

(B) They hate snowboarders.

(C) They don't like to share the mountain with snowboarders.

(D) They think snowboarders lack a high level of skill.

Subtest 4: Mathematics Knowledge

TIME: 24 minutes for 25 questions

DIRECTIONS: This section is a test of your ability to solve general mathematical problems. Select the correct answer from the choices given and then mark the corresponding space on your answer sheet. Use scratch paper to do any figuring. Calculators are not allowed.

1. $(-5)^3 =$
   - (A) −125
   - (B) −15
   - (C) 15
   - (D) 125

2. If $42 < 2x$, which is true about the value of x?
   - (A) x is less than 21.
   - (B) x is greater than 21.
   - (C) x is less than or equal to 21.
   - (D) x is greater than or equal to 21.

3. $473 + 220 + 27 =$
   - (A) 710
   - (B) 620
   - (C) 720
   - (D) 711

4. In the decimal 45.21, which digit is in the tenths place?
   - (A) 4
   - (B) 5
   - (C) 2
   - (D) 1

5. What are the coordinates of point P?

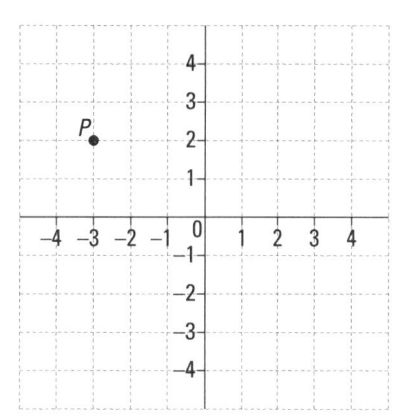

   © John Wiley & Sons, Inc.

   - (A) $(-3, -2)$
   - (B) $(3, -2)$
   - (C) $(-3, 2)$
   - (D) $(2, -3)$

6. Express $\frac{11}{4}$ as a decimal.
   - (A) 2.25
   - (B) 2.5
   - (C) 2.75
   - (D) 3.25

7. If $-2 + y = 8$, then $y =$
   - (A) −10
   - (B) −6
   - (C) 6
   - (D) 10

GO ON TO NEXT PAGE

CHAPTER 26 AFQT Practice Exam 2 571

8. A circle has a circumference of 9.24 centimeters. What is the diameter of the circle?

(A) 1.5 cm
(B) 3 cm
(C) 3.14 cm
(D) 6 cm

9. What is 28 percent of 40?

(A) 9.4
(B) 10.2
(C) 11.2
(D) 12.5

10. Which is equal to $10^3 \times 10^{-6} \times 10^2$?

(A) 10
(B) 100
(C) 0.1
(D) 0.01

11. Simplify: $2 + 2y + 4 + y$

(A) $3y + 6$
(B) $3y + 8$
(C) $8y$
(D) $2y^2 + 6$

12. What is the value of x?

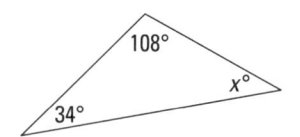

© John Wiley & Sons, Inc.

(A) 54°
(B) 34°
(C) 58°
(D) 38°

13. $(5-2)! =$

(A) 118
(B) 12
(C) 6
(D) 3

14. $\frac{1}{2} + \frac{1}{16} + \frac{1}{4} =$

(A) $\frac{3}{22}$
(B) $\frac{13}{22}$
(C) $\frac{13}{16}$
(D) $\frac{7}{16}$

15. How many factors does the number 51 have?

(A) Four
(B) Three
(C) Two
(D) One

16. The number 0.405 is what percent of 0.9?

(A) 4.5 percent
(B) 45 percent
(C) 25 percent
(D) 50 percent

17. The measure of angle P is m°. What is the measure of the complement of angle P?

(A) $(180 - m)°$
(B) $(90 - m)°$
(C) $(m - 90)°$
(D) $(m - 180)°$

18. What is the length b in the right triangle?

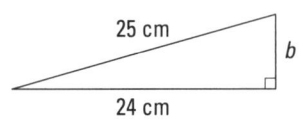

© John Wiley & Sons, Inc.

(A) 4 cm
(B) 5 cm
(C) 6 cm
(D) 7 cm

19. Translate the following sentence into an equation: "x decreased by 11 is twice x."

(A) $11 - x = 2x$
(B) $x - 11 = 2$
(C) $11 - x = 2$
(D) $x - 11 = 2x$

20. The mean of 5, 7, 8, 10, 4, and x is 7.5. What is the value of x?

(A) 7
(B) 8
(C) 10
(D) 11

21. $(9 - 3 \cdot 2)^2 - 0.5(-2) =$

(A) 10
(B) 145
(C) 8
(D) 143

22. Simplify: $9 - 4(5x - 2)$

(A) $17 - 20x$
(B) $25x - 2$
(C) $7 - 20x$
(D) $25x - 10$

23. The height, h, of a cylinder is twice the radius r. What is the volume of the cylinder?

(A) πr^3
(B) $4\pi r^3$
(C) $2\pi r^3$
(D) $8\pi r^2$

24. Find the area of the entire region shown.

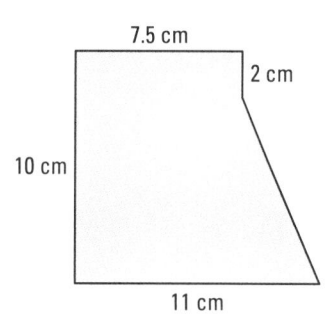

© John Wiley & Sons, Inc.

(A) 85 cm²
(B) 89 cm²
(C) 125 cm²
(D) 719 cm²

25. Of 260 students at a local elementary school, 140 are boys. Express the ratio of girls to boys as a simplified fraction.

(A) $\frac{6}{7}$
(B) $\frac{7}{6}$
(C) $\frac{13}{7}$
(D) $\frac{7}{13}$

Chapter 27
AFQT Practice Exam 2: Answers and Explanations

Did you do well on this practice exam? I sure hope so! Use this answer key to score the practice exam in Chapter 26.

The AFQT isn't scored based on number correct, number wrong, or even percent of questions correct. Instead, the score is derived by comparing your raw score with the raw score of others who have taken the test before you. In determining the raw score, harder questions are worth more points than easier questions. (For more on scoring, turn to Chapter 1.)

Don't waste time trying to equate your score on this practice test with your potential score on the actual AFQT. It can't be done. Instead, use the results of this practice test to determine which areas you should devote more study time to.

Subtest 1: Arithmetic Reasoning Answers

How'd you do on this subtest? If you don't feel so good about the results, you may want to put off taking the real ASVAB until you feel more confident about your math skills. In addition to reviewing Part 3, you may want to find a tutor or a class that can help you brush up on the basics. I can't stress enough how important it is to score well on this subtest.

1. **C.** If Mike has 15 dimes, he has $(15)(\$0.10) = \$1.50$ in dimes. Subtract that from the total to find out how much he has in quarters: $\$5.25 - \$1.50 = \$3.75$. Then, divide that result by $\$0.25$ to determine how many quarters he has: $\$3.75 \div \$0.25 = 15$.

2. **B.** The percent increase is the amount of increase, $25, divided by the original amount, $500: $25 \div 500 = 0.05$. Convert 0.05 to a percent by multiplying 0.05 by 100 to get 5 percent.

3. **B.** The probability of randomly selecting a dime is equal to the number of dimes in the bag, 5, divided by the total number of coins in the bag, 20: $5 \div 20 = \frac{1}{4}$.

4. **B.** If 1 gallon contains 4 quarts, 2 gallons contain 8 quarts. Multiply that number by the number of pints per quart, 2, to get 16 pints in 8 quarts.

5. **B.** Use the interest formula $I = Prt$, where I is the interest, P is the principal, r is the interest rate (as a decimal), and t is the time in years.

    $I = \$2,000(0.04)(1) = \$80$

6. **D.** Convert miles to feet by multiplying 1.2 miles by the conversion factor, 5,280 feet: $1.2(5,280) = 6,336$ ft.

7. **D.** According to the chart, 53 percent of the attendees were women. Multiply the percent of women (0.53) by the number of attendees (200): $0.53(200) = 106$.

8. **B.** Subtract the purchase amounts ($22 and $8) from the amount in your checking account: $\$88 - \$22 - \$8 = \$58$. Then add the amount of the deposit: $\$58 + \$38 = \$96$.

9. **B.** The probability of choosing one of the six left-handed students in the class (remember, it's a class of 30, and 24 students are right-handed) is easy to find. Because $\frac{6}{30}$ students are left-handed, reduce the fraction to come up with the probability. $\frac{6}{30} = \frac{1}{5}$. You have a one-in-five chance of randomly choosing a leftie.

10. **D.** Each total load costs $3.25 ($1.75 + $1.50). Multiply that by 4 to get the total cost of all your laundry: $\$3.25 \times 4 = \$13$. You might be better off taking it to your parents' house, where it's free (and your mom feeds you)!

11. **B.** Convert the minutes to hours by dividing 12 by 60: $12 \div 60 = 0.2$ hours. Use the distance formula, $d = rt$, to find the distance in miles that she walked: $d = 2.5(0.2) = 0.5$ mile.

12. **A.** Use the Pythagorean theorem, $a^2 + b^2 = c^2$, to find the length of the diagonal, c:

    $6^2 + 8^2 = c^2$
    $36 + 64 = c^2$
    $100 = c^2$
    $\pm\sqrt{100} = c^2$
    $\pm 10 = c$

    Use the positive answer because length is always positive.

13. **C.** For the first picture to be hung on the wall, there are three choices. After he hangs the first picture, there are two choices left for the second picture, and then one choice left for the last picture. Multiply to find the number of different ways he can arrange the three pictures: $(3)(2)(1) = 6$ ways.

14. **D.** The easiest way to figure out how much the cleaning company would charge is to first determine how much it charges per square foot. Divide $600 by 4,800 to find that out: $\$600 \div 4,800 = \$0.125$ per square foot. You want the company to clean 12,000 square feet, so multiply that number by the per-square-foot rate: $12,000 \times \$0.125 = \$1,500$.

15. **A.** Kendra earned $\$12(40) = \$480$ for the 40 hours she worked. Her overtime pay rate is $1.5(\$12) = \$18$ per hour. She earned an additional $\$18(4) = \$72$ in overtime pay. Her total pay last week was $\$480 + \$72 = \$552$.

16. **B.** Seventy-five percent of the total amount of water the tub will hold, *x*, is equal to 600 gallons. You can represent this fact with the equation $0.75x = 600$. Solve the equation to determine how many gallons the tub holds when full:

$$\begin{aligned} 0.75x &= 600 \\ x &= \frac{600}{0.75} \\ x &= 800 \end{aligned}$$

The full hot tub holds 800 gallons of water. Half of 800 gallons is 400 gallons.

17. **A.** Let *q* equal the number of quarters and *d* equal the number of dimes. The value of the quarters is 25*q*, and the value of the dimes is 10*d*. So the value of dimes and quarters is $25q + 10d = 255$.

You also know that the total number of coins is 15, so $q + d = 15$. You can rearrange this equation to isolate *q*: $q = 15 - d$. Now you can substitute that for the *q* in the first equation and solve for *d*:

$$\begin{aligned} 25(15 - d) + 10d &= 255 \\ 375 - 25d + 10d &= 255 \\ 375 - 15d &= 255 \\ 15d &= -120 \\ d &= 8 \end{aligned}$$

18. **B.** Use the formula for a rectangle, $A = lw$, to find the area of the tabletop: $A = (48)(36) = 1{,}728 \text{ in.}^2$ The formula for the area of a square is $A = s^2$, where *s* is the length of one side. Use it to find the area of the game board: $A = 18^2 = 324 \text{ in.}^2$ Then you can find the amount of area not covered by the game board by subtracting the area of the game board from the area of the tabletop: $1{,}728 \text{ in.}^2 - 324 \text{ in.}^2 = 1{,}404 \text{ in.}^2$

19. **C.** Let *x* represent the distance between the cities on the map. Write and solve an equation to find *x*:

$$\begin{aligned} \frac{x}{440} &= \frac{1}{11} \\ 11x &= 440 \\ x &= 440 \div 11 \\ x &= 40 \end{aligned}$$

20. **C.** Let *x* represent Kenneth's age. You can then write Jake's age as *x* + 4 and Alicia's age as *x* − 2. The sum of their ages is 38. Write and solve an equation to find *x*:

$$\begin{aligned} x + x + 4 + x - 2 &= 38 \\ 3x + 2 &= 38 \\ 3x &= 36 \\ x &= 12 \end{aligned}$$

21. **A.** The area of a circle is $A = \pi r^2$. If the radius is 10 feet, then the area is $A = \pi r^2 \approx 3.14(10)^2 \approx 3.14(100) \approx 314 \text{ ft.}^2$ Multiply the area by the cost per square foot: $3.14(\$0.50) = \$157$.

22. **C.** John took six quizzes in science class. To find his average, first add all his scores together: $8+6+10+7+9+5=45$. Then, divide that number by 6 (the number of quizzes John took):

$$\frac{45}{6}=7.5$$

His average score was 7.5.

23. **C.** Subtract the $15 base fee from $75 to find Robert's total hourly earnings: $75 - $15 = $60. Divide $60 by $20 to find the number of half-hours that he worked: $60 ÷ $20 = 3 half-hours. Three half-hours equal 1.5 hours, so add this amount of time to 8:45 a.m. to discover that he finished the job at 10:15 a.m.

24. **D.** If two angles are supplementary, the sum of their measures is equal to 180°. To find the supplement of angle P, subtract its measure from 180°: 180° − 44° = 136°. Angle Q is 12° less than half the supplement of angle P, so divide 136° by 2 and then subtract 12°:
$\frac{136°}{2} - 12° = 68° - 12° = 56°$.

25. **C.** Write the fraction of points scored by Rose as a percent: $\frac{3}{5} = 0.6 = 60\%$.

    Together, Rose and Carla scored 60 percent + 16 percent = 76 percent of the points scored by the team. So the percentage of points not scored by either player is
    100 percent − 76 percent = 24 percent.

26. **C.** This problem uses the distance formula: $d = rt$. John's distance is the product of his rate (3.5 mph) and the time (2 hours): $d = 3.5(2) = 7$ miles. Garret's distance is the product of his rate (4.25 mph) and the time (2 hours): $d = 4.25(2) = 8.5$ miles. After 2 hours, they're 8.5 miles − 7 miles = 1.5 miles apart. You can solve this problem another way, too: Figure out John and Garret's speed difference, which is 0.75 mph. Multiply that by 2 hours of running and you can see that they're 1.5 miles apart.

27. **B.** Use the formula $\frac{a \times b}{a+b}$, where a is the amount of time Jim takes to repair the unit and b is the amount of time Kyle takes to repair the unit:

$$\frac{2 \times 3}{2+3} = \frac{6}{5} = 1\frac{1}{5}$$

To figure out how many minutes are in $\frac{1}{5}$ of an hour, multiply that fraction by 60 minutes:

$$\frac{1}{5}\left(\frac{60}{1}\right) = \frac{60}{5} = 12$$

An alternate way to solve this problem is by finding out how much Jim and Kyle can do in the same unit of time, such as 1 hour. Jim can do half of a heating unit in 1 hour, while Kyle can do one-third of a heating unit in 1 hour. Adding their times in a formula like this can be very useful:

$$\frac{\frac{1}{2}}{1} + \frac{\frac{1}{3}}{1} = \frac{\frac{5}{6}}{1}$$

Together, they can do $\frac{5}{6}$ of a unit in 1 hour, leaving $\frac{1}{6}$ of the unit to go. It takes 12 minutes longer for them to finish the unit (1 hour = 60 minutes; 60 ÷ 5 = 12), which tells you that they need 12 more minutes.

28. **D.** To find the length of one side of the square, find the square root of the area: $\sqrt{121} = 11$. Multiply the side length by 4 to find the perimeter: $4 \times 11 = 44$.

29. **C.** Let *x* represent the amount of water to be added to the 20 percent mixture, and then make a chart to help solve the problem.

	# gallons	% water	Amount water
Water	x	100	100x
Juice	4	20	4(20)
Mixture	x + 4	50	50(x + 4)

© John Wiley & Sons, Inc.

From the table, you know that the amount of added water is 100x, and the amount of juice is $4(20)$. The sum of these two amounts is equal to the amount of mixture, $50(x+4)$. Write and solve an equation to find *x*:

$$100 + 4(20) = 50(x + 4)$$
$$100x + 80 = 50x + 200$$
$$50x = 120$$
$$x = 2.4$$

30. **B.** The number of different trucks David can choose from is the product of the number of colors (3) and the number of drive options (2). So he has $3(2) = 6$ choices of trucks.

Similarly, the number of sedans he can choose from is the product of the number of colors (4) and drive options (2). So he has $4(2) = 8$ choices of sedans.

The total number of options is the sum of the number of choices of trucks and sedans: $6 + 8 = 14$.

Subtest 2: Word Knowledge Answers

As with all AFQT subtests, the Word Knowledge subtest determines whether you qualify for enlistment. If you're not seeing improvement in your scores, work with a partner who can quiz you on vocabulary words. I also recommend reviewing the tables in Chapter 4 and the appendix several times a week.

1. **B.** *Kindle* is a verb that means to light or set on fire. It also means to arouse or inspire an emotion or feeling.

2. **C.** *Burnout* is a noun that means physical or mental collapse due to overwork or stress.

3. **A.** *Blatant* is an adjective that refers to something that's very obvious or completely lacking in subtlety.

4. **C.** *Hasten* is a verb that means to be quick to do something, to move or travel in a hurry, or to make something happen sooner than it otherwise would.

5. **C.** *Objective* is an adjective that means not influenced by opinions or personal feelings when considering and representing facts. It's also a noun that refers to a goal.

6. **B.** *Headstrong* is an adjective that means self-willed and obstinate.

7. **A.** *Cringe* is a verb that means to bend the head or body in fear or in a servile manner.

8. **B.** *Domestic* is an adjective that means of or relating to the running of a home or family relations.

9. **D.** *Frugal* is an adjective that means sparing or economical when it comes to money or food.

10. **B.** *Curtail* is a verb that means to reduce in quantity or extent or to impose a restriction on something.

11. **A.** *Accolade* is a noun that means an award or privilege granted as a special honor or as an acknowledgment of merit.

12. **C.** *Covert* is an adjective that means not openly acknowledged.

13. **D.** *Abhor* is a verb that means to regard with disgust and hatred.

14. **C.** *Mandate* is a noun that means an official order to do something. It's also a verb that means to give someone authority to act in a certain way.

15. **D.** *Assortment* is a noun that means a miscellaneous collection of things or people, so the word most opposite in meaning is *consistency*.

16. **C.** *Credible* is an adjective that means able to be believed or convincing.

17. **A.** *Reprieve* is a verb that means to cancel or postpone someone's punishment. It's also used as a noun to refer to the cancellation or postponement of a punishment.

18. **B.** *Tedious* is an adjective that means too long, slow, or dull. It can also mean tiresome or monotonous.

19. **C.** *Oblivious* is an adjective that means not concerned about or not aware of what is happening.

20. **D.** *Bolster* is a verb that means to support, strengthen, or prop up.

21. **B.** *Abstract* is an adjective that means existing in thought or as an idea but without a physical or concrete existence.

22. **D.** *Hamper* is a verb that means to hinder or impede movement or progress of someone or something.

23. **C.** *Cower* is a verb that means to crouch down in fear.

24. **A.** *Tangent* is a noun that means a completely different line of thought or action. It also means a straight line or plane that touches a curve (or curved surface) at a point but, if extended, doesn't cross it at that point.

25. **B.** *Nullify* is a verb that means to invalidate or to make legally null and void. It also means to cancel out something or make something useless or valueless.

26. **D.** *Tangible* is an adjective that means perceptible by touch.

27. **D.** *Absolution* is a noun that means a formal release from guilt, punishment, or obligation.

28. **B.** *Abrogate* is a verb that means to do away with or repeal.

29. **C.** *Temper* is a verb that means to serve as a neutralizing or counterbalancing force to something. It's also a noun that refers to a person's state of mind as it relates to being angry or calm.

30. **D.** *Plethora* is a noun that means a large or excessive amount of something.

31. **C.** *Tentative* is an adjective that means done without confidence or hesitant. It also means not certain or fixed, or provisional.

32. **B.** *Retaliation* is a noun that refers to the action of harming someone in an act of revenge. It also refers to a counterattack. The word most opposite in meaning is *forgiveness.*

33. **D.** *Admonish* is a verb that means to warn or reprimand someone firmly or to advise or urge someone earnestly.

34. **B.** *Diatribe* is a noun that refers to a forceful and bitter verbal attack against someone or something.

35. **A.** *Memento* is a noun that means an object kept as a reminder or souvenir of a person or event, so the word most opposite in meaning is *rubbish.*

Subtest 3: Paragraph Comprehension Answers

If you're struggling with this subtest, remember to take your time when you read the passages. Then read the question and go back and skim the passage to confirm that you're choosing the correct answer. Check out Chapter 5 for more review on this subtest.

1. **C.** The author doesn't explicitly state that California changed Terry, but you can infer the correct answer from the phrase "too much for their beach bum mentality." Based on that phrase and the distinction between sunny California and the worst winter, you can determine that the weather in California had ruined her ability to handle cold weather. The other answer choices can't be inferred from the limited information given in the paragraph.

2. **B.** You may think that the paragraph is about the increased number of pets in American households, but that's only a small piece of information. The other information about pets in shelters and rescue facilities dominates the rest of the paragraph, with the main idea presented in the last sentence. All the information supports the idea that Americans need to adopt more rescue pets.

3. **D.** You'll notice that all the percentage numbers fall within the middle two sentences. You may be tempted by Choice (A), but read carefully and you'll see that it's the total number of households with pets, not the number with rescue pets.

4. **A.** The paragraph describes how the artists were known for their preference, or inclination, for undertaking these large and unconventional projects.

5. **C.** The passage states that shoes last six months for average use, so that's the only information that could lead to a logical assumption about Tara or her shoes. The other answers aren't related to the presented information.

6. **C.** The passage says that De Niro was nominated for six other awards in addition to the Oscar he won in 1975. That makes seven nominations in all.

7. **B.** Although Tiffany certainly seems to have bad luck with flights, the passage describes the different inclement weather conditions for her region. The use of "sometimes" at the end signifies its unpredictability.

8. **D.** The passage states that the thunderstorm caused her flight to be delayed for five hours, which is the meaning of *postponed.*

9. **B.** The term *centennial* means 100 years, but even if you didn't know this fact, you read that the people gathered in 1961 to celebrate a war that started a hundred years earlier, in 1861.

10. **B.** The passage provides safe driving tips for snowy conditions in order to prevent safety hazards. The first part of the first sentence states the focus.

11. **A.** The passage describes what to do and what not to do when driving in snow. The author explains the results of each action. Therefore, you can infer that knowing what actions are dangerous in the snow will help you drive more safely.

12. **D.** If back-to-school shopping has begun, the beginning of school must be around the corner. Nothing in the passage suggests any of the other answers is correct.

13. **A.** The passage states that 532 of his designs were developed.

14. **D.** The last sentence of the passage says that Frank Lloyd Wright is as famous as Bruce Springsteen. You can infer that his career is famous as well.

15. **C.** The passage states that sailors and skiers share similar feelings toward their respective fellow athletes. Sailors don't like to share the water with motorboaters, so the inference you can draw is that skiers don't like to share the mountain with snowboarders.

Subtest 4: Mathematics Knowledge Answers

If you're missing too many math questions, keep studying (see Chapters 6, 7, and 8 for more information on each subject), and consider asking someone who excels in math to help you grasp the basic concepts. If your scores are improving, keep doing what you're doing right up until test day.

1. **A.** The value of $(-5)^3$ is equal to -5 multiplied by itself three times:

   $$(-5)^3 = (-5)(-5)(-5) = 25(-5) = -125$$

2. **B.** To get *x* alone on one side of the inequality, divide both sides of the inequality $42 < 2x$ by 2:

   $$42 < 2x$$
   $$\frac{42}{2} < x$$
   $$21 < x$$
   $$x > 21$$

3. **C.** This one is simple addition.

4. **C.** The digit 4 is in the tens place, the digit 5 is in the ones place, the digit 2 is in the tenths place, and the digit 1 is in the hundredths place.

5. **C.** Locate point P by starting at the origin and moving along the x-axis until you're even with point P. That's the −3 mark, so −3 is your x coordinate. Now move along the y-axis until you reach point P. It's at the 2 mark, so 2 is the y coordinate.

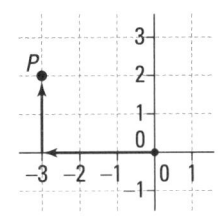

© John Wiley & Sons, Inc.

6. **C.** Divide 11 by 4 using long division.

$$\begin{array}{r} 2.75 \\ 4\overline{)11.00} \\ \underline{-8} \\ 30 \\ \underline{-28} \\ 20 \\ \underline{-20} \\ 0 \end{array}$$

7. **D.** To get y by itself on one side of the equal sign, add 2 to both sides of the equation: $-2 + y + 2 = 8 + 2$. The −2 and 2 on the left side cancel each other, so $y = 10$.

8. **B.** The formula for the circumference of a circle is $C = \pi d$. Substitute 9.24 for C and 3.14 for π and then solve for d by dividing both sides by 3.14.

$$9.42 = 3.14d$$
$$\frac{9.42}{3.14} = d$$
$$3 = d$$

9. **C.** Write 28 percent as a decimal: 28 percent $= 28 \div 100 = 0.28$. Multiply: $0.28(40) = 11.2$.

10. **C.** To multiply terms with the same base, add the exponents:

$$10^{3+(-6)+2} = 10^{-1}$$

Simplify:

$$10^{-1} = \frac{1}{10} = 0.1$$

11. **A.** This expression has two pairs of like terms. First, 2 and 4 are like terms and have a sum of 6. The terms 2y and y are also like terms and have a sum of 3y (remember that y is the same as 1y).

12. **D.** The sum of the angles of a triangle is always equal to 180°. To find the value of x, subtract 34° and 108° from 180°: $180° - 34° - 108° = 38°$.

13. **C.** Using the order of operations, simplify inside the parentheses first: $(5-2)! = 3!$. The expression 3! is the product of all whole numbers from 3 down to 1: $3! = (3)(2)(1) = 6$.

CHAPTER 27 **AFQT Practice Exam 2: Answers and Explanations**   583

14. **C.** To add these fractions, you have to find their common denominator, which is the least common multiple (LCM) of all three denominators. In this case, the common denominator is 16. Multiply the numerator and denominator of each fraction by the number that makes each denominator 16. (You don't have to do anything to the middle fraction because it already has the common denominator.)

$$\frac{1\times 8}{2\times 8}+\frac{1}{16}+\frac{1\times 4}{4\times 4}=\frac{8}{16}+\frac{1}{16}+\frac{4}{16}$$
$$=\frac{8+1+4}{16}$$
$$=\frac{13}{16}$$

15. **A.** The factors of a number are all the numbers, including the number and 1, that divide into the number without a remainder. The number 51 has four factors: 1, 3, 17, and 51.

16. **B.** Write this sentence as an equation, using x to represent the percent you're trying to find: $0.405 = 0.9x$. Divide both sides by 0.9 to get x alone on one side of the equal sign.

$$0.405 = 0.9x$$
$$\frac{0.405}{0.9} = x$$
$$x = 0.45$$

You convert the decimal 0.45 to a percent by multiplying 0.45 by 100: $0.45(100) = 45$ percent.

17. **B.** If two angles are complementary, the sum of their measures is 90°. Because the measure of angle P is $m°$, you find the complement of angle P by subtracting its measure from 90°.

18. **D.** Because the triangle is a right triangle, you need the Pythagorean theorem: $a^2 + b^2 = c^2$. You know the lengths of side a and the hypotenuse (c), so plug those values into the theorem and solve for b:

$$24^2 + b^2 = 25^2$$
$$576 + b^2 = 625$$
$$b^2 = 49$$
$$b = \pm 7$$

Use the positive answer because a length is never negative.

19. **D.** When you decrease something, you're subtracting from it. In this instance, you're taking 11 away from x; that means you have $x - 11$. "Is" means "equals" in mathematical terms (and you know that every equation must have an equal sign). "Twice x" means $2x$. Your equation will look like this: $x - 11 = 2x$.

20. **D.** The mean is the sum of all values divided by the number of values, or the average. First, find the sum of the values: $5 + 7 + 8 + 10 + 4 + x = 34 + x$. Because there are six values, you'll set this side of the equation up as a fraction:

$$\frac{34 + x}{6}$$

You already know the answer to the equation is 7.5, so your equation will look like this:

$$\frac{34 + x}{6} = 7.5$$
$$34 + x = 45$$
$$x = 11$$

21. **A.** Use the order of operations: Simplify inside the parentheses first, compute all exponents next, multiply and divide from left to right after that, and then add and subtract from left to right:

$$\begin{aligned}(9-3\cdot 2)^2 - 0.5(-2) &= (9-6)^2 - 0.5(-2) \\ &= (3)^2 - 0.5(-2) \\ &= 9 - 0.5(-2) \\ &= 9 - (-1) \\ &= 9 + 1 \\ &= 10\end{aligned}$$

22. **A.** First, use the distributive property to remove the parentheses: $9 - 20x + 8$. Then simplify by adding 9 and 8 to get $17 - 20x$.

23. **B.** The formula for the volume of a right cylinder is $V = \pi r^2 h$. Substitute $h = 2r$ into the formula:

$$\begin{aligned}V &= \pi r^2 h \\ &= \pi r^2 2r\end{aligned}$$

Reorder the terms:

$$\begin{aligned}V &= 2\pi \cdot r^2 \cdot r \\ &= 2\pi r^3\end{aligned}$$

24. **B.** You can break the figure down into a rectangle on the left with dimensions 7.5 cm by 10 cm and a right triangle on the right whose base is $11 - 7.5 = 3.5$ cm and whose height is $10 - 2 = 8$ cm.

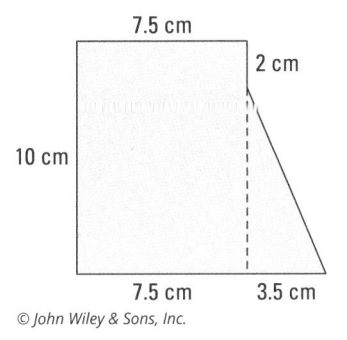

    The area of the rectangle is $A = lw = (10)(7.5) = 75$ cm², and the area of the triangle is $A = \frac{bh}{2} = \frac{(3.5)(8)}{2} = 14$ cm². Add the two areas to find the total area: $75 + 14 = 89$ cm².

25. **A.** The problem only gives you the number of boys, so first you must find the number of girls by subtracting 140 from 260: $260 - 140 = 120$. When you need to express the number of girls to boys as a fraction, there are 120 girls for every 140 boys; that means 120:140 or $\frac{120}{140}$, which simplifies to $\frac{6}{7}$.

    On the ASVAB, you have to pay close attention to wording; if the question had asked for the ratio of boys to girls, Choice (B) would've been correct. If the question had asked for the ratio of boys to total students, Choice (D) would've been correct.

The Part of Tens

IN THIS PART . . .

Find out what mistakes to avoid as you prepare to take the ASVAB on testing day.

Get hints for maximizing your score on the all-important AFQT.

Discover ways to improve your English and math skills.

IN THIS CHAPTER

» Avoiding common ASVAB-preparation mistakes

» Using your prep time wisely

» Testing smarter, not harder

Chapter **28**

Ten Surefire Ways to Fail the ASVAB

Technically, you can't fail the ASVAB — it's not a pass/fail test. It's a tool the military uses to measure your potential for learning military jobs and military duties. But realistically, each of the branches has established minimum Armed Forces Qualification Test (AFQT) scores applicants need to qualify for enlistment and minimum line scores to qualify for certain military jobs. (The test is the same regardless of the branch you want to join; how each branch uses scores is what differs.) If you don't qualify to join the service branch of your choice or don't qualify for the job you want, you haven't technically failed, but you have to take the test again (after a few study sessions) and pass to get into the branch of service you want to join.

If you avoid the mistakes outlined in this chapter, you can improve your chances of qualifying for enlistment and getting the military job of your dreams.

Choosing Not to Study at All

Many people think that they don't need to study for the ASVAB. They assume that because they studied many of the subjects in high school, they'll do fine if they just wing it.

This train of thought isn't correct (and it's kind of off the tracks). Why wouldn't you study? At the very least, brushing up on vocabulary and math concepts definitely helps you score higher on the ASVAB. Using a calculator is a no-go on the ASVAB, so you may want to revisit some math tricks for doing calculations by hand. Auto, Shop, and Mechanical Comprehension aren't required high school courses, so these subjects may be completely new to you and require additional attention.

Using study guides like this one gives you an idea of what to expect *and* allows you to sharpen some skills that may have gotten a little dull. Even better, you won't have to retake the ASVAB if you want to change jobs a few years down the road.

Failing to Realize How Scores Are Used

The military powers that be use the subtests on the ASVAB to determine which military jobs you qualify for. If you don't know how the scores are used, you can't decide which parts of the exam are most important for you to study.

Check out Chapters 1 and 2 for an explanation of how the military uses ASVAB subtest scores to determine your qualifications.

Studying for Unnecessary Subtests

If you don't want to be a mechanic in the military, why would you study Auto & Shop Information? You should be spending your time on the subjects you need to score well on to land your dream job. Don't forget the math and vocabulary review, because the military uses those ASVAB subtests to compute the all-important AFQT score, which determines whether you can join the branch of your choice.

TIP: It's easier to study subject areas that you find easy or have an interest in, but if you're already an electronics whiz, don't waste your time studying for that subtest. Spend your time studying subject areas that you know you need to work on.

Losing Focus

I'm not going to sugarcoat this: The ASVAB is tiring. You have to take nine or ten subtests (depending on the version) that cover some really diverse subjects. You have about three hours to complete the actual test, which is plenty of time for most people. If you lose focus while you're taking the test, time can slip away, and you may not get to all the questions. It's hard, but stay focused on the task at hand throughout the whole test. It'll be over soon.

TIP: Here are some tips that can help you maintain focus:

- **Arrive at the test location with time to spare.** This gives you a few minutes to sit and relax before you have to dive into the test questions. (Most recruiters bring their recruits directly to the testing location, so you'll arrive early enough.)
- **Leave your baggage at the door.** Don't worry about whether you'll get the military job you want or whether you'll pass the physical when you see a military doctor. You'll have plenty of time to worry about that after you finish the test.
- **Concentrate on one subtest at a time.** Don't waste time rehashing the questions on the previous subtest or trying to anticipate the questions on the next subtest. Focus on the subtest you're taking at the time.
- **Take a few moments to relax and refocus between subtests.** If you finish a subtest with time to spare, close your eyes for a bit and take some deep breaths before you begin the next subtest.

When you answer the final question on one subtest on the CAT-ASVAB, you move immediately to the next subtest. If the timer on the computer screen says you have a few minutes of time left on the subtest, use that time to relax and refocus before submitting that final answer.

Panicking over Time

Yes, you have only a limited time to take the test, but don't worry about it. The more you panic, the more likely you are to make mistakes. Just work at a steady pace, and you'll do fine. Most people have plenty of time to answer all the questions in each subtest.

REMEMBER

Don't spend too much time on any single question. If you're drawing a blank, make a guess and move on. (See "Making Wild Guesses or Not Guessing at All" later in this chapter.)

The CAT-ASVAB shows both a timer on the computer screen, counting down the number of minutes you have to finish that subtest, and the number of questions you have remaining. If you're taking the pencil-and-paper version of the test, check the clock on the wall. The proctor will generally write the start and finish times for the current subtest on a whiteboard. Keep your eye on the time remaining, but don't panic over it.

Deciding Not to Check the Answers

You should always double-check your answers before you commit to them — you don't want silly mistakes to trip you up. Don't mark your answer and then check your work. Check your work first.

Do not second-guess yourself (see "Changing Answers" later in this chapter). Just check for accuracy (like in mathematical equations). Be sure to mark your answer sheet correctly, too, verifying that the number of the question matches the number on your answer sheet (you don't have to worry about this with the computerized version of the ASVAB). Getting just one question off can mess up the rest of your answer sheet.

TIP

If you're taking the paper-and-pencil version of the test, mentally say to yourself, "The answer to Question 22 is Choice (C)" as your pencil moves. That can help you avoid filling in the wrong circle.

Making Wild Guesses or Not Guessing at All

Take the time to eliminate answers you know are incorrect before choosing among the remaining answer options. And here's the number one rule: Don't leave any blank spaces. In most cases, guessing if you have to is the way to go — at least you have a higher chance at getting the right answer, as opposed to a 0 percent chance if you leave the answer blank. If you can eliminate answers you know are wrong before guessing, you increase your chances of answering correctly even more. For tips on smart guessing, see Chapter 3.

WARNING

Even though you've likely read this before, I'm still going to say it again: If you're running out of time at the end of a subtest while taking the CAT-ASVAB, be careful about guessing your way through the last questions. If you don't finish a subtest, you'll be scored as if you'd guessed randomly on the remaining questions. It's in your best interest to guess smart if you're running out of time.

CHAPTER 28 **Ten Surefire Ways to Fail the ASVAB**   591

Changing Answers

After you double-check your math, decide that Choice (C) is correct, and mark it on the answer sheet, don't change your answer on the paper version of the ASVAB! You're almost certain to change a right answer to a wrong one when you play that game. Plus, you can drive yourself crazy by second-guessing (and third- and fourth-guessing) your decision. Mark the answer and move on.

WARNING: You can't change an answer on the CAT-ASVAB. After you submit an answer, that's it; the computer moves you on to the next question, and you can't go back.

Memorizing the Practice Test Questions

Don't waste your time trying to memorize the practice questions in this book. I can almost guarantee you won't see any of the practice questions in this book (or any other study guide) on the actual ASVAB. Military test materials are highly controlled items, and no author of an ASVAB preparation book has access to them. In fact, military members and military civilian employees who disclose actual ASVAB test questions or answers can go to jail — and I'm not planning on doing time!

Just use the practice questions in this book as a measurement tool of which subject areas you should spend your time concentrating on.

Misunderstanding the Problem

Make sure that you know what the question wants from you and then give the question what it wants. Pay close attention to detail, because you can easily confuse a division sign for an addition sign or miss a key element that can lead you to the wrong answer. By familiarizing yourself with the types of questions on the ASVAB, you'll be able to zero in on what you're supposed to do a lot more quickly than those poor folks who didn't have the brilliant idea to buy this book.

> **IN THIS CHAPTER**
> » Using your scratch paper wisely
> » Reading carefully
> » Performing math operations
> » Making sure your answers make sense

Chapter 29
Ten Tips for Doing Well on the AFQT

Commonly (and mistakenly) referred to as the ASVAB score, the Armed Forces Qualification Test (AFQT) score is actually computed only from the reading and math skills subtests of the ASVAB. The AFQT score determines whether you're even qualified to enlist in the service of your choice. (For the full scoop, see Chapter 1.) The ten concepts presented in this chapter help you score better on the four subtests of the ASVAB that are used to calculate your AFQT score. If you still need help boosting this score, check out *1,001 ASVAB AFQT Practice Questions For Dummies* by yours truly (and published by Wiley).

As Soon as the Test Starts, Write Down What You're Likely to Forget

TIP You can't bring your own scratch paper to the test, but the test proctors will give you as many sheets of scratch paper as you want. Not only is your scratch paper useful to take the place of the calculator you're not allowed to use, but you can also use it to write notes at the very beginning of the test — things that you're worried you may forget. For example, if you're worried that you'll forget the math order of operations, write it down first thing.

Read All the Answer Choices before Deciding

I think the people who write ASVAB test questions must go through a special course that tells them they have to keep you on your toes. Many of the answer choices given on the ASVAB are "close, but no cigar." In other words, question-writers try to sneak in incorrect answers that are *almost* correct . . . but not quite. You may even notice that the practice exam questions in Chapters 18, 20, 22, 24, and 26 have those types of answers. The military has found that realistic training is the most effective.

The best defense against this type of trickery is to read each answer choice completely, even if you think the first or second choice looks plausible. You're looking for the answer that's *most correct.*

Don't Expect Perfect Word Matches

REMEMBER

The Word Knowledge subtest of the ASVAB contains questions that ask you to find the word that is *closest in meaning* to a given word. Don't get confused and think that you have to find the word that means *exactly* the same thing as the given word. Just follow the directions. Because some of the answer options may have similar meanings, you need to choose the answer that's closest in meaning to the given word — the answer that's *most* right.

Read the Passages before the Questions

Some of the Paragraph Comprehension questions can be tricky. Often, a question asks you to come to a conclusion based on the information presented in a paragraph. The only way to do this effectively is to understand the entire paragraph and what the author wants to convey. If you instead read the question first, you may find yourself wasting time by looking for information that isn't directly stated.

Reread to Find Specific Information

The Paragraph Comprehension subtest often asks you to find specific information in a passage. Go back and reread the paragraph. You shouldn't have to guess what this information is — it's in the passage, or you can easily deduce it from the passage. For instance, if a paragraph includes the sentence, "Six out of ten smokers will contract some form of cancer," and a question asks, "How many smokers *won't* contract some form of cancer?" you can easily deduce that four is the correct number.

Base Conclusions Only on What You Read

You may have to draw inferences or conclusions from what you've read. You must use only the information presented in the paragraph to reach this conclusion instead of relying on your own ideas and opinions. In other words, ask yourself, "Would the author agree with this statement, based on what they've written in this paragraph?" Apply this test to each answer option to choose the best answer.

Change Percents to Decimals

To perform math operations, you often have to change a percent to a fraction or a decimal.

To change a percent to a fraction, multiply the percent by $\frac{1}{100}$ and drop the percent sign:

$$5\% = 5 \times \frac{1}{100} = \frac{5}{100}$$

To change a percent to a decimal, move the decimal point two places to the left and drop the percent sign:

$$5\% = 0.05$$

Understand Inverses

Inverse operations are opposite operations. The opposite of addition is subtraction, and vice versa. And the opposite of multiplication is division, and vice versa.

But when it comes to numbers, the term *inverse* is not the same as *opposite*. The *opposite* of 5 is −5, but the *inverse* of 5 is $\frac{1}{5}$. When you deal with numbers, think of writing the inverse of a number as standing the number on its head: The inverse (reciprocal) of 5, or $\frac{5}{1}$, is $\frac{1}{5}$.

Remember How Ratios, Rates, and Scales Compare

You need to understand the differences among ratios, rates, and scales:

- **Ratio:** A ratio represents any relationship between two objects. If Luis invests $10 in Lotto tickets and Joe invests $20 in Lotto tickets, then for every dollar Luis invests, Joe invests two. That's a ratio of 1:2.

- **Rate:** Rate is an expression of the relationship between two unlike elements. For example, if Anna's car can travel a distance of 450 miles per tank of gas and her gas tank holds 15 gallons, then her car consumes gas at a rate of 30 miles per gallon, or 30 mpg (miles and gallons being unlike elements). Mathematically, 450 (miles) ÷ 15 (gallons in the tank) = 30 miles to the gallon.

- **Scale:** A scale expresses a relationship between two like elements, although the units of measure may differ. A map drawn to scale may use 1 inch to represent 1 mile. Although an inch and a mile aren't the same unit of measure, they measure the same thing (distance).

Make Sure Your Answers Are Reasonable

On the Mathematics Knowledge and Arithmetic Reasoning subtests, you have very limited time to answer each question (flip to Chapters 6 and 9, respectively, for more on the exact timings). If you use your time wisely, you should have plenty of time to double-check and make sure you've chosen the correct answer.

REMEMBER: Your answers should make sense, or they're probably wrong. For example, if you're required to compute the average speed that a car maintains during a 2,000-mile trip and your answer is 2,000 mph, your answer is probably not correct. If a question includes a formula (such as $2 + x = 10$), plug in your answer for the variable and see whether both sides are equal. If you answered 8, plug in 8 for x and find that $10 = 10$. That means your answer checks out.

The people who design ASVAB test questions often include wrong answers that you may choose if you make a common mistake when solving the problem, such as using a formula incorrectly. Double-checking your answers allows you to catch your errors.

IN THIS CHAPTER

» Getting used to doing math correctly by hand

» Knowing key rules and formulas

» Expanding your vocabulary

» Becoming a better reader

Chapter 30
Ten Ways to Boost Your Math and English Skills

The ASVAB includes two math and two English subtests: Mathematics Knowledge, Arithmetic Reasoning, Word Knowledge, and Paragraph Comprehension. These four subtests are probably the most important subtests of the ASVAB, because they make up your AFQT score, which is the score that determines whether you qualify to join the branch of your choice. (Check out Chapter 1 for more info on the AFQT and Chapters 24 and 26 for sample AFQTs. You can also peruse the latest editions of *ASVAB AFQT For Dummies* and *1,001 ASVAB AFQT Practice Questions For Dummies*, both published by Wiley.)

Because these four subtests are so important, this chapter includes ten surefire ways to build your skills in these critical areas before you take the test.

Practice Doing Math Problems

The best way to get a firm grasp of certain types of math is by doing math problems and not simply reading them. Take advantage of the practice math questions in this book, and visit the public library to see what kind of high school math textbooks it has to lend. The more you do math, the better you'll get at it.

Put Away Your Calculator

You're not allowed to use a calculator when you take the ASVAB, so now is the time to get used to solving basic math problems without one. Practice working out problems by hand, and make sure you know your multiplication tables and other basic calculations. Make sure your handwriting is clear, too. It's easy to rush through and mistake a 4 for a 9 or miss a decimal point — and simple errors can lead you to a wrong answer (and waste your time).

TIP As you solve math problems by hand, you can get a feel for what works and what doesn't. For instance, some questions ask you to find the square root of a number, which you may find hard without a calculator. But a little logic can help. If you know the square root of 9 is 3 ($3 \times 3 = 9$) and you know the square root of 16 is 4, then you can conclude that the square root of 12 falls between 3 and 4.

Memorize the Order of Operations

Mathematical equations with multiple steps must be solved in a specific order. Otherwise, you won't get the correct answer. Memorize the order in which you do certain calculations when you're solving equations, and practice applying these rules well before test day.

REMEMBER When solving an equation involves multiple steps, the correct order of operations is

1. **Whatever's within parentheses (and other grouping symbols)**

   If you have multiple parentheses nested inside each other, do the innermost set first. On the ASVAB, the other grouping symbols you run across are the fraction bar and the square root sign. Do what's beneath the square root bar before taking the root. Do any operation above the fraction bar and any operation below the fraction bar before dividing.

2. **Exponents**

3. **Multiplication and division**

   Operate from left to right.

4. **Addition and subtraction**

   Again, work from left to right.

For example, $3 + 2 \times 3$ isn't equal to 5×3, or 15. The correct answer is 9. You first do the multiplication and then the addition. You can remember the order of operations as "Please Excuse My Dear Aunt Sally," or PEMDAS. Check out Chapter 6 for more explanation.

Know Your Geometry Formulas

You encounter some math questions that require you to calculate area, perimeter, and volume on the ASVAB. Memorize the following area formulas:

» **Area of a rectangle:** For any rectangle, Area = Length × Width: $A = lw$.

» **Area of a triangle:** For triangles, Area = Base × Height (or altitude) divided by 2: $A = \frac{1}{2}bh$.

» **Area of a circle:** For circles, area is π (approximately 3.14) times the radius squared: $A = \pi r^2$.

Know these perimeter and circumference formulas:

» **Perimeter of a polygon (a shape with straight sides):** Calculate the perimeter of any quadrilateral (four-sided figure) or triangle by adding the lengths of all the sides together.

» **Circumference of a circle:** Find the circumference of a circle by multiplying π times the diameter: $C = \pi d$. **Note:** Diameter equals 2 times the radius.

And know these formulas for the volume of 3-D solids:

> » **Volume of a box:** Find the volume of a rectangular solid by multiplying Length × Width × Height: $V = lwh$.
>
> » **Volume of a cylinder:** Find the volume of a cylinder by multiplying the area of the circular base (π times the base's radius squared) by the cylinder's height: $V = \pi r^2 h$.

Keep a Word List

The English language is packed with words, and nobody expects you to know them all. However, the ASVAB writers do expect you to have a good grasp of many vocabulary words. One way to improve your vocabulary is to keep a word list.

TIP How does a word list work? As you read, write down the words that you don't know. Quickly look them up in the dictionary (you can even look them up from your smartphone). You can then apply your word list in your day-to-day life. Of course, you can't remember every single word, but you can focus on mastering one new word every day and using it in conversation. Check out Chapter 4 for more tips on building your vocabulary.

REMEMBER Don't waste your time by choosing little-known words, such as *absquatulate* (which means to leave hurriedly or secretly). You're unlikely to see obscure words on the ASVAB, but you should make a practice of learning the meaning of as many common English words as possible.

Study Latin and Greek

You can skip the grammar and pronunciation, but you should get to know some of the roots, prefixes, and suffixes that English has borrowed from Latin and Greek. These word parts are the building blocks of much of the English language, and they can give you clues about what words mean.

If you see an unfamiliar word on the Word Knowledge section, try to figure out its root. For example, if you know the meaning of *mercy*, you can figure out the meaning of *merciful*. Remember that prefixes and suffixes can be added onto a root to change the word's meaning or function. Here are some examples:

> » **Changing meaning:** The prefix *a-* usually means *opposite*, so the word *atypical* means the opposite of *typical*, not a typical thing.
>
> » **Changing parts of speech:** *Establish* is a verb meaning *to make stable* or *to prove*, whereas *establishment* (with a suffix) is a noun meaning *a thing that has been established*.

For a list of common word parts you should know, check out Chapter 4 and the appendix.

Use Flashcards

Flashcards help you remember important facts through the process of spaced repetition. Learning psychologists agree that this is one of the most effective methods of memorizing new information. Plus, it's cheap — all you need is a set of blank index cards and a pen to create your very own studying machine.

You can use flashcards to improve both your mental math and vocabulary — write down vocab words, roots, prefixes, and suffixes; practice matching square roots and square numbers; or just make sure you know your math formulas.

Read More, Watch TV Less

The best way to improve your reading comprehension is simple: Read more. If you spend two hours a day watching TV and posting pictures on social media, you can instead use those two hours to read a novel or the newspaper or a book about car repair — whatever interests you the most. You'll be surprised at how fast your reading speed and comprehension improve with just a little daily practice.

Practice Finding Main and Supporting Points

All writing should have a point. The main point is the thing that the writer wants you to take away from their words. Some passages include more than one point. Usually, such passages have one main point and one or more subpoints that support the main idea. As you're reading passages on the ASVAB (and in real life), you want to be able to easily identify the main point. You should practice identifying the points during your own reading sessions. Read each paragraph and then ask yourself what information the author is trying to convey to you.

Use a Study Guide

In my humble opinion, there is no better commercial ASVAB study guide available than this one. Read the chapters carefully and then use the practice tests to determine where you need more study.

WARNING Use the practice questions only to test your own knowledge of the subject. Don't expect to see the same questions on the actual ASVAB. The people who write the actual ASVAB tests keep a close eye on commercial study guides, like this one, and try to avoid having the same questions. What they can't do is defeat a well-prepared applicant like you, so commit yourself and knock it out of the park!

IN THIS APPENDIX

» Unearthing word roots

» Pinning down prefixes

» Scouting out suffixes

Appendix
Word Knowledge Resources

Word Knowledge makes up a big chunk of your overall ASVAB score — and it's part of the AFQT, or Armed Forces Qualification Test, so it determines whether you're even eligible to enlist in any branch of the U.S. Armed Forces. Your Word Knowledge score also factors into many military jobs.

This appendix gives you exhaustive lists of word roots, prefixes, and suffixes that you can study to ace the Word Knowledge subtest on the ASVAB. Use the far-right column to jot down your own words, which may help you remember specific word parts on test day.

Digging Down to Word Roots

Not all the words you'll see on the ASVAB have their roots in Greek or Latin, but because so many do, you're likely to see at least a handful of them on the test. Knowing the word roots in Table A-1 can help you figure out what words mean, helping boost your Word Knowledge score.

TABLE A-1 Word Roots

Word Root	Meaning	Examples	Your Words
ac or acr	sharp, bitter, or sour	acid	
		acute	
		exacerbate	
act or ag	to do, to force, or to lead	activate	
		agitate	
		enact	

(continued)

TABLE A-1 *(continued)*

Word Root	Meaning	Examples	Your Words
al, ali, or alter	other or another	alias	
		alien	
		alternative	
am	love	amiable	
		amorous	
		enamored	
ambi or amphi	both, on both sides, or around	ambidextrous	
		ambiguous	
		amphibian	
ana	up, back, against, again, or throughout	analysis	
		analytic	
		anatomy	
anim	of the life, mind, soul, or breath	animal	
		animosity	
		unanimous	
anthro or andr	man or human	android	
		anthropologist	
		philanthropy	
aqua or aque	water	aquarium	
		aquatic	
		aqueduct	
arch, archi, or archy	chief, ruler, or principal	anarchy	
		architect	
		monarch	
astro or aster	stars	astronaut	
		astronomer	
		asterisk	
auto	self, same, or one	autocrat	
		autograph	
		automatic	
bell or belli	war	bellicose	
		belligerent	
		rebel	
ben or bene	good or well	benefactor	
		beneficial	
		benevolent	

Word Root	Meaning	Examples	Your Words
bio	life or living matter	biography biohazard biology	
cant or chant	to sing	cant enchant recant	
capt, cept, or ceive	take or hold	captor intercept perceive	
carn	flesh	carnage carnivore reincarnation	
caust or caut	to burn	cauterize caustic holocaust	
cede, ceed, or cess	go or yield	access exceed recede	
centr	center	central concentrate eccentric	
cern, cert, cret, crim, or crit	to separate, to distinguish, to judge, or to decide	ascertain certainty hypocrite	
chron	time	chronic chronology synchronize	
cis	to cut	incision precise scissors	
claim or clam	shout or speak out	clamor exclaim proclaim	
corp	body	corporation corps corpse	

(continued)

TABLE A-1 *(continued)*

Word Root	Meaning	Examples	Your Words
cred	to believe or trust	credit credo incredibly	
crypt or crypto	hidden or secret	crypt cryptic encrypt	
dem	people	academy democracy epidemic	
di	day	dial diary dismal	
dole	to suffer or grieve	condolences doleful indolence	
don, dot, or dow	to give	antidote donate pardon	
dur	to harden, to last, or lasting	durable duration endure	
equ	equal or even	adequate equation equivalent	
esce	becoming	adolescent coalesce incandescent	
fab or fam	to speak	defame fable famous	
fac, fic, fig, fait, feit, or fy	to do or make	configure deficient factory	
fer	to bear, bring, or carry	confer ferry transfer	

Word Root	Meaning	Examples	Your Words
fi or fid	faith or trust	confide fidelity infidel	
fin	end	confine final infinity	
fus	to pour	diffuse infuse profuse	
gen	birth, production, or formation	genealogy generation genes	
geo	earth or soil	dungeon geography geology	
gn or gno	to know	agnostic ignorant ignore	
grad or gress	to step	aggressive digress progress	
gram or graph	to write or draw	diagram grammar graph	
hap	by chance	happen happy mishap	
her or hes	to stick	adhere coherent inherent	
herb or herbi	grass or plant	herbicide herbivorous herbal	
idio	peculiar, personal, or distinct	idiosyncrasy idiot idiotic	

(continued)

APPENDIX Word Knowledge Resources 605

TABLE A-1 *(continued)*

Word Root	Meaning	Examples	Your Words
it or iter	way or journey	ambition	
		itinerary	
		reiterate	
ject	to throw or throw down	eject	
		inject	
		project	
jud	to judge	judgment	
		judicial	
		prejudice	
jur	law or to swear	jurisdiction	
		jury	
		perjury	
lab	work	collaborate	
		elaborate	
		labor	
lang or ling	tongue	bilingual	
		language	
		linguistics	
lav, lau, or lu	to wash	dilute	
		laundry	
		lavatory	
lec, leg, or lex	to read or speak	lecture	
		legend	
		legible	
lect or leg	to choose or select	collect	
		elect	
		select	
lev	to lift, rise, or lighten	alleviate	
		elevate	
		relevant	
liber	free	deliver	
		liberal	
		liberty	
loc, log, or locu	word, speech, or thought	colloquialism	
		dialogue	
		prologue	

Word Root	Meaning	Examples	Your Words
luc, lum, or lus	light	lucid	
		illuminate	
		translucent	
mag or max	big or great	magnify	
		magnitude	
		maximum	
mand or mend	to command, order, or entrust	commend	
		demand	
		mandatory	
mob, mot, or mov	to move	automobile	
		demote	
		movable	
mut	to change	commute	
		mutation	
		transmute	
nau or nav	ship or sailor	astronaut	
		nautical	
		navy	
noc or nox	harm	innocent	
		noxious	
		obnoxious	
pac or peac	peace	appease	
		pacify	
		pact	
pas, pat, or path	feeling, suffering, or disease	compassion	
		empathy	
		sympathetic	
ped	child or education	encyclopedia	
		pediatric	
		pedagogy	
ped or pod	foot	pedal	
		pedestrian	
		podium	
pel	to push or drive	compel	
		expel	
		propel	

(continued)

TABLE A-1 *(continued)*

Word Root	Meaning	Examples	Your Words
pet	to seek or strive	appetite compete petition	
phob	fear	claustrophobic phobia xenophobia	
phys	nature, medicine, or the body	physical physician physique	
ple or plen	to fill or be full	complete implement supplement	
port	to carry	export import portable	
pri or prim	first	primary primal pristine	
put	think	computer dispute input	
que or quis	to seek	acquire inquisition query	
rect	straight or right	correct erect rectangle	
salv	to save	salvage salvation salve	
sci	to know	consciousness omniscient science	
sed, sess, or sid	to sit or settle	dissident preside residue	

Word Root	Meaning	Examples	Your Words
sens or sent	to feel or be aware	resent	
		sensory	
		sentinel	
sol	alone	desolate	
		isolated	
		solitary	
sourc, surg, or surrect	to rise	insurgents	
		resurrect	
		source	
spec or spic	to look or see	inconspicuous	
		retrospect	
		spectrum	
sum	total	sum	
		summary	
		summit	
tact, tag, tam, or tang	to touch	contact	
		contaminate	
		intact	
tain, ten, tent, or tin	to hold	abstain	
		detain	
		tenacious	
test	to bear witness	attest	
		contest	
		testament	
tor, torq, or tort	to twist	contort	
		distort	
		torque	
ult	last or beyond	ultimate	
		ultimatum	
		ultraviolet	
vail or val	strength, worth, or use	avail	
		equivalent	
		invalid	
ver	truth	veracious	
		verdict	
		verify	

(continued)

TABLE A-1 *(continued)*

Word Root	Meaning	Examples	Your Words
vid or vis	to see	adviser	
		video	
		visual	
voc or vok	word or calling	advocate	
		evoke	
		vocation	
volu or volv	to roll or turn	evolve	
		revolution	
		volume	
vor	to eat	carnivore	
		omnivore	
		voracious	

Pointing Out Prefixes

Not all words have prefixes, but those that do put them right in the front of the word (and suffixes go at the end). A prefix can change the entire meaning of a word, as Chapter 4 demonstrates. Understanding the relationships between the prefixes in Table A-2 and the root words listed in Table A-1 can help you settle on the correct answers when you're taking the Word Knowledge subtest.

TABLE A-2 Prefixes

Prefix	Meaning	Examples	Your Words
a- or an-	not or without	agnostic	
		anomaly	
		atypical	
ab-	away from, apart from, or down	abnormal	
		abolish	
		abstract	
ad-	toward or near	address	
		adjacent	
		advocate	
ambi- or amphi-	both, or on both sides	ambidextrous	
		ambiguous	
		amphibian	
ant- or ante-	before	antecedent	
		antenatal	
		anteroom	

Prefix	Meaning	Examples	Your Words
anti-	against	antibiotic	
		antidepressant	
		antifreeze	
bi-	two	bilingual	
		binoculars	
		bipartisan	
cent- or centi-	hundred or hundredth	centiliter	
		centimeter	
		centipede	
circu- or circum-	around	circuit	
		circumference	
		circumstance	
co-, col-, com-, or con-	together or with	collaborate	
		cooperate	
		compatible	
contra-, contro-, or counter-	against	contradict	
		controversial	
		counterculture	
de-	away from, off, down, or reversal	defrost	
		derailed	
		devalue	
deca-	ten	decade	
		decahedron	
		decathlon	
dis-	opposite of	disagree	
		disappear	
		disintegrate	
dys-	faulty or abnormal	dysfunction	
		dystopian	
		dystrophy	
e- or ex-	out of or from	evade	
		exclude	
		expire	
em- or en-	cause to or put into	embed	
		encode	
		engulf	

(continued)

TABLE A-2 *(continued)*

Prefix	Meaning	Examples	Your Words
extra-	outside or beyond	extract, extracurricular, extraordinary	
fore-	before	forecast, foremost, foresight	
hex- or sex-	six	hexagon, hexadecimal, sextet	
hyper-	over or above	hyperactive, hyperbole, hyperventilate	
hypo-	beneath, less than, or under	hypochondriac, hypocrite, hypothesis	
in- or im-	not or without	immoral, inactive, innocuous	
in- or im-	inside or into	implicit, indigenous, intrinsic	
inter-	among or between	interim, intermittent, interstate	
mal- or male-	bad or wrong	malady, malfunction, malicious	
med- or medi-	middle	medieval, mediocre, medium	
mega-	very large	megabyte, megalomania, megaphone	
mis-	wrongly	misinterpret, mistake, misunderstand	

Prefix	Meaning	Examples	Your Words
mono-	one	monologue	
		monopoly	
		monotone	
multi-	many	multiple	
		multiply	
		multitude	
non-	not or without	nonabrasive	
		noncarcinogenic	
		nonsense	
nov-, neo-, or nou-	new	neoclassical	
		neonatal	
		neophyte	
oct-	eight	octagon	
		octane	
		octopus	
omni-	all	omnipotent	
		omnipresent	
		omnivore	
para-	beside	paradox	
		parallel	
		paranoid	
pan- or pant-	all or everyone	pandemic	
		panorama	
		pantheon	
pent-	five	pentagon	
		pentagram	
		pentathlon	
poly-	many	polygamy	
		polygon	
		polytheist	
post-	after	posterior	
		post-mortem	
		postpone	
pre-	before or in front	predetermined	
		prefix	
		premonition	

(continued)

TABLE A-2 *(continued)*

Prefix	Meaning	Examples	Your Words
pro-	to go forth or put forth	proceed proclaim proponent	
quad-, quar-, or quat-	four	quadrant quart quartet	
quin- or quint-	five	quintet quintile quintuplet	
re-	back or again	recline rediscover reunite	
se-	apart or away	seduce segregate separate	
semi-	half	semicircle semiconscious semifluid	
sept-	seven	septennial septet septuplet	
sub- or sup-	under	submarine subterfuge subtitle	
super- or sur-	above or over	supersede surpass surveillance	
sym- or syn-	together or the same	symmetry synonym synthetic	
trans-	across or beyond	transaction transcontinental transit	
un-	not	undone unknown unseen	

Spotting Hard-Working Suffixes

Thousands of words have suffixes that change their meaning. Suffixes always come at the end of a word, as I explain in Chapter 4. Suffixes can also help you identify what type of word (a noun, a verb, or something else) you're working with. When you understand how suffixes hitch themselves to root words, you'll have an easier time answering tough questions on the ASVAB. Table A-3 shows you some of the most common suffixes in the English language.

TABLE A-3 Suffixes

Suffix	Part of Speech It Indicates	Meaning	Examples	Your Words
-able	adjective	able to be	agreeable, available, portable	
-ac	adjective	pertaining to	cardiac, insomniac, maniac	
-acity or -ocity	noun	quality of	audacity, incapacity, ferocity	
-age	noun	action or process	advantage, blockage, pilgrimage	
-al	adjective	relating to	bacterial, frugal, natural	
-an or -ian	adjective or noun	relating to or one who is skilled at	comedian, theologian, urban	
-arian	noun	a person who	Aquarian, librarian, vegetarian	
-ate	adjective or verb	state or quality of; can make a word a verb	affectionate, fixate, medicate	
-ative	adjective	tending to	creative, fixative, talkative	

(continued)

TABLE A-3 *(continued)*

Suffix	Part of Speech It Indicates	Meaning	Examples	Your Words
-cide	noun	killing	homicide insecticide suicide	
-cy	noun	condition or state	efficiency lunacy privacy	
-dom	noun	condition of or state of	boredom freedom kingdom	
-ed	verb	past tense	chased laughed zipped	
-en	verb	makes a word a verb	frighten sweeten thicken	
-ence	noun	state or condition	absence negligence sequence	
-ent	adjective or noun	causing or one who performs or causes	competent correspondent incident	
-escence	noun	process or state	adolescence evanescence florescence	
-est	adjective	most	craziest healthiest stillest	
-ful	adjective	having the quality of	disrespectful hopeful thoughtful	
-ible	adjective	able to be	convertible flexible legible	
-ic	adjective	relating to or having the quality of	apologetic genetic magnetic	

Suffix	Part of Speech It Indicates	Meaning	Examples	Your Words
-ify	verb	to transform something into something else	magnify objectify simplify	
-ing	noun or verb	materials or an action or process	bedding dancing writing	
-ity	noun	state of or quality of	density fertility plausibility	
-ive	adjective or noun	having a quality, or a person or thing with the quality of	competitive explosive negative	
-ize	verb	cause or become	characterize hospitalize personalize	
-less	adjective	without	directionless heartless senseless	
-ly	adverb	makes a word into an adverb	bravely motherly quickly	
-ment	noun	action or result	establishment movement shipment	
-ness	noun	state or quality	fullness kindness thinness	
-or	noun	a person who	advisor inventor translator	
-ous	adjective	full of	dangerous hazardous porous	
-tion or -sion	noun	act or process, result of a process, state, or condition	motion navigation tension	

(continued)

TABLE A-3 *(continued)*

Suffix	Part of Speech It Indicates	Meaning	Examples	Your Words
-tude	noun	state, condition, or quality	fortitude gratitude solitude	
-ty	adjective or noun	state, condition, or quality	ability meaty scanty	
-uous	adjective	state or quality of	arduous strenuous voluptuous	
-y	adjective	having or resembling	dirty guilty sporty	

Index

A

A-arms, 286
AC power supply, 353
acceleration, 315
action forces, 315
action-reaction force pairs, 235
acute angle, 148
adding/addition, 94–95, 97–99, 124
adjective, 52
Administrative (ADM) line score, 22, 23
adverb, 52
AFCT (Armed Forces Classification Test), 8. *See also specific practice tests*
AFQT (Armed Forces Qualification Test). *See also specific practice tests*
  about, 19
  history of, 17
  score, 12–14, 23
  test-taking tips for, 593–595
air density, 256
Air Force. *See* U.S. Air Force
air pressure, 36
air-injection system, 284
algebra
  about, 121
  answers and explanation, 138–145
  practice questions, 134–137
Algebra I For Dummies (Sterling), 108
algebraic expression, 121
Allen wrench, 302
all-wheel drive, 285
alternate exterior angles, 149
alternate interior angles, 149
alternating current (AC), 350–352, 357
alternator, 282
ammeters, 342
amperes (amps), 340, 342
amplifier, 353, 355
amplitude, 238
angiosperms, 212, 214
angles, 148–150
animal cells, 215
animals, 205
answer sheets, 28, 377–378, 429–430, 479–480, 531, 559

answers
  changing, 592
  importance of checking, 591
  reading, 593–594
  reviewing, 179, 595
  reviewing options for, 28–29
  ruling out wrong, 51
answers and explanations, for practice questions
  Arithmetic Reasoning (AR) subtest, 189–195
  Assembling Objects (AO) subtest, 371–372
  Auto & Shop Information (AS) subtest, 295–297, 312
  Electronics Information (EI) subtest, 361–362
  General Science subtest, 222–224, 246–248, 272–274
  Mathematics Knowledge (MK) subtest, 115–119, 138–145, 169–174
  Mechanical Comprehension (MC) subtest, 336–338
  Paragraph Comprehension (PC) subtest, 86–88
  Word Knowledge (WK) subtest, 62–63
antenna, 353, 355
antilock brake system (ABS), 287
antonyms, 48
AO subtest. *See* Assembling Objects (AO) subtest
applied force, 316, 317
approximation symbol, 153
AR subtest. *See* Arithmetic Reasoning (AR) subtest
arc, 147
archaebacteria, 206
Archaeology For Dummies (White), 249
area, 148
area, of shapes, 150, 154, 598
argon, 255
Arithmetic Reasoning (AR) subtest
  about, 9, 175–176
  in AFQT, 12
  answers and explanations, 189–195
  example questions, 176–178, 181
  guessing strategy, 179–181
  handling word problems, 176–179
  practice questions, 182–188
  Q&A for Practice Exam 1 (AFQT), 533–536, 547–550
  Q&A for Practice Exam 1 (ASVAB), 381–384, 409–412
  Q&A for Practice Exam 2 (AFQT), 561–564, 575–579
  Q&A for Practice Exam 2 (ASVAB), 433–436, 461–463
  Q&A for Practice Exam 3 (ASVAB), 484–486, 511–514
Armed Forces Classification Test (AFCT), 8

Index 619

Armed Forces Qualification Test (AFQT). *See also specific practice tests*
  about, 19
  history of, 17
  score, 12–14, 23
  test-taking tips for, 593–595
Armed Services Vocational Aptitude Battery (ASVAB). *See also specific topics*
  about, 7
  history of, 17
  retaking, 15–17
  scores, 10–14
  subtests, 8–9
  versions of, 7–8
Army. *See* U.S. Army
arteries, 207
arteriole, 207
AS subtest. *See* Auto & Shop Information (AS) subtest
asnethosphere, 251
Assembling Objects (AO) subtest
  about, 9, 363–364
  answers and explanations, 371–372
  practice questions, 369–370
  Q&A for Practice Exam 1 (ASVAB), 404–405, 423–426
  Q&A for Practice Exam 2 (ASVAB), 456–457, 473–476
  Q&A for Practice Exam 3 (ASVAB), 506–507, 525–527
  question types on, 364–367
  test-taking techniques for, 367–368
asteroid belt, 266
asteroids, 265–266
astronomy, 262–266
Astronomy For Dummies (Maran), 249
ASVAB. *See* Armed Services Vocational Aptitude Battery (ASVAB)
atmosphere, 253–259
atom, 227, 341
atomic number, 227
atomic weight, 228
auger bits, 304
Auto Repair For Dummies (Sclar), 288, 420
Auto & Shop Information (AS) subtest
  about, 9, 277
  answers and explanations, 295–297, 312
  antilock brake system (ABS), 287
  brake system, 287
  cooling system, 283
  drive system, 284–285
  electrical and ignition systems, 282–283
  emissions-control systems, 284
  engines, 278–282
  example questions, 288, 308–309
  exhaust system, 284
  fasteners, 306–308
  lubrication system, 283
  octane ratings, 281
  practice questions, 289–294, 310–311
  Q&A for Practice Exam 1 (ASVAB), 396–398, 420–421
  Q&A for Practice Exam 2 (ASVAB), 448–450, 470–471
  Q&A for Practice Exam 3 (ASVAB), 498–500, 522–523
  suspension and steering system, 285–286
  tips for, 287–288
  tips for taking, 308–309
  tools, 299–306
autumnal equinox, 264
average, 96–97
axles, 328

B

bacteria, 210
ball and socket joints, 209
Barnhart, Roy (author), 420
barometer, 256, 316
base, 92, 232
basic operation, 93
basins, ocean, 254
battery, 353
bays, 254
bell, 353, 354
belts, 324–328
bench planes, 305
bench vise, 306
bevel gears, 326–327
biochronology, 262
biodiversity, 203
biology, 202–206
Biology For Dummies (Kratz), 199
bits, drill, 303–304
block and tackle systems, 324–326
block diagrams, 352
blocks of time, studying in, 31
boiling, 229–230
bolt cutters, 304
bolts, 307
bone marrow, 208
box wrench, 301–302
boxes, 599
brackish water, 254
brads, 307
brake fluid, 287
brake system, 287
breaker, 342–343, 353

breaker points, 282
bronchioles, 208
bryophytes, 212, 214
bucking bar, 308
butt chisel, 304, 305
buzzer, 353, 354

C

calculators, 597–598
calipers, 300
calories, 227
Calvin cycle, 213
camshaft, 280
cap nut, 307–308
capacitive reactance (capacitance), 351, 357
capacitors, 350–352, 353, 355
capillaries, 207
Car Hacks & Mods For Dummies (Vespremi), 288
carbohydrates, 211
carbon dioxide, 255
carburetors, 279
cardiac muscle, 209
cardiovascular system, 206
Carey, James (author), 420
Carey, Morris (author), 420
carnivores, 202
Carter, Ash (Secretary of Defense), 15
catalytic converter, 284
C-clamp, 306
cell membrane, 214
cells, 214–216, 344, 353
cellular respiration, 216
Celsius (°C), 258
Centigrade (°C), 258
central nervous system, 207
centrifugal force, 318
centripetal force, 318
ceruminous glands, 211
chassis, 278
Cheat Sheet (website), 2
chemical bonds, 227
chemical effect, 349
chemical reactions, 231–232
chemistry, 226–232
Chemistry For Dummies (Moore), 225
chisels, 305
chlorophyll, 213
chromosomes, 216
circle snips, 304
circles, 147, 153–154, 598

circuit breaker, 345, 353
circuits, 344–348, 352–356, 357
circulatory system, 206, 207–208
circumference (C), 153–154, 598
cirrus clouds, 258
clamping tools, 306
clamps, 306
class, 204, 205
classification system, 203–206
Clerical (CL) line score, Army and, 21
climate, 257
clouds, 257–258
clue words, 177
clutch, 285
Coast Guard. *See* U.S. Coast Guard
coasts, 254
coefficient, 122
coil, in ignition systems, 282
cold chisel, 304, 305
cold fronts, 256
Combat (CO) line score, Army and, 21
combat roles, for women, 15
combination reactions, 232
combined figures, 157–158
combustion chamber, 280
combustion reactions, 232
comets, 265–266
common denominators, 97–99
common factors, 99–100
common nails, 307
common sense, 217, 331
compare and contrast, 50–51
comparisons, showing with ratios, 104–106
complementary angle, 148
complex systems, 352
composite number, 92
composite score (line score), 12, 21–23
compound, 227, 230–231
compression, 278–279
compression ignition engines, 281–282
computerized-adaptive testing ASVAB (CAT-ASVAB), 25–27
conclusions, 594
condensation, 229–230
condenser, 282
conduction, 240
conductors, 342
condyloid joints, 210
confidence, building, 76
confirmation test, 29

conjunction, 52
connecting rods, 280
connectors, 364–366
consecutive interior angles, 149
constant, 122
context, creating, 49
contrails, 256
contrast, compare and, 50–51
control arms, 286
convection, 240
conventional current, 344
cooling system, 283
coordinate grid, 159
coordinates, 159–160
coping saws, 304
core, of the Earth, 250
corresponding angles, 149
coulomb, 342
countersink, 304
Cox, John D. (author), 249
crankshaft, 280
crosscut saws, 304
crosswords, 56
crust, of the Earth, 250
cube, surface area of, 154–158
cube root, 108
cubic meter, 227
cumulus clouds, 258
current, 253, 340, 342, 343, 357
curved-nose pliers, 303
cutting pliers, 303
cutting tools, 303
cylinder head, 280
cylinders (engine), 280, 281
cylinders (shape), 154–158, 599
cytoplasm, 214

D

DC power supply, 353
decimals, 101–103, 594–595
decomposition reactions, 232
deep ocean currents, 253
degrees
  in geometry, 147
  in temperature, 258
denominator, common, 97–99
density, 314
depth gauges, 300
diagrams, drawing, 178–179
diameter (d), 153–154

Dictionary.com (website), 56, 76
diesel, 281–282
difference
  defined, 94
  of potential, 343–344
diffuse reflection, 239
diffusion, 207
digestive system, 206, 208–209
digital thickness gauges, 300
dihydrogen oxide, 226
dinosaurs, 260–261
diode, 353, 355
direct current (DC), 350–352
directions, reading, 28
disc brakes, 287
distance, 105–106, 317
distractions, reducing, 31
distributor, 282
dividend, 103
dividing/division, 94, 100, 103, 125
divisor, 103
domain, 204, 205
dominant gene, 217
double-cut file, 305
double-headed nails, 307
drag, 320
drawing diagrams, 178–179
drawings, scale, 104–105
drill bits, 303–304
drilling tools, 303–305
drills, 303–304
drive shaft, 284–285
drive system, 284–285
drum brakes, 287
dual on/off switch, 353, 354
dummy scores, 21

E

earphone, 353, 354
Earth, 263–264
earthquake, 251–252
ecology, 202–203
ecosystem, 202
educated guesses, 217
effort arm, 322–323
EFI computer, 280
EI (Electronics Information) subtest. *See* Electronics Information (EI) subtest
EL line score. *See* Electronics (EL) line score
elastic recoil, 319

electric vehicles (EVs), 282
electrical system, 282–283
electric-arc welding, 303
electricity
  about, 340–350
  circuits, 352–356, 357
  current, 340, 342, 343, 357
  effects, 349–350
  example questions, 347–348
  measuring power, 348
  measuring voltage, 343–344
  Ohm's law, 357
  resistance, 321, 342–343, 351, 357
electrolytic decomposition, 349
electromagnetic induction, 349
electromagnetic spectrum, 238–239
electron, 341
electron flow, 344
Electronics For Dummies (Shamieh), 351
Electronics Information (EI) subtest
  about, 9, 339
  answers and explanations, 361–362
  current, 350–352
  electrical circuits, 352–356
  electricity, 340–350
  practice questions, 359–360
  Q&A for Practice Exam 1 (ASVAB), 394–395, 418–419
  Q&A for Practice Exam 2 (ASVAB), 446–447, 469–470
  Q&A for Practice Exam 3 (ASVAB), 496–497, 520–521
  test-taking techniques for, 357–358
Electronics (EL) line score, 21, 22, 23
electrons, 227
electroplating, 349
elements, 227
elimination, process of, 110, 180
ellipse, 263
emissions-control system, 284
endocrine system, 206, 210
endoskeleton, 209
energy, 236–237, 239–241, 357
engine knock, 281
Engineering and Electronics (BEE) line score, Navy/Coast Guard and, 22
Engineman (ENG) line score, Navy/Coast Guard and, 22
engines, 278–282
English skills, improving, 597–600
enlisted jobs, AFQT score requirements for, 12–14
Enlistment Screening Test (EST), 8
Enlistment version, 8
epiglottis, 208

equal sign (=), 132
equations
  balancing, 124–127
  defined, 122
  simplifying, 126–127
  two-variable, 127–129
equator, 253
equidistant, 149
equilateral triangle, 150
equilibrium, 235, 315–320
estuaries, 254
eubacteria, 205
evaporation, 230, 239
evapotranspiration, 257
Example icon, 2
example questions
  Arithmetic Reasoning (AR) subtest, 176–178, 181
  Auto and Shop Information (AS) subtest, 288
  electricity, 347–348
  General Science subtest, 217, 237, 267
  Mathematics Knowledge (MK) subtest, 104–105, 108–110, 151, 154–158, 159–160
  Mechanical Comprehension (MC) subtest, 331–332
  Paragraph Comprehension (PC) subtest, 67–71, 74–75
  Word Knowledge (WK) subtest, 43, 47, 49–54
excretory system, 206
exhaust, 279
exhaust manifold, 284
exhaust system, 284
exhaust valves, 280
exhaust-gas-recirculation system, 284
exocrine system, 207
exoskeleton, 209
exosphere, 255
explanations and answers. *See* answers and explanations, for practice questions
exponents, 92–93, 94, 122, 129
expressions, algebraic, 121, 129–130

F

factorial, 93
factoring algebraic expressions, 121, 129–130
factors, 92
Fahrenheit (°F), 258
failing, 589–592
family, 204, 205
fasteners, 306–308
fastening tools, 301–303
fats, 211
faults, 251–252

ferns, 212, 214
fiber, 211
Field Artillery (FA) line score, Army and, 21
files, 305
finishing nails, 307
finishing tools, 305
fixed joints, 209
flashcards, 600
flat file, 305
flat washer, 308
flathead screwdriver, 302
focus, losing, 590–591
FOIL, 127
foot-pound, 322
force, 236–237, 315–320
formulas, 160–161
formulas, for geometry, 598–599
fossils, 260–261
four-cycle engines, 279
four-stroke engine, 279
fourth root, 108
four-wheel drive, 285
fractions, 97–106
frame, of vehicles, 278
framing chisel, 305
freezing, 229–230
frequency, 350–351, 357
friction, 317, 319
front-wheel drive, 285
fuel injectors, 280
fulcrum, 322–323
functional groups, 230
fungi, 205
fuse, 345, 353

G

Galilean satellites, 265
gases, 229
gears, 324–328
gender, 216–217
General line score, Air Force and, 23
General Maintenance (GM) line score, Army and, 21
General Science (GS) subtest
  about, 9, 199–200
  answers and explanations, 222–224, 246–248, 272–274
  astronomy, 262–266
  biology, 202–206
  cells, 214–216
  chemistry, 226–232

example questions, 217, 237, 267
forms of measurement, 201–202
genetics, 216–217
geology, 249–252
human body systems, 206–212
oceanography, 252–254
paleontology, 259–262
physics, 233–241
plant physiology, 212–214
practice questions, 218–221, 242–245, 268–271
Q&A for Practice Exam 1 (ASVAB), 379–380, 407–408
Q&A for Practice Exam 2 (ASVAB), 431–432, 459–460
Q&A for Practice Exam 3 (ASVAB), 481–483, 509–510
scientific method, 200–201
tips for, 266–267
General Technical (GT) line score, 21, 22, 23
genes, 216–217
genetics, 216–217
genus, 204, 205
geologic eras, 261
geology, 249–252
Geology For Dummies (Spooner), 249
geometry
  about, 147
  angles, 148–150
  area, 148
  calculating volume, 154–158
  circles, 153–154
  coordinates, 159–160
  formulas for, 160–161, 598–599
  perimeter, 148
  quadrilaterals, 147, 151–152
  triangles, 150–151, 598
Geometry For Dummies (Ryan), 108
geophysicists, 250
germs, 260–261
gigawatt, 340
gliding joints, 210
gouging tools, 303–305
gram (g), 201
graphical computer games, 368
gravity, 316, 317
greatest common factor, 130
Greek, 266–267, 599
ground, 353, 354
ground state, 227
grounding, 350
GS subtest. *See* General Science (GS) subtest
guessing
  about, 54

on Arithmetic Reasoning (AR) subtest, 179–181
educated, 217
on Electronics Information (EI) subtest, 358
in Mechanical Comprehension (MC) subtest, 332
as a test-taking technique, 29–30
tips for, 591
gymnosperms, 212, 214

H
hacksaws, 304
half-round file, 305
Halley's Comet, 266
Hamilton, Gene (author), 420
Hamilton, Katie (author), 420
hammer, 301
hand screw vise, 306
Health (HM) line score, Navy/Coast Guard and, 22
heart, 207
heat, 239–241
heat effect, 349
heater, 353, 354
herbivores, 203
hertz (Hz), 350
hinge joints, 209
holiday lights, 346
Holzner, Steven (author), 225, 313
Home Improvement All-in-One For Dummies (Barnhart, Carey, Carey, Hamilton, Hamilton, Prestly and Strong), 420
homeostasis, 208
Hooke, Robert (scientist), 317
horsepower, 322, 329
human body systems, 206–212
humans, 260–261
hybrid vehicles, 282
hydraulic jacks, 330
hypotenuse, 150

I
ichnology, 260
icons, explained, 2
igneous rock, 251
ignition system, 282–283
immune system, 207, 210–211
impedance, 351
implication questions, on Paragraph Comprehension (PC) subtest, 70–71
improper fractions, 100
inclined plane, 323–324
indicator lamp, 353, 354

inductive reactance (inductance), 351, 357
inductors, 350–352, 353, 354
inequalities, solving, 132–133
inertia, 321
inside calipers, 300
insulators, 342
intake, 278
intake valves, 280
integer, 92
integumentary system, 207, 211
interest, simple, 105
interjection, 52
inverse operation, 93
inverses, 595
ionosphere, 255
irrational numbers, 106, 107, 122
isosceles triangle, 150

J
jigsaw puzzles, 368
Johnston, Angela Papple (author), 92
joined wires, 353
joules, 227, 322
Jovian, 264

K
Kelvin (K), 227, 258
kilogram, 227
kilowatt-hours (kWh), 340, 348
kinetic energy, 237, 320–321
kingdom, 204, 205–206
Kratz, René Fester (author), 199
Kuiper Belt, 264

L
lag screws, 307
lagoons, 254
larynx, 208
last-minute preparations, 37–38
Latin, 266–267, 599
law of inertia, 234
law of thermodynamics, 240–241
law of universal gravitation, 236, 317
leveling tools, 300–301
levels, 300–301
levers, 322–323
ligaments, 210
light dependent resistor, 353
light-dependent reactions, 213

light-emitting diode (LED), 353
lighting lamp, 353, 354
light-year, 262
like terms, 122
line score (composite score), 12, 21–23
Linnaeus, Carl (botanist), 203–206
liquids, 229
liter (L), 201, 227
lithosphere, 251
Local Group of Galaxies, 262
long-nosed pliers, 302
lowest terms, 99
lubrication system, 283
lunar eclipse, 264
lymphatic system, 207, 210–211

M

machine screws, 307
machines
  about, 322
  axles, 328
  belts, 324–328
  gears, 324–328
  hydraulic jacks, 330
  inclined plane, 323–324
  levers, 322–323
  pulleys, 324–328
  vises, 329–330
  wheels, 328
macroscopic, 226
magma, 250
magma chambers, 250
magnetic effect, 349
magnetic flux, 349
magnetic lines of force, 349
magnetism, 241, 317, 319–320
magnetosphere, 255–256
main point/main idea, 68–69, 71–73, 600
mallet, 301
mantle, of the Earth, 250
maps, reading, 368
Maran, Stephen P. (author), 249
Marine Corps. *See* U.S. Marine Corps
mass, 233, 317
math skills, improving, 597–600
Mathematics Knowledge (MK) subtest
  about, 9, 91–92
  in AFQT, 12

algebra, 121–145
answers and explanations, 115–119, 138–145, 169–174
example questions, 104–105, 108–110, 151, 154–158, 159–160
fractions, 97–106
geometry, 147–174
operations, 93–97
practice questions, 111–114, 134–137, 162–168
Q&A for Practice Exam 1 (AFQT), 544–545, 553–555
Q&A for Practice Exam 1 (ASVAB), 391–393, 415–418
Q&A for Practice Exam 2 (AFQT), 571–573, 582–585
Q&A for Practice Exam 2 (ASVAB), 443–445, 466–469
Q&A for Practice Exam 3 (ASVAB), 493–495, 518–520
scientific notation, 106
square roots, 106–108
terminology for, 92–93
test-taking techniques for, 108–110
matter, particles of, 228–229, 314
Mauna Kea, 254
MC subtest. *See* Mechanical Comprehension (MC) subtest
mean, 96–97
measurement, forms of, 201–202
measuring tools, 300
mechanical advantage, 322
Mechanical Comprehension (MC) subtest
  about, 9, 313–314
  answers and explanations, 336–338
  example questions, 331–332
  force, 315–320
  machines, 322–330
  practice questions, 333–335
  Q&A for Practice Exam 1 (ASVAB), 399–403, 421–423
  Q&A for Practice Exam 2 (ASVAB), 451–455, 472–473
  Q&A for Practice Exam 3 (ASVAB), 501–505, 523–525
  test-taking tips for, 331–332
  work, 320–322
Mechanical line score, Air Force and, 23
Mechanical Maintenance 2 (MEC2) line score, Navy/Coast Guard and, 22
Mechanical Maintenance (MEC) line score, Navy/Coast Guard and, 22
Mechanical Maintenance (MM) line score, 21, 23
median, 96–97
megawatt, 340
meiosis, 216
MEPCOM regulation, 29
Merriam-Webster online (website), 56
mesosphere, 250, 255

metabolism, 216
metal-cutting chisels, 305
metamorphic rock, 251
meteors, 265–266
meter (m), 201, 227
metric system (SI), 201–202
micrometers, 300
micropaleontology, 260
microphone, 353, 354
microscopic, 226
Milky Way, 262
minerals, 211
minor planets, 266
minutes, in geometry, 147
mirroring, 365
misunderstandings, 592
mitosis, 216
mixed numbers, 100
mixture, 231
MK subtest. *See* Mathematics Knowledge (MK) subtest
mode, 96–97
molecules, 227
moons, 264–265
Moore, John T. (author), 225
mortising chisel, 304, 305
motor, 353, 354
muffler, 284
multimeter, 344
multiple-choice questions, 28–29
multiplying/multiplication, 94, 99–100, 102, 125
multistep equations, solving, 125–126
muscular system, 206, 209

N

nails, 306–307
naming angles, 150
National Oceanic Atmospheric Administration (NOAA), 257
Navy. *See* U.S. Navy
needle-nosed pliers, 302
negative numbers, 133
nervous system, 206, 207
neutrons, 227, 341
Newton, Isaac (scientist), 317
newtons, 227
Newton's laws of motion, 234–236
nitrogen, 255
notes, making, 593
noun, 52

Nuclear Field (NUC) line score, Navy/Coast Guard and, 22
nucleus, 214, 227, 341
number sequences, 95–96
numerator, 97
nuts, 307–308

O

observations, using as a test-taking technique, 331
obtuse angle, 148
obtuse triangle, 150
ocean basins, 254
oceanography, 252–254
octane ratings, 281
offset screwdriver, 302
ohms, 340, 343, 357
Ohm's law, 343, 357
oil filter, 283
oil galleries, 283
oil pan, 283
oil pump, 283
omnivores, 203
1,001 ASVAB AFQT Practice Questions For Dummies (Johnston), 92
1-week study strategy, 37
one-step equations, solving, 124
online test bank, 32
on/off switch, 353, 354
open-end wrench, 301–302
operations, 93–97, 598
Operations (OPS) line score, Navy/Coast Guard and, 22
Operators and Food (OF) line score, Army and, 21
orbit, 263
order, 204, 205
order of operations, 94–95, 598
osmosis, 216
ossification, 209
outside calipers, 300
oxyacetylene welding, 303
oxygen, 255

P

paleobotany, 259
paleoclimate, 257
paleoecology, 260
paleomagnetism, 262
paleontology, 259–262
palynology, 260
paper test, 25–28

Paragraph Comprehension (PC) subtest
   about, 9, 65
   in AFQT, 12
   analyzing paragraphs, 74–75
   answers and explanations, 86–88
   breaking down paragraphs, 71–73
   components of, 66
   example questions, 67–71, 74–75
   importance of, 65–66
   practice questions, 78–85
   Q&A for Practice Exam 1 (AFQT), 540–543, 552–553
   Q&A for Practice Exam 1 (ASVAB), 388–390, 414–415
   Q&A for Practice Exam 2 (AFQT), 568–570, 581–582
   Q&A for Practice Exam 2 (ASVAB), 440–442, 465–466
   Q&A for Practice Exam 3 (ASVAB), 490–492, 516–518
   question types, 66–71
   slow readers, 76–77
   test-taking tips for, 77
parallel circuit, 346
parallel lines, 149
parallelograms, 152
parentheses, in order of operations, 94
parts of speech, 52–53
pascals, 227
passages, 72–73, 594
patterns, finding, 96
PC subtest. *See* Paragraph Comprehension (PC) subtest
penny system, 306–307
pepsin, 208
percentile score, 12
percents, 101–102, 104, 594–595
perfect squares, 106–107
perimeter, 148, 150, 598
periodic table, 227–228
permutations, 93
pH, 232
phagocytosis, 216
phanerozoic, 261
pharynx, 208
Phillips screwdriver, 302
photosynthesis, 213, 216
phylum, 204, 205
physics, 233–241
Physics I For Dummies (Holzner), 225, 313
Physics II For Dummies (Holzner), 225
physiological effect, 350
pi, 153
pickup tube/screen, 283
pipe cutters, 304
pipe vise, 306

pipe wrench, 302
piston rings, 280
pistons, 280
pivot joints, 209
planes, 305
planets, 250–252, 263–264
plant cells, 215
plant physiology, 212–214
plants, 205, 259–262
plasma membrane, 214
plastic flow, 251
pliers, 302–303, 306
plumb bob, 300–301
Pluto, 264
polarization, 241
polarized capacitor, 353
polygon, 598
polynomial, 122
pop rivets, 308
positive numbers, 133
positive-crankcase ventilation, 284
potential, difference of, 343–344
potential energy, 237, 320–321
potentiometer, 353, 355
power, 236–237, 321–322, 348, 357
Practice Exam 1 (AFQT)
   about, 529, 547
   answer sheet for, 531
   Arithmetic Reasoning subtest Q&A, 533–536, 547–550
   Mathematics Knowledge subtest Q&A, 544–545, 553–555
   Paragraph Comprehension subtest Q&A, 540–543, 552–553
   Word Knowledge subtest Q&A, 537–539, 550–552
Practice Exam 1 (ASVAB)
   about, 375, 407
   answer sheet for, 377–378
   Arithmetic Reasoning subtest Q&A, 381–384, 409–412
   Assembling Objects subtest Q&A, 404–405, 423–426
   Auto & Shop Information subtest Q&A, 396–398, 420–421
   Electronics Information subtest Q&A, 394–395, 418–419
   General Science subtest Q&A, 379–380, 407–408
   Mathematics Knowledge subtest Q&A, 391–393, 415–418
   Mechanical Comprehension subtest Q&A, 399–403, 421–423
   Paragraph Comprehension subtest Q&A, 388–390, 414–415
   Word Knowledge subtest Q&A, 385–387, 412–414

Practice Exam 2 (AFQT)
  about, 557, 575
  answer sheet for, 559
  Arithmetic Reasoning subtest Q&A, 561–564, 575–579
  Mathematics Knowledge subtest Q&A, 571–573, 582–585
  Paragraph Comprehension subtest Q&A, 568–570, 581–582
  Word Knowledge subtest Q&A, 565–567, 579–581
Practice Exam 2 (ASVAB)
  about, 427, 459
  answer sheet for, 429–430
  Arithmetic Reasoning subtest Q&A, 433–436, 461–463
  Assembling Objects subtest Q&A, 456–457, 473–476
  Auto & Shop Information subtest Q&A, 448–450, 470–471
  Electronics Information subtest Q&A, 446–447, 469–470
  General Science subtest Q&A, 431–432, 459–460
  Mathematics Knowledge subtest Q&A, 443–445, 466–469
  Mechanical Comprehension subtest Q&A, 451–455, 472–473
  Paragraph Comprehension subtest Q&A, 440–442, 465–466
  Word Knowledge subtest Q&A, 437–439, 463–465
Practice Exam 3 (ASVAB)
  about, 477, 509
  answer sheet for, 479–480
  Arithmetic Reasoning subtest Q&A, 484–486, 511–514
  Assembling Objects subtest Q&A, 506–507, 525–527
  Auto & Shop Information subtest Q&A, 498–500, 522–523
  Electronics Information subtest Q&A, 496–497, 520–521
  General Science subtest Q&A, 481–483, 509–510
  Mathematics Knowledge subtest Q&A, 493–495, 518–520
  Mechanical Comprehension subtest Q&A, 501–505, 523–525
  Paragraph Comprehension subtest Q&A, 490–492, 516–518
  Word Knowledge subtest Q&A, 487–489, 515–516
practice questions
  Arithmetic Reasoning (AR) subtest, 182–188
  Assembling Objects (AO) subtest, 369–370
  Auto and Shop Information (AS) subtest, 289–294, 310–311
  Electronics Information (EI) subtest, 359–360
  General Science subtest, 218–221, 242–245, 268–271
  Mathematics Knowledge (MK) subtest, 111–114, 134–137, 162–168
  Mechanical Comprehension (MC) subtest, 333–335
  memorizing, 592
  Paragraph Comprehension (PC) subtest, 78–85
  Word Knowledge (WK) subtest, 58–61
practicing, 31, 597
prefixes, 43–45, 610–614
preposition, 52
pre-screening internet-delivered Computerized Adaptive Test (PiCAT), 8, 26, 27
preset variable resistor, 353, 355
pressure, 316
Prestly, Donald R. (author), 420
prime number, 92
primeval seas, 253
primordial ocean, 252–253
prism, surface area of, 154–158
process of elimination, 110, 180
product, 94
pronoun, 52
protein, 212
proterozoic, 261
protists, 205
protons, 227, 341
pulleys, 324–328
punches, 304–305
punching tools, 303–305
push switch, 354
push-to-break switch, 353, 354
push-to-make switch, 353
puzzle games, 368
Pythagorean theorem, 151

Q

quadrants, 160
quadratic equations, solving, 131–132
quadrilaterals, 147, 151–152
questions
  on Assembling Objects (AO) subtest, 364–367
  difficulty level of, 10
  example. See example questions
  on Paragraph Comprehension (PC) subtest, 66–71
  practice. See practice questions
  understanding, 28
  on Word Knowledge (WK) subtest, 42–43
quotient, 94

R

radiation, 240
radiator, 283
radical sign, 106
radiometric dating, 262

radius (r), 153–154
ramp, 323–324
range, 96–97
rates, 105–106, 595
rational number, 122
ratios, 104–106, 595
raw score, 11
reactants, 232
reaction forces, 315
reading, 28, 55, 75, 368, 593–594, 600
real number, 122
rear-wheel drive, 285
recessive gene, 217
reciprocal, 93
recoil, 317, 319
rectangles, 151, 598
rectangular prisms, 154–158
rectifiers, 352, 357
reflection, 239
reflex angles, 148
refraction, 239
relative dating, 262
relativity, 314
relay, 353, 354
Remember icon, 2
renal system, 206, 208
repeating decimals, 101
rephrasing passages, 72–73
reproductive system, 207, 211
rereading, 594
resistance, 321, 342–343, 351, 357
resistance arm, 322–323
resistor, 353, 354–355
resources, for Word Knowledge (WK) subtest, 601–618
respiratory system, 206, 208
retaking ASVAB, 15–17
rheostat, 343, 353, 355
rhombuses, 152
ribosomes, 214
Richter magnitude scale, 252
right angle, 148
right triangle, 150
ripsaws, 304
rivets, 308
rolling friction, 319
root, 108
root words, 45–46
round chisel, 305
round file, 305
rounding, 93
Ryan, Mark (author), 108

S

saddle joints, 209
SAT Math For Dummies (Zegarelli), 108
satellites, 264–265
scale drawings, 104–105
scalene triangle, 150
scales, 595
scientific disciplines. *See specific disciplines*
scientific method, 200–201
scientific notation, 106
Sclar, Deanna (author), 288, 420
scores
    about, 10–11
    AFQT, 12–14
    composite score (line score), 12, 21–23
    as determinants of military training programs and jobs, 20–21
    dummy, 21
    how they are used, 590
    percentile score, 12
    raw score, 11
    standard score, 11
screwdrivers, 302
screws, 307
sebaceous glands, 211
seconds, in geometry, 147
sedimentary rock, 251
seismologists, 250
semiconductor diodes, 352
semiconductors, 342
series circuit, 345–346
series-parallel circuit, 346
sex chromosome, 216–217
shake-proof washers, 308
Shamieh, Cathleen (author), 351
shapes, 366–367
shears, 304
shock absorbers, 286
shooting star, 265
shores, 254
short circuit, 347
shunt, 346
SI derived units, 233–234
SI system, 227, 233–234
signal words, 50–51
simple interest, 105
simplifying equations, 126–127
single-cut file, 305
6-week study strategy, 35–36
skeletal muscle, 209
skeletal system, 206, 209–210

sketching, 368
Skilled Technical (ST) line score, Army and, 21
sledge, 301
slide calipers, 300
sliding friction, 319
slip-joint pliers, 303
slope-intercept, 159
slow readers, 76–77
smallpox, 210
smooth muscle, 209
snips, 304
socket chisel, 304, 305
socket wrench, 302
soft-iron coils, 349
solar cell, 353
solar eclipse, 264
solar wind, 263
soldering, 303
soldering tools, 303
solids, 155–157, 228–229
sonic boom, 237
sound reflection, 237
sound waves, 237–238
sounding it out, 56–57
sounds, 254
Space Force. See U.S. Space Force
spatial skills, 368
speaker, 353, 354
special programs, AFQT score requirements for, 14
species, 204, 205, 206
specular reflection, 239
speech, parts of, 52–53
spheres, 154–158
spikes, 306
split lock washer, 308
Spooner, Alecia M. (author), 249
spring constant, 319
spring force, 319
springs, 286
square file, 305
square roots, 93, 106–108
squares, 151, 300–301
squaring tools, 300–301
standard scores, 11, 20, 23
stapler, 301
starter, 282
states, changing, 228–229
static electricity, 317, 320
static equilibrium, 316
steering knuckle, 286

Sterling, Mary Jane (author), 108
stigma, 214
stop nut, 307–308
straight line, 148
strategies, for Word Knowledge (WK) subtest, 49–54
stratosphere, 255
stratus clouds, 258
striking tools, 301
Strong, Jeff (author), 420
struts, 286
Student version, 8
study breaks, 31
study guides, 600
study plans, personalizing, 32–33
study strategies, outlining, 33–37
study techniques, 25, 30–32, 589
subatomic particles, 227
subject areas, concentrating on specific, 31
sublimation, 230
subpoints/supporting points, 71, 73, 600
substitution, 127–128
subtests, 8–9, 31, 590
subtracting/subtraction, 94–95, 97–99, 124
suffixes, 43–45, 615–618
sum, 94
summer solstice, 264
sun, 262–263
supercontinents, 252
supplementary angle, 148
surface area, 155–157
surface ocean currents, 253
Surveillance and Communications (SC) line score, Army and, 21
suspension and steering system, 285–286
switch, 354
symbols, 28, 133
synonyms, 48

T

tachometer, 279
tailpipe, 284
taphonomy, 260
Technical Stuff icon, 2
tectonic plates, 251–252
temperature conversions, 258–259
tendons, 210
tension, 316, 318
tension force, 318
terminology, 23, 92–93
terms, 121

terrestrial, 264
test-taking techniques, 25–32, 77, 108–110, 308–309, 331–332, 357–358, 367–368, 593–595
thermal energy, 239–241
thermal equilibrium, 239–241
thermosphere, 255
Thesaurus.com (website), 56
thickness gauges, 300
thread gauges, 300
3-week study strategy, 36–37
three-term equations, factoring, 130
throttle, 280
tides, 254
tie rods, 286
time, 591
Tip icon, 2
tires, 286
tools, for automobiles, 299–306
topic sentences, 71–72
torque, 285, 328–329
torque converter, 285
torque wrench, 302
trachea, 208
trade winds, 254
training programs/jobs, scores and, 20–21
transducer, 354
transformer, 353, 354
transistors, 352, 353, 355, 357
transmission, 285
transversal, 149
trapezoids, 152
treasure hunt questions, on Paragraph Comprehension (PC) subtest, 67–68
triangles, 150–151, 598
troposphere, 255
tube cutters, 304
12-week study strategy, 34–35
twist drills, 303
two-variable equations, 127–129
two-way switch, 353, 354

U

unbalanced force, 235
universal donor, 208
universal joint, 284
universal recipient, 208
unjoined wires, 353
urinary system, 206
urinary tract, 208

U.S. Air Force
  AFQT score requirements for enlistment in, 14
  line scores and, 22–23
  Paragraph Comprehension (PC) subtest score and, 66
  retest policy for, 16
  training programs/jobs and, 20
  Word Knowledge (WK) subtest score and, 42
U.S. Army
  AFQT score requirements for enlistment in, 14
  line scores and, 21
  Paragraph Comprehension (PCS) subtest score and, 66
  retest policy for, 16
  Word Knowledge (WK) subtest score and, 42
U.S. Coast Guard
  AFQT score requirements for enlistment in, 14
  line scores and, 22
  Paragraph Comprehension (PC) subtest score and, 66
  retest policy for, 17
  training programs/jobs and, 20
  Word Knowledge (WK) subtest score and, 42
U.S. Marine Corps
  AFQT score requirements for enlistment in, 14
  line scores and, 22–23
  Paragraph Comprehension (PC) subtest score and, 66
  retest policy for, 16
  training programs/jobs and, 20
  Word Knowledge (WK) subtest score and, 42
U.S. Navy
  AFQT score requirements for enlistment in, 14
  line scores and, 22
  Paragraph Comprehension (PC) subtest score and, 66
  retest policy for, 16
  training programs/jobs and, 20
  Word Knowledge (WK) subtest score and, 42
U.S. Space Force
  AFQT score requirements for enlistment in, 14
  guaranteed jobs/aptitude/career areas and, 20
  lines scores and, 22–23
  Paragraph Comprehension (PC) subtest score and, 66
  retest policy for, 16
  training programs/jobs and, 20
  Word Knowledge (WK) subtest score and, 42

V

variable capacitor, 353
variable resistor, 355
variables, 122
vector quantities, 316

verb, 52
Vernal equinox, 263
vertex, 148
Vespremi, David (author), 288
vise, 306, 329–330
vise-grip pliers, 302, 303
vitamins, 212
vocabulary, improving, 54–57, 76
Vocabulary.com (website), 56
voltage, 343–344, 357
voltage drop, 343–344
voltmeter, 344
volts, 340, 357
volume, 154–158, 599

W

warm front, 256
Warning icon, 2
washers, 307–308
water jackets, 283
water pumps, 283
watt-hour, 340, 357
watts, 340, 357
wavelength, 238
Weather For Dummies (Cox), 249
weather patterns, 257
websites
  Cheat Sheet, 2
  dictionary, 76
  Dictionary.com, 56, 76
  Merriam-Webster online, 56
  online test bank, 32
  Thesaurus.com, 56
  Vocabulary.com, 56
wedge, 324
weight, 233, 314
welding, 303
welding tools, 303
wheel-and-axle machine, 328
wheels, 328
White, Nancy Marie (author), 249
whole numbers, dividing decimals by, 103
wing nut, 308
winter solstice, 264
wire gauges, 300
wires, 353, 356–357

WK subtest. *See* Word Knowledge (WK) subtest
women, combat roles for, 15
Women's Armed Services Integration Act (1948), 15
wood screws, 307
wood-cutting chisels, 305
word families, 46–47
Word Knowledge (WK) subtest
  about, 9, 41
  in AFQT, 12
  answers and explanations, 62–63
  antonyms, 48
  deciphering word meanings, 43–48
  example questions, 43, 47, 49–54
  importance of, 42
  improving vocabulary for, 54–57
  practice questions, 58–61
  Q&A for Practice Exam 1 (AFQT), 537–539, 550–552
  Q&A for Practice Exam 1 (ASVAB), 385–387, 412–414
  Q&A for Practice Exam 2 (AFQT), 565–567, 579–581
  Q&A for Practice Exam 2 (ASVAB), 437–439, 463–465
  Q&A for Practice Exam 3 (ASVAB), 487–489, 515–516
  question format in, 42–43
  resources for, 601–618
  strategies for, 49–54
  synonyms, 48
  timing for, 43
word lists, 55–56, 599
word matches, 594
word meanings, 43–48, 69–70
word problems, 105–106, 176–179
word roots, 601–610
words, 47–48, 49–50, 51–52, 53–54
work, 236–237, 320–322
wrench, 301–302
wrench pliers, 303
wrist pins, 280

X

x, solving for, 123

Z

Zegarelli, Mark (author), 108
Zener diode, 355
zero, 132
zeroth law of thermodynamics, 240

About the Author

Angie Papple Johnston joined the U.S. Army in 2006 as a Chemical, Biological, Radiological, and Nuclear (CBRN) Specialist, ready to tackle chemical weapons in a Level-A HAZMAT suit. During her second deployment as part of Operation Iraqi Freedom, Angie became her battalion's public affairs representative, covering breaking news from Tikrit to Kirkuk. She has earned a Combat Action Badge, several Army Commendation medals and Army Achievement medals, and numerous accolades for her work in Iraq.

Angie also served as the Lead Cadre for the Texas Army National Guard's Recruit Sustainment Program (RSP), teaching brand-new privates how to survive Basic Combat Training, Advanced Individual Training, and the Army before becoming the CBRN noncommissioned officer-in-charge in an aviation battalion in Washington, D.C. She currently resides in Washington, D.C.

Dedication

This book is for everyone brave enough to stand up, raise your right hand, and put on a uniform.

Author's Acknowledgments

Lindsay Berg, I appreciate everything you do and the opportunities you've given me to help our military. I salute you, but not the way they do it in the stock photos.

Chrissy Guthrie, you are the pinnacle of professionalism, the epitome of expertise, and the apex of awesomeness. I know that sounds dramatic, but thank you so much for always keeping everything running smoothly every step of the way.

MAJ Jonathan Kralick, I'm deeply humbled by your exceptional service to this nation. Thank you for combing through every word to make sure we get it right as you climb literal mountains between edits.

Megan Knoll, thank you for your exceptional eye for detail over the past several years. I can always count on you to catch everything, and your contributions have made this book better each time.

Bonnie Swadling, I love you. Your turn!

Mom, Dad, Darl, Tina, and Jesse, I love you guys. I'll give Jesse a break this year to tell Tina something: Congratulations. Best thing you've ever done. (Also, I lied. Jesse, Mom said she loves me more.)

Publisher's Acknowledgments

Executive Editor: Lindsay Berg
Development Editor: Christina Guthrie
Copy Editor: Megan Knoll
Technical Editor: MAJ Jonathan Kralick, P.E.

Senior Managing Editor: Kristie Pyles
Cover Image: © Katarzyna Hurova/Shutterstock

Take dummies with you everywhere you go!

Whether you are excited about e-books, want more from the web, must have your mobile apps, or are swept up in social media, dummies makes everything easier.

Find us online!

dummies.com

dummies
A Wiley Brand

Leverage the power

Dummies is the global leader in the reference category and one of the most trusted and highly regarded brands in the world. No longer just focused on books, customers now have access to the dummies content they need in the format they want. Together we'll craft a solution that engages your customers, stands out from the competition, and helps you meet your goals.

Advertising & Sponsorships

Connect with an engaged audience on a powerful multimedia site, and position your message alongside expert how-to content. Dummies.com is a one-stop shop for free, online information and know-how curated by a team of experts.

- Targeted ads
- Video
- Email Marketing
- Microsites
- Sweepstakes sponsorship

20 MILLION PAGE VIEWS EVERY SINGLE MONTH

15 MILLION UNIQUE VISITORS PER MONTH

43% OF ALL VISITORS ACCESS THE SITE VIA THEIR MOBILE DEVICES

700,000 NEWSLETTER SUBSCRIPTIONS TO THE INBOXES OF **300,000** UNIQUE INDIVIDUALS EVERY WEEK

# of dummies

Custom Publishing

Reach a global audience in any language by creating a solution that will differentiate you from competitors, amplify your message, and encourage customers to make a buying decision.

- Apps
- Books
- eBooks
- Video
- Audio
- Webinars

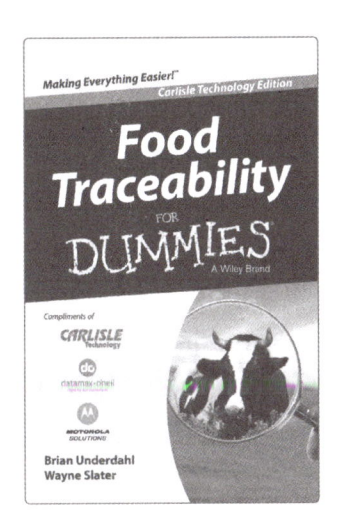

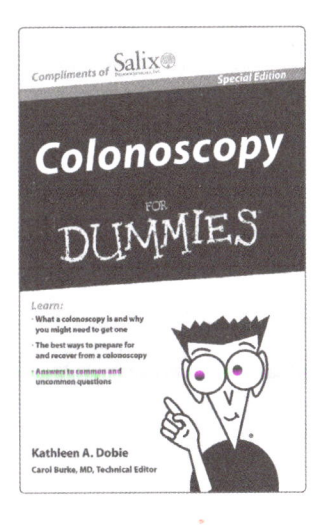

Brand Licensing & Content

Leverage the strength of the world's most popular reference brand to reach new audiences and channels of distribution.

For more information, visit dummies.com/biz

dummies
A Wiley Brand

PERSONAL ENRICHMENT

Staying Sharp	Facebook	Guitar	Investing	Beekeeping	Digital Photography
9781119187790	9781119179030	9781119293354	9781119293347	9781119310068	9781119235606
USA $26.00	USA $21.99	USA $24.99	USA $22.99	USA $22.99	USA $24.99
CAN $31.99	CAN $25.99	CAN $29.99	CAN $27.99	CAN $27.99	CAN $29.99
UK £19.99	UK £16.99	UK £17.99	UK £16.99	UK £16.99	UK £17.99

Meditation	Pregnancy	Samsung Galaxy S7	iPhone	Crocheting	Nutrition
9781119251163	9781119235491	9781119279952	9781119283133	9781119287117	9781119130246
USA $24.99	USA $26.99	USA $24.99	USA $24.99	USA $24.99	USA $22.99
CAN $29.99	CAN $31.99	CAN $29.99	CAN $29.99	CAN $29.99	CAN $27.99
UK £17.99	UK £19.99	UK £17.99	UK £17.99	UK £16.99	UK £16.99

PROFESSIONAL DEVELOPMENT

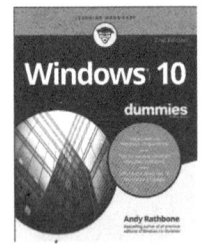

Windows 10	AutoCAD	Excel 2016	QuickBooks 2017	macOS Sierra	LinkedIn	Windows 10 All-in-One
9781119311041	9781119255796	9781119293439	9781119281467	9781119280651	9781119251132	9781119310563
USA $24.99	USA $39.99	USA $26.99	USA $26.99	USA $29.99	USA $24.99	USA $34.00
CAN $29.99	CAN $47.99	CAN $31.99	CAN $31.99	CAN $35.99	CAN $29.99	CAN $41.99
UK £17.99	UK £27.99	UK £19.99	UK £19.99	UK £21.99	UK £17.99	UK £24.99

SharePoint 2016	Fundamental Analysis	Networking	Office 2016	Office 365	Salesforce.com	Coding
9781119181705	9781119263593	9781119257769	9781119293477	9781119265313	9781119239314	9781119293323
USA $29.99	USA $26.99	USA $29.99	USA $26.99	USA $24.99	USA $29.99	USA $29.99
CAN $35.99	CAN $31.99	CAN $35.99	CAN $31.99	CAN $29.99	CAN $35.99	CAN $35.99
UK £21.99	UK £19.99	UK £21.99	UK £19.99	UK £17.99	UK £21.99	UK £21.99

dummies.com

dummies
A Wiley Brand